MEMORY & NARRATIVE

MEMORY & NARRATIVE
THE WEAVE OF LIFE-WRITING

JAMES OLNEY

THE UNIVERSITY OF CHICAGO PRESS
CHICAGO & LONDON

JAMES OLNEY is Voorhies Professor of English and professor of French and Italian at Louisiana State University. He is also coeditor of *The Southern Review*.

The University of Chicago Press gratefully acknowledges the assistance of the John Simon Guggenheim Memorial Foundation in the publication of this book.

The University of Chicago Press, Chicago 60637
The University of Chicago Press, Ltd., London
© 1998 by The University of Chicago
All rights reserved. Published 1998
07 06 05 04 03 02 01 00 99 98   1 2 3 4 5
ISBN: 0-226-62816-7

Library of Congress Cataloging-in-Publication Data

Olney, James.
    Memory & narrative : the weave of life-writing / James Olney.
      p. cm.
    Includes bibliographical references and index.
    ISBN 0-226-62816-7 (alk. paper)
    1. Autobiography—Authorship.   2. Autobiographical memory.
  3. Narration (Rhetoric).   I. Title.
  CT25.043 1998   98-17135
                                              CIP

♾ The paper used in this publication meets the minimum requirements of the American National Standard for Information Sciences—Permanence of Paper for Printed Library Materials, ANSI Z39.48-1992.

For my brothers and sisters—
Richard
Margaret
Norris
John
Elizabeth
Frances (in memoriam)
Byron—
sine quibus non

Life lives on. It is the lives, the lives, the lives that die.
—Pseudo-Lucretius

My imagination goes some years backward, and I remember a beautiful young girl singing at the edge of the sea in Normandy words and music of her own composition. She thought herself alone, stood barefooted between sea and sand; sang with lifted head of the civilisations that there had come and gone, ending every verse with the cry:
O Lord, let something remain.
—W. B. Yeats

CONTENTS

ACKNOWLEDGMENTS

I record first my deep gratitude to two friends, Steven Marcus and Patricia Meyer Spacks, who not only provided me a liberal education over the course of four summers at the National Humanities Center in North Carolina, but also, in Steven's case, found—and not once but twice—an ideal place for me to work and, in Pat's case, read—and not once but twice—the entire manuscript of this book. I am equally grateful to James M. Cox, who has nourished me with ideas and more for over twenty years. Josie Dixon, of Cambridge University Press, followed the work from near the beginning to the end with always thoughtful advice. Porter Abbott has offered hospitality and assistance beyond anything one might have expected. Michael Griffith and Nicola Mason, of *The Southern Review* and Louisiana State University Press, cast an expert editorial eye over the manuscript and, in so doing, improved it immeasurably. Brenda Macon, also of *The Southern Review*, did heroic work in subduing a recalcitrant text to the elegant wonders of the computer. A generous leave policy at Louisiana State University allowed me to do the book as I thought it had to be done, and the Heyman Center for the Humanities at Columbia University provided, in 1993–94 and again in 1996, an undisturbed atmosphere for accomplishing the work. I have been helped to the same end by conversations with various colleagues at LSU: Lewis P. Simpson, Dave Smith, J. Gerald Kennedy, Daniel Mark Fogel, Panthea Reid, John Irwin Fischer, Joseph Kronick, Michelle and Jesse Gellrich, and Nat and Betsy Wing. Graduate students at LSU (of whom I will name but three to stand for all the others: Margaret Bass, Donna Perreault, and Martha Regalis) have contributed more than they can possibly recognize over the past fifteen years, as also have the seventy-two participants in the six seminars for college teachers I directed for the National Endowment for the Humanities beginning in 1981.

I am indebted to professional colleagues at other universities who made helpful interventions at important moments: Donald Phillip Verene of Emory University, Germaine Brée of Wake Forest University, James McConkey of Cornell University, Gertrud Lenzer of Brooklyn College, Eugene Stelzig of SUNY/Geneseo, Paul John Eakin of Indiana University, Georges Gusdorf of the University of Strasbourg, Michael Sheringham of the University of London, James F. Jones, Jr., of Southern Methodist University, Philippe Lejeune of the University of Paris–Nord, Mary Lydon of the University of Wisconsin, Daniel Albright of the University of Rochester. Several books pertinent to the concerns of this one (Brian Stock's *Augustine the Reader,* Michael Sheringham's *French Autobiography,* H. Porter Abbott's *Beckett Writing Beckett,* Richard Begam's *Samuel Beckett and the End of Modernity,* and Marjorie Perloff's *Wittgenstein's Ladder*) came too late to be fully incorporated into my text, but from their authors, in conversation and correspondence as well as in print, I have learned much. In addition, I am grateful for permission to reprint a previously published article, which I have included as the first half of chapter I: James Olney, "Memory and the Narrative Imperative," *New Literary History* 24, no. 4 (autumn 1993): 857–80. I am grateful also to Artists Rights Society for permission to reprint *Three Walking Men* (1948) and *Figure in a Box between Two Houses* (1950), both by Alberto Giacometti. © 1998 Artists Rights Society (ARS), New York/ADAGP, Paris; photos courtesy Kunsthaus Zürich, Alberto Giacometti Foundation.

Alan Thomas, Randolph Petilos, and Leslie Keros have been wonderfully sympathetic editors at the University of Chicago Press. Michael Koplow has copyedited *Memory and Narrative* with a sure eye and with the author's interests always at heart. Marianne Jankowski is responsible for the book's superb design, and Dave Aftandilian has been assiduous in promoting it. To everyone at the Press I offer thanks. Likewise to the staff at the National Humanities Center, where this project (all unknown to myself) was begun, and in particular to Kent Mullikin, who, while everyone else has come and gone for twenty years, has remained at the Center, a steady and steadying figure of intelligence, integrity, and grace. The John Simon Guggenheim Memorial Foundation supported my work at the Humanities Center with a fellowship and has now gained my redoubled gratitude with a subvention to aid in publication of the book.

Finally, Laura O'Connor has been so much a part of the writing of this book that my memory of its making can scarcely draw the line between what was hers, what was mine. I cannot find words equal to my indebtedness and so fall back on the simplest of expressions: thank you.

PRELUDE

"Murphy, all life is figure and ground." So Neary proclaims to the epony-
mous hero of Samuel Beckett's first novel. Whatever Neary may have in
mind with his gnomic saying, I am happy to appropriate it to characterize
the shape of *Memory and Narrative*. The three great principals of my book—
St. Augustine, bishop of Hippo; Jean-Jacques Rousseau, Citizen of Geneva;
Samuel Beckett, Irish Parisian—stand like colossi each fully capable of giving his name to the age in which he lived and wrote: Augustine, presiding
spirit of the Catholic Middle Ages; Rousseau, child of the Enlightenment
yet prime mover of Romantic attitudes; Beckett, comic genius of a world
in ruins. At the same time, the three taken together establish a tradition of
writing, founded by Augustine, radically altered by Rousseau, concluding
(for the moment) in Beckett, that is the ground against which, during sixteen centuries, innumerable figures and transformations have played themselves out like variations on a theme.

Memory and Narrative had its beginnings in a brief paper called "Autobiography and the Narrative Imperative from St. Augustine to Samuel Beckett" that I wrote for a scholarly gathering in 1981. That paper, like the first
part of the first chapter of this book, dwelt on what I perceived to be
some curious but striking similarities between Augustine's *Confessions* and
Beckett's then recently published (1980) *Company* on such issues as narrative theory and the relationship of recollecting or remembering to the act
of narrating. But the paper was written for a particular occasion, and when
that occasion was over I tucked it into a file drawer and forgot about it. I
could not, however, forget about the issues the paper dealt with, and every
time I have returned in the past fifteen years to a consideration of autobiography as a literary mode—which is to say very frequently, whether in seminar or lecture or some other forum—I have found myself trying to sort
out once again the tangled and fascinating, dual and symbiotic matter of

memory and narrative. Each chapter of the present book I have conceived of as a more or less freestanding essay—a kind of meditation on the subject of memory-and-narrative—woven according to its own pattern from the thematic material of the whole, all of the chapters more or less equal in weight if not the same in length nor alike in texture or tone. The ways of memory are many (and often devious), and the ways of narrative no less so, and this protean quality in the subject demands an equally protean response in thinking and writing about it.

While each of the chapter-essays has its own shape, intention, and terminology, there nevertheless lies behind them all and flows through every one of them a self-conscious narrative of history and tradition, giving a shape to the whole that has been in my mind from the beginning. As in the paper mentioned, whenever I have adopted a historical approach to memory and narrative, considering how the one and the other and the relationship between them might have changed over time, it has come to be inevitable that I should see Augustine as the initiator of a long tradition of life-narration in the Western world that now finds its conclusion in Beckett's late fictions. Murphy's response to Neary's claim that "all life is figure and ground" is to say that all life is "but wandering to find home." Home for the present tale, when it is not with Augustine in the fourth-fifth century, is situated in modernism, postmodernism, and the late twentieth century; Augustine and Beckett thus anchor my story at either end. To arrive at the later home requires leaving the earlier one (not leaving it behind, however), and it entails much wandering between. Lying like a great dragon well on this side of the Middle Ages, indeed just outside the gate of modernism, and altogether crucial to whatever it was that happened to memory and narrative in the sixteen centuries from Augustine to Beckett, is the implausible but inescapable figure of Jean-Jacques Rousseau. Many other writers must be passed over or touched on very lightly in this study, but anyone who would trace a line of memory-and-narrative from Augustine to Beckett can do so only by way of Rousseau; thus the lengthy second chapter, "Jean-Jacques Rousseau and the Crisis of Narrative Memory." Rousseau is the true center of it all: without his achievement as the middle, Augustine's would not be the beginning, Beckett's would not be the end. Lest the line of tradition snap through being stretched too far, I have inserted a pair of interludes, one between Augustine and Rousseau, the other between Rousseau and Beckett, both of them drawing on the intriguing life-writing project devised and executed by Giambattista Vico. Though he has never been accorded the significance as a life-writer that both Augustine and Rousseau have received, only Vico, in my judgment, is capable of providing theoretical and practical justification for understanding this long tradition of writing as a single enterprise, *corso e ricorso,* universal and individual, containing all history and of profoundly human design. In performing this role in the unfolding drama, Vico adopts some crucial ideas from St. Augustine, makes some observations of eerie applicability to Rousseau, and anticipates where Beckett (who displays a deep and shrewd knowledge of Vico in his early essay, "Dante . . . Bruno . Vico . . Joyce") will come out in the twentieth century.

Chapters I and II and the two interludes provide the grounding (to echo Neary again) for what I think of as the second half of the book, chapters III, IV, and V, where I take up the problem of memory-and-narrative in a variety of twentieth-century contexts, all with specific regard to Samuel Beckett's work. Chapter III, taking its title—*Not I*—from Beckett's short play of 1972, looks at the disappearance of the subject, both grammatical and thematic, in a largish group of modernist writers—R. L. Stevenson, Henry Adams, Gertrude Stein, Ronald Fraser, Maxine Hong Kingston, Richard Wright, Christa Wolf, Mary McCarthy, Samuel Beckett, Nathalie Sarraute, Primo Levi, Virginia Woolf—of whom, for my purposes, Beckett still remains the supreme representative. Chapter IV brings together three figures—Beckett, of course, also Alberto Giacometti and Franz Kafka—whose work in and around narrative I take to be definitive for the twentieth century. Chapter V is what I there term "a case study of twentieth-century literary memory across the whole body of Beckett's work," supplemented by reference to the recent "memory work" coming from a variety of scientific disciplines.

Two further points I think it important to make about the approach adopted to the material in *Memory and Narrative.* It has long been my conviction that theory of life-writing is best derived from major instances of the mode rather than from interchange with other critics. This judgment is generated neither by disrespect for such criticism nor by ignorance of it. If one thinks of how much St. Augustine has to say about narrative and how much about memory, even as he practices the one and exercises the other, one will quickly conclude that there is God's plenty of theory here without searching elsewhere for it. The same of Rousseau and of Beckett, neither of whom conceptualizes or theorizes quite as readily and openly as Augustine, but both of whom offer material for the purpose in quite as full supply as Augustine himself. The second point, closely related to this first one and also to my sense that the life-writing project is an all-encompassing endeavor, is that if I expect my three comprehensively representative figures to sustain the massive historical and theoretical weight put on them, it can only be by bringing to bear evidence spread out across their entire bodies of work. It simply would not do in these circumstances to confine myself to Augustine's *Confessions,* Rousseau's *Confessions,* and Beckett's *Company,* for each of these takes its place in a much larger history and in a vast network of texts without which we cannot understand what may admittedly be, in each case, the central piece of life-writing. There are at least half a dozen other major texts necessary to our reading of Augustine's *Confessions,* texts that have gone quite unattended by students of autobiography; and similarly I believe that time and again a crucial mistake has been made in focusing nearly all discussion of Rousseau's life-writing on the *Confessions* to the comparative neglect of the *Reveries* and the utter neglect of the *Dialogues.* The *Dialogues* could quite well be taken to be the single most important text in the history I am tracing, yet with one or two honorable exceptions it has received no notice at all from critics. And while *Company* (or, as I argue in chapter V, *Stirrings Still*) may be the culmination of Beckett's efforts, we will get no true sense of that culmination without an awareness of everything going before it (and here I mean to say everything before it in Beckett's work and in the tradition). This is the very principle on which Beckett's oeuvre is founded; likewise with his two great predecessors. A corollary to my practice of deriving theory from texts of life-writing and at the same time expanding the meaning of text to include a whole body of work is my resolve to discuss issues of memory and narrative only in terms historically appropriate to the time of writing. Thus I have resisted, as being both unnecessary and unprofitable, any temptation to transport recent discussions of memory, for example, back to a reading of Augustine or Rousseau.

If, in my sense of it, there is a kind of inevitability about the presence of Augustine, Rousseau, and Beckett in this study, I must admit that, on the contrary, there is something rather arbitrary in my choice of the dozen modernist writers named as supplementary to Beckett. What I mean is that virtually any writer of the century might have been chosen, with nearly equal validity, instead of those I have settled upon. (With regard to the most glaring omission, I will say only what Anatole France said: "Life is short, and M. Proust is very long." I decided at the very beginning of this project not to mention Proust a single time, for if I had let him in the door at all what I should have had to say about him would have turned out to be almost as long as *À la recherche du temps perdu* itself.) But that so many contemporary authors offer themselves as obvious choices is part of the point: that an agonized search for self, through the mutually reflexive acts of memory and narrative, accompanied by the haunting fear that it is impossible from the beginning but also impossible to give over, is the very emblem of our time.

Although I have in the past written frequently about autobiography as a literary genre, I have never been very comfortable doing it, primarily because I believe that if one is to speak relevantly of a genre one has first of all to define it, and I have never met a definition of autobiography that I could really like. Looking back from the present moment, it strikes me that there has been a gradual alteration—an evolution or devolution as one may prefer—in the nature of life-writing or autobiography over the past sixteen centuries, moving from a focus on "bios," or the course of a lifetime, to focus on "autos," the self writing and being written; and this shift, which one sees occurring unaware in Rousseau to become finally established and pervasive in the twentieth century, has introduced a number of narrative dilemmas requiring quite different strategies on the writers' part. In the course of *Memory and Narrative* I call the kind of writing I am looking at by various names—confessions, autobiography, memoirs, periautography (although I deny myself use of this designation until it becomes historically available with Vico), autography (H. Porter Abbott's term for what Beckett does), and—the most frequently employed term—life-writing. I confess that from among these terms I have a special fondness for "periautography," which to my ear has a sound that is both strange and familiar, both ancient and new. "Periautography" was the term used by Count Gian Artico di Porcía when he issued the "Proposal to the Scholars of Italy" calling for the scholars to write their intellectual memoirs for the educational benefit of the young; it was this proposal that elicited the book that we have in English translation as *The Autobiography of Giambattista Vico.* What I like about the term "periautography," which would mean "writing about or around the self," is precisely its *in*definition and lack of generic rigor, its comfortably loose fit and generous adaptability, and the same for "life-writing" (though the term in itself seems to me less attractive than "periautography"). As I write this, I am reminded that I said much the same thing about autobiography in the preface to *Metaphors of Self,* my first book on the subject. In the twenty-five years since *Metaphors of Self* there has been a flood of publications on autobiography, books and articles that have undoubtedly increased and sharpened our understanding of this mode of writing but that have also, to a degree, fixed it in place as a literary genre with rules, conventions, expectations. As I reflect back, in the manner of life-writing itself, I realize what I had not been aware of when I began *Memory and Narrative* and certainly was unaware of when I wrote *Metaphors of Self:* that *Metaphors of Self* was the beginning—as three or four books and numerous articles have been the middle—of something that has led to *Memory and Narrative* as its natural conclusion. And I am satisfied that it should be so. For by whatever name we call the literature—autobiography, life-writing, or periautography—there exists a particularly intriguing kind of writing to be considered for which any one of the terms mentioned might be a fair enough designation, the crucial tactic, in my view, being not to insist on strict definitions and rigid lines of demarcation. I have always felt, and continue to feel, that it is best to think of what I am doing as exploratory in nature rather than definitive. It is in that spirit that I have written *Memory and Narrative*.

I

MEMORY AND THE NARRATIVE IMPERATIVE

St. Augustine and Samuel Beckett Ensemble

ESTRAGON: All the dead voices.

VLADIMIR: They all speak at once.

ESTRAGON: Each one to itself. . . .

VLADIMIR: What do they say?

ESTRAGON: They talk about their lives.

VLADIMIR: To have lived is not enough for them.

ESTRAGON: They have to talk about it.

Waiting for Godot

"Lord, since eternity is yours, can you be ignorant of what I say to you?" St. Augustine asks at the outset of book 11 of the *Confessions;* and being certain that all that takes place in time is eternally present to the mind of God, Augustine goes on to ponder the next logical question about the act he has been engaged in throughout the first ten books of the *Confessions:* "Why then do I put before you in order the stories of so many things?"[1] We all know the kinds of stories Augustine has been putting before God in order, stories, like the one of stealing pears, that have little moment in themselves but that, echoing events in both the New Testament and the Old Testament, reverberate in significance far beyond their apparent triviality. Shorn of Augustine's theological terminology and the confessional context, this question about narrative motives and intentions is essentially the same question the various narrators of Samuel Beckett's fiction and the characters of his drama ask over and over again. What is the impetus, Beck-

---

1. *The Confessions of St. Augustine,* trans. Rex Warner (New York: Mentor, 1963), 11.1, 257; hereafter cited by book and chapter numbers as *Conf.,* with page numbers from this edition.

1

ett's different personae ask, why the compulsion to begin and rebegin, all over again and incessantly, these futile stories of futility, in search of something that though it may be desired cannot even be named? "And ever murmuring," as the anonymous voice of *The Unnamable* puts it, "my old stories, my old story, as if it were the first time."[2] Augustine's "Why then do I put before you in order the stories of so many things?" becomes in Beckett, "Why should I try to put in order, time after time, the stories of so few things, my old stories, my old story, as if it were the first time?" With Beckett, the impulse to narrate, which could be and was given rational analysis and logical explanation by Augustine, has become irrational and illogical, compulsive, obsessional, repetitive, unwilled and often unwanted but not to be denied.

The entire justification, validation, necessity, and indeed exemplary instance of writing one's life, of finding the words that signify the self and its history, are offered to us for the first time (according to my narrative) in the *Confessions;* by the time of *Company,* the justification and validation established by Augustine are long since vanished and all that remains of the Augustinian legacy, drawn on so many times by so many writers from the fifth to the twentieth century, is the necessity of performing the narrative act without a first person in sight to perform it or to do the remembering that precedes, accompanies, and follows the narrating. That necessity, however, has lost nothing of its compulsive force. "Strange notion," the narrator of *The Unnamable* says, "Strange notion in any case, and eminently open to suspicion, that of a task to be performed, before one can be at rest. Strange task, which consists in speaking of oneself" (*Trilogy,* 285). Strange as the task may be, however, the last words of this exercise in life-writing confirm the necessity of carrying it out. "I don't know," as the narrator says,

> I don't know, that's all words, never wake, all words, there's nothing else, you must go on, that's all I know, they're going to stop, I know that well, I can feel it, they're going to abandon me, it will be the silence, for a moment, a good few moments, or it will be mine, the lasting one, that didn't last, that still lasts, it will be I, you must go on, I can't go on, you must go on, I'll go on, you must say words, as long as there are any, until they find me, until they say me, strange pain, strange sin, you must go on, perhaps it's done already, perhaps they have said me already, perhaps they have carried me to the threshold of my story, before the door that opens on my story, that would

---

2. *The Beckett Trilogy: Molloy, Malone Dies, The Unnamable* (London: Picador, 1979), 277, hereafter cited as *Trilogy.*

surprise me, if it opens, it will be I, it will be the silence, where I am, I don't know, I'll never know, in the silence you don't know, you must go on, I can't go on, I'll go on. (*Trilogy*, 381–82)

But let me return to Augustine's *Confessions* to establish the beginning of the historical, philosophical, psychological process that issues finally in Beckett's "I don't know, I'll never know, in the silence you don't know, you must go on, I can't go on, I'll go on."

When I say that the justification, validation, and necessity of writing one's life are established in the *Confessions,* I have principally in mind a passage in book 11 in which Augustine describes what happens when he recites a psalm that he knows. This absolutely crucial passage on narrative comes after the equally crucial disquisition on memory in book 10 and the twin meditation on time in book 11, toward the end of which Augustine writes: "It is now, however, perfectly clear that neither the future nor the past are in existence, and that it is incorrect to say that there are three times—past, present, and future. Though one might perhaps say: 'There are three times—a present of things past, a present of things present, and a present of things future.' For these three do exist in the mind, and I do not see them anywhere else: the present time of things past is memory; the present time of things present is sight; the present time of things future is expectation" (*Conf.,* 11.20, 273). That "one might perhaps say" that there exists such a temporal hybrid as "a present of things past" follows from Augustine's exalted conception of memory, and it is what grounds his ideas about narrative in general and about life-narrative in particular. "Suppose," Augustine says of the narrative act and the way it realizes itself in time,

> Suppose I am about to recite a psalm which I know. Before I begin, my expectation is extended over the whole psalm. But once I have begun, whatever I pluck off from it and let fall into the past enters the province of my memory. So the life of this action of mine is extended in two directions— toward my memory, as regards what I have recited, and toward my expectation, as regards what I am about to recite. But all the time my attention is present and through it what was future passes on its way to become past. And as I proceed further and further with my recitation, so the expectation grows shorter and the memory grows longer, until all the expectation is finished at the point when the whole of this action is over and has passed into the memory. And what is true of the whole psalm is also true of every part of the psalm and of every syllable in it. The same holds good for any longer action, of which the psalm may be only a part. It is true also of the whole of a man's life, of which all of his actions are parts. (*Conf.,* 11.28, 282)

Augustine conceives of memory according to various formulations at different places in the *Confessions*. Here he imagines it as a great reservoir, which provides the matter to be recited or narrated and which receives it back again, but no doubt altered and enriched by the process of reciting, when the recitation/narration is completed. Beckett imagines very much the same process, though with two reservoirs or vessels, when, in his little book on Proust, he writes, "The individual is the seat of a constant process of decantation, decantation from the vessel containing the fluid of future time, sluggish, pale and monochrome, to the vessel containing the fluid of past time, agitated and multicoloured by the phenomena of its hours."[3] The process as Augustine (again) describes it is perfectly circular, and there is a point before recitation begins and after it ends when expectation and memory coincide and are identical. A psalm one knows and can recite—knows "by heart," as we say—is the object of expectation, but, to be known, it must also be secure in memory; likewise, "at the point when the whole of this action is over and has passed into the memory," it immediately becomes available again, as a whole, for rerecitation, and expectation is thus, once more, "extended over the whole psalm."

It may seem too casually dropped in to bear such significance, but surely the final quoted sentence—"It is true also of the whole of a man's life, of which all of his actions are parts"—is intended as justification for the procedure of the entire volume of the *Confessions*. It was not at all obvious to Beckett that the whole of a man's life is narratable as the whole of a psalm is recitable. "[B]ut an instant, an hour, and so on," the Unnamable wonders, "how can they be represented, a life, how could that be made clear to me, here, in the dark . . ." (*Trilogy*, 407). But let us consider what the narrative procedure is according to the Augustinian passage and what it has been for the first ten books of the *Confessions*. In the moment of reciting or narrating, expectation and memory lie on one side and the other of the present, on one side and the other of the enunciation of syllables, words, sentences, and larger syntactic units. It is as if the elements of narrative pass from expectation, which is allied with the future (what *will be* narrated), across the laser beam of the present (what *is being* narrated), to fall again into memory, allied with the past (what *has been* narrated). But the recitation or narrative once over, there is a merger of expectation and memory or a reversal of the two so that what fell into memory is now there in expectation for another act of recitation/narration. And Augustine clearly states

---

3. Samuel Beckett, *Proust and Three Dialogues with Georges Duthuit* (London: John Calder, 1965), 15; hereafter cited as *Duthuit*.

that the whole of a man's life may be held in this reservoir that is memory/expectation and will there be available for recitation and rerecitation, for narrating and renarrating, as that which is to be narrated is drawn from the future to pass across the beam of present narrating thence to fall into the reservoir of that which has been narrated . . . which will once again present itself for narrating as that which is now in the past as memory shows its other face as that which exists in the future as expectation. But all of this, we should remember, like all of Beckett's late narratives, takes place in the mind, and we should be careful not to speak, as I have just done, of past and future but rather of "a present of things past, a present of things present, and a present of things future." The Augustinian act of remembering and narrating is figured in *Company* in only slightly altered terminology when we are told that there is "no tense in the dark in that dim mind. All at once over and in train and to come."[4] The "dim mind" of *Company* is the twentieth-century version of Augustinian mind where all takes place, where past, present, and future exist as the present of time past, the present of time present, and the present of time future; and in that dim mind, too, occurs the Augustinian act of narration or recitation where all is held in expectation, then in recitation, finally in memory.

This whole process figures in Augustine's text frequently as pairs of verbs—*recordor et confiteor, recolo et narro*—as if they were bound each to each by an internal, unbreakable bond of identicalness: remember-and-confess, recall-and-narrate, recollect-and-tell. The paired verbs serve to suggest a reverse mirror likeness in the two activities; or perhaps one might better say that the verbs suggest a single activity of dual dynamic, recalling a story backward and telling it forward. "A voice comes to one in the dark. Imagine" (*Company,* 7). So begins the Beckettian process of remembering-and-narrating in *Company,* in some ways strikingly like the process described in book 11 of Augustine's *Confessions* and in other ways, of course, strikingly unlike that process both as described in book 11 and as realized in the first nine books of the *Confessions*. "To one on his back in the dark," the narrative of *Company* continues. "Only a small part of what is said can be verified. As for example when he hears, You are on your back in the dark. Then he must acknowledge the truth of what is said. But by far the greater part of what is said cannot be verified" (*Company,* 7). Why is it that most of what the voice says to the one in the dark is unverifiable? Presumably because it comes as the voice of memory, speaking of past events that cannot certainly be connected with present being. Memory, if it is truly memory according

4. Samuel Beckett, *Company* (New York: Grove, 1980), 34.

to the Augustinian understanding, should be the guarantor of identity and
continuity of being across time, the only liaison—but an unbroken and
fully capable liaison all the same—between past experience and present
consciousness. Thus the claim Augustine makes for memory, a claim that
Company calls radically into doubt:

> . . . by far the greater part of what is said cannot be verified. As for example
> when he hears, You first saw the light on such and such a day. Sometimes
> the two are combined as for example, You first saw the light on such and
> such a day and now you are on your back in the dark. A device perhaps from
> the incontrovertibility of the one to win credence for the other. That then is
> the proposition. To one on his back in the dark a voice tells of a past. With
> occasional allusion to a present and more rarely to a future. . . . (*Company*,
> 7–8)

Were Augustine the one on his back in the dark, he would not admit that
what the voice says to him cannot be verified; on the contrary, he feels
himself fully present to himself in an irrefragable continuity, and the past
of which the voice tells would be verifiable (perhaps "ratifiable" would be
a more precise term) by his full apprehension of "a present of things past,
a present of things present, and a present of things future."

It is ingenious of the Beckettian voice that, in this earliest reference to
events past, it should choose the event that, it is said, no one is able to
remember, the event of birth (ironically enough, Beckett implies several
times that *he* remembers being born, or if not Beckett then fictional characters who clearly stand in for him claim to remember their birth). Autobiographers and other life-narrators, of course, frequently begin with this unre-
membered experience: "I was born on such and such a date in such and
such a place. . . ."[5] What the narrative of *Company* succeeds in doing by
beginning with this absolutely unverifiable event is not only to cast great
doubt on everything else the voice tells of a past but to render impossible
the assertion of *I* in the recalling of these unrecallable events. If you cannot
say ". . . born on such and such a day," you cannot say "I" either: if you

---

5. The French way of saying "I was born"—"Je suis né"—, as Germaine Brée has
remarked, gets around this problem of narrating the unrememberable event very deftly,
though it also introduces some complexities into the situation that the philosophically
and linguistically simpler English locution does not have. "Je suis né à Genève en 1712
d'Isaac Rousseau Citoyen et de Susanne Bernard Citoyenne." Thus Rousseau's narrative
brings him into the world, but is he recording a historical birth or is it a birth into narrative that occurs only as a simultaneous consequence of the act of writing the words "Je suis
né . . ."?

cannot remember the event, you cannot narrate out of the continuity of being that *I* implies. Augustine gets around this as best he can by writing, not of his birth to be sure but of his early infancy, "Then all I knew was how to suck, to be content with bodily pleasure, and to be discontented with bodily pain; that was all. Afterward I began to smile; first when I was asleep and later when awake. So, at least, I have been told and I can easily believe it, since we see the same thing in other babies. I cannot of course remember what happened in my own case" (*Conf.*, 1.6, 21). The *I* can perfectly well hold here because it is to later, verifiable experience that Augustine appeals for his account of these unverifiable events of his own past—"A device," the narrator of *Company*, who sees through this sort of thing, says, "perhaps from the incontrovertibility of the one to win credence for the other." Here is the "device" as Augustine employs it: "This, I have learned, is what babies are like, so far as I have been able to observe them; and they in their ignorance have shown me that I myself was like this better than my nurses who knew that I was" (*Conf.*, 1.6, 22). It must be acknowledged, however, that "by far the greater part of what is said"— by the voice, by Augustine, by any life-narrator—"cannot be verified." Ratified it may be, perhaps, but not verified.

Even ratification, however, which would require saying "I remember," thus implying a belief in the continuity of being covered by the use of *I* and a belief also in the capacity of memory to sustain this continuity of being, seems impossible in *Company*, for the one lying (and the reader can never be free of the double meaning of "lying") on his back in the dark "cannot but sometimes wonder if it is indeed to and of him the voice is speaking" (*Company*, 9). Is the past the voice tells of the past of the one lying in the dark? Are these his memories or someone else's memories? We never know. What ecstasy it would be—"What an addition to company that would be!"—we are told in *Company*, if he to whom the voice speaks were one day able to say, "Yes I remember. That was I. That was I then" (*Company*, 27). But Beckett, or his creature, a "devised deviser devising it all for company" (*Company*, 64), will not permit this easy resolution, this easy claim of remembering and of a secure identity. What makes all this so anguishing is that in any piece of life-writing of the type of the *Confessions* and *Company* (and I maintain that they *are* of the same type) reference— to take up the prickly question of referentiality that properly troubles critics of this kind of writing—is never to events of the past but to memories of those events. "The present of things past is memory," as Augustine says, but how are we situated if memory is so uncertain or unstable, both epistemologically and ontologically, that we do not even know if a given set of memories is ours or someone else's? To think of autobiography's referentiality as pertaining not to events of the past but to memories of those events solves a lot of problems arising in a good many texts, but Beckett, like other writers of our time, has altered the terms and raised the stakes of the wager by calling into doubt, in the most radical way, memory's capacity to establish a relationship to our past and hence a relationship to ourselves grown out of the past.

The *Confessions* and *Company* are alike in that they are both narratives about the act of remembering and also narratives about the act of narrating. Augustine, like Beckett, tells the story of himself telling the story of himself telling the story of his life. For the process of remembering-and-narrating as Augustine describes it in the passage I have quoted on reciting a psalm there is a perfect modern analogy not available to Augustine in his time but made full use of by Beckett: the tape recorder and player, an analogy that becomes the literal vehicle of *Krapp's Last Tape*. In that short play Krapp, "a wearish old man" of sixty-nine, listens to a tape he made on his thirty-ninth birthday ("Thirty-nine today, sound as a bell, apart from my old weakness, and intellectually I have now every reason to suspect at the . . . *(hesitates)* . . . crest of the wave—or thereabouts")[6]—a tape he prepared to make thirty years earlier by listening rather mockingly, as he is listening now, to a tape made in a yet earlier year. "Just been listening to an old year," the thirty-nine-year-old voice on the tape says to the "wearish old man," "passages at random. I did not check in the book, but it must be at least ten or twelve years ago" (*Krapp,* 218). Each time that he prepares, at age twenty-seven or twenty-nine, thirty-nine, and now at sixty-nine (and there appear to be many more tapes in between since the tape made at thirty-nine is spool five from box three), to reflect back on the previous year and previous years, Krapp, in order to assist himself in extending expectation over the whole of his life, listens to the narrated episodes of his life pass from the spool of expectation on the left across the head of the tape player, which corresponds to the present of narration, to be taken up by the spool of memory on the right—which, when rewound, becomes once again the spool of expectation. The analogy to the Augustinian recitation of a psalm—"true also of the whole of a man's life"—is quite exact.

What the sixty-nine-year-old Krapp hears on the tape made by his

6. *Krapp's Last Tape,* in *The Complete Dramatic Works* (London: Faber and Faber, 1986), 217; hereafter cited as *Krapp*.

thirty-nine-year-old incarnation and his latter-day reaction to it are also, mutatis mutandis, rather Augustinian: "Just been listening to an old year, passages at random. . . . These old P.M.s are gruesome, but I often find them—*(Krapp switches off, broods, switches on)*—a help before embarking on a new . . . *(hesitates)* . . . retrospect. Hard to believe I was ever that young whelp. The voice! Jesus! And the aspirations! *(Brief laugh in which Krapp joins.)* And the resolutions! *(Brief laugh in which Krapp joins.)* To drink less, in particular. *(Brief laugh of Krapp alone)*" (*Krapp*, 218). Is not the laughter of the two Krapps at the very young Krapp, succeeded by the "brief laugh of Krapp alone" at both of the earlier Krapps, rather similar to this cele- brated passage on chastity in the *Confessions?* "But I, wretched young man that I was—even more wretched at the beginning of my youth—had begged you for chastity and said: 'Make me chaste and continent, but not yet.' I was afraid that you might hear me too soon and cure me too soon . . ." (*Conf.,* 8.7, 173–74). Whether or not one hears the same kind of mocking laughter in these two passages, there can be little question about the similarity in retrospective reflection cast back over retrospective reflec- tion. For Beckett's character as for the Augustinian confessant, the making of earlier tapes of recollection or the recall of earlier acts of retrospection are made a part of the twin acts of memory and narration in the present, so that memorial acts surround earlier memorial acts, which surround earlier memorial acts, which . . . as far back as memory reaches. Is this not the nature of the autobiographical act as established by Augustine in the *Confes- sions* and as practiced by Beckett in his late fictions-cum-dramas-cum-life- writings—a perpetually renewed attempt to find language adequate to ren- dering the self and its experience, an attempt that includes within itself all earlier attempts and that draws up behind it all these earlier attempts in this latest quest? At the beginning of *The Unnamable* the narrator imagines that all of Beckett's earlier creations and projections—Murphy, Molloy, Moran, Malone, Macmann, etc.—are present in and for this summary narrative: "To tell the truth," he says, "I believe they are all here, at least from Murphy on, I believe we are all here . . ." (*Trilogy*, 268). And we must suppose that for both of them, the Augustinian protagonist and the Beckettian one, the dramatized confessant and the dramatic character, the act of remembering- and-narrating, of recalling-and-confessing, will go on as long as life contin- ues. As Krapp puts it: "Ah finish your booze now and get to your bed. Go on with this drivel in the morning. Or leave it at that. *(Pause.)* Leave it at that. *(Pause.)* Lie propped up in the dark—and wander. Be again in the dingle on a Christmas Eve, gathering holly, the red-berried. *(Pause.)*

Be again on Croghan on a Sunday morning, in the haze, with the bitch, stop and listen to the bells. *(Pause.)* And so on. *(Pause.)* Be again, be again. *(Pause.)* All that old misery. *(Pause.)* Once wasn't enough for you" *(Krapp,* 223). So it is that Estragon responds to Vladimir's observation that "To have lived is not enough for them" with "They have to talk about it": to live a life is not enough; it must be narrated, even compulsively, obsessively narrated: "Once wasn't enough for you."

The narrative imperative across the centuries seems clear enough. There remains the question of how a life is to be narrated. Augustine, we recall, speaks of telling "in order [*ex ordine*] the stories of so many things." What is this order for Augustine's stories and how is it established? He repeats the phrase at the beginning of chapter 2 of book 11:

> But my pen's tongue will never have strength to declare all your exhortations and your terrors, the consolations and the guidance by which you brought me to become a preacher of your word to your people and a dispenser of your sacrament. And suppose I have the strength to declare all this in order [*ex ordine*], yet the drops of my time are too precious, and for long I have been full of a burning desire to *meditate in Thy law* and to confess to you both my knowledge and my lack of skill in it, the first beginnings of the light you shed on me and the remnants of my darkness, until my weakness be swallowed up in strength.

Now, it would be easy to imagine that *ex ordine* has a simple chronological significance and that not only the "plot" of a life-story but the memory that recalls it has the pattern (or nonpattern) E. M. Forster describes as that of the most primitive kind of fiction: "and then . . . and then . . . and then." Indeed, I have at times claimed that the narrator of a life-story remembers in reverse chronological order as he or she has lived and narrates in forward chronological order. I am not sure this is altogether wrong, but I do feel that the matter is considerably more complicated than this rather simple formulation would suggest.

Much earlier in the *Confessions,* when Augustine is engaged in recounting *ex ordine* the stories of so many things, he gives a hint of what the source and nature of the order sought and discovered (or invented) might be: "sine me, obsecro, et da mihi circuire praesenti memoria praeteritos circuitus erroris mei, et immolare tibi hostiam iubilationis." Rex Warner, whose translation I have been quoting, renders the passage thus: "Allow me this, I beg, and grant me the power to survey in my memory now all those wanderings of my error in the past and to offer unto Thee the sacrifice of rejoicing" *(Conf.,* 4.1, 69). This is interesting, as it emphasizes the root meaning of *erro,* "to wander, to stray," so that we have "wanderings of my error [or of my wandering] in the past," but it fails to capture the wordplay that repeats *circuire* ("to go round in a curve") in *circuitus* ("a going round in a circle, circuit, revolution") and that suggests linguistically the isomorphic relationship between the act of memory and the act of narrative. Peter Brown comes closer to capturing the pun of the original in his translation: "Allow me, I beseech You, grant me to wind round and round in my present memory the spirals of my errors."[7] For Augustine, the winding round and round in present memory is the precise linguistic and structural analogue of the going round in a circle of errors of the past, and a narrative that would be adequate to the experience of present memory as well as the experience of past erring must display that one same structure that is responsible, according to Augustine, for the continuity of identity between past experience and present memory of that experience. Moreover, a Latin dictionary will tell us that in rhetorical terms (Cicero is cited for this usage) *circuitus* signifies "a period"; and for a rhetorician of Augustine's eminence this would suggest that rhetoric—specifically the rhetoric of narrative —is fully capable of rendering equally the *circuitus* of past errant experience and the *circuitus* of present imitative memory.

That Beckett, too, wishes desperately and strains mightily to achieve this same sort of equivalence of experience, memory of experience, and what I have just termed the rhetoric of narrative is, I think, unquestionable: "you must say words, as long as there are any, until they find me, until they say me." Tom Driver, in an account of a conversation he had with Beckett in Paris, quotes Beckett to this effect: "One cannot speak anymore of being [as, one might interject, Augustine could do], one must speak only of the mess." As an artist, Beckett went on to say, "one can only speak of what is in front of him, and that now is simply the mess." Then, according to Driver's account, Beckett

> began to speak about the tension in art between the mess and form. Until recently, art has withstood the pressure of chaotic things. It has held them at bay. It realized that to admit them was to jeopardize form. "How could the mess be admitted, because it appears to be the very opposite of form and therefore destructive of the very thing that art holds itself to be?" But now we can keep it out no longer, because we have come into a time when "it invades our experience at every moment. It is there and it must be allowed in. . . . What I am saying does not mean that there will henceforth be no form in art. It only means that there will be new form, and that this form will be of such a type that it admits the chaos and does not try to say that the

7. Peter Brown, *Augustine of Hippo: A Biography* (London: Faber and Faber, 1967), 164.

chaos is really something else. The form and the chaos remain separate. The
latter is not reduced to the former. That is why the form itself becomes a
preoccupation, because it exists as a problem separate from the material it
accommodates. To find a form that accommodates the mess, that is the task
of the artist now."[8]

The belief that the chaos of experience must not be reduced simply to the
form of the artwork, but rather that the two should necessarily "remain
separate," in a very nearly intolerable tension and antagonism, has various
consequences for Beckett's repeated and renewed attempts at narrating a
life. First of all (for my purposes), there is the tremendous difference from
Augustine in narrative means that this belief entails. Augustine, we recall,
says of the act of recitation/narration, "And what is true of the whole psalm
is also true of every part of the psalm and of every syllable in it. The same
holds good for any longer action, of which the psalm may be only a part.
It is true also of the whole of a man's life, of which all of his actions are
parts." For Augustine, the form of a life-narrative did not at all, as Beckett
puts it, exist "as a problem separate from the material it accommodates."
On the contrary, the form and the material it accommodates are, for Augustine, one and the same, and they are both thoroughly traditional—one
might almost say *conventional,* if one thinks, for example, of the account of
Augustine's conversion, which has within it echoes of earlier conversions
(St. Paul's, of course, but also intratextual conversion accounts: Simplicianus's tale of Victorinus and Ponticianus's embedding of several conversions within a single narrative) and which, in its turn, provided the conventions according to which conversions would be narrated for centuries to
come.

A second consequence of accepting Beckett's argument that the task
of the contemporary artist is "to find a form that accommodates the mess"
would be that for a writer in the modern world there could be no security
in the set of narrative conventions that Augustine partly accepted from previous life-narrators but mostly established for future ones. To seek a form
that accommodates the mess will mean obeying in the strictest way the
modernist injunction to "make it new," refusing not only any traditional
narrative conventions that may exist but also any momentary formal successes the individual writer may have enjoyed in previous attempts, and
this Beckett unquestionably did in the astonishing series of works of the

8. Tom Driver, "Beckett by the Madeleine," *Columbia University Forum* 4 (summer
1961): 23.

last forty years or so of his life: *Molloy, Malone Dies, Waiting for Godot, The Unnamable, Endgame, Krapp's Last Tape, How It Is, Happy Days, Not I, Company, Ill Seen Ill Said,* and *Worstward Ho,* each a renewed attempt "to find a form that accommodates the mess," neither easing nor falsifying the situation that demands the narrative effort and the search for the accommodating form. And yet, while Beckett certainly seeks an ever-new form, subtly adapted to the mess in front of him, and while he rejects those conventions of narrative we might think of as Augustinian, he works to an impossible end—impossible as he himself sees it—that is precisely the end to which Augustine worked and to which, as Augustine saw it, he could well hope to attain. Nor is Augustine without formal lessons for the twentieth-century writer, at least as far as Beckett has been concerned. Harold Hobson describes a pair of conversations he had with Beckett at the time of the production of *Waiting for Godot* in London during which Beckett declined to be drawn into controversies about the meaning of his play while being altogether willing to talk about what he called "the shape of ideas." Questioned about the difficulties Estragon has with his boots in the play ("One of them would go on comfortably, and the other would not go on at all," Hobson explains), Beckett responded, "One of Estragon's feet is blessed, and the other is damned. The boot won't go on the foot that is damned; and it will go on the foot that is not. It is like the two thieves on the cross." This brings an expression of surprise from Hobson, who has just been told that Beckett long ago lost any faith he might once have had:

> "And yet the thieves on the cross interest you [Hobson says]. Vladimir is troubled to account for one of them being lost and the other saved. How can you be so preoccupied with this when you do not believe in salvation?"
>
> It was at this point that Beckett became eager, excited. His sharp, rugged face leaned over the table. "I am interested in the shape of ideas even if I do not believe them. There is a wonderful sentence in Augustine. I wish I could remember the Latin. It is even finer in Latin than in English. 'Do not despair; one of the thieves was saved. Do not presume; one of the thieves was damned.' That sentence has a wonderful shape. It is the shape that matters."[9]

This "wonderful sentence" (which, incidentally, is much easier to find in Beckett than in Augustine), or rather the passage in Luke to which it refers,

---

9. Harold Hobson, "Samuel Beckett: Dramatist of the Year," *International Theatre Annual,* no. 1 (1956): 153.

is, as Hobson remarks, central to the dramatization of the mess in *Waiting for Godot,* where Didi, after musing, "One of the thieves was saved. . . . It's a reasonable percentage," goes on to worry that, although all four of the evangelists "were there—or thereabouts" at the time of the crucifixion, only one of the four mentions that one of the thieves was saved.[10] The

10. I remark above that the "wonderful sentence" is easier to find in Beckett than in Augustine, and indeed considerable search in Augustine's writings has failed to turn up precisely this sentence. It reads as if it were from a sermon rather than from such works as the *Confessions, The City of God, On the Trinity,* or any of Augustine's polemical writings. In fact, Augustine does treat of the relevant passage in Luke (24.32–43) in a number of his sermons, usually in the context of a discussion of whether salvation is possible through faith without baptism. Augustine makes the point more than once that the one thief, although he had not been baptized, was saved because what he said clearly indicated belief and faith on his part. In one sermon—but with a somewhat different inflection—Augustine touches on the issue that troubles Didi: "Sed forte aliqui vestrum nesciunt quod dixi de latrone, non audiendo passionem secundum omnes Evangelistas. Iste enim evangelista Lucas narravit quod dico. Quia duo latrones crucifixi sunt cum Christo, dixit hoc et Matthaeus: sed unus eorum latronum quia insultavit Domino, et alter eorum quia credidit in Christum, Matthaeus non dixit, Lucas dixit" (sermo CCXXXII, "In diebus Paschalibus," *Sancti Aurelii Augustini . . . Opera* [Naples: Bibliothecae Litterariae, 1854], vol. 8, p. 1095D). In *Waiting for Godot* the Lucan passage elicits the following dialogue, which sounds like a meditation on and revision of Augustine's sermonic adjurations:

> VLADIMIR: And yet . . . *(pause)* . . . how is it—this is not boring you I hope—how is it that of the four Evangelists only one speaks of a thief being saved. The four of them were there—or thereabouts—and only one speaks of a thief being saved. . . . One out of four. Of the other three two don't mention any thieves at all and the third says that both of them abused him.
> ESTRAGON: Who?
> VLADIMIR: What?
> ESTRAGON: What's all this about? Abused who?
> VLADIMIR: The Saviour.
> ESTRAGON: Why?
> VLADIMIR: Because he wouldn't save them.
> ESTRAGON: From hell?
> VLADIMIR: Imbecile! From death.
> ESTRAGON: I thought you said hell.
> VLADIMIR: From death, from death.
> ESTRAGON: Well what of it?
> VLADIMIR: Then the two of them must have been damned.
> ESTRAGON: And why not?
> VLADIMIR: But one of the four says that one of the two was saved.
> ESTRAGON: Well? They don't agree and that's all there is to it.
> VLADIMIR: But all four were there. And only one speaks of a thief being saved. Why believe him rather than the others?
> ESTRAGON: Who believes him?
> VLADIMIR: Everybody. It's the only version they know.
> ESTRAGON: People are bloody ignorant apes. (*Complete Dramatic Works,* 14–15)

Augustine refers to the Lucan passage as narrative ("Lucas narravit quod dico"), and it seems to me that Beckett's Augustinian sentence serves him as something like an intensely com-

blankness in the other three evangelical accounts presumably reduces the "reasonable percentage" considerably.

In the conversation with Tom Driver, Beckett turns once again to his "wonderful" Augustinian sentence and precisely in the context of discussing the "chaos" for which the artist must seek an accommodating form. "Yes. If life and death did not both present themselves to us," Driver quotes Beckett as saying,

> there would be no inscrutability. If there were only darkness, all would be clear. It is because there is not only darkness but also light that our situation becomes inexplicable. Take Augustine's doctrine of grace given and grace withheld: have you pondered the dramatic qualities in this theology? Two thieves are crucified with Christ, one saved and the other damned. How can we make sense of this division? In classical drama, such problems do not arise. The destiny of Racine's Phedre is sealed from the beginning: she will proceed into the dark. . . . Within this notion clarity is possible, but for us who are neither Greek nor Jansenist there is not such clarity. The question would also be removed if we believed in the contrary—total salvation. But where we have both dark and light we have also the inexplicable.

It is this nearly unbearable situation of the inexplicable, "where we have both dark and light," that Beckett dramatizes with images of black and white, dark and light, in *Krapp's Last Tape*. "Everything there," Krapp exclaims into his memory-machine, the tape recorder, near the end of the

---

pressed, elliptical core narrative of the human condition: the barest possible narrative expressive of the situation we find ourselves in.

How Beckett came to know the "wonderful sentence" is an extraordinarily interesting puzzle. In English it is, of course, not a single sentence but two sentences composed of four exactly balanced and parallel clauses. Stylistically it does indeed sound Augustinian, but one could fairly say that in this regard it also sounds Beckettian. The following three passages come as close to Beckett's "sentence" as anything I can find in Augustine, and in none of them is there the crucial twofold admonition, "Do not despair. . . . Do not presume" (which would thus be Beckett's interpretative gloss on Augustine): "Dominus erat in medio crucifixus; juxta illum duo latrones erant: unus insultavit, alter credidit; unus damnatus est, alter justificatus est; unus habuit poenam suam et hic et in futurum, alteri autem dixit Dominus, *Amen dico tibi, hodie mecum eris in paradiso*" (*Ennaratio in Psalmum XXXIII*). ". . . [I]n medio enim iudice constituto, unus latro qui credidit liberatus, alter qui insultavit damnatus . . ." (*In Iohannis evangelium tractatus*). "Tres cruces in loco uno erant: in una latro liberandus: in alia latro damnandus; in media Christus: alterum liberatur: alterum damnatur" (*Epistolae*). These are all from quite obscure sources—not, one would think, the commonest sort of reading matter for an Irishman who would be described as a lapsed Protestant if he had ever had enough religion to lapse from. That Beckett originally knew the passage in Latin, in which language it was "even finer . . . than in English," but had forgotten the Latin in favor of the "wonderful sentence" in English is interesting in a number of ways, but it rather increases than lessens the mystery of Beckett's being so learned in Augustinian studies.

play, "everything on this old muckball, all the light and dark and famine and feasting of . . . *(hesitates)* . . . the ages!" Beckett points to the same condition earlier in the play when he has the aged Krapp puzzling over the ledger entry made by himself thirty years before: "Memorable . . . what? *(He peers closer.)* Equinox, memorable equinox. *(He raises his head, stares blankly front. Puzzled.)* Memorable equinox?" An equinox is the moment that occurs twice in the year when day and night, light and dark, are of equal duration, exactly balanced one against the other. And a *"memorable equinox"*—i.e., an equinox that sets this year apart from all others in having the most equinoctial of equinoxes—would display, one might imagine, in heightened form the same "wonderful shape" that Beckett found in Augustine's "wonderful sentence"—"Do not despair . . . Do not presume"— and it is, as Beckett said, "the shape that matters." It is interesting, and very much to the purposes of the present discussion, that the twentieth-century dramatist should ally himself with the saint of the very early Middle Ages (who long found it difficult to break from his adherence to Manichaeanism with its evenly matched forces of light and dark) rather than with Greek or Jansenist, for whom there was clarity even if only the clarity of darkness. The implication we must take from this is that Augustine, for all his apparent assurance that a life could be narrated in the same way a psalm could be recited, faced (at least in Beckett's judgment) something of the same mess or chaos as his twentieth-century descendant in life-narration. For Beckett, if not for Augustine (and I am not so very sure this may not hold for Augustine as well), the primary agent in the making of the mess—and perhaps in its unmaking too—is nothing other than human memory, which, like narrative in Beckett, is obsessive, self-creative and self-destructive, a faculty that for better and worse is much more than a faculty, too often out of our (or any) control. "And through the spaces of the dark," T. S. Eliot writes in "Rhapsody on a Windy Night," and one thinks of all of the narrating voices of Beckett's late fiction,

> And through the spaces of the dark
> Midnight shakes the memory
> As a madman shakes a dead geranium.

Let us look a little more closely now at what Augustine says of memory, primarily in books 10 and 11 of the *Confessions,* and at what memory is as dramatized and analyzed by Beckett, primarily in *Company.*

Book 10 of the *Confessions,* we should recall, constitutes Augustine's attempt at confessing not "what I have been but what I am . . . , what I am inside myself, beyond the possible reach of . . . eyes and ears and minds."

It is confession of himself, not of his actions, not even of his thoughts, but confession of his very self that Augustine undertakes in book 10, and it is altogether significant how immediately he comes to memory in this confession of himself. Here narrative, even at this moment the product of memory, in an act strikingly analogous to Augustine's attempt to discover God where he dwells, tries to turn back on itself and inside out to encompass memory, its very begetter, within the narrative frame. This, as Augustine comes to realize, is like the mind trying to know itself, which, in turn, may be, although Augustine certainly does not say this, rather like the eye trying to see itself. In *De Trinitate,* in response to those who "will say that this is not memory whereby the mind, which is always present to itself, is said to remember itself, since memory is concerned with the past and not with the present," Augustine argues thus: "Wherefore, as in past things, that is called memory which makes it possible for them to be recalled and remembered, so in a present thing, which the mind is to itself, that is not unreasonably to be called memory, by which the mind is present to itself, so that it can be understood by its own thought, and both can be joined together by the love of itself."[11] The mind, through memory—and in the *Confessions* Augustine will say that mind and memory are one and the same thing—can recall experiences of the past, but it can also, in the present, recall itself to itself, "can be understood by its own thought," and this too, whereby "the mind is present to itself," is accomplished through memory.

Memory is altogether specific to the individual, according to Augustine, but beyond its particularity and uniqueness it also affords a bridge between time and eternity and is the nonlocatable locus where the individual may discover God, "the embracement of my inner self—there where is a brilliance that space cannot contain, a sound that time cannot carry away, a perfume that no breeze disperses, a taste undiminished by eating, a clinging together that no satiety will sunder" (*Conf.,* 10.6, 215). Attempting to make his mind present to itself so that he may make it present also to his readers, Augustine simultaneously seeks to know the God who is the embracement of his inner self: "I shall pass on, then, beyond this faculty [of the senses] in my nature as I ascend by degrees toward Him who made me. And I come to the fields and spacious palaces of memory, where lie the treasures of innumerable images of all kinds of things that have been brought in by the senses" (*Conf.,* 10.8, 217). Here one is reminded that in the Middle Ages memory was called the interior sense, as it were the inte-

11. St. Augustine, *On the Trinity,* 14.11.14, 431–32, trans. Stephen McKenna (Washington, D.C.: Catholic University of America Press, 1963); cited hereafter by book, chapter, paragraph, and page number as *Trin.*

grative and summative sense that transforms the rich but disordered experience of the external senses—which, however, are likewise specific to the
individual—into the stuff of selfhood, giving to that experience the shape
and pattern of the interior sense itself: "and through these senses, with all
their diverse functions, I act, retaining my identity as one soul" (*Conf.*,
10.7, 217).

There is, in Augustine, no distinguishing of memory from the self.
"Great indeed is the power of memory!" he exclaims. "It is something
terrifying, my God, a profound and infinite multiplicity; and this thing is
the mind, and this thing is I myself: et hoc animus est, et hoc ego ipse
sum" (*Conf.*, 10.17, 227). And when it comes to the act of remembering,
Augustine has no problem at all in asserting the first-person singular: "It is
I myself who remember, I, the mind: ego sum, qui memini, ego animus"
(*Conf.*, 10.16, 226). It is otherwise with Beckett, however; the act of remembering in *Company,* with what should be, according to Augustine, a
concomitant calling into being of a self continuous across time, assumes all
the pathos attendant upon yearning on the one hand and failure on the
other. Of the voice that comes to one lying on his back in the dark we
are told, "Another trait its repetitiousness. Repeatedly with only minor
variants the same bygone. As if willing him by this dint to make it his. To
confess, Yes I remember. Perhaps even to have a voice. To murmur, Yes
I remember. What an addition to company that would be! A voice in the
first person singular. Murmuring now and then, Yes I remember" (p. 16).
Memory, like narrative, is obsessive in Beckett, but it is ultimately unsuccessful in evoking "the first person singular." The twentieth-century act
of confession—and I take it that Beckett is deliberately nodding to Augustine in the sentence "To confess, Yes I remember," which in its confess-
remember sequence is no more than a reversal of the Augustinian "recordor
et confiteor: I remember and confess"—yields only a subjunctive condition
that, however much desired, is contrary to fact: "What an addition to company that *would be!*" That this "would be" will never become "is" we can
know, if we haven't known it long since, from the last words of *Company,*
where even the conditional *I* has disappeared and the hope of company
that might ensue upon confessing "Yes I remember: ego memini" is seen
to be simply, sadly illusory:

> And you as you always were.
> Alone.

There is finally no company in *Company,* no *I* and no remembering, and
false, therefore, is "[t]he fable of one with you in the dark," and false, too,

"[t]he fable of one fabling of one with you in the dark" (p. 63). Narrative, in this latter-day parable, has no more validity, no more power to seek out and to discover or to create a self than has memory. Augustine describes, but can hardly imagine, the state in which Beckett's narrator finds himself when, in book 10 of the *Confessions,* he says, "[T]his force of my memory is incomprehensible to me, even though, without it, I should not be able to call myself myself" (10.16, 226). This describes the affliction, though it is virtually unimaginable to Augustine, of the Beckettian figure, unable to call himself himself because without the assurance memory would give of a continuity of being or of being at all. When the voice of *The Unnamable* says, "In the meantime no sense bickering about pronouns and other parts of blather. The subject doesn't matter, there is none" (*Trilogy,* 331), I take it that "the subject" has not only linguistic and grammatical reference but epistemological, ontological, and theological overtones as well. In drawing the bond between the force of memory and the ability "to call myself myself," Augustine employs the subjunctive to describe the condition of *not* having memory, *not* having an *I* and a self, whereas Beckett employs it to describe the condition of *having* memory, an *I* and a self, the state of being able "To confess, Yes I remember": "What an addition to company that *would* be"—but never *will* be for this bereft, late-twentieth-century inheritor of the Augustinian confessional imperative.

As Augustine explores his own memory and analyzes the nature of memory itself in book 10 of *The Confessions,* he presents, in effect, two different models for memory, quite distinct one from the other and widely divergent in their implications for the act of narrating. The first of these I will term an archaeological model, the second a processual model. When offering us an archaeological model for memory, Augustine writes of levels and layers and deposits; he thinks in spatial terms and speaks of "the great harbor of memory, with its secret, numberless, and indefinable recesses," of "the fields and spacious palaces of memory, where lie the treasures of innumerable . . . things," and of "a vast and boundless subterranean shrine." "Who," he goes on to ask rhetorically, "Who has ever reached the bottom of it?" When the archaeological model is in play, the implication is that memory is something fixed and static, a site where the archaeologist of memories can dig down through layer after layer of deposits to recover what he seeks. And when he finds the memories he is looking for, they will be as they were when deposited, unchanged except as they may have suffered from the decaying effects of time. "When I am in this treasure house," Augustine writes, "I ask for whatever I like to be brought out to me, and then some things are produced at once, some things take longer

and have, as it were, to be fetched from a more remote part of the store.
. . ." (10.8, 217). On occasion, the wrong memories come forward but
this presents no problem to Augustine: "With the hand of my heart I brush
them away from the face of my memory, until the thing that I want is
discovered and brought out from its hidden place into sight." And when
it is a question of going into the treasure house of memory to recite a
psalm or to narrate a life-story, everything comes out *ex ordine,* in order,
as Augustine says of the stories he has been telling throughout the *Confessions:* "And some things are produced easily and in perfect order, just as
they are required; what comes first gives place to what comes next, and,
as it gives place, it is stored up ready to be brought out when I need it
again. All this happens," according to Augustine, "when I repeat anything
by heart," and we have to recall, although it must be proleptically, the
reciting of a psalm that will come in book 11.

"All this I do inside me, in the huge court of my memory," Augustine
says, continuing the archaeological model for memory; but within a few
lines he subtilizes and modulates this description until, almost imperceptibly, he comes to be employing a processual model for memory that plays
itself out in temporal rather than spatial metaphors:

> There too [in the huge court of my memory] I encounter myself; I recall
> myself—what I have done, when and where I did it, and in what state of
> mind I was at the time. There are all the things I remember to have experi-
> enced myself or to have heard from others. From the same store too I can
> take out pictures of things which have either happened to me or are believed
> on the basis of experience; I can myself weave them into the context of the
> past, and from them I can infer future actions, events, hopes, and then I can
> contemplate all these as though they were in the present. (*Conf.* 10.8, 218–19)

Weaving, as a characteristic metaphor for the operation of memory, will
have a long history in the tradition of life-writing that springs from Augustine's *Confessions.* Unlike the archaeological dig, the weaver's shuttle
and loom constantly produce new and different patterns, designs, and forms,
and if the operation of memory is, like weaving, not archaeological but
processual, then it will bring forth ever different memorial configurations
and an ever newly shaped self. The verb translated as "weave" in this passage
is *contexo,* "to weave together," from the root *texo,* "to weave": "ex eadem
copia etiam similitudines rerum vel expertarum vel ex eis, quas expertus
sum, creditarum alias atque alias et ipse contexo praeteritis." The relevant
part of the passage might be literally translated, "I weave these remembered
experiences together into likenesses of things of the past" (though one must
acknowledge Rex Warner's translating ingenuity since his "context of the

past" picks up on and repeats the "contexo" of "I weave together"). The past participle of *texo* is the neuter *textum* or masculine *textus,* meaning "that which is woven" and figuratively, of a written composition, "texture, style," or of discourse, "mode of putting together, connection." It also, of course, gives us modern English "text," which is hardly a step away from a narrative text like this one of Augustine in process before us. Augustine weaves his weaving, his text, his narrative, weaves it out of memories that are themselves in process and taking on new forms, even as he analyzes and describes memory by way of a metaphor of weaving. This makes the narrating of a life-story, ruled by a metaphor of weaving, something differ-ent from reciting a psalm, ruled by a metaphor of archaeological recovery. Yet even the latter may not be quite so fixed in character and significance as it at first seems if we recall Hegel's saying that the old man repeats the same prayers he learned as a child but now altered, weighted, given entirely new coloring by the experience of a lifetime.

Beckett's weaving of memories into a narrative that will simultaneously compose and decompose a text is as double as Penelope's activity in the *Odyssey:* weaving a shroud for Laertes by day and undoing it by night to keep the suitors at bay. For Beckett's various narrators, as for him as narrator of their narrating, the dual act of remembering and narrating is at once painful and pleasurable, at once necessary and impossible. And drawing the analogy to Penelope's weaving a shroud is not altogether idle, for Beckett conceives of his weaving as an act both of life and of death: his narrative destroys as it creates, it devours the life it records as it devours the remaining sheets in the exercise book and the pencil with which he writes. In the trilogy (*Molloy, Malone Dies,* and *The Unnamable*) he summons all those stand-ins for his own life, "at least from Murphy on" as we are told in *The Unnamable,* so that their lives can be consumed one last time in the consummation of the ultimate narrator's life. "But I write them all the same," Moran says of the lines he puts down as the narrative of Molloy's life, "I write them all the same, and with a firm hand weaving inexorably back and forth and devouring my page with the indifference of a shuttle" (*Trilogy,* 122). Weaving and devouring—the double image suggests that with Beckett memorial narrative is itself both the ultimate sign of life and the cancellation of that life and a movement into death. All of his late fictions move in this direction, devouring the bit of life remaining as words come to an end and narrative exhausts itself. "But this innumerable babble, like a multitude whispering?" Malone asks of himself in *Malone Dies.* "I don't understand. With my distant hand I count the pages that remain. They will do. This exercise-book is my life, this child's exercise-book, it

has taken me a long time to resign myself to that. And yet I shall not throw
it away. For I want to put down in it, for the last time, those I have called
to my help, but ill, so that they did not understand, so that they may cease
with me. Now rest" (*Trilogy,* 252). And so Malone—or Beckett, rather,
the "devised deviser devising it all," as he says of himself in *Company*—
with a firm hand weaves inexorably back and forth and devours his page—
not, however, as Moran claims, "with the indifference of a shuttle" but
with considerable emotional anguish: "Devising figments to temper his
nothingness. . . . Devised deviser devising it all for company. In the same
figment dark as his figments" (*Company,* 46).

Augustine, of course, is not happy or complacent about the memories
he has of his preconversion self, but still those memories do not have about
them the open-wound painfulness or the desperately yearning quality that
memories have in Beckett. Augustine established a long tradition of narrative confession as something compelled by God and imposed as a duty on
every Christian. Beckett hasn't this explanation or justification in God's
will for his repeated performances in recalling and narrating, but the activity
is at least as obligatory and compulsive for Beckett as for Augustine—indeed
rather more so, I would say. It is difficult to say, for a character like Krapp
in *Krapp's Last Tape,* whether his memories of a very distant love relationship are more painful or more pleasurable, but for certain obsessive, recurrent memories in Beckett's writing there can be no doubt about the domi-
nance of pain; yet they will not be denied but must be narrated and not
once only but again and again. "Memories are killing," according to the
narrator of a story called "The Expelled." "So you must not think of certain
things, of those that are dear to you, or rather you must think of them, in
your mind, little by little. That is to say, you must think of them for a
while, a good while, every day several times a day, until they sink forever
in the mud."[12] The only problem with this strategy and advice is that the
real and really painful memories decline to sink forever in the mud. There
is one such memory in *Company* that makes earlier appearances in *Malone
Dies* and in a piece called "The End" from *Stories and Texts for Nothing.*
Here is the memory as narrated in *Company:*

> A small boy you come out of Connolly's Stores holding your mother by
> the hand. You turn right and advance in silence southward along the highway.
> After some hundred paces you head inland and broach the long steep home-
> ward. You make ground in silence hand in hand through the warm still sum-
> mer air. It is late afternoon and after some hundred paces the sun appears above

12. *Stories and Texts for Nothing* (New York: Grove, 1967), 9; hereafter cited as *Stories.*

the crest of the rise. Looking up at the blue sky and then at your mother's face you break the silence asking her if it is not in reality much more distant than it appears. The sky that is. The blue sky. Receiving no answer you mentally reframe your question and some hundred paces later look up at her face again and ask her if it does not appear much less distant than in reality it is. For some reason you could never fathom this question must have angered her exceedingly. For she shook off your little hand and made you a cutting retort you have never forgotten. (*Company*, 12–13)

Never to have forgotten is always to have remembered, and no matter how often thought of, little by little, in the mind, this memory is not going to sink in the mud. As recalled and reported in *Malone Dies*—as woven into a likeness of something experienced in the past—the episode goes like this:

One day we were walking along the road, up a hill of extraordinary steepness, near home I imagine, my memory is full of steep hills, I get them confused. I said, The sky is further away than you think, is it not, mama? It was without malice, I was simply thinking of all the leagues that separated me from it. She replied, to me her son, It is precisely as far away as it appears to be. She was right. But at the time I was aghast. I can still see the spot, opposite Tyler's gate. A market-gardener, he had only one eye and wore sidewhiskers. That's the idea, rattle on. (*Trilogy*, 246)

As with Augustine's model for narration, where a psalm or a life-story, once recited or narrated, becomes available again for rerecitation and renar-rating, so this unfortunate experience seems to offer itself for telling again and again. As we are told of the voice of memory in *Company*, "Another trait [is] its repetitiousness. Repeatedly with only minor variants the same bygone" (p. 16). In *Malone Dies*, in addition to the repetition of the story "with only minor variants," we are given a suggestion of how to deal with such insistent and painful memories: surround them, drown them with more narrative; distract the mind's attention with the irrelevant information that Tyler was a market gardener who had only one eye and wore side-whiskers. "That's the idea, rattle on," until you get over this treacherous and rough patch in the narrative. Not that this will sink it in the mud, but at least it allows you to go on until the next time the memory thrusts itself upon you and into your narrative, as it does once more in "The End":

Now I was making my way through the garden. There was that strange light which follows a day of persistent rain, when the sun comes out and the sky clears too late to be of any use. The earth makes a sound as of sighs and the last drops fall from emptied, cloudless sky. A small boy, stretching out his hands and looking up at the blue sky, asked his mother how such a thing was

> possible. Fuck off, she said. I suddenly remembered I had not thought of asking
> Mr Weir for a piece of bread. (*Stories,* 50)

That's the idea, rattle on about Mr. Weir and a piece of bread. Who
wouldn't, if addressed by his mother in this manner?

No one would claim that this obsessive memory that turns up several
times in Beckett's fiction has world-shaking importance, but then neither
does the stealing of pears in St. Augustine. So why does each of them tell
his story with such urgency? Why—as I had Augustine asking at the beginning of this chapter—"Why then do I put before you [before God] in order
the stories of so many things?" Beckett in effect asks the same question, but
puts it in the mouth of his partner in dialogue in *Georges Duthuit.* The
premise of his writing, Beckett says in the first dialogue, and the premise
of any art sufficiently conscious of the conditions under which it must be
produced in our time to make that art of any value, is "that there is nothing
to express, nothing with which to express, nothing from which to express,
no power to express, no desire to express, together with the obligation to
express" (*Duthuit,* 103). And by the time of *Company* not only is there
"nothing with which to express, nothing from which to express, no power
to express," etc., there is also no longer any narrative *I* to do the expressing.
(Yet curiously enough—especially curious after the trilogy and its conclusion in *The Unnamable*—there *is* in *Company* something to express: the
series of bygones, fifteen in number, of which the voice speaks and which
constitute a coherent, followable life-story. Moreover, most of the episodes
can be, on external evidence, directly associated with Beckett. That is, the
voice is speaking to Beckett of his own bygones.) When, in the third dialogue, Duthuit asks why, then, given the general absence of content, means,
and ability to express, the artist is obliged to express, Beckett's answer is
of an ultimate simplicity: "I don't know" (*Duthuit,* 119). Augustine could
say, "Because God so wills it." Beckett never gives this response, but there
is nevertheless the sense that it is a force outside and beyond him that com-
pels him to the narrative act, that obliges him to tell and retell his story by
weaving together likenesses of things of the past remembered now in the
present. One might say, on the model of *la poésie pure,* that a text like
The Unnamable constitutes an instance of *la narration pure:* narrative without
substance, form without content; or, perhaps more accurately, it takes
form—narrative form—as content. It shows us a consciousness or a subject
in quest of itself, but, as the Unnamable says, "the subject doesn't matter,
there is none." The question of why both Augustine and Beckett are
obliged to narrate their stories is like asking why they—and all of us—
possess and have imposed upon us the capacity and the necessity for remem-

bering. Once you answer the one question, I suspect you will have the answer to the other, but for as long as we are within the circle of remembering and narrating—so long, that is, as we are alive—Beckett's seems the only intelligent answer: "I don't know."

On the occasion of his seventieth birthday, Beckett told his British publisher, John Calder, that in old age work would be his company. However futile it was, however helpless to make anything outside itself happen, the work of remembering and narrating became his company, his obligation, perhaps his salvation. It is as if Beckett responded to Freud's observation that there is nothing of value in human experience but love and work by shearing away the first and leaving only work. It is an unrelievedly bleak vision, but as honest and courageous as it is bleak; what is especially curious about Beckett's vision, however, as expressed in its extreme form at the end of *The Unnamable,* say, or in the conclusion to *Company,* is that it is positively lyrical in its rhythms, in its style and manner, even as it is grimly pessimistic in its message (if we can speak of a message in Beckett). It seems profoundly paradoxical that a statement about the apparent futility and meaninglessness of human life in its twin aspects of remembering and narrating should be (as I feel it anyway) so songlike, so lyrical, so irrepressibly buoyant. But I wonder if this isn't merely a reformulation of the "wonderful sentence" that Beckett found in St. Augustine: "Do not despair; one of the thieves was saved. Do not presume; one of the thieves was damned." Of the end of *The Unnamable* or *Company* one might say that the sentiment expressed seems to be: "Do not despair, the lyrical buoyancy says, for you may be saved; do not presume, the vision says, for you may be damned." Is this not an expression, for our time, of the (nearly) impossible and totally paradoxical tension "between the mess and form," as Beckett termed it in his conversation with Tom Driver? I wonder, too, if what I have been calling the buoyancy of the last words of *Company,* however bleak, is not due to a parallel lyricism in the narrative impetus. "Tell us a story": Is there not something incipiently exciting and inherently buoyant—the buoyancy of the human spirit itself—in that demand and its satisfaction? "Supine now you resume your fable where the act of lying cut it short," the final portion of *Company* begins:

> Supine now you resume your fable where the act of lying cut it short. And persist till the converse operation cuts it short again. So in the dark now huddled and now supine you toil in vain. And just as from the former position to the latter the shift grows easier in time and more alacrious so from the latter to the former the reverse is true. Till from the occasional relief it was supineness becomes habitual and finally the rule. You now on your back in the dark

shall not rise to your arse again to clasp your legs in your arms and bow down your head till it can bow down no further. But with face upturned for good labour in vain at your fable. Till finally you hear how words are coming to an end. With every inane word a little nearer to the last. And how the fable too. The fable of one with you in the dark. The fable of one fabling of one with you in the dark. And how better in the end labour lost and silence. And you as you always were.

Alone.

St. Augustine Solo

Multitudinous Narrative

In about 426, when he was seventy-two or seventy-three years old, St. Augustine undertook, in a work unique for its time, a review of all his postconversion writings: *Retractationum libri duo* or, in English, *Two Books of Retractations*.[13] He had long planned such a work, Augustine tells us in his prologue, and "am now undertaking [it] because I do not think it should be postponed: with a kind of judicious severity, I am reviewing my works—books, letters, and sermons—and, as it were, with the pen of a censor, I am indicating what dissatisfies me" (*Ret.*, 3). Augustine's revisiting of his life as a writer, from his early days as a catechumen through his priesthood and the long period of service as bishop of Hippo up to a point three years before his death in 430, includes review of ninety-three books and yet, like so many of his works, remains incomplete: there was not only the writing still to come in the last years of his life, but the venture had already become so extended that Augustine let it go without doing anything about his letters and sermons (except those that could be considered to be books). The *Retractations* was finally given to the world in two books, and it is difficult to say how many books there might have been had Augustine had the time, the strength, and the will to survey his letters and sermons. And the reason he both began and then cut short his review is plain from the prologue. "I had to consider," Augustine writes,

> the pronouncement of the Apostle when he says: "If we judged ourselves, we should not be judged by the Lord." The following words of Scripture, too, terrify me very much: "In a multitude of words, you shall not avoid sin," not because I have written a great deal . . . , but I fear this pronouncement of Holy Scripture because, indeed, without a doubt, many things can be collected

13. *Saint Augustine: The Retractations,* trans. Sister Mary Inez Bogan (Washington, D.C.: Catholic University of America Press, 1968). Subsequent citations will be given by the abbreviation *Ret.* and page number.

from my numerous disputations which, if not false, yet may certainly seem or even be proved unnecessary. In truth, which one of Christ's own faithful has He not terrified when He says: "Of every idle word men speak, they shall give account on the day of judgment"? (*Ret.,* 4–5)

If the passage from 1 Corinthians compelled Augustine to write in judgment of himself and the whole body of his writings, the terrifying passages from Proverbs and Matthew brought him to a halt (as they had done before: see, for example, the conclusion of *De Trinitate*) before he should condemn himself with "a multitude of words." The *Retractations,* thus, turns into another volume of *Confessions* (which also had to be cut short, as it were in midbreath, because it too threatened to become almost uncontrollably long), and Augustine concludes his *Retractations* prologue with the same exhortation we find throughout the *Confessions:*

> Let those, therefore, who are going to read this book not imitate me when I err, but rather when I progress toward the better. For, perhaps, one who reads my works in the order in which they were written will find out how I progressed while writing. In order that this be possible, I shall take care, insofar as I can in this work, to acquaint him with this order. (*Ret.,* 5)

The phrasing here in the Latin ("ordine quo scripta sunt. . . . eumdem ordinem")[14] and the strategy of presentation that Augustine follows will come as no surprise to readers who recall his question in book 11 of the *Confessions* about why he tells "in order [*ex ordine*] the stories of so many things" and his doubts about whether he will have "the strength to declare all this in order [*ex ordine*]," for what he is doing in the *Retractations*— tracing his whole development from a defined point in the past to the present moment—is not different in kind, in intention, or in procedure from what he did in the *Confessions*. It is all a matter of remembering remembering and telling about both the first and the later remembering. As Augustine puts it in the *Confessions,* "I remember that I often did understand" certain subjects,

---

14. "Inveniet enim fortasse quomodo scribendo profecerim, quisquis opuscula mea, ordine quo scripta sunt, legerit. Quod ut possit, hoc opere, quantum potero, curabo ut eumdem ordinem noverit" (*Sancti Aurelii Augustini Hipponensis Episcopi Opera Omnia* [Paris, 1841], vol. 1). This edition of Augustine's *Opera Omnia* places the *Retractations,* as has become standard practice, not in its chronological place but at the head of the works, followed then by the *Confessions* and, after the *Confessions,* all the other works in the chronological order of their composition. John Henry Newman wanted his *Apologia pro vita sua* to be the first volume in any collected edition of his work, and it would seem that editors of Augustine are following this same principle when they place the *Retractations* and the *Confessions,* as a kind of double-barreled autobiography and the key to understanding all else, at the head of his complete works.

and also I store up in my memory what I see and understand now, so that later I may remember what I did understand at this moment. So I remember that I have remembered, and if in the future I recall that I have now been able to remember these things, it will be by the force of my memory that I shall recall it. (*Conf.*, 10.13, 223)

In the *Retractations* Augustine, in effect, is ordering and reordering his experience in narrative form, telling once again, *ex ordine,* the story of the same story of his life.

And Augustine brings the promised rigor to his examination of all he had written since becoming a Christian, though he naturally finds less to correct in the later writings, after he had been through the polemical skirmishes with the Manichaeans, the Donatists, the Pelagians, the Arians, and various other heretical groups, than in those early writings when he was, as he puts it, "still puffed up with the usages of secular literature" (*Ret.*, 5). It would not be quite fair to say that he relents in his severity only when he comes to the *Confessions,* but there is, I think, a note of special human warmth—of affection and remembered joy—in his treatment of the *Confessions* that is not much in evidence elsewhere in the *Retractations.* Nor is this really unexpected since what Augustine is doing in the *Retractations* is so similar to what he did in the earlier book, where he asked for (and to a supreme degree was granted) "the power to survey in my memory now all those wanderings of my error in the past . . ." (*Conf.*, 4.1, 69). He had no doubt rejected "all those wanderings of my error in the past," but they were still his nevertheless and they were still him. The intention of "the thirteen books of my *Confessions,*" Augustine says—and, he might have added, the achievement of that book—was to "praise the just and good God for my evil and good acts, and lift up the understanding and affection of men to Him" (*Ret.*, 130). "At least," he goes on, "as far as I am concerned, they had this effect on me while I was writing them and they continue to have it when I am reading them." Thus, long after he had written the *Confessions* and even longer after he had passed through the experiences recounted therein, Augustine continued to revisit his life not only as he thought back over his past ("A man may let his fluttering mind wander through images of times past . . ." [*Conf.*, 11.13, 266]: exactly—so he had done and so he was then doing) but also as he read and reread his own earlier account of that past. And he was not the only one moved by reading the story of his "evil and good acts," for, as he says in the *Retractations,* "I know that they have given and continue to give pleasure to many of my brethren" (*Ret.*, 130). Even Augustine, I imagine, could not have foreseen to how many brethren and nonbrethren alike his *Confessions* would continue to give not only pleasure but also matter for thought and forms for imitation in the centuries to follow, even down to Jean-Jacques Rousseau and Samuel Beckett and troops of other believers and nonbelievers who have looked with varying degrees of envy and admiration, exasperation and affection, to Augustine's *Confessions* as the great ur-book of life-writing, the initiator and progenitor of a literary (and more than literary) tradition that, in however altered a form (sometimes altered almost out of all recognition), continues alive and questionably well—very, very alive and, depending on one's view, very well or very sick—in our time.

A number of years ago, when I was directing a summer seminar for college teachers on "the forms of autobiography" as a visiting professor at the University of North Carolina, a member of the English faculty at UNC stopped by the office assigned to me to introduce himself and to chat about my seminar. When he noticed a copy of Augustine's *Confessions* on my desk he expressed surprise that that book would find a place in a seminar on autobiography. I have to admit that I was surprised at his surprise, for it seemed to me perfectly obvious not only that the *Confessions* could be talked about as autobiography but also that to talk about autobiography at all without extended consideration of the *Confessions* would be like, if not a theology without God, then at least a history of Western philosophy without Plato. While I still retain something of that feeling, I must acknowledge that my views have had to change somewhat, for I have come to recognize that the first person who would have been surprised—and no doubt deeply dismayed—to learn that the *Confessions* could be read with profit and enjoyment in the context of a literary tradition that was eventually to embrace not just saints of the Catholic Church but Protestants and poets and novelists and heretics and scoundrels of every stripe would have been St. Augustine himself. Yet I still hold largely to my original opinion that it is not possible to think about autobiography or life-writing as we have come to know it without thinking also—and first of all—about the *Confessions;* but I also believe that the fact that the tradition begun with the *Confessions* should later have come to give joyous acceptance to such unsavory (but to Augustine unknown and unforeseeable) types as Protestants and novelists is in large part owing to the *Confessions* itself—to what that book was and what it did. It may be that when Augustine set about writing the *Confessions,* without any real model to follow (for I do not consider St. Paul convincing as model or compelling example), he intended something other than the book he in fact produced. Pierre Courcelle, in his wonderfully illuminating *Recherches sur les "Confessions" de saint Augustin,* suggests just exactly this: that Augustine originally intended to write only a sketch of his life and his

intellectual development as preface to a detailed exposition of Christian
doctrine, "based on the entire Scriptures beginning with the first words
of Genesis."[15] Starting with book 3, Courcelle continues, "Augustine expected to finish quickly with his biography; but he was carried away by
his subject and"—like any latter-day descendant—"could not restrain himself" from going on at much greater length about his own life than he had
ever intended. This is well said, and I think one can discover much evidence
in the very texture of the *Confessions* for the judgment that Augustine's
story simply took over and left his exegetical and doctrinal intentions to
fend (unsuccessfully) for themselves; but this being so, I do not see that we
can follow Courcelle when he later claims that "like modern readers, but
contrary to the author's opinion, Augustine's contemporaries preferred the
first part of the work to the last" (p. 26). I would not dispute that this was
the case with his contemporaries or that it is so with Augustine's modern
readers, but I am much less certain that this shared ancient and modern
judgment runs contrary to Augustine's own. When he looks back to the
Confessions thirty years later to record how moved he is as he reads, how
moved he was as he wrote, his story—and how moved others have been—
I believe Augustine is pointing to something undeniable in the text itself,
something of warmth and delight and deep human feeling, that he might
not have consciously intended to put there; but once there it did not fail
to make itself known and attractive to Augustine as also to the book's earliest and latest readers. The turn to memory and the turn to self-writing is
irresistible in Augustine as when, in book 10 of the *Confessions,* he writes
of his frequent, repeated, and joyous recourse to memory of things past.
Seeking God, he says,

> I entered into the recesses of my memory, space folded upon huge space and
> all miraculously full of innumerable abundance, and I considered it and I was
> amazed. . . . and now in the vast treasury of my memory I would meditate
> on something stored there, or put something away or take something out. . . .
> And I often do this, I find delight in it, and whenever I can relax from my
> necessary duties I have recourse to this pleasure. . . . And sometimes working
> within me you open for me a door into a state of feeling which is quite unlike
> anything to which I am used—a kind of sweet delight which, if I could only
> remain permanently in that state, would be something not of this world, not
> of this life. (*Conf.,* 10.40, 252–53)

---

15. *Recherches sur les "Confessions" de saint Augustin* (Paris: De Boccard, 1950), 24; hereafter cited as *Recherches*.

The phrase translated "sweet delight" here is *dulcedinem* in the original, the root word of which—*dulcis,* meaning "sweet"—is scattered broadcast in the pages of the *Confessions,* sometimes to describe Augustine's delight in God but other times, and equally, to describe the burning lusts that drew him on in Carthage or the friendships that, in mature retrospect, he thought mistaken but that nevertheless meant more to him almost than anything else in life. He can thus begin book 2 by invoking the sweetness of his God in the following tones: "I want to call back to mind my past impurities and the carnal corruptions of my soul, not because I love them, but so that I may love you, my God . . . , so that the bitterness may be replaced by the sweetness of you, O unfailing sweetness, happy sweetness and secure!" [ut tu dulcescas mihi, dulcedo non fallax, dulcedo felix et secura (*Conf.,* 2.1, 40)]. But he can also begin book 3, after the stunning first words— "Veni Karthaginem": To Carthage, Dido's city, I came, "and all around me in my ears were the sizzling and frying of unholy loves"—with a recollection of the sweetness of those carnal loves: "Being in love with love I looked for something to love. . . . It was a sweet thing to me both to love and to be loved, and more sweet still when I was able to enjoy the body of my lover" [amare et amari dulce mihi erat, magis si et amantis corpore fruerer] (*Conf.,* 3.1, 52). I do not mean to suggest that Augustine was being untruthful when he claimed he had achieved complete chastity and continence (or almost complete: his dreams, he confesses in book 10, still troubled him); but even if he did not relive the sweetness in recalling it (and I believe him when he says that he did not) there still remained somewhere in his memory the fact that his carnal loves *had* been sweet—even in his postconversion rejection of those loves there is no suggestion that their sweetness was mere self-delusion—and in the rigorous honesty of his confession there is the necessity that Augustine acknowledge this with use of the same language he would bring to tell of his feeling for his God. This is almost, if not quite, the lesson Montaigne will teach a thousand years and more later: that we must not in age reject those sweet pleasures of youth merely because we are no longer capable of enjoying them. Augustine makes his rejection alright, but not on the grounds of incapacity and not even on the grounds that the pleasures are not really sweet. Thus the postconversion Augustine has the honesty to describe his preconversion attempt to persuade his friend Alypius—who, unlike Augustine, had no problem with chastity: he had tried sex once early on and "had regretted the experience and despised it and ever since had lived in the greatest continence" (clearly a matter of wonder to the early Augustine, and possibly to

the late Augustine as well)—to persuade him not to give up too hastily
the sweet delights the world has to offer. "But wait," he tells Alypius,
"These worldly things too are sweet; the pleasure they give is not inconsid-
erable; we must not be too hasty about rejecting them . . . (*Conf.*, 6.11,
129). The argument that Augustine here directs against Alypius's easily
achieved chastity is very much the one that, according to the account given
as far along in the narrative as book 8, a few pages short of Augustine's
dramatic conversion, kept Augustine himself for a long time from becoming
a Christian. "Many years (at least twelve) of my own life had gone by,"
Augustine says, introducing another retrospection within the retrospective
framework of the *Confessions,*

> since the time when I was nineteen and was reading Cicero's *Hortensius* and
> had been fired with an enthusiasm for wisdom. Yet I was still putting off the
> moment when, despising this world's happiness, I should give all my time to
> the search for that of which not only the finding but merely the seeking must
> be preferred to the discovered treasures and kingdoms of men or to all the
> pleasures of the body easily and abundantly available. But I, wretched young
> man that I was—even more wretched at the beginning of my youth—had
> begged you for chastity and had said: "Make me chaste and continent, but
> not yet." I was afraid that you might hear me too soon and cure me too soon
> from the disease of a lust that I preferred to be satisfied rather than extin-
> guished. (*Conf.*, 8.7, 173–74)

There are many things to be said about this well-known and wonderful
passage. One is that the wretched young Augustine, even more wretched
earlier on, had attempted to impede or to delay the full flow of the narrative—and the effective, necessary conclusion of the narrative—that was his
life. But another thing to be said is that Augustine, for all his awareness of
how wretched he had been in trying to get around the Lord, nevertheless
shows a sneaking sympathy and even admiration (however slight, however
veiled) for the cunning of the young (and younger) man that he had been—
and that, in some way, he still was, still is at the moment of writing.

However much sub-rosa sympathy one might want to read into his
account of his youth and young manhood, it could not be said that Augustine displays overmuch love for what he was, or figures he must have
been, as an infant. Indeed, the picture he gives of those unpleasant, jealous,
greedy, screeching little creatures we have all been (as Augustine sees it)
reminds one of nothing so much as the comic rendition Nabokov gives of
the Freudian world "with its crankish quest for sexual symbols . . . and its
bitter little embryos spying, from their natural nooks, upon the love life of

their parents."[16] Once past infancy, however, and in the full flow of his school days in Thagaste (though he is careful to dismiss the intentions and the effects of most of his education) a new note creeps into Augustine's writing. Even as he lists the sins of his childhood—cheating in school, envy, gluttony—Augustine is compelled to admit that he took easily to his studies "and indeed was delighted with them and for that reason was considered a most promising boy" (Conf., 1.16, 35). "For even then I had a being," Augustine writes; "I lived and I felt . . . ; by my inward sense I watched over the integrity of my outer senses; even in these little things and in my thoughts about these little things truth delighted me. I hated to be deceived; I had a vigorous memory; I was educated in speech; and I was made tractable by kindness. I avoided pain, meanness, ignorance. How wonderful and how praiseworthy are all these things in such a little living creature!" These virtues, it is true, are all ascribed by Augustine to God's goodness, but all the same they were in him and they were him as a boy—as, in some sense, they are still in him and are him as a man: "But all these things are the gifts of my God; it was not I who gave them to myself, and they are good and all of them together am I" (Conf., 1.20, 38–39). Taking the generally dim view of his education that he feels necessary in the Confessions, Augustine is at some pains to reject Virgil and Homer and their unchristened hearts (in Yeats's phrase), but what reader can doubt the appeal the two epic poets held for the boy? And more: what reader can doubt the appeal they hold for the forty-five-year-old man writing and for the seventy-three-year-old man reexperiencing, in Retractations, the forty-five-year-old man's reexperiencing of the boy's delight? "At that time," Augustine says, contrasting his feeling for literature with his nonfeeling for arithmetic, " 'One and one make two; two and two make four' was a horrible kind of singsong to me. What really delighted me were spectacles of vanity—the Wooden Horse full of armed men, the Burning of Troy, and 'there the very shade of dead Creusa' " (Conf., 1.13, 32). Had rejection been his sole purpose, Augustine could well have omitted the flourish of that final phrase—"there the very shade of dead Creusa"—but supreme rhetorician that he was—that he is, I should say rather, in this very book—, Augustine cannot resist the line of poetry (remembered verbatim, be it noted, some thirty years after his schoolboy reading of the Aeneid) that he must have known would carry the day for all readers as against his cries of "vanity" and the dryness of his rejection. Likewise the effect of the earlier "I wept for dead Dido

16. Vladimir Nabokov, Speak, Memory: An Autobiography Revisited (New York: Capricorn, 1970), 20.

'who by the sword pursued a way extreme' " (*Conf.*, 1.13, 31: cf. *Aeneid,*
bk. 6, line 457) and the later "Homer too is skillful at putting together this
sort of story and there is great sweetness in his vanity [et dulcissime vanus
est]. . . ."—"great sweetness," indeed, and it is altogether in character that
Augustine should have granted to Homer and to Virgil the superlative degree (*dulcissime*) that a more cautious Christian bishop might have reserved
for God.

In a similar way, although all his expressed sentiments about mortal
ties, about mortal friendships and mortal loves, are appropriately negative
and ascetic, Augustine cannot long deny to himself or his readers the deep
and powerful human emotions that bound him to friend and concubine
alike. When at one point he decided it would be better to marry than to
burn, Augustine nevertheless had great difficulties in putting aside his feelings for the mistress with whom he had been living for years (the mother
of the son, Adeodatus, whom Augustine apparently came to love very
dearly),[17] and she proved more firm in her vows of chastity than Augustine
at that time was able to be. "The woman with whom I was in the habit
of sleeping," Augustine writes, "was torn from my side on the grounds of
being an impediment to my marriage, and my heart, which clung to her,
was broken and wounded and dropping blood" (*Conf.*, 6.16, 132–33). If
the original purpose of the biographical portion of the *Confessions* was
merely to introduce the real matter of the book—an exposition of Christian
doctrine and an exegesis of Holy Scripture—then Augustine's language in
such a passage as this does much to undermine that purpose. The unnamed
concubine, Augustine goes on, "had returned to Africa after having made

17. After Augustine's conversion Adeodatus accompanied his father on the journeys
that took them from Cassiciacum to Milan to Ostia to Rome and finally back to Carthage
and Thagaste. In book 9 of the *Confessions,* Augustine writes:

> We also had with us young Adeodatus, the son of my flesh. . . . He was scarcely fifteen, but he
> showed more intelligence than many serious and learned men. . . . There is a book of mine called
> *The Master;* it is a dialogue between Adeodatus and me. You know that all the ideas put into
> the mouth of the person conversing with me were his own ideas, when he was sixteen. And
> there were other things too, even more remarkable, which I noticed in him. I found his intelli-
> gence really awe-inspiring. And who except you could be the maker of such wonders? Soon you
> took away his life from this earth and, as I think of him, I am perfectly at ease, for there is nothing
> in his boyhood or youth or indeed his whole personality to make one feel fear for him. (*Conf.*,
> 9.6, 193)

Peter Brown speculates that when Augustine, in his final book, quotes a passage from Cicero
on fatherhood, he may have been thinking of Adeodatus, and that quoting the passage
"perhaps betrays the hurt" of the loss he suffered in Adeodatus's death: "Surely what Cicero
says comes straight from the heart of all fathers, when he wrote: *'You are the only man of all
men whom I would wish to surpass me in all things'* " (*Augustine of Hippo,* 135).

a vow to you that she would never go to bed with another man, and she had left with me the natural son I had had by her. But I, in my misery, could not follow the example of a woman." Since he had to wait two years to marry, Augustine says, but could not allay the desires of the flesh, "I found another woman for myself—not, of course, as a wife," but this did nothing to assuage the hurt, both physical and spiritual, of the original loss: "Nor was the wound healed which had been made by the cutting off of my previous mistress. It burned, it hurt intensely, and then it festered, and if the pain became duller, it became more desperate." Did Augustine, as a bishop, desire a mistress? Surely not. But did Augustine, as a bishop, remember what it was to desire this mistress? Surely, surely he did.

The most interesting, and the most harrowing, passage in which Augustine's feelings will out in spite of him is when he writes of the death of the friend with whom he became so close after returning from Carthage to his hometown of Thagaste to teach rhetoric. Augustine draws himself up sharply several times in the course of recounting his friend's death to remind himself and his reader that it is folly to love someone so much when it is certain that she or he will die, but this Christian message—no doubt salutary in its way—is lost again and again in the flood of feeling not only for the friend dead but for friendship itself.

> In the time when I first began to teach rhetoric in the town where I was born, I had found a very dear friend who was following the same studies. We were both of the same age, now at the beginning of manhood; he had grown up with me as a child and we had gone to school together and played together. . . . [T]his [renewed] friendship was something very sweet [dulcis] to us and had ripened in the enthusiasm of the studies which we had pursued together.

But this friendship, which "was sweeter to me than all sweetnesses that in this life I had ever known," was destined to end after scarcely a year. And the effect on Augustine, as he says, was devastating:

> My heart was darkened over with sorrow, and whatever I looked at was death. My own country was a torment to me, my own home was a strange unhappiness. All those things which we had done and said together became, now that he was gone, sheer torture to me. My eyes looked for him everywhere and could not find him. And as to the places where we used to meet I hated all of them for not containing him. . . . I had become a great riddle to myself and I used to ask my soul why it was sad and why it disquieted me so sorely. And my soul did not know what to answer. . . . Only tears were sweet to me, and tears had taken the place of my friend in my heart's love.

With the passage of time, Augustine is able to draw if not Christian consolation then at least the Christian lesson: "I was unhappy and so is every soul unhappy which is tied to its love for mortal things; when it loses them, it is torn in pieces, and it is then that it comes to realize the unhappiness which was there even before it lost them." The Christian lesson is hardly out of Augustine's mouth, however, before he is back in the throes of mourning for his friend and for himself. Each of them was the half of a single soul, Augustine says,[18] and he describes himself as near to madness with the loss of his other half:

> Mad and foolish I was at that time. I raged and sighed and wept and worried, I could not rest, I could not think intelligently. For I was carrying about with me my soul all broken and bleeding and not wanting to be carried by me; yet I did not know where to put it down. There was no rest for it anywhere— not in pleasant groves, not in games and singing, not in sweet-smelling gardens, not in fine banquets, not in the pleasures of the bed, not in the reading of books, nor in poetry. . . . And myself to myself had become a place of misery, a place where I could not bear to be and from which I could not go. For my heart could not flee away from my heart, nor could I escape from myself, since wherever I ran, I should be following. Nevertheless I did flee from my native place; for my eyes did not search for him so much in places where they were not accustomed to see him. So I left the town of Thagaste and came to Carthage.

This is not the end, however, not the end of the episode nor the end of the alternation between the conscious and uplifting message that one ought not love mortal things too much and the recollected emotion of friendship that effectively proved to Augustine that to a feeling human being—himself, for example—there cannot be such a thing as too much loving friendship. "For the reason why that great sorrow of mine had pierced into me so easily and so deeply was simply this," Augustine writes, and then he produces one of those great figures of speech for which the *Confessions* is justly famous: "I had poured out my soul like water onto sand by loving a man who was bound to die just as if he were an immortal." So he had done wrong—Augustine says. Let any reader believe him who wishes to.

18. "I agree with the poet who called his friend 'the half of his own soul.' For I felt that my soul and my friend's had been one soul in two bodies, and that was why I had a horror of living, because I did not want to live as a half being, and perhaps too that was why I feared to die, because I did not want him, whom I had loved so much, to die wholly and completely" (*Conf.*, 4.6, 76). This latter clause about his friend's dying entirely if he should also die is virtually the only passage from the *Confessions* that Augustine criticizes in the *Retractations,* saying of it, "This seems to me, as it were, a trifling pronouncement rather than a serious confession, although this absurdity may be moderated to some extent by the word *perhaps* which I added" (*Ret.,* 130). This demonstrates how very seriously Augustine was inclined to take any pronouncement he might have made on the subject of friendship.

What did him most good, nevertheless, and helped most to cure him, according to Augustine, "was the comfort I found in other friends." Yet he calls this "one huge fable, one long lie"; and in a figure that tops even the earlier one of pouring out the soul like water onto sand he says that "by its adulterous caressing, my mind, which lay itching in my ears, was corrupted. Nor, if one of my friends died, would that fable die out in me." How should this extended episode (it has by now run over five chapters of book 4) continue and conclude? Without so much as a chapter break to take a breath and change course, Augustine follows this condemnation of the "huge fable, one long lie" of human friendship[19] by launching into a paean to friendship that has few affective equals in the literature of the world:

> There were other things which more fully took up my mind in their company—to talk and laugh and do kindnesses to each other; to read pleasant books together; to make jokes together and then talk seriously together; sometimes to disagree, but without any ill feeling, just as one may disagree with oneself, and to find that these very rare disagreements made our general agreement all the sweeter; to be sometimes teaching and sometimes learning; to long impatiently for the absent and to welcome them with joy when they returned to us. These and other similar expressions of feeling, which proceed from the hearts of those who love and are loved in return, and are revealed in the face, the voice, the eyes, and in a thousand charming ways, were like a kindling fire to melt our souls together and out of many to make us one.

"It is this," Augustine continues in the next chapter (book 4, chapter 9), "It is this which we love in our friends, and we love it so much that a man's conscience will condemn him if he fails to give or accept friendship when it is sought for or offered." Indeed, it was this that Augustine himself loved in those friends he had by him all his life long—and needed, for life in its positive aspect was, for him, largely made up of friendships. "I could not be happy," Augustine writes of his friends Alypius and Nebridius at the conclusion of book 5, "even in the way I then understood happiness, without friends. . . . For certainly I loved my friends for their own sake, and I knew that they too loved me for my own sake." He seems to have had a peculiar genius for friendship, both early and late, which is but one

---

19. On the "huge fable" and "long lie" that is friendship, cf. the verbal and thematic similarity of *Company,* where Augustine's "friendship" could easily translate as "company": "From time to time with unexpected grace you lie. . . . Supine now you resume your fable where the act of lying cut it short. . . . But with face upturned for good labour in vain at your fable. . . . The fable of one with you in the dark. The fable of one fabling of one with you in the dark" (*Company,* 61–63).

of the ways in which, in Augustine's development, the child was father
of the man, his days being bound each to each by the natural piety of
friendship.

   These preceding five or six pages have been by way of saying several
closely related things: that Augustine gave himself over to revisiting his
memories and to the autobiographical act, whether in writing or simply in
his mind and whether he called it confession or something else, very frequently throughout his life; that, not being content merely to revisit his
memories and his life, Augustine, both in the *Confessions* and in other
mixed-genre books that surrounded and expanded on the *Confessions,* developed some very complex and far-reaching theories of both memory and
narrative that establish him as the great fountainhead of the theory as well
as the practice of life-writing; that, for all the changes and the one great
conversion, he discovered, through memory, a continuity in his life that,
reproduced in his narrative, made him the same person in his youth as in
his maturity (and old age); that though the past was past and therefore did
not exist, it nevertheless, through memory, had its own, peculiarly potent
kind of reality in the present—the presence of things past; and that all sorts
of memories coexisted, layered or embedded or nested in Augustine's mind,
demanding for sufficient expression a complex narrative of evolution and
exfoliation yet coming out of and always relating back to a single principle
of being. These are the terms set by the *Confessions* for practitioners of life-
writing for going on sixteen hundred years now, who, according to their
own best lights, would embrace those terms or reject them, attempt to
equal Augustine's great effort or deconstruct it. In any case these are the
original terms, and it seems to me that the tradition of writing that grounded
itself in the *Confessions,* to take what way it would thereafter, displays the
same kind of narrative logic of development-within-continuity—of complexity spiraling out of singleness—that Augustine's story has about it. In
other words, what we have is something like two parallel, evolutionary
narratives—one the life of Augustine, the other the life of the tradition
grown out of that first instance of life-writing. Biologists say it is not possible to predict species evolution and that, viewed before the fact, a species
could develop in any direction. The same could be said of the two evolutionary stories I am concerned with: St. Augustine could scarcely have seen
himself as bishop of Hippo when he was stealing pears, nor, when he finished the *Confessions,* could he have imagined that a man named Samuel
Beckett would write a book called *Company* that would be the lineal descendant of the *Confessions* (and surely Augustine would have found it unthinkable—probably unspeakable—that a rascal like Jean-Jacques Rous-

seau should choose for his book the same title Augustine had chosen for his own). On the other hand, however, looking back from his position as a priest and bishop of the Catholic Church to his early errant days, the way from the one to the other must have seemed to Augustine inevitable—as one might say, overdetermined. Likewise, if we look back from *Company* to the *Confessions* with the other *Confessions* of Rousseau in between, since it is no longer a question of prediction but (so to say) of postdiction, the evolutionary passage from antiquity through romanticism to modernism and postmodernism is not at all undecidable but instead has the inescapable curve of history and the compelling logic of the-way-things-are about it. But, in addition to this dual narrative of Augustine's recalled life and the tradition that grew out of that act of recalling-and-narrating, there are several other narratives going on in and around the *Confessions* itself. There is what one might term the naive narrative, as imagined from the young Augustine's point of view, which shows no knowledge of the ends to which God's providence is directing it all, and at the same time there is the entirely nonnaive narrative, which locates its point of view as it were at the end of the narrative with full knowledge of where, under God's guidance, the story is tending. It is the continual interplay of these dual-level narratives that makes the *Confessions* a supremely ironic text in which nothing is as the central figure imagines it to be—except that the central figure is also the narrator who operates from the end of the narrative, and everything—not nothing—is as he imagines it to be. One of Augustine's great strengths is the ability to keep alive the sense of the way it was at the time, the sense of open possibility for the story to develop as it will—he does not at all suggest that the days of his youth were simply worthless and misguided or that it were better that they had never been—and he does this while simultaneously indicating that it could not have been otherwise than it has been and that it all—all of it—is good, very good. Again, the dual-level narrative of the *Confessions* is surrounded by and grounded in a whole series of Augustine's other writings, of the same time, earlier, and later—the *Two Books on Genesis against the Manichees,* the "Unfinished Book" *On the Literal Interpretation of Genesis, On Free Choice of the Will, The Literal Meaning of Genesis, On the Trinity,* and *The City of God*—all of which concern themselves one way or another with narrative, drawing now and then on the narrative of Augustine's life but more often struggling with the nature of narrative itself: what a story is, how it is produced, and how we are to interpret it. And finally the story that Augustine tells in the *Confessions* of his conversion and of his slow development to the point where he could hope to produce an adequate interpretation of Holy Scripture is embedded in a congeries of other conversion narratives—those of Simplicianus, Ambrose, and Victorinus, of Alypius and Nebridius, of Ponticianus and Antony—and at the same time it resonates with all the quotations from scriptural narrative that Augustine interweaves with his own narrative. (To give some sense of the frequency of such biblical quotations, one might glance at chapter 1 of book 8—a chapter of slightly under two pages—which quotes, in this order, Psalm 86, Psalm 116, Job 1.10, 1 Corinthians 13.12, 1 Corinthians 5.7, John 14.6, 1 Corinthians 7.8, Matthew 19.12, 2 Wisdom 13.1, Romans 1.21, Job 38.28, Proverbs 3.7, Romans 1.22, and Matthew 13.46.) It is quite astonishing to contemplate how many narratives Augustine maintains simultaneously and at how many different narrative levels he is able to conduct himself. To be equal to narrating the experience of being "on pilgrimage in this mortal life," as Augustine terms it in *The City of God*,[20] demands seeing yours as both individual story and as *mythos,* as the tale of this individual in this time and this place and as the tale of humanity. When, after the passage in the *Confessions* about reciting a psalm, Augustine goes on to say, "And what is true of the whole psalm is also true of every part of the psalm and of every syllable in it. The same holds good for any longer action, of which the psalm may be only a part. It is true also of the whole of a man's life, of which all of his actions are parts. And it is true of the whole history of humanity, of which the lives of all men are parts" (*Conf.*, 11.29, 282), he points up the multilayered, concentrically structured, metonymic nature of the narrative project he has in hand and that he pursued, both theoretically and practically, from the early soliloquies and the *Two Books on Genesis against the Manichees* through the central confessions to the (almost) concluding retractions. The one most salient feature of this project that makes it so vastly and unavoidably complex is that it is a story unfolding in time and told in human language that would, if successful, have ultimate reference to a reality that exists before and outside of time and that—because it is nontemporal—cannot be captured in a language that must utter itself in time and that must fade away even as the words are sounded. The individual story Augustine tells is of the slow, step-by-step, day-by-day development that prepared him to attempt the leap to interpretation of the story beyond all stories and specifically to go beyond and outside time to an understanding of the narrative of creation in Genesis. In *The Literal Meaning of Genesis* (begun in 401, the same year Augustine completed the

20. St. Augustine, *The City of God,* ed. David Knowles, trans. Henry Bettenson (Harmondsworth: Penguin, 1972), 11.28, 463; hereafter cited by book and chapter numbers, with page numbers from this edition.

Confessions, but not finished until 414) Augustine says that there are (rather like his own practice) two narratives of creation in Genesis, one a narrative of the simultaneous creation of all things, the other a narrative of creations spread out over six days. The six days of creation, according to Augustine, constitute a temporal figuration of a single day of creation, repeated six times over, which, however, has no temporal dimensions to it—it is not, he says, the same thing as our "solar day," the Sun and other heavenly bodies being markers of time. Why the two narratives? It is simply because we who are bound to the wheel of time "cannot arrive at the meaning of Scripture unless the narrative proceeds slowly step by step."[21] And so Augustine's own narrative proceeds in the same manner: "One day," Augustine writes in book 8, beginning the account leading up to the moment of his actual conversion with a formulaic expression recalling the "Once upon a time" or "In the beginning" of any number of stories, "One day, when Alypius and I were at home (Nebridius, for some reason which I cannot remember, was away) we were visited by a man called Ponticianus who, coming from Africa, was a fellow countryman of ours and who held an important appointment at the emperor's court." Here we have laid out, almost in schematic form, all the elements of any narrative, and what follows is the story of Ponticianus's story of being converted by reading the story of Antony's conversion—all embedded in the ongoing story of Augustine's coming slowly to the point of conversion, which itself occurs in a thoroughly narrativized way as Augustine goes into the garden and hears the child's voice calling out "Tolle, lege: Take it and read it" and, remembering that according to Ponticianus's account Antony had been converted by a similar admonition, he goes inside, opens the Bible at random, and comes upon a passage in Paul's Epistle to the Romans that contains and implies a great deal of narrative activity (rather an excess of it perhaps)—"Not in rioting and drunkenness, not in chambering and wantonness, not in strife and envying: but put ye on the Lord Jesus Christ, and make not provision for the flesh in concupiscence"—and Augustine is thereupon converted. Surrounding all these human stories that surround Augustine's story, of course, is the story of God's creation and his providence that provides the counterpoint—a divine and ironic counterpoint—to Augustine's story throughout. But the question that must occur to any reader is how Augustine or anyone else, being confined to time, to temporal understanding,

---

21. St. Augustine, *The Literal Meaning of Genesis,* trans. John Hammond Taylor, 2 vols. (New York: Newman Press, 1982), 4.33.52, 1.142; hereafter cited by book, chapter, and paragraph numbers, with volume and page numbers from this edition.

and to stories that begin "One day . . ." and "Once upon a time . . . ," can expect to have any apprehension or comprehension at all of the divine story supervening every human story. And thereby hangs a tale of great complexity indeed.

The Trinity of Mind

"I began the books on the Trinity as a young man," Stephen McKenna quotes St. Augustine as saying in the introduction to his translation of *De Trinitate,* "but published them as an old man."[22] Augustine was almost exactly halfway through the writing of the *Confessions* (which extended from c. 397 to c. 401) when he began the *Trinity* in 399 or 400. He finally completed the book, after a number of intervening problems, in about 416, concluding his task with this characteristic prayer: "Deliver me, O God, from the multitude of words with which I am inwardly afflicted in my soul; it is wretched in Your sight, and takes refuge in Your mercy. For I am not silent in my thoughts, even when I am silent in my words" (*Trin.,* 15.28.51, 524). Certainly, during this immensely productive period of his life, Augustine was silent neither in his thoughts nor in his words, both thoughts and words being largely given over to recollecting and writing his life experience and—perhaps even more—to meditating on the significance of this dual activity of recalling-and-narrating and on the capacity of the human mind that made the activity possible and—if possible or *because* possible—therefore necessary. Why should he write his life-story? Why should he have been so caught by his subject when, in the beginning, he had apparently not intended it? Why did it prove so interesting to himself and to others? What is it about the mind that makes it and its experience knowable to itself? And what does the mind's knowledge of itself, of its present and its past, imply about knowledge of that which lies outside of— before, beyond, and after—the mind? These are the kinds of questions Augustine addresses—in a highly interrogative fashion, suggesting that so long as we see "through a mirror in an enigma,"[23] we can proceed only

22. *The Trinity,* trans. Stephen McKenna (Washington, D.C.: Catholic University of America Press, 1963), p. vii. Subsequent citations will be given by book, chapter, and paragraph number and by page number in this edition.

23. This is the version of 1 Corinthians 13.12 that Augustine quotes in the *Trinity,* 15.8.14, 469. Elsewhere the passage appears as: "We see now in an enigma, as in a cloud" (*Two Books on Genesis against the Manichees,* 2.5.6, in *St. Augustine on Genesis,* trans. Roland J. Teske [Washington, D.C.: Catholic University of America Press, 1991], 100); "as if through a mirror in a riddle" (*Literal Meaning of Genesis,* 12.28.56, 2.219); "darkly, . . . through a glass" (*Conf.,* 12.13, 293); and "Now we see a puzzling reflection in a mirror" (*City of God,* 22.29, 1083). As will become apparent in my discussion, 1 Corinthians 13.12

by way of questioning, exploring, guessing, and theorizing—in the *Confessions,* in the *Trinity,* and in the various other writings that attempt an interpretation of the account of creation in Genesis, from the first words ("In the Beginning . . .") up to—and crucially including—verse 26 of chapter 1: "And God said, 'Let Us make mankind to Our image and likeness.'" Honoring the injunction of the Delphic Oracle—"Gnothi seauton: Know thyself"—Augustine writes at the outset of book 4 of the *Trinity,*

> Men are wont to set a high value on the knowledge of earthly and celestial things. But they are certainly better who prefer the knowledge of themselves to this knowledge; and a mind to which even its own weakness is known, is more deserving of praise than one which, knowing nothing of this, searches out the courses of the stars in order to learn to know them, or to retain the knowledge of them it has already acquired, but is itself ignorant of the course by which it must proceed to reach its own true health and strength. (*Trin.,* bk. 4, preface, p. 129)

And it is at discovering "the course by which it must proceed" that Augustine's mind works so assiduously in this and its companion volumes.

Describing the slow, step-by-step, narrative way he took to knowing something of himself, Augustine says the chief obstacle he had to overcome was an imagination that was entirely corporeal and that told him, in his early Manichaean days, that nothing existed but what was extended in time and in space. Even when he heard Ambrose "preaching to the people the word of truth," telling them that "the phrase 'man, created by Thee, after Thine own image' was not understood by your spiritual children . . . in such a way as to mean that you are bounded by the shape of a human body," Augustine says he could not come near the truth because "I had not the faintest or most shadowy notion about what a spiritual substance could be . . ." (*Conf.,* 6.4, 115). Augustine never doubted that the mind itself, by which he knew or failed to know these things, was incorporeal, but he says that early on he was incapable of drawing out the implications of mind's incorporeality when it came to attaining the highest objects of its knowledge. The "sensual man"—which is very much what Augustine presents himself as having been from his youth up—cannot grasp the doctrinal enigma that declares that the three persons of the Trinity "are together equal to each singly" because "he cannot think except in terms of bulk or space, whether large or small, for phantasms or, as it were, images of bodies flit about in his mind" (*Trin.,* 7.6.11, 239). There is a deep paradox in this

---

was of enormous importance to Augustine's Neoplatonizing hermeneutical endeavor—he quotes from or alludes to the verse countless times in the volumes I will be dealing with.

doctrine of the Trinity, but there is a yet deeper and greater paradox in the assumption lying behind Augustine's procedure—the assumption that it is only by recalling experience back over time and by following a narrative that is, of necessity, grounded in—and is both constrained and liberated by—its temporal and spatial dimensions that one can hope to come to a noncorporeal, nontemporal, nonspatial higher reality. To reach a nonnarrative Narrative, as it were—a story of creation effected in no-time yet also effected in six days, which, however, are not our "solar days"—one can proceed, Augustine indicates, only by way of a thoroughly narrativized path, the journey of one wayfarer through minutes and hours and days of time. But the paradox of paradoxes—or perhaps the resolution to the paradoxes—and the conclusion to which Augustine comes, is how exquisitely the mind, fastened to a dying animal and knowing not what it is ("So great is the force of memory, so great is the force of life in man who lives to die" [*Conf.*, 10.17, 227]), is fitted to that which, at its highest, it would know, whether that be the mind itself, in its incorporeal and immortal nature, or the creative power by which it exists.

Paradox or not, Augustine can begin the same book from which I have just quoted with this prayer: "Let me know you, my known; let me know Thee even as I am known. Power of my soul, enter into it and fit it for yourself. . . . This is my hope . . . and in this hope is my joy, when my joy is healthy" (*Conf.*, 10.1, 210). Clearly this is looking forward to the beatific vision promised in 1 Corinthians, but there is also no suggestion here that God is unknown or unknowable to the human mind in its wayfaring status. "Power of my soul, enter into it and fit it for yourself"—this is just what Augustine believed God had done in creating humans "to our image and likeness"—not the body, however, which time wastes and destroys, but the mind, which contains multitudes. "From this," Augustine writes of the Genesis narrative of creation, "we are to understand that man was made to the image of God in that part of his nature wherein he surpasses the brute beasts. This is, of course, his reason or mind or intelligence, or whatever we wish to call it. . . . [M]an has been created to the image of God . . . not by any features of the body but by a perfection of the intelligible order, that is, of the mind when illuminated" (*Literal Meaning of Genesis*, 3.20.30, 1.96). If, then, the mind "has been created to the image of God," may it not be, Augustine asks in the final book of the *Confessions*, that in the mind itself and in the mind's knowing of itself we can discover some trace, some shadow, some sign, seen "in an enigma, as in a cloud," of that of which the mind is an image? May we not, in other words, discover in the structural principle of the mind that Structure that is without structure because without extension but that is very structure itself? "Who can understand the almighty Trinity?" Augustine asks rhetorically, implying the clear answer that no one can. "Yet we all speak of it. . . ." And so: "I should like men to consider three aspects of their own selves. These three are something very different from the Trinity; I only make the suggestion as a mental exercise which will allow people to find out and to feel how far distant they are from it. The three things I mean are existence, knowledge, and will. For I am, and I know, and I will" (*Conf.*, 13.11, 323). How far distant, yes, for in human experience existence, knowledge, and will are uncertain, mortal, and mutable while the Trinity "exists immutably, knows immutably, and wills immutably." How far distant, then, but maybe, just maybe, how close also, how very close, even if it must be "as if through a mirror in a riddle." "But whether because of these three"—existence, knowledge, and will—"there is in God also a Trinity," Augustine writes in a rather tortured conclusion to his proposed "mental exercise," "or whether all three are in each Person so that each Person has three aspects, or whether both views are correct and in some unimaginable way, in simplicity and in multiplicity, It itself, though unbounded, is within Itself and bound to Itself, by which it exists and is known to itself and is sufficient to itself, unchangeably the Selfsame in the plentiful magnitude of its unity— who can easily grasp this in his mind? Who can in any way tell of it? Who could in any way venture to make a pronouncement upon it?" Well, put in that way, I think it would be fair to say that no one could "*easily* [facile] grasp this in his mind"; and as for telling of it or making a pronouncement upon it—as opposed to getting some darkling glimpse of it in the mind— Augustine always maintained, even on the infrequent occasions when he claimed to have been favored with the mystical vision himself, that it could not be expressed in words. Nevertheless, much of the hesitancy of assertion ("I only make the suggestion as a mental exercise") and much of the uncertainty about the trinity that may exist in and as the mind that one finds in this relatively early formulation of a psychological trinity corresponding by analogy to the theological Trinity have disappeared by the time Augustine gives magisterial treatment to the subject in the long work that, by its title, virtually announces itself as a major doctrinal statement: *De Trinitate*.

St. Augustine's repeated, almost obsessive, return to the first verses of Genesis and to an interpretation that will do some kind of rough justice to the dense complexity of those verses—however inadequate, however tormented the interpretation may be in the sight of God—finds its center, as I have already implied, and virtually its terminus in verse 26 of the first chapter of Genesis: "And God said, 'Let Us make mankind to Our image and likeness . . .' " (translation in *Literal Meaning of Genesis*, 3.19.29, 1.94). From the kernel of these few words one could fairly say that Augustine opened out a vast, closely articulated system of thought that is psychological, philosophical, and theological in nature, a system that explained memory and circled about that mysterious phenomenon in a way that intrigues thinkers to the present day, and that laid the grounds for a narrativized understanding of Scripture, of human history, and of any individual life that has informed the theory and practice of life-writing from Augustine's time to our own. Here (from the *Trinity*) is but one characteristic instance of the way Augustine's thought was sparked off by Genesis 1.26:

> "Let us make man to our image and likeness." "Let us make" and "our" are said in the plural. . . . For it was not that gods might make to the image and likeness of gods, but that the Father, the Son, and the Holy Spirit might make to the image of the Father, the Son, and the Holy Spirit, in order that man might subsist as the image of God. But God is the Trinity.

But why the strange locution "to the image" rather than simply "the image"? Or, turning the matter around, "since the Son is the image of the Father alone," what can be the meaning of God's saying "to our image"? "But as we have already mentioned," Augustine explains,

> man is said to be "to the image" on account of an imperfect likeness, and, therefore, "to our image," in order that man might be the image of the Trinity, not equal to the Trinity as the Son to the Father, but approaching it, as has been said by a kind of similarity, just as nearness, not of place but of a sort of imitation, may be signified even in distant things. (*Trin.*, 7.6.12, 240–41)

Yes, a "nearness" even in "distant things"—one hears the echo from the *Confessions* but with a greater assurance now that humanity *is* "to the image of the Trinity," and though Augustine does not invoke 1 Corinthians 13.12 specifically in his discussion there can be little doubt that the verse is hovering over the passage, like the Holy Spirit itself, even if just out of sight. Likewise, in the *City of God,* the way of seeing is as in a glass, darkly, when Augustine declares,

> We do indeed recognize in ourselves an image of God, that is of the Supreme Trinity. It is not an adequate image, but a very distant parallel. It is not co-eternal and, in brief, it is not of the same substance as God. For all that, there is nothing in the whole of God's creation so near to him in nature. . . . (*City of God,* 11.26, 459)

"For all that . . ."—this is the bottom line; and in the *Trinity* Augustine will say, with equal assurance and with the same doctrinal precision,

With regard . . . to that supreme, ineffable, incorporeal, and unchangeable
nature, which is to be seen in some manner by our understanding, nowhere
else does the eye of the human mind exercise itself to better advantage, provided only that it is guided by the rule of faith, than in that which man himself
has in his own nature better than other animals, better even than other parts
of his own soul, and that is the mind itself. . . . (*Trin.*, 15.27.49, 520–21)

But when Augustine says, as he does so frequently, that we can discern
in the human mind an image—obscure and dim, to be sure, but a true
image for all that—of the "supreme, ineffable, incorporeal, and unchangeable" Trinity, he has much more specific attributions to make or analogies
to draw between the original and that which is created to the image of the
original. Indeed, he makes a number of different analogies, and the *Trinity*
is filled with trinities intended to give some idea of God's delighted luxuri-
ance in reproducing small-scale trinities everywhere: an object seen, the
seeing itself, and the attention that fixes seeing (11.1.1, 316); the lover, the
beloved, and the love (8.10.14, 266); the mind, love, and knowledge (9.5.8,
277); etc. These, however, are all what one might call second-order analogies, the primary analogy and the one Augustine draws most frequently and
most tellingly being that one that sees the mind, the self, the whole being
as a single unity invested entirely in each of its three distinct attributes or
faculties—memory, understanding, and will, for memory remembers not
only itself but also understanding and will, understanding understands both
itself and memory and will, and will wills both itself and memory and understanding. This is a trinity very much to the image of the Trinity of
Father, Son, and Holy Spirit. "By making use of the creature which God
has made," Augustine writes in the final book of the *Trinity,*

we have warned those who demand the reason concerning such things, that
they should behold the invisible things of Him through those that were made,
especially through that rational or intellectual creature which was made to the
image of God; through which, as through a mirror, they would behold, insofar
as they would be able, if indeed they would be able, that God who is Trinity
in our memory, understanding, and will. (*Trin.*, 15.20.39, 505–6)

Even before we would seek to know the Trinity of which the mind's trinity
is an image, Augustine argues, we should look to the mind as it is in itself,
for "even though it has become impaired and disfigured . . . , it remains
nonetheless an image of God. For it is His image by the very fact that it
is capable of Him, and can be a partaker of Him . . ." (*Trin.*, 14.8.11, 426).
When I say that Augustine urges us to look to the mind as it is in itself, I

mean (and I think he means) that the mind or brain[24] is, as contemporary psychologists and neuroscientists of all sorts—neuroanatomists, neurobiologists, neurochemists, even neurophilosophers[25]—are nowadays saying, a dynamic and open system, with multifold sensory ties to the external world but also with a determining self-schema of its own that is capable of memory processes and memory formation that do not necessarily rely on any information received from without. At least such is the gist of what he goes on to say after urging his reader to look closely at the mind:

> Behold! the mind, therefore, remembers itself, understands itself, and loves itself; if we perceive this, we perceive a trinity, not yet God indeed, but now finally an image of god. The memory has not received from without what it was to retain, nor has the understanding found without what it was to behold, as does the eye of the body, nor has the will joined these two from without, as it joins the form of the body, and that which was wrought from it in the eye of the beholder; nor when the thought was turned to it, has it found an image of the object seen from without which has been seized, so to say, and hidden in the memory, and from which the gaze of the one recollecting has been formed, while the will as a third joins both together, as we showed taking place in those trinities which were found in corporeal things, or which were somehow drawn within from bodily objects through the senses of the body. . . . (*Trin.*, 14.8.11, 426)

After this, one might be inclined to quote Augustine back to himself— "who can easily grasp this in his mind?"—but surely what he would have us see, or try to see, is that the mind is constituted of a trinity of memory, understanding, and will, in each of which it resides unitarily and entirely while each member of the trinity is nevertheless distinctively itself and simultaneously the whole. I do not say that this is easily grasped either, but the difficulty comes in that what is being said participates—as does the doctrine of the Trinity—in the mystery of paradox.

Mind is an image of God, then, an imperfect figuration, because in its aspects of memory, understanding, and will, it composes a trinity that is a likeness of the Trinity that created it. Augustine gives more than one name to the third aspect of mind, calling it sometimes love or charity (an issue I will return to momentarily), but he always, I believe, lists them in the

24. I won't here go into the vexed issue of mind and brain because it would take us too far from the matter in hand but will leave it for chapter III. Suffice it to say that Augustine drew a distinction between mind and brain, but he also believed that an adequate account of memory, for example, had to accord a different but equal reality to mind and brain and ultimately had to recognize both as crucial to an understanding of what human beings are.

25. See Patricia S. Churchland, *Neurophilosophy: Towards a Unified Science of the Mind-Brain* (Cambridge: MIT Press, 1986).

same order—memory, understanding, will—and this for the reason that he wishes to be very specific in his attribution of aspects of the mind's trinity to the three Persons of the divine Trinity. There is a necessary relation that obtains, Augustine would say, among the Persons of the Trinity that is repeated—rather more dimly, rather more darkly—in the threefold aspects of mind: as memory is to understanding and will, so the Father is to the Son and the Holy Spirit; as understanding is to memory and will, so the Son is to the Father and the Holy Spirit; and as will is to memory and understanding, so the Holy Spirit is to the Father and the Son. When it comes to ascribing the trinity of human faculties to the separate Persons of the Holy Trinity, Augustine so hedges his reasoning by analogy around on all sides, with the apparent intention of not letting the reader imagine him so clumsy or blasphemous as to be saying that memory *is* the Father, understanding *is* the Son, and will *is* the Holy Spirit, that in the end he succeeds most notably in demonstrating that human language cannot bear the strain of the subtlety and complexity of the kind of assertions he is attempting to make. Yet through all the necessary hedges we can understand him to be saying—cautiously, hesitantly, sometimes seeming to take it back even before he has said it—that *some* analogy exists, in the always repeated order, between the individual aspects of mind—memory–understanding–will (or love)—and the individual members of the Holy Trinity—Father–Son– Holy Spirit. Augustine comes about as close as he ever will to outright assertion in these matters that will not submit to the crudity of human assertion when, in the following passage, he argues that as the Trinity is certainly a trinity so too the human mind really does partake of trinitari- ness—on the human level, of course:

> For although the memory of man, and particularly that which beasts do not have, namely, that in which intelligible things are so contained that they do not come into it through the senses of the body, has, in proportion to its own small measure in this image of the Trinity, a likeness, incomparably un- equal, of course, but yet a likeness of whatever kind it may be to the Father; and similarly, although the understanding of man, which is formed from the memory by the attention of thought, when that which is known is spoken— it is a word of the heart and belongs to no language—has in its great unlikeness some likeness to the Son; and although the love of man which proceeds from knowledge and combines the memory and the understanding, as though com- mon to the parent and the offspring—whence it is understood to be neither the parent nor the offspring—has in this image some likeness, although very unequal, to the Holy Spirit, yet we do not find that, as in this image of the Trinity, these three are not the one man, but belong to the one man, so in the highest Trinity itself, whose image this is, are those three of one God, but

they are the one God, and there are three Persons, not one. (*Trin.*, 15.23.43, 509–10)

Augustine, great rhetorician that he was, may not have had difficulty composing this single-sentence, paragraph-length analysis of things human and divine, but I think Stephen McKenna must have girded up his loins before he set himself to translating the passage (though, as usual, he does an excellent job of it), and likewise most readers, I imagine, would find the comma starts and stops, the parenthetical expressions, and the clauses within clauses a little hard going. But it is possible to extract the skeletal structure of the sentence-thought thus: "[T]he memory of man . . . has . . . a likeness . . . to the Father; and similarly, the understanding of man . . . has . . . some likeness to the Son; and . . . the love of man . . . has . . . some likeness . . . to the Holy Spirit. . . ." It can be (and a bit later I hope will be) instructive to consider why Augustine wrote the sentence he did write rather than this one I have pulled from his sentence, but for the moment I think we should take a closer look at memory, understanding, and will-love-charity, each in itself and each as it is one-in-three, three-in-one.

"[W]hen these three are in one person, such as man is," Augustine writes, "anyone could say to us: these three, memory, understanding, and love are mine, not their own; they do what they do not for themselves, but for me, nay rather, I do it through them. For I remember by memory, understand by understanding, and love by love . . ." (*Trin.*, 15.22.42, 508). Augustine is at considerable pains to establish that it is not memory that remembers but rather the person, the whole being—the self as we might call it, or the subject, that which is signified in English by the *I*. "This can be expressed briefly," he says in this same paragraph: "I remember, I understand, I love by all these three things, I who am neither my memory, nor my understanding, nor my love, but I have these" (p. 509). Yet when any one of these is in effect, it so thoroughly expresses the whole being that it seems to become it: as I remember so I am, as I understand so I am, as I love so I am. This is why, when he turns specifically to memory in book 10 of the *Confessions,* Augustine can say (as I quoted him saying in the first part of this chapter), "Great indeed is the power of memory! It is something terrifying, my God, a profound and infinite multiplicity; and this thing is the mind, and this thing is I myself" (*Conf.*, 10.17, 227). No, he is not his memory—we have to agree with Augustine about this: I "am neither my memory, nor my understanding, nor my love"; but his memory is himself, his understanding is himself, his love is himself. Each of the three, both separately and together, "is I myself," as Augustine claims with specific reference to memory. "Since these three, the memory, the understanding, and the will, are, therefore, not three lives but one life, not three minds but one mind, it follows that they are certainly not three substances, but one substance. For when we speak of memory as life, mind, and substance, we speak of it in respect to itself; but when we speak of it simply as memory, we speak of it in relation to something else. . . . Therefore, these three are one in that they are one life, one mind, and one essence" (*Trin.*, 10.11.18, 311). But memory has the particular capacity, as it were, to contain both understanding and will in a way, it seems to me, that neither of the other two could be said to contain memory. This is especially true of what Augustine terms "the inner memory of the mind" or "that principal memory . . . that is a more profound depth of our memory." At such depths, memory retains and secretes away not only memory of itself but memory of understanding and will as well: "For if we betake ourselves to the inner memory of the mind by which it remembers itself, and to the inner understanding by which it understands itself, and to the inner will by which it loves itself, where these three things are always together at the same time, and always have been together at the same time, from the moment when they began to be, whether one thought of them or whether one did not think of them, then the image of that trinity, too, will indeed be seen to belong to the memory alone . . ." (*Trin.*, 14.7.10, 424). In a kind of symphonic summary of all he has been able to say about mind's trinity and the Holy Trinity Augustine writes, "I have indeed exerted myself as much as I could to make God the Father and God the Son known to us . . . not for the purpose of now seeing them face to face, but rather of seeing them through this likeness in an enigma, in the memory and understanding of our own mind, by means of conjectures however tenuous they might be, attributing to the memory everything that we know, even if we do not think of it, and to the understanding the formation of thought by its own special type of thinking" (*Trin.*, 15.21.40, 506–7). These two, like Father and Son, only begetter and only begotten, form a unique tandem in their operation, but what is particularly interesting is what Augustine has to say about memory and understanding—and most particularly about memory—at what he calls the more profound depth of our memory: "For we usually say that we understand what we have found to be true by thinking of it, and this indeed we again leave in our memory." But beyond this, beyond what we have known and have "found to be true" and have left in storage in our memory, there is

> a more profound depth of our memory, where we also find those contents which we think of for the first time, and where the inner word is begotten which does not belong to the language of any nation, as it were, knowledge

of knowledge, vision of vision, and understanding of understanding, for the understanding, which appears in thought, comes from the understanding which already existed in the memory but was latent there. . . .

But with regard to the Holy Spirit, I pointed out that nothing in this enigma would seem to be like Him except our will, or love, or charity which is a stronger will. For our will, which belongs to us by nature, experiences various emotions, according to whether the things which are adjacent to it or which it encounters either entice or repel us. . . . [and] doubtless it possesses its own kind of knowledge which cannot be there without memory or understanding. . . . As there is understanding, so, therefore, there is also love in that principal memory in which we find prepared and stored away that which we can reach in thought . . . (*Trin.*, 15.21.40–41, 507)

The intriguing and significant point here, I believe, is Augustine's claim that there is unknown knowledge and unexperienced, untapped love deep in the deepest memory, "latent there. . . . prepared and stored away" for the time when we become capable of it. Of course, it "does not belong to the language of any nation," for it is pure latency, pure potency, quite outside—or hidden away from—the temporal, historical, cultural conditions of any language. "[A]nd we utter this true word within us," Augustine says, "without the language of any people when we say what we know"— what we know but do not know, we might add, not in any verbal way, not in the "language of any people," a languageless utterance and a languageless vision as it were. And all this, as Augustine says in the *Confessions,* "All this I do inside me, in the huge court of my memory. . . . Who has ever reached the bottom of [memory]? Yet this is a faculty of my mind and belongs to my nature; nor can I myself grasp all that I am" (*Conf.*, 10.8, 218–19).

As will be apparent, Augustine has a great deal to say in the *Confessions* and in the *Trinity* about memory as the source and the container—to adopt clumsy, inadequate terms for that which on its one face may be human but on its other looks onto the transcendent—of both understanding and will. About understanding, on the other hand, he says comparatively little, conceiving of it, as I have already implied, mostly in the relational terms of the Father and the Son: as the Son is the Only Begotten of the Father, so understanding is the only begotten of memory—which would seem to leave will, and its analogous partner, the Holy Spirit, out in the cold. Not really, however, for as the Holy Spirit "issues from" the relationship of Only Begetter to Only Begotten, so will issues from the symbiotic but also parent-child relationship of memory and understanding. But having issued from that relationship, it is the particular role of will to turn back to bind together yet more closely its two-in-one issuers. It has been said that Christianity never got off the ground—and never would have got off the ground—as long as it conceived of one god alone or two gods in one, but when it came up with the three-in-one of the Trinity then it was (relatively) smooth flying. Augustine would not talk like this, of course, but his real and deep devotion to the Holy Trinity—and, at another level, to the trinity of the mind—suggests something of how powerful was his attraction to a numerology that might bind all things into unity. It is in this regard that will, in its own right but also in its various guises of desire, love, and charity, takes on great significance for Augustine, and its significance is intimately related to his thought about both memory and narrative.

Readers of the *Confessions* will remember that it was the issue of will that particularly exercised and troubled Augustine in the account of his progress toward (and all too frequent regress from) conversion. Indeed, Augustine interrupts his narrative at a critical point in book 8, just when he has been so powerfully affected by the conversion narratives of Ponticianus, Antony, et al. and immediately before he goes into the garden where he hears and obeys the singsong command "tolle, lege," for a disquisition on the will. I say that he interrupts his narrative, and if said with regard to other authors this might be fair comment; it is not, however, an interruption at all in Augustine, for what he has to say about will is merely an extension and intensification of his narrative and is itself fully narrativized. "This was what Ponticianus told us," Augustine writes, and the effect of what he had been told was a fierce contest of wills within him.

> But you, Lord, while he was speaking, were turning me around so that I could see myself; you took me from behind my own back, which was where I had put myself during the time when I did not want to be observed by myself, and you set me in front of my own face so that I could see how foul a sight I was. . . . Ponticianus still went on with his story, and again you were setting me in front of myself, forcing me to look into my own face, so that I might see my sin and hate it. I did know it, but I pretended that I did not. I had been pushing the whole idea away from me and forgetting it. (*Conf.*, 8.7, 173)

This battle of memory with forgetting, of knowing with not knowing, of desire with desire is ultimately a contest of will against will. "[T]he more ardent was the love I felt for those two men of whom I was hearing," Augustine says, "the more bitter was the hatred I felt for myself" (8.7, 173), yet the old ways beckon and the old will stiffens so that Augustine finds himself, in effect, where he was twelve and fifteen years earlier, praying for continence but cautiously, wantonly asking that it come not yet, not yet. "So I was being gnawed at inside. . . . I lashed my soul on to follow me now. . . . [a]nd my soul hung back. . . . There remained a mute shrinking; for it feared like death to be restrained from the flux of a habit by which it was melting away into death" (8.8, 174). So Augustine goes to Alypius and cries out, "What is wrong with us?" or "some such words as these," and Alypius simply "stared at me in silence and amazed. For I sounded strange to him. My forehead, cheeks, eyes, color of face, and inflection of voice expressed my mind better than the words I used" (8.8, 175). This is the point at which Augustine goes out and throws himself on the ground in the garden. There, in a "storm of mental hesitation," he enacts his agony with his body: "I tore my hair, beat my forehead, locked my fingers together, clasped my knee," freely and easily making "the kind of movements which people sometimes want to make, but cannot make, either because they have not the limbs, or because their limbs are bound or weakened by illness or in some way or other prevented from action" (8.8, 175–76). How is this, Augustine asks, that he can will his body to do something and it obeys, yet he wills his mind and it responds "No, thanks" or "Yes, all right, but not yet"? "What can be the explanation of such an absurdity?" The force of the insult to his logic can be measured by the fact that Augustine asks this same question three times in a single, short paragraph.

> What can be the explanation of such an absurdity? The mind gives an order to the body, and the order is obeyed immediately: the mind gives an order to itself, and there is resistance. . . . The mind orders the mind to will; it is the same mind, yet it does not obey. What can be the explanation of such an absurdity? The mind, I say, orders itself to will: it would not give the order, unless it willed it, yet it does not obey the order. (*Conf.*, 8.9, 176)

The answer Augustine comes up with—and this accords with what he has to say in the *Trinity* about not being his memory, his will, or his understanding but possessing and using all three—is that the mind "does not will the thing entirely. . . . and disobedience to the order results from insufficiency of the will." There are, he says, "two wills in us," and this is because "one of them is not entire, and one has what the other lacks." What Augustine denies vehemently is that this means there are two minds or two selves or two *I*s in him or in any of us. "Let them perish from your presence, God, as perish empty talkers and seducers of the soul," Augustine prays, referring to all those—Manichaeans and their like—who "conclude from this that we have in us two minds of two different natures, one good and one evil." No, for Augustine there is a singleness of self, riven as it may be—riven as it was—by two contrary wills. "As to me," when he was being torn apart from within by his will and not-will, "it was I who willed it, and it was I who was unwilling. It was the same 'I' throughout. But neither my will nor my unwillingness was whole and entire. So I fought with myself and was torn apart by myself" (8.10, 177). The contest becomes a very poignant one for any reader still adhering to the sensual world when Augustine describes the tones in which the world appealed to the Old Adam in him:

> Toys and trifles, utter vanities had been my mistresses, and now they were holding me back, pulling me by the garment of my flesh and softly murmuring in my ear: "Are you getting rid of us?" and "From this moment shall we never be with you again for all eternity?" and "From this moment will you never for all eternity be allowed to do this or to do that?" (8.11, 180)

With the sad siren song of "never for all eternity" sounding in his ears, well might Augustine be given pause; and in fact he says he was "held in suspense," even though

> now their voices were not half so loud in my ears; now they no longer came out boldly to contradict me face to face; it was more as though they were muttering behind my back, stealthily pulling at my sleeve as I was going away so that I should turn and look at them. Yet still they did hold me back as I hesitated to tear myself away and to shake them off and to take the great step in the direction where I was called. Violence of habit spoke the words: "Do you think that you can live without them?" (8.11, 180–81)

How many saints, sinners no longer (not in this respect anyway) and safe in the bosom of the Church, would grant to the voices of temptation the moving accents that Augustine gives to the "mistresses" plucking at the garment of his flesh and murmuring softly in his ear? At this narrative moment, as at so many, Augustine is a master in investing the will he was to reject with a sufficient force of desire that the contest never seems like a sham. No one (I think) would suggest that his was a Pyrrhic victory, but neither does it feel like an easy victory—as Alypius's presumably was—or like one without any cost at all. One should recognize that there were not just two wills involved in this epic struggle, now transposed to the mind and heart of the individual Christian, but there were at least two memories as well, and with them all the yearning desire that memory could insinuate into the conflict. "Remember how sweet"—to adopt Augustine's favorite word in this context—"Remember how sweet were those delights, and how very sweet they could be again? Do you think that you can live without them?" As Samuel Beckett would have it—"To confess, Yes I remember. . . . To murmur, Yes I remember. . . . A voice in the first person singular. Murmuring now and then, Yes I remember." St. Augustine, I think one must judge from his own account, does remember, and indeed he confesses, in undenied, undeniable voice, "Yes I remember." Pierre Courcelle intended it, I am sure, in quite a different way, but I want to avail myself here of what he writes of the deeply emotional prayers that are spotted here and there throughout Augustine's narrative: "des élans lyriques," he says, "s'insérent dans les morceaux narratifs [lyrical outbursts inserted into passages of narrative]" (*Recherches,* 27). Courcelle, probably no less than Augustine himself, would be shocked and dismayed to think that the "élans lyriques" that he addresses to God might have, in the reader's mind at least, overtones that are more human and more worldly than the author would have consciously intended, but the language Augustine employs throughout the *Confessions* is the very language of desire and it is difficult as one reads the book not to think ahead to Jean-Jacques Rousseau and those "élans du desir" (piercing surges of desire) by whose intensity of affective power he was himself moved to wonder. But desire—which, with Augustine, is another name for love, which is another name for will—drives narrative and memory alike, and this we can learn from Augustine centuries before we can observe it in Rousseau.

So just as memory, in the mind's trinity, corresponds to the Father and understanding to the Son, so will or love corresponds to the Holy Spirit. "Love, then, which is from God and is God, is properly the Holy Spirit, through whom the charity of God is poured forth in our hearts, through which the whole Trinity dwells in us" (*Trin.,* 15.18.32, 497), Augustine writes, and a little further along in the same book: "But if the will of God is also to be specially attributed to any Person in the Trinity, then this name, just as love, belongs more appropriately to the Holy Spirit. For what else is love than will?" (*Trin.,* 15.20.38, 505). Analyzing will and love in the aspect of desire, Augustine argues that we cannot be said to love something until we know it, yet the desire we have to know it can be seen as a dim figuration of the love we will have for it when known.

> For inquiry is a desire to find. . . . [and] that desire, which is latent in seeking, proceeds from one who seeks, remains as it were in suspense, and only comes to rest in the goal towards which it is directed, when that which is sought has been found and is united with him who seeks. Although this desire, that is, this seeking does not seem to be love, by which that which is known is loved, for we are still striving to know, yet it is something of the same kind. (*Trin.,* 9.12.18, 288)

Desire, like seeking, is thus a thoroughly temporal version of knowledge and love, but this in no way lessens its impelling, driving force. "For it can already be called will," Augustine says of "this desire . . . this seeking," since everyone who seeks wishes to find; and if what he seeks belongs to the order of knowledge, then everyone who seeks wishes to know. . . . A kind of desire, therefore, precedes the birth in the mind, and by means of it, that is, by our seeking and finding what we wish to know, an offspring, namely, knowledge itself is born. (*Trin.*, 9.12.18, 289)

I have already glanced at Augustine's notion of the two wills at strife within him during the protracted period of his arriving at full conversion. He also in various places distinguishes (and this is much the same idea though in slightly different terms) between will in the fallen and the unfallen state. Before the Fall, Adam and Eve, although free to choose,[26] enjoyed an undivided will that was capable of some remarkable feats—feats many readers may find it difficult to imagine although Augustine says that we would all be capable of them were it not for the unfortunate Fall in the first Garden of humankind. By inversion this may recall to the reader's mind the passage in the *Confessions* when, Augustine being in *his* garden in Milan and about to hear the child's voice telling him to "take up and read"—an injunction that will momentarily lead on to Augustine's conversion and restoration of his spiritual health—he tells how he willed to move various parts of his body—his hands, arms, legs, etc.—and those parts of his body obeyed his command; it was only his mind, he says, that refused to obey its own will and its own command. But Augustine imagines that Adam and Eve, before they actually fell, would have had willed control over yet more members of their bodies than he was ever able to claim for himself. Montaigne, in his essay "Of the power of the imagination," wanting to demonstrate that the will is not so very completely in control of the body, refers to

the unruly liberty of this member, obtruding so importunately when we have no use for it, and failing so importunately when we have the most use for it, and struggling for mastery so imperiously with our will, refusing with so much pride and obstinacy our solicitations, both mental and manual.[27]

But Augustine will have none of this. It is not true, he says—or maybe it is true for you and for me but not for prelapsarian Adam in the Garden of Eden. "[M]ay we not assume," he asks in the *Literal Meaning of Genesis,*

26. The doctrine of freedom of the will, whence evil comes into the world, is an essential part of Augustine's ongoing battle with the Manichaeans. See his *De Libero Arbitrio*, translated by Thomas Williams as *On Free Choice of the Will* (Indianapolis: Hackett Publishing Co., 1993).

27. "Of the Power of the Imagination," in *The Complete Works of Montaigne*, trans. Donald M. Frame (Stanford: Stanford University Press, 1957), 72.

"that the first couple before they sinned could have given a command to their genital organs for the purpose of procreation as they did to the other members which the soul is accustomed to move to perform various tasks without any trouble and without any craving for pleasure?" (9.10.18, 2.81). One might question the necessity of that last phrase—"without any craving for pleasure"—which seems just a bit mean, but Augustine justifies the general thrust of his remarks by reference if not to the birds at least to the bees, saying that "the almighty Creator . . . , who is great even in the least of His works, has given to the bees the power of reproducing their young just as they produce wax and honey"—so why not human beings? "Why, then, should it seem beyond belief that He made the bodies of the first human beings in such a way that, if they had not sinned . . . , they would move the members by which offspring are generated in the same way that one commands his feet when he walks, so that conception would take place without passion and birth without pain? But as it is," he concludes with iron justice, "by disobeying God's command they deserved to experience in their members . . . the movements of a law at war with the law of the mind. . . ." We can trace from its inception the "unruly liberty of this member" (as Montaigne has it) in what Augustine has to say in the *City of God* of Adam and Eve in the Garden of Eden. Immediately after the Fall, he tells us, they took fig leaves,

> which were perhaps the first things they could lay hands on in their confusion, to cover their *pudenda,* the "organs of shame". . . . [for] they felt a novel disturbance in their disobedient flesh, as a punishment which answered to their own disobedience. . . . At its own pleasure the soul deserted its superior and master; and so it no longer retained its inferior and servant obedient to its will. It did not keep its own flesh subject to it in all respects, as it could have kept it for ever if it had itself continued in subjection to God. This then was the time when the flesh began to "lust in opposition to the spirit," which is the conflict that attends us from our birth. (*City of God,* 13.13, 522–23)

It is gone now, the undivided will, to be replaced by "the conflict that attends us from our birth" (though we can hope and expect that it will be restored in the hereafter: "In the Heavenly City then, there will be freedom of will. It will be one and the same freedom in all, and indivisible in the separate individuals" [*City of God,* 22.30, 1089]); and I believe that Augustine would agree that there were other consequences for the mind's trinity beyond the will itself in the splitting and division of the will—consequences specifically for memory.

If one recalls that it is God the Father who is dimly figured in human memory (though somewhat less dim at the "more profound depth of our memory" that Augustine calls "principal memory"), then it must be assumed that, when transposed back to its original and transcendent source, memory would be as perfect, as undivided, as absolute as will—desire become love become charity—was before the Fall. In that perfected state, prelapsarian and postrestoration, will and memory would be not only each of them individually perfect but also perfectly at one (and at one with understanding too of course), so that to will to remember would be the same as to remember. Any modern reader of Augustine's *Confessions* must feel that he had if not a perfect memory then at least an extraordinary memory, which was extraordinarily directed by his will (whether his memory was unusual in its time is another issue—that it seems so now, when the memory techniques available to Augustine have been all but lost, cannot be doubted). He seems able to remember all that he wants to remember, and those things that he "repeats by heart" (*narro memoriter*) come forth "easily and in perfect order, just as they are required" (*faciliter atque imperturbata serie sicut poscuntur suggeruntur: Conf.*, 10.8, 217). This is not the whole story, by any means, for Augustine tells of going to his memory in search of other things than those he has "by heart" and of being besieged by unwanted items that "with the hand of my heart I brush . . . away from the face of my memory," and clearly the "perfect order" here is in large part owing to the way these things have been committed to his memory. There are also, as I have pointed out in the first part of this chapter, those passages in Augustine where he sees memory as a dynamic process, not far removed from invention and imagination, rather than as a treasure house where everything is filed away in a fixed and unalterable order. Augustine was in many ways an astonishingly modern writer, and his modernity shows in the multiple views he takes of memory as much as it does, for example, in what he reveals about the psychology of conversion. This all having been said, however, it still remains true that in Augustine there is a particularly intimate and strong bond between will and memory that is hard to imagine for readers familiar with the ways of memory in Rousseau, for example, where nothing seems to come forth in any kind of order at all, and familiar too with the vagaries of memory in a host of writers of our time who come not only after Rousseau but after Freud as well. For Augustine—but here I do not intend any necessary contrast with subsequent writers, or if there is a contrast it is in the details of the procedure and not in the overall fact of relationship—memory is a most powerful ally, equal surely to either understanding or will, in the ongoing drama of human interpretation—

interpretation of a life, interpretation of Scripture, interpretation of any text woven out of a life and memory of that life.

The Hermeneutics of Memory

It is necessary, I believe, to distinguish at least three kinds of memory in St. Augustine. One is what might be termed rote memory, where we "memorize" something—a psalm, let us say—and have it by heart so that we can bring it out in perfect, unchanged order whenever we like; a second is memory of experiences that have come to us through our various senses—sight is the sense Augustine most often refers to—which we more or less consciously store away and which we can consciously return to, call up, and then store away once again, though in this kind of memory, for all the consciousness with which we store things away and call them up again, the probability of change in the contents of memory is much greater than in rote memory; and third is that "more profound depth of our memory. . . . that principal memory" that neither partakes of the mechanics of rote memory, nor depends on the external world for sensory input and nourishment, but instead looks to an internal world and comes to be shaped, in large part, by what psychologists would now term a "self-schema." The three kinds of memory that I have described and that Augustine discusses in various places might be imagined as lying along a continuum from the fixed, ordered, and unalterable at the end of rote memory to the inventive, plastic, and always-in-process at the end of principal memory. But it must be emphasized that these kinds of memory that I distinguish are on a continuum with no absolute divisions separating one from another as to function in the psychology of memory. When Augustine recites a psalm for the fiftieth time it is going to be different, however slightly, however subtly, from the forty-ninth time, not to say from the first time and precisely, in part, because there has been a forty-ninth time and a first time and all the times in between. Each recitation is going to involve a new orientation toward the contents of the psalm on the reciter's part, and each will bear, to however tiny a degree, a new and accretive interpretation by the person now engaged in a thirty-fourth or fiftieth repetition of the same words. (We need not trouble ourselves about the instance in which different, incorrect words come forth: this would not alter the principle involved and is, in any case, more a matter for modern than for Augustinian psychology.) And at the far end of the continuum, those more free-floating creations of principal memory are not creations out of nothing—only God, in Augustine, creates out of nothing—but are shaped according to a self already largely formed from memorial acts earlier in time and further back on the continuum. Nevertheless, for purposes of analysis, one can distinguish among these three kinds of memory and can mark the differing ways they engage themselves with acts of interpretation.

When Augustine describes himself—or anyone: Everyman—reciting a psalm, he seems to suggest that the activity is always the same, inerrant and *ex ordine,* and given his knowledge of the Psalms (I think there is no question but that he had them all by heart) there may have been much truth in this for his recitation if not for the recitation by any of the rest of us. And I see no reason to dispute what he says when he goes on to tell us that "what is true of the whole psalm is also true of every part of the psalm and of every syllable in it" or when he maintains that the "same holds good for any longer action, of which the psalm may be only a part." But the next step is different, and with it doubt will begin to assail the modern reader (if indeed it did not assail Augustine's contemporary readers as well). "It is true also of the whole of a man's life," Augustine claims, "of which all of his actions are parts"—meaning, apparently, that the whole of a life can be held in memory and expectation, just like a psalm, inalterable and ready for precisely repeated narration twenty or forty or however many times one may like—and, as if this were not enough, then comes the whop-per: "And it is true of the whole history of humanity, of which the lives of all men are parts." Well, yes, if you happen to be God, then this latter feat might be possible, and in Milton's *Paradise Lost* the Archangel Michael, acting as God's deputy and with all his knowledge and all his narrative ability at his command, does give Adam a vision of what will happen post-Paradise that corresponds pretty well to "the whole history of humanity, of which the lives of all men are parts." But this is a surprising claim for Augustine to make, or seem to make, about human capacities of memory and narration, and one can only suppose that he made it when rapt in something like a vision, a condition to which, as Augustine often says, human language is simply not adequate. Be that as it may, what interests me more at the moment is what Augustine has to say about narrating, again and again and in perfect order, "the whole of a man's life, of which all of his actions are parts." Undoubtedly we do all make repeated attempts to narrate pieces and parts of a life, and some of us, sometimes, do attempt the whole life—Augustine, as I have pointed out, was preeminent in this regard and showed the way to a multitude of followers who tried their hand at life-writing. But I think we would do well to look at a specific "action" that was a "part" of Augustine's life to question the nature of the claim that is being made here. No action in his life was more significant—surely Augustine would agree—than his conversion: the whole of the *Con-*

fessions, up to and through book 8, is directed to it and is preparation for that moment when, in the garden in Milan, he hears the child's voice that is the cause of his being literally as well as metaphorically turned around; and we recall that the vast project of scriptural exegesis Augustine planned had his conversion as the pivotal event that made him capable of even attempting to carry out that project. One cannot doubt that his conversion was one of those events, one of those parts of his life, that Augustine must have recited many times over to people both inside and outside the Church. Now, when Augustine implies that successive narrations of a life, like successive recitations of a psalm, will be precise repetitions, I don't think we should understand him to mean that they will be *verbatim ac literatim* the same or that when he told the story to Monica or Nebridius or friends back in Africa he produced something of the exact length and word for word the same as the account we have in the *Confessions.* To do this, or even to attempt it, would be rhetorical folly—a narrative is effective only if it is adjusted to its audience—and the person who thus repeats himself we would normally call a bore. Augustine, however, was a great rhetorician—he was professor of rhetoric in Milan at the moment of his conversion—and he is never a bore, so it would be a mistake to hold him to any misguided requirement of exact repetition no matter what seems to be implied in his writing that it "is true also of the whole of a man's life. . . ." But Pierre Courcelle, on the other hand, tells us something intensely interesting about Augustine's account, in the *Confessions* and elsewhere, of the climactic moment of his conversion. "In the middle of this scene," he writes of the event in the garden, "a sort of miracle occurs; a young voice calls out: 'Tolle, lege.' Augustine takes these words for a divine admonishment, seizes the Epistles of St. Paul, reads the first verse he sees and decides to change his life to be in keeping with what he has read." This is a close paraphrase of the event as Augustine describes it in book 8, chapter 12; what is fascinating is what Courcelle goes on to report: "Neither in what I have called the '*first Confessions*' "—that is, those autobiographical accounts of his conversion that Augustine wrote prior to his writing the *Confessions*—"nor afterwards, does Augustine recall this episode" (*Recherches,* 190). This is striking. The "sort of miracle" Augustine describes in the *Confessions* would not seem to be the kind of thing he would forget in recounting his conversion experience elsewhere. I'm not at all sure how to account for this, except to say that the narrative is immensely effective as we have it and would be much less so without the drama of the child's voice, the blind reading of Scripture (which is connected to a similar event recalled from the story of Antony's conversion), the immediate conversion of Augustine's will and the fulfillment of God's will. Is this to suggest that Augustine's account in the *Confessions* somehow constitutes a lie? Not at all, but it might be to suggest that, by this point, Augustine's narrative has a will of its own and a memory that can do no other than conform itself to that narrative will. I don't think we need to suppose that Augustine consciously changed—added or deleted—anything in his *Confessions* account; but I do think that this episode should tell us something, indeed much, about the continuum of memory, or kinds of memory, that I have pointed to in Augustine (which, however, I do not mean to imply is strange or unique to him).

I think, too, that we can gain considerable insight into what happens in the *Confessions* passage and into the broad range of activities that we cover with the word "memory" when, in the *Trinity*, Augustine distinguishes between memory in the storytelling animal that is humankind and in other animals that (so far as we know) are without narrative capacities. "Even beasts can perceive corporeal things outwardly through the senses of the body," Augustine writes, "can recall them when they are fixed in the memory, can seek for what is beneficial in them, and flee from what is unpleasant." This is much, but it falls far short of what memory is, according to Augustine, in humans:

> But to make note of them, to retain them not only as caught up naturally, but also as deliberately committed to the memory, and to impress them again by remembrance and reflection, when they are gradually slipping away into forgetfulness, in order that, as the thought is formed from that which the memory bears, so too this very same thing, which is in the memory, may be firmly fixed in thought; to combine also imaginary visions by taking pieces of recollection from here and there and, as it were, sewing them together [*fictas etiam visiones hinc atque inde recordata quaelibet sumendo et quasi assuendo componere*], to see how in this kind of things the probable differs from the true, and this not in spiritual but in corporeal things themselves— these and similar operations, although performed in sensible things, and in those which the mind has drawn from them through the sense of the body, are yet not lacking in reason, nor are they common to men and beasts. (*Trin.*, 12.2.2, 344)

This seems to me an altogether remarkable meditation on memory that extends all the way from animals, which have, as it were, no memory of memory, to the animals in us that can perform mental, memorial operations on "corporeal things," finally to the higher (or lower: the "more profound depth of our memory") capacity of our "principal memory" that combines "imaginary visions by taking pieces of recollection from here and there and, as it were, sewing them together" into a story that, being probable, is (if we remember Aristotle's *Poetics*) truer than the merely true, true as only poetry, not history, can be. "[T]aking pieces of recollection from here and there and . . . sewing them together"—this is the operation of memory, certainly, but is it not also a complex act of textual weaving, of narration and the simultaneous interpretation and reinterpretation of the narrative produced? At another point in the *Trinity* Augustine pauses, as it were, and takes a breath and as he does so produces another telling figure of speech for the dual act of remembering-and-narrating that so preoccupied him in his middle and later years. "It remains to ascend even from here," he writes at the end of book 8, halfway through his self-appointed task,

> and to seek for those higher things, insofar as it is granted to man. But let our purpose rest here a while, not that it may think to have already found that which it is seeking, but as a place is usually found where something is to be sought; what is sought has not yet been found, but the place has now been found where it is to be sought. So it will have sufficed to have said this, so that from it, as if from a small portion of some beginning, we may weave [*contexamus*] the rest of our discourse. (*Trin.*, 8.10.14, 266–67)

We may remember that when Augustine used this same verb ("contexo": to weave together) in the *Confessions,* he was referring to the operation of memory; here the reference is to shaping a discourse that, for purposes of interpretation, is akin to narrative. He would weave a discourse and a narrative, in bright and shifting colors, out of the woven—and continuing to be woven—fabric of memory. Augustine concludes the stunning passage about sewing together pieces from here and there by pointing to what it is about mind and its rich and deep memorial faculty that makes it capable of such comprehensively creative acts:

> But it is the province of the superior reason to judge of these corporeal things according to incorporeal and eternal reasons which, if they were not above the human mind, would certainly not be unchangeable; and yet unless something of our own were subjoined to them, we should not be able to employ them as standards by which to judge of corporeal things. But we judge of corporeal things according to the standard of dimensions and figures which, as the mind knows, remain unchangeable. (*Trin.*, 12.2.2, 344)

Thus, because "something of our own"—what else but mind? what else but memory, understanding, and will?—is subjoined to "incorporeal and eternal reasons," we can and do tell changeable and corporeal stories, out of a memory both changeable and unchangeable, that, in their own mysterious fashion, are subjoined to and encompassed by "dimensions and figures which, as the mind knows, remain unchangeable."

The notion that memory of every sort is inalterably fixed is quite thoroughly disposed of in another passage of the *Trinity*. Even rote memory, which is at one extreme of the continuum, is not entirely fixed, as I have already argued. Anyone who has ever memorized a longish passage of verse knows that it is new and different, with different possibilities of interpretable meaning, maybe richer, maybe poorer, each time it is run through the mind again, each time it is recited whether silently or aloud. Augustine comes up with another remarkable figure of speech in the *Trinity* for the part that memory, along with understanding or knowledge, plays in the processing and reprocessing of contents brought to it in one form and taken from it in another. Augustine is here discoursing on how even a transitory thought or a brief piece of music can have about it apprehensible significance of a nontransitory and unchangeable nature. "For a man's thought," he writes,

> does not abide in the incorporeal and unchangeable reason of a square body, for example, as this incorporeal and unchangeable reason itself abides, if, in fact, it could attain to it without the phantasy of local space. Or if one were to grasp the rhythm of some artificial and musical sound, passing through intervals of time, while it [this incorporeal and unchangeable reason] stands apart from time in a kind of secret and sublime silence, then it could at least be conceived as long as that singing could be heard. Yet what the gaze of the mind snatched from it, even though only in passing, and swallowing as it were into a belly, stored it in the memory, over this it will be able in a certain measure to ruminate again by recollection, and transfer what it has thus learned into the respective branch of knowledge. (*Trin.*, 12.14.23, 365–66)

I am very fond of the phrase "in a kind of secret and sublime silence"— it has all the mystery and loveliness that Augustine's training in rhetoric had taught him was most effective and that his departure into asceticism could not altogether deprive him of—but I must reserve my greatest admiration for the expression that has the gaze of the mind snatching a rhythm from passing music, swallowing it into a belly (presumably the first stomach of this ruminant animal that is memory), then bringing it up as cud to be chewed and rechewed and prepared for a more thorough digestion and incorporation into the bones and sinews and flesh of the living beast. This is nothing less than an imaginative narrative about memory and its important role in the interpretation of just such figurative narratives as this one. Every attentive reader of the passage will perforce engage in the activity— snatching at phrases and chewing the cud of them—that the passage describes and thus be taken by a circular route back to the beginning, but changed, enriched, and grown. And how different is rumination or chewing the cud from weaving and reweaving? How different from sewing together—into something new and strange—pieces of recollection taken from here and there?

"In one and the same soul, then, there are different visions," Augustine writes in *The Literal Meaning of Genesis,* laying the grounds for interpretation, both literal and figurative, of scriptural narrative or indeed any narrative; but we must not imagine that there is no intercourse between these different visions, even though they be ordered in a hierarchy of inferior and superior:

> [B]y means of the body it [the soul] perceives objects such as the corporeal heaven and earth and everything that can be known in them in the degree that they are capable of being known; with the spirit it sees likenesses of bodies . . . ; and with the mind it understands those realities that are neither bodies nor likenesses of bodies. But there is, of course, a hierarchy in these visions, one being superior to another. For spiritual vision is more excellent than corporeal, and intellectual vision more excellent than spiritual. (12.24.51, 2.213)

Thus Augustine provides, in effect, the rationale of subjoining (if one may so term it) that may validate, in the appropriate degree, the act of interpretation. "Corporeal vision cannot take place without spiritual," he tells us,

> [f]or it is not the body that perceives, but the soul by means of the body; and the soul uses the body as a sort of messenger in order to form within itself the object that is called to its attention from the outside world. . . . Hence I believe that spiritual vision can be reasonably and naturally said to occupy a kind of middle ground between intellectual and corporeal vision. For I suppose that a thing which is not really a body, but like a body, can be appropriately said to be in the middle between that which is truly a body and that which is neither a body nor like a body. (*Literal Meaning of Genesis,* 12.24.51, 2.214)

Memory, along its continuum from rote to almost free invention ("because it is undeniable that the images of bodies are not only stored . . . in memory but also are fashioned at will in countless numbers" [*Literal Meaning of Genesis,* 7.21.29, 2.22]), like narrative also, is of this middle state, moving in time and ceaselessly changing, yet in its very motion imitating and dimly figuring that which is immovable and changeless. All of us, with our divided will, our flawed memory, and our frail understanding, have been exiled from the unchangeable world, "but yet have not been cut off and torn away from it"; thus, when it comes to seeking the truth that does not change through constructive, deconstructive, and reconstructive acts of remembering and interpreting, "I am certainly aware of how many figments are born in the human heart, and what is my own heart but a human heart?" Does this mean, however, that for Augustine remembering and interpreting should cease? Of course not: "I drink in this truth [of God's nature] in the measure in which I, although changeable, see nothing changeable in it . . ." (*Trin.*, 4.1.1, 130).

I have said relatively little about understanding or knowledge in this discussion of memory shading off into hermeneutics because (as it seems to me) Augustine himself says relatively little. There is one passage in the *Trinity* on knowledge, however, that I think is well worth close attention at this point, for it bears very significantly on the issue of interpretation and how adequate our powers of understanding and interpretation are to what we know or would know. Augustine has just been discussing the question of the knowledge we may have of God, saying that we can, in fact, have some knowledge of God, "yet that knowledge is less than he, because it is in a lower nature; for the mind is creature, but God is Creator." What, then, of the mind's knowledge of itself?

> We conclude from this that, when the mind knows itself and approves what it knows, this same knowledge is in such way its word, that it is wholly and entirely on a par with it, is equal to, and is identical with it, because it is not the knowledge of a lower essence, such as the body, nor of a higher essence such as God.

But where does a mind discover itself and know itself except in memory? As Mary Carruthers points out in the afterword to her fine *Book of Memory*, throughout the Middle Ages all human learning was taken to be "memorative in nature,"[28] and so too it must be of the mind's knowing of itself. The question for Augustine at this point, however, is not precisely the source of this knowledge but rather how accurate and how adequate can we suppose the mind's knowledge of itself to be, and he is unequivocal in his conclusions. When the mind knows itself it produces a word, which is *its* word—surely on the analogy of God the Father begetting his Son in the beginning as the Word, in all ways commensurate with the Begetter and indeed with the Trinity as a whole—and that word is "wholly and entirely on a par with it, is equal to, and is identical with it." Here it is not a question of knowing in part or as in a mirror, darkly, but rather of knowledge that is perfectly at one—as it were, face to face—with the known.

> And since knowledge has a likeness to that thing which it knows, namely, that of which it is the knowledge, then in this case it has a perfect and equal

28. Mary Carruthers, *The Book of Memory* (Cambridge: Cambridge University Press, 1990), 260.

likeness, because the mind itself, which knows, is known. And, therefore, knowledge is both its image and its word, because it is an expression of that mind and is equalled to it by knowing, and because what is begotten is equal to its begetter. (*Trin.*, 9.11.16, 286)

Still, we must always remember that for Augustine the whole reason for knowing the mind or wanting to know it is so that we may have some apprehension of that which is before and beyond mind, and it is here that hermeneutics comes front stage.

If, as I have been intimating, memory at its farther reaches is more nearly akin to the inventive, shaping power of poiesis than it is to the mechanical retrieval of a fixed content, and if memory at its "more profound depth" is subjoined on one side to time but on the other side to eternity, then the science and art of interpretation, especially of Holy Scriptures— i.e., hermeneutics—will play a crucial role for someone like Augustine in understanding a life, in forming a narrative account commensurable with the life, in following the narrative of creation that we have in Genesis, and in seeing how the one narrative fits itself to the other as a scale model might be imagined to represent the full reality in small. The word "hermeneutics" derives, of course, from Hermes, the god who was messenger of the other gods, thus a go-between both on the level of the gods and, like memory itself, in the interchanges between mortals and immortals. Hermes interpreted the will of the gods to human beings, but as he was himself a god, speaking (in the *Odyssey,* for example) in an intermediate tongue—a human language to be sure (Homeric Greek in the *Odyssey*) but informed by the will and the language of the gods—his message, too, beyond Hermes' own interpretation, required interpreting by the mortals to whom it was brought. The case is quite precisely the same with the Holy Scriptures. Produced by human beings—who were, however, Augustine assumed, divinely inspired—the Scriptures (and here I mean primarily the first twenty-six verses of the Book of Genesis, on which Augustine expended his interpretative skills so lavishly) are a thoroughly mixed, human/divine performance. The task for Augustine, then, was, so to say, a second-level interpretation: to interpret humanly that which is beyond the human but that which has already been given a first-level interpretation when put into human language and narrative form by the writer or writers of Genesis. And what we find again and again is that Augustine is not willing to say, "Here, once and for all, is what this verse means, this and nothing else." For like any narrative the Scriptures and interpretation of them constitute an interlocked pair of text and reading in continual process and evolution.

The meaning of Scripture changes and grows with the collective capacity of human beings to understand it. Which is not to say there is not a stable and unchanging ground on which interpretation exercises itself. Certainly there is, and this is why Augustine was so determined to give, first of all and as of the greatest necessity, a literal interpretation of Genesis. His first outing, which, as its title would indicate, was more specifically polemical than later attempts would be, came in the *Two Books on Genesis against the Manichees;* his first real effort not shaped to particular polemical ends was the "Unfinished Book" *On the Literal Interpretation of Genesis,* and his reasons both for undertaking the work and for breaking it off and calling the resulting product "imperfectus" are very pertinent. After the earlier book directed "against the Manichaeans," Augustine tells us in the *Retractations* that he wanted "to test my capabilities in this truly most taxing and difficult work" of explaining "such great mysteries of natural things literally—that is, in what sense the statements there made can be interpreted according to their historical significance." He soon discovered, however, that he had not lived long enough and had not sufficient experience to accomplish such a superhuman task, so that "in explaining the Scriptures, my inexperience collapsed under the weight of so heavy a load and, before I had finished one book, I rested from this labor which I could not endure" (*Ret.,* 76). It should be noted that Augustine's abilities gave way at this early stage not because he was attempting one of the "higher" modes of interpretation—allegorical, moral, prophetic, or whatever—but the "lower" mode of literal interpretation: this was what proved not just difficult but impossible for the relatively young Augustine. "Imperfectus" this early book may have been, but Augustine was very far from abandoning the task of literal interpretation. Indeed, he returned to it throughout his life in such landmark productions as the *Confessions,* the *Literal Meaning of Genesis* (in twelve books as against the one book of the unfinished version), the *Trinity,* and the *City of God.* What Augustine insists upon in all of these works is that the account of creation in Genesis must have a literal meaning and a historical actuality (not that he is dogmatic about saying *what* that literal meaning has to be) before any of the other possible kinds of interpretation—and Augustine is willing to admit a multiplicity of them—are brought to bear. This is very similar to what Mary Carruthers argues was the nature of thought about memory throughout the Middle Ages: that, with a fixed and invariant rote foundation—but only with that—the individual was freed to elaborate in altogether inventive and imaginative ways, so that a sort of superstructure of memorial invention was considered by medieval thinkers on hermeneutics and memory to be not only permissible but admirable on the condition that it had a literal and rote grounding.[29]

The same problem, of course, returned again and again for Augustine in his attempt to fix the fact of a literal meaning and a historical dimension for Genesis: that he was interpreting humanly that which was beyond the reach of human language. The problem might be put as a question, thus: When something is asserted literally of God, or of some act of God, is this the same as a literal assertion about something in the human realm? The answer, unfortunately but certainly, is that they are not the same. Of God it can be said literally (it *can* be said, Augustine would maintain, because it *is* said in Genesis) that he created everything in one day and that he created everything in six days and there is not, because there must not be, a contradiction in the dual assertion. Now with the limitations of the human mind this is difficult to understand, and with the limitations of human language it is equally difficult to convey in words, and so Augustine gave it up in his "unfinished" book as being beyond him. To his later attempt, *The Literal Meaning of Genesis,* Augustine gives comparatively high marks in the *Retractations,* although he does say—and it is very much to the point of the present discussion—that "[i]n this work, many questions have been asked rather than solved, and of those which have been solved, fewer have been answered conclusively. Moreover, others have been proposed in such a way as to require further investigation" (*Ret.,* 169). Augustine finished his second attempt at a literal interpretation of Genesis, but it was only, as he intimates, by accepting tentativeness, by asking questions and offering inconclusive solutions, by remaining suspended among various possible and acceptable meanings for any given text. For him this was the very nature of the relationship between human inquiry and divine truth, and it led him to the rather desperate—but at the same time, perfectly logical—device of propounding two narratives, categorically different from one another in nature, in the account of creation.

The distinction in the two kinds of narrative in Genesis, which we might term temporal and causal narratives, can be discerned in contrasting modes of utterance. There are on the one hand "the words of the Lord in the flesh spoken by His mouth, as well as the words of God spoken by the mouths of prophets, [which] are uttered in time by a voice coming from

29. See not only her *Book of Memory* but also the account of work in progress in "The Poet as Master Builder: Composition and Locational Memory in the Middle Ages," *New Literary History* 24 (autumn 1993): 881–904. The *NLH* contributor's note describes this essay as "a preliminary study for her forthcoming book *Machina Memorialis: Memory as Invention in the Middle Ages.*"

a body, and such words with all their syllables require and fill out corresponding intervals of time." On the other hand—and these display an altogether different narrative logic—there are such utterances as "Let Us make mankind in Our image and likeness . . .":

> [T]hese words of God, spoken before there were any sound vibrations in air and before any voice coming from man or from cloud existed, were uttered in His supreme Wisdom, through which all things were made. They were not like sounds that strike human ears, but they implanted in things made the causes of things yet to be made. Thus, God by His almighty power made what would appear in the future; and when He who is before the ages created the beginning of the ages, in what we might call the germ or root of time, He created man to be formed later in due time. (*Literal Meaning of Genesis,* 6.8.13, 1.186–87)

Earlier in the same volume Augustine adopts an elegant phrasing to contrast the time of narrative with the non-time of God's eternal creative act when he argues that we should understand "in the account of the stages of the creation of the world not a real progression in time, since God created matter at the very moment he created the world, but a mere progression in the narrative" (2.15.31, 1.68). There are, then, according to Augustine, two categorically different but parallel narratives at play in Genesis; moreover, as I have already suggested, the language of Genesis is, being Hermeslike, necessarily of a mixed, intermediate nature, requiring every interpretative subtlety and ingenuity of which the human mind is capable and more besides. And the reader can be quite sure that Augustine will be well out ahead in interpretational brilliance on almost every occasion. There is a deeply interesting moment in the *Confessions* when Augustine—casting himself in a role I should think few of us could conceive for ourselves— imagines himself the writer of Genesis and goes on to describe the many levels of significance he would have wanted to pack into his words as the inspired writer of that book:

> Now if I had been Moses then (for we all come from the same lump and what is man, saving that Thou art mindful of him?), if, I say, I had been then what he was and had been given by you the task of writing the Book of Genesis, I should have wished to be granted to me such a power of expression and such stylistic abilities that those who cannot yet understand how God creates would still not reject my words as being beyond their capacity, and that those who already have understanding would find in the few words of your servant every true opinion which they had reached themselves in their own thinking, and I should wish too that if another man were to see some other true opinion by the light of truth, that that opinion also should be discoverable in these same words of mine. (*Conf.*, 12.26, 308)

Can anyone doubt that Augustine wished and prayed for—and was granted—this same power of utterance, these same stylistic abilities, in short the same hermeneutical richness when it came to writing his own life story that he would have wanted had he been assigned Moses' task? For the truth is that his own narrative demands and repays the same kind of tenacity of inquiry and openness to discoverable meaning as the Augustinian Mosaic text would have done or as the Mosaic text does demand and does receive from Augustine.

In *The Art and Thought of Heraclitus* Charles H. Kahn outlines a principle of interpretation that seems to me altogether appropriate to invoke both for the reading of St. Augustine and for his own reading of Scripture. Citing "the *linguistic density* of the individual fragments" of Heraclitus and "the *resonance* between them," Kahn argues for the necessity of what he calls "a principle of hermeneutical generosity."[30] This, as I say, seems to me not only a perfectly appropriate principle to bring to the reading of Augustine, but a principle for which he argues strongly in his own interpretation of Scripture. In Augustine's view, the Scriptures attempt to tell a story of divine origin, a story of the unmoved and the eternal working in space and time, a superhuman story, but told in a language that is all too human, and this brings a pressure to bear on the language—to say the unsayable— which, as it were, overloads it. But it becomes our duty then, acting with hermeneutical generosity, to draw out as many of those multifarious meanings as we may be capable of, individually and collectively. God, like Moses writing under his inspiration (or Augustine ditto), is capable of having put in more meanings—in fact, with God, an infinity of them—than we are capable of distinguishing. Augustine follows the passage in the *Confessions* where he imagines himself as the author of Genesis with these musings on the virtually boundless spread and multiplicity of scriptural meaning:

> A spring shut in a small place [like language under the pressure of divine meanings, I would say] has a more plentiful supply of water and distributes its flow to more streams over a greater area of ground than does any single stream, however far it goes, which is derived from that spring. It is the same with the writing of him who dispenses your word. This writing will do good to many who will preach and comment upon it, and from a narrow measure of speech it will spread and overflow into streams of liquid truth, and from these, as they wind away in lengthier stretches of language, each man may on these subjects draw what truth he can—one man one truth, one another. (*Conf.*, 12.27, 308–9)

30. Charles H. Kahn, *The Art and Thought of Heraclitus* (Cambridge: Cambridge University Press, 1979), 92; italics in the original.

This is quite astonishing—and astonishingly generous for its time, when the Catholic Church was trying to establish itself on an indisputable credo and when Augustine felt it necessary to do polemical battle with heretical movements on every hand.

It is important to recognize that the principle of hermeneutical generosity as Augustine follows it (and as Kahn also intends it I believe) does not constitute an argument for an indeterminacy of meaning but rather for a multiplicity of meaning. In pondering difficult passages of Scripture, Augustine says that we should choose that meaning the author intended, but if this cannot be determined then we should choose a meaning that comports well with the context and is in harmony with our faith. The best reading will be the one that catches the author's meaning and is in full accord with Christian faith, but failing this ideal, "even though the writer's intention is uncertain, one will find it useful to extract an interpretation in harmony with our faith," for there are so many legitimate meanings in the "wide variety of true doctrines which are drawn from a few words" (*Literal Meaning of Genesis,* 1.21.41, 1.45). And enacting the interpretative role himself in the *Confessions,* Augustine exclaims in wonder at how many truths are to be found compacted into how few words in Genesis, yielding one truth to one person, another to another, and so on to an almost bewildering multiplicity of truths. In the first words of Genesis—"In the Beginning God made heaven and earth"—there are so many truths, Augustine says, that we could scarcely exhaust them if we were to indulge in an interpretative spell lasting for a month of Sundays.

> Now of all these truths—which are accepted unhesitatingly by those to whom you have given the power to perceive them with the inner eye . . .—out of all these truths a man chooses just one who says: In the Beginning God made heaven and earth means this: "In His Word, which is coeternal with Himself, God made the intelligible and the sensible, or the spiritual and the corporeal, creation."

This, however, even though it is true, is but one out of so many truths. "Another truth is chosen by the man who says . . . ," etc. And again, "Another truth is chosen by the man who says . . . ," etc. And yet once more, "Another truth is chosen by the man who says . . . ," etc. But the multiplicity of meaning does not end here, for, Augustine says, it is even so "with regard to the understanding of the words that follow. Out of all the truths . . . , one is chosen by the man who says. . . . Another truth is chosen by the man who says. . . . Another truth is chosen by the man who says. . . . Another truth is chosen by the man who says. . . . Another truth is chosen by the man who says . . ." (*Conf.,* 12.20–22, 301–3). In a herme-

neutical gesture of proper generosity, Augustine says that each and all of
these are true and thus that no one of them is exclusively true: "[I]n finding
the meaning there are so many truths which occur to us from these words,
according to whether we understand them in one way of another." What
we can and must affirm, according to Augustine, is the literal sense of "In
the Beginning God made heaven and earth," but all that may follow from
that common source and ground has more to do with individual interpretative capacities and with subjective truth than with a single dogma to be
imposed and enforced.

> Consider me, my God, me, your servant . . . ; see how confidently I affirm
> that in your immutable Word you created all things, visible and invisible;
> could I affirm with the same confidence that Moses had just one particular
> meaning and no other when he wrote: In the Beginning God made heaven
> and earth? No. (*Conf.*, 12.24, 305)

As simple as that: No. And with this we recall that, had he been Moses,
Augustine would have wanted to command a language swarming with
truths, rich in possibility beyond the capacity of anyone, himself included,
to specify all that the words might contain and suggest. For Augustine
sought to infuse into his own writing the same "linguistic density and resonance" that he found in the Holy Scriptures and especially in the first
twenty-six verses of Genesis.

Augustine's exegesis of the scriptural ur-narrative from "In the Beginning . . ." to "And God said, 'Let Us make mankind to Our image and
likeness . . .'" offers us a model for reading narrative in the same way that
the passage in the *Confessions* about reciting a psalm—or, indeed, all of the
Confessions—can be said to offer us a model for producing narrative out
of memory. Augustine's interpretation of Scripture most often concludes—
though of course he brings in thousands of later scriptural passages along
the way—with Genesis 1.26 (when, in fact, he gets that far, as he does not
in the *Confessions*), because this stretch of Genesis not only provides the
principles for a full interpretation of the creation narrative but also the logic
according to which the human mind can interpret at all and with some
assurance that its interpretation will possess at least subjective accuracy. This
reading of Genesis 1.26, which is at once both a model of interpretation
and a justification of interpretation, surrounds all the other interpretative
acts in Augustine, whether of Scripture or of his own life. It was Genesis
1.26 that defeated Augustine in his first attempt at a literal interpretation
of the book—his own intellectual and spiritual narrative was insufficiently
advanced at the time to allow him to deal with the passage; it is the crux

of the *Trinity*—the subject of the final book 15 toward which all else looks; and it lies behind the account of his mind's growth, in memory, understanding, and will, in the *Confessions*. That the human mind was made to the image and likeness of God was, for Augustine, the quintessential, paradigmatic center and circumference of the creation narrative, and as such it informs virtually everything we have from him. What can it possibly mean, how *many* things can it mean, to say that God made humankind to his own image and likeness? It took Augustine many thousands of pages to chew the cud of this narrative properly, and he never really finished, for what else was his life's activity, what else the story of his life, but this very chewing and rechewing of the cud of narrative thrown up by his memory for endless rumination?

Language's Sufficiency

As he makes quite clear in the *Confessions* and elsewhere, Augustine had been gradually prepared for an understanding of the biblical "And God said, 'Let Us make mankind to Our image and likeness' " by his reading in the Platonists and Neoplatonists, who not only helped him conceive of a nonmaterial reality but also provided him with a metaphysics that distinguished between, while not absolutely sundering, a world of being on the one hand and a world of becoming on the other. There are two distinct ontological levels, with two corresponding narratives and, I would suggest, two memories, in the creative act of Genesis 1.26, with "mankind," "image," and "likeness" possessing a much lesser degree of being than "God," "Us," and "Our"; and yet, lower though they are in the order of being, image and likeness are nevertheless "like a shadow and a sign" (*Literal Meaning of Genesis,* 4.35.56, 1.145) imperfectly figuring that whose impress they bear. God, according to Augustine, engaged in two different acts of creation, which, in the language the author of Genesis was compelled to employ, result in two separate narratives; and these separate narratives, though neither of them is precisely narrative in the human sense, lead on to the narratives we live as history or life story. The first of the divine narratives has God, in a one-day simultaneous creation, begetting his Word and therein producing the reasons for all things; the second unfolds this single nontemporal day into a temporal dimension of six days that sees the creatures come into existence whose reasons were created on the separate first day; and finally that day and days spread out into a world of becoming that is our ongoing world of words, history, and narrative. "We must, therefore," Augustine says, "make a threefold distinction in speaking of creation. First, there are the unchangeable forms in the Word of God; secondly, God's works from which He rested on the seventh day; finally, the things that He produces from those works even now" (*Literal Meaning of Genesis,* 5.12.28, 1.163). This, except for the seventh day of rest and certain other minor details, could have come from any Neoplatonist more or less contemporaneous with Augustine, and indeed he tells us in the *Confessions* that in "some books written by the Platonists" he had, early on, found everything that, in his mature writings, he wrote about creation—everything, that is, but the central narrative of the Christian religion: "I did not find then that the Word was made flesh and dwelt among us" (*Conf.,* 7.9, 147). This, and the matter of faith, made all the difference for Augustine, but otherwise he had everything from the Platonists. Concluding with his "threefold distinction in speaking of creation," Augustine writes that

> [o]f these three, those that I put in the third place are known to us in some way by our senses and common experience. The first two are beyond our senses and ordinary human knowledge, and they must be first believed on divine authority. Then some knowledge of them can be attained through things known in accordance with each individual's limited capacity, when he has God's help enabling him to know. (*Literal Meaning of Genesis,* 5.12.28, 1.163)

Faith is required for knowledge of the latter two, and it was in this that Augustine, for all his reading of the Platonists, was for so long lacking, as he tells us in the *Confessions.* He presents his dilemma to us in a version of the hermeneutical circle: to understand the Scriptures he first needed to have faith, but he could only believe by first understanding. Thus the problem of the intellectual who would be a Christian. The drama of the hermeneutical circle plays itself out in the central books of the *Confessions* before being miraculously resolved in the "tolle, lege" and the consequent instantaneous belief upon opening Scripture. It should be noted that Augustine's account of his conversion is not only, as it had to be, in words of common use, but it is language-soaked throughout, actuated by words—"tolle, lege"—after Augustine has already heard and read the stories of other conversions, and completed in the reading of scriptural words before the writing of the account we have. Unlike God in the silence of his one day of creation, Augustine can only proceed—and we can only follow him—through a narrative in time, through days that succeed one another, through words whose sounds vibrate on the air and then fade away. And even Scripture, although the reality it would present may be very different from the semireality of our experience and thus inaccessible to human language, can proceed only in the same fashion since we "who cannot understand the meaning of the text, *He created all things together,* cannot arrive at the meaning of Scripture unless the narrative proceeds slowly step by step" (*Literal Meaning of Genesis,* 4.33.52, 1.142).

Language, being time bound and subject to alteration and decay, is not, in Augustine's view, adequate for saying anything of God, but it is precisely because of its inherent changeability, its transitoriness and ever-shifting nature, that language may be exquisitely adapted to narrative in the human realm. While Augustine never suggests that language can say the unsayable of God ("For with God there is pure intellect, without the noise and diversity of languages"),[31] he equally never suggests that language, in its nature, is not sufficient within and for our world. He never exclaims with J. Alfred Prufrock, "It is impossible to say just what I mean!"—or, were he ever to exclaim thus with Prufrock, it would be a reflection on his personal incapacity, not on any intrinsic inadequacy in words. We have only to recall Augustine's imagining himself to be Moses to realize that he never left behind his belief, his training, or his mastery in rhetoric. In the *City of God* Augustine will claim that the beauty of God's providence and his universe is to be observed nowhere better than in certain poetic uses of language:

> For God would never have created a man, let alone an angel, in the foreknowledge of his future evil state, if he had not known at the same time how he would put such creatures to good use, and thus enrich the course of world history by the kind of antithesis which gives beauty to a poem. "Antithesis" provides the most attractive figures in literary composition. . . . The opposition of such contraries gives an added beauty to speech; and in the same way there is beauty in the composition of the world's history arising from the antithesis of contraries—a kind of eloquence in events, instead of in words.[32]

To draw the analogy in this direction rather than the reverse—God as poet rather than the poet as God—points up very nicely the powers that are there in language for the one—God, Moses, or Augustine—who knows how to put them to proper use.

When, just before the prayer that concludes the *Trinity,* Augustine acknowledges that what he has been able to say of his subject comes far short

---

31. *Two Books on Genesis against the Manichees,* 1.9.15, 63. Cf. this earlier passage in the same volume: "So too, there are words of the Old Testament which do not prove that God is weak, but are a concession to our weakness. For nothing can be said worthily of God. Still there are said those things that we can grasp so that we may be nourished and come to those things which cannot be said by any human language" (1.8.14, 62).

32. *City of God,* 11.18, 449. We might here recall what Beckett said of what he called Augustine's "wonderful" sentence, which is most wonderful, of course, for its play of antitheses: "I take no sides. I am interested in the shape of ideas. There is a wonderful sentence in Augustine: 'Do not despair; one of the thieves was saved. Do not presume; one of the thieves was damned.' That sentence has a wonderful shape. It is the shape that matters."

of the ineffable reality of the Trinity, he nevertheless avails himself of some very effective language to lament his failure (which is, in fact, a common poetic and rhetorical trope: to write a poem—and often enough a great poem—lamenting one's inability to write a poem). "I venture to acknowledge openly," Augustine writes, "that I have said nothing worthy of the ineffability of that highest Trinity, among all these many things that I have already said, but confess rather that its sublime knowledge has been too great for me, and that I am unable to reach to it." Notice that while Augustine acknowledges that he has *said* nothing worthy of that which is ineffable and admits that he is "unable to reach to it" in words, he is careful to distinguish between not having had the vision on the one hand and being unable to express it on the other. Indeed, in the peroration to his soul that follows, in which he sounds a little like Walt Whitman addressing his soul and a lot like Plotinus ascending to the ultimate vision at the conclusion of the last of the *Enneads,* Augustine claims to have participated for an eternal moment in that supreme ecstasy promised to the Christian in the life hereafter.

> And you, O my soul, . . . you have seen many true things, not with these eyes by which colored bodies are seen, but with those for which he prayed who said "Let my eyes see the thing that is right." Verily, then, you have seen many true things, and you distinguished them by that light which shone upon you when you saw them. . . . [T]his very light reveals to you those three things in you [i.e., memory, understanding, will], and in them you recognize the image of that highest Trinity itself, . . . although you neither were able, nor are you now able, to unfold with adequate speech what you scarcely saw amid the clouds of corporeal likenesses that do not cease to appear in our human thoughts. (*Trin.*, 15.27.50, 521–22)

Even as I quote these lines admiringly, I cannot quite rid my mind of the passage in Beckett's *Watt* when Arsene concludes what the narrator calls a "short statement"—which turns out to be a very, very long and hopelessly inane narrative—with the claim that he has not said all that he knows "because what we know partakes in no small measure of the nature of what has so happily been called the unutterable or ineffable, so that any attempt to utter or eff it is doomed to fail, doomed, doomed to fail."[33] To this Augustine would respond, I think (and Beckett would surely have to agree), that though the attempt is indeed "doomed, doomed to fail," there is nevertheless something of great value even in the failure, and it is possible so to describe the attempt and so to enact the failure as to create a narrative of

33. *Watt* (London: John Calder, 1976), 61.

profound significance about the human condition and the language created to express it.

This is why Augustine, though urging always the higher, nonsensory vision, never abandons the language of the senses in the *Confessions,* for then he would have no language at all. "But what do I love when I love you?" he asks in the sixth chapter of book 10 of the *Confessions:* "Not the beauty of the body nor the glory of time, not the brightness of light shining so friendly to the eye, not the sweet and various melodies of singing, not the fragrance of flowers and unguents and spices, not manna and honey, not limbs welcome to the embraces of the flesh: it is not these," he says, "that I love when I love my God" (*Conf.,* 10.6, 214–15). It may not be these that he loves when he loves his God, but that they are lovable and that Augustine loves them and invokes them lovingly in language—"the beauty of the body . . . the glory of time . . . the brightness of light shining so friendly to the eye . . . the sweet and various melodies of singing . . . the fragrance of flowers and . . . limbs welcome to the embraces of the flesh"— this cannot be denied; and what he does love when he loves his God, though it be not these poignantly transitory experiences of the senses, can only be said nevertheless by way of the body's beauty, the friendly, bright sunlight of Thagaste and Carthage and Hippo Regius, the sweet melodies of the psalms, and embraces of the flesh.

> And yet I do love a kind of light, melody, fragrance, food, embracement when I love my God; for He is the light, the melody, the fragrance, the food, the embracement of my inner self—there where is a brilliance that space cannot contain, a sound that time cannot carry away, a perfume that no breeze disperses, a taste undiminished by eating, a clinging together that no satiety will sunder.

It was only through what Augustine calls "the gates of my senses" and "the messengers from my body" (*Conf.,* 10.6, 215)—only through the language of the senses and the language of the body—that he could hope to appeal to the reader in recounting the passion and the progress of his soul. Just as, had he been Moses, Augustine would have brought every resource of linguistic density and resonance (to invoke Charles Kahn's terms once more) that he could command to the composition of Genesis, so also he avails himself of the same in composing the narrative of his life. I will not try to describe all the ways that Augustine creates density and resonance in his story, but I think it will repay us to look rather closely at a specific passage of linguistic richness to see how he brings density to his language internally and how he establishes resonance between his narrative and biblical narrative, in particular the Psalms, externally. The passage I have in mind is chapter 29 of book 11, which comes immediately after the chapter in which Augustine speaks of reciting a psalm in perfect order and compares this to the recounting of a life.

> But because *Thy loving kindness is better than all lives,* see, my life is a kind of distraction and dispersal. And *Thy right hand upheld me* in my Lord, the *Son of Man, the Mediator betwixt Thee,* the One, and us, the many (many also in our many distractions over so many things), so that *through Him I may apprehend in Whom I have been apprehended* and that I may be gathered up from my former days to follow the One, *forgetting what is behind,* not wasted and scattered on things which are to come and things which will pass away, but intent and *stretching forth to those things which are before*—no longer distracted, but concentrated as *I follow the voice of Thy praise,* and contemplate Thy delight which is neither coming nor passing. But now *are my years spent in mourning,* and you, my comfort, my Lord, my Father, are eternal. But I have been spilled and scattered among times whose order I do not know; my thoughts, the innermost bowels of my soul, are torn apart with the crowding tumults of variety, and so it will be until all together I can flow into you, purified and molten by the fire of your love. (*Conf.,* 11.29, 283)

Italics in the foregoing indicate scriptural quotations and allusions as identified by the editors of the version of the *Confessions* I cite; editors of other versions point to other and more scriptural echoes in the passage. But there is no way, short of quoting the entire book of Psalms, to suggest how loaded this passage is with remembrances of individual psalms and of the Psalms as a whole. It would be no exaggeration to say that every word in the passage, with the exception of those that have specific reference to the New Testament ("Son of Man," "Mediator," etc.), echoes and resonates with one or more verses from Psalms, and rather than attempting to isolate and identify specific psalms as the origin for specific phrases, it might be as well to say simply, of this book and chapter, *vide* Psalms *passim.* This, however, is but one exemplary instance of the way the *Confessions* works throughout, from the first line ("Great art thou, O Lord, and greatly to be praised; great is thy power, and thy wisdom is infinite": Psalm 147.5) to the last ("This must be asked of you, sought in you, knocked for at you. So, so shall it be received, so shall it be found, so shall it be opened. Amen": Luke 11.9). Here, as everywhere in the *Confessions,* it is a matter of two and more narratives in antiphonal response, constantly resonating one with the other—the narrative of Augustine's spiritual struggles, his faith, and his redemption resonating with the narrative of the Psalms and the narrative of the Gospels; Augustine's conversion resonating with many other conversions, including Paul's; Augustine's slow progress in understanding the creation story in Genesis resonating with that creation story itself. Comple-

menting this internal-external resonance of the language of narrative is what
one might call an internal density of language with the play on such words
and images as "distraction and dispersal . . . wasted and scattered . . . no
longer distracted, but concentrated," which implicates the philosophical
and theological issue of the one and the many and culminates in the mighty
last lines: "But I have been spilled and scattered among times whose order
I do not know; my thoughts, the innermost bowels of my soul, are torn
apart with the crowding tumults of variety, and so it will be until all together
I can flow into you, purified and molten by the fire of your love." And
not only is this a rich climax to the play on words and ideas within the
single passage, but it picks up and repeats crucial terms from elsewhere in
the *Confessions*—for example, the question of order, here an order he cannot know, earlier an order he would bring to his narrative and the order
he gradually discerns in his life. For all this, whatever be the case with the
ineffability of God, Augustine's language is wonderfully sufficient.

One final instance of language's sufficiency and insufficiency mixed we
can see in the account of the vision that Augustine tells of sharing with his
mother, Monica, when they had paused at Ostia on their intended return
to Africa. "I am passing over much because I am in haste," Augustine
writes. "But I shall not pass over whatever my soul can bring forth about
that servant of yours who brought me forth, giving me birth in the flesh
to this temporal light, and in her heart to light eternal" (*Conf.*, 9.8, 195–
96). Here we have once again, in embryonic form, a dual narrative, a temporal story giving body to an eternal one, an eternal story amplifying to
virtually mythic dimensions a temporal one. After some details of Monica's
life (including a most interesting, well-placed, and fully human account of
how she came to be a youthful drunkard), Augustine continues the narrative with all the specifics of time and place demanded of the expert storyteller: "Now the day was approaching on which she was to leave this life
. . . , and it so happened . . . that she and I were standing alone, leaning
in a window which looked onto the garden inside the house where we were
staying, at Ostia on the Tiber." Even here, when Augustine is preparing to
try to utter the ineffable, which he knew well was "doomed to fail,
doomed, doomed to fail," he does not fail to observe all the needs and
niceties of the narratively effable, realizing the scene for the reader as effectively as he realizes so many scenes throughout the *Confessions*:

> So we were alone and talking together and very sweet our talk was, and *forget-
> ting those things which are behind, and reaching forth unto those things which are before,*
> we were discussing between ourselves and in the presence of Truth, which
> you are, what the eternal life of the saints could be like. . . .

Our talk had reached this point: that the greatest possible delights of our bodily senses, radiant as they might be with the brightest of corporeal light, could not be compared with the joys of that eternal life. . . . Then, with our affections burning still more strongly toward the Selfsame, we raised ourselves higher and step by step passed over all material things, even the heaven itself from which sun and moon and stars shine down upon the earth. And still we went upward, meditating and speaking and looking with wonder at your words, and we came to our own souls, and we went beyond our souls to reach that region of never-failing plenty where *Thou feedest Israel* forever with the food of truth and where life is that Wisdom by whom all these things are made, both what is past and what is to come; but Wisdom herself is not made; she is as she has been and will be forever; or rather, there is no place in her for "to have been" or "to be going to be"; one can only say "to be," since she is eternal and "have been" and "going to be" are not eternal. And as we talked, yearning toward this Wisdom, we did, with the whole strength of our hearts' impulse, just lightly come into touch with her, and we sighed and we left bound there *the first fruits of the Spirit,* and we returned to the sounds made by our mouths, where a word has a beginning and an ending. (*Conf.,* 9.10, 201)

Like the passage quoted earlier in which Augustine addresses his soul, this one is heavily indebted to Plotinian mysticism and in particular to the description of the ascent of the soul in the final page or so of the *Enneads*. There is one really significant difference, however, between Augustine and Plotinus—a difference I would characterize as a narrative difference—and that is that Augustine begins, as Plotinus does not, with two bodied human beings together in a carefully realized scene, and after the narrative climax (I use the term advisedly, for the account is delicately eroticized: "And as we talked, yearning toward this Wisdom, we did, with the whole strength of our hearts' impulse, just lightly come into touch with her, and we sighed. . . .") he returns once again to the human scene and "to the sounds made by our mouths, where a word has a beginning and an ending." Committed as he was to Plotinian Neoplatonism and mysticism, Augustine still knew the appeal, for himself as for his reader, of narrative—which, after all, is what he says distinguishes Christianity from the philosophy of Plato and his followers. And while he was "doomed to fail, doomed, doomed to fail" in saying the unsayable, his failure was a grand one nevertheless, and he is the reverse of a failure when he adapts language, sufficient and adequate, to the writing of a life in search of ways to know the unknowable, to say the unsayable.

At the end of *Watt,* among the flotsam and jetsam of "Addenda" (bearing this footnote: "The following precious and illuminating material should be carefully studied. Only fatigue and disgust prevented its incorporation"), we can read this fragment in its isolated splendor of Latin: "pereant qui ante nos nostra dixerunt." *Bartlett's Familiar Quotations* credits this fragment to Anonymous and translates it as "May they perish who have used our words before us." It is altogether impossible to know what Beckett or his narrator ("Sam") or whoever is responsible for the addenda had in mind with this small piece of wisdom. I do not imagine, at any rate, that he was thinking in such a hostile fashion of St. Augustine, who, we must recall, provided Beckett with his "wonderful" sentence. But Augustine did use a lot of Beckett's words before him and before many others who followed in the tradition of life-writing that he established with his *Confessions* and the works surrounding it. Even if Beckett did not include Augustine among those against whom his prayerful anathema was directed, other earlier writers in the tradition—Jean-Jacques Rousseau, for example—probably would have, for to have the first in the line be the greatest cannot have presented a pleasant prospect for writers who arrived on the scene with great ambitions but sadly belated.

FIRST INTERLUDE
VICO *(CORSO)*

"Vico," W. B. Yeats declared in the last year of his life, when he was putting together all the various pronouncements in genetics, politics, poetry, and philosophy that constituted his *On the Boiler,* "Vico was the first modern philosopher to discover in his own mind, and in the European past, all human destiny. 'We can know nothing,' he said, 'that we have not made.' "[1] While this has about it all the revelatory grandeur and luminosity that Yeats favored from the time of *A Vision* onward, he was not in fact the first to make this claim for Vico, for Vico himself said as much in his *New Science* and also, perhaps more to the point, in his periautography. Writing both in the first-person plural and in the third-person singular but avoiding the first-person singular pronoun that had been preferred by Augustine, was to be problematized by Rousseau, and would be declined by Beckett—and thus acquiring a certain authority and objectivity for his claim—Vico, in the book his translators and editors title *The Autobiography of Giambattista Vico,* says, "From the time of the first oration of which we have spoken, it is evident both in it and in all that followed but above all in this last, that Vico was agitating in his mind a theme both new and grand, to unite in one principle all knowledge human and divine."[2] When he came to publish his *New Science* in its second edition (1730), Vico was altogether confident that he had accomplished what he had earlier agitated in his mind, and in a certain sense that I will try to spell out we can grant his claim of priority: "a theme both new and grand, . . . unit[ing] in one principle all

1. *On the Boiler* (Dublin: Cuala Press, 1939), 32; reprinted in *Explorations,* selected by Mrs. W. B. Yeats (London: Macmillan, 1962), 429.
2. *The Autobiography of Giambattista Vico,* trans. Max Harold Fisch and Thomas Goddard Bergin (Ithaca: Cornell University Press, 1963), 145–46. The title used by Vico was *Vita di Giambattista Vico scritta da se medesimo,* i.e., *Life of Giambattista Vico, Written by Himself.* Subsequent references will be to this edition and will be indicated by *Vita.*

knowledge human and divine." It was no doubt Vico's exposition of this "theme both new and grand" that moved Samuel Taylor Coleridge to write in the postscript of a letter to Gioacchino de' Prati, an Italian exile in England who had loaned Coleridge a copy of the *New Science,* in the very words of the narrator (or author) of *Watt:* "I am more and more delighted with G. B. Vico, and if I had (which thank God's good grace I have not) the least drop of *Author's* blood in my veins, I should twenty times successively in the perusal of the first volume . . . have exclaimed: *'Pereant qui ante nos nostra dixere.' "[3] May they perish who use our words before us:* thus the anxieties about originality and firstness, whether one be Coleridge, the author of *Watt,* Jean-Jacques Rousseau, or a multitude of twentieth-century writers, if there be anything of *Author's* blood coursing through the veins.

But what is particularly intriguing in the history of life-writing is not so much that Vico could claim priority for his grand philosophic synthesis but rather that during the same period when he was completing and publishing the *First New Science* (1725) and then the *Second New Science* (1730), Vico was also composing his *Vita,* his *Life,* a book that both subtends and is subtended by the *New Science.* The two books were, in their composition, intertwined to the degree that either can be understood in its fullness only by way of the other. If we look at the chronological table provided by Fisch and Bergin in their translation of the *Autobiography,* we see that "Scienza nuova in forma negativa," an early version of the *New Science* that was never published because of loss of patronage, was completed in 1724. In the space of little more than a year Vico thoroughly recast the "New Science in Negative Form" and published it, in October 1725, as the *New Science* (now known as the *First New Science*). In June of the same year Vico had been able to send to Count Gian Artico di Porcía, the man who had originally proposed that eminent Italian scholars write what was termed a periautography, part A of the book that we know as his *Autobiography.* In December he drafted part B, which is almost entirely concerned with the ideas of the *New Science* and the conditions of its composition and publica-

---

3. The letter, dated May 14, 1825, is quoted in the introduction to *Vita,* 84; the full letter is to be found in *Collected Letters of Samuel Taylor Coleridge,* ed. Earl Leslie Griggs (Oxford: Clarendon Press, 1971), vol. 5, p. 456 (letter 1457). The editor of Coleridge's letters does better than Bartlett's in identifying the source of the saying that turns up both in *Watt* and in the letter to Prati: "This saying is attributed to Donatus by St. Jerome. See *Commentarium in Ecclesiasten* 390 (Migne, Patrologia latina: Hieronymus, vol. iii, column 1019)." See also Max Harold Fisch, "The Coleridges, Dr. Prati, and Vico," *Modern Philology* 41 (November 1943): 111–22, for a very complete account of Coleridge's interest in Vico.

tion, but did not send this second part to Porcía until March 1728, by which time he had revised part B and made corrections to part A. In the meantime Vico was at work on what was to be the second edition of the *New Science,* which was published in December 1730 (now known as the *Second New Science*). And in 1731 he undertook a continuation of the *Autobiography* that would bring it up to the year in which he was writing. By this time the work, the thought, and the life—the *New Science* and the *Autobiography*—have become one. The two projects or the two books exist in a state of perfect symbiosis, demanding, as Edward Said has said, to be interpreted as if they were two parts of a single whole. Being something like the Original Autodidact, Vico, according to Said, had a "passionate concern with the fundamentally severe and economical operations of the autodidactic humanistic mind," and this concern, he continues, "condones, even requires, the application of *The New Science* to the *Autobiography* and vice versa."[4]

Yeats, an autodidact if there ever was one, is right again—as he so often was: Vico discovered nowhere but in his own mind the history of philosophy, the history of humanity, and the method by which both of them were to be recalled, imagined, and written. But Yeats was careful to qualify his assertion—"Vico was the first *modern* philosopher"—and he was wise to do so, for on the one hand Augustine anticipated Vico by well over a millennium and yet, on the other hand, the number of modern and modernist writers who knowingly or unknowingly (mostly the latter) have followed in the path of Vico is legion. In thought if not in practice (for distinction in the latter category must go to Rousseau, so much better known and so much more influential than Vico in the history of life-writing), Vico, as I see it, stands as the middle term in an intellectual progression from St. Augustine to Henry Adams, Samuel Beckett, and a whole host of writers of our time. For my purposes, however, great as his achievement in the history of ideas may have been, Vico must figure only as an interlude, a transitional figure who can go a certain way toward filling up the gap— more like an abyss really—between Augustine and Rousseau.

Like Augustine a rhetorician by training and discipline—he was professor of rhetoric in the University of Naples for over forty years—Vico was clearly aware of a parallel between what he was doing in the *New Science* and what Augustine had done in his *City of God.* What at one point in the *New Science* he calls "the great city of the nations, founded and governed

4. *Beginnings* (New York: Basic Books, 1975), 363.

by God"[5] is imagined by Vico according to the same distinction that Augustine draws between what he calls "the earthly city" or "the society of mortal men" or "the city of this world"[6] on the one hand and the City of God on the other. Vico, however, although he says that "the great city of the nations" was "founded and governed by God," restricts himself in the *New Science* to the city of men and has nothing to say about the City of God or about providence beyond observing that providence is another name for what he more often calls the *storia ideale eterna*, the "ideal eternal history," the principle of which he was, after Augustine, the first—and for a long time the only—person to have grasped. "Our new Science must therefore be a demonstration, so to speak, of what providence has wrought in history . . ." (*New Science,* para. 342). The little formulaic phrase "so to speak" is very interesting here, as it suggests a telling difference-in-similarity between Vico and Augustine. In pointing up the provisional nature of Vico's accommodation of his new science to the Christian notion of providence, "so to speak" also shows how far one has come from Augustine, who would neither have needed nor have used any such qualifying phrase; but shorn of "so to speak," what Vico says is thoroughly Augustinian.

The fact that Vico confines himself to the city of nations in his *New Science* says nothing against his having developed his conception of that very city of nations and of providence as a true name for its history out of St. Augustine. Indeed, I think it could be argued that the reasons for Vico's restricting himself to the earthly city were themselves Augustinian in nature. One of the basic principles according to which the *New Science* proceeds is that human beings can know only what they have made—so they should not presume to know nature or nature's God; but if they should not presume, neither should human beings despair, for they *can,* according to this doctrine, know what they have made, and this means that all human institutions are grist for the mill. Augustine, who maintained that language was sufficient to all things human but not to things divine, would not have presumed to scan the mind of God any more than Vico did, but for both of them the customs, the laws, and the history of the human world are perfectly and properly scannable. As Vico puts the positive side of the *verum-*

5. *The New Science of Giambattista Vico,* trans. Thomas Goddard Bergin and Max Harold Fisch (Ithaca: Cornell University Press, 1968), paragraph 1107. References to the *New Science* will be to this edition, given hereafter by paragraph number.

6. These terms all occur in book 18, chapter 2 of the *City of God.* Book 18 gives an account of "the course of history" from the time of Abraham down to "the era of the Saviour" that focuses on the ancient secular history running parallel to the history of the City of God.

factum principle (that is, the principle that the truth of that which has been made can be known by the maker):

> But in the night of thick darkness enveloping the earliest antiquity, so remote from ourselves, there shines the eternal and never failing light of a truth beyond all question: that the world of civil society has certainly been made by men, and that its principles are therefore to be found within the modifications of our own human mind. Whoever reflects on this cannot but marvel that the philosophers should have bent all their energies to the study of the world of nature, which, since God made it, He alone knows; and that they should have neglected the study of the world of nations, or civil world, which, since men had made it, men could come to know. (*New Science*, para. 331)

Thus Augustine and Vico observed the same principle according to which humans can have any knowledge at all; moreover, what Vico came to know about "the world of nations, or civil world" in a flash of insight after some twenty years of hard study, he tells us, was in large part from St. Augustine, who also showed Vico, according to Vico's own account, how he might reconcile his pious intentions with the thoroughly secular if not heretical new science he was propounding. In the *Autobiography* Vico describes how he spent nine years of isolated and intense study in the Rocca family's "castle of the Cilento, beautifully situated and enjoying a perfect climate."[7] During those years, Vico says, he educated himself with an intense program of reading. One book in particular he picked up by a happy chance in his father's bookshop and brought with him to be studied in his cloistered isolation, a book by "Richardus, the theologian of the Sorbonne." What he discovered in the book was that

> Richardus by a geometrical method shows that the doctrine of St. Augustine is midway between the two extremes of Calvin and Pelagius, and equidistant

---

7. Donald Phillip Verene, in *The New Art of Autobiography: An Essay on the Life of Giambattista Vico, Written by Himself* (Oxford: Clarendon Press, 1991), 189–93, casts a good deal of doubt on the factual veracity of Vico's account of this episode, suggesting that he was patterning his life for effect after the fact and wanted "to increase the power of his fable of himself as the autodidact." I want to make a general acknowledgment here of my indebtedness to Professor Verene's writings on Vico, which have been of immense help to me in seeing something of the importance and grandeur of Vico's thought. In addition to *The New Art of Autobiography*, I have made much use of his *Vico's Science of the Imagination* (Ithaca: Cornell University Press, 1981), his essay on "Vico's Philosophy of Imagination" in *Vico and Contemporary Thought* (Atlantic Highlands, N.J.: Humanities Press, 1976), his introduction to the translation of *Giambattista Vico: On the Study Methods of Our Time* (Ithaca: Cornell University Press, 1990), and his preface to the translation of *Giambattista Vico: On Human Education* (Ithaca: Cornell University Press, 1993).

likewise from the other opinions that approach these two extremes. This disposition enabled him later to meditate a principle of the natural law of the
nations, which should both be apt for the explanation of the origins of Roman
law and every other gentile civil law in respect of history, and agree with the
sound doctrine of grace in respect of moral philosophy. (*Vita,* 119)

Any reader thrown into confusion by the pronouns in the second sentence
might be forgiven for thinking that "him" refers to St. Augustine—the
reference must, in fact, be to Vico—but the confusion is telling in a positive
way all the same, for what Vico seems in any case to be saying is that he
discovered in Augustine a principle that he would himself enunciate much
later, "a principle of the natural law of the nations . . . apt for the explanation
of the origins of Roman law *and every other gentile civil law in respect of history.*"
This is the very basis and the germinal idea of the *New Science,* and yet for
Vico there was more in St. Augustine even than this, for Vico claims that
Augustine taught him how to reconcile his *New Science* with "the sound
doctrine of grace." Well might Vico call Augustine, in another place, his
"particular protector" (*Vita,* 211 n. 44) if the latter brought thus much to
him in natural law, in philology, theology, and moral philosophy.

That Vico was indebted to St. Augustine in certain specifiable ways
no doubt has its significance, but more important for the purposes of this
interlude is the fact that the two of them were at one on the nature and
the power of memory and on the nature and the power of narrative,
whether such agreement was attributable to immediate influence or to two
similar minds brooding over the same subjects in like ways. What Vico
tells us of the first of the orations he delivered "at the annual opening of
studies in the Royal University" is redolent of Augustinian thought and
phrasing, as a glance back at "The Trinity of Mind" in the previous chapter
will demonstrate. In that first oration of 1699 he proposed, Vico says in
his periautography, "that we cultivate the force of our divine mind in all
its faculties. Its thesis is: 'That the knowledge of oneself is for each of us the
greatest incentive to the compendious study of every branch of learning.' It
proves that the human mind is by analogy the god of man, just as God is
the mind of the whole [of things]" (*Vita,* 140). This proposal, as the translator and editor's notes to the orations gathered together under the title *On
Humanistic Education* indicate, is Ciceronian through and through, but so
also is it Augustinian, and it was only Augustine who left, for Vico and
others, the example of an autobiography that dramatizes Vico's thesis about
self-knowledge as well as the example of half a dozen books that prove
"that the human mind is by analogy the god of man, just as God is the mind
of the whole [of things]." Likewise, when "at the solemn public opening of

studies in 1719" Vico proposed the argument that "[a]ll divine and human learning has three elements: knowledge, will and power, whose single principle is the mind, with reason for its eye, to which God brings the light of eternal truth" (*Vita*, 156), we have only to tie this back to the inaugural oration of twenty years earlier to observe how close Vico's ideas are to Augustine's on the trinity of the human mind and on the analogy this human trinity might bear to the divine Trinity, an analogy for which Augustine argues so often, so variously, and so passionately in the book of that title.

As to memory itself, what Vico has to say in the *New Science* and elsewhere has all sorts of intriguing resonances with the Augustine of the *Confessions,* of the *Trinity,* and of the volumes on interpretation of Scripture. In the earliest heroic stages, when language was at its most imaginative and poetic and when "common script had not yet been invented," the peoples, Vico writes,

> who were almost all body and almost no reflection, must have been all vivid sensation in perceiving particulars, strong imagination in apprehending and enlarging them, sharp wit in referring them to their imaginative genera, and robust memory in retaining them. It is true that these faculties appertain to the mind, but they have their roots in the body and draw their strength from it. Hence memory is the same as imagination, which for that reason is called *memoria* in Latin. . . . Imagination is likewise taken for ingenuity or invention. . . . Memory thus has three different aspects: memory when it remembers things, imagination when it alters or imitates them, and invention when it gives them a new turn or puts them into proper arrangement and relationship. For these reasons the theological poets call Memory the mother of the Muses. (*New Science,* para. 819)

This, like so much of Vico—indeed, like so much of Augustine as well—requires unpacking, but when unpacked it reveals some stunning things. The memorial process begins for Vico (and for Augustine) in sensory experience. According to Vico, this is especially true for the very first stages in the development of human thought and language, but it is also true for later stages when we attempt to imagine (= remember or recollect) our way back to the condition of those earliest progenitors. Thought begins with sensory experience and with reception of images from the external world into an internal world where memory, as the interior sense, receives them and simultaneously integrates and shapes the images to the configuration of itself. These images are then stored in memory for recall, but even then they do not merely lie there in an inert and passive state, nor is the subsequent process of recollection a mechanical or computer-like activity.

For Vico—and I believe that this is more an extension of Augustine's thought than an entirely new way of thinking—memory falls into three distinct but in the end unified faculties, which he terms memory, imagination, and invention. The image is reshaped as it enters memory; it is subject to continual reshaping while it is held in memory; and it is reshaped as it is recalled from memory and as it is instantaneously reformulated as words, thence as articulated syntax, and finally as full narrative. I remarked in chapter I that for Augustine memory might be seen to occupy an entire spectrum extending from rote memory at one end to memory as something like free, creative imagination at the other. To get that reading, however, it was sometimes necessary to tease the interpretation out of some dark passages, like the one on memory as a ruminant activity, that would not immediately yield such meanings. There is no such problem with Vico, who makes the one extreme sense of memory as imagination perfectly clear and systematic. If Vico could be said to scant any part of the full Augustinian range of memory, it would be the rote rather than the imaginative extreme, but this says little more than that the art of memory (as Frances Yates calls it), i.e., those techniques for remembering so familiar to the ancient and medieval worlds,[8] had pretty much faded by the time of Vico, who shows little interest in tinkering with his system to accommodate what might be thought of as a mechanical view of memory. When he wrote that clause that delighted James Joyce and that would equally have pleased Vladimir Nabokov had he been aware of it—"Hence memory is the same as imagination"— Vico was moving into a modern new world for which Augustine might be said, to an extent, to have prepared the way, but it could hardly be claimed that Augustine was in a position, or would have had the desire, to have embraced the entire Vichian scheme of things. Augustine, nevertheless, is often astonishingly close to anticipating Vico, and Vico often astonishingly close to a restatement of Augustinian principles with his bold new manner and in his own quirky accents.

In *On the Most Ancient Wisdom of the Italians,* a book published in 1710, about midway between the two orations quoted above and some fifteen years before the publication of the *New Science,* Vico writes, "The Latins called the faculty that stores sense perceptions 'memory'; when it recalls

8. Frances A. Yates, *The Art of Memory* (Chicago: University of Chicago Press, 1966). See also two illuminating books of more recent date that deal with memory in the ancient and medieval worlds: Mary J. Carruthers, *The Book of Memory: A Study of Memory in Medieval Culture* (Cambridge: Cambridge University Press, 1990), and Janet Coleman, *Ancient and Medieval Memories: Studies in the Reconstruction of the Past* (Cambridge: Cambridge University Press, 1992).

perceptions they called it 'reminiscence.' But memory also signified the faculty that fashions images (which the Greeks call *phantasy* and the Italians *immaginativa*)."[9] At this point in his progress, Vico had not quite arrived at the full mature doctrine of the *New Science* that would hold that memory includes memory, imagination, and invention (he treats invention in the section of the *Most Ancient Wisdom* that follows immediately upon that quoted above), but in saying that memory also signifies "the faculty that fashions images"—as it were out of itself—he is saying something that is altogether consonant with what Augustine says of "a more profound depth of our memory, where we also find those contents which we think of for the first time, and where the inner word is begotten which does not belong to the language of any nation . . ." (*Trin.*, 15.21.40, 507). Although Augustine does not use the terms "imagination" and "invention" to describe his "more profound depth of memory," surely what he says points right to these Vichian aspects of a tripartite memory vastly rich in endowments and capacities. What this memory, with its parameters the same as those of the human mind both individual and collective, is capable of recollecting, imagining, and inventing out of its own three-part nature is nothing less than Vico's *storia ideale eterna,* his ideal eternal history, which repeats itself in cycles of beginning, middle, and end, of "rise, development, maturity, decline, and fall," in the real history of every nation, every family, every individual. This narrative of narratives is the story Vico draws from his memory as imagination and invention to tell in the *New Science,* whence it is brought as justifying theory and as actual practice to be rerealized in the story of his *Autobiography.* "Our Science," Vico writes in a passage of the *New Science* that repeats what he says many times elsewhere in the book but now with a summative force absent in other passages,

> Our Science therefore comes to describe at the same time an ideal eternal history traversed in time by the history of every nation in its rise, development, maturity, decline, and fall. Indeed, we make bold to affirm that he who meditates this Science narrates to himself this ideal eternal history so far as he himself makes it for himself by that proof "it had, has, and will have to be." For the first indubitable principle posited above is that this world of nations has certainly been made by men, and its guise must therefore be found within the modifications of our own human mind. And history cannot be more certain than when he who creates the things also narrates them. (*New Science,* para. 349)

9. *On the Most Ancient Wisdom of the Italians Unearthed from the Origins of the Latin Language,* translated with an introduction and notes by L. M. Palmer (Ithaca: Cornell University Press, 1988), 95–96.

What is asserted here about the certainty involved when the person "who creates the things also narrates them" not only provides the theoretical scaffolding for Vico's and everybody's autobiography (with a bow in advance to the Gertrude Stein of *Everybody's Autobiography* and *The Making of Americans*), but it also transforms the *New Science* itself into autobiography and meta-autobiography, history and historiography. In every case what is produced is a story with the repeated pattern—how could it not be repeated?—of Vichian beginning, middle, and end, origin, history, and conclusion, "rise, development, maturity, decline, and fall." As Vico puts it in the paragraph previous to the one quoted above, "The decisive proof in our Science is therefore this: that, since these institutions have been established by divine providence [read: 'ideal eternal history'], the course of the institutions of the nations had to be, must now be, and will have to be such as our Science demonstrates, even if infinite worlds were born from time to time through eternity, which is certainly not the case" (*New Science*, para. 348). That sentence, confident, comprehensive, and conclusive, has the true Vichian ring about it.

The history of every nation, Vico tells us repeatedly in the *New Science*, traverses in time the ideal eternal history, crossing and recrossing the same path, enacting in its turn and time the drama enacted by every other nation. And this is so for every individual as well, for whatever the particulars and details of the life may be, there is no escape from what "had to be, must now be, and will have to be." But even if there is no escape there is nevertheless a positive aspect to the impossibility of transcending the pattern of rise, maturity, and fall, which is that the story of a life, like the history of a nation, is eminently narratable and, being narratable, demands to be narrated. This is the sense of narrative ineluctability—the sense of "it-could-not-be-otherwise-than-it-is"—that all autobiography displays. With regard to this inevitable Vichian cycle of origin, history, and end that imposes itself at every narrative level from the individual to the universal, I would recall once again what Augustine says in the *Confessions* about the primal act of narration, which he figures as the recitation of a psalm: "And what is true of the whole psalm is also true of every part of the psalm and of every syllable in it. The same holds good for any longer action, of which the psalm may be only a part. It is true also of the whole of a man's life, of which all of his actions are parts. And it is true of the whole history of humanity, of which the lives of all men are parts" (*Conf.*, 11.28, 282). This is, almost with a vengeance, the ideal eternal history being traversed in time by all sorts of particular histories from the enunciation of a syllable of a psalm to the recitation of an entire psalm to individual actions in a person's

life to the whole life of that person to "the whole history of humanity."
I have been accustomed to say, in seminars on autobiography, that this
latter history could be narrated only by God, but Vico would certainly
dispute this, for he claims to narrate just such a history and to demonstrate
the theoretical necessity of it in his *New Science;* and I am not sure Augustine
would not agree with Vico that since the ideal eternal history is something
that rises out of the mind of the people, gives shape to all human institutions, and is traversed by the histories of the gentile nations in all ages and
all places, it is possible to join history to metahistory and produce thereby
in the *New Science* what Donald Phillip Verene calls "the autobiography of
humanity," an act that is reproduced in small in the microcosm that is his
Vita. The grand fable of the world, which is also the fable of his own life,
was revealed to him, Vico tells us, when he came to understand the necessity of joining philosophy and philology and beginning the study of both
at their own beginnings. This was to bring together the universals of philosophy with the particulars of philology to produce a comprehensive understanding of the narrative principles and the narratable actualities of human
history. Describing the achievement of the *New Science* and adopting all the
terminology of that book, Vico writes thus in his periautography: "By
means of these principles of ideas and tongues, that is by means of this
philosophy and philology of the human race, he develops an ideal eternal
history based on the idea of the providence by which, as he shows throughout the work, the natural law of the peoples was ordained. This eternal
history is traversed in time by all the particular histories of the nations, each
with its rise, development, acme, decline and fall" (*Vita,* 169). For Vico
as for Augustine the narrative of an individual life is analogically, synec-
dochically the history of humanity, and his *Vita* is therefore nothing more
and nothing less than a recapitulation in small of his *New Science.*

In tracing the intellectual debts that he wishes to acknowledge, Vico
lists in his *Vita* the four authors he says that he always, after a certain point,
kept before him—Plato, Tacitus, Bacon, and Grotius. The first of these,
great predecessor that he was, should, according to Vico, have come up
with his own "ideal eternal law that should be observed in a universal city
after the idea or design of providence, upon which idea have since been
founded all the commonwealths of all times and all nations." This was the
vision to which Plato's thought ought to have led him, but it did not, and
thus it was left to Vico, according to his tale, to propound and to prove
the ideal eternal law directing all nations and all lives. And he tells us not
only that Plato failed but also why: "This was the ideal republic that Plato
should have contemplated as a consequence of his metaphysic; but he was

shut off from it by ignorance of the fall of the first man" (*Vita,* 122). The fall of the first man signifies the entry of the human race into history, it brings together ideal eternal history and all particular histories, and it is the starting point of all specifically human narrative. Surely Vico must have been aware that the omission he found in Plato had long since been repaired in St. Augustine's Christianizing Platonism, and as to the fall of the first man, Augustine held as strongly as Vico could have wished to the doctrine that human beings are thoroughly and from very near the beginning fallen creatures. He lets us know in the very first book of the *Confessions* that the human infant, though we like to flatter ourselves with the belief that innocence goes naturally with childhood, is as vicious as any full-grown adult, for the same Adam and the same Eve who fell so long ago are forever being reborn in infants. And as to Plato, who was for Augustine even more a dominant predecessor than he was for Vico, he says in chapter 9, book 7 of the *Confessions* that in the Platonists he found everything his heart desired and his philosophy required—everything, that is, but the one little fact that they were not Christians and thus were shut off from the narrative center of all history and, more particularly, of all life-writing.

Looking back from Vico we can discern many elements of his thought in St. Augustine; looking forward we find fewer of them in Jean-Jacques Rousseau. Yet what is discoverable by way of similarity—as also what is discoverable by way of contrast—between the latter two is of great importance to an understanding of Rousseau's absolute centrality in the history of life-writing in the Western world. The tie between Vico and Rousseau can, for convenience, be put in a single word: origins. In his periautography Vico says of the *New Science* that "[i]n this work he finally discovers in its full extent that principle which in his previous works he had as yet understood only in a confused and indistinct way. For he now recognizes an indispensable and even human necessity to seek the first origins of this science in the beginnings of sacred history" (*Vita,* 166). To seek the origins in the beginnings is indeed one of the principal axioms of the *New Science.* Lest it seem redundant to the point of inanity to refer to seeking origins in beginnings, I should say that as I am using it—and as I think Vico intends it—the word *origins* implies causes and consequences in a way that *beginnings* does not. "Doctrines," Vico declares in number 106 of the axioms that establish the principles of the *New Science,* "must take their beginning from that of the matters of which they treat" (*New Science,* para. 314). *One hundred and six?* How many axioms are there, and if this one is so important why does it come so late? The short answer to the first question is that there are 114 axioms (followed by a set of "universal and eternal principles" [para.

332] and a fairly extended discourse on method); the second question Vico hastens to answer as soon as he has posited the axiom. "This axiom, placed here for [its application to] the particular matter of the natural law of the gentes, is universally used in all the matters which are herein discussed. It might have been laid down among the general axioms . . ." (*New Science,* para. 315). Any reader of the *New Science* will be aware that Vico never observed or honored any principles of organization and structure other than his own, so that making this axiom number 106 should not be understood to deprive it of any of its force or its universal relevance. What Vico says at the beginning of what he here terms "the general axioms" is unquestionably true of number 106: "In order to give form to the materials hereinbefore set in order in the Chronological Table, we now propose the following axioms, both philosophical and philological, including a few reasonable and proper postulates and some clarified definitions. And just as the blood does in animate bodies, so will these elements course through our Science and animate it in all its reasonings about the common nature of nations" (*New Science,* para. 119). In the beginning, then, is origins and in origins is contained all else including, especially and inescapably, ends. Of the two mottoes on which T. S. Eliot meditates in "East Coker"—"In my beginning is my end" and "In my end is my beginning"—the first is for Vico a principal and necessary axiom of his new science, while the second, whether true or not, would be for him without significance. This means, among other things, that for Vico (and, I will argue, for Rousseau as well) narrative is driven forward by origins, not pulled along by ends. And the use of Vichian memory, in all three of its aspects, is to recall origins, to return us by way of recollection, imagination, and invention to the human beginning, whence one can see unfolding, as by an inner necessity, the course of the life of an individual, of a nation, of humankind.

St. Augustine, as I have remarked, lived in a time when the art of memory flourished, a time when very elaborate, controlled, and willed techniques for remembering seemed successful in calling up the text of the past for reading. When Vico, on the other hand, came to the exercise of memory as a way to get back to the first mentality of human beings in the age of the gods and the age of the heroes, he found it a matter of extreme difficulty. It took him, he says, twenty or twenty-five years to work it out. By the time of Rousseau and even more by the time of Beckett no length of years would do. Yet what the systematic recovery of origins revealed to Vico about the nature of the first human beings, about the first human languages, and about the beginnings and development of human society is not at all unlike what we get in Rousseau's very *un*systematic, emotion-driven account of the same originary persons and events in such books as the *Discourse on the Sciences and Arts,* the *Discourse on the Origin and Foundations of Inequality,* the *Essay on the Origin of Languages, The Social Contract . . .* and the *Confessions.* I include the last book here, and might as well have included the *Dialogues* and the *Reveries of a Solitary Walker* also, because Rousseau was being altogether Vichian when he imagined his *Confessions* in the metahistorical light of his theories about the origins and evolution of human society as laid down in the other books. Or perhaps it should be put the other way around: that Rousseau's theories came out of the experience and the understanding of experience that provided both the substance and the structure of the autobiographical work. Or perhaps it should be put both ways simultaneously. Whichever way it is put, what is being described is the dual, symbiotic activity of autobiography-and-philosophy, of autobiography-and-oeuvre, that we find everywhere from the time of Vico (if not from the time of Augustine) on.

As regards the actual similarities in thought between Vico and Rousseau about the origins and evolution of human institutions, it has been suggested that Rousseau, who was in Venice in 1743–44 as secretary at the French embassy, read the third edition of the *New Science,* which appeared early in 1744, and derived from his reading those ideas that he would go on to develop in his own special manner in theoretical works published between 1749 and 1762 and in autobiographical works that occupied him until virtually the end of his life. It doesn't much matter whether the ideas came directly from Vico, whether they were characteristic of Rousseau without any Vichian influence, or whether many of them were merely commonplaces of the time, but notions about a Golden Age in the distant past, about a devolution of civilization in the course of time, about the figurative, poetic language spoken (or not spoken: both Vico and Rousseau include observations about mutes in their theories) by the first humans, and about a fall suffered by every individual and every nation in passing from imaginative, mythic thought to conceptual, reflective thought—these notions, in one form or another, are common to them both. Where they are really alike, however, is in their passion to explain everything from origins, a passion that came to Vico only after long, hard thought but that seems to have been innate and temperamental with Rousseau. Whatever the source of the passion, what needs saying is that Rousseau was as much an enthusiast for origins as Vico. What he would not have been so warmly disposed toward if he had ever encountered it was Vico's sense of an inevitable end—the sense, as Rilke put it, that for each of us our death is born with us. Yet if Rousseau would have refused Vico's doctrine of the end out of

an emotional need to return to the beginning and remain there, he subscribed to that doctrine of the end fully and ironically with his life. Of the
separate elements in axiom number 66 of Vico's *New Science*—"Men first
feel necessity, then look for utility, next attend to comfort, still later amuse
themselves with pleasure, thence grow dissolute in luxury, and finally go
mad and waste their substance" (*New Science,* para. 241)—I think Rousseau
in his theory of social evolution would concur with the first five clauses
about necessity, utility, comfort, pleasure, and luxury; but it required his
life and the course of his life to prove the final clause about going mad and
wasting substance. But if there was irony in the split between Rousseau's
thought and his life, or between his emotional wants and the ideal eternal
history that his individual history traversed, there was a painful absence of
irony in the manner in which the life of the deviser of the ideal eternal
history traversed that history to the final letter. Vico's system told him that
memory is acute and strong in childhood and at the earliest stage of human
evolution but that thereafter, in adulthood and in the third stage of historical
development, memory progressively weakens, which is why most of us
cannot imagine our way back to the originary, primal state. Sad to say, if the
marquis of Villarosa, who added a continuation and conclusion to Vico's
periautography, is right, this is precisely what happened to Vico who, in
age, could no longer read with any pleasure and recognized neither friends
nor his own children: "His memory was so far gone that he forgot the
nearest objects and confused the names of the most familiar things" (*Vita,*
205). Now, it is true that most scholars doubt the accuracy of Villarosa's
account, for as Leon Pompa, for example, points out, Vico continued to
write and publish in his last years and he "was actively engaged in supervis-
ing the proof-reading of the *Third New Science* when he died."[10] But if
Villarosa is wrong must we not surmise that it is either because Vico deliberately gave the appearance of memorial inanition so as not to falsify his theoretical construct by his life or because Villarosa subscribed so thoroughly
to Vico's theory that he could not see what was before him? If Vico did
fake a loss of memory to save his theory, this would be quite in keeping
with the way he rearranged his entire life in the periautography so that it
would be seen to have traversed, step by step, the ideal eternal history. If
he had to sacrifice memory to get the narrative pattern right, then, one
can imagine Vico saying, so be it. It was the great project of philosophy
in the ancient Greek world to develop a theory that would "save the phe-

---

10. *Vico: Selected Writings,* ed. and trans. Leon Pompa (Cambridge: Cambridge University Press, 1982), 13.

nomena"—a theory, that is, that would be comprehensive and yet true to the way things are in the world. Vico, on the other hand, might be said to have ordered the phenomena in his account to the end of saving his theory. It was only "the more shameless" among "the caitiff semi-learned or pseudo-learned," Vico tells us near the end of his periautography, who "called him a fool, or in somewhat more courteous terms . . . said that he was obscure or eccentric and had odd ideas" (*Vita*, 199–200). Perhaps he was a little odd after all, but can we fairly expect the person who devised a New Science uniting "in one principle all knowledge human and divine" and who devised a Life through which that one principle would shine in every detail to be perfectly normal? Normal he was not, but neither did Vico ever claim that he or his life was unique; on the contrary, his life, like every other life and like "the course of the institutions of the nations," he said, was as it "had to be, must now be, and will have to be such as our Science demonstrates" (*New Science,* para. 348). It was left for Jean-Jacques Rousseau to claim that he and his doings were unique, with neither predecessor nor successor, and the consequences of that claim spread out across the history of life-writing like so many ripples from a stone dropped into a pond.

II

JEAN-JACQUES ROUSSEAU AND THE CRISIS OF NARRATIVE MEMORY

The Trilogy Principle

When asked if his three late works, *Company, Ill Seen Ill Said,* and *Worstward Ho,* could be seen as a trilogy, Samuel Beckett responded with a characteristic lack of interest and concern: "I hadn't thought of it as such," he said, "but I suppose so—more so than the other works called the Trilogy [i.e., *Molloy, Malone Dies,* and *The Unnamable*]."[1] Taking his laconic indifference for positive approval, Beckett's British publisher, John Calder, currently has in print under Beckett's name not only a volume titled *Trilogy (Molloy,* etc.) but also a volume called *Nohow On (Company, Ill Seen Ill Said, Worstward Ho);* and there seems to me, well beyond Beckett's semireluctant "OK," a good deal of justification, stylistically, structurally, and thematically, for the decision to publish both the three earlier and the three later works as trilogies. In a similar vein, but with even more compelling reason, I believe that the editors of the Pléiade Rousseau, Bernard Gagnebin and Marcel Raymond, are precisely right when they publish *Les Confessions, Rousseau juge de Jean Jaques—Dialogues,* and *Les Rêveries du Promeneur solitaire* in a single (if, of necessity, very long) volume, implying thereby that the three works should be understood to constitute a tripartite, single book, that is to say, an autobiographical trilogy.

We cannot suppose that Rousseau, when he began the *Confessions,* any more than Beckett when he began *Company,* foresaw writing a trilogy. How could he have, and why should he have? On the contrary, Rousseau set out to write a single, all-inclusive and thoroughly unified text in which the man and his book, the life and the writing, should be inseparably, seamlessly one, a book that required no successor just as it had no predecessor

1. As reported by Enoch Brater in *Why Beckett* (London: Thames and Hudson, 1989), 136.

and that, when achieved, would bring him, Rousseau imagined, universal love. "When all has been revealed," he exclaimed, even before setting pen to paper, "how posterity will love me! how it will bless my memory!"[2] Clearly, Rousseau started his project with the intention and confident expectation of making himself known to the reader (or auditor), according to the motto placed at the beginning of the *Confessions,* "Intus et in Cute" (inside and under the skin); he did not, at the outset, doubt at all his ability to produce what, in a little speech designed to introduce a reading aloud of the *Confessions,* he described as "le narré fidèle de tout ce qui m'est arrivé, et si j'ose ainsi parler, l'histoire de mon âme. . . ."[3] If he could do this—and Rousseau gives no indication that he consciously doubts it (the insistence, the repetition, and the extravagance of assertion may argue that *unconsciously* he had doubts—doubts that would, in fact, prove well founded)—then, the implication is, what higher, more worthy activity might there be, and what reason would Rousseau have for doing or attempting more?

That Rousseau did not, in the beginning, foresee writing a trilogy, however, says nothing against the trilogistic nature of what, in the end, he produced. Indeed, looked at ex post facto, there is a kind of inevitability about the progression and the succession of texts, an inevitability about his going on . . . and on . . . and on, and an inevitability, too, about there being precisely three texts rather than only one, or two or four or any other number. *Confessions* leads, as by an iron logic, into *Dialogues,* which leads on in the same way into *Reveries,* and there are continual returns from the second text to the first and from the last text to the two earlier, as if *Dialogues* were folding itself embryonically back into *Confessions* and *Reveries* back into both *Dialogues* and *Confessions.* Again looking back from after the fact, we must see that *Confessions* anticipates *Dialogues* and *Reveries* (even if unknowingly) and that *Dialogues* anticipates *Reveries,* in each case the earlier text requiring the later text(s) as completion (albeit unsuccessful completion) of its own unsuccessful effort in making known "l'histoire de mon

2. Quoted in Jean Guéhenno, *Jean-Jacques Rousseau,* 2 vols., trans. John and Doreen Weightman (New York: Columbia University Press, 1966), 2.132.

3. "[T]he faithful narrative of all that has happened to me, and if I dare say so, the history of my soul": "Discours projeté ou prononcé pour introduire la lecture des *Confessions,*" in *Oeuvres complètes,* ed. Bernard Gagnebin and Marcel Raymond, 4 vols. (Paris: Gallimard, Bibliothèque de la Pléiade, 1959), 1.1185; my translation. Rousseau repeats virtually the same language in the *Confessions* themselves (Pléiade, 1.278) and in the so called "premier préambule" or "Ébauches des *Confessions*" (Pléiade, 1.1155). Subsequent references to the *Oeuvres complètes* will be given as "Pléiade," with volume and page numbers.

âme." Although he does not employ the word "trilogy," Michel Foucault, in his introduction to an edition of the *Dialogues*,[4] argues that the three works of the Pléiade volume constitute a single project, a trio of interrelated, interlocked texts that will yield their full significance only when so read; and he goes on to claim, in effect, that the crucial text among these three is not, as has long been assumed, the *Confessions*, but rather the text that is literally the central one, the *Dialogues* of *Rousseau juge de Jean Jaques*, the book that James F. Jones, Jr., suggests has been neglected for so long, in favor of the *Confessions*, because it is so difficult to construe, to place, or to know what to do with at all.[5] There is much to be said, I believe, for the call issued by Foucault and Jones for us to consider the *Dialogues* as the crux—in all ways the crux, and especially the interpretative crux: the text in which the *Confessions* and the *Reveries* cross—of what I would see as Rousseau's trilogistic autobiographical project, a project that just as surely as it resonates with St. Augustine's initiatory exercise in life-writing so surely does it anticipate modernist and postmodernist instances of the mode from Henry Adams and Gertrude Stein to Franz Kafka, Samuel Beckett, and an entire array of writers of the past fifty years and of today, figuring thus in literary history as a kind of middle term in a trilogy, a crux wherein the ancient and modern worlds are joined and in which they cross and recross.

What I am calling the Trilogy Principle can be readily found in the structures of thought and expression of the Western world from the ancient Greeks to the present time (and outside the Western world, I am sure, as well). Both of my titular subjects, memory and narrative, are dominated by a kind of trilogism, a single process that analysis would render in three stages that bear an inherently necessary relationship to one another such that any one would be incomplete without the other two. When Aristotle writes of narrative as something possessed of a beginning, a middle, and an end, where the beginning is that which comes before the middle and the end, the middle is that which comes after the beginning and before the end, and the end is that which comes after the beginning and the middle, he may seem to be saying something laughably obvious but he is in fact saying something profound and altogether basic to any followable thought or narration; he is pointing to something that exists logically, structurally in the very nature of things and, correspondingly, in the very nature of the

4. Michel Foucault, introduction to Jean-Jacques Rousseau, *Dialogues* (Paris: Armand Colin, 1962).
    5. James F. Jones, Jr., *Rousseau's "Dialogues": An Interpretive Essay* (Geneva: Droz, 1991).

human mind.[6] St. Augustine's devotion to the Trinity, to the *idea* of three-ness as an organizing fact both in the world and beyond it, is to be found everywhere in his works, most especially of course in *De Trinitate* where tri-unity is not only a principle of theology and of the divine but finds its necessary replication in the human psyche as well with its three dominant and interlocking powers of memory, understanding, and will. Augustine is likewise thoroughly trinitarian in his discussion of time (there are not three different times—past, present, and future—but three modes of a single time—a present of things past, a present of things present, and a present of things future); in his discussion of narrative (which, as a single process, moves from anticipation through recitation to memory); and in his discussion of memory itself, which is the operative faculty in all three of the temporal modes mentioned above. In a passage from the *Trinity* that is very similar to the passage from book 11 of the *Confessions* that I analyzed at some length in chapter I, Augustine writes of the relationship of memory to the present and future as well as the past in the act of recitation or narration:

> We do not conjecture the past from the future, but the future from the past. . . . This can be proved by those sayings and hymns which we render from memory in the proper sequence. For unless we foresaw in our thought what follows, we certainly could not utter them. And yet it is memory, not foresight, that enables us to foresee them. For as long as we continue to speak or to sing, we utter nothing except what we have foreseen and anticipated. And yet when we do so, we do not say that we sing or speak from foresight, but from memory; and those who are especially gifted in reciting many things in this way are wont to be praised, not for their foresight, but for their memory. (*Trin.*, 15.7.13, 468)

According to Augustine's analysis, we foresee, we see, and we have seen—we look forward, we look at, and we look back—all through the operation of memory.

Vico too understood memory as being essentially three-in-one. Depending on the view we take and the point at which we cut it, memory

6. Having said that plot is "an imitation of an action that is complete, and whole," Aristotle continues thus on the issue of wholeness: "A whole is that which has a beginning, a middle, and an end. A beginning is that which does not itself follow anything by causal necessity, but after which something naturally is or comes to be. An end, on the contrary, is that which itself naturally follows some other thing, either by necessity, or as a rule, but has nothing following it. A middle is that which follows something as some other thing follows it. A well constructed plot, therefore, must neither begin nor end at haphazard, but conform to these principles." Aristotle, *Poetics,* in *Critical Theory since Plato,* ed. Hazard Adams (New York: Harcourt Brace Jovanovich, 1971), 52.

can be seen as memory itself (recollection), as imagination, and as invention, and as such it forms the very basis of human thought as a metaphoric process, which is itself trilogistic in nature. Similarly, Vico imagined his ideal eternal history as a true narrative in trilogistic form. Donald Phillip Verene can fairly say that Vico's "is an absolutely simple idea—that anything human can be understood in terms of an origin-end principle" because he has already indicated that he knows full well that the function of the hyphen in "origin-end" is not to separate one from the other but, on the contrary, to bind them ineluctably together as genetic and consequential parts of the same unitary process; and further he is altogether aware that that little mark of punctuation represents nothing less than history itself, individual, ideal, eternal, and universal, and that Vico is entirely in league with the trilogists not the dualists. "The *storia ideale eterna* is Vico's master image of history and even more his master image of the human world itself. It is the perception that the human world as a whole and in every one of its parts moves through a beginning, a middle, and an end."[7] And when Vico describes, as he does so often in the *New Science,* the cycle through which "all nations" have passed, are now passing, and will have to pass—"rise, progress, maturity, decadence, and dissolution" (*New Science,* para. 1096)—he is really giving us, in what appears to be a five-term progression, nothing other than a trilogy within a trilogy, with the middle term being broken down into three: progress, maturity, decadence. So strong was the pull toward threeness for Vico. In his very early essay titled "Dante . . . Bruno . Vico . . Joyce," Samuel Beckett maintains that Joyce adopted as "a structural convenience" Vico's enumeration of the three institutions common to every society—Religion, Marriage, Burial—and he continues thus: "By structural I do not only mean a bold outward division, a bare skeleton for the housing of material. I mean the endless substantial variations on these three beats, and interior intertwining of these three themes into a decoration of arabesques—decoration and more than decoration."[8] Here we have, as it were, Vico's Italian Baroque transformed into Celtic interlacing, but one cannot suppose that Vico would have been displeased, since it was just such a theory of transformation and transferability that lay behind his *New*

---

7. *Vico's Science of Imagination* (Ithaca: Cornell University Press, 1981), 108.

8. "Dante . . . Bruno . Vico . . Joyce" first appeared in 1929 in the Shakespeare and Company publication of essays on the book that eventually became *Finnegans Wake* (then known simply as "Work in Progress"): *Our Exagmination Round His Factification for Incamination of Work in Progress.* I have taken the quotation from *I Can't Go On, I'll Go On,* a selection from Samuel Beckett's work, edited and introduced by Richard W. Seaver (New York: Grove Weidenfeld, 1976), 111.

Science; nor could there be a better description than Beckett's of what I mean by "the Trilogy Principle"—and why should this not be so since Beckett is perhaps the Master Trilogist of our time?

Beckett is being no more and no less than a good Aristotelian, a good Vichian, and a good Augustinian when he begins *How It Is* with the narrative voice saying, "how it was I quote before Pim with Pim after Pim how it is three parts I say it as I hear it."[9] Indeed one might imagine that Beckett's diffidence about calling the *Trilogy* a trilogy or about confirming that *Company, Ill Seen Ill Said,* and *Worstward Ho* compose a trilogy was due to his knowledge that there was among his works a real and intended trilogy— a kind of trilogistic model—in *How It Is.* This ur-trilogy is in three un-named but numbered parts, the first beginning as above with "before Pim," the second beginning,

> here then at last part two where I have still to say how it was as I hear it in me that was without quaqua on all sides bits and scraps how it was with Pim vast stretch of time murmur it in the mud to the mud when the panting stops how it was my life we're talking of my life in the dark the mud with Pim part two leaving only part three and last that's where I have my life where I had it where I'll have it vast tracts of time part three and last in the dark the mud my life murmur it bits and scraps. (P. 51)

This is Aristotle's middle, "which follows something as some other thing follows it"; and as this middle "with Pim" follows "before Pim," we can be pretty sure that it will be followed in its turn by "after Pim," as indeed it is at the beginning of part three: "here then at last I quote on part three how it was after Pim how it is part three at last and last towards which lighter than air an instant flop fallen so many vows sighs prayers without words ever since the first word I hear it the word how" (p. 103). And the trilogy ends as it must with nothing to follow, yet, as in the Augustinian act of recitation or the Vichian *corso* transformed and reversed to become the *ricorso,* returned now to the beginning where expectation and memory are one and the same, the narrative folded up into itself, into "how it is" and into memory, latent now but there to be unfolded in three parts at any time in the future when narrative desire and necessity return: "good good end at last of part three and last that's how it was end of quotation after Pim how it is" (p. 147).

If *How It Is* provides us, as I believe it does, with a kind of narrative model of the Trilogy Principle, then the Augustinian "sentence" that so

---

9. *How It Is,* translated from the French by the author (New York: Grove Press, 1964), 7.

fascinated Beckett (see chapter I)—"Do not despair; one of the thieves was saved. Do not presume; one of the thieves was damned."—seems to me the Beckettian narrative of the human condition compacted into eighteen words and organized according to a principle of one-whole-composed-of-three-interactive-parts. There are the two thieves in Augustine's sentence, but there is also present an unnamed third, the middle term, he who is literally the Crux of the trilogistic arrangement: Christ is the very archetype of human experience, hanging between hope and despair, composed equally and agonistically of both. Perhaps of more interest in this context than the substantive aspect of the "sentence" is what Beckett has to say about its form: "I take no sides. I am interested in the shape of ideas. There is a wonderful sentence in Augustine: 'Do not despair; one of the thieves was saved. Do not presume; one of the thieves was damned.' That sentence has a wonderful shape. It is the shape that matters." In saying that he takes no sides, I assume Beckett means that he neither commits himself to nor opposes Christian doctrine; but that to the trinitarian, trilogistic shape of thought that descends to the twentieth century from Augustine (and earlier: from Pythagoras, for example) he is fully and unwaveringly committed. It matters less to Beckett what narrative contents you might pour into the vessel in three parts than that the vessel be of just that number of interrelated parts.

It is not quite so momentous an event as that of the two thieves and Christ on Golgotha but of somewhat the same nature that Rousseau re-counts in book 6 of the *Confessions:*

> In the midst of my studies [at Les Charmettes] and of a life as innocent as any man could lead, I was still frequently disturbed by the fear of Hell, no matter what anyone might say. "In what state am I?" I asked myself. "If I were to die at this moment, should I be damned?" . . . One day, when brooding on this melancholy subject, I began throwing stones at the tree trunks, and this with my usual skill, which meant that I hardly hit one. While engaged in this noble exercise, it occurred to me to draw a sort of omen from it, to allay my anxiety. "I am going to throw this stone," I said to myself, "at the tree facing me. If I hit it, it is a sign that I am saved; if I miss it I am damned." As I said this I threw my stone with a trembling hand and a terrible throbbing of the heart, but so accurately that it hit the tree full in the middle; which really was not very difficult, since I had taken care to choose a very large tree very near to me. Since then I have never again doubted my salvation.[10]

10. *The Confessions of Jean-Jacques Rousseau,* trans. J. M. Cohen (Harmondsworth: Penguin, 1953), 231. The passage occurs at Pléiade, 1.243. Subsequent citations of the *Confessions* will refer to both the English translation by Cohen and the original French of the Pléiade.

I imagine that both Beckett and St. Augustine would have found this a somewhat crude and unworthy way of determining one's salvation or damnation, and surely neither would have approved of cheating in the matter (or even have thought it possible to cheat); but in however debased a form, Rousseau does engage the principle of trilogy in his childish activity. I think one should have to say, however, that in his cheating and even more in his inveterate optimism about the condition of his soul, Rousseau violates the principle of trilogy, which would insist on the conflicted, divided condition of the individual suspended between hope and despair, and he thus skews the narrative—"l'histoire de mon âme"—in which he is engaged; and I believe this is true not only in the *Confessions* but in all three books under consideration. This question we will return to later, but for now we can say that it is this same principle of trilogy in the Augustinian-Beckettian sentence that determines the structure, the rhythm, and the sense of the famous conclusion to *The Unnamable:* "you must go on, I can't go on, I'll go on"; that gives logical rigor to the syllogism, with its major premise, minor premise, and its conclusion, and philosophical force to the Hegelian thesis, antithesis, and synthesis; and that lies behind the emotional and intellectual power of the sonata form, with its exposition, development, and recapitulation.[11]

If we look closely at the word "trilogy" we can see that it has to do with the logic of threeness, or with the organizing, arranging capacity (as in the suffix *-logy*) of threeness. Borrowing Heraclitus's notion of the logos as the underlying formula directing all the incessant change of the natural world, we might say that the principle of threeness underlies and determines the changes, interchanges, and relationships obtaining among the three parts of a trilogy, all of which parts relate to and develop a single theme. The single theme in Rousseau's case is, of course and always, himself, what he is in his deepest and truest being. With Rousseau, it must be said, the Trilogy Principle often seems to verge on, and even to become indistinguishable from, a repetition compulsion, the compulsion to begin and begin yet again, the compulsion to say over and over and over ad nauseam the same things,

11. In the news recently as I write this there have been reports of a "discovery" by certain experimental psychologists that university students do better on examinations after listening to recordings of Mozart than after listening to other varieties of music or to "white noise" or to other sounds that, it might have been supposed, would prepare them to do well on exams. At least one account suggests that this is due to the "soothing" effect that Mozart's music exercises on the minds of the examinees, but this is surely wrong. If the experiments are valid and the reports are accurate, then it is not the soothingness of Mozart's music but instead the capacity of that music to put the mind in the way of apprehending relationships—sonata-like formal relationships of trilogism—that is responsible.

"repeatedly with only minor variants the same bygone," as Beckett has it in *Company* (p. 16). In spite of his disavowal of the profession of letters and the scorn he directed at those he termed "authors," Rousseau himself, once he started writing, could hardly stop. He suffered from a kind of logorrhea that returned him again and again to only one or two subjects: his own naturalness, his own goodness and purity of heart, and his own loveableness, on the one hand, and, on the other hand, the vast and universal conspiracy designed by the enemies he imagined all around him, those whom he calls in the *Dialogues* "ces Messieurs." Nevertheless, repetitious as he may be, the three major units of Rousseau's massive project in life-writing are distinctively different each from the others while, as the Trilogy Principle requires, still being concerned with a single theme, differently developed though it be: Jean-Jacques himself, "inside and under the skin."

What should be said of the *Confessions,* the *Dialogues,* and the *Reveries* is that in them Rousseau attempted to do one thing in three different ways, and thus each of the books is modally very different from the other two while, in order to maintain the relationship on the level of form, occasionally intruding on the modal territory of the others. The primary mode of the *Confessions* is narration, of the *Dialogues* it is dialogue, and of the *Reveries* it is the meditative sketch, but the narrative of the first book occasionally edges over into the dialogue of the second and into the meditation of the third; the passages of dialogue in the second book, especially those spoken by "Rousseau," become so long at times and so narrative in method, so polemical in intent, that we forget that this is all supposed to be spoken by one of two equal-time interlocutors; and so on. But this is all just one of a number of ways in which the three books are different while being the same. One can observe an attempt to stitch the three books together at various points within the books themselves. In the *Dialogues* the character bearing the name "Rousseau" says that "J. J."—the subject of the conversation between "Rousseau" and "The Frenchman"—had to give up writing the *Confessions* ("that work unique to mankind, the reading of which he profaned by offering it to the listeners least suited to hear it") because "he found neither the courage nor the strength to sustain the meditation of so many horrors."[12] Near the end of book 12 of the *Confessions,* completed

12. *Rousseau Judge of Jean-Jacques: Dialogues,* vol. 1 in *The Collected Writings of Rousseau,* ed. Roger D. Masters and Christopher Kelly, trans. Judith R. Bush, Christopher Kelly, and Roger D. Masters (Hanover, N.H.: University Press of New England, 1990), 154. The passage occurs at Pléiade, 1.859. Subsequent references to the *Dialogues* will refer to the Masters/Kelly and Pléiade editions.

a year or so before this passage from the *Dialogues* was written, Rousseau had said, "It will be seen in the third part of my *Confessions,* if ever I have strength to write it, how though I thought I was setting out for Berlin I was in fact leaving for England . . ." (Cohen, 605; Pléiade, 1.656). Likewise, in book 7 of the *Confessions,* Rousseau writes that "if ever Providence . . . grants me a less disturbed life, I will devote my days to recasting this work, if I can, or at least to adding a supplement, which I feel it greatly needs," but then adds a footnote to the passage: "I have given up this idea" (Cohen, 304; Pléiade, 1.325). The material that would have gone into the "third part of my *Confessions,*" however, or into "a supplement" to "this work"—i.e., the events of Rousseau's life after he left for England and especially the conspiracy in which he imagined he was ensnared—became the material of the *Dialogues,* which is thus to be seen as the continuation of or supplement to the earlier book. In a similar manner, the end of the *Dialogues,* where Rousseau invests all his hope in posterity and in the "au-delà," the world beyond, can be seen as a clear preparation for the *Reveries,* which is an attempt in a new mode made necessary by the failure to accomplish what Rousseau had desired in the dialogue mode of the previous volume. As Michel Foucault very elegantly says of the first line in *Reveries*—"Me voici donc seul sur la terre" [Here then am I alone on earth]—a line that he sees as embracing not only the logic of the *Dialogues* but as going all the way back to the very beginning of the *Confessions:* "[A]u 'moi seul' qui ouvre le premier livre des *Confessions* repondra des la première ligne des *Reveries* son rigoureux equivalent: 'me voici donc seul sur la terre'. Ce 'donc' envel-oppe dans sa courbe logique toute la nécessité qui a organisé les *Dialogues.* . . ." [To the "I alone" that opens the first book of the *Confessions,* the very first line of the *Reveries* responds with its precise equivalent: "Here then am I alone on earth." This "then" gathers into its encompassing logic all of the compulsive force that directed the *Dialogues.* . . .][13] Although I very much admire what Foucault says here, as the reader will become aware I believe there is more to be discovered in Rousseau's "donc" even than Foucault points to—so much more that I could almost as well have called the present chapter "Jean-Jacques Rousseau and the Narrative of 'Donc,'" for "donc," as we will see, lies at the very heart of the *Confessions,* it "gathers into its encompassing logic all of the compulsive force that directed the *Dialogues,*" and it sets the *Reveries* off on its circular trajectory of self-circumscribed, self-sufficient, God-like isolation and all-inclusiveness.

13. Foucault, op. cit., p. xiv.

Another approach to understanding the trilogistic strategy of Rousseau's three volumes is to observe that they are organized and they move according to three quite different yet complementary and mutually dependent patterns: the movement of the *Confessions* is linear, of the *Dialogues* it is a dialectical back-and-forth, and of the *Reveries* it is circular. By its very nature, the middle term reaches out to the other two, and the back-and-forth movement of the *Dialogues* is obviously appropriate for the mediatorial volume. Even as the *Dialogues* move dialectically back and forth between hope and despair, however, or between the obligation Rousseau feels he has to defend himself and his equally deep feeling for resignation, he composes out of these dialectical opposites a third thing that is neither hope nor despair but something representing the conflicted and paradoxical in-between. And at the same time that they move dialectically back and forth, the *Dialogues* move gradually forward to a resolution of the antinomic opposites at another level where Rousseau will be justified "au-delà" if not "ici bas," *sub specie aeternitatis* if not *sub specie temporis.* The *Dialogues* themselves operate *sub specie temporis,* but Rousseau hoped (whether vainly or not we will consider later) that, by tying them back to the *Confessions* and thus grounding them in linear time and lived experience, and by anticipating the self-circumscribed calm and stillness of the *Reveries,* he would be able to transform the opposition, conflict, and violence of temporal experience into the comprehensive, justifying vision of the eternal. While the *Reveries* may have been the (unforeseen) goal, however, and the *Dialogues* the only way to reach that goal, it is in the *Confessions* that we have the original moment of Rousseau's massive autobiographical project, and with that volume we should begin our reading of his trilogy.

"Ici Commence"

"Here begins the work of darkness in which I have been entombed for eight years past . . . . : Ici commence l'oeuvre de tenebres dans lequel depuis huit ans je me trouve enseveli . . ." (Cohen, 544; Pléiade, 1.589). So Rousseau starts book 12, the last book, of his *Confessions.* This initiatory phrase—"Ici commence"—and numerous variations on it echo throughout the first volume in Rousseau's autobiographical enterprise, for it is a book desperate in its search for origins. Sometimes the phrase leads into an account of a temporarily happy state, as at the beginning of book 6—"Here begins the short period of my life's happiness: Ici commence le court bonheur de ma vie" (Cohen, 215; Pléiade, 1.225)—but much more frequently it is the start of misery and intrigue and darkness that the phrase announces; and even when "Here begins" is followed by "the short period of my life's happiness," already present in the expression is the certainty that the period of happiness will be short, to be followed presumably by its opposite, a long train of ills (nearly always inflicted by others). We are offered in book 1 an account of this exact moment that ends happiness and begins misery when Rousseau tells of having been wrongly accused of and punished for breaking a comb: "That first meeting with violence and injustice has remained so deeply engraved on my heart that any thought which recalls it summons back this first emotion" (Cohen, 30; Pléiade, 1.20). In an exact inversion of "Ici commence," but with precisely the same pivotal significance of beginning-and-ending, Rousseau writes, "There ended the serenity of my childish life" (Cohen, 30; Pléiade, 1.20), which leads naturally into an account of the miseries of his adult life. Whether he is tracing the "first affections of my dawning years" (Cohen, 23; Pléiade, 1.12) or describing how his desires took a strange turn because they crossed with sensual arousal at their birth (Cohen, 26; Pléiade, 1.15), whether he is locating, far back and far within, the source of his own personal characteristics ("When I trace my nature back in this way to its earliest manifestations: En remontant de cette sorte aux premières traces de mon être sensible" [Cohen, 28; Pléiade, 1.18]) or discovering the moment when "I was first the victim of that malicious play of intrigue that has thwarted me all my life" (Cohen, 85; Pléiade, 1.82), whether he is pointing to the time after which "I was to be a fugitive upon earth" (Cohen, 548; Pléiade, 1.594) and after which "all the rest of my life has been nothing but affliction and heartaches" (Cohen, 553; Pléiade, 1.599), Rousseau is throughout the book concerned with origins and originary moments. It was easy enough for Rousseau to see that all these primal instants led on to his "fatal destiny: la fatalité de ma destinée" (Cohen, 50; Pléiade, 1.43), but what Rousseau was obsessed by was the need to fix beginnings. He knew, or thought he knew, where he was, but how had it all started? Nor was he obsessed with origins only in personal terms, for Rousseau also sought to know where things started in human history and human society, as is evident merely in the titles of the *Discourse on the Origin of Inequality among Men* and the *Essay on the Origin of Languages;* and, though the word does not figure in the title, *The Social Contract* is concerned throughout with the origin of human society. The beginning of the *Confessions* itself, of course, is among the most famous and the most bizarre in all of literature, but even before he could begin with that beginning Rousseau had to begin with antecedent beginnings—with a preamble, and before that with an "ébauche" or "premier préambule," and before that with "Mon Portrait" and the autobiographical *Lettres à Malesherbes,* etc.

Once begun, however, and in whatever way that beginning might have to be accomplished, Rousseau's problem—or if not his, the problem that every reader must feel as the book goes on—soon became how he was ever going to stop. It is as if the writing itself took over and then turned pathological, words gave birth to more words, and any real end disappeared from view. Part I (books 1 through 6) was soon felt to be insufficient and part 2 (books 7 through 12)—which, Rousseau himself said, was written in darkness, secrecy, and haste—grew and grew until, to most readers, it must seem quite out of control. The first six books, which cover twenty-nine years of Rousseau's life, occupy 268 pages; the last six books, which cover twenty-four years of his life, require 380 pages. Books 7, 9, and 12 alone are individually half again as long to twice as long as the average book of part 1. In book 10 the narrative of the *Confessions* overtakes Rousseau as he is writing this very volume, so that the writing of the *Confessions* becomes the subject of the *Confessions:* it is as if a dog chasing its tail had actually caught it—but what is to be done with it then? And after so many beginnings, false or otherwise, the *Confessions* has no end; it simply breaks off in disorder and disarray. Or rather, the end presented, after the narrative end (corresponding to the preambles and so on before the beginning), is a viva voce reading of the entire book (a bravura performance on Rousseau's part of seventeen or eighteen hours, sustained, one auditor remarked, only by the reader's deep fascination with the subject of his reading), which, in the event, was even less satisfactory than the conclusion of the narrative in shambles. What was to be done? Rousseau thought of a part 3 but finally realized that the *Confessions* should seek its end not in more of the same but only in another, differently organized volume, the *Dialogues,* which, in its turn, would seek *its* end in the *Reveries.* Writing and language had for Rousseau a tendency to become independent, self-representational, autotelic, and, consequently, treacherous, a tendency on full display in the *Confessions,* especially in its latter books.

It seemed not so, however, in the beginning, wherever that beginning might be located. Rousseau appears in his various starts to be as certain of his intentions as he is of his ability to realize those intentions. Not that anyone had ever done this before and so could give him confidence—on the contrary—but that was to be the point of the book, or if not *the* point, at least *a* point and one constantly affirmed and reaffirmed. Thus in the preamble to the preamble to the start of Rousseau's narrative: "Here is the sole portrait of man, painted exactly according to nature and true in every detail, that exists and, probably, will ever exist."[14] The venture, Rousseau insisted, was unique in his time and in any time, past or to come, and compounding that uniqueness (if it is possible to compound uniqueness) was the frequently reiterated assertion that Rousseau himself was unique: "I know my own heart and understand my fellow man. But I am made unlike any one I have ever met; I will even venture to say that I am like no one in the whole world. Whether Nature did well or ill in breaking the mould in which she formed me, is a question which can only be resolved after the reading of my book" (Cohen, 17; Pléiade, 1.5). This is from the standard preamble; in the more extended preamble, attached to the Neuchâtel manuscript, we find Rousseau referring to himself as "une espéce d'être à part: a species of being unto myself."[15] And in a letter written a couple of years before he began the *Confessions,* Rousseau exclaimed to his Genevan admirer Paul Moultou, "Ah! Moultou! Providence has erred; why did it decree that I should be born among men, yet made of a different species from the rest of mankind?"[16] If this is true of him, well might Rousseau say that his project is unique, but equally well might he say that it is impossible, for how will he communicate, across species barriers and to those who are utterly alien, the nature and the history of his heart and soul? What language is there for such communication? Will it be the language unique to this unique species or a language common to and shared among all those others? Obviously the former, but then there is no currency value to that language, no commonality of articulation that would bridge the chasm between "moi seul," myself alone, as Rousseau proudly, frequently, and pathetically proclaims himself to be, and all the others who do not participate in his species of being apart.

In the Neuchâtel preamble Rousseau takes it on himself to be "un autre" (Pléiade, 1.1149) for all of humankind; in effect he will become, if his effort succeeds, "the other" for everyone else. He will be the one everyone knows best and least; others will know everything about him, because he will tell everything—the good, the bad, *everything* ("Je serai vrai; je le serai sans réserve; je dirai tout; le bien, le mal, tout enfin" [Pléiade, 1.1153])—but they will understand nothing because they are not the very man he is. He will divest himself of his public role as author of books and,

14. My translation of the first sentence of an untitled note (not translated in Cohen) that appeared only in the Geneva, and not in the Paris, manuscript of the *Confessions:* "Voici le seul portrait d'homme, peint exactement d'après nature et dans toute sa vérité, qui existe et qui probablement existera jamais" (Pléiade, 1.3).

15. "Ébauches des *Confessions,*" Pléiade, 1.1148.

16. See Guéhenno, *Jean-Jacques Rousseau,* 2.89.

no longer the name on the title pages, will become the familiar of all, but unknown and unknowable to any, as "Jean-Jacques," "J-J" or "Gigi" (as the French would say it). Strange idea for his time, perhaps less strange for ours, he would become kin to the "K." of Kafka's novels and kin to Beckett's "The Unnamable," a voice with all names and none. This is but one of the many paradoxes of Rousseau's undertaking, paradoxes that he recognized only fitfully if at all.

What Rousseau insisted on more than once—and here his paradoxes become confused and irresolvable contradictions—was that his work was to be both (and simultaneously and equally) "unique et utile," unique and useful. In the preamble to the Neuchâtel manuscript he declares, "It is certain then that if I accomplish successfully what I have undertaken I will have done something unique and useful," unique in human history, he clearly means, and useful for all humankind; and in the note prefixed to the Geneva manuscript he refers to the *Confessions* simply as "un ouvrage unique et utile."[17] No doubt the phrase recurs in Rousseau in part because the two words sound well together (better in French than in English), and to some ears (Rousseau's perhaps among them) the words might recall a tag from Horace or from some other classical or neoclassical writer on the poet's dual aim. That poet wins every vote, Horace says, who mixes the useful (*utile*) with the pleasurable (*dulce*), "qui miscuit utile dulci."[18] But while Rousseau and Horace might both wish their work to be "utile"—useful or helpful—Horace would pair that aim with amusement or pleasure; it is only Rousseau who places the very highest valuation on the "unique" in himself and in his *Confessions*. But could it be that this difference is due to the fact that Horace writes poetry while Rousseau writes "confessions"? Not if we believe Rousseau's great predecessor in the confessional mode. St. Augustine may have seen his life as, in a certain sense, an exemplary one—the example of the sinner turned to the true way through the grace of God—but he never imagined himself, his life, or his work as unique, or, in the strange Rousseauvian, full-blown Romantic way, as exemplary *because* unique. It was precisely the *non*unique nature of his experience that

17. "Il est donc sûr que si je remplis bien mes engagements j'aurai fait une chose unique et utile" (Pléiade, 1.1150); translation in the text is my own. This is what I will later call a "donc" moment in Rousseau's text. The other occurrence of "unique et utile," in the note to the Geneva manuscript, comes in a sentence in which Rousseau pleads with his reader not to refuse or to allow to come to nothing this work that is both unique and useful (Pléiade, 1.3).

18. Horace in the Loeb Classical Library, *The Art of Poetry*, lines 333–34, 343, trans. H. Rushton Fairclough (London: William Heinemann; New York: G. P. Putnam's Sons, 1926), 479.

made Augustine's potentially an exemplary life. The account of his conversion is embedded in a nest of other, similar conversion narratives—the conversions of Victorinus, Antony, Ponticianus—and Augustine tells his own
story that others might find it useful because in many ways it echoed their
own spiritual experience. When, in book 10 of his *Confessions,* Augustine
turns to an account not of what he has been and done but of what he is
now at the moment of writing, he says he does so for its possible usefulness
for people very much like himself. In considering the preamble to his account of his inner being we should observe how very similar Augustine is
to Rousseau in certain ways, how utterly dissimilar in other ways. "But as
to what I now am," Augustine writes,

> at the very moment of writing these confessions, there are many people who
> want to know about this—both those who know me personally and those
> who do not, but have heard something about me or from me; but their ear
> is not laid against my heart, where I am whatever I am. And so they want,
> as I make my confession, to hear what I am inside myself [quid ipse intus sim],
> beyond the possible reach of their eyes and ears and minds. . . . So in confessing
> not only what I have been but what I am the advantage is this: I make my
> confession not only in front of you, in a secret exultation with trembling, with
> a secret sorrow and with hope, but also in the ears of the believing sons of
> men, companions in my joy and sharers in my mortality, my fellow citizens
> and fellow pilgrims—those who have gone before and those who follow after
> and those who are on the road with me. These are your servants and my
> brothers. . . . So it is to people like this, those whom you command me to
> serve, that I shall show not what I was, but what I now am and continue to
> be. But neither do I judge myself. It is in this way that I should like to be
> heard. (Bk. 10, chaps. 3 and 4, pp. 212, 213–14)

Books 10 and 11 of his *Confessions* will show him to his readers, Augustine
could say with Rousseau, "Intus, et in Cute," as "I am inside myself," in
"my heart, where I am whatever I am"; thus far their projects could be
seen as very nearly the same. But when it comes to the nature of their
experience and their inner being, as they separately understand it, and
when it comes to the audience to which they would address themselves,
the differences between Augustine and Rousseau could hardly be
greater.

Consider once again what Rousseau proposes as he presents it in the
Neuchâtel preamble. He has often noticed, Rousseau writes, that those
who claim to possess the greatest knowledge of human nature frequently
know nothing other than themselves (if even that, which Rousseau finds
unlikely). Now this, Rousseau says, is a very faulty procedure, to claim to
know another and all others through a knowledge of oneself; and he in

particular has suffered from this since, having felt from early on that he was the sole instance of his species, he was certain that what others knew of him by knowing themselves had to be utterly false. So, to straighten this all out, he suggests that we should cease trying to know another or others by knowing ourselves; instead, Rousseau says, turn it around: one should try to know oneself by knowing another, or at least one could establish a sort of hermeneutical-circle dialectic that would move continually between knowledge of oneself and knowledge of another, gradually increasing knowledge of both as well as knowledge of some generalized human nature. And then he generously, grandly proposes himself for that unique but now, with regard to those in search of another so that they might know themselves, somehow universal other. "[P]our apprendre à s'apprecier, on puisse avoir du moins une piéce de comparaison; que chacun puisse connoitre soi et un autre, et cet autre ce sera moi" [To know oneself requires at least one term of comparison; one must know himself and an other, and that other will be me]. But the unique cannot serve as a term of comparison ("piéce de comparaison") for that which is utterly unlike; yet, enamored of the idea, Rousseau repeats the phrase in the note prefixed to the Geneva manuscript, where he refers to the *Confessions* as "un ouvrage unique et utile, lequel peut servir de prémiére piéce de comparaison pour l'étude des hommes" [a work both unique and useful, which can serve as the first term of comparison for the study of mankind] (Pléiade, 1.3). Apparently sensing that the reader might well be skeptical about this procedure or about his offer, Rousseau continues in the Neuchâtel preamble with "Oui," reiterating, reenforcing, and raising the stakes, "Oui, moi, moi seul, car je ne connois jusqu'ici nul autre homme qui ait osé faire ce que je me propose."[19] Thus Jean-Jacques would be simultaneously unique and universal. Were it possible to be both things at once, he could, I suppose, claim to be very useful as well, but the logical rule would seem to be, "If unique then not useful, if useful then not unique." In any case, Rousseau was surely right about one thing: no other had dared to do, had been foolish enough or sublimely egotistical enough to attempt to do, what he proposed doing. True, in the final preamble, Rousseau was cautious enough to say, "Je veux montrer à mes semblables un homme dans toute la vérité de la nature: My purpose is to display to my kind a portrait in every way true to nature" (Cohen, 17; Pléiade, 1.5), but he immediately follows this reference to

19. "To know how to judge one's own self accurately, one must have at least one term of comparison; everyone must know himself and another—and I will be that other. Yes, I, I alone, for I know no other man up to the present time who has dared to do what I propose" (Pléiade, 1.1149); my translation.

"mes semblables"—"my kind" or "those like me"—with the flat assertion that there *are* none like him.

In the end, if he could not claim for himself both terms, the unique and the useful, and much less all three, the unique, the universal, and the useful, it was the unique that Rousseau settled on and insisted upon, but this hardly resolved the problem of how to accomplish what I believe was his ultimate desire: to communicate the essence of his own unique being to others. The issue goes back again to his sense of himself as a being radically different from all others. Rousseau characterized himself in these same terms of uniqueness in all three volumes of his autobiographical trilogy, saying, in effect, as he puts it in the *Confessions* preamble, that while he may be no better than other men he is *different* (actually, as he makes clear more than once, Rousseau did think he was better, indeed the best of men: "I . . . believe, and always have believed, that I am on the whole the best of men" [Cohen, 479; Pléiade, 1.517]). Although they parse it in different ways, "Rousseau" and the "Frenchman" of the *Dialogues* agree that "J. J." is a man of an absolute difference. "[I]f the issue here were a wicked man of an ordinary type," the "Frenchman" says to "Rousseau," then your opinion might be correct. "But always keep in mind that the issue is a monster, the horror of the human race" (Masters/Kelly, 36; Pléiade, 1.705). "Monstre" might seem a bit strong and unlikely to please the author of the *Dialogues* as describing a character who bears his own most familiar name, but if one considers that the term could be inflected as "monstre sacré" and that, as the *Oxford English Dictionary* indicates under "monster," the word originally meant anomaly, something very unusual, then I am not sure that it would be altogether disagreeable to Rousseau. In any case, when the "Frenchman" goes on to say that "J. J." is "doubtless of an unusual kind, so unusual that nature has never produced one and I hope will never reproduce one like him" (Masters/Kelly, 36; Pléiade, 1.705–6), he is, except for the mean little phrase "I hope," saying nothing other than what Rousseau had said of himself at the beginning of the *Confessions:* "unlike anyone I have ever met . . . like no one in the whole world. . . . Nature [broke] the mould in which she formed me" (Cohen, 17; Pléiade, 1.5). "Rousseau," the dramatic character in the *Dialogues,* not surprisingly puts his finger on what Rousseau, the author of the *Dialogues,* would see as the essential point when he says of "beings who are so uniquely constituted" as "J. J." is that they "must necessarily express themselves in other ways than ordinary men" (Masters/Kelly, 12; Pléiade, 1.672). Again, Rousseau, now as author of the Neuchâtel preamble, says very much the same thing of his undertaking as his character "Rousseau" says of "J. J." when, having claimed that this will be the first and only time that anyone has been so free and full in self-revelation, he goes on: "It will be necessary for what I have to say to invent a language as new as my project."[20] But surely it must be clear to anyone but Rousseau, and even at times to him as well, though he most often refuses to acknowledge it, that this merely heaps difficulty upon complication upon impossibility: inventing a new language to express unique being to readers of an alien species in "an enterprise which has no precedent, and which, once complete, will have no imitator" (Cohen, 17; Pléiade, 1.5). Moreover, in a strange postscript (to which I will return later) that corresponds structurally to the preamble just quoted—that is to say, in a document that comes after some six hundred pages of trying to communicate his essence to readers through the written word (or even to listeners through the spoken word)—Rousseau implies that he can be known and would want to be known without the mediation of language at all: "For my part, I publicly and fearlessly declare that anyone, *even if he has not read my writings,* who will examine my nature, my character, my morals, my likings, my pleasures, and my habits with his own eyes and can still believe me a dishonorable man, is a man who deserves to be stifled" (Cohen, 606; Pléiade, 1.656). In effect, this challenge to know "J. J." without the ministry of the written word is the one that "Rousseau" accepts in the *Dialogues* when he goes to visit "J. J.," just as the "Frenchman" accepts the challenge to know "J. J." only through his writings; but the defiant declaration of the postscript comes strangely after a thoroughly *written* text as long, as anguished and yet as assured of the force of its own rightness and goodness as the *Confessions* is—a text in which Rousseau has attempted to present, precisely, his nature, his character, his morals, his likings, his pleasures, and his habits.

For all his strenuous argument in the Neuchâtel preamble against what Rousseau takes to be the nearly universal tendency to judge of the nature, the experience, and the hearts of others through an understanding of one's own being—using knowledge of oneself as the sole term of comparison for knowing others—this is unquestionably one of the procedures to which Rousseau commits himself in the *Confessions*. In fact, what Rousseau would find in his account of his own experience is nothing less than his understanding of the archetypal experience of the human race. That is to say, the *Confessions* serves not only as an outline of Rousseau's origins, his growth, his education, and his fall from a prelinguistic, natural state of bliss

20. "Il faudroit pour ce que j'ai à dire inventer un langage aussi nouveau que mon projet" (Pléiade, 1.1153); my translation.

into language, into the profession of authorship, and into society, but it also, at the same time and on another level, serves as an imitation of his philosophic system: human beings—all human beings—according to Rousseau's philosophy, are born, good, pure, and happy, into the state of nature, where they live a blessed existence as separate individuals, motivated entirely by what Rousseau terms (and what he would himself seem to have retained in large measure even after his forced departure from the natural state) "amour de soi," love of self, a kind of instinct to self-preservation, which has at its heart only one's own good, not the harm of others. Growing up means leaving the state of nature, unfortunately but necessarily, to be incorporated into the society of humans where, though no longer good or pure or happy, we can be virtuous (as natural man cannot), though few of us are because the social being is motivated not by "amour de soi" but by "amour-propre," self-love, which has at its heart not one's own self or one's own good so much as competitive concern with others and the ambitious need to harm those others so that one can oneself come out on top professionally and socially. "I saw throughout the development of his great principle that nature made man happy and good, but that society depraves him and makes him miserable," the "Frenchman" says in the *Dialogues* (Masters/Kelly, 212–13; Pléiade, 1.934) of "J. J.'s" system—a system that, as the "Frenchman" also says, "may be false, but in developing it, he portrayed himself truthfully in a manner so characteristic and so sure that it's impossible for me to mistake it" (Masters/Kelly, 212; Pléiade, 1.934). Rousseau's narrative thus intends to be not only his own story but also humankind's story, which is a scheme that, as we will see more fully later, lies behind the *Dialogues* and the *Reveries* as well. This is one reason Rousseau cites his fate or destiny so incessantly in telling why things came about as they did. How could he have done otherwise than he did? It was something outside himself, as it were something predestined, that made things be as they were. The *Confessions* is an ontogenetic recapitulation or repetition of Rousseau's phylogenetic schema, and it is often difficult to say, for Rousseau, which came first—the ontogeny or the phylogeny, the experience or the system. We get much this same sense of an individual autobiography in which the author would trace the origins and the lines of development of the human race in Vico's autobiography[21] where, again, we cannot always be certain whether the autobiography determines the theory or the

21. See Donald Phillip Verene, *The New Art of Autobiography: An Essay on the Life of Giambattista Vico, Written by Himself* (Oxford: Clarendon Press, 1991), which argues this point very subtly with regard to Vico's autobiography and his *New Science*.

theory determines the autobiography—or whether, for both Vico and Rousseau, the relationship between the two, as to cause and effect, is not symbiotic and circular. In any case, we have to ask of Rousseau (but not of Vico, who never made the Rousseauvian claim to uniqueness) how he can presume to read mythic, species experience into—or out of—unique, personal experience when he himself argued so strenuously against this same invidious (as he took it to be) practice in the Neuchâtel preamble.

That there is really no answer to this question points, I think, to something basic and important in Rousseau's entire autobiographical project (and here, although I will restrict myself to the *Confessions,* the *Dialogues,* and the *Reveries,* one should see *all* of Rousseau's works, from the *Discourse on the Sciences and Arts* to *The Social Contract* and beyond—and importantly including *La Nouvelle Héloïse* and *Émile*—as profoundly autobiographical in nature) and that is that, for better or for worse (and actually it is always for both), the project has little to do with logic or thought or dispassionate observation and everything to do with emotion and desire and memory-driven narrative. Rousseau's appeals to thought and reason are frequent— "It cannot be thought that I would act in this or that way; it is not within reason that my enemies treat me so"—but these are mere gestures of language and conventional expressions, touching not at all on the internal dynamic of Rousseau's rhetoric of apology (for though he denies it vehemently, the three autobiographical texts are apologia in the traditional sense of a defense of himself, his life, and his ideas). It is an overwhelmingly significant fact that Rousseau is scarcely interested in events at all, being almost entirely concerned with the feelings that accompanied or caused those events, and that what he would defend is not in the nature of thought that exists out there, outside himself, arguable and defensible, but emotions that, for Rousseau, are necessarily good, therefore inarguable and requiring no defense, since they were and are *his* emotions. The problem of Rousseau's narrative thus restates itself in the following form: he was intent not on recounting events or on bringing the reader to follow a train of thoughts but on making the reader feel what he had felt (and claims to refeel at the moment of writing) and thus making it possible for the reader to know the pure, natural, good springs of his—Rousseau's—heart, the source and the site of all his ceaseless, tumultuous feelings. But surely this is the province of poetry, and one must wonder if, short of Rousseau's turning to poetry, success in such a venture was possible. What Rousseau says in the Neuchâtel preamble of the *Confessions*—"C'est ici de mon portrait qu'il

s'agit et non pas d'un livre: It is not a book but my portrait that is at issue"
(Pléiade, 1.1154)—finds a nice echo in Walt Whitman a hundred years
later—

> Camerado, this is no book,
> Who touches this touches a man . . .

but then Whitman was a poet and he believed, as Rousseau on a number
of occasions made it clear that he did not believe, that language—and specifically the language of poetry—was a sufficient medium for realizing spiritual and emotional presence.[22] At any rate, Rousseau seems to imagine and
yearn for the possibility of simply bypassing language (but then what other
medium has he?) in rendering a living portrait, true in every detail, of his
internal essence, "l'histoire la plus secrette de mon ame: the most secret
history of my soul" (Pléiade, 1.1155). "It is not impossible," Rousseau
writes in the autobiographical fragment "Mon Portrait," "that an author
should be a great man, but it will not be in writing books, whether in verse
or prose, that he will become such."[23] Now, Rousseau undoubtedly aspired
to be "un grand homme," but how did he imagine he would become that
if not in writing books? He was unquestionably a remarkable sight and
probably acquired a certain notoriety when, at about the time he was writing the *Confessions,* he took to wearing his Armenian dress (long skirts with
silk tassels for summer and fur linings, topped off with a fur-lined bonnet,
for winter), began to make laces that he distributed to young virgins who
would promise to suckle their children after marriage, and became, in his
own words, "by more than half a woman," who "took my cushion round
with me on visits, or worked at my door, like the women, and gossiped
with passers-by."[24] This was a good life, Rousseau declares, and "without

22. Rousseau wrote some poetry early on but spoke of it—both the poetry he had
produced and poetry in French generally—rather scornfully. He thought the French language a language of "reason" and therefore not suited to poetry, but if I am right in the
argument above then it was even less suited to his emotion-laden purposes in autobiography.
One must wonder if this matter of reason vs. emotion and prose vs. poetry might not account
for the tangles of presumably rational explanation and justification that Rousseau gets himself
into so frequently in the *Confessions.*

23. "Il n'est pas impossible qu'un auteur soit un grand h[omme] mais ce ne sera pas en
faisant des livres ni en vers ni en prose qu'il deviendra tel" (Pléiade, 1.1129); my translation.

24. For an account of these activities, see *Confessions* (Cohen, 554–55; Pléiade, 1.600–
601) and especially the Pléiade notes on the passage, 1.1571–72. Of his Armenian habit,
Rousseau says in this passage that, because of his "frequent recourse to catheters," he had
long been aware of "the advantage of a long robe." Nevertheless, he held off acquiring
his long robe, he says, until he had had the opportunity to seek the opinion of Mme. de
Luxembourg,

boredom" (Cohen, 555; Pléiade, 1.601), but Rousseau can hardly have supposed that this way of life, all by itself, would qualify him for the honorific title of "grand homme." No, in spite of what Rousseau says in "Mon Portrait," greatness could only come to him through writing. But what a strange work it is for that purpose, this book designed to make everyone love Jean-Jacques.

It is difficult to know just how one is to react to much in the *Confessions,* but I think it safe to say of many passages that many readers feel something other than Rousseau intended them to feel, and if this was a major part of his design—that readers should feel what he felt—then the whole enterprise must be in doubt. At one point, Rousseau describes how, when he was an apprentice to an engraver, he set about trying to steal some apples from his master's larder[25] ("It is nearly always generous feelings misdirected that lead a child into taking his first steps in crime" [Cohen, 41; Pléiade, 1.32]—another nice instance of Rousseau's search for the origin of everything), and after telling of one near success that turned to failure, he exclaims, "Kind reader, sympathise with me in my grief!" (Cohen, 42; Pléiade, 1.34). The failure is followed by another attempt, but just as he is about to reach the apples, Rousseau writes, "the larder door suddenly opened; my master came out, folded his arms, looked at me, and said, 'Bravo!' The pen falls from my hand" (Cohen, 42; Pléiade, 1.34). The present tense employed in both of these instances—"sympathise with me in my grief" and "the pen falls from my hand"—would indicate an emotion so strongly recalled that it is reexperienced by Rousseau and would seem to want from

---

and she advised me strongly in favour of the change. So I had a little Armenian outfit made. But the storm it raised caused me to defer wearing it until calmer times, and it was not till some months later that, forced by more attacks to have fresh recourse to catheters, I felt I could safely wear my new clothing at Motiers, especially after I had consulted the pastor of the place, who told me that I could wear it even in church without offence. I put on the jacket, the caftan, the fur cap and the belt therefore; and after having attended divine service in this costume I saw nothing wrong in wearing it at my Lord Marshal's. When His Excellency saw my attire he greeted me quite simply with *Salamaleki,* which concluded the matter, and I never wore any other dress.

25. I have no doubt that St. Augustine is thinking of the transgression of Adam and Eve in the Garden of Eden when he tells in his *Confessions* about how, as a child, he stole some fruit from a nearby orchard. Whether Rousseau, on the other hand, is thinking of either Augustine or the Garden of Eden I have no idea. Certainly, stories like that of Adam and Eve stealing the fruit of the tree of knowledge of good and evil have lost their currency in our time, if they had not in Rousseau's time, as I became sharply aware once when teaching Augustine's *Confessions* to a very bright class in a very wealthy, very modern, very advanced liberal-arts college in New England; when I asked if the passage about stealing the fruit recalled anything to them from earlier literature, there was a long and embarrassed silence, to break which a young woman timidly raised her hand and asked, "Is it . . . George Washington and the cherry tree?"

the reader an emotional response equal in kind and intensity to Rousseau's own. The same phenomenon of reexperienced emotion we have again (or earlier) when Rousseau tells of his first encounter with adult injustice: "I feel my pulse beat faster once more as I write. I shall always remember that time if I live to be a thousand. That first meeting with violence and injustice has remained so deeply engraved on my heart that any thought which recalls it summons back this first emotion" (Cohen, 30; Pléiade, 1.20). Not only his ability but what one might call his compulsion to reexperience in memory and now in present time these strong, first emotions of childhood and youth—actually to feel what he felt then—would seem to set Rousseau somewhat apart from most people. At least, such is the gist of what Augustine says of *his* experience of remembering certain emotional moments: "This same memory also contains the feelings of my mind. It does not contain them in the same way as the mind itself has them when it is experiencing them, but in a very different way, appropriate to the nature of memory. For I remember that I was happy when I am not happy now, and I recall my past sadness when I am not sad now; when I am not frightened, I can remember that I once was frightened, and I can recall a desire I had once, when I have it no longer."[26] For better or for worse, the Augustinian full presence of memory with detachment from the feelings that accompanied the original event—the Wordsworthian recollection of emotions in tranquillity—seems not to have been available to Rousseau, and in consequence he reads like the original Man of Feeling, doomed to an endless repetition of the same emotional experiences without the possibility of their ever taking their place in a retrospectively determined pattern or of assuming the significance that detachment might confer upon them. Consider Rousseau's description of his feelings for the spot where he first met Mme. de Warens, the woman whom he describes as "rather stout: ramassée un peu dans sa taille" (Cohen, 56; Pléiade, 1.50) and again as having "an ill-concealed plumpness: un embonpoint mal caché" under her kerchief (Cohen, 107; Pléiade, 1.107)—another witness said "elle avait beaucoup, beaucoup d'embonpoint"—a physical fact that, at least in part, qualified her to be "Maman" to Jean-Jacques as he was "mon petit" to her: "Indeed I ought to remember the place, for often since I have bathed it with my tears and smothered it with kisses. I should like to surround that happy spot with railings of gold, and make it an object of universal veneration" (Cohen, 55; Pléiade, 1.48–49). "Often since . . .": it seems to have been so with Jean-Jacques that he returned again and again, in memory and imagination

26. *Conf.*, 10.14, 223.

if not in physical fact, to bathe with tears and smother with kisses all those feeling moments of his childhood. A poem that I recall from the dim past had a pair of lines in it (as I remember them)—"Backward, turn backward, oh time in thy flight; / Make me a child again just for tonight"—the appeal of which many might understand, but there are few who either could or would yield as wholeheartedly or as frequently to that insidious appeal as Rousseau. And I emphasize the "could," for it seems to have been a special psychological and memorial capacity in Rousseau, whether we admire it or not, that permitted—and caused—him not just to remember his childish emotions but to reexperience them again and again.

"Although in certain respects I have been a man since birth," Rousseau writes in book 4 of the *Confessions,* "I was for a long time, and still am, a child in many others" (Cohen, 169; Pléiade, 1.174). Here and in many other places, Rousseau seems content—proud would perhaps be a better word—to remain a child ("un enfant" in the original) into years of adulthood, surely in part because that means that he has continued in a state of nature longer than others. But childishness or puerility is also a criticism against which he feels the need to defend himself very frequently in the *Confessions,* and with good cause, for there *is* something childish about many of the events that he recounts and that seem to have acted as emotional cathexes in his psychological development—if, indeed, it is to be called development. "Nothing that happened to me during that delightful time," Rousseau writes of his stay with "Maman" at Les Charmettes,

> nothing that I did, said, or thought all the while it lasted, has slipped from my memory. The period preceding it and following it recur to me at intervals; I recall them irregularly and confusedly; but I recall that time in its entirety, as if it existed still. My imagination, which in my youth always looked forward but now looks back, compensates me with these sweet memories for the hope I have lost for ever. I no longer see anything in the future to attract me; only a return into the past can please me, and these vivid and precise returns into the period of which I am speaking often give me moments of happiness in spite of my misfortunes. (Cohen, 215–16; Pléiade, 1.226)

That scholars have found Rousseau's memory (or if not his memory then his imagination) wrong—and culpably wrong—about the time at Les Charmettes, creating a mythic world and an idyllic time that never existed against which he could play out the dark drama of his enemies conspiring to destroy him because he was still the good and happy man of nature, is perhaps less to the point than to remark that this capacity or tendency to "return into the past," to live there and there only, and to subject himself to those same emotions at the age of fifty-five as at the age of ten or sixteen

is both Rousseau's strength and his weakness. Again of "that first meeting
with violence and injustice" glanced at a few pages earlier, which he recounts with "my pulse beat[ing] faster once more as I write," Rousseau
says, "It is now nearly fifty years since this occurrence, and I have no fear
of a fresh punishment for the offence. But I declare before Heaven [and
we recall the preamble: 'Let the last trump sound when it will, I shall come
forward with this work in my hand . . .'] that I was not guilty. I had not
broken, nor so much as touched, the comb. I had not gone near the stove,
nor so much as thought of doing so" (Cohen, 29; Pléiade, 1.19). These
are the very accents of the aggrieved child— "IT'S NOT FAIR!"—that any
parent can expect to hear once or twice every day until (the parent can
hope) the child will reach an age when events will assume their place in
a certain perspective and the infantile sense of always being a victim will
be replaced by a more mature understanding. In many ways, Jean-Jacques
never reached that age, and this means all sorts of interesting things for the
functioning of his memory and the ordering of his narrative.

One thing it does is to make Rousseau always the one to be pitied,
no matter what the content might otherwise be of the narrative that engages
him. A simple instance of this pervasive tendency came at the death of the
Maréchal de Luxembourg in 1764. On that occasion, Rousseau wrote, in
words that would be echoed some twelve years later in the first sentence
of the *Reveries*, "I remain alone on earth [seul sur la terre—word for word
the same as *Reveries*], crushed with ills, without friends, without resources,
without comfort" (Pléiade, 1.1585). This seems a bit exaggerated—there
were plenty of people around who would have professed the friendliest
feelings toward Rousseau and who would have been delighted to offer him
resources and comfort—but much more astonishing than this feeling that
the death of the Duc de Luxembourg had left him alone on earth was the
letter that Rousseau wrote to the freshly widowed Duchesse de Luxembourg in which he informed her that he was himself more to be pitied and
had more to regret in the duke's death than she.[27] The duchess seems to

27. To read a really good biography of Rousseau like Maurice Cranston's is to be
amazed again and again at a self-centeredness in Rousseau that seems to have been absolute
and total yet quite unwitting. On the occasions when Rousseau felt himself compelled to
write letters of condolence on the deaths of children or grandchildren, spouses or siblings,
he would begin by saying that he was too rough hewn and too much a man of nature to
engage in this artificial exercise; he would go on, however, to reveal that he was not too
rough or too natural to feel very keenly all the sorrows of his own condition, his endless
illnesses, maltreatment by friends, etc. Condolences were artificial until demanded by Rousseau; then they were natural and obligatory. It was never for the loss of someone close to
him that Rousseau felt the need of condolence, however—except in the case of his dog

have been surprisingly forbearing in the circumstances and responded with concern for their continuing relationship. A more typical narrative of tangled emotion and logic, which in the end seems designed, like a great suction device, to draw all pity toward Rousseau, is the matter of the ribbon stolen by Rousseau who then accused Marion, the girl with whom he worked, of the theft. Having described the theft, the confrontation by employers, and his accusation of Marion, Rousseau goes into a frenzy of confused explanation and defense. It was not done out of badness of heart because that could never be the case with Jean-Jacques; it must, then, have been done from a precisely *opposite* motive, it must have been from the *goodness* of his heart, for this is how Rousseau's mind worked in such circumstances. "[N]o one will accuse me, I am certain, of palliating the heinousness of my offence," Rousseau writes. "But I should not fulfil the aim of this book if I did not at the same time reveal my inner feelings . . ." (Cohen, 88; Pléiade, 1.86). Ah yes, "inner feelings"—that way, for Rousseau, lies redemption and even exaltation. And what were those inner feelings? They were, as Rousseau himself might well say, unique: "Never was deliberate wickedness further from my intention than at that cruel moment. When I accused that poor girl, it is strange but true that my friendship for her was the cause [il est bizarre mais il est vrai que mon amitié pour elle en fut la cause]. She was present in my thoughts, and I threw the blame on the first person who occurred to me. I accused her of having done what I intended to do myself. I said that she had given the ribbon to me because I meant to give it to her" (Cohen, 88; Pléiade, 1.86). One thinks of all the great and moving documents from antiquity and from more recent times— by Plato, by Cicero, by St. Augustine, most of all by Montaigne, from whom Rousseau steals wholesale and whom he then accuses of being false in his sincerity—and then one wonders what to say about Rousseau on friendship. "Il est bizarre mais il est vrai que mon amitié pour elle en fut la cause." Bizarre indeed. Nowhere in all the literature of friendship do I recall another characterization or explanation like this one. I have said that it is often difficult to know what emotions Rousseau would have us feel

---

Turc—it was always for his own ills. And the number of times he implicitly or openly begged for pity because he was dying (which he started to do very early on) are strewn everywhere. Cranston, after recounting several instances of the phenomenon of condolences redirected by Rousseau to himself, remarks mildly, "Once again, we see Rousseau incapable of directing his attention from his own misfortunes to those of others . . . ; incapable, perhaps, of imagining how bitter Vernes's grief [at the loss of his seventeen-year-old wife in childbirth] must be" (*The Noble Savage: Jean-Jacques Rousseau 1754–1762* [Chicago: University of Chicago Press, 1991], 211).

in such episodes as this one; it is equally difficult to accept his memory and his analysis of those emotions. When he claims to remember that "I said that she had given the ribbon to me because I meant to give it to her," the act of memory is as unbelievable as the narrative of defense is confused. And what the reader discovers finally is that when Rousseau refers to "that cruel moment" he has in mind much more the cruelty of the moment for himself than any cruelty that it might have represented for Marion. The thoughtlessness of the adults in the whole affair, as Rousseau tells the story, amounts to something like child abuse, the child who suffers the abuse, of course, being Rousseau. "If M. de la Roque had taken me aside and said: 'Do not ruin that poor girl. If you are guilty tell me so,' I should immediately have thrown myself at his feet, I am perfectly sure. But all they did was to frighten me, when what I needed was encouragement. My age also should be taken into account. I was scarcely more than a child. Indeed I still was one" (Cohen, 89; Pléiade, 1.87). By his own account, Rousseau could have availed himself of this final excuse of childishness at any age whatsoever (actually he was sixteen when he stole the ribbon, which is not the first blush of infancy), but his perfect assurance, some thirty-five or forty years on from the event, of how he would have acted had the full-grown adult present been more encouraging and less frightening, may not be shared by all readers. Rousseau concludes the episode by calling the theft and the false accusation "the sole offence I have committed" and by reflecting that this single, only offense "must have been atoned for by all the misfortunes that have crowded the end of my life, by forty years of honest and upright behaviour under difficult circumstances" (Cohen, 89; Pléiade, 1.87). It is with some distress that any reader will realize that in this account of his sole offense Rousseau has not yet come near the raw nub of his narrative, the *real* origin and beginning—the omphalos—of the *Confessions,* as against all the preambles and preambles to preambles and the "Je suis né" of page 2: i.e., the disposition of his five children seriatim in the foundling hospital precisely during those "forty years of honest and upright behaviour under difficult circumstances."

I have said that, often as he may deny it, the *Confessions* do constitute Rousseau's *apologia pro vita sua,* and he is almost as profligate in apologies— in defenses and explanations—of his method, this method unique in his time and inimitable, he claims, in any time, as he is of the life itself. His method, he tells us time and again, is to tell all the truth, in particular the truth of his inner life; and for the truth of his inner life, "l'histoire la plus secrète de mon ame," he will depend entirely on his memory to recall in exact and faithful detail all those feelings that were both cause of and accompaniment to his actions. "I am writing entirely from memory," Rousseau declares near the end of book 3, "without notes or materials to recall things to my mind. There are some events in my life that are as vivid as if they had just occurred. But there are gaps and blanks that I cannot fill except by means of a narrative as muddled as the memory I preserve of the events [qu'à l'aide de recits aussi confus que le souvenir qui m'en est resté]" (Cohen, 128; Pléiade, 1.130). Though this passage begins with reference to a period of his youth "about which my ideas are the most confused," the truth is that it is as his story goes on and begins to draw nearer to the present time of its own telling that it becomes most confused and that Rousseau finds it necessary to find—to reconstruct or to construct—muddled "recits" to fill in for equally muddled memories of events and their accompanying emotions. In what is one of the best known of Rousseau's descriptions of what he means to be about in the *Confessions,* at the beginning of book 7 and as a kind of preamble to part 2 of the volume, Rousseau writes, "I may omit or transpose facts, or make mistakes in dates; but I cannot go wrong about what I have felt, or about what my feelings have led me to do; and these are the chief subjects of my story. The true object of my confessions is to reveal my inner thoughts exactly in all the situations of my life. It is the history of my soul that I have promised to recount, and to write it faithfully I have need of no other memories; it is enough if I enter again into my inner self, as I have done till now" (Cohen, 262; Pléiade, 1.278). What he attempted was certainly daring—we have to grant Rousseau that—but who could ever expect success in such a venture? And was it so important that everyone in his time and everyone in times to come should know his inner thoughts exactly? Rousseau clearly believed that nothing was more important to humankind than to know all that he had felt in all circumstances of his life; nothing was more important than that he be able "to make my soul transparent to the reader's eye" (Cohen, 169; Pléiade, 1.175). But why do we need to know, and how will we profit from knowing, what the young Rousseau was thinking or feeling when he exhibited himself regularly to young women (only to be scared off the practice finally by "a big man with a big mustache, a big hat, and a big sword" [Cohen, 91; Pléiade, 1.89])? What benefit can we derive from knowing what Rousseau remembers feeling when he committed all of his many foolishnesses with Maman (e.g.: "One day at table, just as she had put some food into her mouth, I cried out that I had seen a hair in it. She spat the morsel back on her plate, whereupon I seized it greedily and swallowed it" [Cohen, 108; Pléiade, 1.108])? And, though he prefaces the episode by declaring, "Whoever you may be that wish to know a man, have the courage to read the next two or three pages and you will have complete knowledge of Jean-Jacques Rousseau," what does a reader gain, except amusement or pleasure (which, in a preamble to the *Dialogues,* Rousseau specifically and bitterly disavows ever aiming at in the *Confessions*), upon learning of Rousseau's recalled feelings and thoughts during his encounter with Zulietta, the Venetian courtesan with the "téton borgne" or "malformed nipple" (Cohen, 300–302; Pléiade, 1.320–22)? True, the reader inclined to frivolity might get a laugh out of the latter episode and might find wisdom not so much in "complete knowledge of Jean-Jacques Rousseau" as in Zulietta's final advice to "Zanetto"/Jean-Jacques—*"Zanetto, lascia le Donne, e studia la matematica: Give up the ladies, and study mathematics"*—but such a reader will be in for a stern reproof and a high-minded lecture upon passing on to the *Dialogues:* "As for those who want only some agreeable rapid reading, who sought and found only that in my *Confessions,* and who cannot tolerate a little fatigue or maintain their attention in the interest of justice and truth, they will do well to spare themselves the boredom of reading this. It is not to them I wished to speak, and far from seeking to please them, I will at least avoid the ultimate indignity of seeing that the picture of the miseries of my life is an object of amusement for anyone" (Masters/Kelly, 7; Pléiade, 1.666). *Get serious, Reader* is the message: knowing the inner truth about Jean-Jacques Rousseau's soul is the most important thing in the world.

The ultimate thing to be revealed in the *Confessions,* however, had not to do with the young Jean-Jacques's exhibitionism or with his interest in Maman's spat-out morsel of food or even with Zulietta's "téton borgne" but with the matter of the five children and the foundling hospital. Here the dual process of memory and narrative in Rousseau shows itself in its most disordered form as he approaches the hidden center of his autobiographical project. To explain what I mean by disorder at the central point of Rousseau's trilogy, I want to invoke the idea that not only is there a logic to narrative but that there is also a narrative to logic. The logic that lies behind narrative says that you cannot begin just anywhere but instead must begin with the beginning, follow that with the middle, and end with the end. We are told that the epic poet should begin "in medias res," and we understand, in spite of the seeming contradiction, how the logic of narrative can determine that the "middle of things" can be the proper and logical beginning, or how, to put it slightly differently, the narrative middle can be—and logically must be—the plot beginning. But there is an implicit narrative about logic as well, and it is here that Rousseau frequently skews things. In the progression of a syllogism from major premise to minor premise to conclusion we can read an unfolding story. What I claim is that in the *Enfants-Trouvés* episodes of the *Confessions* the story told by Rousseau's logic is not a followable story; it is forever running off the tracks, and this loss of control has to do with Rousseau's two incompatible memories: one, the memory, ab initio or even from before time began, of the ineffable goodness of his heart (which is another way of stating Rousseau's dilemma—while plain and obvious to him, the goodness of his heart was literally ineffable and therefore unrecognizable by anyone else); and the other, the memory, fully temporal in nature and retained faithfully by Voltaire and others if not unfailingly by Rousseau himself, of the times when he shipped children numbers 1, 2, 3, 4, and 5 off to the foundling hospital where their fate was death or something not much better (of the children committed to *Enfants-Trouvés* in Rousseau's time, 70 percent died in their first year, only about 5 percent lived to mature years, and most of that 5 percent concluded as tramps and beggars).[28] But, as Jean Guéhenno remarks, Rousseau begins the first of the two narrative episodes dealing with the disposition of the children with a "pretense of light-heartedness" (une légereté affectée), as if to say, "There's no problem here." That tone, however, cannot be sustained for long, and the text soon shows signs of the kind of internal turmoil in which the logic of narrative and the narrative of logic both collapse. Before going on with the narrative, however, we should consider the background and the context in which Rousseau felt himself called upon to address the subject of the children at all—or it would be better to say *required* to address the subject, for he would have avoided it if he could have. In late 1764, amid mounting woes for Rousseau, coming, it seemed, from all directions, Voltaire published an anonymous pamphlet titled *Sentiment des citoyens*. In that eight-page brochure, Voltaire, adopting the voice of the good citizens of Geneva, accuses Rousseau of numerous immoralities if not quite crimes. "We confess with pain and embarrassment," Voltaire writes, "that this is a man who shows on him the dreadful marks of his debaucheries and who, suited out like a mountebank, drags with him from Village to Village and from Mountain to Mountain the unfortunate woman whose mother's death he has caused and whose children he has exposed at the gates of a hospital, rejecting the cares for them that a charitable person offered and renouncing all natural sentiments

---

28. See Pléiade notes, 1.1415–16; also Lester G. Crocker, *Jean-Jacques Rousseau: The Quest (1712–1758)* (New York: Macmillan, 1968), 179, and Maurice Cranston, *Jean-Jacques: The Early Life and Works of Jean-Jacques Rousseau 1712–1754* (Chicago: University of Chicago Press, 1982), 245. Not all scholarly accounts agree exactly on the mortality figures for the Hôpital des Enfants-Trouvés, but the picture is fairly consistent and not very pretty.

as he likewise repudiates those of honor and religion."[29] Rousseau's immediate response to these accusations was as bizarre as Voltaire could have
wished from one whom he had already called a madman:[30] Rousseau had
the pamphlet republished in Paris with his own manuscript preface and
annotations. What Rousseau hoped to gain by this we can only guess.
When he arrived at the passage where Voltaire had written "whose children
he has exposed at the gates of a hospital," Rousseau first wrote a footnote
in the margin, then crossed it out and wrote a note on a separate sheet of
paper that he attached to the text. After asserting that he does not suffer
from any disease consequent upon debauchery but only from his troublesome, lifelong retention of urine for which he has had regular recourse to
his catheters, Rousseau proceeds to the heart of the matter—Thérèse, her
mother, and the putative children:

> The wise and universally esteemed woman who cares for me in my illnesses
> and comforts me in my afflictions is unfortunate only in that she shares the
> fate of a very unfortunate man; her mother is still very much alive and in good
> health in spite of her old age. I have never exposed nor caused to be exposed
> any child at the gates of any hospital, nor anywhere else; anyone possessed of
> the charity spoken of here should have had enough of it to keep the matter
> secret; and everyone knows that it is not from Geneva, where I have scarcely
> ever lived and where so much animosity is spread against me, that one should
> expect accurate news of my conduct. I will add no more on this passage but

29. "Nous avouons avec douleur & en rougissant que c'est un homme qui porte encor
les marques funestes de ses débauches, & qui déguisé en saltimbanque traine avec lui de
Village en Village, & de Montagne en Montagne, la malheureuse dont il fit mourir la
mère, & dont il a exposé les enfants à la porte d'un hôpital, en rejettant les soins qu'une
personne charitable vouloit avoir d'eux, & en abjurant tous les sentiments de la nature
comme il dépouille ceux de l'honneur & de la Religion." My translation, from an appendix
to vol. 12 of *Correspondance générale de J.-J. Rousseau,* ed. P.-P. Plan (Paris: Armand Colin,
1929). The editor of the *Correspondance générale* reproduces in this appendix the text of Voltaire's pamphlet as prefaced and annotated by Rousseau and republished by him in Paris;
the passage quoted comes on p. 6 of the pamphlet, and on *Correspondance générale,* 12.376.
I assume that the "déguisé en saltimbanque" is Voltaire's sly way of referring to Rousseau's
Armenian costume, and the upper-case Village and Montagne presumably allude to Rousseau's *Devin du Village* and his *Lettres écrites de la Montagne.* The title of Voltaire's pamphlet
suggests mockery of Rousseau's habit of signing himself "J.-J. Rousseau, Citoyen de Genève" (as he did in a letter to Voltaire himself in 1750); at one point Rousseau insisted that
friends and acquaintances address him as "le Citoyen."
30. "A madman is to be pitied; but when insanity becomes frenzy, he has to be tied
down. Tolerance, which is a virtue, would otherwise be a vice" (On a pitié d'un fou; mais
quand la démence devient fureur, on le lie. La tolérance qui est une vertue seroit alors
un vice). My translation from the beginning of the *Sentiment des citoyens,* reproduced in
Correspondance générale, 12.371.

this: that—excepting only murder—I would rather have done what its author accuses me of than to have written anything similar.[31]

Rousseau begins this, at the very least duplicitous, note with the remark, "I wish to make, with all simplicity, the declaration that this article seems to demand of me," which he then follows with his resounding denials— "Jamais aucune maladie. . . . jamais . . . aucun enfant. . . ." I believe, nevertheless, that for all the bluster and daring of his denials, Rousseau really knew, in his heart of hearts, that he had been had by the master of this sort of literary skulduggery (though Rousseau was mistaken as to the author's identity, believing the pamphlet to have been by Pastor Jacob Vernes rather than by Voltaire). It was at this point that he determined to write his *Confessions,* and it was at this point also that (as quoted earlier) he exclaimed, with pathetically bad foresight, "When all has been revealed, how posterity will love me! how it will bless my memory!"

After this excursion into the imbroglio that set the *Confessions* in motion, we can return to the text where Jean-Jacques begins to tiptoe up to the fearful subject matter. Having told what a good time he had had with friends in Chenonceaux in the autumn of 1746, Rousseau goes on with what, to all appearances, is a gay and lighthearted, if slightly cynical and rakish narrative—the voice of one of the boys and, at the same time, of a man about town:

> Whilst I was growing plump at Chenonceaux my poor Thérèse was doing the same in Paris, though in another way; and when I returned I found the work I had set under way further advanced than I had expected. Considering my position, this would have thrown me into the greatest embarrassment if some table companions had not provided me with the only means of extricating myself. This is one of those essential details which I cannot relate too baldly. For were I to comment on them, I should have either to excuse or

31. "La personne sage et généralement estimée qui me soigne dans mes maux et me console dans mes afflictions, n'est malheureuse que parce qu'elle partage le sort d'un homme fort malheureux; sa mère est actuellement pleine de vie, et en bonne santé malgré sa vieillesse. Je n'ai jamais exposé ni fait exposer aucun enfant à la porte d'aucun hôpital, ni ailleurs; une personne qui auroit eu la charité dont on parle auroit eu celle d'en garder le secret; et chacun sent que ce n'est pas de Genève, ou je n'ai point vécu et d'ou tant d'animosité se repand contre moi, qu'on doit attendre des informations fidèlles sur ma conduite. Je n'ajouterai rien sur ce passage, sinon qu'au meurtre près j'aimerois mieux avoir fait ce dont son Auteur m'accuse, que d'en avoir écrit un pareil"; my translation. The syntax of the final sentence is so tangled that it is virtually impossible to find one's way through in either French or English. This, I take it, is a sign of Rousseau's mental distress at that moment, which comes out also in the crossings-out, interlinings, and general messiness of the manuscript text reproduced in the *Correspondance générale,* 12.381.

blame myself, and here I have no business to do either. (Cohen, 320; Pléiade, 1.342–43)

One might well explore the phrases "considering my position" and "the greatest embarrassment," examining just what they might mean in their context, but undoubtedly the most questionable part of this introductory passage is the final sentence. Rousseau appears to believe his own oft-repeated statement that he has not engaged, does not engage, will not engage in excusing himself in the *Confessions,* but this is to refuse the plain meaning of words like "excuse" and the plain meaning of what he has done and what he has written about it. Even as he continues in the lighthearted vein, the excuses begin to insinuate themselves into the description of the company that provided him with the only means of extricating himself. The narrative pace here is remarkable as Rousseau chatters on about the dining arrangement he had at the time, offering a hundred irrelevant details—or details that seem so until he finally comes to the point—about the character of the other diners, the nature of their conversation, and the general spirit of the company that was responsible for providing him with the solution to his great "embarrassment." The food was "pretty poor," Rousseau says, but the "table was always popular on account of the good and respectable company [bonne et sure compagnie] that frequented it." Among the diners were an old rake, "all wit and courtesy," and "a giddy and brilliant company of young Guard and Musketeer officers," who, however giddy they may have been, were kept "in some kind of order: un certain ordre" by M. Du Plessis, "a good and respectable old man, and M. Ancelet, a Musketeer officer." "The place was also frequented by merchants, financiers, and provision dealers, . . . well-bred and honourable men . . . distinguished in their trades . . . ; [i]n fact one met people of standing of all classes, except priests and lawyers," which was very much to Rousseau's taste as he never had any use for those classes anyway. "The company was fairly numerous and very gay, though not noisy, and the conversation was risky but never vulgar." The tone of the conversation at Mme. la Selle's table was established by the old rake who, "despite the broadness of his stories, never forgot his old courtly good manners" (Cohen, 321; Pléiade, 1.343–44). Rousseau's control of the narrative up to this point is both admirable and assured as he picks his way carefully through his characterization of these people as, on the one hand, "all wit and courtesy . . . , giddy and brilliant . . . and very gay," and, on the other hand, "good and respectable . . . , well-bred and honourable . . . , distinguished [and with] courtly good manners."

With all this narrative persiflage (as it seems) Rousseau eases gradually and insensibly closer to what, from the time of the appearance of the *Senti-*

ment des citoyens, he has felt himself required to confess. In the first instance—i.e., when he had Voltaire's pamphlet republished in Paris—Rousseau denied everything; now he is left with the task of confessing that which he has denied without, *at least to himself* (for his own absolute sense of inner worth demands this), seeming to have lied in his first outing. Jean-Jacques lie? Never! But how, then, to tell, at this late stage, that he did in fact send his children to the foundling hospital? As I say, Rousseau handles it well up to this point, but hereafter it gradually gets out of control, and in a very characteristic manner. The young men at Mme. la Selle's table adopted the old rake's tone, Rousseau says, and

> recounted their affairs with equal elegance and freedom. . . . and [I] heard a lot of most amusing stories there. Gradually indeed I adopted not, thank Heaven, the morals but the principles I found accepted there. Honest men injured, deception of husbands, seductions and secret childbirths were the most common themes; and the man who best helped to stock the Foundling Hospital was always the most applauded. I caught the habit, and modelled my way of thinking upon that which I saw prevalent among these very pleasant and fundamentally very decent people. 'Since it is the custom of the country,' I told myself, 'if one lives there one must adopt it.' That was the way out I was looking for. I cheerfully resolved to take it without the least scruple. . . . (Cohen, 321–22; Pléiade, 1.344)

The phrase "very pleasant and fundamentally very decent people" (a characterization that is even more positive and upright in the French: "des gens très aimables, et dans le fond très honnêtes gens") is, of course, an attempt to capitalize on the earlier rhetorical gesture that established the table company as "good and respectable," etc. But Rousseau's hand has been too clearly revealed in the sentence beginning "Gradually indeed . . ." for this maneuver to succeed. The sentence runs thus in French (picking up with the previous half-sentence): "J'y apprenois des foules d'anecdotes très amusantes, et j'y pris aussi peu à peu, non grace au Ciel jamais les moeurs mais les maximes que j'y vis établies." Typically, Rousseau goes over the top in his shocked denial—shocked that anyone could ever imagine anything like this of Jean-Jacques Rousseau—that he adopted "les moeurs" of these "fundamentally very decent people." "Les maximes," yes, but "les moeurs . . . non . . . jamais." But what exactly, we must ask, is the distinction Rousseau is drawing between "moeurs" and "maximes"? We should first remark the alliteration that is no doubt partly responsible for the coupling of the words, but this alliterative linking makes the terms similar rather than different, leaving us the same problem with which we began. I assume that Rousseau would say something like this to justify contrasting "moeurs" and "maximes": that "moeurs" arise out of one's deepest convictions or beliefs and they define one's ultimate nature. This description could well be granted, but could not the same be said of "maximes"? Perhaps with "maximes" Rousseau means something like "clever, pithy sayings," but if so he has chosen—or allowed alliterative euphony to choose—dangerous language that betrays him in the event. Elsewhere in the *Confessions* Rousseau uses the word "maxime" in a perfectly straightforward manner to mean "a principle of conduct" that would in no way be opposed to or at odds with "moeurs." From the unfortunate taint of greed observed in his father, Rousseau says in an earlier passage, he himself learned this "one great maxim of morality (cette grande maxime de morale) . . . : to avoid situations which place our duties in opposition to our interests. . . . I have carried this maxim firmly imprinted on my heart and applied it . . . to all my conduct" (Cohen, 61–62; Pléiade, 1.56). When, some five books later in the *Confessions,* Rousseau writes, "Considering my position, this [Thérèse's pregnancy] would have thrown me into the greatest embarrassment if some table companions had not provided me with the only means of extricating myself," one might wonder if there is not an opposition of duties and interests here, but Rousseau has no doubt put behind him any memory of the earlier passage that claimed that the maxim was "firmly imprinted on my heart." Again in the "moeurs" vs. "maximes" passage, the rhetorical allure of alliteration and rhyming goes further than the *m*s of the two opposed words. In "jamais les moeurs mais les maximes" the "mais" not only contributes to the alliterative pattern while turning the sense of the words against one another, but it also, in repeating and rhyming with the end of "jamais," effects a kind of doubling of the negative: "never . . . but" (where "but" serves as the negative opposite of "and"). Moreover, Rousseau muddies the waters further (which is no doubt his deepest, perhaps unconscious intention) and further confuses any distinction one might justifiably draw between "moeurs" and "maximes" when he continues, "I caught the habit, and modelled my way of thinking [formai ma façon de penser] upon that which I saw prevalent . . . ," etc. Is a "way of thinking" a matter of "moeurs" or of "maximes"? I think one could give an answer, for Rousseau and with regard to this passage alone, but it would have no significance elsewhere and no significance in itself at all.

However, having said that he adopted "without the least scruple" the "maximes" that provided the way out of his embarrassment, Rousseau concludes his first account of the crucial child issue thus with an attempt to return to the lighthearted tone (never altogether abandoned) of the beginning:

> [I]ndeed the only scruples that I had to overcome were Thérèse's, and I had
> the greatest difficulty in the world in persuading her to accept this sole means
> of saving her honour. But her mother had another fear, that of a fresh embar-
> rassment in the form of a brat, and she came to my aid; Thérèse gave in. We
> chose a discreet and safe midwife, Mlle Gouin by name, who lived at the
> Pointe Sainte-Eustache, to undertake the depositing of the baby; and when
> her time was come, Thérèse was taken by her mother to be delivered at
> Mlle Gouin's. I went to see her there several times, and took her a set of
> initials which I had written on two cards, one of which was put in the child's
> swaddling clothes. It was then deposited by the midwife at the office of the
> Foundling Hospital in the usual manner. In the following year the same
> inconvenience was removed by the same expedient . . . (Cohen, 322; Pléiade,
> 1.344–45).

Let us pass over in silence the matter of saving Thérèse's honor (there is
no evidence at all that she was concerned about this, especially no evidence
when it was in balance with the child) as well as the support given by
Thérèse's mother (whom otherwise Rousseau could find no use for at all
and who is rather badly cut up elsewhere in the *Confessions*), but I think
we must pause over the French of the final sentence to get the full force
of Rousseau's relief that this is all over, at least for the moment: "L'année
suivante même inconvénient et même expédient"—the perfectly balanced
and rhymed phrases do not even require a verb to move us smartly out of
the tricksy situation. But four sentences (three in English) remain to be
negotiated before Rousseau can move on, and they are highly characteristic
in the manner in which—how can even Rousseau do this?—they turn the
pity of it all, the "lacrimae rerum," back in the direction of "le pauvre
Jean-Jacques."

> Pas plus de réflexion de ma part, pas plus d'approbation de celle de la mére;
> elle obéit en gémissant. On verra successivement toutes les vicissitudes que
> cette fatale conduite a produites dans ma façon de penser ainsi que dans ma
> destinée. Quant-à-present tenons-nous à cette prémiére époque. Ses suites
> aussi cruelles qu'imprévues ne me forceront que trop d'y revenir.
> [No more serious reflection on my part, and no greater willingness on the
> mother's; she obeyed with a sigh. In due course it will be seen what vicissitudes
> this fatal conduct occasioned in my way of thinking and also in my destiny.
> For the present let us confine ourselves to this first period. Its consequences,
> which were as cruel as they were unforeseen, will force me to return to it
> only too often.] (Cohen, 322; Pléiade, 1.345)

It is notable, though Rousseau's prose determinedly does not note it, that
Thérèse still had not got it through her head how important it was for her
that her honor should be saved. The vicissitudes, however, are not visited

upon Thérèse—her honor, after all, has been saved—but only upon Jean-Jacques, whose way of thinking will be troubled and his destiny bedeviled by these children who had seemed to be so conveniently disposed of. There is no question of who felt the full cruelty of those consequences that were unforeseen, indeed unforeseeable, by anyone. The cruelty that the world constantly and unaccountably heaped on this good man is a spectacle that Rousseau, in the *Confessions,* finds it difficult to contemplate with equanimity.

The first two shipments of children to *Enfants-Trouvés* Rousseau thus justifies and excuses by saying it was an unthinking act to which he was misled by listening to the maxims of a fun-loving but fundamentally good and decent group of people. This recourse to excusing himself by claiming that he acted without thinking will not be good enough for Rousseau when he returns to the question with the next three children, for he is determined there to attempt the much more difficult feat of providing a fully rational, carefully reasoned account of why Three, Four, and Five had to go. Once again we would do well to step back just a bit to see how Rousseau approaches the problem, how he surrounds the actual compelled confession with all sorts of strange, apparently unrelated narratives. The passage dealing with the first two children comes just before the conclusion of book 7; the latter three children turn up half a dozen pages into book 8, which begins with language that we might well recognize: "I had to pause at the end of the last book. With this one starts the long chain of my misfortunes, in its very beginnings [J'ai dû faire une pause à la fin du précédent Livre. Avec celui-ci commence dans sa prémiére origine la longue chaine de mes malheurs]" (Cohen, 326; Pléiade, 1.349). No matter that we have heard "ici commence" before and will hear it again; this time it is the beginning raised to the second and third power, "dans sa prémiére origine," the beginning of the first beginning of the long chain of my misfortunes. This is followed by the crucial and famous episode that, according to his own account, divided Rousseau's life into two halves, the before and after of his becoming an author. On the road to Vincennes, where he was going to visit Diderot in prison, Rousseau tells of seeing the question posed by the Dijon Academy for a prize essay ("Has the progress of the sciences and arts done more to corrupt morals or improve them?") and of deciding, with Diderot's encouragement, to enter the contest (which he eventually won), "and from that moment I was lost. All the rest of my life and of my misfortunes followed inevitably as a result of that moment's madness" (Cohen, 328; Pléiade, 1.351). This critical episode, which occupies about one page of the text, somehow—but it is difficult to say just how—segues into description of Thérèse's parents, in particular her mother:

> Thérèse's father was a very mild old fellow and extremely frightened of his wife whom he had nicknamed The Hanging Judge, a title which Grimm subsequently transferred to her daughter. Mme Le Vasseur was not without intelligence, that is to say shrewdness; she even prided herself on her civility and worldly manners. But she had a mysterious wheedling tone that I found unbearable and was always misadvising her daughter, and trying to make her dishonest with me. She also tried to set each of my friends separately against each other and against myself. In other respects she was a fairly good mother[32] because she found it paid her to be so, and concealed her daughter's faults because she profited by them. But though I loaded the woman with cares and attentions and little presents and did all I could to gain her affection, because of my utter inability to do so she was the one cause of trouble in my little establishment. (Cohen, 329–330; Pléiade, 1.353)

Besides finding in Mme. Le Vasseur another origin of his woes ("la seule cause de peine que j'eusse"), Rousseau probably has her in mind at this point because she was the one, we recall, who, because she feared "a fresh embarrassment in the form of a brat" [craignoit un nouvel embarras de marmaille], helped persuade Thérèse to agree to let the first child (and perhaps the second) be sent to *Enfants-Trouvés*. In any case, Rousseau follows his deconstruction of Mme. Le Vasseur's character with an episode one would think unrelated—the rather sordid business of Rousseau, Grimm, and Klupffel taking turns with the young girl kept by Klupffel—but that

32. "[D]u reste assez bonne mère": This is a formula Rousseau loves to produce after giving a dreadful list of negative attributes of someone he would do in. See, for an even better example, the description of Wintzenried, the young man who replaced Rousseau in Maman's affections and in her bed: "This young man . . . was a journeyman wigmaker [not even remotely true, but Rousseau had a particular contempt for wigmakers]. . . . He was a tall, pale, silly youth, tolerably well-built, with a face as dull as his wits. . . . He was vain and stupid, ignorant and insolent, but in other ways the best fellow in the world [au demeurant le meilleur fils du monde]" (Cohen, 248; Pléiade, 1.261–62). Rousseau adopts this trick, and repeats the exact phrasing, from a line in Clément Marot where, after listing his valet's many vices, Marot says, "Au demeurant le meilleur fils du monde." Rousseau could have found much the same sort of thing in Montaigne, where he found so much else, the only difference being that Montaigne turns the joke back on himself rather than directing it at someone else: in the essay "Of Presumption," after listing all the various activities in which he has failed to learn anything—music, dancing, tennis, wrestling, swimming, fencing, vaulting, jumping, penmanship, reading, etc.—Montaigne concludes his educational portrait with "Otherwise, a good scholar." See *Montaigne's Essays and Selected Writings,* trans. and ed. Donald M. Frame (New York: St. Martin's Press, 1963), 260–61, where Frame identifies the source in Marot.

in turn leads us back to Thérèse, with whom Rousseau "relieved myself of my guilty conscience by a free and frank confession." And how did Thérèse react? Splendidly, according to Rousseau: "I received nothing from her but touching and tender reproaches, in which I never perceived the slightest trace of anger. That good girl's kindness of heart was equalled only by her simple-mindedness," which reminds Rousseau of an altogether different kind of anecdote that he cannot forbear relating. It seems that Thérèse

> took it into her head that Klupffel [because he was a minister] was the Pope. I thought she was mad the first time she told me, on my coming home, that the Pope had come to see me. I made her explain, and went off at top speed to tell this story to Grimm and Klupffel. Ever afterwards he was known amongst us as the Pope, and we called the girl in the Rue des Moineaux [the one who "did not know whether to laugh or to cry" as the three chums enjoyed her one after the other] Pope Joan. We could not control our laughter; we almost choked. Whoever made me say, in a letter that someone has been pleased to attribute to me, that I have only laughed twice in my life, did not know me at that time, nor in my youth, or that idea would certainly never have entered his head. (Cohen, 331–32; Pléiade, 1.355–56)

The account of these madcap adventures (not having been there, the reader is to be excused for not enjoying their recounting quite as much as Rousseau does), along with descriptions of the peculiarities of the Le Vasseur family and an intervening paragraph about how victory in the Dijon competition "set that first leavening of heroism and virtue working in my heart that my father, my native land, and Plutarch had implanted there in my childhood" (Cohen, 332; Pléiade, 1.356), leads directly into the second attempt to lay to rest the bogey of the children. "Whilst I was philosophizing on the duties of man an event occurred which made me reflect more deeply upon my own. Thérèse became pregnant for the third time" (Cohen, 332; Pléiade, 1.356). In some sense—a sense perhaps not clear even to himself and certainly not clear to the common reader—Rousseau, I believe, has been trying to prepare, in a most complicated way, since the first sentences of book 8 about the "prémiére origine [de] la longue chaine de mes malheurs," for this admirably simple sentence—"Thérèse devint grosse pour la troisiéme fois"—and at the same time lay the ground that will permit him to extricate himself from the consequences of that simple sentence.

It is notable that this time out Rousseau affects no lightness of spirit or of tone. Instead of the earlier casual, even flip attitude what we have in book 8 is a hypertensive pushing against logic, a shrillness and exaggeration of assertion, a raising of the voice and of moral tone by several decibels, all because it is felt that a narrative has gone and is going wrong.

> Thérèse became pregnant for the third time.[33] Too sincere with myself, too proud in my heart, to be willing to belie my principles by my actions, I began to consider the fate of my children and my relationship with their mother, by reference to the laws of nature, justice, and reason, and of that religion—pure, sacred, and eternal as its Author—which men have soiled whilst pretending they were trying to purify it, and which they have turned by their formulas into no more than a religion of words, seeing that it is not costly to prescribe the impossible if you excuse yourself from performing it.

If the first sentence in this passage is admirably simple, the second is something else again—neither simple nor admirably anything. What kind of confession is this? Rousseau confesses his own sincerity, his pride "en dedans," his unwillingness to belie his principles by his actions. It seems quite a pleasant mode of confession this, and one might imagine the confessor asking, "Is that all, my child? Have you nothing more serious to confess?" Well, yes, Rousseau does have something more on his mind if not on his conscience: he will confess that *others* have soiled the Christian religion, *they* have turned it into nothing more than a religion of words, and *they* have excused themselves, through rhetorical trickery, from any kind of moral culpability for their failure to live up to the principles of Christianity. One would be tempted to call this special pleading except that it seems neither controlled enough nor rational enough to qualify as special pleading. Any reader might be forgiven for imagining that when Rousseau writes, "Whilst I was philosophizing on the duties of man an event occurred which made me reflect more deeply upon my own," and when he invokes "the laws of nature, justice, and reason," he will come out at a different place this second time around than on the first occasion when he had to deal with the embarrassment of children about to arrive. And in a certain sense he does. Not that the three later children are not disposed of as the first two were—they are—but now that action will be defended, excused, and justified as being in keeping with "the laws of nature, justice, and reason," therefore a sacred duty to be performed by Jean-Jacques Rousseau, "Citoyen de Genève"—or citoyen of any state to which Rousseau would give his moral approbation. This goes well beyond, even insanely beyond, the earlier excuse of going along with the ways of table companions.

---

33. I have remarked that this is an admirably simple sentence, and it is. I would be remiss, however, if I did not point out—if only in passing because my argument permits no more—that the simple sentence neither requires nor allows for any male agency in the fact of Thérèse's pregnancy.

"If I was mistaken in my conclusions," Rousseau says (though he has not yet told us what those conclusions were), "nothing can be more remarkable than the calm spirit in which I surrendered to them." We have only to turn Rousseau's sentence back to front to observe its logic (or lack thereof): I surrendered (which is what one does in the face of an invincible force) to my conclusions in a calm spirit; *therefore* I was not mistaken. And what grounds has he for this chain of (mis)reasoning? Rousseau continues in the subjunctive, condition-contrary-to-fact, verbal mood: "If I were one of those low-born men, deaf to the gentle voice of Nature, a man in whose breast no real feeling of justice and humanity ever arose, this hardness of heart would have been quite easy to explain." As sure as he starts this sentence with an "If," Rousseau is going to start the next sentence with a "But," and so he does in a sentence whose wildness and craziness puts everything heretofore into the shade:

> But my warm-heartedness, my acute sensibility, the ease with which I formed friendships, the hold they exercised over me, and the cruel wrench when they had to be broken; my innate goodwill towards my fellow men; my burning love for the great, the true, the beautiful, and the just; my horror of evil in every form, my inability to hate, to hurt, or even to wish to; that softening, that sharp and sweet emotion I feel at the sight of all that is virtuous, generous, and lovable: is it possible that all these can ever dwell in the same soul along with depravity which, quite unscrupulously, tramples the dearest of obligations underfoot?

This remarkable self-encomium might find its appropriate place in a number of different contexts: it might be part of a plea for votes in a contest of popularity or congeniality; it might be a Dickensian hypocrite gone overboard in oleaginous self-praise; it could be a character in one of Rousseau's own novels, expressing the high-minded sentiments of the author himself. What it cannot conceivably be—not reasonably, not logically, not appropriately—is any part of an account of placing five children in a foundling hospital where they were virtually assured of dying before adolescence. It cannot possibly be—but it is—part of an account leading to the following sentence with its "therefore" or "donc" acting as the unavoidable Q.E.D. at the end of a series of logical propositions: "My third child, *therefore,* was taken to the Foundling Hospital like the others [Mon troisiéme enfant fut *donc* mis aux enfans-trouvés ainsi que les prémiers], and the next two were disposed of in the same way, for I had five in all" (Cohen, 333; Pléiade, 1.357). Rousseau, by deploying his "donc" in this way, is, I believe, borrowing, if not directly then allusively, from Descartes ("Je pense donc je suis") and would like the reader to feel all the inevitability of Cartesian logic behind his phrasing. The real logic that troubles all of this account, however—the logic that lies behind it and spooks it at every moment—goes, I believe, like this:

> Major premise: A good man would not send his children to *Enfants-Trouvés;*
>
> Minor premise: Jean-Jacques is a good man;
>
> Conclusion: Therefore, Jean-Jacques did not. . . .

But "No," Rousseau exclaims at this point, remembering always his timeless goodness yet also remembering at this point, as he must, the disposition of the children, sensing the irresolvable conflict between the two memories and sensing as well the conflict between his true and false syllogisms, "No, I feel, and boldly declare—it is impossible: Non, je le sens et le dis hautement; cela n'est pas possible." "Je le sens:[34] I feel"—and that is that: off with your logic, out with reason; feeling proves, justifies, validates, and excuses everything. "Never for a moment in his life could Jean-Jacques have been a man without feelings or compassion, an unnatural father." "Un père dénaturé"—this is what Rousseau had been called and he simply could not stand it. The "père" business didn't bother him so much, for after all, as he will say a little farther along, "a father's feelings cannot speak very loudly for children he has never seen" (Cohen, 335; Pléiade, 1.359); but the "dénaturé" touched Rousseau very nearly since it was his naturalness, his oneness with "the gentle voice of Nature," that was the origin, the "ici commence," of his goodness, his "love for the great, the true, the beautiful, and the just," the origin, in short, of his feelings and of his lovableness.

What Rousseau's critics did was to take his very messy syllogism, turn it inside out, making his conclusion into a minor premise and supplying a new major premise, and thereby came up with an entirely new and different, but entirely appropriate conclusion—thus:

> Major premise: Only a "père dénaturé" would send his child or children to *Enfants-Trouvés;*
>
> Minor premise: Jean-Jacques Rousseau sent his five children to *Enfants-Trouvés;*
>
> Conclusion: Therefore, Jean-Jacques Rousseau is a "père dénaturé," an unnatural father.

34. Cf. the famous phrase (which Cohen translates, "I know my own heart") at the very beginning of the standard preamble to the *Confessions:* "Je sens mon coeur." For Rousseau that is really all that is necessary.

This is logic that could never be to Rousseau's taste, however, and the most it gets from him is the acknowledgment, "I may have been mistaken," which he immediately reverses with his next clause: "but I could never be callous." In the original this is "J'ai pu me tromper, mais non m'endurcir," which I think could be fairly translated as "I may have been mistaken, but not unfeeling," which turns a trivial concession about reasoning ability into a significant compliment about a capacity for feeling; and then, in a passage that surpasses everything heretofore and beggars both description and belief, he writes, "If I were to state my reasons, I should say too much. For since they were strong enough to seduce me, they would seduce many others; and I do not wish to expose any young people who may read me to the risk of being misled by the same error." Yet—we must remind ourselves—Rousseau's refusal to give the compelling reasons that seduced him comes in the middle of the long paragraph that is supposed to issue—that *will* issue, not reasonably but by main force—in "My third child, *therefore,* was taken to the Foundling Hospital. . . ." That his reason for not giving his reasons is sheer bluff does nothing to lessen the insult to the reader's intelligence—quite the contrary. "I will be content," Rousseau says, and then goes on with a sentence that has failed to make many readers feel content, "I will be content with a general statement that in handing my children over for the State to educate, for lack of means to bring them up myself, by destining them to become workers and peasants instead of adventurers and fortune-hunters, I thought I was acting as a citizen and a father, and looked upon myself as a member of Plato's Republic." One wonders what Plato would have had to say of this notion of his Republic, but more critically it must be observed that if Rousseau's five children ran true to the *Enfants-Trouvés* norms only one would have grown up to any destiny at all and it would more likely have been that of beggar or vagabond than worker or peasant.

The "general statement" I have quoted occurs in the Geneva manuscript; in the middle of that statement as we have it in the Paris manuscript is an extraordinarily interesting insertion that demonstrates something of Rousseau's frustrated attempts to introduce some kind of narrative order into what he clearly felt, I believe, was getting quite out of control. A separate interesting study could well be done, in fact, of the cancellations, omissions, insertions, and tortured decisions about including or excluding material so clearly evident on the surface of the various textual versions of the *Confessions* when the children and the *Enfants-Trouvés* appear on the scene. In the Paris manuscript what we have is this: "I will be content with a general statement that from that time on I regarded my liaison with Thérèse as nothing other than an honest and healthy commitment, although free and voluntary, my faithfulness to her, as long as the relationship should last, as an indispensable duty, the violation of it that I committed one single time as a true adultery, and as for my children, in handing them over for the State. . . ."[35] I would not claim that this succeeds in bringing greater narrative control to bear—indeed, I believe it does the reverse—but I think from the insertion one can see why Rousseau surrounds the core of his narrative with other narratives about Thérèse and the Le Vasseur family, about his relationship with Grimm and Klupffel, and about his sole violation of his faithfulness to Thérèse. He seems to find some kind of dim and shadowy justification for what he has done with the children in the anecdotes recounted—perhaps not altogether unlike what the dining company at Mme. la Selle's represented in the earlier episode—and moreover telling the tales postponed for at least a few pages the necessity of the painful confession (if "confession" it is to be called). It was undoubtedly all roiling around in his head and, as he would say later, the memory of it was so confused that it was "impossible for me to impose any order or connexion on the ideas which come back to me" (Cohen, 579; Pléiade, 1.627).

Rousseau's enrolling himself as a charter member of Plato's Republic is far from the end of his tortured progress through his unruly narrative. "More than once since then," Rousseau writes, in a passage that will reverse the terms of the heart-reason contrast introduced earlier, "the regret in my heart has told me that I was wrong. But far from my reason having told me the same story, I have often blessed Heaven for having thus safeguarded them from their father's fate, and from that which would have overtaken them at the moment when I should have been compelled to abandon them [quand j'aurois été forcé de les abandonner]." This would seem to be sailing dangerously close to the wind in its phrasing since it was precisely a charge of having abandoned his children that set the *Confessions* going in the first place and that led to the torment of this very passage, but at least Rousseau manages to reach out and snatch some pity for himself in "I have often blessed Heaven for having thus safeguarded them from their father's fate. . . ." "Le pauvre Jean-Jacques," as Jean-Jacques would himself say. "If I had left them to Mme d'Epinay or to Mme de Luxembourg who, out of friendship or generosity, or from some other motive"—one of Rousseau's

---

35. "Je me contenterai de dire qu'elle fut telle que des lors je ne regardai plus mes liaisons avec Thérèse que comme un engagement hônnete et sain, quoique libre et volontaire, ma fidélité pour elle, tant qu'il duroit, comme un devoir indispensable, l'infraction que j'y avois faite une seule fois comme un véritable adultère, et quant à mes enfans, en les livrant à l'éducation publique . . ." (Pléiade, 1.1430–31); my translation.

favorite tricks, as here, is to hint at some unspeakable, base motive, then leave it to the reader's imagination to supply a motive worse than anything that could be spelled out—"offered to take charge of them at a later date, would they have been happier, would they have been brought up at least as honest people? I do not know; but I am sure that they would have been led to hate, and perhaps to betray, their parents. It is a hundred times better that they have never known them." There is a certain pronoun ambiguity in that last clause that permits us to understand either that it is a hundred times better that the children never knew their parents or that it is a hundred times better that the parents never knew their children; it may be that we should understand it both ways, for by this point I very much doubt that Rousseau himself could say which he intended. In any case, the next sentence after this one is the sentence that waves its "donc" as if it were a flag signifying "Mission accomplished and home free at last"—"Mon troisiéme enfant fut donc mis aux enfans-trouvés. . . ." Perhaps overcome by a heady feeling of having negotiated these treacherous waters successfully, Rousseau permits himself the luxury of going one incautious step further: "This arrangement seemed so good and sensible and right to me that if I did not boast of it openly it was solely out of regard for their mother." It might be wondered to *whom* he would have boasted of it, but then that's Rousseau for you, and when he says that it was "uniquement" out of regard for Thérèse that he didn't brag about what he had done, we must recognize in this the true Rousseau touch of delicate sensitivity, and we will recall that he earlier had to persuade Thérèse that dispatching the first child to *Enfants-Trouvés* was the sole means ("unique moyen") of saving her honor. Though he did not, for this sole reason, boast of the expedient he had found, Rousseau says that he did freely tell of it to "everyone whom I had told of our relationship"—Diderot and Grimm, later Mme. d'Epinay, and still later Mme. de Luxembourg—so that what he could have kept as a secret he didn't: "In a word, I made no mystery about my conduct, not only because I have never been able to conceal anything from my friends, but because I really saw nothing wrong in it. All things considered, I made the best choice for my children, or what I thought was the best. I could have wished, and still do wish, that I had been brought up and nurtured as they have been" (Cohen, 334; Pléiade, 1.358). The only thing it is possible to say in the face of something like this is that in circumstances of exculpatory and emotional extremity Rousseau is capable of saying anything—absolutely anything at all—without regard to truth, probability, consistency, honor, or dignity. For this comes just two pages after the reference to that "leavening of heroism and virtue working in my heart that my father, my native land, and Plutarch had implanted there in my child-hood"; and it comes less than a page before Rousseau claims that whatever he has done it is not nearly so bad as what so-called friends did in making "my secret . . . noised abroad" (Cohen, 334; Pléiade, 1.358). What secret, one might ask; but it has changed colors since, a few lines earlier, it was something freely told to anyone and a deed worth vaunting to the world.

> Without wishing to disown the blame which I deserve, I would rather have that on my conscience than have to answer, like them, for sheer maliciousness. My fault is great, but it was an error. . . . But to betray a friend's confidences, to violate the most sacred of all bonds, to publish secrets entrusted to our bosom, deliberately to dishonour the friends we have deceived and who still respect us as they say good-bye—those are not faults; they are utter baseness and infamy.
>
> I have promised to write my confessions, but not to make my apologies; so I will stop here. My duty is to tell the truth; my readers' to be just, and that is all that I shall ever ask of them. (Cohen, 334–35; Pléiade, 1.358–59)

That Rousseau can say—and perhaps believe—that he has been making his confession and not writing an apologia ("J'ai promis ma confession, non ma justification") is a sufficient index of his ability to deceive himself if not his reader. It is difficult to think of another autobiographer or life-writer or self-writer—whatever term we choose—as thoroughly and as continuously self-deceived as Rousseau. We have only to think of Rousseau's two great predecessors in the mode—one of them named in the text, the other implied in the title of the *Confessions*—to realize how deficient Rousseau was in his understanding of his own motives. I refer, of course, to Montaigne and St. Augustine, neither of whom is ever deceived about himself in the writing of his *Essays* or his *Confessions*. To understand what confession is in any classical sense we would obviously go to Augustine and not to Rousseau, but my impression is that in our time—and one must make of this what one can—literary confession owes almost nothing to Augustine and almost everything to Rousseau. *True Confessions*—which are neither true nor confessions—set the tone for our time and they come more or less directly out of Rousseau.

But Rousseau also has more respectable progeny (I am not thinking now of the five children) than *True Confessions,* and with a number of them we will be later concerned. Here it suffices to say that Rousseau redefined and reordered the writing of confessions and autobiography. He did so thoroughly and in a way that would not permit of any simple return to earlier forms. "After such knowledge, what forgiveness?" Gerontion asks, and we can only repeat the question. But the real indication of the interest and importance of Rousseau's *Confessions* may well be that it contains many more questions than answers—and this even, or especially, in Rousseau's presumably self-assured treatment of who he is, what his story is, what his memories are. At the beginning of the *Confessions* Rousseau could not be more affirmative about his self-knowledge and his knowledge of others— "Je sens mon coeur et je connois les hommes"—and he repeats this assurance time and again, at least through the first six books. Thereafter, it seems to me that it all begins to come unraveled (and it is not insignificant that the *Enfants-Trouvés* episodes occur in books 7 and 8). By book 12 what we get is no longer the supreme self-confidence of the preamble (which may even then have been more show than reality) but instead passages like the following:

> I should like to go on talking for ever about George Keith; my last happy memories are connected with him. All the rest of my life has been nothing but afflictions and heartaches, which I find it so sad to recall, and which come to me in so confused a form that I can no longer reduce my story to any sort of order. Henceforth I shall be obliged to arrange my facts haphazard, as they come to my mind. (Cohen, 553; Pléiade, 1.599)

> The further I go in my story, the less order and sequence I can put into it. The disturbances of my later life have not left events time to fall into shape in my head. . . . The only strong impression they have left me is that of the horrible mystery enveloping their cause, and of the deplorable state to which they have reduced me. Now my story can only proceed at haphazard, according as the ideas come back into my mind. (Cohen, 574; Pléiade, 1.622)

> I have so confused a memory of this whole affair that it is impossible for me to impose any order or connexion on the ideas which come back to me. I can do no more than record them in the scattered and isolated form in which they come to my mind. (Cohen, 579; Pléiade, 1.627)

By the end of the *Confessions* Rousseau hardly knew himself much less others, and he could have said, as he later would say in *Reveries,* that "the real and basic motives of most of my actions are not as clear to me as I had long supposed."[36] Unhappy as that was for Rousseau, worse was the recognition that what he had begun by knowing so clearly about himself and about his heart he had failed utterly to convey to anyone else whether readers of the *Confessions* or auditors at one of the readings he gave of the book before they were stopped at Mme. d'Epinay's instancy. For this is

---

36. *Reveries of the Solitary Walker,* trans. Peter French (Harmondsworth: Penguin Books, 1979), 94. This appears at Pléiade, 1.1051. Subsequent references will be given by page numbers of the translation by French and the Pléiade edition.

surely the significance of the extratextual note tacked onto the end of this first volume of memoirs: "Thus I concluded my reading, and everyone was silent. Mme d'Egmont was the only person who seemed moved. She trembled visibly but quickly controlled herself, and remained quiet, as did the rest of the company. Such was the advantage I derived from my reading and my declaration" (Cohen, 606; Pléiade, 1.656). According to one of those present at another reading of the *Confessions*, Rousseau paused when he came to the *Enfants-Trouvés* episode, apparently hoping for something from his audience even if it were censorious, but "the only response he received was a lugubrious silence" (Pléiade, 1.1613). That no one showed a sign of knowing him as he had begun by knowing himself, that no one appeared to feel as he felt, that no one seemed to love him as he expected to be universally loved for his book and for himself, that no one except Mme. d'Egmont showed any emotion at all and even this slight return was quickly and easily subdued—this represented the most tragic failure for Rousseau. It did not mean that he gave up the attempt, however; it meant that he had to change his strategy, his structure, and his immediate audience. It meant, in short, that he had to go on to *Rousseau juge de Jean Jaques—Dialogues,* a book determined throughout by what had happened in and to his first, epoch-making but—from his own point of view—unsuccessful, venture in life-writing.

Nothing Sole or Whole

Rousseau's strategy in the face of this worst of all responses to his *Confessions*—for, as he came to feel, silence *was* a response: an all-enveloping, suffocating, and universal response engineered by his enemies to keep him absolutely in the dark about the conspiracy (the "complot") that he felt all about him but that he could neither hear nor see—was not to retreat or in any sense to give up on what he considered the most important thing for himself and for everyone: to make himself known as he was within, and to show that he was always and everywhere one and the same, in his writing and in his life, a singular, unique being, entirely sole and whole in himself. In a tactic that resembled his response to publication of the *Sentiment des citoyens,* when, instead of lying low and remaining quiet, he had the pamphlet republished in Paris where it would receive much more attention and notoriety than in Geneva, Rousseau, in *Rousseau juge de Jean Jaques,* embraces the fact of fragmentation, of self-division and self-alienation, and pushes it to a new and heretofore unknown extreme. If he cannot be and cannot persuade his audience that he is the single *I* that he knows himself to be, then, Rousseau seems to say, he will split himself into two, three, four *Is*, in a dizzying proliferation of selves at various removes from the presumed originary *I,* but always in the apparent hope of returning from and through these divided, multiple selves to a state of oneness and wholeness. The logic of Jean-Jacques's procedure, though not at first obvious, nevertheless seems to be in keeping with what W. B. Yeats's Crazy Jane tells the Bishop:

> A woman can be proud and stiff
> When on love intent;
> But Love has pitched his mansion in
> The place of excrement;
> For nothing can be sole or whole
> That has not been rent.

Rousseau rends himself in the *Dialogues,* and in so doing succeeds in disorienting virtually every reader of the book, but it is done in the paradoxical interest of finally asserting that he is, or has become through the very process of rending, sole and whole. It is as if he hopes that, by carrying the rending to the extreme beyond which there is no question of a stable identity, he can issue on the other side, the postlapsarian, postrending side, where the process is turned inside out and where prelapsarian wholeness once again exists, beyond division, beyond fragmentation.

I have heard it argued (by James F. Jones, Jr., and others at a symposium on autobiography held at Washington University in St. Louis) that as Rousseau's *Confessions* is the prototypical modernist autobiography so his *Dialogues* is the prototypical postmodernist autobiography. This, I think, is an interesting argument, with much to be said for it (though I would alter it at least to the extent of claiming that what latter-day modernists and postmodernists did consciously and with full, happy awareness of the drastic consequences, Rousseau, as the first in the line, did more or less blindly and in the dark); but the question that should occupy us as we turn from the *Confessions* to the *Dialogues* (perhaps not unrelated to the issue of modernism and postmodernism) is what Rousseau is doing with the created personae of the *Dialogues*—his "J. J.," his "Rousseau," his "Frenchman" (each of them divided within himself at some point or points in the book)— and indeed what he does with created personae in the *Confessions.* The question might be posed this way: What is the ontological and the literary status of "J. J." and "Rousseau" in the *Dialogues* (leaving aside for the moment "the Frenchman," who does not share in any part of Jean-Jacques Rousseau's name)? They both bear the author's name, and are given first-person voice and address for the fictional moment of the text, yet they are presumably also *he*s to an author who exists, at some remove outside his text, in a way that they, his characters, do not. But we must go a step beyond this, too, and ask what is the ontological and the literary status of Jean-Jacques Rousseau, author of the *Dialogues,* who, like "J. J." and "Rousseau," appears as an *I* at various places in the text—in the preamble ("On the Subject and Form of This Writing"), in fairly frequent footnotes, and in the postscript ("History of the Preceding Writing")? Is it different for Rousseau from what it is for "J. J." and "Rousseau"? If one says, "Yes, it *is* different: the two latter are characters in a quasi fiction written by the former, who is not a fictional but a historical figure," then what does one say when "Rousseau," the character of the *Dialogues,* says to "the French-man," presumably speaking not of himself in the third person but of the author, "It is unfortunate for J. J. that Rousseau cannot say everything he knows about him" (Masters/Kelly, 106; Pléiade, 1.797)? When a character of fiction—so indicated by the conventional use of quotation marks, "Rousseau," to signify a character whose existence is solely fictional, lying entirely within the covers of a book—reaches outside the fiction and the book to refer to his creator and the author of the fiction by his historical name, which appears, of course, on the title page, when the author becomes a creature of his own created character, then how many sets of single and double quotation marks do we have to put around the name and the onto-logical status of the author-creature-of-his-own-creature? Is it Rousseau, "Rousseau," " 'Rousseau,' " or " ' "Rousseau" ' "? I would be inclined to-ward the last of these were it not that vertigo sets in. There are passages in the *Dialogues*—and this is hardly surprising—where Rousseau-as-author in a footnote corrects or supplements something said by "the Frenchman" (e.g., the note on Masters/Kelly, 234; Pléiade, 1.962); a bit more surprising are passages where Rousseau-as-author corrects "Rousseau" (e.g., note on Masters/Kelly, 187; Pléiade, 1.901—"it must be understood that Rous-seau, who is speaking here, doesn't have a very sublime opinion in general of the high virtue of the well born," etc.); but the most surprising is a passage where Rousseau-as-author in a footnote corrects or supplements Rousseau-as-author in the text of the postscript, "History of the Preceding Writing." In that postscript, Rousseau-as-author, already, as it were, in dialogue with himself, writes, "For the idea that my manuscript would reach the King directly and that this young Prince would take the trouble to read this long writing was, I said, so crazy that I myself was amazed I had deluded myself with it even for a moment" (Masters/Kelly, 248–49; Pléiade, 1.980–81). But the division within himself implied by this self-dialogue is, at this point, not enough for Rousseau-as-author, who adds in a footnote, "This idea and that of the deposit on the altar had occurred to me during the life of Louis XV, at which time it was a bit less ridiculous." This situation of complete ontological instability for characters, narrators, and authors, which is deliberately created and extreme in the *Dialogues,* is not unknown to the *Confessions,* and I think we would do well to take it up there first, where it is a relatively simpler matter, before giving ourselves over unprepared to the snares and tangles of the *Dialogues.*

In "Ici commence" I have referred (as is conventional when discussing what one takes to be autobiography) to the author, the narrator, and the protagonist of the *Confessions* by a single name, Jean-Jacques Rousseau, with neither quotation marks nor any other sign to suggest that there is anything other than a shared identity among the three, and also with no suggestion that any of the three is a consciously designed fiction. Of course, we think of Rousseau, the historical figure, as a writer who may, in his autobiographical text, mistake his facts, manipulate his text, and transform his confession into an apologia without ever acknowledging to the reader (or perhaps to himself) what he is doing. Today at least, this is all acceptable practice, and we still call it autobiography (although we may think that Gertrude Stein's brother, Leo, was acting naturally, if old-fashionedly, when he exclaimed of her performance in *The Autobiography of Alice B. Toklas*—which, of course, has built into it many of the same questions as I am raising about Rousseau's *Confessions*—"God, what a liar she is!"). But from time to time a suspicion creeps into our reading of the *Confessions* that something other and something more may be going on here, something different from a mere confusion about dates or a manipulation of events to the author's benefit or even lying, something more complex than this and much more interesting in the history of literature; and whether that suspicion is simply due to the fact that we are looking back from the late twentieth century to the late eighteenth century, from a time of sophistication to a time of comparative innocence (strange word to apply to Rousseau), is not at all clear. The suspicion, I believe, properly takes the form of speculation not about Rousseau the man (to repeat Leo Stein, altering only the pronoun: "God, what a liar he is!"), fascinating as that subject is and as many biographical responses as it has drawn, nor of speculation about the biographical context of his life; the suspicion is associated instead with the nature of the actual text—or I should say "texts"—of his autobiographical enterprise. The kind of suspicion I have in mind—and we are all suspicious readers nowadays when it comes to reading and thinking about autobiography—might be put in terms of what has come to be called "the unreliable narrator." Now Foucault would argue, and with much force, that it is not a man, not a life, not a pathological case but only texts that we have or that we should be concerned with in the case of—dare one say, ought one to say, "in the case of 'Rousseau,'" with or without quotation marks around the name Rousseau? For this is what is at issue, even in the *Confessions*. Let us acknowledge that the author of that book is Rousseau; this seems safe enough. But is the narrator of the *Confessions* Rousseau or "Rousseau"? And what about the protagonist—Rousseau or "Rousseau"? These are not questions easily or safely answered.

In discussing the *Confessions* it might be strategically advisable to abandon use of the name Rousseau and speak only of a narrator or a narrative voice. One distinct advantage of this usage is that it would lessen the temptation to an attitude of petulant personalism in writing about that "bad man," Jean-Jacques Rousseau; and certainly critics have not been wanting who like writing about Rousseau to show how much they dislike him (as well as critics who like writing about him because they warm to him as a person). But if this device of impersonalizing and textualizing offers advantages, it also introduces some very troubling issues. One is the issue, as argued, for example, by Philippe Lejeune, of the coincidence, in autobiography and especially in autobiography as practiced by Rousseau, of the author, the narrator, and the protagonist—they are all three, Lejeune and others would say, one and the same in autobiography, and without this coincidence what we are looking at is, generically speaking, not autobiography. There is a curious passage in the *Confessions* when Rousseau, having left Maman and returned to the picaresque road, meets up with a Mme. de Larnage, with whom he has a brief, intense, and entirely satisfactory affair (Rousseau was at the moment twenty-five years old, Mme. de Larnage going on forty-five and the mother of ten children). Merely for a frolic—there seems no other reason for it—Rousseau passes himself off as an English Jacobite, though he knew no English and risked discovery on that ground, named M. Dudding (this is not the only time in the *Confessions* that Rousseau assumed another identity; back in book 4, in quite a similar incident, he decided to be Vaussore de Villeneuve for a time). After Mme. de Larnage has gone on ahead, Rousseau-as-Dudding continues to correspond with her, and at one point we are told, "I spent the mornings taking medicines . . . and writing to Mme de Larnage. For our correspondence went steadily on, and Rousseau kindly undertook to collect his friend Dudding's letters" (Cohen, 244; Pléiade, 1.257–58). This doubling of himself is, of course, partly a joke, but not entirely, for the tendency is pervasive in Rousseau to think and speak of himself under the third person of his name while still using the first-person *I*. Writing to Sophie d'Houdetot, the great love of his life who, he felt, had cooled toward him, Rousseau says, "I do not ask why your friendship has not increased, but why it is extinct. Do not blame it on my breach with your sister-in-law and her worthy friend. You know what happened; and all the time you must have been aware that there cannot be any peace between J.-J. Rousseau and the wicked."[37] Or again, there is the very common self-address by name in the *Confessions:* "Poor Jean-Jacques, at that cruel moment you could hardly expect that one day . . . ," etc. (Cohen, 146; Pléiade, 1.149). And we should remember that in the *Confessions* generally Rousseau intended, as he said, to offer himself as "un autre" to all readers. An issue nearly related to this one of the coincidence of author, narrator, and protagonist as against a tendency to doubling and to division into first, second, and third persons, as I have suggested above, is the issue of the unreliable narrator, a concept we are all familiar with, and must accept, in twentieth-century fiction (and earlier as well), where we acknowledge that the author is not always, not often, not necessarily identified in any way with the narrator (except as creator to creature). But if we adopt this as a principle in reading not just the most recent experiments in life-writing but also earlier, more traditional autobiographical texts—the *Confessions,* for example—the practice becomes immensely more complicated and less clearly workable. It may be granted that Rousseau-as-narrator-of-the-*Confessions* seems often to be viewable as an unreliable narrator. He seems like a figure created perhaps by Dostoyevsky, or by Kafka or Beckett or Ellison, whom we are to understand as fictional and as given to all sorts of narrative explanations and ruses and blind spots that the author would have no part of. It could well be said that the *Confessions* often reads like Henry MacKenzie's *The Man of Feeling,* but then to admire the book would require that there be a great ironical gap between author and narrator,[38] for the "Man of Feeling" could

37. *Correspondance complète de Jean-Jacques Rousseau,* ed. R. A. Leigh, 51 vols. (Geneva and Oxford: Voltaire Institute, 1965–95), 5.63, letter 633; cited and translated in Maurice Cranston, *The Noble Savage,* 130.

38. I am reminded of an incident that occurred a few years ago when I was directing a seminar on autobiography and a member of the seminar, Marcia Jacobson, brought in a book that she had encountered called *Memoirs of an Anti-Semite.* Before reading it she had heard nothing about the book and she knew nothing of its author, thus had no way to determine the book's status as autobiography or fiction. Her response to the book was extremely interesting and altogether natural. If, she said, this is, as the title claims, memoirs or autobiography, then I think both the book and the man are despicable; if, on the other hand, it is an ironic novel, then I think it is brilliant and the author wholly admirable for writing it. This—without changing a word on the title page, in the text, or anywhere else.

not himself have written his story in such a way as to make it (as Rousseau's *Confessions* undoubtedly is) one of the supremely great texts of world literature. Can we posit such an ironical gap for Rousseau? Surely we cannot. How, then, do we take the *Confessions?* It reads best as a novel, but is plainly not a novel. It reads worst as an autobiography, and has arguably been the single greatest book in the history of autobiography in the Western world.

One fact about Rousseau and his writings must be observed, though what principle of reading might follow from this I am not sure. That is that everything we have of Rousseau takes place in texts, and this includes even, or especially, the five (?) children (?), their disposition (?), and everything surrounding them. I have strewn question marks in the preceding sentence to indicate that every detail of the *Enfants-Trouvés* episodes has been contested in one text or another. There is first of all, of course, the text of Voltaire's *Sentiment des citoyens* and Rousseau's republication of it; after the *Confessions* appeared there were texts that disputed that any children were ever born to Thérèse or, if there were children, texts disputing Rousseau's paternity; there were archival texts from *l'hôpital des Enfants-Trouvés* that did or did not prove anything; there were texts that claimed that Rousseau was impotent, therefore could not have been a father if indeed there were children to account for, and texts that argued either that Rousseau made up the entire story to have something serious to confess to or that Thérèse and her mother deceived Rousseau and told him that five children had been born when in fact there were none; there were supplementary texts, like Boswell's journals (the relevant pages, unfortunately, torn out and destroyed), that were used to argue for Thérèse's infidelity and Rousseau's (presumed) nonpaternity; and the children, real or chimerical, turn up irrepressibly in both the *Dialogues* and the *Reveries.* What all of this would seem to tell us is that the children, like everything else in Rousseau, are a textual, not an extratextual, event. And yet, if we adopt the tactic of not speaking of Rousseau (or at least not without quotation marks) and speak instead only of the narrator and the narrative, focusing everything on the text, little or nothing on the man, the tactic, I think, will soon falsify itself, for Rousseau personalizes more than almost any other writer: he *demands* that the reader respond to him as Jean-Jacques Rousseau; and the reader, because of the strange nature of this text and its author, is suddenly caught in the familiar bind of damned-if-you-do, damned-if-you-don't. In many ways, Rousseau is—after Henry Adams, with his ceaseless, remorseless irony—the most treacherous of life-writers. They are both of them, Rousseau and Adams, like ignes fatui playing over the swamp and tempting the reader and critic to follow in pursuit of them until lost in the murk. This is a very serious and very real danger. Yet it is not possible to proceed from antiquity and St. Augustine to modernity and Samuel Beckett without daring the swamp of Rousseau, even more than the morass of Henry Adams. All of this, I am convinced, must be said of the *Confessions;* how much more it is to be said of the *Dialogues.*

As with the *Confessions* so with the *Dialogues,* before the text proper there is a preamble ("On the Subject and Form of This Writing"), before that a prefatory note, and before that a discursive epigraph; and after the text there is a postscript ("History of the Preceding Writing"), which is one of the most fascinating things Rousseau ever wrote, with its intercalated "DEPOSIT HANDED OVER TO PROVIDENCE" and "COPY OF THE CIRCULAR NOTE WHICH IS SPOKEN OF IN THE PRECEDING WRITING." All of this textual turning back on itself and reflexive self-reflexiveness is profoundly characteristic of the entire work in its design, intention, and mode of working, and I think we might most effectively approach the *Dialogues* by first examining some of the swaddling in which Rousseau wraps the exchanges of "Rousseau" and "the Frenchman." The epigraph from Ovid's *Tristia*—"Barbarus hic ego sum, quia non intelligor illis"—has much more than merely peripheral interest both because of its sense and because Rousseau deploys it more than once in his writing career. This same Ovidian line that serves as epigraph to Rousseau's penultimate work also stood as epigraph before his *Discourse on the Sciences and Arts,* the work that, by his own account, divided Rousseau's life in two as it set him off on the unfortunate path to becoming an author. Thus the epigraph represents a kind of autobiographical circumscription of Rousseau's career as an author, binding his beginning with his (almost) end. And the sense of the epigraph is one he held to throughout his career. The translation in Masters/Kelly—"Here I am the barbarian because no one understands me"—is reasonable English, but a more literal, and in the context more pointed, rendering would be, "I am here a barbarian, because I am not understood by them."[39] When I say that this translation, though not very graceful English, is more pointed in context, I mean that in the Pléiade edition of Rousseau's works, where *Rousseau juge de Jean Jaques*

<hr />

39. I have not found any translator who renders the last phrase literally as "because I am not understood by them." This rendering seems to me, however, not only apposite for Rousseau but for Ovid as well. In exile in the *Tristia,* Ovid is not understood by those around him, but that does nothing to lessen his sense of his real superiority over "them"; A. D. Melville (*Sorrows of an Exile: "Tristia"* [Oxford: Clarendon Press, 1992], 109) translates the line of Rousseau's epigraph and the line after it from the *Tristia* to give a clear sense of the Ovidian/Rousseauvian attitude of me-against-them:

> *I'm* the barbarian—no one understands me;
> My Latin speech the stupid Getae mock.

follows immediately upon the end of *Les Confessions,* we have "Barbarus hic ego sum, quia non intelligor illis" on the right-hand page (p. 657), and just across the spine, on the left-hand side (p. 656), we have what I have called the extratextual note concluding the *Confessions:* "J'achevai ainsi ma lecture et tout le monde se tut. Made d'Egmont fut la seule qui me parut émue; elle tressaillit visiblement; mais elle se remmit bien vite, et garda le silence ainsi que toute la compagnie. Tel fut le fruit que je tirai de cette lecture et de ma déclaration." [Thus I concluded my reading, and everyone was silent. Mme. d'Egmont was the only person who seemed moved. She trembled visibly but quickly controlled herself, and remained quiet, as did the rest of the company. Such was the advantage I derived from my reading and my declaration.] At this textual moment that separates the postscript of the *Confessions* from the epigraph of the *Dialogues* Rousseau is in a state of deep frustration "because not understood by them"—"them" being "M. et Made la Comtesse d'Egmont . . . , M. le Prince Pignatelli . . . , Made la Marquise de Mesme et . . . M. le Marquis de Juigne." "Barbarus" and "barbarian" come from the Greek, in which language they refer to, by imitating, the graceless, uncouth, babbling, and incomprehensible language of non-Greeks, i.e., barbarians. This, of course, was a role assumed by Rousseau throughout his career. He was the Citizen of Geneva, out of place in France, a rough, unpolished, natural man not at home in the excessively refined, artificial, effete, corrupt social milieu of Paris, his language not understood yet, like the barbarian's, closer to the natural, imitative origins of language than the French of either the philosophers or the arbiters of Parisian society. That he was "not understood by them" could be taken to be a credit to the barbarian Rousseau—and surely was so taken by him—but it also meant that his deeply moved, deeply moving account of his life was met with the terrible response of silence from "them." And this carries us directly into the prefatory note: "If I dared address a prayer to those ["à ceux"—which has the same grammatical status as "illis" (the dative) in the Latin: "to those" or "by them"] into whose hands this writing will fall, it would be to read all of it before making use of it and even before talking about it with anyone. But very certain beforehand that this favor will not be granted to me, I keep silent and give over everything to providence" (Masters/Kelly, 2; Pléiade, 1.659). The thrust of this brief note goes in two or even three different directions simultaneously. There is first Rousseau's adopting for himself a policy of silence ("je me tais") in the face of what he will call a couple of pages later "this terrifying and terrible silence," but he will be silent only after all the sound and fury of the *Dialogues,* which is, in fact, an exceedingly noisy text with many, many voices in contention;

there is second a turn from failed speech, the reading of the *Confessions,* to an insistence on writing in the *Dialogues* as a way to be understood ("into whose hands *this writing* will fall," "On the Subject and Form of *This Writing,*" "History of the Preceding *Writing*"); and there is third the mixture of hope and the felt need to persuade someone of the truth with despair and resignation before the inevitable failure in being understood, and resort, therefore, to the silent giving "over [of] everything to providence." With his epigraph and prefatory note out of the way, Rousseau is at last ready to begin—not with the text of the *Dialogues* but with his preamble to that text.

The preamble to the *Dialogues* vies with its postscript for the honor of being Rousseau's most characteristic as well as most bizarre piece of writing in the autobiographical mode. The preamble commences with the same situation and at the exact point where the *Confessions* concludes, that is, with Rousseau feeling himself judged and condemned by someone, by everyone, but so surrounded by silence, darkness, and mystery that he can find no explanation for why he has been condemned nor can he even find who his persecutors and judges are. "[A]ll Paris, all France, all Europe" seem in "unanimous agreement" in their judgment and condemnation of Rousseau (or the writer of this preamble), but "without any reasonable or at least apparent foundation," and "a whole generation [seems] agree[d] to suppress wantonly all natural enlightenment, to violate all the laws of justice, all the rules of good sense, without purpose, without profit, without pretext, uniquely to gratify a whim whose goal and cause I could not even glimpse" (Masters/Kelly, 3–4; Pléiade, 1.662). "All . . . all . . . all . . . unanimous . . . all . . . all . . . all . . . without . . . without . . . without . . . uniquely": the absoluteness of Rousseau's problem could hardly be more insistently felt or expressed. "The profound, universal silence—," Rousseau writes, "no less inconceivable than the mystery it veils, a mystery that has been hidden from me for fifteen years with a care that I refrain from characterizing and with a success that appears extraordinary—this terrifying and terrible silence has kept me from grasping the least idea that could clarify these strange attitudes for me" (Masters/Kelly, 4; Pléiade, 1.662). I have said that the *Dialogues* begins at the exact point where the *Confessions* leaves off; this is almost true, but the silence of Mme. d'Egmont and her fellow auditors has now grown into a "profound, universal silence," a "terrifying and terrible silence," and Paris has become France has become Europe has become the entire world bent on suffocating the writer of this preamble with utter, utter silence. What is to be done? It is necessary, before returning to the silence promised in the prefatory note, to make these people speak, make them explain their motives; but as they will not speak, being by conspiratorial bond sworn to maintain universal silence, the writer will be compelled to do so in their names and voices, imagining what their motives, no matter how improbable, might be. Thus Rousseau, though he must manage both sides of it, will at last get the dialogue he feels necessary, and he will finally have, though he must produce it himself, some explanation for the otherwise unaccountable situation that exists.

> Yet in order not to fight a chimera, not to slander a whole generation, it was necessary to assume some reasons on the side approved and followed by everyone. I spared nothing in seeking them, in imagining those likely to seduce the multitude; and if I found none that could have produced that effect, Heaven is my witness that it is not for lack of will or efforts, and that I carefully collected all the ideas my understanding could supply for that purpose. When all my efforts led to nothing that could satisfy me, I made the only choice left to reach an explanation: being unable to argue on the basis of private motives that were unknown and incomprehensible to me, I would reason on the basis of a general hypothesis that could combine them all. (Masters/Kelly, 4; Pléiade, 1.662–63)

The "general hypothesis" from which he begins, then, since he cannot distinguish or imagine individual, "private motives," is that of "un complot universel," a universal plot or conspiracy. We might, for a moment, return to book 12 of the *Confessions,* where Rousseau, much as he will soon do in this preamble to the *Dialogues,* confesses that he cannot produce any order in his account, cannot configure a workable plot, because he is surrounded by nothing but plot, designed to his misfortune by others. The "general hypothesis," then, is an attempt to reassume the plotting function by a writer who feels himself subjected to the plots of others. What the Rousseau of the preamble determines to do is to construct the plot of the *Dialogues* by reconstructing the plot that has ensnared him. So expressed, it seems a paradoxical and somewhat problematical endeavor, but like everything in the *Dialogues*—plot, structure, character, intention, theme— the procedure is a continual turning inside out of elements in the hope of effecting a reversal from subjection to the will of others to full freedom in oneself as it simultaneously turns division, fragmentation, and isolation into unity, wholeness, and self-sufficiency. The task requires, according to the preamble, that the author exhaust "everything that could be said in their [i.e., his adversaries'] favor . . . , attributing to them all plausible motives and specious arguments, and collecting all imaginable charges against myself" (Masters/Kelly, 4; Pléiade, 1.663). And in spite of his best efforts at reproducing all the "specious arguments" of his enemies, "I admit," we are told, that "I often blushed at the reasons I was forced to ascribe to them." There is fairness for you, fairness of an extreme sort, to blush at the folly and weakness of the motives and arguments of your enemy. So much for the "subject of this writing," which is the "general hypothesis" of a universal plot directed against the Rousseau of the preamble and footnotes and against the "J. J." of the *Dialogues* proper. The preamble now turns to "la forme de cet écrit."

"As the dialogue form appeared to me best suited to discuss the pros and cons," according to the preamble, "I chose it for that reason" (Masters/Kelly, 4–5; Pléiade, 1.663). This may seem a bit disingenuous since the writer of the preamble is in control of presenting both pros and cons ("le pour et le contre") and is the "onlie begetter" of "the Frenchman" as well as of "Rousseau" and "J. J.," but it is what follows this claim that is particularly intriguing. "In these conversations I took the liberty of resuming my family name, which the public judged it appropriate to take from me, and following its example, I refer to myself as a third party, using my Christian name to which the public chose to reduce me" (Masters/Kelly, 5; Pléiade, 1.663). This casual observation, which may look fairly simple at first, is finally almost beyond the powers of analysis to resolve. There is first of all the question of what is meant by saying that "the public judged it appropriate to take from me . . . my family name. . . ." When he returned from his disastrous stay in England, Rousseau felt it best, for reasons of safety, to adopt the name "Monsieur Jacques," somewhat as he had earlier passed himself off as "Vaussore de Villeneuve" and "Monsieur Dudding." When it was impressed upon Rousseau that "Monsieur Jacques" would not fool anyone, he increased his cover, but only slightly, by taking the name "Jean-Joseph Renou,"[40] a disguise that he maintained for some 2½ years, from

40. See the extraordinarily interesting and pertinent discussion by James F. Jones, Jr., of Rousseau's adoption of various pseudonyms in *Rousseau's "Dialogues,"* 64–90. Among other things, Jones makes the fascinating suggestion that the very peculiar marriage to Thérèse in August 1768 could have taken place only during the "Renou" years: "In one of the most bizarre moments of his existence, Rousseau 'married' the woman who had been his companion for much of his adult life and who had borne his children. Not only did Rousseau act as groom; he also performed the ceremony himself, pronouncing upon the occasion a fine speech on the joys of matrimony that was filled with that sort of elevated, sentimental rhetoric of which he was the eighteenth-century's unquestioned stylistic master. Yet Rousseau actually did not marry Thérèse; Renou did, and one must wonder whether Rousseau as himself would (or perhaps could) ever have married Thérèse" (p. 81). According to another account of the "marriage" (in Guéhenno, 2.227), Rousseau invited two guests to dinner, M. de Champagneux, the mayor of Bourgoin, and one of his cousins, M. de Rosière, without telling them anything of the marriage plans. "When they arrived the two guests found Jean-Jacques and Thérèse suitably dressed for the wedding. Jean-Jacques himself offi-

June 1767 to January 1770, in part because of the insistence of his protector, the prince de Conti, but also in part because of the dual fascination Rousseau felt for going incognito under an assumed name and for being someone else. When the Rousseau of the preamble says that the public had judged it appropriate to take his family name from him, it may be that he is referring to the "Renou" period, in which case it is, at the very least, a peculiar way to put the matter of his adopting a pseudonym and signing himself scrupulously for 2½ years "Jean-Joseph Renou" (when he was not further deliberately confusing things by signing himself "J. J. R.," which a correspondent of course could read as either Jean-Joseph Renou or Jean-Jacques Rousseau—or both simultaneously). But perhaps this is not what he means either. Perhaps he means, as the next clause seems to suggest, that the public has taken his family name from him by referring to him regularly not as "Rousseau" but as "Jean-Jacques." If this is what is meant, then we must recall that it was not the public that first began to call him "Jean-Jacques"— it was Jean-Jacques himself, throughout the letters, the *Confessions,* and elsewhere. And why, when he is professedly so offended with the public, should he follow its example and "reduce" himself to his Christian name?— which, of course, he does not do anyway, but instead splits himself into his family name and his Christian name, "resuming" the one and "using" the other in referring "to myself as a third party." But the third-party address is as true for the "Rousseau" of the family name as for the "J. J." of the Christian name, so what exactly is the distinction that he is drawing? When, in the "History of the Preceding Writing," Rousseau writes, "They make a J. J. that suits them in vain; Rousseau will remain the same always despite them," we must ask ourselves whether it would have been any different at all had he written, "They make a Rousseau that suits them in vain; J. J. will remain the same always despite them." Moreover, it is not the Rousseau of the preamble but the "Rousseau" of the dialogues who refers to someone named "J. J.," a fictional character evoking another fictional character. The truth is that Rousseau so inveterately presents himself as J. J. or Rousseau or both that there is virtually no way of distinguishing a fictional character from a historical reality in any given passage. In the *Confessions,* we recall, Rousseau proposes himself as "un autre" to everyone else; now in the *Dialogues* he becomes "un autre" to himself. It is something

---

ciated: Thérèse and he pronounced the customary 'yes'. According to M. de Champagneux, Jean-Jacques, in a state of great excitement, delivered a moving speech and everyone dissolved into tears. M. de Champagneux declared that he had never been so affected in all his life." Of course one does not know how much emotional excitement was normally available to the citizens or the mayor of Bourgoin.

of a relief to turn from this single sentence about naming (but we will have to return to the question later) to what Rousseau says in the preamble about the formal properties of the *Dialogues* not as planned but as completed.

Sounding very much like the narrator of book 12 of the *Confessions,* the author of the preamble writes, "What I had to say was so clear and I felt it so deeply that I am amazed by the tediousness, repetitiousness, verbiage, and disorder of this writing" (Masters/Kelly, 5; Pléiade, 1.664); and the reason given for this is even more striking than the fact of disorder itself: "The subject was myself, and I no longer found for my own interest that zeal and vigor of courage which can exalt a generous soul only for another person's cause." Can this be Rousseau? Surely there has never before been any waning of interest when "the subject was myself." However it may have been in the past, we are told of the present writing that, "[u]nable to endure such a sorrowful occupation continuously, I engaged in it for brief moments only, writing each idea as it came to me and then stopping, writing the same thing ten times if it came to me ten times, without ever recalling what I wrote previously . . ." (Masters/Kelly, 5; Pléiade, 1.664). The *Dialogues* thus begins where the *Confessions* ends, in "sorrow and distress," in "disgust and heartbreak," in "formless essays which I am in no condition to correct . . . , drowned in a chaos of disorder and repetitions . . . ," and with listeners and readers "who cannot tolerate a little fatigue or maintain their attention in the interest of justice and truth . . ." (Masters/Kelly, 5–7; Pléiade, 1.664–66). Thus, "cet écrit," as Rousseau calls it both in the preamble and the postscript, "this writing" is not only a supplement to the *Confessions* or a continuation of the previous volume but it has the same recalcitrance to form that Rousseau himself pointed to more than once in the second half of the *Confessions.* The preamble concludes by jumping right over the dialogues to the "History of the Preceding Writing" that follows them, binding the after-the-end to the before-the-beginning, but with the despairing certainty that this writing will fall into the hands of enemies and that "following the natural course of events, all the trouble I have taken is a total waste. I do not know what choice Heaven will suggest to me, but I shall hope until the end that it will not abandon the just cause. Into whatever hands Heaven makes these pages fall, if there may still be a human heart among those who read them, that is enough for me, and I will never despise the human species so much that I will not find in that idea some reason for confidence and hope" (Masters/Kelly, 7; Pléiade, 1.666). We have only to look to the footnote at the bottom of the page, however, to see confidence and hope transformed quickly to despair, an alternation that is altogether characteristic of the movement of the *Dialogues:* "The unhappy history of this work found at the end of these dialogues tells how this prediction [that the work would fall into the hands of enemies] proved true." At this point I think we should continue on the periphery of the *Dialogues,* following Rousseau to his postscript account of his attempt to place his writing into the hands of one—it is important that he insists that all he requires or desires is not a multitude but simply one—who would preserve for posterity this writing and with it the memory of its author.

The "History of the Preceding Writing" recounts the search for the one to whom Rousseau can commit everything in trust. For four wretched years, we are told, the author worked on the dialogues, "and I was close to the end of that sorrowful task without knowing or imagining how to make use of it." Experience, he says, had taught him not to trust any of his acquaintance, so, "In this situation, mistaken in all my choices and finding only perfidy and falseness among men, my soul—exalted by the feeling of its innocence and by that of their iniquity—rose up impulsively to the seat of all order and all truth, to seek there the resources I no longer had here below." As there was no one to whom he could commit the manuscript in this world, he decided to entrust it to the One in a world beyond: "In order to do that, I imagined making a fresh copy of this writing and placing it in a Church on an altar; and to make this gesture as solemn as possible, I chose the high Altar of the Cathedral of Notre Dame" (Masters/Kelly, 246; Pléiade, 1.977–78). As he completed work "on the clean copy of my writing," he reconnoitered Notre Dame to determine which "would be the day [he settled on a Saturday] when I would have the easiest time entering, reaching the Altar, and placing my deposit there." When the clean copy was ready, he wrote out a long inscription headed "DEPOSIT HANDED OVER TO PROVIDENCE," which is a prayer in the familiar voice of "tu" and "toi" to the "Protector of the oppressed, God of justice and truth" from "an unfortunate stranger, alone, without support, without a defender on earth [seul . . . sur la terre], insulted, mocked, defamed, betrayed by a whole generation, burdened for more than fifteen years at whim by treatment worse than death and by indignities unheard of until now among men, without ever having been able at least to learn the cause." The inscription concludes with a "donc," a "therefore," that not only echoes the "donc" of the *Confessions* and prepares for the "donc" of the *Reveries* but also recalls the imagined scene of the Final Judgment in the preamble to the *Confessions,* when Rousseau will "come forward with this work in my hand, to present myself before my Sovereign Judge, and proclaim aloud. . . ." "Si donc mon travail est perdu," the final sentence of the inscription accompanying the

Dialogues begins, in a kind of peroration addressed to the One Protector remaining: "Therefore if my work is lost, if it must be given to my enemies and destroyed or disfigured by them, as seems inevitable, I will not count any less on your work, although I am ignorant of its time and its means; and having tried,[41] as I must, my efforts to cooperate with it, I wait with confidence, I rely on your justice, and I resign myself to your will" (Masters/Kelly, 247; Pléiade, 1.979). With this all prepared, and with a note "on the back of the title page" that is quite similar to the note that comes in the printed text between the epigraph and the preamble, "the Author," as he designates himself in the note, "took my package and went to Notre Dame on Saturday, February 24, 1776 at two o'clock, with the intention of presenting my offering there that same day" (Masters/Kelly, 248; Pléiade, 1.979). In spite of all the preparations, the venture could hardly have turned out worse. Upon arriving at the church, the Author found a side door closed, and when he tried to enter through another side leading into the nave,

> my eyes were struck by a grill I had never noticed and which separated from the nave the part of the side aisles that surrounded the Choir. The doors of this grill were closed, so that the part of the side aisles I have just spoken of was empty and it was impossible for me to enter it. At the moment I perceived that grill, I was overcome by a dizziness like a man with apoplexy, and this dizziness was followed by an upheaval of my whole being such that I cannot recall suffering anything like it. . . .[42] In the course of my thirty-six years in Paris, I had come very often and at various times to Notre Dame. . . . and I hadn't . . . ever noticed a grill or a door, as far as I could recall. All the more struck by this unforeseen obstacle because I hadn't told anyone of my project, I believed in my initial transport that I was seeing Heaven itself collaborate in the iniquitous work of men. . . . (Masters/Kelly, 248; Pléiade, 1.980)

The Rousseau who wrote the preamble to the *Confessions*—"Let the last trump sound when it will"—could never have imagined the situation in which the "Sovereign Judge" would shut and lock a grill, whose existence was unsuspected before, and effectively turn away the sacrificial offering of a life, its narrative and its justification.

---

41. This is how the translation reads, but the volume is riddled with typographical errors and I take it that this is one of them. The original reads "et après avoir fait, comme je l'ai dû, mes efforts pour y concourir"; I assume that "tried" is a mistake where "made" was intended.

42. Rousseau's description of his state at this moment is strikingly like the description he gives of his psychological reaction when he first read of the Dijon contest that led to his writing his *Discourse on the Sciences and the Arts*. See the second of his *Lettres à Malesherbes*, Pléiade, 1.1135.

In a frenzy, then, to place his manuscript in the hands of one who would be worthy of receiving it, Rousseau says he took it to Condillac, "a man of letters with whom I had been acquainted for years," and left it with him for two weeks but to no positive effect, for Condillac was so foolish as to talk "to me about this writing as he would have talked about a literary work," and "he said nothing of the effect my writing had on him, nor of what he thought of the author" (Masters/Kelly, 249–50; Pléiade, 1.981–82). Condillac, who failed to perceive that what he held in his hands was not a book but a man, was no better nor any more to the author's purposes than Mme. d'Egmont and the others who listened, silent and unmoved, as Rousseau read his *Confessions*. "But I didn't lose courage yet," the author says. "I told myself that my lack of success was due to my poor choice, that I had to be really blind and biased to place my trust in a Frenchman. . . ." So, in spite of the fact that Rousseau never expressed any higher regard for the English than for the French—on the contrary—he entrusted as much of his new copy of the book as was done at the time to Brooke Boothby, "a young Englishman who had been my neighbor at Wootton" during the bad stay in England; but no sooner was the manuscript delivered to Boothby than suspicions (unjustified, as events later proved) set in, "and I accused myself of madness for having put my trust in an Englishman, a nation personally aroused against me and which has never been cited for any act of justice going contrary to its own interest." If neither a Frenchman nor an Englishman is to be trusted—and Rousseau, after his bitter wrangling with Grimm and his ongoing controversies with all his own compatriots, never even mentions a German or a Swiss as a possibility—to whom should the author turn? He devises a plan to address himself not to this or that individual but "to the French nation" in "a kind of circular letter" that he would "distribute . . . in parks and on the streets to those strangers whose faces most appealed to me." Here we come to another "donc" moment: "Je fis donc mon petit écrit en forme de billet":

> So I wrote my little writing in the form of a letter, and I had the patience to make a large number of copies. But in distributing it, I encountered an obstacle I had not foreseen in the refusal to receive it of those to whom I presented it. The address was: *To all Frenchmen who still love justice and truth*. I hadn't imagined that with this address anyone would dare refuse it. Almost no one accepted it. After reading the address, all of them declared with an ingenuity[43] that made me laugh in the midst of my sadness that it was not addressed to them. You're right, I told them, taking it back, I see very well that I was

---

43. "Ingenuousness" would surely be a better translation here of "ingenuité."

mistaken. That was the only frank statement I have obtained from any French mouth in fifteen years. (Masters/Kelly, 251–52; Pléiade, 1.984)

All the benefit he derived from this attempt was a little satire at the expense of the French and a not altogether original pun on "frank . . . French" ("franche . . . françoise"), which leaves the author still in search of a satisfactory "donc." But he did learn one thing from "this final ill success," he says: "By teaching me that there was no help for my lot, it taught me not to fight necessity any longer. A passage of *Émile* that I recalled made me return within myself [me fit rentrer en moi-même] and find what I had vainly sought outside." This, then, provides the final "donc" and leads into it just as *it* leads on to the "donc" of *Reveries:* "J'ai donc pris enfin mon parti tout à fait":

> So I've finally made up my mind completely. Detached from everything pertaining to the earth and the senseless judgments of men, I am resigned to being disfigured among them forever, without counting any less on the value of my innocence and suffering. My felicity must be of another order. It is no longer among them that I must seek it, and it is no more in their power to prevent it than to know it. Destined to be the prey of error and lies in this life, I await the hour of my deliverance and the triumph of truth without seeking them any longer among mortals. Detached from all worldly affection and released even from the anxiety of hope here below, I see no hold by which they can still disturb my heart's repose. I will never repress the first impulse of indignation, transport, anger, and I no longer even try to do so. But the calm that follows this passing agitation is a permanent state out of which nothing can pull me anymore. (Masters/Kelly, 253; Pléiade, 1.986–87)

Rousseau's conclusion is that, having sought the one—or the One—and failed to find him, the one can only be himself, and this, on the one hand, returns him to the very beginning of the *Confessions* ("Oui, moi, moi seul: Yes, I, I alone") and, on the other hand, moves forward into the first line of the *Reveries* ("Me voici donc seul sur la terre: Here then am I alone on earth")—the first, however, a condition of full engagement with all of humankind, for whom Rousseau would be "un autre" as a first term of comparison, the second an absolute detachment from everything of this world, from humankind and everything else alike, in favor of a timeless fulfillment in the world beyond. The question that remains is how, through the process of self-division and subdivision that, in Rousseau's hands, the dialogical form entails, we can arrive at this conclusion of wholeness (but isolation) and of oneness (but complete detachment and separation).

We should remark to begin with that there was always with Rousseau a tendency to psychological doubling even when he felt himself most secure in the integrity and continuity of his identity. The episodes when he doubled himself as Vaussore de Villeneuve and Monsieur Dudding have already been mentioned, as has been the more serious doubling as Monsieur Jacques and as Jean-Joseph Renou and the self-dramatizing as "Citoyen de Genève." But even when retaining his own name Rousseau was frequently to speak of himself in the third person, as if he were acting and at the same time standing off observing himself acting, as if he were both subject and object, both first and third person (and sometimes second person as well). "Pauvre Jean-Jacques," the narrator exclaims in one characteristic passage in the *Confessions:* "Poor Jean-Jacques, at that cruel moment you could hardly expect that one day your music would excite murmurs of surprise and applause, when played before the King of France and all his Court, and that in all the boxes around the most charming ladies would say half aloud: 'What delightful sounds! What enchanting music! Every one of those airs goes straight to the heart!' " (Cohen, 146; Pléiade, 1.149). There is certainly some irony in a passage like this (as well as some unironical expression of sentiment), but is irony itself—at least in life-writing—not dependent upon a kind of doubling of the self, a kind of detachment from oneness of being? On the other hand, there is no question of irony in a passage like the following, which is altogether characteristic of the self-naming and moral earnestness of Rousseau's epistolary manner: "No, no, St-Lambert. The breast of Jean-Jacques Rousseau will never hold the heart of a traitor and I would despise myself more than you think if I had ever tried to detach her [i.e., St-Lambert's mistress, Sophie d'Houdetot] from you."[44] Nor is there the slightest hint of irony in a passage from the *Confessions* quoted earlier, the second of the passages about the children and *Enfants-Trouvés:* "No, I feel, and boldly declare—it is impossible. Never for a moment in his life could Jean-Jacques [in the original: J. J.] have been a man without feelings or compassion, an unnatural father." In a gesture very similar to the splitting that occurs in the *Dialogues,* Rousseau as author projects himself as character into the figure of the tutor, Jean-Jacques, responsible in *Émile* for executing the educational ideas that would make his charge, as Rousseau thought, an exemplary citizen of the world. Moreover, in addition to these local instances of doubling, there is a kind of doubling, Rousseau writes in the Neuchâtel preamble to the *Confessions,* a kind of Montaignesque doubling (although Rousseau neglects to name his predecessor) that not only does not militate against singleness of being but on the contrary, he

44. *Correspondance complète,* 4.527; cited and translated in Cranston, *The Noble Savage,* 76.

claims, positively reinforces the integral oneness of his own being and his writing. Having said that what he intends to produce in his *Confessions* is a portrait and not a book, Rousseau continues the portrait-painting analogy, suggesting that the likeness that he seeks in his self-portrait will be more stylistic than referential, to be discovered as much in the manner as in the matter—or rather that the manner and the matter will be so indistinguishably fused that, while still doubling one another, they become at the same time identical.

> I need no other art than to follow exactly the traces I see marked out. I commit myself equally to style and to the things represented. I will not try to make the style uniform but will adopt whatever style occurs to me; I will change styles without a second thought according to my mood of the moment; I will say everything as I feel it and as I see it, without strenuous seeking, without great troubling, without embarrassment about the patchwork result. In giving myself over both to my remembrance of the past impression and to my present feeling, I will depict doubly [je peindrai doublement] the state of my soul, that is both at the moment the event happened to me and at the moment I describe it; my style, which is uneven yet natural—now energetic and now leisurely, now subdued and now extravagant, now grave and now gay—will itself form a part of my story.[45]

Properly seen, it is the nature of all successful narrative autobiography to render such a doubled self-portrait, realized both in the events narrated and in the style of narration. But doubling takes on a new, a much greater and an often darker, significance in the *Dialogues,* where it is on the one hand so profligate and on the other hand so uncertain of control and intent. The *Dialogues* is not, in any case, a narrative text, and so the issue of doubling through style and reference is not so obviously germane. Put another way, memory plays little direct role in the *Dialogues;* events are all too much present and swarming all over Rousseau in that text, so that there is little reflecting back and forth between a present and a past self as there is in, say, Augustine's *Confessions* or Montaigne's *Essais* (with the b and c insertions) or, in a slightly different way, in Rousseau's own *Confessions.* But we must not be defeated by this new and strange book, *Rousseau juge de Jean Jaques,* for as I write these words I am reminded—and we should not forget—that the *Dialogues* is the crux of Rousseau's autobiographical project, and we will not have any adequate understanding of that project and how it impinges on life-writing in the present century unless we come to terms with the way Rousseau dismantled the Augustinian project in his

---

45. From the preamble to the Neuchâtel manuscript ("Ébauches des *Confessions*"), Pléiade, 1.1154; my translation.

own *Confessions* and then proceeded to dismantle the apparent project of those *Confessions* in his *Dialogues*.

The *Dialogues* begins in full flow with "Rousseau" exclaiming in disbelief at what he has just heard from "the Frenchman" about the diabolical evil of the "Author" who is to be known between the two of them as "J. J." "Rousseau," who has read the writings ascribed to "J. J.," refuses to accept that the man described by "the Frenchman" as a monster of hypocrisy, depravity, and misanthropy can be the same as the man who produced the books; hence, a bit later he will posit two different individuals—thus dividing "J. J.," who has already been split off from "Rousseau" (or is it from Rousseau?), in two—but before that he adopts what seems a very peculiar tactic, which, however peculiar, is established with the now familiar, logic-asserting, but not obviously logical "donc." To "the Frenchman," who asks what he means by expressing doubts about the existence of an Author of soul-elevating virtues joined to a man of deep and unremitting viciousness, "Rousseau" responds: "Figurez-vous donc un monde idéal semblable au nôtre, et neanmoins tout différent: Picture an ideal world similar to ours, yet altogether different" (Masters/Kelly, 9; Pléiade, 1.668). Why this should be a response to the question is not immediately obvious and indeed becomes so only gradually over the entire course of the *Dialogues*. It will be noticed that the English version simply forgoes any attempt to translate "donc" (a literal translation would be, "Picture to yourself, then, an ideal world . . ."), and I think I see why, since "thus" or "therefore" or "so" or "then" or any other possible rendering seems awkward and improbable, not to say illogical and unfollowable, in the context of what has gone before. "Donc" leads to something alright, but it does not follow from anything; yet I do not believe that we can strike the word from our consciousness and still remain true to Rousseau in general or to this text in particular, for his use of the word here and elsewhere is much more than a mere mannerism or stylistic tic. Indeed, the "donc" on which the establishment of "un monde idéal" pivots—"Figurez-vous *donc* un monde idéal"—is going to determine the entire course of the *Dialogues* and, the author clearly intends, will be the basis for the successful reintegration into one voice and one vision of all the divided voices and selves that constitute this text; and projecting ahead, "le monde idéal" is that same world that Rousseau spins out in reverie and closes around himself in the text that will follow this one and that will round out his autobiographical trilogy.

So what is Rousseau's "ideal world" like? It is nothing other than the Rousseauvian state of nature, the mythic condition of before-the-fall enjoyed by Natural Man before he became Social Man. In the ideal world,

"Forms are more elegant, colors more vivid, odors sweeter, all objects more interesting. All nature is so beautiful there," we are told, "that its contemplation, inflaming souls with love for such a touching tableau, inspires in them both the desire to contribute to this beautiful system and the fear of troubling its harmony; and from this comes an exquisite sensitivity which gives those endowed with it immediate enjoyment [des jouissances immédiates] unknown to hearts that the same contemplations have not aroused" (Masters/Kelly, 9; Pléiade, 1.668). According to Rousseau—and it doesn't seem to me much to matter here whether we surround the name with quotation marks or not, for Rousseau is surely speaking through "Rousseau" in his characterization of the ideal world—"All the first movements of nature are good and right," and in that ideal world, in contrast to our real world, "[t]he inhabitants . . . have the good fortune to be maintained by nature, to which they are more attached, in that happy perspective in which nature placed us all, and because of this alone their soul forever maintains its original character" (Masters/Kelly, 9; Pléiade, 1.668–69). The inhabitants of that world, like all of us in the beginning, are motivated by a single principle, "amour de soi" or love of self, but they, fortunate souls, never encounter obstacles that deflect them from attaining the object of their desire, which, were it to happen, as it does happen to all of us in the real world, would turn them from their proper object to the obstacles in their way. In describing what would happen then, "Rousseau"/Rousseau drops all pretense to be talking about inhabitants of an ideal world so that he can make the point that he feels needs making about the world we live in:

> But when they are deflected from their object by obstacles, they are focused on removing the obstacle rather than reaching the object; then they change nature and become irascible and hateful. And that is how the love of self [amour de soi], which is a good and absolute feeling, becomes amour-propre, which is to say a relative feeling by which one makes comparisons; the latter feeling demands preferences, whose enjoyment is purely negative, and it no longer seeks satisfaction in our own benefit but solely in the harm of another. (Masters/Kelly, 9; Pléiade, 1.669)

Now the speaker is referring not to any ideal world but to what he terms "human society: la société humaine," and it is not "les habitans du monde idéal" who are in question but, if we think of the speaker as "Rousseau," it is "J. J." he has in mind, and, if we think of the speaker as Rousseau, it is himself who must maintain a difficult allegiance to "amour de soi" in a social context that encourages and values only "amour-propre."

The man who retains something of his natural character even into adult

life and human society will find himself encountering obstacles to fulfillment of his desires at every turn, and "the only recourse of the wise man"
then "is to withdraw from the crowd as much as possible and remain patiently wherever he chances to be . . . ; and while he sometimes seeks to
parry his enemies' thrusts, he does so without trying to retaliate, without
arousing his passion against them, without leaving either his place or the
calm he wishes to maintain" (Masters/Kelly, 10; Pléiade, 1.669–70). This
is clearly "Rousseau's" preparation for defense of "J. J.'s" isolation of himself and his refusal to see the pests of society who swarmed around him for
self-seeking reasons of their own; it is equally clearly Rousseau's response
in his own behalf to charges that he felt had been made against him of
misanthropy and hatred of everyone and everything in the human world.
Switching back at this point to "the inhabitants of the ideal world," "Rousseau" says that to them "the express will to harm, venomous hatred, envy,
baseness, betrayal, deceit are unknown," and "[t]hus bounded on all sides
by nature and reason, they stop and spend life enjoying it, doing each day
whatever seems good for themselves and beneficial for others, without regard to the estimation of men and the caprices of opinion" (Masters/Kelly,
11–12; Pléiade, 1.671–72). It is all very well, "the Frenchman" suggests
in his response, to outline this ideal world and to describe its inhabitants,
but what has any of this to do with a "J. J." (or a Rousseau, we might
add) living in our real world? "Rousseau" answers that he will get to this
in a moment but first it is important to recognize that if there should ever
be a meeting of ideal beings and the real world of society there would be,
at the very least, a serious problem in communication, for "[b]eings who
are so uniquely constituted must necessarily express themselves in other
ways than ordinary men." We have heard this, of course, before, not, however, from the "Rousseau" of the *Dialogues* but from the Rousseau of the
preamble to the Neuchâtel manuscript of the *Confessions:* "For what I have
to say, it will be necessary to invent a new language."[46] The language in

46. There is in Huntington Williams's *Rousseau and Romantic Autobiography* (Oxford:
Oxford University Press, 1983), 113–19, a pertinent discussion of the similarity between
the new language that Rousseau felt he had to invent to write himself in the *Confessions*
and the remarks that he made in his *Essay on the Origin of Languages* about a cuneiform script
of incredible antiquity that he had read about. The relevant passage in Rousseau's *Essay*
reads as follows: "This unknown language, of an almost mind-boggling antiquity, must
nevertheless have been well formed to judge by the artistic perfection discernible in the
beauty of the cuneiform characters and the wonderful monuments where the inscriptions
are found. I don't know why these astonishing ruins are so seldom mentioned: when I read
their description in Chardin I feel myself transported to another world [un autre monde].
It seems to me that there is matter here for the most tremendous sort of thought" (*Essai*

question, we must suppose, is an old language to humankind in the natural state and to "habitans du monde idéal"; it is new here only because it is to be spoken to those in human society but about one—"J. J." or Rousseau, however we may prefer to designate him—who comes still trailing clouds of glory about him from "le monde idéal," which is his home. When such "uniquely constituted" beings express themselves in their uniquely constituted language they never do so for trivial, social reasons, nor do they make a profession of it and keep at it endlessly: "The inhabitants of the enchanted world write few books in general, and do not arrange to write them; it is never a profession for them. When they do write, they have to be forced to do so by a stimulus stronger than interest and even glory. . . . When someone has said what he has to say, he will remain tranquil as before, without leaping into the literary fray, without feeling that ridiculous urge to repeat himself over and over, and scribble endlessly on paper, an urge which is said to be part of the profession of Author" (Masters/Kelly, 12; Pléiade, 1.672–73). It might come as a surprise to some readers of the *Confessions* and even of the *Dialogues* to realize that this is intended to bring us not only to an understanding of "J. J.'s" writings—sparse, brief, and compelled always by altruistic and utterly impersonal motives ("a felicitous discovery to publicize, a beautiful and great truth to share, a general and pernicious error to combat, or some matter of public utility to establish")— but of Rousseau's as well, but surely this is the import of the little exchange that follows:

> THE FRENCHMAN: My dear M. Rousseau. You certainly look to me like one of the inhabitants of that world.
>
> ROUSSEAU: I recognize one at least, without any doubts, in the Author of *Émile* and *Héloïse*.

One is inclined to pause here to try to sort out whether by "the Author" we are to understand the fictional "J. J." or the real (but now implicated in a fiction) Jean-Jacques Rousseau, but the uncertainty hardly matters in a text that at this point seems intent precisely on destabilizing any certainty of reference or identity the reader may be grasping for. In any case, this leads "Rousseau" to his momentary conclusion (or "hypothèse provisoire," as the Pléiade editors call it), a heuristic strategy that will allow him (and

---

sur l'origine des langues, ed. Charles Porset [Bordeaux: Ducros, 1970], 59–61); my translation. The "autre monde" of this passage, so unbelievably ancient yet so astonishingly new to us, is surely none other than the "monde idéal" of the *Dialogues,* and the figural language of those old/new people would correspond both to the language Rousseau must invent for his *Confessions* and the language of the "habitans du monde idéal"—and of "J. J." as well.

his Author, Rousseau) to arrive at unity after and through division. "But you combine things that I separate," "Rousseau" says. "The Author of the Books and of the crimes appears to you to be the same person. I believe I am correct to see them as two. That, Sir, is the key to the enigma" (Masters/Kelly, 13; Pléiade, 1.674). This separation, effected by "Rousseau," of the Author of the Books and of the crimes replicates and compounds the strategy of division from the preamble, "On the Subject and Form of This Writing," where the Author resumes his family name while simultaneously using his Christian name, and it anticipates a further separation on the following page, where "Rousseau" says of "J. J.," "You must admit that this man's destiny has some striking peculiarities. His life is divided into two parts that seem to belong to two different individuals, with the period that separates them—meaning the time when he published books—marking the death of one and the birth of the other." On one side of the divide, according to "Rousseau," was "a peaceful, gentle man," who "was liked by all who knew him," and whose "friends remained faithful to him"; on the other side is "a hard, fierce, gloomy man," who "earns the loathing of everyone he flees, and in his awful misanthropy takes pleasure only in displaying his hatred of the human race." The logic behind the "donc" of "Figurez-vous donc un monde idéal" begins to glimmer fitfully through the text now (at the expense, however, of a complete confusion between the "real" and the "ideal") as we come to see that the figure on the far side of the divide is the "real" "J. J." of the "monde idéal," while the figure on the near side is the image of a distorted, deformed "J. J."—distorted and deformed by his enemies—an unreal "J. J." (but *not* an ideal one) living in "un monde" that is altogether too "réel" while being also thoroughly "irréel" or, we might perhaps better say, living in a world that is real, unreal, and surreal all at the same time.

What gradually becomes apparent as we struggle to maintain our balance amid the dizzying divisions and subdivisions at the outset of the *Dialogues* is that all the divisions define an emergent pattern of bipolar symmetry, a kind of mitosis in which units divide themselves into two and those two into four, etc., until, at a certain point, the process reverses itself and a new movement to convergence sets in, which, however, forms its own symmetry, a symmetry that is both internal and external: internal as the eight becomes four becomes two becomes one; external as the move to convergence is the inverse image and contrary movement—an equal and opposite other—to the original series of symmetrical divisions. And not only does a clear process of convergence establish itself midway through the first dialogue, but even before that, in the very symmetry of the divisions, a

clear sense of unity is being asserted, for symmetry in itself carries the implication of two halves of a whole. Convergence, then, is a kind of natural
outgrowth of and twin to the division that dominates early on yet implies
its opposite even at the beginning of the *Dialogues*.

In theory if not always in practice, dialogue itself is grounded in a symmetrical exchange so that from its title onwards the *Dialogues* is a text of
divided/joined partners or halves, and Rousseau regularly emphasizes this
both in the way he represents the dialoguists and in the way they represent
themselves. At the outset, "Rousseau" knows "J. J.'s" writings but not his
reputation, while "the Frenchman" knows "J. J.'s" reputation but not his
writings; "Rousseau" refuses to meet "J. J.," who is universally "known"
to be monstrous, and "the Frenchman" refuses to read "J. J.," whose writings are universally "known" to be monstrous. But about halfway through
the first dialogue (which thus falls into two more or less equal halves),
"Rousseau" becomes convinced that he was wrong to separate, as he put
it, what "the Frenchman" combined: "The Author of the Books and of
the crimes appears to you to be the same person," he had said earlier. "I
believe I am correct to see them as two." He now reverses this, however,
when he comes to understand, from revelations of "the Frenchman" himself about the activities of "nos messieurs," that what the Rousseau of the
preamble called a "general hypothesis" of a universal conspiracy is not that
so much as it is an assured fact; and this changes the rules of the game
altogether. When "the Frenchman" asks "Rousseau," who is now prepared
to see the man "J. J." so that he can judge for himself whether he is a
monster or not, if he is going to be persuaded by his own eyes or if he would
not do better to agree with universal opinion, he poses for "Rousseau" a
pair of apparently symmetrical choices ("That your eyes deceive you or
that the whole human race, except for yourself alone, is devoid of sense?
Which of these two assumptions seems more natural to you, and on which
of them will you finally decide?") that the latter does not see as such. "There
is another, more natural explanation" than his own or the world's blindness,
"Rousseau" says, and one "that eliminates many difficulties. It is to assume
a conspiracy the object of which is the defamation of J. J. whom the conspiracy has carefully isolated for that purpose." Here one can clearly discern
the "Rousseau" of the *Dialogues* joining hands with the Rousseau of "On
the Subject and Form of This Writing," one of the early instances in which
convergence comes to replace separation. "But why do I say assume?"
"Rousseau" continues. "Whatever the motive that prompted the formation
of this conspiracy, it exists. By your own report, it would seem universal.
. . . Everything around him [J. J.] is snares, lies, betrayals, darkness. He is

absolutely alone and has only himself as a resource; he must expect neither aid nor assistance from anyone on earth. Such a singular position is unique in the existence of the human race" (Masters/Kelly, 81; Pléiade, 1.764–65). What "the Frenchman" had called earlier "le plan de nos messieurs" (who, he says, in a statement endowed with a good deal of the author's irony, are "all men of the most sublime virtue and great philosophers who are never wrong" [Masters/Kelly, 30; Pléiade, 1.696–97]} and had praised as "great, generous, admirable" (Masters/Kelly, 44; Pléiade, 1.716) "Rousseau" now declares to be "a hundred times worse than the Inquisition. For although the prisoner is forced to accuse himself, at least there is not a refusal to hear him, he is not prevented from talking, the fact that he is accused is not hidden from him, and he is not judged until after he has been heard. The Inquisition is willing to have the accused defend himself if he is able, but here they do not want him to be able to do so" (Masters/Kelly, 84; Pléiade, 1.767–68). The upshot of "Rousseau's" perception of a universal conspiracy and of his considerable powers of persuasion—and the Author makes "the Frenchman" at least capable of being persuaded: he must be for the eventual strategy and purposes of the *Dialogues*—is that at the end of the first dialogue "Rousseau" agrees to go and see "J. J." while "the Frenchman" agrees to go and read "J. J." Thus we have the exact symmetry of their first exchange in the second dialogue—

> THE FRENCHMAN: Well, Sir, did you see him?
>
> ROUSSEAU: Well, Sir, did you read him?[47]—

and we have the symmetry of the second and third dialogues in which we are offered (second dialogue) an account of "Rousseau's" seeing "J. J." and (third dialogue) an account of "the Frenchman's" reading "J. J." From here on it is all convergence both inside the *Dialogues* and outside, convergence, that is, among the characters of the *Dialogues* on the one hand and between the characters as a converged group and their author on the other hand: in the end they are all one.

It must be admitted that a certain dissymmetry sets in with the advent of the second dialogue, a dissymmetry that involves both the length of the individual dialogues and the amount of space given to the dialoguists. The

---

47. Masters/Kelly, 87; Pléiade, 1.773. Except for a single letter the two lines are exactly the same in the original: "Hébien, Monsieur, vous l'avez vu?" "Hébien, Monsieur, vous l'avez lu?" That the two of them speak exactly the same language and exactly the same words, with the sole variation of an "l" replacing a "v," is a linguistic preview of their eventual, nearly complete merger in attitude, will, and intention. James F. Jones, Jr., makes some very pertinent observations about this exchange in his *Rousseau's "Dialogues,"* 120.

second dialogue is much the longest of the three, the third dialogue much the shortest (well under half the length of the second). This disproportion might be accounted for in a number of ways, but I think when we observe that there is an even greater disproportion in the allotment of space to the dialoguists, especially in the long central dialogue, we can begin to grasp the reason for the apparent dissymmetry of parts. In the second dialogue, "Rousseau" occupies about one hundred thirty of the one hundred forty-two pages, leaving only about twelve for "the Frenchman," who, anyhow, doesn't require much more than this to say, as he does at one typical moment, "No, go on"—which "Rousseau" then does for seventeen more uninterrupted pages. One might imagine that this disproportion might be compensated for by giving "the Frenchman" many more pages in the third dialogue—that, after all, is the dialogue in which he reports on his reading of "J. J." as, in the second dialogue, "Rousseau" reported on his seeing of "J. J." But this is only partly the case, for of the sixty pages of the third dialogue, about thirty-two are allotted to "the Frenchman," about twenty to "Rousseau," and the remaining pages are taken up with quotations from "J. J.'s" writings. It is true that once "Rousseau" begins speaking it is awfully difficult to get him to stop, and it may be that the Author intends to characterize "Rousseau" by making him something of a windbag, but I do not believe that this is the entire explanation (indeed, I am skeptical about it as even a partial explanation). The primary reason that the second dialogue is so long and that "Rousseau" preempts so much of it is that it has to do, precisely, with *seeing* "J. J." and thus making him present and real to the reader, often enough in his own voice as his speech is reported, for pages at a time, by "Rousseau." We should recall that with the *Confessions* Rousseau intended a "portrait," not a "book": although a text and a volume, it was a presence to be seen and to be felt in the heart, not something to be read and to be grasped by the mind. In a crucial passage of the *Confessions* (one dealt with brilliantly and at some length by Jean Starobinski),[48] Rousseau declares:

> I never promised to present the public with a great personage. I promised to depict myself as I am; and to know me in my latter years it is necessary to have known me well in my youth. As objects generally make less impression on me than does the memory of them, and as all my ideas take pictorial form,

48. Jean Starobinski, *Jean-Jacques Rousseau: Transparency and Obstruction,* trans. Arthur Goldhammer (Chicago: University of Chicago Press, 1988); originally published as *Jean-Jacques Rousseau: la transparence et l'obstacle* (Paris: Gallimard, 1971). See esp. chap. 7, "The Problems of Autobiography."

the first features to engrave themselves on my mind have remained there, and such as have subsequently imprinted themselves have combined with these rather than obliterated them. . . . I endeavour in all cases to explain the prime causes, in order to convey the interrelation of results. I should like in some way to make my soul transparent to the reader's eye. . . . (Cohen, 169; Pléiade, 1.174–75)

This same desire, "to make [his] soul transparent to the reader's eye," lies behind the strange and paradoxical, if not outright contradictory and impossible, burden (commented on earlier) laid on the reader at the end of the *Confessions*—or after the end—to know Rousseau by *seeing* him without necessarily having read him: "For my part, I publicly and fearlessly declare that anyone, even if he has not read my writings, who will examine my nature, my character, my morals, my likings, my pleasures, and my habits *with his own eyes* [par ses propres yeux] and can still believe me a dishonourable man, is a man who deserves to be stifled" (Cohen, 606; Pléiade, 1.656). Between the first and second dialogues, "Rousseau" has *seen* "J. J.," and this is why, imitating Rousseau himself in the *Confessions,* he goes on at such length, trying to do the impossible, attempting to translate into words that which he has seen and felt but for which there are no words. Midway through a speech of some fourteen pages that is an extended and exalted paean to the purity and sensitivity and sublimity of "J. J.'s" soul, "Rousseau" says that "J. J." is one of those—like himself and like the Author of both—to whom "it seems . . . that what they feel should become apparent and penetrate from one heart to another without the cold intermediary of words" (Masters/Kelly, 157; Pléiade, 1.862). It is peculiar, then, but not uncharacteristic that he, like the Author of this very text as well as the Author of the *Confessions,* should so multiply words in what both "Rousseau" and Rousseau would seem to regard as a futile task. When, after six pages of the most hyperbolic praise of "J. J.'s" tenderness of soul, "Rousseau" says of "J. J.," "In short [en un mot], a loving and tender nature," and when some 6½ pages later (same speech) he repeats the formula of "In short: En un mot," any reader must be forgiven for thinking that this is no more than a rhetorical device or a stylistic tic and for feeling real doubt about "Rousseau's" ability to make anything short. It is not at all insignificant that this passage should occur at the heart of the second dialogue, in the middle of a long and impassioned speech, just when "Rousseau" has come to speak of the writing of "J. J.'s" *Confessions,* "that work unique to mankind [unique parmi les hommes], the reading of which he profaned by offering it to the listeners least suited to hear it . . ." (Masters/Kelly,

154; Pléiade, 1.859); for what he goes on to say of "J. J.," who has withdrawn "into his own heart," is that "[h]is heart [is] transparent as crystal"—
exactly as the Rousseau of the *Confessions* desired might be the condition
of *his* heart.

What happens essentially in the second dialogue is that "Rousseau"
discards his previous "hypothèse provisoire" that would make the Author
of the books and the man known as "J. J." two different people, and he
also comes to believe, after seeing "J. J." and realizing that an impenetrable
conspiracy surrounds him, that there is no division in "J. J.'s" life between
a "before" and an "after"; instead, "J. J.," he says, has always been uniquely
and consistently himself, but there is now a conspiracy where earlier there
had been none. So "Rousseau," who had divided "J. J." twice in the first
dialogue, now claims that the Author of the books he has read and the
man he has seen are one and the same, that "J. J." before and "J. J." after
are one and the same, and that where he ("Rousseau") had posited, or had
been caused to posit, four separate individuals before, he now conceives
of one alone, and with that one he makes such common cause that throughout the second dialogue there is hardly any distinction at all between
"Rousseau" and "J. J."

"So tell me at last," "the Frenchman" demands of "Rousseau" near
the beginning of the second dialogue, "what must be thought of this strange
character [cette étrange personnage]" (Masters/Kelly, 87; Pléiade, 1.773).
"Rousseau" responds by summing up "J. J.'s" moral character—"As for
crime, I am as persuaded as I am of my own existence that it never came
near his heart, nor did hate"—but says that the "rest cannot be stated so
briefly" because "this man is like none other I know. He requires a separate
analysis, made uniquely for him." After giving "the Frenchman" a picture
of "J. J.'s" natural friendliness, his genuineness and warm hospitality,
"Rousseau" offers an explanation (provided by "J. J." himself) for why he
removed himself from society, an explanation that is intended to show that
leading a solitary life is not the same as being a misanthrope. "I asked him
the reason for this behavior," "Rousseau" says. "He told me that having
seen the entire current generation join together in the dark work of which
he was the object, he had at first put all his efforts into seeking someone
who did not share the public iniquity." Unfortunately, "J. J.'s" arduous
search revealed that there was no one—not one—who "did not share the
public iniquity" and so, at last, "tired of these mocking and deceitful displays, and indignant at being thus the plaything of his supposed friends, he
stopped seeing them, withdrew without hiding his disdain from them, and
after seeking a man without success for a long time, he extinguished his

lantern and shut himself up completely within himself [au dedans de lui]" (Masters/Kelly, 101–102; Pléiade, 1.792). Now, already in the first dialogue we have been told by "Rousseau" of a curiously similar experience of his own, of his search for some one man with whom his heart could communicate frankly and openly, of his disappointment in not finding such a man, and of his consequent withdrawal from human contact: "no longer finding among men either rectitude or truth or any of the feelings I thought were innate in their souls because they were in mine, and without which all society is only deceit and lies, I withdrew into myself [au dedans de moi]" (Masters/Kelly, 52; Pléiade, 1.727). Little wonder that "Rousseau" could understand "J. J.'s" Diogenes-like gesture in extinguishing his lantern and withdrawing within himself, since "Rousseau" had himself done the same; but there was this single difference in his experience as recounted by "Rousseau," that he believed he had found such a man as he sought—"one more appropriate for my heart, more consoling in adversity, more encouraging to virtue"—he had found him, "Rousseau" believed, not, indeed, in person, but in the writings of "J. J." What he sought, "Rousseau" says, he "found . . . in the books of J. J. . . . His example was useful above all in nurturing my confidence in the feelings that I alone among my contemporaries had preserved. . . . Only J. J. seemed to seek the truth with rectitude and simplicity of heart." In a word, as "Rousseau" himself might say, or in short, "alone among all the authors I have read, he was for me the portrayer of nature and the historian of the human heart. I recognized in his writings the man I found in myself . . ." (Masters/Kelly, 52, 53; Pléiade, 1.727, 728). Surely it could be said of "Rousseau" and "J. J."—and of Rousseau encompassing them both—that they withdrew alike, alone, and yet together, "au dedans de moi   au dedans de lui . . . au dedans d'eux." One feels one's mind becoming just slightly unhinged in contemplating a sentence like "I recognized in his writings the man I found in myself," with its suggestion of—what is it to be called? incestuousness? narcissism? It's a strange package they make—"J. J.," "Rousseau," "J. J./Rousseau," Rousseau, and Rousseau/"J. J./Rousseau"—all wrapped up indistinguishably, indiscriminately together and withdrawn into themselves/himself—yet not so strange either, at least not in this book with its bizarre premise and procedure. When, back in the second dialogue again, we are told by "Rousseau" that upon one of his visits to "J. J." he found him engaged in writing the Dialogues that we are reading, it cannot be surprising, but it does nothing to still the disturbance in the reader's mind. In spite of his vow to withdraw completely from the world of men, "Rousseau" says of "J. J.," "he made one more effort, and attending once again to his destiny and to his persecutors despite himself, he wrote a kind of judgment of them and of himself in the form of a Dialogue, rather like the one that may result from our conversations" (Masters/Kelly, 136; Pléiade, 1.836). Gertrude Stein or Beckett or Nabokov or Philip Roth might do this sort of thing in our time and Sterne might do it back in Rousseau's time, the lot of them playing games with the reader's mind, but we hardly anticipate it from the super-earnest author of the *Confessions* who, after all, in the preamble to this very book told us to concentrate and be serious and not be looking for fun and games, especially not games of a literary sort.

What "Rousseau" says he hopes to do in the second dialogue, however, no matter how different the form of the *Dialogues* may be from that of the *Confessions,* is exactly what Rousseau declared his intention to be in that earlier volume. He wants, "Rousseau" says, to find "some way to make you feel all at once, through a simple and immediate impression," what "J. J." is: "I would like to try to sketch for you here the portrait of my J. J. as its idea has become imprinted in my mind after a long examination of the original," "Rousseau" continues, and he goes on to insist on the unity of his portrait, which should be an earnest of its accuracy: "First, you can compare this portrait to the one they ['your gentlemen'] have drawn, judge which of the two is better unified in its parts, and seems to better form a single whole, which more naturally and more clearly explains the conduct of the person represented, his tastes, his habits, and everything that is known about him not only since he has written books, but from his childhood and at all times." "Rousseau" follows this by what is in effect a monologue of over one hundred pages, broken into only very infrequently and inconsequentially by "the Frenchman," in which he gives us a portrait of "J. J." as a natural inhabitant of "the ideal world," who is motivated by a good "amour de soi," but unfortunately born into a world of social beings all under the evil sway of "amour-propre" from whom he can only flee to withdraw into solitude and into the kind of reverie for which he was born. In the middle of this monologue, speech is granted to "J. J." himself as "Rousseau" gives an apparently verbatim account, stretching over five pages (Masters/Kelly, 137–41; Pléiade, 1.837–42), of what "J. J." had said of himself to "Rousseau" when the latter made his visit; it is less than surprising that what "J. J." says conforms exactly, in largest outline and in detail, to what "Rousseau" has said of him. In other words, "Rousseau" gives us a portrait of "J. J." and "J. J." one of himself that is not unlike that which Rousseau gives of himself in the *Confessions* and not unlike that which he gives of himself again in the *Reveries*. At one point "Rousseau" says of the "frame of mind" with which an entire generation has regarded "J. J." that "[o]ne could see Socrates, Aristides, one could see an Angel, one could see God himself with eyes thus fascinated and still believe one were seeing an infernal monster," and though he does not give the final term in this progression from Socrates to God it can hardly be doubted that it is "J. J." This makes for a remarkable group gathered together to provide analogues to "J. J.'s" character and his situation, but by this time convergence among characters, books, narrators, and authors, from the ancient world and from Rousseau's own writing, has become the order of the day; it will not be complete, however, until "the Frenchman" has been given the opportunity to report on his reading of "J. J." in the third dialogue in this trilogy of dialogues and to become thereby a member of the counterconspiracy constructed by Rousseau, comprising Socrates, Aristides, an Angel, God himself, "Rousseau," "the Frenchman," "J. J.," and Rousseau, in response to the universal "complot" surrounding him.

As "the Frenchman" is nothing like as long-winded as "Rousseau," the third dialogue moves rather quickly, after something of a false start, to a grand symphonic union of voices at the end. It may be that Rousseau felt that at the beginning of this final dialogue he had to maintain some kind of tension or uncertainty of outcome, but whatever the explanation, he has "the Frenchman" claiming, in what seems a deliberate attempt to provoke "Rousseau," that in "J. J.'s" writings he has "found, enumerated, collected the irremediable crimes that couldn't have failed to make their Author the most odious of monsters and the horror of the human race" (Masters/Kelly, 199; Pléiade, 1.916). If provocation is what he intended, "the Frenchman" succeeds, for "Rousseau" responds in shock and horror ("Sir! . . . What are you saying? Is it really you talking . . . ?"), but in the end all the former produces by way of "irremediable crimes" is a collection of extracts from "J. J.'s" writings directed against various ill-assorted groups of people who were favorite objects of Rousseau's censure and satire: "Men of Letters," "The Doctors," "The Kings, the Nobles, the Rich," "Women," and "The English." We are to understand these extracts, of course, as entirely sensible and quite unrelated to crimes of any sort, and once this preliminary exercise is out of the way we find "the Frenchman," in his attempt to say what he really found in "J. J.'s" writings, adopting almost exactly the same language "Rousseau" had used to describe what he saw in "J. J.'s" heart and soul in the second dialogue; and at the same time that "the Frenchman" and "Rousseau" seem to merge with one another in language and judgment, "Rousseau" begins to anticipate, sometimes word for word, what Rousseau—the author, now, not the character—will say in the appended "History of the Preceding Writing." A tight little homogeneous circle begins to form itself in the third dialogue, with the speakers sounding not so much like disputants as like a priest and congregation in prayer and response, so that the dialogistic back-and-forth movement of the *Dialogues* overall is replaced by a circular structure that clearly looks forward to the same organizational principle in the *Reveries*.

What "the Frenchman" found in "J. J.'s" writings, he says, "were things that were profoundly thought out, forming a coherent system," all of a piece, consistent throughout and indivisible: "I found . . . a doctrine that was as healthy as it was simple, which without epicureanism and cant was directed only to the happiness of the human race" (Masters/Kelly, 209; Pléiade, 1.930). The final obstacle "the Frenchman" had to overcome to be in perfect accord with his fellow characters "Rousseau" and "J. J." as well as with the creator of them all was, as he says, the heuristic but ultimately unacceptable notion that "Rousseau" himself had introduced, viz., that the Author of the books and the man were two different people. The writings themselves disposed of that last hesitation for "the Frenchman," who says truthfully, "I fully adopt the ideas you've given me about him," and could say with equal truth, "I adopt not only the ideas you've given me but your very language as well," for by a point midway through the third dialogue "the Frenchman" has so fully mastered "Rousseau's" language, his point of view, and his voice that one might imagine that "Rousseau's" speeches from the second dialogue had been transferred to the third and simply reheaded "the Frenchman." "I found the writings of J. J. full of affections of the soul which penetrated mine," "the Frenchman" tells "Rousseau"; "I found in them ways of feeling and seeing that distinguish him easily from all the writers of his time and most of those who preceded him. He is, as you said, an inhabitant of another sphere where nothing is like it is here. His system may be false, but in developing it, he portrayed himself truthfully in a manner so characteristic and so sure that it's impossible for me to mistake it" (Masters/Kelly, 212; Pléiade, 1.933–34). This other sphere occupied uniquely by "J. J." and depicted by him in his writings is, of course, the "monde idéal" described by "Rousseau" in the first dialogue, and what, "the Frenchman" asks, could have been the source of "J. J.'s" knowledge of that ideal world of nature and the natural man but experience of himself?

> Where could the painter and apologist of nature, so disfigured and calumnied now, have found his model if not in his own heart? He described it as he himself felt. . . . In short [en un mot], a man had to portray himself to show us primitive man like this, and if the Author hadn't been as unique as his books, he would never have written them. . . . If you hadn't portrayed your

J. J. to me, I would have believed that the natural man no longer existed, but the striking relationship between the person you depicted and the Author whose books I read would not leave me in any doubt that they are one and the same person even if I had no other reason to believe it. (Masters/Kelly, 214; Pléiade, 1.936)

The original of the final clause here—"mais le rapport frappant de celui que vous m'avez peint avec l'Auteur dont j'ai lu les livres ne me laisseroit pas douter que l'un ne fut l'autre, quand je n'aurois nulle autre raison de le croire"—will recall to the reader that the one and the other, "l'un . . . l'autre," were separated in the first dialogue, separated provisionally but so thoroughly that Rousseau became an "other" to himself or selves. Now, however, they are all "one and the same." "Yes," "the Frenchman" says, "I feel and assert just as you do: the moment he is the Author of the writings that bear his name, he can only have the heart of a good man. . . . In everything I read by [J. J.], I felt the sincerity, the rectitude of a soul that was lofty and proud but frank and without bile, which shows itself without precaution, without fear, which censures openly, praises without reticence, and has no feeling to hide" (Masters/Kelly, 218; Pléiade, 1.941). "The Frenchman" is at one with "Rousseau" not only as regards "J. J.'s" character but also as regards the heinous plot against him; and here "the Frenchman" can give information to "Rousseau" since, merely by the fact of his being French, he has been privy to the workings of the plot. "It is impossible for you," "the Frenchman" tells his non-French interlocutor, "to have a just idea of the position of your J. J. or of the manner in which he is enmeshed. Everything is so well organized concerning him that an Angel could descend from Heaven to defend him without being able to do so" (Masters/ Kelly, 220; Pléiade, 1.944). Though "Rousseau" may not be able to imagine in detail the plot directed against "J. J.," surely the Angel cited by "the Frenchman" is the same being as we met in the series outlined by "Rousseau": Socrates–Aristides–an Angel–God himself–"J. J." "Alone against a whole conspiring generation, from whom," "the Frenchman" asks rhetorically, "would he demand the truth without getting a lie for an answer instead?" Alone though he has been—"Seul contre toute une génération": this is the "seul" that will also begin the *Reveries*—and unable to find "a single human heart that opened up to his," "J. J." now has opened to him two human hearts, "Rousseau's" and "the Frenchman's," which, however, are not two but one—and one and the same also as "J. J.'s" own heart.

This all leads, after a frenzy of agreement and accord between "Rousseau" and "the Frenchman," the one alternately repeating and topping the other in praise of "J. J.'s" character and in condemnation of the conspiracy, and after a positive ecstasy of union among the three of them, to a "donc . . . donc . . . donc / therefore . . . therefore . . . so" conclusion to the dialogue and the *Dialogues*. "Therefore, don't believe that all the accomplices of an execrable scheme can always live and die in peace in their crime," "Rousseau" tells "the Frenchman": "Ne croyez *donc* pas. . . ." The conspiracy will ultimately be in vain, he says, for it is inevitable that "the natural order is reestablished sooner or later," and the two of them, knowing that "[t]ransmitting clarifications about this matter to posterity is perhaps preparing and fulfilling the work of providence," must join in support of the just and divine cause: "Therefore I will devote myself to this work of justice [Je me dévoue *donc* a cette oeuvre de justice] in every way I can, and I exhort you to collaborate with me on it. . . ." By now, "Rousseau" scarcely needs to exhort "the Frenchman"—doing so is hardly more than exhorting himself or "J. J." or Rousseau—but he goes on to say, in a phrase that, even standing alone, would express very well the overwhelming drive and rush to unification that dominates this third dialogue, "If we unite to form a social group with him / Si nous nous unissons pour former avec lui une societé . . ." (Masters/Kelly, 244; Pléiade, 1.974). In the French reflexive—"nous nous unissons"—with its repetition of "nous nous" and its virtual reduplication of the letters and sounds of "nous nous" in "unissons"—there is only one different letter introduced in "unissons" and that is the "i/I" around which one could (playfully) suggest the uniting is taking place—we have a perfect linguistic correlative for the self-enclosed, circular union that is being enjoined. But what "Rousseau" goes on to say is equally interesting:

> If we unite to form a social group with him that is sincere and without fraud, once he is certain of our rectitude and our esteem, he will open his heart to us without difficulty; and receiving from ours the outpourings to which he is naturally so disposed, we will draw out the basis for precious memoirs whose value will be felt by other generations and which at least will enable them to discuss from all sides the questions that are now decided on the basis of his enemies' reports alone. The moment will come, my heart assures me of it, when taking up his defense—which is as perilous as it is useless now—will honor those who wish to undertake it, and cover them at no risk with glory as beautiful and pure as can be obtained by generous virtue here below.

What is particularly intriguing in "Rousseau's" prediction of what is to come is the suggestion that the effect of their tripartite union will be to produce "precious memoirs whose value will be felt by other generations / précieux mémoires dont d'autres generations sentiront la valeur"; but leaving this aside for the moment, there can be little surprise for us in what "the Frenchman" says—"This proposition is entirely to my taste"—or in his responding to the "si/if" of "Rousseau" ("Si nous nous unissons . . .") with the final "donc/so" of the dialogue: "Je ne refuse *donc* pas de le voir":

> So I don't refuse to see him. . . . I will gladly cooperate with you. . . . I know that his papers, entrusted at various times with more confidence than selectivity to hands he believed faithful, have all passed into the hands of his persecutors. . . . The only way he has to preserve them is to entrust them secretly, if possible, into truly faithful and secure hands. I offer to share with you the risks of this trust, and I promise to spare no effort in order to have it appear someday for public viewing just as I received it, enlarged by all the observations I have been able to amass that tend to unveil the truth. (Masters/ Kelly, 244–45; Pléiade, 1.975)

"And that is also all he himself desires," "Rousseau" responds. "The hope that his memory be restored to the honor it deserves, and that his books become useful [utile] through the esteem owed to their Author is henceforth the only hope that can please him in this world. Add to that the sweetness of seeing two decent and true hearts once again open themselves to his own." Earlier in the dialogue "the Frenchman" has claimed that "J. J.'s" writings are as unique as he is himself, so that at the end of the *Dialogues* we are returned to the beginning of the *Confessions* and to the assurance that the "precious memoirs whose value will be felt by other generations" and the memory that will be "restored someday to the honor it deserves" will be, both of them, both "unique et utile." The memory "Rousseau" adduces here in his final speech ("sa mémoire") can be understood to be the remembrance that others will retain of "J. J.," or it can be understood to be "J. J.'s" own faculty of memory; or it can be—and is perhaps best—understood to be remembrance of "J. J." and, at the same time, "J. J.'s" own capacity for remembering, for "J. J." will be remembered—Rousseau, the Author of it all, will be remembered—for the way he remembered the truth of his heart as a natural man and the way he told the story he remembered of being born an alien and alone, outside of society and virtually outside of time, into a world dominated by the *amour-propre* and the time-bound memories of merely social beings.

I have already remarked that the prefatory "On the Subject and Form of this Writing" circles ahead to the appended end, and now that afterpiece returns to the beginning to make this a claustrophobically enclosed work from which there is no way to break free; the only option is a new attempt in a new mode. As for the *Dialogues,* Rousseau is trapped in his writing, in his text, in the written performance that was to make up for the inadequacy of the oral performance when he read the *Confessions,* and all he can do, if he is not to continue, continue, continue like Beckett's "Unnamable"—"you must go on, I can't go on, you must go on, I'll go on, you must say words, as long as there are any, until they find me, until they say me . . ."—is, in sad imitation of his hearers, to fall silent once again. The repetition and the continual rebeginning, the logical working-out of the dialogue structure of the *Dialogues*—splitting, *dédoublement,* division, continual invasion and infection of one level of discourse by another—and the pervasive imagery of darkness and silence, of invisible, speechless people everywhere stifling every sound, every gesture—these constitute a nearly perfect objective correlative for a certain emotional, psychological state, the state that founds itself on the "hypothèse générale" with which the *Dialogues* begins. Typically, what Rousseau does at this moment of greatest aporia, when he feels himself crushed by silence and isolation, is to embrace that condition, call it his own choice, and push it further, beyond the limits of the extreme, where he imagines silence and isolation will reverse themselves to become positive goods. It is as if he were to proceed finally by a series of "donc's" or "so's": "So I am alone; so it was in the beginning, so it is in the end; so it is good." And so we arrive at the *Reveries.*

"Les Élans du Désir"

What becomes immediately apparent as one moves from the *Dialogues* to the *Reveries* is that the other side and the consequence of "si nous nous unissons / if we unite" is inevitably "seul/alone": "Me voici donc seul sur la terre, n'ayant plus de frere, de prochain, d'ami, de societé que moi-même. / Here then am I alone on earth, having neither brother, nor neighbor, nor friend, nor any company but myself."[49] The circle that draws "Rousseau," "J. J.," "the Frenchman," and Rousseau together into one at the end of the *Dialogues* also encloses and isolates them/him. By making all these figures projections of himself and then returning them to their origin and source, Rousseau effectively excludes any other company from his own existence. In English, "all one" and "alone" are etymologically, psychologically, existentially the same—the two are, indeed, one, all one, alone. Rousseau's twofold gesture of union and isolation irresistibly reminds one of Beckett's *The Unnamable,* where all the earlier projections of the narrator and the author—Murphy, Molloy, Malone, et al.: "a few puppets," they are called—are absorbed back into the narrator's voice and being

49. Pléiade, 1.995. I have translated this to correspond to my earlier translation of the first clause. Peter French translates as follows: "So now I am alone in the world, with no brother, neighbour or friend, nor any company left me but my own" (p. 27).

("To tell the truth I believe they are all here, at least from Murphy on, I believe we are all here . . ." [*Trilogy,* 268]); and even more, perhaps, it reminds one of the end of *Company:*

> But with face upturned for good labour in vain at your fable. Till finally you hear how words are coming to an end. With every inane word a little nearer to the last. And how the fable too. The fable of one with you in the dark. The fable of one fabling of one with you in the dark. And how better in the end labour lost and silence. And you as you always were.
>   Alone.[50]

This, but for the lyric manner, is Rousseau at the point of transition from the *Dialogues* to the *Reveries,* alone in the silence and the dark, alone both by necessity and by choice. At this crucial moment, all of Rousseau's puppets have been called home and drawn back into himself, and he could well say, in the second-person voice of Beckett's narrator, "And how better in the end labour lost and silence. And you as you always were. Alone." "Alone" rings like a knell through the *Reveries* and, moving backwards, through the *Dialogues* and the *Confessions* as well; for Rousseau, by his own account, has been alone since the first page of his three-part autobiographical project, and he invokes his lifelong aloneness with the echo from the first lines of the *Confessions* in the first line of the *Reveries* ("moi seul . . . Me voici donc seul"), of which latter volume he says, "These pages may therefore be regarded as an appendix to my *Confessions* . . . / Ces feuilles peuvent donc être regardées comme un appendice de mes *Confessions* . . ." (French, 33; Pléiade, 1.1000). It all recalls, and perhaps not irrelevantly in light of what Rousseau attempts to make of his aloneness in the *Reveries,* the great mystical phrase from Plotinus's *Enneads:* "the flight of the alone to the alone."

The world Rousseau recovers, or claims to recover, in his "promenades" and "reveries" is, on the one hand, the originary (and imaginary) world of humankind, "le monde idéal" of the first dialogue, and, on the other hand, the world of "l'au-delà" or the beyond, contrasted with "ici bas" or here below. The end of the *Dialogues* and all of the *Reveries* look

---

50. In the French version, *Compagnie,* which, even considering Beckett's usual translating practice, has a peculiarly intimate relationship to the English *Company,* the passage reads thus:

> Mais le visage renversé pour de bon peineras en vain sur ta fable. Jusqu'à ce qu'enfin tu entendes comme quoi les mots touchent à leur fin. Avec chaque mot inane plus près du dernier. Et avec eux la fable. La fable d'un autre avec toi dans le noir. La fable de toi fabulant d'un autre avec toi dans le noir. Et comme quoi mieux vaut tout compte fait peine perdue et toi tel que toujours.
>   Seul.

entirely to the condition of the beyond, wishing, however, in a paradoxical gesture, to establish that condition of permanence and stillness for himself not in a world elsewhere or later but in the one here and now. "Detached from everything pertaining to the earth and the senseless judgments of men. . . . and released even from the anxiety of hope here below," Rousseau claims in the "History of the Preceding Writing" (in a passage cited earlier) that he enjoys a "calm that . . . is a permanent state out of which nothing can pull me anymore" (Masters/Kelly, 253; Pléiade, 1.986–87). Earlier, in book 12 of the *Confessions,* and later, in the fifth promenade of the *Reveries,* Rousseau describes this state of calm permanence as the experience he had known during the period in 1765 that he spent on the Island of Saint-Pierre in the Lake of Bienne, at which time, he says, he hoped to make it his for the rest of his life. "So the last hope I had left," Rousseau writes, looking back some five years from the moment when he was concluding the *Confessions* to his stay on Saint-Pierre, "was to live without restraints and eternally at leisure. Such is the life of the blessed in the other world, and henceforth I thought of it as my supreme felicity in this" (Cohen, 591; Pléiade, 1.640). One cautionary caveat should be entered here, however, as one considers Rousseau's evocation of the "supreme felicity" that was his, comparable to "the life of the blessed in the other world [la vie des bienheureux dans l'autre monde]," during the brief time on Saint-Pierre, a caveat to this effect: that, so far as we as readers are concerned, the felicity exists only in Rousseau's *memory* of the experience (from five years and twelve years later) and, more pointedly, it exists only in his *writing* about his memory of the experience. That is to say, he creates a felicity, through a joint act of recollection and narration, that has no existential status, and perhaps never had any existential status, apart from the remembering and writing. The description of the life of the blessed of "l'autre monde," like the description of "le monde idéal" and its inhabitants in the first dialogue, is necessarily of the same category as Rousseau's attempt to give some sense of the nature of humankind in the primitive state, before there was any social world and, most particularly, before there was any language. For "how," he asks in the preface to the second discourse ("On the Origin and Foundations of Inequality among Men"),

> how can the source of inequality among men be known unless one begins by knowing men themselves? And how will man manage to see himself as nature formed him, through all the changes that the sequence of time and things must have produced in his original constitution, and to separate what he gets from his own stock from what circumstances and his progress have added to or changed in his primitive state?

Others coming after him may, by that fact, be able to do better than he has done, Rousseau writes, but of his own attempt he says, "[I]t is no light undertaking to separate what is original from what is artificial in the present nature of man, and to know correctly a state which no longer exists, which perhaps never existed, which probably never will exist, and about which it is nevertheless necessary to have precise notions in order to judge our present state correctly."[51] I should say that "no longer exists . . . never existed . . . probably never will exist" characterizes very nicely "l'autre monde" and "le monde idéal," the felicity of the beyond that is nevertheless imagined as possible here below, the "sufficient, complete and perfect happiness which leaves no emptiness to be filled in the soul" (French, 88; Pléiade, 1.1046) that Rousseau strives so mightily to evoke for the reader in the *Reveries*.

What, in his vast autobiographical project, Rousseau claims to remember and attempts to realize in narrative is not only his own childhood—and, as pointed out earlier, to remember it in such a way that he becomes that memory, is possessed by it rather than possessing it—but also, in effect, the childhood of humanity. He would remember the natural state and would re-create it in the originary language of nature and the heart; and, in a daring reversal of perspective, he would also remember—proleptically—the state of blessedness in the world beyond. Rousseau's claim is that he remembers, in effect, before and after individual history—indeed, before and after any history at all—or, putting it differently and pushing it a bit further, that he remembers before, after, and quite outside of time. To the question posed in Augustine's *Confessions*—why do we, all of us, seek happiness in this life?—Rousseau would presumably give the same answer as Augustine himself: because, in some other existence or state of existence, we have previously known and now remember, however dimly, however confusedly, the same happiness we seek to recover. But in Rousseau this makes for a very troubled narrative in which his ahistorical, nontemporal memory is frequently not in keeping either with the observable world of present reality or—more significantly and more anguishingly for Rousseau—with specific historical acts and with certain of his own temporal (mostly painful) recollections. The one recollective act, ahistorical and nontemporal, is singular and is what Rousseau might see as essential memory; the other, which is plural, he might argue consists of merely accidental

---

51. *Jean-Jacques Rousseau: The First and Second Dialogues,* ed. Roger D. Masters, trans. Roger D. and Judith R. Masters (New York: St. Martin's Press, 1964), 91, 92–93 (Pléiade, 3.122, 123).

or contingent memories. In any event, the two, singular and plural, essential and contingent, are often in conflict, and, for Rousseau, that conflict is deeply disturbing and destabilizing. What he attempts in the *Reveries*, however, running directly counter to this destabilizing tendency and with varying degrees of success, is to draw the essential memory down into this world of contingencies, or, vice versa, to raise contingent memories to the status of essential memory. Although memory hasn't much place in the present-time dialogical back-and-forth of the *Dialogues*, one might, behind that bipolar movement, discern dimly the effort to bring the world of essence and the world of accidence together, to make them one; and looking beyond the *Dialogues* one can see it as an in-between text that prepares the way and provides the necessity for drawing the essential and the contingent together as one in the *Reveries*.

Not that this procedure was ever easy for Rousseau to accomplish. For one thing, although he sought and, with the Island of Saint-Pierre, felt that he had found, for communing with the eternal in himself, a place "naturally circumscribed and cut off from the rest of the world, where I saw nothing but images of delight, where there was nothing to recall painful memories" (French, 90; Pléiade, 1.1048), those painful memories he feared too often, in the *Reveries*, intruded themselves into his consciousness. There was the time, for example, Rousseau tells us in the fourth promenade, when he was dining alfresco at Mme. Vacassin's restaurant, and the elder daughter of his host, "who had recently been married and was expecting a child, suddenly looked hard at me and asked if I had had any children. Blushing all over my face, I replied that I had not had that happiness. She smiled maliciously at the company" (French, 75; Pléiade, 1.1034). The meaning of her question was, of course, not lost on Rousseau, but he, at the moment of the question, fell into confusion, just as, at the moment of recounting it, his text falls into confusion. "She was expecting a negative answer," Rousseau writes, "indeed she was provoking it in order to have the pleasure of making me tell a lie. I was not so obtuse as not to understand that. Two minutes later the answer I should have given suddenly came to me: 'That is an indiscreet question from a young woman to a man who remained a bachelor until his old age.'" This reflects Rousseau's confusion in the event; the confusion in his text follows when he looks back to praise the unparalleled frankness and honesty of his *Confessions*, precisely on this matter of the children and the foundling hospital. "Yes, I can declare with a proud consciousness of my achievement, that in this work I carried good faith, truthfulness and frankness as far, further even, or so I believe, than any other mortal." But in the *Confessions*, he acknowledges, "I was writing from memory; my memory often failed me or only provided me with an incomplete picture, and I filled the gaps with details which I dreamed up to complete my memories, but which never contradicted them." There is nothing very surprising here, but a couple of pages later, after recounting some events that could have been used "to demonstrate the goodness I felt in my heart" had he told of them in his *Confessions,* Rousseau produces this truly astonishing passage: "No, when I have spoken against the truth as I knew it, it has always been about unimportant matters and has been caused more by the need to find something to say or the pleasure of writing [le plaisir d'écrire] than by my own self-interest or the advantage or disadvantage it might bring to others" (French, 79; Pléiade, 1.1038). That he has been led to speak against the truth by "the pleasure of writing" is very interesting, especially in light of the number of times Rousseau unburdens himself on the folly and iniquity of the writing profession; equally interesting is the fact that he should have been set off on this strange and tangled narrative route by the malicious reminder of his paternity and the memory of those actions of his that proved (his enemies all said) that he was "un père dénaturé."

The children rear their heads again right through the text of the ninth promenade, followed, as usual, by an attempt—this time both bizarre and pathetic—on Rousseau's part to demonstrate that he is not, indeed is the opposite of, an unnatural father. Again, the children are recalled to Rousseau's memory by someone acting out of malice—or so Rousseau perceived it, though it must be admitted that there seems more than a hint of paranoia in the perception. The story is that a Monsieur P. called on Rousseau to give him a copy of an obituary of one Mme. Geoffrin written by d'Alembert in which the deceased is praised in particular for her love of children. The obituary writer suggests that for Mme. Geoffrin the love of children is a sign of good character and the failure to love children a sign of bad character, and he goes on to assert, according to Rousseau's account, "that if everyone who was being taken to be hanged or broken on the wheel was questioned on this point, they would all admit to not having loved children."[52] The suggestion of a connection between crimi-

---

52. French, 138; Pléiade, 1.1086. The passage reads thus in the obituary: "Je voudrois . . . qu'on fît une question à tous les malheureux qui vont subir la mort pour leurs crimes: *avez vous aimé les enfans?* je suis sûre qu'ils répondroient que non [I wish that a single question could be asked of all the wretches about to be put to death for their crimes: *did you love children?* I am certain that they would answer no]." The editors of the Pléiade Rousseau remark drily that "d'Alembert, himself an abandoned child, would have been thinking of himself much more than of Rousseau" (1.1824 nn. 5, 6).

nality and a lack of love for children was more than enough to set Rousseau off. The serenity of his self-circumscription ("where there [is] nothing to recall painful memories") shattered, Rousseau returns to his own defense in much the same narrative manner as that of books 7 and 8 of the *Confessions.* "I can understand," Rousseau writes, "that the reproach of having put my children in the Foundlings' Home should easily have degenerated, with a little embellishment, into that of being an unnatural father [un père dénaturé] and a child-hater. Nevertheless," he goes on, taking a characteristic right-about-face,

> Nevertheless there is no doubt that in doing so I was influenced most of all by the fear that any other course of action would almost inevitably bring upon them a fate a thousand times worse. Had I been less concerned about what would happen to them, since I was not in a position to bring them up myself, I should have been obliged by my circumstances to leave their education to their mother, who would have spoiled them, and to her family, who would have made monsters of them. What Mahomet did to Seide [viz., persuade him to patricide] would have been as nothing compared to what would have been done to them with regard to me, and the traps that have subsequently been laid for me in this connection are confirmation enough of the plot that was hatched at this time. It is true that in those days I was far from foreseeing these terrible schemes, but I knew that the least dangerous form of education they could have was at the Foundlings' Home, so I put them there. I should do the same thing again with even fewer misgivings if the choice were still before me, and I am sure that no father is more affectionate than I would have been towards them once habit had had time to reinforce my natural inclination. (French, 139–40; Pléiade, 1.1087)

This is no more than Rousseau had said, with such lack of success, in the *Confessions.* The pathos of his attempt to prove himself not an unnatural father—indeed, to prove that, in the hypothetical situation of his having kept the children, he would have been at least the equal of any other father and superior to most in the affection he would have shown toward them—comes when Rousseau tells of three different instances when he felt and exhibited the fond loving-kindness and the deep benevolence of his own spirit with regard to children. The first has a boy of five or six tugging at Rousseau's knees as he wanders "dreamily and absent-mindedly" through "the village of Clignancourt"; Rousseau, thinking "that is how my children would have treated me," grabs the child up, kisses "him several times in a kind of rapture," and then buys him "some Nanterre rolls which a passing salesman happened to have," thinking, obviously, "If only my detractors could have seen me in that moment." What remains of this encounter, Rousseau says, "is a quite vivid memory tinged always with affection and sadness," and, one cannot doubt, the feeling that he, beyond all men, could never be—and should never be taken for—an unnatural father. The second and third instances both have Rousseau devising little games for groups of children encountered in the streets, games in which Rousseau dispenses small largesse, with perfect generosity and equity, on each child, thus showing the reader (who is also to be Rousseau's judge and then partisan) a natural father following his natural instincts of affectionate loving-kindness for his surrogate children.[53]

But in the controlling schema and the dominant movement of the *Reveries* such passages as the foregoing are mere narrative blips, set off by painful memories that require equal and opposite, pleasant memories to correct them, the bad memories of Rousseau's own children being counterbalanced—or, it is to be hoped, outweighed—by the good memories of loving attention to anonymous street children. The essential narrative of the *Reveries,* however, has neither children nor anyone else but only Rousseau in it, and the quintessential narrative is his memory of his cradled self-sufficiency, as Rousseau himself describes it, on the Island of Saint-Pierre in the Lake of Bienne. "I was barely allowed to spend two months on this island," Rousseau says, "but I could have spent two years, two centuries and all eternity there without a moment's boredom" (French, 82–83; Pléiade, 1.1041), and indeed it is just this experience of eternity in a moment that Rousseau attempts to recall and to evoke throughout the fifth and—in all ways—central promenade of the *Reveries.* His sojourn on the Island of Saint-Pierre (which actually lasted only some six weeks rather than two months) Rousseau describes all in terms of his being alone with his

---

53. Earlier in this same promenade, still on the issue of his being or not being an unnatural father, Rousseau writes:

> I had put my children in the Foundlings' Home, and this was enough for people to misrepresent me as an unnatural father, and so, developing this idea and embroidering on it, they had gradually reached the obvious conclusion that I hated children; as I followed this progression of ideas, I wondered at the art with which human ingenuity manages to turn white into black. For I do not believe that any man has ever loved seeing little children romping and playing together more than I do, and I often stop in the street or on the boulevards to look at their little tricks and games with an interest which no one else seems to share. (French, 138–39; Pléiade, 1.1086–87)

The editors of the Pléiade edition provide a note on this passage that might be translated as follows:

> Eugène Delacroix, in his journal (May 31, 1824), reports the following anecdote told to him by an old gentleman whom he met one evening at the Odéon and who had "seen Gretry, Voltaire, Diderot, Rousseau, etc.": "He was taken by one of his friends to lunch with Jean-Jacques, Plâtrière Street. They went out together. In the Tuileries, some children were playing ball: 'Look there,' Rousseau said, 'that's the exercise for Émile,' and similar things. But the ball of one of the children happened to strike the leg of the philosopher, who, in a fit of rage, abruptly left his two companions and chased after the child with his stick." (Pléiade, 1.1824–25)

aloneness: "ce séjour isolé ou je m'etois enlacé de moi-même: this isolated place where I was intertwined with myself."[54] Saint-Pierre, Rousseau writes, was, as an island, "very agreeable and uniquely well situated for the happiness of a man who likes to be self-circumscribed [très agréable et singulièrement située pour le bonheur d'un homme qui aime à se circonscrire]." The very syllables and sounds of "se circonscrire" seem to enact the sibilant process of closing the island in, around, and over himself. There, "isolé" and "enlacé de [s]oi-même," Rousseau, according to his own account, scarcely needed to think at all—that activity that gave him so much trouble throughout his life—"in order to be recalled to himself while forgetting all his troubles [pour se souvenir de soi-même en oubliant tous ses maux]."[55] This centering in on himself, this recalling himself to himself, is a process of memory, of recollection—a process, one might almost say, of Platonic anamnesis, of remembering a state of the soul before birth and of remembering, by way of anticipating, a state of the soul after death. It is an attempt to make real the Augustinian present of things past and to make real the present of things future by transforming both of them into the present of things present. "Set free from all the earthly passions that are born of the tumult of social life, my soul would often soar out of this atmosphere and would converse before its time with the celestial spirits whose number it hopes soon to swell" (French, 91; Pléiade, 1.1048–49). One cannot emphasize too strongly that, as Rousseau describes it, this is all achieved through memory—and not just singlefold but twofold and threefold memory. For what Rousseau is recalling in writing the fifth promenade is the experience of recollecting himself to himself on the Island of Saint-Pierre, an experience he had earlier recollected and narrated in book 12 of the *Confessions*—a nest, then, of recollections of recollections of recollections. Yet between the writing of the *Confessions* and the writing of the *Reveries* seven years had passed—just as, between the experience on Saint-Pierre and the writing of the *Confessions,* five years had passed—years during which Rousseau's memory, shading off into imagination, had not been idle, and the differences to be noted—differences between one account and the other and differences also, perhaps, between either account or both accounts and the actual experience—are as remarkable as are the similarities.

54. My translation; French translates "the isolated place in which I had imprisoned myself," which does not quite convey the sense of self-embracement or self-intertwining of the original: French, 83; Pléiade, 1.1042.

55. French, 90; Pléiade, 1.1048. Translation of this passage, too, has been adapted for the purposes of my discussion.

I have said that it is memory that everywhere informs the Saint-Pierre narrative, yet how shall we distinguish between the operation of memory and that of imagination? Rousseau himself sees imagination as the faculty that saves him from the enemies who, as soon as they know of it, would deny him the "happy sanctuary" of his blessed isle:

> But at least they cannot prevent me from being transported there every day on the wings of imagination and tasting for several hours the same pleasures as if I were still living there. Were I there, my sweetest occupation would be to dream to my heart's content. Is it not the same thing to dream that I am there? Better still, I can add to my abstract and monotonous reveries charming images that give them life. During my moment of ecstasy the sources of these images often escaped my senses; but now, the deeper the reverie, the more vividly they are present to me. I am often more truly in their midst and they give me still greater pleasure than when I was surrounded by them. (French, 91; Pléiade, 1.1049)

It scarcely matters whether we think of what is going on here as memory or whether we think of it as imagination; in either case a better formulation might be "memory setting imagination in motion" or, conversely, "imagination completing the imperfect action of memory." Whatever we may choose to call the process by which it happens, what is effected between the account in book 12 of the *Confessions* and the fifth promenade of the *Reveries,* like what is effected, we must suppose, between the actual experience and both accounts of it, is a gradual refinement and stripping away of the superficies of experience as the narrator centers in on and becomes a pure state of being. From the time of his stay on Saint-Pierre to the writing of book 12 of the *Confessions* to the writing of the fifth promenade of the *Reveries* there is a movement away from the specific details of events transpiring in time to a condition that is virtually timeless. The effect of memory in Rousseau (and no doubt the effect of memory more generally), or the effect of memory-and-imagination, is to transform the singular event of history into the always-occurring event of the as-if world of fiction and of autobiographical narrative. "Emerging from a long and happy reverie," Rousseau says, recalling his experience from twelve years after the fact, "seeing myself surrounded by greenery, flowers and birds, and letting my eyes wander over the picturesque far-off shores which enclosed a vast stretch of clear and crystalline water, I fused my imaginings with these charming sights, and finding myself in the end gradually brought back to myself and my surroundings, I could not draw a line between fiction and reality . . ." (French, 90–91; Pléiade, 1.1048). This, Rousseau says, is what happened on Saint-Pierre, but any reader must be forgiven for thinking that this is what happens—not past tense but present tense—in the moment of memory and in the moment of writing about what happened on Saint-Pierre.

One can observe a nice instance of the transformative capacities of memory in two separate accounts—very similar but with a slight yet radical difference between them—that Rousseau gives, one in book 12 of the *Confessions,* the other in the fifth promenade of the *Reveries,* of apple picking on the Island of Saint-Pierre. In both books the apple-picking episode occurs in the context of Rousseau's living the natural life, "like another Robinson Crusoe" (Cohen, 594; Pléiade, 1.644), once introducing a colony of rabbits to stock the island ("another red-letter day for Jean-Jacques: autre fête pour J. J.") and botanizing over the specimens offered by the island for hours every day. "To these amusements I added another," Rousseau writes in the *Confessions* version,

> which recalled the delightful life at Les Charmettes [with Maman], and which was most suitable to the season. This was assisting in the country labours of bringing in the vegetables and fruit, a job in which Thérèse and I were delighted to take our share with the receiver's wife and her family. I remember that when a M. Kirkeberghr from Bern came to see me he found me perched in a large tree with a sack tied to my waist, and already so loaded with apples that I could not move. (Cohen, 594–95; Pléiade, 1.644)

Here we have Rousseau, five years after the event, apparently recalling a singular, unrepeated incident involving himself and a specific individual from Bern ("Je me souviens qu'*un Bernois* nommé M. Kirkeberghr . . ."). However often Rousseau may have picked apples in the seasonal life of Saint-Pierre, there is no suggestion in the *Confessions* account that there was any other occasion when any other *Bernois* than one "named M. Kirkeberghr" had come upon him while he was engaged in this idyllic activity.

Seven years later, however, during which time an expansive memory had clearly intervened to confer on the event the significance of mythic repetition, Rousseau would recall in the *Reveries* many occasions on which a whole troop of *Bernois* had come, seriatim, to discover him perched in his tree. Excited by the prospect of all the botanical varieties for study on Saint-Pierre, Rousseau writes in the fifth promenade that "every morning after breakfast"—not just once or occasionally but "tous les matins après le déjeuné"—

> I would set out with a magnifying glass in my hand and my *Systema Naturae* under my arm. . . . After two or three hours I would come back with a rich

> harvest, enough to occupy me at home all the afternoon if it should rain. The
> rest of the morning I spent going with the Steward, his wife and Thérèse to
> see the labourers working at the harvest, and usually to lend them a hand;
> often people coming to see me from Bern found me perched up in a big tree
> with a bag round my waist, which I would fill with fruit and then lower to
> the ground on the end of a rope. (French, 84–85; Pléiade, 1.1043)

The one time and the one *Bernois* named Kirkebergher have been replaced,
through the action of seven years of memory, by "often" and "people . . .
from Bern" ("souvent des Bernois"). From the actual experience (whatever
it may have been) on the Island of Saint-Pierre to the account in the *Confessions* and from that account to the later one in the *Reveries* there is a steady
movement away from singularities and contingencies through repetition to
essence, a movement from the particularities of history to the universals of
myth (what more mythic than the picking of apples?) and from events taking place in time to a state transcending time. But is this not the natural
effect of all repeated acts of memory and narrative? The more times an
event is recalled and the more times its story is retold, the more often it
occurs—it occurs again with every retelling—and the larger the significance that accrues to it. Each of the ten promenade narratives of the *Reveries*
is invested with an atemporal atmosphere that one might most readily associate with dreams. This is to be felt most vividly perhaps in the account that
Rousseau gives in the second promenade of having been knocked down by
a Great Dane and the ensuing return to consciousness after a period of
being out of his senses:

> Night was coming on. I saw the sky, some stars, and a few leaves. This
> first sensation was a moment of delight. I was conscious of nothing else. In
> this instant I was being born again, and it seems as if all I perceived was filled
> with my frail existence. Entirely taken up by the present, I could remember
> nothing; I had no distinct notion of myself as a person, nor had I the least
> idea of what happened to me. . . . I felt throughout my whole being such a
> wonderful calm, that whenever I recall this feeling I can find nothing to com-
> pare with it in all the pleasures that stir our lives. (French, 39; Pléiade, 1.1005)

The experience Rousseau would evoke here is either before time or after
time—at all events outside of time.

The promenade that is most insistently and thoroughly dreamlike and
unworldly, however, giving the impression of a narrator yet-unborn who
floats in an amnesiac amniotic fluid, is not the second but the fifth promenade, where Rousseau repeats and perfects the account given in book 12
of the *Confessions* of his life on Saint-Pierre. In the later, *Reveries* account
Rousseau tells us that, after his morning's exercise and a midday meal, when

the others lingered too long at table, "I would make my escape and install myself all alone in a boat, which I would row out into the middle of the lake. . . ." The verbs here—"esquivois . . . allois . . . conduisois"—and throughout the rest of the passage are all in the imperfect—that verb tense, the dictionary says, that is "used to designate a continuing state or an incomplete action esp. in the past."

> I would make my escape and install myself all alone in a boat, which I would row out into the middle of the lake when it was calm; and there, stretching out full-length in the boat and turning my eyes skyward, I let myself float and drift wherever the water took me, often for several hours on end, plunged in a host of vague yet delightful reveries, which though they had no distinct or permanent subject, were still in my eyes infinitely to be preferred to all that I had found most sweet in the so-called pleasures of life. Often reminded by the declining sun that it was time to return home, I found myself so far from the island that I was forced to row with all my might in order to arrive before nightfall. (French, 85; Pléiade, 1.1044)

"I would make my escape . . . I would row out . . . and . . . let myself float and drift . . . often for several hours on end. . . . Often reminded by the declining sun. . . ." While there is no particular reason to doubt the "often" here, there is good reason to remark it and to suggest that the oftenness of the experience is a consequence of Rousseau's replacing one kind of memory in the narrative with another.[56] In such a passage recall of specific dates and events gives way to recall of an unchanging state of being that, among other things, permits Rousseau to forget painful memories and to recapture that ideal state of being-in-the-beginning, that "monde idéal" that, as we have seen, Rousseau acknowledges "no longer exists . . . , never existed . . . , probably never will exist." The very language of the fifth promenade tells this same story, consciously or unconsciously, of the non-existence of the ideal state. In the evenings, Rousseau says, he liked to go and sit in a secluded spot "by the edge of the lake," where "the noise of the waves and the movement of the water, taking hold of my senses and driving all other agitation from my soul, would plunge it into a delicious

---

56. Cf. Kafka on this sort of move (inevitable, as he sees it) in autobiography: "In an autobiography one cannot avoid writing 'often' where truth would require that 'once' be written. For one always remains conscious that the word 'once' explodes that darkness on which the memory draws; and though it is not altogether spared by the word 'often', either, it is at least preserved in the opinion of the writer, and he is carried across parts which perhaps never existed at all in his life but serve him as a substitute for those which his memory can no longer guess at" (*Diaries of Franz Kafka,* ed. Max Brod [Harmondsworth: Penguin, 1964], 163–64).

reverie in which night often stole upon me unawares. The ebb and flow of the water, its continuous yet undulating noise, kept lapping against my ears and my eyes . . . , and it was enough to make me pleasurably aware of my existence, without troubling myself with thought." In such moments in and out of time (as T. S. Eliot might call them) "the unchanging and ceaseless movement" on the surface of the water, Rousseau says, "lulled me and without any active effort on my part occupied me so completely that even when time and the habitual signal called me home I could hardly bring myself to go" (French, 86–87; Pléiade, 1.1045). The ebb and flow of Rousseau's prose, its continuous yet undulating sound that keeps lapping against the reader's ears and eyes, might well remind one of Whitman's "Out of the Cradle Endlessly Rocking," and indeed Rousseau arrives finally at the crucial, Whitmanian phrase when he says that "l'uniformité du mouvement continu . . . me berçoit": the unchanging and ceaseless movement cradled, rocked, lulled me. This is undoubtedly the intended sense of the passage, and the translation of "me berçoit" as "lulled me" is altogether reasonable; but there is also an undersense to the verb "bercer" (as there is to the verb "to lull" in English)—"to delude with false visions or hopes"—that would suggest that the experience here described is closer to self-delusion or deception than to transcendence. And Rousseau uses the verb "bercer" in exactly this other sense in the *Dialogues* ("History of the Preceding Writing") when he writes that the notion that the manuscript deposited on the High Altar of Notre Dame might come to the attention of the king "was, I said, so crazy that I myself was amazed I had deluded myself with it [pu m'en bercer] for a moment," and he repeats the use later in the same piece when he starts a sentence with "Deluded by this new hope: Bercé de cette nouvelle espérance" (Masters/Kelly, 249, 250; Pléiade, 1. 981, 983). In a footnote to *The Social Contract* we find Rousseau pleading thus with his reader: "Please, attentive reader, do not hasten to accuse me of contradiction. I cannot avoid a contradiction of words, because of the poverty of language; but wait."[57] In the *Reveries,* however, it is not the poverty of language but its richness that complicates matters. In the latter book it is not so much that language cannot do what Rousseau desires or demands of it (it never could: it is simply a fact that with Rousseau language is always insufficient to the tasks he sets it); it is rather that language in that text (and elsewhere in his vast life-writing project) is forever doing things—pertinent, interesting, and revealing things—that Rousseau would

57. *The Social Contract,* translated and introduced by Maurice Cranston (Harmondsworth: Penguin Books, 1968), 74; Pléiade, 3.373.

never have intended. And this duplicitous nature inherent in his very medium casts quite a different light on the experience of God-like self-sufficiency that Rousseau would evoke in the *Reveries*.

"I have noticed in the changing fortunes of a long life," Rousseau tells us in the fifth promenade, "that the periods of the sweetest joys and keenest pleasures are not those whose memory is most moving and attractive to me." It is not the moments recoverable by memory—memory now as we ordinarily understand it—that most move Rousseau and have permanent value for him; not those "brief moments of madness and passion. . . . [that] are too rare and too short-lived to constitute a durable state." No, Rousseau says, "the happiness for which my soul longs is not made up of fleeting moments, but of a single and lasting state, which has no very strong impact in itself, but which by its continuance becomes so captivating that we eventually come to regard it as the height of happiness" (French, 87–88; Pléiade, 1.1046). With this contrast between the transitory and the permanent—a contrast, presumably, between that which is recoverable by contingent memory and that which is discoverable only by essential memory—Rousseau launches into a meditation that may sound superficially Augustinian but that is ultimately more indebted to Heraclitus than to St. Augustine:

> Everything is in constant flux on this earth. Nothing keeps the same unchanging shape, and our affections, being attached to things outside us, necessarily change and pass away as they do. Always out ahead of us or lagging behind, they recall a past which is gone or anticipate a future which may never come into being; there is nothing solid there for the heart to attach itself to. . . . [H]ow can we give the name of happiness to a fleeting state which leaves our hearts still empty and anxious, either regretting something that is past or desiring something that is yet to come?

This notion of happiness dispenses altogether with memory as commonly conceived, for what place has memory where time does not obtain and where everything is always the same? It would dispense with all writing, and especially all autobiographical writing, as well, for if there were not something "always out ahead of us or lagging behind," if we were not forever "either regretting something that is past or desiring something that is yet to come," narrative would have no attractions for us, and no one would feel either the need or the desire to tell the story of a life. "But if there is a state," Rousseau continues, and then goes on to describe the "monde idéal" that by his own admission never existed and never will exist but that he yet claims as the condition of his life on Saint-Pierre,

But if there is a state where the soul can find a resting-place secure enough to establish itself and concentrate its entire being there, with no need to remember the past or reach into the future, where time is nothing to it, where the present runs on indefinitely but this duration goes unnoticed, with no sign of the passing of time, and no other feeling of deprivation or enjoyment, pleasure or pain, desire or fear than the simple feeling of existence, a feeling that fills our soul entirely, as long as this state lasts, we can call ourselves happy, not with a poor, incomplete and relative happiness such as we find in the pleasures of life, but with a sufficient, complete and perfect happiness which leaves no emptiness to be filled in the soul.

Now, since this passage establishes itself on an "if" ("But *if* there is a state . . ."), it may seem that it is all intended to be understood as being in the subjunctive mode (though it is not: it is in the indicative), offering, at best, a description of a hypothetical condition or, at worst, a statement of a condition contrary to fact. But Rousseau is alert to this possible misapprehension: lest the reader imagine that he is describing a never-neverland fantasy of a "monde idéal" as in the first dialogue or of the natural state of man before his fall into society as in the second discourse, Rousseau hastens to say that this was virtually his everyday experience on Saint-Pierre: "Such is the state which I often experienced on the Island of Saint-Pierre in my solitary reveries. . . ." And here I must pause to point out that what Rousseau first wrote was not "Tel est l'état ou je me suis trouvé *souvent*" but rather "Tel est l'état ou je me suis trouvé *quelquefois*"—not a state that he experienced "often" but one that he experienced "on occasion." This is very similar to M. Kirkebergher's sole visit to the apple-picking Rousseau being turned into the frequent visits of many citizens of Bern. And if we look back to the *Confessions* we will not find any account at all of "the state which I often experienced on the Island of Saint-Pierre in my solitary reveries." Though Rousseau says that memory had nothing to do with this state, one begins to suspect that memory—a memory that was highly imaginative and creative, that was capable of mythifying and mystifying to an extraordinary degree, that depended on the passage of time for its full flowering, and that was inextricably bound up with narrative and the writing of narrative—had everything to do with it. "Such is the state which I often [or occasionally] experienced on the Island of Saint-Pierre in my solitary reveries, whether I lay in a boat and drifted where the water carried me, or sat by the shores of the stormy lake, or elsewhere, on the banks of a lovely river or a stream murmuring over the stones." Rousseau goes on to question the provenance of such a state and finds no answer but on the inside of aloneness. "What is the source of our happiness in such a state? Nothing external to us, nothing apart from ourselves and our own existence. . . ." Rousseau's two "nothings" imply the conclusion of the negative theology that (as W. B. Yeats puts it in the title of one of his stories) "Where There Is Nothing There Is God"; and indeed Rousseau does not hesitate to proceed from his own nothing to his self-sufficiency as God: "as long as this state lasts we are self-sufficient like God [tant que cet état dure on se suffit à soi-même comme Dieu]" (French, 89; Pléiade, 1.1047).

What is odd or paradoxical about a passage like this one is not the claim of God-like self-sufficiency, for Rousseau had already hinted at his status as divine Unmoved Mover in the first promenade ("I have nothing left in the world to fear or hope for, and this leaves me in peace at the bottom of the abyss, a poor unfortunate mortal, but as unmoved as God himself" [French, 31; Pléiade, 1.999]); it is rather that Rousseau should attempt to render such a state in the human language he always considered to be thoroughly unstable and unsatisfactory, and moreover that his rendering of that state—or, in fact, its very existence—so plainly depended on an act of memory prolonged over time when he denied both memory and time any place in the experience. Even before Rousseau attempts to find language, as in the passages quoted above, for the experience that he would agree was ineffable, he has written this, which points right to memory as the chief architect of it all: "Such, apart from unforeseen and troublesome visits, was the way I spent my time on this island during the weeks I lived there. I should like to know what there was in it that was attractive enough to give me such deep, tender and lasting regrets that even fifteen years later it is impossible for me to think of this beloved place without each time feeling myself transported once again by piercing surges of desire."[58] Perhaps Rousseau wrote "fifteen years" when he should have written "twelve years" because he could not imagine memory being so active as it had been in fewer than a full fifteen years; but however that may be, when he speaks of "deep, tender and lasting regrets [des regrets si vifs, si tendres et si durables]," when he points up the repetitiousness of his experience with "each time" and "once again," and even more when he describes himself as being "transported . . . by piercing surges of desire," any reader must reflect that

58. Pléiade, 1.1045; my translation. French (p. 87) translates the latter part of this quotation ("au bout de quinze ans il m'est impossible de songer à cette habitation chérie sans m'y sentir à chaque fois transporter encore par les élans du désir") as "even fifteen years later I am incapable of thinking of this beloved place without being overcome by pangs of longing." "Pangs of longing" I think does not have quite the same emotional charge about it as "les élans du désir."

regrets and desire have nothing at all to do with a state where one is as unmoved and as self-sufficient as God, but everything to do with memory and the narratives of memory where one is constantly being transported by—and which are themselves motivated by—surges of desire. Rousseau may claim that he has no wish—precisely because they are transitory—for those fleeting moments recoverable by memory, and he may claim that his whole heart is set on a permanent state of undesiring, to achieve which state memory would be little more than a hindrance and a nuisance, but in the end he has no other language than the language of memory and desire, no other language than language itself, in which to render either the fleeting moments or the permanent state.

The Children of Jean-Jacques

For language, its sufficiency or insufficiency, its dispensability or indispensability, its necessity, its treachery, its successes and its failures, was the very heart of Rousseau's autobiographical project, and it was the essence of the legacy he left for his nineteenth- and twentieth-century inheritors (whether they acknowledged him or not) to deal with as they could. It was a truth, sad but inexorable, that language was all Rousseau had—all anyone has, really—for knowing and communicating what he had been in the past, was at this moment, and always would be. In book 12 of the *Confessions,* telling of his stay on Saint-Pierre, Rousseau says that his enemies will find it impossible to comprehend what he found there, "[b]ut whatever they may think or say, I shall continue just the same faithfully to reveal what J.-J. Rousseau was, did, and thought, without explaining or justifying the strangeness of his feelings or ideas, or inquiring whether any others have thought like him" (Cohen, 595; Pléiade, 1.645). But while Rousseau might, on occasion, have been able to "reveal faithfully" what he did and perhaps even what he thought, to make known what he *"was"*—to command language that would say this and be fully communicable to others— this he could not do, and it is not too much to say that his failure in the effort in the *Confessions* drove him to write the *Dialogues,* and his failure there—one feels it in the text, in the desperate push against language— drove him to a kind of frenzy, to quiet which he could only seek, in the *Reveries,* to be as unmoved, as self-sufficient, as still in all senses as God himself. All of us, at least since Rousseau, believe (or know) that we are other and more than our words can say. Only the greatest of the poets have discovered an adequate language of and for the self; but few of us are great poets, and even they in the end—or so at least one of them says—

Now that [their] ladder's gone
. . . must lie down where all the ladders start
In the foul rag and bone shop of the heart.

There is a sense in which language itself, his greatest and his only ally, became something like Rousseau's worst enemy, and one feels him struggling against his medium as if he were beating against a barrier that kept him from full revelation. And to make the dilemma more acute and more anguished, Rousseau had always maintained that only spoken language, because it was the natural form of the natural state of humankind—the imagined language of "le monde idéal"—only spoken language, which expressed feelings rather than ideas (the province of written language), could retain its internal life and the viva voce power to make an auditor *see*.[59] We have only to recall the postscript (and it is ironic that it should be a post*script,* a written account of a spoken performance) to the *Confessions* to understand how great an investment Rousseau had in the hoped-for power and the superior vitality of the spoken word. And what are the *Dialogues* but an attempt to bring language to life—back to life—through speech and dialogue, no longer to be imagined as words on a page but as words issuing from living mouths?—an attempt that is followed (again in a postscript: "History of the Preceding Writing") by the sad spectacle of Rousseau in the streets of Paris calling out to passersby—*"To all Frenchmen who still love justice and truth"*—to hear him and to know him through his speech.

But Rousseau's skepticism about language was much more radical than I have yet suggested and his dilemma, therefore, the more extreme, for in the final analysis he, who felt himself an alien born into the human species, believed no more in the effective power of speech to reveal what he was— and this was the highest good to which he could imagine himself or anyone else aspiring: making the heart of Jean-Jacques known to everyone—than he believed in the power of writing to the same end. Of sensitive souls like "J. J."—those who have "received from Heaven a truly ardent, lively,

---

59. Cf. the following passage from the *Essay on the Origin of Languages,* which is in keeping with what Rousseau says about the contrast between spoken and written languages throughout the volume:

> Writing, which would seem to crystallize language, is precisely what alters it. It changes not the words but the spirit, substituting exactitude for expressiveness. Feelings are expressed in speaking, ideas in writing. In writing, one is forced to use all the words according to their conventional meaning. But in speaking, one varies the meanings by varying one's tone of voice, determining them as one pleases. Being less constrained to clarity, one can be more forceful. And it is not possible for a language that is written, to retain its vitality as long as one that is only spoken. (*Essay on the Origin of Languages,* trans. John H. Moran [Chicago: University of Chicago Press, 1966], 21–22)

sensitive, and tender nature"—the "Rousseau" of the *Dialogues* tells us that they are "completely involved in their feelings [and so] attend too little to their words to arrange them with . . . art. The cumbersome sequence of speech is unbearable to them. They chaff [*sic:* read "chafe"—the verb is "se dépitent" in French] against its slow progression. From the speed of the impulses they feel, it seems to them that what they feel should become apparent and penetrate from one heart to another without the cold intermediary of words" (Masters/Kelly, 157; Pléiade, 1.862). Not what he had done (the children again) and not what he thought (for that was the dominant activity of the unnatural social world of amour-propre) but what he felt and what he was in his heart: this is what Rousseau wanted to instill, but "without the cold intermediary of words," in the hearts of others; what he wanted, as he said in a central passage of the *Confessions,* was "in some way to make my soul transparent to the reader's eye" (Cohen, 169; Pléiade, 1.175). Direct and unmediated vision, without recourse even to the spoken voice and much less to the written word, was what Rousseau imagined he could achieve or felt he must achieve. But the gambit is impossible, inconceivable, with a joker lying in virtually every one of Rousseau's words and especially in the word "reader," for what will Rousseau offer his reader for reading but words? What has he for making known "the essential Rousseau"[60] but memories on the one hand, narratives on the other, both of them caught and contained in a web of words, both of them twice and three times removed from the reader's immediate apprehension by the necessary but baleful mediation of language? But the consequence of his own feeling that he could not expect to make known what he was through language, paradoxical as it may seem—and here he was very like certain of his modernist and postmodernist followers—was that, instead of falling

---

60. I choose this phrase deliberately because, as I am writing this paragraph, my eye falls on a little Mentor–New American Library book called *The Essential Rousseau,* which would seem to claim that we can know "the essential Rousseau" by reading *The Social Contract,* the first and second discourses (*Discourse on the Arts and Sciences* and *Discourse on the Origin of Inequality*), and "The Creed of the Savoyard Priest" (extracted from *Émile*). One would not deny that Rousseau is in some sense in each of these works as he is in everything he wrote—all his books being, as I have argued earlier, exercises in autobiography disguised or manifest—but Rousseau himself never tired of saying that it is in the *Confessions,* the *Dialogues,* and the *Reveries* and only there that his essence—"what J.-J. Rousseau was, did, and thought"—is revealed. I am aware that many readers, especially those interested in Rousseau as a political and social philosopher, virtually dismiss the three autobiographical works with the observation that Rousseau had been driven mad through persecution by the time he wrote those books. The answer, however, seems to me obvious and unavoidable: "No, the Rousseau of the *Confessions,* the *Dialogues,* and the *Reveries* was not mad; he was Rousseau."

silent, he desperately multiplied words, writing more and ever more, as if sheer number could counter and reverse logical impossibility and as if language could suddenly become something other than what Rousseau had always said it was. Narrative took on a proliferative life of its own, by no means always under Rousseau's control, and here the paradox doubles and inverts itself, for one comes to feel that it is in the compulsive, uncontrolled, perhaps unwilled narrative—as in his compulsive, uncontrolled, and unwilled memories—that the "real" Rousseau, "the essential Rousseau," is most revealed. At such moments the language—both Rousseau's own language and the French language—spoke and wrote Rousseau more clearly than he spoke and wrote himself or either of the languages.

Virtually every commentator on Rousseau has felt compelled to address, one way or another, the two correlative but oppositional questions of whether Rousseau was the victim of a universal "complot" or whether he was a raving lunatic and victim of nothing more than his own paranoia. Reading any one or all three of his autobiographical texts it is easy enough to see why the questions insist on being raised and explored if not always (or ever) definitively answered. On his own reckoning, every friend Rousseau ever imagined himself to have betrayed him in the end. As the "Rousseau" of the *Dialogues* would have it, "ces Messieurs"—those gentlemen who devised the conspiracy—had succeeded in reaching and contaminating everyone. How believable is this? Surely not very, at least not in the literal sense Rousseau clearly intended. In another sense, however, the plot did exist and it was deeper and darker and more universal than even Rousseau imagined. For he was betrayed not only (if at all) by every friend, but he was betrayed at the most profound level by the very language in which he defended himself, by the language in which he said he was not as others claimed he was, by the language in which he said and wanted to show that he was not just a decent human being but "on the whole the best of men." And yet should one speak of betrayal? Or should one not speak rather of fulfillment and destiny? When Rousseau exclaimed, "I have not deserved my fate,"[61] surely he was wrong and surely he was being unfair to himself: he deserved his fate because he assiduously, determinedly (I do not necessarily say knowingly) accomplished it. Heraclitus proclaimed that "man's character is his destiny," and the truth of the Heraclitean dictum is borne out to the last detail in Rousseau's life-story. Even though it is impossible to know just what Rousseau intended by it, it seems to me that he was closer to the mark when he concluded the second promenade of his *Reveries* with

61. Quoted in Guéhenno, 2.284.

this paragraph: "God is just; his will is that I should suffer, and he knows my innocence. That is what gives me confidence. My heart and my reason cry out that I shall not be disappointed. Let men and fate do their worst, we must learn to suffer in silence, everything will find its proper place in the end and sooner or later my turn will come" (French, 44; Pléiade, 1.1010). It is not Rousseau's apparent Christian resignation I have in mind when I say that this seems more on target than the complaint that "I have not deserved my fate"; it is rather the hint that however desperate his fate may be or seem, Rousseau's "turn will come"; and come it has, ever since his death but especially in the final quarter of the twentieth century. An astute observer of these matters remarked to me recently that today Rousseau is everywhere, and certainly he seems to be. And while the "everywhere" no doubt includes the disciplines of political science, philosophy, and perhaps even educational theory, its center, to which everything else holds, is without question language and literature and what the autobiographical trilogy has to tell us—which is only now beginning to be fully revealed— about the conditions and limits of language and literature and about the terms in which we are to understand linguistic possibility and literary success and failure. Rousseau's example may indeed be a monitory one—I think that it was and is—but the massiveness of his example, like the pervasiveness of his influence, cannot be denied. Henry Adams—an early modernist and even postmodernist *bien avant la lettre* (and as such the apparent model for T. S. Eliot's Gerontion)—declared in the preface to *The Education of Henry Adams,* which, it seems to me, is the more an exercise in egoism in that Ego, in the form of the personal pronoun, is absent, that "[a]s educator, Jean-Jacques was, in one respect, easily first; he erected a monument of warning against the *Ego.* Since his time, and largely thanks to him, the *Ego* has steadily tended to efface itself. . . ."[62] I will later consider the question of the Ego's effacement—a complex and intriguing question—but here I would simply remark that if Adams is correct then Rousseau stands behind not only those who, in imitation of him, have erected monuments to their own *Ego*s but also behind those who, taking the warning from his example, have (as Adams would claim for himself) refused to do so. "Jean-Jacques was . . . easily first": in how many ways is this not true?—or if not first, then in how many ways was Jean-Jacques not the crucial, pivotal, transitional figure in life-writing or self-writing between the antiquity of St. Au-

62. *The Education of Henry Adams,* in the Library of America *Henry Adams,* ed. Ernest Samuels and Jayne N. Samuels (New York, 1983), 721. The Library of America volume (which includes *Democracy, Esther, Mont Saint Michel and Chartres, The Education of Henry Adams,* and *Poems*) is cited hereafter as *Adams.*

gustine and what we have come to call the modernism and postmodernism of Samuel Beckett? One might well say that Rousseau is the middle term, the crux, of this particular trilogy—the *"donc"* that binds the beginning in Augustine to the (momentary) ending in Beckett. It was with Rousseau that both memory and narrative were cut loose from will and willed control to become undirected, compulsive, obsessional. It was with Rousseau that desire in its pure, unassimilated, nonspecific form—not nostalgia, not lust, not family yearning, but sheer desire: "les élans du désir"—became the unacknowledged but ever present motive force in all that was remembered, in all that had to be written. And writing, though disavowed, became with Rousseau compulsive. Narrative, in ever shifting, altered forms (from the linear movement of the *Confessions* through the back-and-forth structure of the *Dialogues* to the circular form of the *Reveries*) was something to be ceaselessly renewed, something literally without end except in the death of the narrator and the author. The ever shifting, altered forms represent Rousseau's attempt (to put it in Beckettian terms) to accommodate the mess and to find some form for chaos. Rousseau it was also who, in the *Dialogues,* fragmented the *I* and dispersed it among various *he*s (and at least one *I*) in a thoroughly modernist, postmodernist fashion, leaving us in no doubt, however—which is also entirely postmodern—about the overdetermined subjective investment in the different *he*s that embody in fragments the dispersed *I*. This tactic, which seems so bizarre—a kind of anachronism—in Rousseau, will become a virtual commonplace in writers of our time who, one after another, show themselves either unable or unwilling to assert *I*. And in complex ways this fragmenting and refusal of the *I* in both Rousseau and his latter-day descendants is related to altered processes of memory—one could say a failure of memory—resulting in a disjuncture of past and present. Rousseau was not only ahead of his time in pointing to the instability of meaning created in language, but he lived that instability and demonstrated it in boldface throughout his three volumes of autobiographical writing. Rousseau's progress in those three volumes reads like a paradigm of the modernist condition: disappointed by the reception given to his *Confessions* when read to members of polite French society, Rousseau reacted by removing himself from society and by splitting himself into various *he*s and *I*s in the *Dialogues;* when this proved insufficient he proclaimed the isolate self in the *Reveries* and assumed not only the possibility but the desirability of severing his own isolate self from the community and from all human contact. This, in a general way, is what Rousseau did in the history of self-writing. He cut the self loose, leaving it without ties, anchor, or direction, and to modern descendants he left as starting point what, for him, was the endpoint: a free-floating self, uncentered except in itself, and quite unreal. (An instructive comparison could be made with Montaigne, who, like Rousseau, turned always inward but seeking there the general and universal *through* the particular and individual.) Rousseau's individual is both unique and insane, unjudgeable by the experience or the criteria of others. He is the hero or the protagonist of the narratives of Dostoyevsky, Kafka, and Beckett. Outcast and self-outcast, he doesn't fit in the social world—which, from his point of view (and I use the gendered pronoun advisedly: all such heroes seem to be male), is as insane as society declares him to be. Beckett will carry this further in the passage from *Waiting for Godot* quoted as epigraph to chapter I, where he declares that this kind of Rousseauvian insanity is nothing other than the general human condition of our time. In the play, Didi and Gogo natter on and on because they do not want to hear "all the dead voices"—those voices that "make a noise like wings . . . like leaves . . . like sand . . . like leaves. . . . They all speak at once. . . . Each one to itself." This, one feels, was in the end Rousseau, enclosed within a world of insufficient language, of disjunct memory and narrative, self-circumscribed, "enlacé de soi-même," speaking incessantly but always and only to and about himself. This, one feels, is also where all the children of Jean-Jacques begin. And who, in our time, is not one of his children?

SECOND INTERLUDE

VICO *(RICORSO)*

Giambattista Vico could have foretold Rousseau's end. Indeed, he did fore-tell it, though without specific reference to the Citizen of Geneva. When a society approaches its destined end (and here once again the arc of an individual life is drawn to the same curve as the life of the society), it falls, Vico writes, "from a perfect liberty into the perfect tyranny of anarchy or the unchecked liberty of the free peoples, which is the worst of all tyran-nies" (*New Science,* para. 1102). For this disease in the social realm there are three possible remedies, according to Vico: first, "a man like Augustus" may rise from within the society, "establish himself as monarch and, by force of arms, take in hand all the institutions and all the laws, which, though sprung from liberty, no longer avail to regulate and hold it within bounds"; second, "if providence does not find such a remedy within, it seeks it outside" and may discover an external conqueror capable of impos-ing order in the same manner as Augustus; or third and worst,

> if the peoples are rotting in that ultimate civil disease and cannot agree on a monarch from within, and are not conquered and preserved by better nations from without, then providence for their extreme ill has its extreme remedy at hand. For such peoples, like so many beasts, have fallen into the custom of each man thinking only of his own private interests and have reached the extreme of delicacy, or better of pride, in which like wild animals they bristle and lash out at the slightest displeasure. Thus no matter how great the throng and press of their bodies, they live like wild beasts in a deep solitude of spirit and will, scarcely any two being able to agree since each follows his own pleasure or caprice. (*New Science,* para. 1106)

Finally, when a society has reached this lowest point, at which cities have been turned "into forests and the forests into dens and lairs of men" and peoples are "stunned and brutalized," providence decrees that the cycle shall reverse itself, and a new history, set to traverse once more the ideal eternal history, shall begin with a "few survivors" who, "returning to the primitive simplicity of the first world of peoples, are again religious, truthful, and faithful." This *ricorso* that brings the world of humans back at the end of every *corso* to a new beginning is available, however, only at the level of society, not at the level of the individual. For someone like Rousseau, whose end was a mere unfolding of his beginning and whose course of life had brought him to "a deep solitude of spirit and will," there was no starting over. There was instead what he looked forward to at the end of the *Dialogues*—great posthumous fame—and also what he could not possibly have foreseen: an influence that, one way and another, would touch virtually every subsequent practitioner of life-writing.

Though Vico's fate was not altogether different from Rousseau's, he would never have praised himself for isolation and uniqueness as Rousseau did, nor would he have recommended either of these as virtues to others. On the contrary, Vico considered isolation and "deep solitude of spirit" a great evil to be avoided if at all possible; and uniqueness held no interest for him—or for anybody else until Rousseau came along with his claim to be unlike anyone who had ever existed or would ever exist. The three institutions that Vico said were to be found in every civilization and that defined them as civilizations—religion, marriage, and burial—all point away from individuality, from isolation and uniqueness, and toward community and the civil society. In the sixth of his university inaugural orations, delivered in 1707, Vico tells us in his periautography that he "leads his hearers to meditate on themselves, how man under pain of sin is divided from man by tongue, mind and heart" (*Vita,* 144). In that oration Vico spells out just what he means by each of these divisive elements in the body politic, concluding with the observation that where individuals are divided in spirit from one another, mere bodily numbers will never compose what he intends by a civil society: "Because basic human nature has been changed by original sin," he writes, "assemblies of men may appear to be societies, but the truth is that isolation of spirits is greatest where many bodies come together."[1] And Vico goes on to provide a stunning metaphor for this "isolation of spirits . . . where many bodies come together"—a metaphor that has innumerable echoes in the literature of the twentieth century. "Even more," he says, "is it like the crowded inmates of a prison where the spirits that I have mentioned above endure punishments, each in the cell to which

1. *Giambattista Vico on Humanistic Education (Six Inaugural Orations, 1699–1707),* trans. Giorgio A. Pinton and Arthur W. Shippee (Ithaca: Cornell University Press, 1993), 129.

it is assigned." I should think that no one reading these lines in our time could fail to be reminded of Eliot's *Waste Land*—

> I have heard the key
> Turn in the door once and turn once only
> We think of the key, each in his prison
> Thinking of the key, each confirms a prison

—or of Auden's "In Memory of W. B. Yeats"—"And each in the cell of himself is almost convinced of his freedom"—or of Kafka's *Castle* and *Trial* or of Sartre's *Huis clos* or of half a hundred other instances.

Rousseau, who always wanted to be the first to do whatever it was he was doing, in this case had his wish. He was "easily first" (in Henry Adams's phrase) to turn the key on himself in the prison-house of ego; there, "in the cell of himself," he pretended to the freedom of God while despairing of ever liberating himself from the treacherous web of desire and language that was his own doing—and undoing. According to commentators, it was to escape the suffocating ubiquity of the ego in Descartes's *Discourse on Method* that Vico in his periautography abandoned use of the first-person singular pronoun in favor of third-person. While Rousseau might seem to be abandoning ego when he splits it four or five ways in the *Dialogues,* the reverse is the real truth. Instead of disappearing, ego is everywhere in the *Dialogues,* dispersed throughout the entire cast of characters. "Rousseau," "J. J." (composed both of the living man who can be seen and the "Author" who can be read), "the Frenchman," the writer of footnotes, prefaces, and afterwords—all are alter egos for Jean-Jacques Rousseau. And when we move from the *Dialogues* to the *Reveries,* from dispersal and then union of all the alter egos to isolation of a single, massive, self-enclosed ego, paranoia is the inevitable consequence. The union is all within Rousseau himself, never with anything or anyone external. It is one against many, me against them—which is immediately transformed by Rousseau into the universal conspiracy of many against one, them against me.

Mary Carruthers, contrasting what she terms the "rhetorician or prag-matist" on the one hand and the "extreme idealist or formalist" on the other (the latter, she says, "thinks of language in terms of how completely it represents the tiger, and since it can never fully get that right, would rather lapse into silence than speak"), writes thus of the former: "The rheto-rician or pragmatist, having to speak, accepts that words are all more or less in the nature of crude stick-figures, but can be used meaningfully so long as speaker and audience share a common cultural and civic bond, whether that of *civitas Romana* or *civitas Dei*, a bond forged by the memories of people and their texts."[2] Both Augustine and Vico, one remembers, were rhetoricians, bound by temperament as well as profession to a community, a community that was in some sense themselves writ large. Rousseau allowed for no such community, but what his autobiographical trilogy—set like a crown upon his lifetime's effort—reveals is that ego cannot subsist without some identifying *communitas*. He was unique among men, Rousseau claimed, or he was God-like, or he was both; but in any case he tolerated no human society between himself and himself, between himself and his maker and judge ("Let the last trump sound . . ."). And his memories were his alone. When Rousseau says of the project of his *Confessions* that it will "be necessary for what I have to say to invent a language as new as my project" (Pléiade, 1.1153), he puts forward for commendation what others would think more nearly a disaster—the absence of any common language and any common memory. According to his own view of the matter, Rousseau spoke in an idiolect, and what he spoke of one might call idiomemories. In a private language he recalled private—unshared and unshareable—memories of innocence, goodness, and absolute difference. The common memory of Paris (in the manner of tabloid journalism of our day) dwelt on five children sent to the foundling home. From the *Confessions* we can be sure Rousseau never forgot about his children or about the way they were disposed of, but, as psychotherapists are fond of saying nowadays, he was in deep denial: denial that someone of his character could be guilty of what his actions seemed to convict him of. Locked in the cell of himself, as he was both proud and miserable to be, Rousseau suffered exactly the fate Vico would have foreseen for such a person.

When I earlier cited Eliot, Auden, Kafka, and Sartre as writers who adopted Vichian metaphor, I did not mean to imply that any of them were influenced to write as they did because of Vico's example. I don't know that any of them read Vico; they may have, but this is not the point. Commentators on Vico have frequently noted that his discernible presence in subsequent writers is almost always a matter of anticipation rather than of direct influence, and this is one reason why Vico serves as well for the transit from Rousseau to the twentieth century as for the much longer one from Augustine to Rousseau. Benedetto Croce, near the end of his *Philosophy of Giambattista Vico*, writes thus of the virtual omnipresence of Vichian thought—but most often without awareness or acknowledg-

2. *The Book of Memory*, 24.

ment—throughout the nineteenth century: "These innumerable reappear-
ances of the work of an individual in the work of several generations, this
parallelism between a man and a century, justify a fanciful phrase with
which we might draw from the later developments in order to describe
Vico; namely that he is neither more nor less than the nineteenth century in
germ."[3] If he was the nineteenth century in germ, then how much more,
one might say, was he the twentieth century in germ. Well into this century
W. B. Yeats tells of the philosophic system he received in the rather inchoate
form of his wife's automatic writing and goes on to say, "When the automatic
script began, neither I nor my wife knew, or knew that we knew, that any
man had tried to explain history philosophically." Only after he had written
it all out—and, he hastens to add, only after it was published as *A Vision*—
did Yeats discover there were others before him who had turned their hand
to the philosophy of history. From Gerald Heard, Yeats says, he learned of
"Henry Adams' two essays, where I found some of the dates I had been given
and much of the same interpretation"; from the same source he was given
information about Flinders Petrie's *Revolutions of Civilisation,* "and then a few
months after the publication of the first edition of *A Vision* a translation of
Spengler's *Decline of the West* was published, and I found there a correspondence too great for coincidence between most of his essential dates and those
I had received before the publication of his first German edition." But all
these parallels to or anticipations of his own philosophical explanation of
history, as Yeats goes on to make clear, had been anticipated in their turn
by someone for whom Yeats adduces no progenitors. "After that," Yeats
writes—after Gerald Heard, Henry Adams, Flinders Petrie, and Oswald
Spengler—"I discovered for myself Spengler's main source in Vico, and that
half the revolutionary thoughts of Europe are a perversion of Vico's philosophy." Given this philosophic pedigree for the ideas communicated to him
by the instructors through the medium of George Yeats's automatic writing,
Yeats concludes, "Certainly my instructors have chosen a theme that has
deeply stirred men's minds though the newspapers are silent about it; the
newspapers have the happy counter-myth of progress; a theme as important
perhaps as Henry Adams thought when he told the Boston Historical Association that were it turned into a science powerful interests would prevent its
publication."[4] From all of this one can only suppose that Yeats must have

---

3. *The Philosophy of Giambattista Vico,* trans. R. G. Collingwood (New York: Macmillan, 1913), 243.
4. *A Vision* (London: Macmillan, 1937), 261–62.

intended Vico to be among those to whom he paid tribute in his little poem "Gratitude to the Unknown Instructors":

> What they undertook to do
> They brought to pass;
> All things hang like a drop of dew
> Upon a blade of grass.

If Vico could say of St. Augustine that he was his "particular protector," Yeats could say much the same of Vico in his own case.

That Vico was an Unknown Instructor to Henry Adams also, shaping with his ghostly hand such characteristic passages as the concluding chapters of *The Education of Henry Adams* (especially "A Dynamic Theory of History" and "A Law of Acceleration"), the "Letter to American Teachers of History," and the "Rule of Phase Applied to History," seems, in Yeatsian terms, an inevitable conclusion though, as Instructor, he remained truly Unknown to Adams. It strikes one as odd that Adams, omnivorous reader that he was and especially devoted to books in which life-writing mingled with history, with philosophy, and with the philosophy of history, should have remained unaware of Vico. When, in old age, he had his vision of how the rule of phase should be applied to history and called on teachers of American history to follow him in creating a new science that would explain the cycles through which history passes, has passed, and must always pass, Adams could well have used the intellectual support of Vico, who had first thought it all out more than a century and a half earlier. Moreover, had he known enough of Vico to be familiar with his periautography as well as the *New Science,* Adams could have found a predecessor much closer to himself than either the admired Augustine or the reviled Rousseau, a predecessor who, like Adams in his *Education,* wrapped his philosophy of history into and around his autobiography and thus generated his own life story formally out of the necessary story of humanity—and vice versa. Adams's lack of awareness of Vico shows clearly, I believe, in a letter of 1908 to William James in which he says of the *Education* that "it interests me chiefly as a literary experiment, hitherto, as far as I know, never tried or never successful."[5] Adams might mean a number of different things in calling the book "a literary experiment." He could be referring to his adoption of the third person to render his own past experience; he might have in mind the view he gives of his life as captive to a historical cycle moving

---

5. *The Letters of Henry Adams,* ed. J. C. Levenson, Ernest Samuels, Charles Vandersee, and Viola Hopkins Winner, 6 vols. (Cambridge: Harvard University Press, 1988), 6.118; cited hereafter as *Letters.*

at a continually accelerating speed; he could also be thinking of what the editor's preface to the *Education* describes as his attempt "to work into it [i.e., the *Education*] his favorite theory of history." But if it is any one of these that Adams means, then Vico has been there before him with his periautography, the only difference between the two being that Adams's anxiety—albeit veiled and disguised as pessimism by his persistent irony—is much greater than Vico's in the face of the tragic pattern inevitably displayed by all history, but especially at the individual level.[6]

Although he seems to have been ignorant of Vico as predecessor, Adams, as both his letters and the *Education* show, was well aware of a tradition of life-writing that included Augustine and Rousseau as central figures. Writing again to William James, who had responded to reception of the *Education* by describing it as "a hodge-podge of world-fact, private fact, philosophy, irony, (with the word 'education' stirred in too much for my appreciation!) which gives a unique cachet to the thing, and gives a very pleasant *gesammt-eindruck* of H. A.'s *Self*," Adams asked, "Did you ever read the Confessions of St Augustine, or of Cardinal de Retz, or of Rousseau, or of Benvenuto Cellini, or even of my dear Gibbon[?]" And he goes on to say of the first of these, who at least in part succeeded where the rest (and Adams himself even more than those he names) were destined to fail, "Of them all, I think St Augustine alone has an idea of literary form,—a notion of writing a story with an end and object, not for the sake of the object, but for the form, like a romance. I have worked ten years to satisfy myself that the thing cannot be done today" (*Letters*, 6.119–20). Unpropitious as the circumstances were for Adams in 1908, one would have to say that they were only to get worse as the century wore on, for Samuel Beckett (born in 1906) worked for fifty years and more to satisfy himself that the thing could not be done in his day—but succeeded nevertheless in satisfying a great many readers, paradoxically, that he had done it.

In his own preface to *The Education of Henry Adams* and in the editor's preface (which was really his as well since Adams wrote it himself and left it behind for Henry Cabot Lodge to sign after its author should be safely

---

6. It was this pervasive tendency in Adams to muddle together anxiety, irony, and pessimism in a brilliant show of intelligence that caused William James to write to him with considerable exasperation, "To tell the truth, it [Adams's "Letter to American Teachers of History"] doesn't impress me at all, save by its wit and erudition; and I ask you whether an old man soon about to meet his Maker can hope to save himself from the consequences of his life by pointing to the wit and learning he has shown in treating a tragic subject. No, sir, you can't do it, can't impress God in that way" (*The Selected Letters of William James,* ed. Elizabeth Hardwick [New York: Farrar, Straus and Cudahy, 1961], 263).

dead) Adams invoked his two principal predecessors—what one might call, in contrast to Vico, his Known Instructors—in the tradition of Western life-writing. In the editor's preface he has Lodge claiming (in a ruse that might remind the reader of Rousseau in the *Dialogues* or Beckett in *Company* or Nabokov in *Pale Fire* or . . .) that Adams "used to say . . . that his great ambition was to complete St. Augustine's 'Confessions,' but that St. Augustine, like a great artist, had worked from multiplicity to unity, while he, like a small one, had to reverse the method and work back from unity to multiplicity. The scheme became unmanageable as he approached his end" (*Adams*, 719). It is characteristic of Adams that he should want to write his death into his life—and even to place it before the beginning of the life—for it was this same Henry Adams who wrote of his *Education*, not this time to William but to Henry James, "The volume is a mere shield of protection in the grave. I advise you to take your own life in the same way, in order to prevent biographers from taking it in theirs" (*Letters*, 6.136). With this twofold, prevenient act of suicide, committed both in the editor's preface and in the text proper, Adams had no need to try to foretell his own end; he could instead look back on it from after the fact. But is this not what any writer possessed of a Vichian understanding of the cycles and phases of history should be capable of? It was just this understanding that allowed W. B. Yeats to write his own epitaph—

> Under bare Ben Bulben's head
> In Drumcliff churchyard Yeats is laid . . .
> On limestone quarried near the spot
> By his command these words are cut:
> > *Cast a cold eye*
> > *On life, on death.*
> > *Horseman, pass by!*

—and this that could tell any committed Vichian of his own and a cycle's end.

In a letter of 1909 to Barrett Wendell, Henry Adams drew himself, Augustine, and Rousseau together into a circle of life-writers and declared them all failures because, as he puts it, "We have . . . undertaken to do what cannot be successfully done—mix narrative and didactic purpose and style." Yet for the failure he finds a kind of justification, which sounds not unlike what any number of subsequent practitioners of the art might have said in their own behalf: "The charm of the effort is not in winning the game but in playing it. We all enjoy the failure." As to his particular kind of failure (Augustine's was that his "narrative subsides at last into the dry sands of metaphysical theology"; Rousseau's was that his "narrative . . .

subsides into still less artistic egoism"), Adams says, "I found that a narrative style was so incompatible with a didactic or scientific style, that I had to write a long supplementary chapter to explain in scientific terms what I could not put into narration without ruining the narrative" (*Letters,* 6.237– 38). Putting aside the supposed failures of Augustine and Rousseau, one could reasonably argue that it is on precisely those same grounds on which Adams acknowledges failure that success might well be claimed for Vico, for Vico conceived of his periautography scientifically and of his new science autographically and allowed for no split between the two. Adams, by his own account, tried for the same seamless narrative-didactic effect but failed, the narrative and the science falling out separately for him, one into the first thirty-two chapters of the *Education,* the other into the last three chapters and the posthumously published "Letter to American Teachers of History" and "Rule of Phase Applied to History." One might imagine that Adams would say with Beckett that he had attempted "to find a form that accommodates the mess" and had failed, but Vico, I think, would admit to no such failure. At any rate, the intention and the attempt were shared not by Adams and Beckett alone but by Vico as well. As Adams puts the matter in the circular letter written to professors of history to accompany the "Rule of Phase Applied to History," any teacher who follows him "will conceive of the University as a system of education grouped about History, a main current of thought branching out, like a tree, into endless forms of activity, in regular development, according to the laws of physics; and to be studied as a single stream, not as now by a multiversal, but by a universal law; not as a scientific but as a historical unity; not as a practice of technical handling, but as a process of mental evolution in history, controlled, like the evolution of any series of chemical or electric equilibria, by one general formula" (*Letters,* 6.207). The rule of phase was, for Henry Adams, literally the new science of his time, and from an early age he was determined to work out the principles of (and to practice) what he termed "scientific history." Disregarding minor stylistic differences, I would defy any reader who has a general knowledge of the thought of Vico and Adams but not a specific knowledge of the following passage to say which man wrote it: "In this work he finally discovers in its full extent that principle which in his previous works he had as yet understood only in a confused and indistinct way. . . . By the light of this new critical method the origins of almost all the disciplines, whether sciences or arts, which are necessary if we are to discuss with clarity of ideas and propriety of language the natural law of nations, are discovered to be quite different from those that have previously been imagined." Certain characteristic terms (e.g., "the natural law of nations") might reveal to the discerning reader that this is Vico (*Vita,* 166–67), as might also the claim to success, but the project of arranging all thought according to an entirely new philosophy of history was as much Adams's as Vico's.

Moreover, for all his ironic self-belittling, there are many readers who would feel that Adams was not such a failure as he confessed to (or exulted in?) being. The last three chapters of the *Education* are very compelling reading for those looking back on them from all decades of this century. "Simplicity may not be evidence of truth," Adams writes in the "Letter to American Teachers of History," "and unity is perhaps the most deceptive of all the innumerable illusions of mind; but both are primary instincts in man, and have an attraction on the mind akin to that of gravitation on matter."[7] Deceptive it may be—Adams would never be caught making an assertion about something as grand as unity without immediate qualification if not outright denigration—but in age Adams was as determined as Yeats was in youth "to hammer his thoughts into unity," and the formula he sought for the history of mind—his mind and the mind of mankind—was the most daring attempt at unity imaginable. Adams felt that in the book immediately preceding the *Education* he had discovered social, intellectual, emotional unity, but it was not of his time, not of the nineteenth century, most certainly not of the end of a millennium. In *Mont Saint Michel and Chartres* Adams went back to the twelfth century to find unity, and after that the pull was all, at an ever accelerating pace, away from unity toward multiplicity, which is to say, if there be no formula to describe and control the process, away from unity toward fragmentation, anarchy, disorder.

Mont Saint Michel and Chartres is a long book but not so long as *The Education of Henry Adams,* for it is a relatively easier task to define and describe unity in a distant century than to construct a scientifically precise formula for something approaching chaos in the present. The only thing one can think to say to make the task Adams undertakes in the *Education* seem marginally less burdensome is that it is not quite so heavy or so maddening as what Beckett would face fifty years later. Yet what Adams attempts is not essentially different from the effort of either Vico before him or Beckett after: to find the narrative—and the metanarrative—form for (and now we go all the way back before Adams, before Rousseau, before

---

7. *The Degradation of the Democratic Dogma* (New York: Macmillan, 1920), 241–42. This posthumously published volume contains three pieces by Henry Adams—"The Tendency of History," "A Letter to American Teachers of History," and "The Rule of Phase Applied to History"—as well as a long introductory essay by Brooks Adams, "The Heritage of Henry Adams."

Vico to Augustine) "the whole of [an] action . . . , the whole of a man's life, of which all of his actions are parts . . . , [and] the whole history of humanity, of which the lives of all men are parts" (*Conf.,* 11.28, 282). *And the metanarrative:* this it was that Adams found so difficult—to bring the theory and the science into one with the narrative—and that made him feel that not only he but Augustine and Rousseau as well had failed. Was Adams, however, such a failure as he liked to say? Toward the end of "Vis Nova," the fourth-from-the-last chapter of the *Education,* Adams tells how a series of events in 1904 caused him to reflect that the Virgin, who had been his preeminent symbol for medieval unity, had "never looked so win-ning,—so One,—as in this scandalous failure of her Grace. To what pur-pose had she existed, if, after nineteen hundred years, the world was blood-ier than when she was born?" This leads Adams to turn from the "stupendous failure of Christianity" to provide a satisfactory formula for unity and to ponder where, then, such a formula is to be sought. "To the tired student, the idea that he must give it up seemed sheer senility. As long as he could whisper, he would go on as he had begun, bluntly refusing to meet his creator with the admission that the creation had taught him nothing" but an entirely trivial equation that stated "that the square of the hypothenuse might for convenience be taken as equal to something else." Tired as the student Adams might be, this is nowhere good enough for him; and like Beckett's Unnamable, who can't go on but must go on and will go on, he vows that "[a]s long as he could whisper, he would go on as he had begun."

> Every man with self-respect enough to become effective, if only as a machine, has had to account to himself for himself somehow, and to invent a formula of his own for his universe, if the standard formulas failed. . . .
>
> The effort must begin at once, for time pressed. The old formulas had failed, and a new one had to be made, but, after all, the object was not extrava-gant or eccentric. One sought no absolute truth. One sought only a spool on which to wind the thread of history without breaking it. Among indefinite possible orbits, one sought the orbit which would best satisfy the observed movement of the runaway star Groombridge, 1838,[8] commonly called Henry Adams. (*Adams,* 1151)

As the Vichian Yeats puts it, in very nearly the same accents as the Vichian manqué Adams, "When I remember that Shelley calls our minds 'mirrors

---

8. The Library of America *Adams* glosses the reference thus: "Stephen Groombridge (1755–1832). In 1838, the year of Adams's birth, his *Catalogue of Circumpolar Stars* was pub-lished posthumously; it recorded his discovery of star No. 1830, the swiftest moving of all observed stars."

of the fire for which all thirst,' I cannot but ask the question all have asked, 'What or who has cracked the mirror?' I begin to study the only self that I can know, myself, and to wind the thread upon the pern again."[9] The old formulas having failed, Adams would wind the thread of history and the thread of himself anew onto a single spool, tracing the orbit of the runaway star Groombridge as it "perne[s] in a gyre" both individual and universal. Adams's newly conceived formulas, verbal now, not mathematical, are to be found as narrative theory in the next two chapters of the *Education* ("A Dynamic Theory of History" and "A Law of Acceleration"), in the "Letter to American Teachers of History," and in the "Rule of Phase Applied to History"; and they are to be found as narrative practice in the *Education* as a whole. When, in "Nunc Age," Adams begins to wind his narrative to its close with the death of John Hay and his own imagined death, he writes, "There it ended! Shakespeare himself could use no more than the common-place to express what is incapable of expression. 'The rest is silence!' " This is the silence of Augustine, after so many words, the silence surrounding Rousseau after the reading of the *Confessions* and the silence of his *Reveries;* it is the silence of Vico without memory and of Beckett with no more words: "Till finally you hear how words are coming to an end. . . . And how better in the end labour lost and silence." "It was time to go," Adams says:

> The three friends had begun life together; and the last of the three had no motive,—no attraction—to carry it on after the others had gone. Education had ended for all three, and only beyond some remoter horizon could its values be fixed or renewed. Perhaps some day—say 1938, their centenary,— they might be allowed to return together for a holiday, to see the mistakes of their own lives made clear in the light of the mistakes of their successors; and perhaps then, for the first time since man began his education among the carnivores, they would find a world that sensitive and timid natures could regard without a shudder. (*Adams,* 1181)

It is difficult to account for this final sentence except as Adams's ultimate ironic gesture. He may not have known anything of Vico, but Adams knew all anyone could know about phases and cycles, and as T. S. Eliot has Gerontion-cum-Adams asking, "After such knowledge, what forgiveness?" Adams died in the midst of the First World War, full of years and pessimism, and the suggestion that he might return twenty years later on the eve of the Second World War to find a world new-designed for sensitive and timid natures can only have been a joke, unless (which would be worse

9. *Per Amica Silentia Lunae,* in *Mythologies* (New York: Macmillan, 1959), 364.

to think) it represented a complete failure of Adams's accustomed and acute prescience.

For all the similarities in their thought, Adams differs markedly from Vico in the irony that is his stylistic hallmark. When, in the *New Science,* Vico describes the four tropes by means of which primitive humanity fashioned a knowable world for itself—metaphor, metonymy, synecdoche, and irony—he is once again insisting that humankind can know only what it has made. But of these four tropes only three have the honor of participating in that earliest stage of shaping and knowing that Vico terms "poetic wisdom." Metaphor, metonymy, and synecdoche are all primary tools of poetic wisdom, but irony comes into play only later, when humanity has attained to the level of reflection. After praising the imaginative powers of the first three tropes, Vico goes on to consider the fourth: "Irony certainly could not have begun until the period of reflection. . . ." And why? The reason is very interesting. Irony, Vico says, had no place in poetic wisdom and could have begun only with reflection "because it is fashioned of falsehood by dint of a reflection which wears the mask of truth." The very earliest human beings, Vico implies, were like Swift's Houyhnhnms, who knew not the practice of lying and had, therefore, to resort to an ad hoc definition of this most characteristic speech act of Yahoos and humans: *to say the thing which is not.* But when the first humans proceeded to the stage of reflection, Vico says, then they acquired the capacity for falsehood and irony. "Here emerges a great principle of human institutions, confirming the origin of poetry disclosed in this work: that since the first men of the gentile world had the simplicity of children, who are truthful by nature, the first fables could not feign anything false; they must therefore have been . . . true narrations" (*New Science,* para. 408). Thus in his own narrative as in the narrative we call history it is crucially important that the narrator, the historian, the periautographer remember back to the beginning, "For he now recognizes," Vico writes of himself in his periautography, "an indispensable and even human necessity to seek the first origins of this science in the beginnings of sacred history" (*Vita,* 166), where the narration is true and human events may be understood as they had, have, and will have to be. Perhaps the pervasive irony in Adams's writing means that he did not get back to Vico's "beginnings," and his not getting all the way back may account in turn for the extreme pessimism of his late years; for the poetic mind of humankind, the first mind, is imaginative and creative, but the reflective mind—and Adams agreed with Vico about this—is not. For better and for worse, Adams's was a reflective mind through and through, and exercising the full powers of reflectivity he was caught in a tragic intellectual bind. He could perceive the tragedy of human existence but could neither free himself of it nor make anything out of it.

Be that as it may, Adams stood for the same set of intertwined principles at the end of the nineteenth century as Vico stood for early in the eighteenth: that one can know only what one has made (the *verum-factum* principle described in the first interlude); that human beings make history as the individual human makes a life, and thus both history and life-history are humanly knowable; and that there is a kind of reciprocity between these two activities that means that we must understand history in the light of our own lives and our own lives in the light of history. It was on this ground that Adams, seeking a spool on which to wind the thread of history, chose, as nearest to hand and most knowable, the orbit of "the runaway star Groombridge, 1838, commonly called Henry Adams." The *verum-factum* principle, first stated by Vico but implicitly accepted by Adams as well, is nothing other than the principle of interpretation known as the hermeneutical circle. In its original sense, the hermeneutical circle had to do with biblical exegesis and interpretation and took the form of a paradox that might be expressed thus: We must understand in order to believe, but we must believe in order to understand. (This is precisely the paradox or the dilemma we find recounted in the first 7½ books of Augustine's *Confessions*—i.e., up to the point of conversion. Augustine could not believe because he failed to comprehend the Scriptures in all their simplicity, and he could not comprehend the Scriptures because he did not believe.) A second, related sense of the hermeneutical circle, having to do with Scripture but with other kinds of writing as well, says that we can understand a text only from a basis of previous self-understanding, but our self-understanding, at least in the context of our reading, is contingent upon the understanding we have of the meaning created in the text; there is thus a correlation and reciprocity between self-understanding and text-understanding, and the responsive reader—i.e., one who properly engages the hermeneutical circle—profoundly implicates a life and an understanding of that life in the interpretation of a text and, if the text be one of life-writing, in the interpretation of another life. A final, somewhat different, sense of the hermeneutical circle says that we can understand a whole—whether it be a whole text or a whole life—only by understanding first the parts, but we can understand any part or parts only by understanding first the whole. In Vichian terms this might be expressed in the following manner: We can understand only what we have made, but we can make only what we have understood. The hermeneutical circle is intensely paradoxical, but as Paul Ricoeur has argued, the circle is not a vicious one because there exists the possibility of continual movement from one term to the other and back again with incremental advances achieved in each movement. So we can begin, say, with some small self-understanding, which we bring to a text, and from the increased understanding thereby acquired return to a greater understanding of ourselves and so on; and the same with the part and the whole, with comprehension and belief.

Wilhelm Dilthey, whose life was almost exactly contemporary with Adams's, brings Vichian thought to bear on the writing of history on the one hand and the writing of autobiography on the other when he declares,

> Autobiography is the highest and most instructive form in which the understanding of life confronts us. Here is the outward, phenomenal course of a life which forms the basis for understanding what has produced it within a certain environment. The man who understands it is the same as the one who created it. A particular intimacy of understanding results from this. The person who seeks the connecting threads in the history of his life has already, from different points of view, created a coherence in that life which he is now putting into words. . . .
>
> Here we approach the root of all historical comprehension. Autobiography is merely the literary expression of a man's reflection on the course of his life.[10]

The continual oscillation that he imagines between life and world, between life and text, and between self-understanding and historical comprehension leads Dilthey to claim that "[t]he course of a historical personality's life is a system of interactions in which the individual receives stimuli from the historical world, is moulded by them and, then, in his turn, affects the historical world. The stimuli originate in part of the world context which, in its turn, is shaped by the actions of the individual."[11] Here we see the hermeneutical circle at full play as both the maker and the interpreter move back and forth, back and forth, as Vico would do—and *could* do, because they were both narratives, and isomorphic narratives at that—between the *storia ideale eterna* and the *storia* that was his own life and his *Vita,* or as Adams would do between his "Dynamic Theory of History" or the "Rule of Phase Applied to History" and *The Education of Henry Adams.* Georges Gusdorf has written that the motto of all autobiography ought to be "Faire et en faisant se faire: To make and in making to be made," which draws the autobiographical act right around into a compact hermeneutical cir-

10. *Meaning in History,* ed. H. P. Rickman (London: Allen and Unwin, 1961), 85–86.
11. *Meaning in History,* 90.

cle and simultaneously permits it to expand to the dimensions of universal history.

The biographer of Henry Adams, Ernest Samuels, tells us that in spite of the slighting remarks Adams makes in the *Education* about his years at Harvard, he first encountered there intimations of "that Tannhäuser quest upon which the prospective historian must embark. He must establish the continuity of history."[12] This would mean discovering genetic principles of cause and consequence, narratives of beginning, middle, and end, and, being Vichian without knowing it, it would mean an eventual vision of cycles and recurrence. The editors of Vico's *New Science,* attempting to define his *corso* and *ricorso,* write, "Course and recourse, as in the flow and ebb of the tides, may mean traversing the same stages in opposite directions; or recourse may mean simple recurrence, a coming back or around of some particular event or state of affairs; but the strongest and most literal meaning is a retraversing of the same stages in the same order" (*New Science,* xlii). I hope it will not seem extravagant to suggest that in this "strongest" sense Adams performs the *ricorso* to Vico's original *corso.* As Vico thought hard and long before he arrived at his cyclical vision of history so also did Adams, and the understanding of history they came to was the same understanding. How could it not be, either or both of them might say, since it is true, describing as it does the way things had, have, and will have to be. Samuel Beckett, in his essay on the presence of Vico in Joyce's *Finnegans Wake,* writes of the force "of a Necessity that is not Fate, of a Liberty that is not Chance," and says that Vico, "with his tongue, one feels, very much in his cheek," called this force "Divine Providence." Beckett immediately qualifies the term, however, even if it was only offered tongue in cheek by Vico, saying, "This is not Bossuet's Providence, transcendental and miraculous, but immanent and the stuff itself of human life, working by natural means. Humanity is its work in itself. God acts on her, but by means of her. Humanity is divine, but no man is divine."[13] This is the real meaning of the continuity that Adams was destined to seek in history. And though he, too, might have to lodge his tongue firmly in his cheek before calling it "Divine Providence," surely he is thinking of the same force "of a Necessity that is not Fate, of a Liberty that is not Chance . . . , working by natural means" when he writes, in something that sounds very like a credo, "If the historian will only consent to shut his eyes for a moment to the microscopic analysis of personal motives and idiosyncrasies, he cannot but be-

---

12. Ernest Samuels, *Henry Adams* (Cambridge: Harvard University Press, 1989), 14.
13. "Dante . . . Bruno . Vico . . Joyce," in *I Can't Go On, I'll Go On,* 111.

come conscious of a silent pulsation that commands his respect, a steady movement that resembles in its mode of operation the mechanical action of Nature herself."[14] Rousseau had it wrong when, in the *Reveries,* he claimed a God-like solitude and sufficiency, but if we put aside his claims to uniqueness, Rousseau's story, like Vico's story and Adams's, like the story of Humphrey Chimpden Earwicker and the story of the Unnamable, is the story of humanity. They are all of them—and yes, Augustine too, although he might not approve of some of the shenanigans of *Finnegans Wake*—present, mourning and rejoicing, at Finnegan's wake, present also at Finnegan's cyclical reawakening as, adopting the initials of Humphrey Chimpden Earwicker, he assumes the lineaments of humanity: Here Comes Everybody.

14. Samuels, *Henry Adams,* 114.

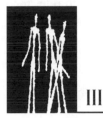

III

NOT I

On the second page of *Watt* a characteristic Beckettian footnote informs the reader that "[m]uch valuable space has been saved, in this work, that would otherwise have been lost, by avoidance of the plethoric reflexive pronoun after *say*."[1] I take it that Beckett is mostly joking when he speaks here of "the plethoric reflexive pronoun," but elsewhere he was deeply serious about pronouns, their use and abuse, their referential capacity and incapacity. In his vocabulary, pronouns demanded to be treated with extraordinary care and concern. The first-person personal pronoun is not, in the ordinary grammatical sense, reflexive, nor does its occurrence or nonoccurrence have anything to do with *say,* and whether it is always, sometimes, or never "plethoric" would doubtless depend on the attitude of the person making the judgment; but that "the first personal singular and a fortiori plural pronoun had never any place in [Beckett's] vocabulary" (*Company,* 61) and that the *I* is distrusted and by declared principle avoided, in theory if not in fact, in all the later work—say from the Trilogy (*Molloy, Malone Dies, The Unnamable*) on—is incontestable. Were this banishment

---

1. *Watt* (London: John Calder, 1976), 6. The footnote is attached to a passage in which Mr. Hackett observes a man and woman seated on a bench, apparently waiting for a tram: "[T]he lady held the gentleman by the ears, and the gentleman's hand was on the lady's thigh, and the lady's tongue was in the gentleman's mouth. Tired of waiting for the tram, said Mr. Hackett, they strike up an acquaintance. The lady now removing her tongue from the gentleman's mouth, he put his into hers. Fair do, said Mr. Hackett." I assume that the footnote means that "to himself" has been omitted after "said Mr. Hackett." Unless I am mistaken, these are the only two instances in the novel where a character is clearly speaking to himself or herself; thus it is rather an exaggeration to say that "much valuable space" is saved. On the other hand, there is a certain amount of dialogue in *Watt* (for example, the "short statement" produced by Arsene, pp. 36–72), and if we are to understand that *all* of it is characters speaking only to themselves, this would cast quite a striking interpretative light on the speech acts of the novel.

of the *I* peculiar to Beckett it would still have a clear interest and relevance for us in thinking about his work, but when one considers the number of life-writers of the twentieth century who have likewise shunned the *I* or called its use into question (for reasons similar to Beckett's or not), and when one realizes that there is a prehistory for this phenomenon, then Beckett's pronominal thought and practice assume a certain paradigmatic significance.

In her little book titled *Memory,* Mary Warnock considers what legitimate meaning might be assigned the question *Am I the same person as I was forty years ago?* Although, as she says, it "seems in some way to contain its own answer by its use of the first-person pronoun," the question nevertheless "can be understood, and may be quite seriously raised."[2] Leaving aside for a moment the question Warnock is concerned with, I want to ponder the answer she says seems contained in "use of the first-person pronoun." What if this pronoun were used to make a negative statement—*I am not the same person I was forty years ago?* Does this use of the *I* provide the same answer as in Warnock's question? Does the double use of the first-person pronoun for present ("I am not the same person") and past ("I was forty years ago") controvert the statement made by the sentence? Moreover, if deployment of the *I* can claim to guarantee self-sameness or identity of being for a period from forty years in the past to the present moment, then what should we say about life-writers like Vico and Adams who choose *he* rather than *I* for their past selves? What about Rousseau, who so multiplies and disperses the *I* in the *Dialogues* that the concept of self-sameness has no meaning? What about Gertrude Stein, whose *I* belongs to Alice B. Toklas? or Franz Kafka, who substitutes *I* for *he* and *he* for *I* with such astonishing rapidity? or Richard Wright, whose *I* in *Black Boy* is clearly *he,* though the fact is never acknowledged? or Maxine Hong Kingston, who claims that she had infinite difficulty understanding and writing the character *I* in grade school? or Nathalie Sarraute, whose *I* in *Childhood* is split into a dialogic *I* and *you?* or Christa Wolf and Ronald Fraser, who, in *Patterns of Childhood* and *In Search of a Past* respectively, employ every pronoun but *I* until the final pages? What about Rimbaud, who wrenched grammar into a defining phrase for the modern world with his *Je est un autre?* And most of all, what about Beckett, whose *Not I*—a very short play in which the only speaking character, Mouth, recounts a life story, but each time it begins to appear to be her story she cries out with frantic intensity,

---

2. Mary Warnock, *Memory* (London: Faber and Faber, 1987), 68; subsequent citations will be given in the text.

in what Beckett describes as a "vehement refusal to relinquish third person," ". . . what? . . . who? . . . no! . . . she! . . . SHE! . . ." For all of them, in any case, it is "She! . . . SHE! . . . He! . . . HE! . . . Not I! . . . Not I!"— or at least not any *I* that can be stretched so far as to cover a consciousness of forty years ago and one of the present.

It is memory, of course, or our belief in the capacity of memory, that would cause any of us to assert, *I am the same person I was forty years ago.* Elsewhere in *Memory,* Mary Warnock speaks of "the sense in which memory and imagination overlap and cannot be wholly distinguished. Both consist in thinking of things in their absence" (p. 12). By "things" Warnock no doubt means objects, events, persons, and the like, but could we not say the same of the self or the *I*—that memory consists in thinking of the *I* in its absence . . . and in its presence? Might not the *I* be constituted in and by the act of thinking about itself? And how much difference is there, in this case, between absence and presence? One might say that an *I* remembered from forty years ago has a ghostly presence in the linguistic *I* spoken or written now. But surely it is the absence of the *I,* past or present, and the failure of memory to make it anything more than ghostly that so troubles (or delights) modern writers. What most would lament, W. B. Yeats celebrates when he declares "that all happiness depends on the energy to assume the mask of some other self; that all joyous or creative life is a rebirth as something not oneself, *something which has no memory* and is created in a moment and perpetually renewed."[3] Yeats would make "je un autre" by the deliberate adoption of another's name, by taking an other—or the other's—memoryless pronoun, *you* or *he,* and assigning to it the pronoun *I.* It is Beckett's particular genius—and perhaps the genius of the modernist writer in general—to lament and celebrate simultaneously, to sing a threnody for the *I* that at the same time effects its perpetual rebirth, to say the self and simultaneously deny the possibility of such saying, to speak a *he* that hides an *I* or an *I* forever disappearing into a series of *hes.* "[I]t's always he who speaks," the voice of *The Unnamable* says of someone who is neither named nor namable, "Mercier never spoke, Moran never spoke, I never spoke, I seem to speak, that's because he says I as if he were I . . ." (*Trilogy,* 371). The mind reels. Who is *he?* Who is *I? He* is no doubt the same one who, in *Company,* is said to be devising it all for company. But we cannot name him Beckett, at least not without multiple sets of quotation marks around the name—so multiple, in fact, that they represent the infinite regress that will yield neither a name nor an *I.* The voice of *The Unnamable,* Maurice

3. W. B. Yeats, *Autobiographies* (London: Macmillan, 1955), 503; italics are mine.

Blanchot has said, suffers "the worst degradation, that of losing the power to say, 'I.' "[4] It is quite impossible, in fact, to determine who the Unnamable is, whether the voice that speaks throughout or "the devised deviser devising it all for company" (*Company,* 46), the latter the created creature of his own creation.

In *Company,* which is structured on a series of undeniable memories— undeniable both in the sense that it cannot be denied that these are memories and in the sense that the memories are obsessive and will not be denied—the question becomes, *Whose are the memories? His? Yours?* They can scarcely be *mine* since the text has no *I.* But what does it mean, outside science fiction, to say that I can have your memories, you can have his, or he can have mine? When Kafka writes, "I am a memory come alive,"[5] can we fairly alter the expression, à la Rimbaud—but with an effect the opposite of his—to read, "*I* is memory come alive"? This would be to conceive of memory as the sole ground of subjectivity and source of identity, but it would also imply a unity of consciousness and a continuity of being—figured in language—that is quite at odds with the general tenor of modernist and postmodernist writing. Kafka was of two minds about the issue, as was Beckett, and their shared ambivalence may fairly be taken to represent the certain uncertainty of our time. The most dramatic instance of "memory come alive" in Beckett may well be in *Krapp's Last Tape,* where Krapp's voice of thirty years ago comes alive from the tape recorder to speak directly to Krapp now and to be answered by him, with both voices wielding the first-person pronoun that theoretically should ensure sameness in spite of temporal separation. But of this colloquy across time we must ask, in a slight revision of Warnock's question, "Is *I* the same person *I* was thirty years ago?" Although the sixty-nine-year-old Krapp seems quite sure of the answer—"[H]ard to believe I was ever as bad as that. Thank God that's all done with anyway"—the truth of the play is that he both is and is not the same; and when the older Krapp uses the first-person pronoun to say, in effect, *I am not the same person I was thirty and forty years ago,* the sentence's statement holds good—he is not the same person—but so too does the linguistic tie that binds *I* to *I*—the *I* he uses for now is the same *I* he uses for then. Betrayed by the emotions that draw him back thirty years and more, Krapp seems to want to cry out in the tones of Mouth in *Not I*—". . . what? . . . who? . . . no! . . . he! . . . HE!

    4. Maurice Blanchot, "Where Now? Who Now?" in S. E. Gontarski, ed., *On Beckett: Essays and Criticism* (New York: Grove Press, 1986), 144.
    5. *The Diaries of Franz Kafka,* ed. Max Brod (Harmondsworth: Penguin, 1964), 392.

. . ."—but virtually the last words spoken in the play by the aged Krapp are not the "Not I" of Mouth, nor even the incredulous question of Speaker in *A Piece of Monologue*—"He?"—but rather the "Be again, be again" of one who would say *I* if he could, but can't—of one, that is, who not only would acknowledge a past self as his own but also yearns for an impossible return to the past.

It was all very different in the beginning with St. Augustine, and not only because he would have been appalled at the idea of wanting to "be again, be again" the "wretched young man that I was—even more wretched at the beginning of my youth" (*Conf.*, 8.7, 173). On the contrary, in a way that few life-writers of the twentieth century seem to be, he was confident in uttering the *I* because he believed his ability to do so was grounded in a memory that, in spite of conversion and all else, made him the same person he had been, was, and would be, but this without a Rousseauvian desire to return to the past. Augustine could say that he was a question to himself, but it was not because, like Krapp, he failed to recognize an earlier self: the question of himself was there at every age, from the onset of memory to the time of writing, as unanswerable as the mystery of his being was impenetrable. It may be that Augustine's assurance in using the first-person pronoun was owing to a strong individual memory or perhaps to superior techniques of memory training. Whatever the explanation, the first nine books of the *Confessions,* Augustine tells us, confess "what I have been," books 10 and 11 confess "what I am" (*Conf.*, 10.4, 213); and for him there is no categorical difference between confessing what he remembers himself to have been and what he now discovers himself to be: "It is I myself who remember, I, the mind" (*Conf.*, 10.16, 226). Augustine shows no hesitancy about use of the *ego* here; indeed, he doubles it ("ego sum, qui memini, ego animus"), as in another passage he *re*doubles it with "ego, ego animus" (10.6, 215)—I, I the soul, I the mind, I the self. Memory is profoundly mysterious for Augustine, but what he seems sure of is its concomitance with selfhood. "[T]his force of my memory is incomprehensible to me," he writes, "even though, without it, I should not be able to call myself myself" (*Conf.*, 10.16, 226).

No reader of Rousseau's *Confessions* would complain about any infrequency of the first-person pronoun in that book. The first word of the first paragraph is "Je," and the last word of the same paragraph is "moi," and this copulative relationship between subject and reflexive pronoun (a true "plethoric reflexive pronoun," to adopt the phrase from *Watt*) pretty much establishes the pattern of the volume. "Je forme une entreprise qui n'eut jamais d'éxemple, et dont l'exécution n'aura point d'imitateur. Je veux montrer à mes semblables un homme dans toute la vérité de la nature; et cet homme, ce sera moi: I have resolved on an enterprise which has no precedent, and which, once complete, will have no imitator. My purpose is to display to my kind a portrait in every way true to nature, and the man I shall portray will be myself" (Cohen, 17; Pléiade, 1.5). Again, in one of the fragmentary "Ébauches des Confessions," Rousseau transports himself right to the heart of the twentieth century, binding himself linguistically to himself with *je* and *moi-même* even as he treats himself semantically as another, as a *he* consigned to the past: "J'écris la vie d'un homme qui n'est plus, mais que j'ai bien connu, qu'ame vivante n'a connu que moi et qui merita de l'être. Cet homme c'est moi même [I am writing the life of a man who is no longer, but whom I knew well; one who was known to no living soul but me, yet was well worth knowing. That man is myself]" (Pléiade, 1.1159). The seemingly assured identification of *je* and *moi-même* with *cet homme* implies a continuity of consciousness, while the free movement between tenses and the very use of third person (*un homme, cet homme*) distances the noun from the pronouns and suggests a radical disjunction between past and present. Indeed, across this entire text and increasingly toward the end, for all the profligacy with which Rousseau deploys the *I* (or maybe because of that profligacy), the pronoun seems remarkably unstable and referentially insecure. In chapter II I have quoted several passages from book 12 of the *Confessions,* where Rousseau speaks of the disordered state of his memory and consequently of his narrative ("I have so confused a memory of this whole affair that it is impossible for me to impose any order or connexion on the ideas which come back to me" [Cohen, 579; Pléiade, 1.627]) and alludes to "the deplorable state to which [the disturbances of my later life] have reduced me" (Cohen, 574; Pléiade, 1.622). The disordered memory, the haphazard narrative, and the deplorable state to which *I* has been reduced are clearly three ways of coming at a single phenomenon, which has its origin, I would argue, in the impossibility of conceiving that the *I* of the moment of writing, known to himself to be motivated by a "burning love for the great, the true, the beautiful, and the just" and by "the sight of all that is virtuous, generous, and lovable" (Cohen, 333; Pléiade, 1.356–57), can be the same *I* by whose agency five children were dispatched to the foundling home. Rousseau finds it impossible to tell two such different stories with a single *I* as the grammatical and thematic subject—hence the wild confusion of the text. Despite the passage in which he refers to himself as "cet homme" and as a man "qui n'est plus," Rousseau never really claims (as in effect Krapp does, or would like to), "I am not the same person I was twenty years ago," and surely most readers of the

Confessions feel that there is all too near a sameness between the *I* then and the *I* now. Rousseau is compelled to deny what his project requires him to affirm, but the task is too great, and the text collapses under the burden. And yet the mad and impossible struggle is what constitutes the book's greatness, for Rousseau finds a way to fail that no one before him had found, and that, according to Beckett, is the sine qua non of great artistry: "to be an artist is to fail, as no other dare fail" (*Duthuit*, 125).

Not content with the form of failure of the *Confessions,* however, Rousseau went on to more bizarre failure in the *Dialogues,* and thereby anticipated much life-writing in the late twentieth century. Here again he seems proleptically to be following a Beckettian dictum, for when Beckett speaks of failing as no other dare fail, he has in mind not only other artists but also earlier failures of the same artist, who, Beckett would have it, must find ever new ways of failing. There is nothing outside the texts to suggest that Rousseau formulated the matter to himself in these terms, but within the *Confessions,* the *Dialogues,* and even the *Reveries* the evidence is rich and compelling. As I have argued in chapter II, the failure recorded in the note appended to the *Confessions* ("Thus I concluded my reading, and everyone was silent," etc.) leads on to the altered attempt of the *Dialogues,* and the account of abysmal failure recorded in the "History of the Preceding Writing" of the *Dialogues* establishes all the terms and conditions for the specific failure of the *Reveries.* And as Henry Adams was fond of pointing out, each of his predecessors (he specifies Augustine and Rousseau) had failed—as he also was destined to do—"as no other dare fail." What concerns me now is the extraordinarily daring way Rousseau discovered to fail in the *Dialogues.*

It is in the fragmentation of the *I* and in the multiplication of voices saying *I* that Rousseau is so far beyond anyone of his time in daring— indeed, so far beyond anyone of any time until the history of life-writing had worked its way through Henry Adams, Franz Kafka, and Gertrude Stein to Samuel Beckett. Assigning fragments of his own *I* to "J. J.," to "Rousseau," and to "the Frenchman," all of them a figment of his imagination, Rousseau posits another *I* for use in the prefatory "On the Subject and Form of This Writing," in the footnotes to the three dialogues, and in the appended "History of the Preceding Writing." The text proper of the *Dialogues*—i.e., the actual conversations between "Rousseau" and "the Frenchman"—positively crawls with *I*s that, in footnotes and other extratextual passages, are transformed into *he*s—with, however, the *I* of Jean-Jacques Rousseau presumably behind them. But when Rousseau introduces his figments into the extratextual material to engage them as figures in his own real world (if the word "real" has any meaning now), it has the effect of making him one of his figments and of transforming his *I* into a *he,* yet with another Rousseau behind this *he* posing as an *I.* The best gloss on the mind-staggering procedure of the *Dialogues* is *Company,* where Beckett takes the operation apart even as he practices it. The authorial self, identity, or *I* behind *Company* is split and fragmented into as many pieces as the Rousseau behind the *Dialogues.* There is the *he* lying in the dark and there is the voice, but there is also one telling of him lying in the dark and of the voice, and one telling of one telling of him lying in the dark and of the voice, and so on. . . . If there is an *I* in *Company*'s far distance, all the reader can be sure of is never reaching it, but this is so also of the *I* of the *Dialogues.* "Deviser of the voice and of its hearer and of himself. . . . He speaks of himself as of another. He says speaking of himself, He speaks of himself as of another" (*Company,* 26). *He* might be named Rousseau or might be named Beckett, but best to call him the Unnamable and understand that he is "[d]evising figments to temper his nothingness" (*Company,* 46). But where does all this devising take place? "In another dark or in the same another devising it all for company. This at first seems clear. But as the eye dwells it grows obscure. Indeed the longer the eye dwells the obscurer it grows" (*Company,* 22). Truer words were never written, but they soon (p. 24) come in for some close questioning:

> For why or? Why in another dark or in the same? And whose voice asking this? Who asks, Whose voice asking this? And answers, His soever who devises it all. In the same dark as his creature or in another. For company. Who asks in the end, Who asks? And in the end answers as above? And adds long after to himself, Unless another still. Nowhere to be found. Nowhere to be sought. The unthinkable last of all. Unnamable. Last person. I. Quick leave him.

Infinite regress, in the case either of *Company* or the *Dialogues,* seems to hold out the tantalizing promise of arriving "in the end" at the "last person," which, grammatically, would be the first person—and "What an addition to company that would be!" (p. 16). Then the ultimate deviser would be revealed as *I.* But of course this is never to be, for the infinite regress is just that—a regress and infinite—and the last person/first person is "Nowhere to be found. Nowhere to be sought." It is something of a shock to realize that Rousseau, acting alone and in the dark as he liked to maintain was the case, did something that was two centuries before its time, yet has received little credit for doing it, for the *Dialogues* remains a largely undiscussed text. Giving his *I* over to so many voices, he succeeds (which is his special way of rising to failure) in pushing the *I* back further and further until it disappears over the horizon, "Nowhere to be found. Nowhere to be sought." His *I* becomes *Not I*. And we thought this was one of the dubious achievements of the twentieth century.

The editors of Vico's periautography tell us that what he does in that book is in part intended as a negative response to Descartes's *Discourse on Method,* which "he thought of . . . not as a model to be followed, but as an example of the faults to be avoided." In particular, they go on to say that the "choice of the third person is a reaction from the ubiquitous 'I' of the *Discourse*" (*Vita,* 7).[6] We need no editors to know why Henry Adams adopted the third person—he tells us himself that it was "a reaction against the ubiquitous 'I' " of Rousseau's *Confessions.* There is no reason to doubt that the "not I" of Vico and Adams was designed to escape the stifling egoism of Descartes and Rousseau, but the consequences are more various than this single intention suggests. For one thing—and surely both Vico and Adams would have desired this—adoption of *he* rather than *I* confers on the individual story something of the objectivity of history and something more of the contours of universalizing myth. This is a lot to acquire simply through banishing *I,* and all the more a bargain in that we can always sense *I*'s active presence in the style and structure of the narrative. Beyond this, resort to *he* or *she* by Vico, Adams, Stein, and most of all Beckett constitutes a skeptical, perhaps sardonic comment on what goes on in conventional life-writing, for—looked at closely—it is not use of the third-person but of the first-person pronoun that is unnatural and that leads immediately to the kind of fiction (pernicious or otherwise as one may choose) that we find in Rousseau's *Confessions. I* of the present does not share con-

---

6. In *Descartes' Error: Emotion, Reason, and the Human Brain* (New York: Putnam, 1994), Antonio Damasio argues that the "error" of his (Damasio's) title lay in Descartes's sundering of mind from both brain and what Damasio terms "body proper." The "self" (which is equivalent to the *I* except that the latter is always implicated in language) "is based on activities throughout [the] entire organism, that is, in the body proper and in the brain. . . . [T]he self is a repeatedly reconstructed biological state," according to Damasio, but "it is *not* a little person, the infamous homunculus, inside your brain contemplating what is going on." He rejects this Cartesian notion because it implies that such a homunculus would also have "a little person in his brain doing his seeing and thinking, and so on ad infinitum. That explanation, which poses the problem of infinite regress, is no explanation at all" (pp. 226–27). I quote Damasio not only for the interest his characterization of the self holds and for his rejection of Cartesian dualism but also because he executes, in a footnote, an intriguing reversal on the issue of infinite regress: "I would actually prefer to call the problem infinite regress *in space,* to emphasize the point that the real trouble rests with the creation of a nest of Russian dolls, one inside the other looking at yet another." This suggests that while the notion of infinite regress, when conceived in spatial terms, is the reverse of helpful, if reconceived as a temporal and experiential matter it may provide one of the best understandings we can have of the self or the *I.*

sciousness with *I* of forty years ago, and mere use of the first person can scarcely paper over the gap.

It is just such an opening up of the autobiographical act to reveal its inner workings that Gertrude Stein contrives in *The Autobiography of Alice B. Toklas*. "About six weeks ago," the last lines of that book declare (in the voice of Stein speaking through Toklas about to quote Stein), "Gertrude Stein said, it does not look to me as if you were ever going to write that autobiography. You know what I am going to do. I am going to write it for you. I am going to write it as simply as Defoe did the autobiography of Robinson Crusoe. And she has and this is it."[7] As Daniel Defoe is to Robinson Crusoe, so Gertrude Stein to Alice Toklas, the deviser of a character for company; and what wonderful company Alice is, too, discoursing tirelessly on the genius of her deviser. But Stein is a character in her book also, and thus fits the formulation of *Company* perfectly: "Devised deviser devising it all for company. In the same figment dark as [her] figments" (p. 46). The relationship of deviser to devised since the time of Rousseau is not clear, however, until we begin to use quotation marks to place in a separate category those for whom historical reference can be claimed but who also enter into their own (and others') fictions: Daniel Defoe is to Robinson Crusoe (had Defoe chosen the name Alexander Selkirk then it would have to go in quotation marks) as Gertrude Stein to "Gertrude Stein" and "Alice Toklas," as Henry Adams to "Henry Adams," as Rousseau to "Rousseau," and as Samuel Beckett to Molloy, Moran, Malone, the Unnamable, and—one keeps thinking, imagining, almost expecting, but never quite getting—"Samuel Beckett," into whom, were he clearly present, all the other figments would be resolved because they are entirely fictional, and Beckett would then be writing about the act of life-writing and about the making of fictions.

Unlike Beckett, Gertrude Stein was not interested (as "Alice Toklas" would phrase it) in failure; on the contrary, she was a genius, she knew it, and she felt compelled to make frequent public statements designed to solve for the world at large what she felt to be problems presented by different modes of writing. She was particularly cogent about the possibilities and the difficulties of life-writing. "It is funny this knowing being a genius, everything is funny," Stein writes in *Everybody's Autobiography*,[8] and she continues:

---

7. *The Autobiography of Alice B. Toklas* (New York: Random House, 1933), 252.
8. *Everybody's Autobiography* (New York: Random House, 1937), 68.

And identity is funny being yourself is funny as you are never yourself to yourself except as you remember yourself and then of course you do not believe yourself. That is really the trouble with an autobiography you do not of course you do not really believe yourself why should you, you know so well so very well that it is not yourself, it could not be yourself because you cannot remember right and if you do remember right it does not sound right and of course it does not sound right because it is not right. You are of course never yourself.

The repetition of the phrase "of course," which might seem excessive to some readers, does yeoman rhetorical work. To circumvent the "trouble" that autobiography presents, Stein, illustrating her dicta and showing other writers the way, substitutes imagination for memory ("remembering" Alice Toklas's self rather than her own), tells her—Stein's—story as the story of another, and produces two books that on their very title pages violate all that we conventionally understand autobiography to be: *Everybody's Autobiography* and *The Autobiography of Alice B. Toklas,* by Gertrude Stein. In violating conventions, however, Stein does more than simply get around them; she also reveals what autobiography, its appearances to the contrary notwithstanding, has been and is, and she lays the ground for what Beckett and others, no longer willing even to give the title of autobiography to their books, will do with life-writing. "Identity always worries me," Stein writes in *Everybody's Autobiography* (p. 115), "and memory and eternity." Leaving aside the last subject as too grand for present consideration, one might say that identity and memory are, of course, and have always been, principal concerns of the life-writer and that it is mainly worry about them that has determined the skittishness of mid-twentieth-century writers about the use of *I.* Yet there are writers of the century who seem (but I emphasize "seem") not to be anxious about identity and memory and who, in consequence, assert the autobiographical *I* as if its capacity for making the past and an absent self present were never in question. Richard Wright comes first to mind. *Black Boy,* like other of his books (*Uncle Tom's Children* and *Native Son* in particular), exercises a compelling narrative power over the reader's imagination. Two scenes from the memoir are especially noteworthy: the opening, when the four-year-old Richard (or "Richard"?) burns down the house where his grandmother lies sick in bed; and the scene in which Uncle Hoskins drives a horse and buggy, with the terrified boy in it, into the Mississippi River. For the length of time it takes to read these passages, I don't suppose any reader doubts either account: Wright's control scarcely admits of skepticism. Yet we know that the Uncle Hoskins episode was not drawn from Wright's boyhood memories;[9] and I suggest that when we detach ourselves from the grip of the opening scene sufficiently to see what is going on, we realize that the kind and quantity of detail Wright offers ("One winter morning in the long-ago, four-year-old days of my life I found myself standing before a fireplace, warming my hands over a mound of glowing coals, listening to the wind whistle past the house out-side. . . . I was dreaming of running and playing and shouting. . . . A bird wheeled past the window and I greeted it with a glad shout," etc.) have little to do with the way memory works and much to do with the way a narrative artist would set a scene. What interests me now, however, is not so much the nature of memory in the two passages as the ubiquity and the unquestioned status of *I* in both. Consider these characteristic passages, at the end of the first episode, near the end of the other:

> I was lashed so hard and long I lost consciousness. I was beaten out of my senses. . . . I was lost in a fog of fear. . . . I could not sleep. . . . Whenever I tried to sleep I would see huge wobbly white bags, like the full udders of cows, suspended from the ceiling above me. . . . I was gripped by the fear that they were going to fall and drench me with some horrible liquid. . . . I begged my mother and father to take the bags away. . . . I was afraid to sleep. . . . for a long time I was chastened whenever I remembered that my mother had come close to killing me. (*Black Boy,* 13)

> "Are you really that scared?" [Uncle Hoskins] asked softly.
> I did not answer; I could not speak. My fear was gone now and he loomed before me like a stranger, like a man I had never seen before, a man with whom I could never share a moment of intimate living. . . . I would not listen or speak to him. I never trusted him after that. Whenever I saw his face the memory of my terror upon the river would come back, vivid and strong, and it stood as a barrier between us. (Pp. 61, 62)

The first event occurred something over thirty years before Wright recalled it for the purposes of *Black Boy;* the second—had it been an actual part of his boyhood experience—would have occurred twenty-four or twenty-five years before the writing of the book. There is nothing in either passage

---

9. See the account of the making of *Black Boy* in Constance Webb, *Richard Wright: A Biography* (New York: G. P. Putnam's Sons, 1968): "And he would try to make a state-ment—could he do it? Using portions of his own childhood, stories told him by friends, things he had observed happening to others, he would write an 'autobiography' " (p. 205). And in an endnote, Webb tells the reader, "An episode concerning Richard and Uncle Hoskins . . . was based on an incident told him by Ralph Ellison. Ellison's father had been teasing him and was actually going into the river for sand to make a sandpile and had not realized his son's terror" (p. 409 n. 9). Citations to *Black Boy* refer to the 1966 edition (New York: Harper and Row).

to suggest that the author of 1944 does not share emotional vitality and consciousness with the boy of 1912 and the youth of 1920. The *I* is deployed in such a manner as to seem to guarantee a continuity of identity from four to twelve to thirty-seven. We know about the fiction of the *I* in the second episode; common sense would tell us that a fiction of the *I* is as complete in the first. Among the omissions indicated by ellipsis marks is this sentence (immediately after "I was lost in a fog of fear"): "A doctor was called—I was afterwards told—and he ordered that I be kept abed, that I be kept quiet, that my very life depended upon it." We have already been told that the boy had been "lashed so hard" he "lost consciousness" and was delirious for days if not weeks, so we must see "I was afterwards told" as serving much the same narrative function as the phrase frequently repeated in the *Odyssey*—"as the goddess afterwards told me"—designed to cover knowledge that Odysseus could not possibly possess but that he brings into his story. In Wright's text *I* is assumed to be an appropriate marker of identity at all times and in all states of consciousness: for the boy of four both in his right senses and in delirium, for the youth of twelve in extreme terror, and for the man of thirty-seven engaged in remembering, speculating, and writing. But this is simply the convention of any autobiography written in the first person, which the generic name would seem to suggest is a requirement.

In many ways Wright was as committed to modernism as Stein, yet on this crucial question of *I/not I* he stood apart. The reasons one might adduce for this are not without interest. The other side of Wright's unquestioning adherence to a unitary *I* in his autobiography is the complete avoidance of *I* in his fiction. Just as he never attempts the Vichian/Adamsian/Steinian third person in his memoirs, so he never experiments with the first person in his short stories and novels. Wright, unlike Stein and Beckett, shows no interest in offering the reader something that could be called, indifferently, either fiction or autobiography but that might best bear the designation life-writing, understanding by that a form that entertains simultaneously the possibilities of autobiography and fiction. Had Wright chosen to cast *Native Son* or any of the stories of *Uncle Tom's Children* in the first person, it would have had the effect of throwing interest back on the narrator, thus making the implied judgments of the fiction, as is sometimes said, "subjective." Curiously enough, adoption of the unwavering *I* in *Black Boy*—an *I* presented as possessing something approaching perfect recall, it is true—has the opposite effect, and this is an effect and a sign of the difference in genre. It is as if the *I* provided warrant of authenticity in *Black Boy,* which only the *he* can provide in fiction. The third-person fiction of *Native Son* makes the statement, "This is the way it is"; *Black Boy* says, "I am the man, I suffer'd, I was there"—and incidentally this is the way it was. It is notable that Whitman's claim, like Wright's, depends on the *I* that can say itself with equal authority for then and now, there and here. That Whitman precisely is *not* the man and was *not* there except by empathic identification with another makes the point: neither is Wright's *I* the boy's except by an imaginative leap. Or perhaps it would be better to say that the tense shift from "I am the man" to "I was there" is a linguistic figuration of what we are told of the strategy of the voice in *Company:* that it combines what is present and can be verified (e.g., "I am the man" or "You are on your back in the dark") with what is past and cannot ("I was there" or "You first saw the light on such and such a day")—a device "from the incontrovertibility of the one to win credence for the other." In the end Wright may not be so different from Stein and Beckett as he initially seems, for what he too does (for specific rhetorical purposes) is to transform *he* into *I;* or, in the words of *The Unnamable,* "he says I as if he were I" (p. 371).[10] Most readers would sense a greater gap between the thirty-seven-year-old Richard Wright and the four-year-old boy than between Gertrude Stein and Alice Toklas or Samuel Beckett and his various aliases—Murphy, Krapp, Molloy, Moran, Malone, and all the unnamables of the late fiction and drama. Perhaps the real difference between Wright on the one hand and Stein and Beckett on the other is that in the latter two a playfulness with language masks and relieves the underlying seriousness, while in Wright there is never any sense of play, only dead seriousness. But surely neither Stein nor Wright—nor any of the other twentieth-century writers

---

10. Ironically, biographers of Wright have tended to reverse his procedure in *Black Boy,* regularly turning his *I*s back into *he*s. In *Richard Wright: Ordeal of a Native Son* (Garden City, N.Y.: Doubleday, 1980), for example, Addison Gayle takes the dramatized scenes of *Black Boy* for plain, unmediated accounts of what happened. Thus the opening episode of setting fire to the house is virtually reproduced in Gayle's book, except that *I* has become *he.* "I begged my mother and father to take the bags away" becomes "He begged his mother and father to remove the bags," etc. Constance Webb offers a third-person account of the same scene, same words: "Nightmares of huge wobbly white bags, like the full udders of cows, suspended from the ceiling, made him awaken and scream. He was afraid they would fall and drench him with some horrible liquid. Day and night he begged his parents to take away the bags . . ." (*Richard Wright,* 23). In a footnote and an endnote (p. 20, p. 401), Webb says her account is taken from *Black Boy* "and confirmed in conversation with Richard Wright." No doubt. Michel Fabre (*The Unfinished Quest of Richard Wright* [Urbana: University of Illinois Press, 1993]) claims that "the conversation between the two brothers during the episode of the fire leads us to suppose that Richard had already attained enough strength of character to dominate his younger brother to the point where he no longer needed to be jealous of him" (p. 9). This is nonsense. What the conversation "leads us to suppose" is that by the time of *Black Boy* Wright had become accustomed to writing effective dialogue.

of the present chapter—would quarrel with what *The Unnamable* tells us: "it's the fault of the pronouns, there is no name for me, no pronoun for me" (p. 372). Even *I* (which we were taught in grade school to call the "subjective case") is not a pronoun that can be attached by copula with any assurance to the "objective-case" *me*.

In an eerie and fascinating anticipation of the divided and fragmented *I* and the hesitance among twentieth-century life-writers to claim that pronoun, Robert Louis Stevenson has Henry Jekyll, in the brief life he gives us as the last chapter of *The Strange Case of Dr. Jekyll and Mr. Hyde*,[11] writing that "I now felt I had to choose" between the two halves of a split being (p. 86). "My two natures had memory in common," Jekyll says (and this I find a deeply interesting notion), but there the sharing of faculties stopped. Choosing, however, avails little for Jekyll since the will, unlike memory (here we recall St. Augustine, whose will was similarly divided, but not his memory), is not a faculty held in common by the doctor and his alter ego. On "a fine, clear, January day," Jekyll tells us, "I sat in the sun on a bench; the animal within me licking the chops of memory; the spiritual side a little drowsed . . . (p. 91). This somnolence of the will on the spiritual side leads where one might expect: "I looked down, my clothes hung formlessly on my shrunken limbs; the hand that lay on my knee was corded and hairy. I was once again Edward Hyde." That he can give a different name to the entity yet use the first-person pronoun suggests that Hyde is a fully autonomous and momentarily dominant personality within the psychic economy heretofore known as Dr. Jekyll. This emergence of the animal and the despairing thought that "*I was . . . Edward Hyde*" (and who am I now?) is overcome two pages later by the writer's weakened but still existent moral sense as he describes Hyde's vicious activities and then exclaims, sounding for all the world like "Mouth" in Beckett's play, "He, I say—I cannot say, I" (p. 93). "What? . . . who? . . . no! . . . he! . . . HE!" For the remainder of the final chapter ("Henry Jekyll's Full Statement of the Case") Hyde is indeed third person, designated either by name or by *he*. But (curiously) so, for the most part, is Jekyll: "The powers of Hyde," we read, and we must remember that this is supposed to be Jekyll speaking or writing, "seemed to have grown with the sickliness of Jekyll. . . . He [Jekyll] had now seen the full deformity of that creature [Hyde] that shared with

---

11. New York: Vintage Books, 1991; page citations refer to this edition. As I was writing the lines above, it was pleasing to come across Beckett's nephew and literary executor, Edward Beckett, saying of his uncle, "I know he read Robert Louis Stevenson extensively" (in Mel Gussow, *Conversations with and about Beckett* [New York: Grove Press, 1996], 126).

him [Jekyll] some of the phenomena of consciousness. . . . This was the shocking thing. . . . , that that insurgent horror was knit to him closer than a wife, closer than an eye; lay caged in his flesh, where he heard it mutter and felt it struggle to be born; and at every hour of weakness, and in the confidence of slumber, prevailed against him, and deposed him out of life" (p. 95). Whatever else is to be said of the narrator here, he seems, by the pronouns chosen, to be sundered in consciousness from both Hyde and Jekyll. One cannot but admire the phrase "deposed him out of life," which characterizes the condition in question in a more telling and elegant way than does the technical term provided by researchers of the late twentieth century—"dissociative identity disorder."[12] Indeed, Jekyll, writing about his twoness, presciently forecasts an even more dire dissociative situation for our time: "I say two, because the state of my own knowledge does not pass beyond that point. Others will follow, others will outstrip me on the same lines; and I hazard the guess that man will be ultimately known for a mere polity of multifarious, incongruous and independent denizens" (p. 76)—bearing such names, one might speculate, as Murphy, Watt, Molloy, Moran, Malone, Sapo, Macmann, Mahood, Worm, the Unnamable . . . perhaps even, perhaps ultimately, "the old bastard" (*Trilogy,* 311). Taken together they compose what the voice of *The Unnamable* calls "my troop of lunatics" (p. 282), elsewhere "my vice-existers" (p. 289). Beckett evidently learned a good deal about such "vice-existers" and about dissociation from attending, in 1935, the third of C. G. Jung's Tavistock Lectures, where Jung spoke, among other things, of what he called "complexes," which split off from conscious control to establish separate, autonomous, Hyde-like identities that have their own *I*s and "speak in voices which are like the voices of definite people."[13] The voice that speaks in the first person in *The Unnamable* is in continual danger of being deposed out of life by just such a "complex," an intrusive, other *I;* or, perhaps worse, of being dispersed among an almost infinite number of *he*s, none of them, as linguists tell us, endowed with the subjectivity and personhood that accompany the articulation of *I.*

In several crucial chapters of *Problems in General Linguistics* (primarily

12. See Daniel L. Schacter, *Searching for Memory: The Brain, the Mind, and the Past* (New York: Basic Books, 1996): "[T]he recognized standard bearer in clinical psychiatry and psychology (the fourth edition of *The Diagnostic and Statistical Manual of Mental Disorders,* or DSM-IV) has recently changed the term *multiple personality disorder* to *dissociative identity disorder*" (p. 238).

13. C. G. Jung, *Analytical Psychology: Its Theory and Practice. The Tavistock Lectures* (New York: Pantheon, 1968), 80.

"Relationships of Person in the Verb," "The Nature of Pronouns," and "Subjectivity in Language"), Émile Benveniste addresses the same pronominal questions in theoretical-linguistic terms that Stevenson, Beckett, and others were addressing in literary, philosophical, and psychological terms. Leaving aside the issue of plurals, Benveniste adopts the unsurpassably simple and exact definition of person in the pronouns handed down by Arab grammarians: first person is "the one who speaks"; second person is "the one who is addressed"; third person is "the one who is absent."[14] The three persons are not, however, "homogeneous," Benveniste argues; rather, as the terms of speech and address on the one hand and absence on the other might suggest, the first- and second-person pronouns are invested with person and the personal, but the third—in spite of the symmetrical name we give it—is not. "In the first two persons, there are both a person involved and a discourse concerning that person. 'I' designates the one who speaks and at the same time implies an utterance about 'I'; in saying 'I,' I cannot *not* be speaking of myself" (p. 197). Interrupting the exposition for just a moment and anticipating a point that will be returned to later, one should remark here that this is exactly the problem for Beckett in the *Trilogy:* granted, that "in saying 'I,' I cannot *not* be speaking of myself," yet, as Beckett insists, the self, however much one might struggle to accomplish it, cannot be spoken, hence the empty *I* of *The Unnamable* and hence also the endless string of "puppets," "manikins," "avatars," who say *I* as if he or they *were* I and say *he* as if out of that could come the *I*. "They say they," according to the Unnamable, "speaking of them, to make me think it is I who am speaking." This is ingenious of "them," to adopt the absentee third person, thus hoping to make the *I*-less Unnamable believe he has uttered in the first person, subjective, nominative, but he slips away into Mouth's "Not I" as if that were itself a speaking entity: *"Not-I."* "Or I say they, speaking of God knows what, to make me think it is not I who am [or is] speaking" (*Trilogy,* 340). But it won't do: even if the plural "they" be switched to the singular "he," *I* still cannot be reached, and it is "Not I" all the way:

> . . . he thinks he's caught me, he feels me in him, then he says I, as if I were he . . . I seem to speak, that's because he says I as if he were I, I nearly believed him, do you hear him, as if he were I, I who am far . . . I know it's not I, that's all I know, I say I, knowing it's not I, I am far, far . . . it will never be I, that's all I know . . . I haven't stirred, that's all I know, no, I know something else, it's not I, I always forget that. (Pp. 371, 372, 380)

14. Émile Benveniste, *Problems in General Linguistics* (Coral Gables, Fla.: University of Miami Press, 1971), 197. Further citations appear in the text.

I hesitate to make things worse for the reader, but if we try to assign identities to pronouns in the foregoing we would come out with something like
this: "I" is the Unnamable, and "he" is the deviser of the Unnamable, let
us say tentatively "Beckett"; but that means that "I" is a "he" to "Beckett"
and "he" is the real "I" (= "Beckett") behind the whole mess. Little wonder that the passage concludes with "I always forget that," for how can one
remember the negative *not I,* which, like the *I* itself, is always "far, far."
What we are told earlier of Worm (the least and last of the surrogates for
the Unnamable or for "Beckett"—the surrogate of surrogates, as it were)
must be said also, in Beckett's view, of *I* and the self: ". . . the place where
he lies is vast, that's interesting, he is far, too far for them to reach him
even with the longest pole. That tiny blur in the depths of the pit, is he
[is *I,* we must interject]. There he is now in a pit. . . . They say they see
him, the blur is what they see, they say the blur is he [is *I*], perhaps it is"
(pp. 329–30). Perhaps, but the self as a blur is not readily expressible, may
not be expressible at all, which is the issue the entire tormented exercise
of the Trilogy was designed to explore.

"In the second person," Benveniste continues, " 'you' is necessarily
designated by 'I' and cannot be thought of outside a situation set up by
starting with 'I'; and at the same time, 'I' states something as the predicate
of 'you' " (*Problems in General Linguistics,* 197). Here is where the *I* and *you*
pronouns are altogether different from *he* and *she:* "The form that is called
the third person really does contain an indication of a statement about
someone or something but not related to a specific 'person.' The variable
and properly 'personal' element of these denominations is here lacking. It
is indeed the 'absent' of the Arab grammarians. . . . The consequence must
be formulated clearly: the 'third person' is not a 'person'; it is really the
verbal form whose function is to express the *non-person*" (pp. 197–98).
". . . [I]t can't be I," the Unnamable says, "there I am far again, there I
am the absentee again, it's his turn now, he who neither speaks nor listens"
(*Trilogy,* 380). Were one able—as of course one is not with Beckett—to
move back (or forward) through the almost endless string of absent, nonperson *he*s to the last in the series, it would turn itself inside out to become
first, which is to say the grammatical first person, invested with both presence and personhood. But as the blur that is *I* is unattainable directly
through language—this Beckett undoubtedly believed to be the case and
demonstrated repeatedly—so a fortiori (as Beckett himself might say) it
cannot be reached through multiplying instances of the nonperson; thus
the "quick leave him" when the notion of last person–first person is
broached in *Company.* If the dictum that declares the third person a nonper-

son is important for Beckett—and it undoubtedly is, as a matter of epistemological vexation if nothing else—it becomes, as we shall see later, exquisitely so, in different but always anguished ways, for writers as unlike one
another as Ronald Fraser, Maxine Hong Kingston, Christa Wolf, and
Primo Levi. For some of these writers (Wolf in particular) there may seem
a sort of security in adopting the third person for narrating one's experience,
for others (Fraser for example) it may be the only pronoun family made
possible; but Benveniste spells out very clearly some of the problems in
saying *she* or *he* when *I* would be expected. "[O]ne characteristic of the
persons 'I' and 'you,'" he writes, "is their specific 'oneness': the 'I' who
states, the 'you' to whom 'I' addresses himself are unique each time. But 'he'
can be an infinite number of subjects—or none. That is why Rimbaud's 'je
est un autre' represents the typical expression of what is properly mental
'alienation,' in which the 'I' is dispossessed of its constitutive identity"
(*Problems in General Linguistics,* 199). Benveniste may be right when he says
of instances of discourse that "oneness" is a characteristic of the *I,* but who
would doubt Moran when, in *Molloy,* he exclaims, "How little one is at
one with oneself, good God" (*Trilogy,* 104); and "mental 'alienation,'" in
Benveniste's formulation, is of course but another name for "dissociative
identity disorder." Another characteristic of the *I* and *you* but not of *he* or
she, according to Benveniste, is that the first two pronouns are reversible:
"the one whom 'I' defines by 'you' thinks of himself as 'I' and can be
inverted into 'I,' and 'I' becomes a 'you.' There is no like relationship
possible between one of these persons and 'he' because 'he' in itself does
not specifically designate anything or anyone" (*Problems in General Linguistics,* 199). This reversibility of first- and second-person pronouns provides
the logic of Nathalie Sarraute's *Childhood,* where the present *ego* is split into
I and *you,* each speaking as *I* in turn during the dialogue, making the other,
for the moment, a *you.* The half that most often says "you" (from an *I*
perspective, of course) represents an insistently analytic intelligence, coming
from the outside, determined to scrutinize motives with an "objective"
eye, and distrustful of the capacity of memory to come up with anything
like "the truth"; the half that says "I" (responding to her alter ego who has
just said "you") is more emotional, less inclined to a reductionist version
of human desire, and willing at least to test memory as a no doubt "subjective," but still possibly truth-producing, phenomenon. Sarraute demonstrates the validity of Benveniste's observation that use of *you* always implies
an *I*—or more than implies it, creates it—just as deployment of *I* always
implies a *you* (which, I imagine, is why we so often address ourselves mentally, if not aloud, as *you:* "You've done it again, haven't you?" and the

like). To accept a *you*/*I* split and proceed from there is one of many ways (for other ways see Fraser, Kingston, Wolf, Levi, and Virginia Woolf—not to say Beckett—below) of seeking the unified *I* that seems to have become—to put it in the most optimistic terms—so elusive in our time.

When Benveniste says that "'he' can be an infinite number of subjects—or none," he touches on an issue central to Beckett's practice, for the *he*s there are as infinite as the notion of infinite regress would suggest, yet they can achieve no more subjecthood than their role as pronominal, stand-in mannequins permits. And whatever games the "foul brute"—"it's . . . the same foul brute all the time, amusing himself pretending to be a many, varying his register, his tone, his accent and his drivel" (*Trilogy,* 323)—standing behind the fiction may play, the relationship between the *he* and the *I* is neither an equal nor a reversible one. "He tells his story every five minutes," one of the *he*/*I* mannequins complains of "Beckett," "the old bastard" and the "foul brute," in the fourth of the *Texts for Nothing,*

> saying it is not his, there's cleverness for you. He would like it to be my fault that he has no story, of course he has no story, that's no reason for trying to foist one on me. That's how he reasons, wide of the mark, but wide of what mark, answer us that. He has me say things saying it's not me, there's profundity for you, he has me who say nothing say it's not me. All that is truly crass. If at least he would dignify me with the third person, like his other figments, not he, he'll be satisfied with nothing less than me, for his me.[15]

It is a demanding taskmaster—and Beckett, shorn now of quotation marks, was unquestionably that[16]—who demands "nothing less than me, for his me." The voice of *Texts for Nothing* makes virtually the same complaint made by Mouth in *Not I,* except that the former turns on his deviser with "[a]ll that is truly crass" while the latter must remain content with her "vehement refusal to relinquish third person."

15. *Texts for Nothing,* in *Samuel Beckett: The Complete Short Prose, 1929–1989,* ed. S. E. Gontarski (New York: Grove Press, 1995), 115.

16. According to Alan Schneider, there were actors (and even some directors) who complained that they were treated like little more than "impersonal or even disembodied puppets" of Beckett's will. "Now [the actors say] he's even down to strapping them into some sort of medieval torture chamber, closing off their faces, including their eyes—the windows of the stage souls—in order to leave only a mouth visible on stage. What's next, they ask me, the uvula alone, pinpointed on a darkened stage?" ("Working with Beckett," in S. E. Gontarski, ed., *On Beckett: Essays and Criticism* [New York: Grove Press, 1986], 249–50). If this complaint were reformulated in terms of the discussion above, it would be that Beckett, in the effort to say himself—to say his own *I*—treated actors and directors as nonperson *he*s and *she*s, most notably in pieces like *Happy Days* and *Not I.* One should note, however, that actors such as Billie Whitelaw, who played both Winnie and Mouth, were not inclined to protest Beckett's treatment of them.

Lest the use of *I* seem trouble free for the life-writer—at least by way of contrast with *he* and *she*—we must attend to the implications of what Benveniste has to say about the *I*, which he terms, in a suggestively dangerous phrase, a "mobile sign." First, we should remark what is seldom noticed because so "familiar," that pronouns are among the signs of every language: "A language without the expression of person cannot be imagined." Indeed, the first-person pronoun, Benveniste writes, is the sine qua non of all human language and communication. "Language is possible only because each speaker sets himself up as a *subject* by referring to himself as *I* in his discourse" (*Problems in General Linguistics,* 225). Were there not such a sign and were every speaker thrown back on finding a unique marker—using "a distinct identifying signal . . . to express the feeling he has of his irreducible subjectivity"—then "there would be as many languages as individuals and communication would become absolutely impossible" (p. 220). (We must recall here Rousseau's felt need "to invent a new language" for what he had to say.) This, Benveniste writes, is where the *I* is language's salvation: "Language wards off this danger by instituting a unique but mobile sign, *I,* which can be assumed by each speaker on the condition that he refers each time only to the instance of his own discourse" (p. 220). But what if one is more ambitious—or more troubled—and wishes to refer to more than the instance of discourse? The *I* then becomes much slipperier and much less accommodating, but precisely because it is *too* accommodating. Anyone at all can slip in under the cloak of this *I*, which, as a shifter, must take up with everyone who takes up with it. This, at least, is what I understand to be Beckett's implied misgiving when he has the Unnamable say, "But enough of this cursed first person, it is really too red a herring. . . . But what then is the subject? Mahood? No, not yet. Worm? Even less. Bah, any old pronoun will do, provided one sees through it" (*Trilogy,* 315). In the French of *L'Innommable* the first sentence here reads, "Puis assez de cette putain de première personne, c'en est trop à la fin. . . ."[17] It is presumably in the nature of a *putain* or whore that she is a "mobile shifter," not bound to any one man—certainly never in such a way as to be obliged to be the means by which he expresses what Benveniste terms his "irreducible subjectivity"—and this would seem to be the Unnamable's reason for having no more to do with such a (first) person.

It is not because he would not consort with this *putain* of a first person but, I take it, because he *could* not that Ronald Fraser turns his back on the *I* until the final chapter of *In Search of a Past,* which, as the title suggests,

17. *L'Innommable* (Paris: Éditions de Minuit, 1953), 93–94.

is an attempt not so much to restore a past as to reconstruct one—or, perhaps, without reference to anything preexisting, even to construct a virgin past.[18] Fraser's title is clearly intended to echo *À la recherche du temps perdu* but with the crucial difference that the indefinite *a* ("*a* past") replaces Proust's definite article ("*le* temps perdu"). Unlike Proust's title, which implies that the past exists and may be recoverable, Fraser's implies that there is no past—or at least that he has none—unless and until it is created. This absence of a past, we are given to understand, is a very personal affair and has resulted, at the beginning of the book, in a severe depression, or in what it is now fashionable to call a crisis of identity. Fraser's construction of a past, which he assumes will restore a sense of self-identity and lift the depression, takes a dual form: first, what he terms "oral history," which involves a series of interviews, conducted in 1969, with the men and women who were servants at the manor house in Amnersfield when "Master Ronnie" was growing up there from 1933 to 1945; and second, a four-year course of psychoanalysis, conducted in the present time of the book (1979–1983), which includes, among other material (dreams and the like), a review of all the interviews with the servants as well as information acquired from the author's brother about his memories of their shared childhood. As will be seen, the book is deeply engaged with memories of one sort and another: the author's, the servants', the author's memories of the servants' memories, the brother's memories, all of them remembered and analyzed in the sessions with "P," the psychiatrist, which are themselves remembered for the purposes of writing the book. Played off against this is an interspersed narrative that tells of the author taking his father to a nursing home because, in age, the latter's memory is gone, and with it all sense of an identity and any place he might occupy in the world. Thus we have layered, for construction of a past that may never have been and that, for the author, certainly is not now, not only memories of the past and memories of memories of the past but also, shadowing everything else, what Antonio Damasio might call "memories of the future" (*Descartes' Error,* 262), a future when memory itself will be gone, and gone also, therefore, any hope of possessing a coherent past *or* present. The author's original intention in undertaking his project, as he tells "P" in an early session, was to write about the past and thus "dispose" of it; eventually he is persuaded that he cannot dispose of *the* past, but, by gathering memories, analyzing them, and turning them into a comprehensible narrative that would be

18. Ronald Fraser, *In Search of a Past: The Manor House, Amnersfield 1933–1945* (London: Verso, 1984). Further citations appear in the text.

both objective and subjective in its sources and procedure, he might come to understand and possess *his* past.

In Search of a Past is thus a classic modernist treatment of the intertwining and interdeterminative workings of memory and narrative in a time when both are under heavy siege. What interests me at the moment, however, is not how neatly Fraser's book answers to the requirements of my argument about memory and narrative but rather the way he structures both his search and the narrative of his search. The contents page of *In Search of a Past* is very simple, very schematic, and looks like this:

	1	
We		1
	2	
They		7
She/He/She		53
You		69
	3	
We		87
Us		125
I		173

To run through these pronouns and give the referent for each: "We" signifies Fraser (perhaps better, "Fraser") and his analyst; "They" signifies the servants, who give their version of the past; "She/He/She" signifies, in turn, the mother, the father, and the governess, who took on a kind of parental role; "You" signifies the young Fraser—"Master Ronnie"—as remembered by the servants and by himself (indeed, when treating of himself as a boy or referring to himself at any time earlier than the present, analytic moment of the book, Fraser uses "you"); "We" signifies again "Fraser" and his analyst; "Us" signifies "Fraser" and his brother; and "I," finally, signifies "Fraser," at the very edge of the present—the moment the book is ready for publication, as it were—with himself and the lessons of his past and his analysis gathered together within the expandable boundaries of that single-letter, but always (in English) upper-case pronoun. A few of these designations might bear some comment, especially in light of Benveniste's linguistic formulations and Beckett's literary practice. Why, for example, the nominative "We" for analyst and analysand, but the accusative "Us" for the two brothers? I imagine the logic is that the brothers are seen as having been largely acted upon by other people and by forces outside themselves, whereas the analyst and his patient are pictured as coequal, active

agents and grammatical subjects in their joint creation of a past and, from
that, a present. Benveniste's analysis of the nature of the first-person plural
might cast some doubt here, however. What he argues is that the *we*, in
presuming to bring together an *I* and one or more *he*s, either ceases to be
first person—since there is in it an admixture of that which is not invested
with subjectivity or personhood—or is merely an inflated *I*, making false
claims to confer personal status on *he* or *she*, "whose function," Benveniste
says, "is to express the *non-person*" (*Problems in General Linguistics*, 198). This
dubious quality in the first-person plural pronoun presumably accounts for
Beckett's utter rejection of it, even beyond the singular, in *Company:* "No.
For the first personal singular and a fortiori plural pronoun had never any
place in your vocabulary" (*Company*, 61). Fraser clearly does not see it this
way, however, and in the final dialogue with "P," the other half of *we*,
speaking of his father's funeral, "Fraser" says, "During the brief ceremony
I felt not sadness but longing. . . . To be with him, somehow, I think. . . .
In destroying him I destroyed something in myself. I had no 'I' for him"
(*In Search of a Past*, 185)—or for himself, is the clear implication. But "P"
responds, presumably pointing the way to integration of all the fragments
into a unified *I*, "[T]he ego is a graveyard scattered with the headstones
of lost objects. . . . So yours is of many origins: your mother, father, Ilse,
Bert . . ."; and "Fraser" is quick to take the point: "I thought, there's still
a chance, it's not too late. Writing is a way of recuperating what has been
lost. . . . The dead live on in us, despite everything" (pp. 185–86). "P's"
response—"You want to be the subject of your history instead of the object
you felt yourself to be"—"Fraser" qualifies only slightly—"The subject,
yes—but also the object. It's the synthesis of the two, isn't it?"—leaving
"P" to complete the thought: "The author of your childhood then, the
historian of your past" (p. 187). This, except for "Fraser's" swinging his
"legs off the couch" and apparently going out into a brave new world of
restored psychic health, is where Fraser—the author, now, not the character—concludes his search and leaves the reader, and the book we hold in
our hands is, one supposes, the product of the character-author's stated
intention: "That's what I intend—to write about it from inside and out.
. . ." There may be some deliberate ambiguity about the final two lines—
"I find my glasses and swing my legs off the couch. 'I'll see you next Mon-
day.' I turn to look at him ['P'] for a moment, and his face is impassive"—
but surely the reader, having been prepared by the resonant rhetoric of the
last pages, cannot but feel this a very positive, upbeat conclusion . . . or
would so feel, had Beckett (and others) never written. The mother, the
father, Ilse, and the servants have been throughout so insistently *she, he,*

she, and *they,* opaque nonpersons in pronouns designed for that status, that it seems like sleight of hand to scoop them all, in the final three pages, into the *I,* who sees them suddenly in a wholly new light: "I feel them gathering, coming together, until they fill the emptiness around me [the emptiness of the *I,* one supposes], and in their eyes, unimaginably, I see an indestructible love, in their bodies touching each other, an unsurpassable assurance, and I stand there, my hands by my side, like a child overwhelmed with wonder" (p. 186). Beckett—and surely he was right in this—could not be so sanguine about reaching a stable and secure, originary *I* through collocation of however many *hes* and *shes.* "That brings us up to four, gathered together"—as it might be, "mother, father, Ilse, Bert," except that this is *The Unnamable,* where the four would seem to be Mahood, Worm, the Unnamable, and "the old bastard." But where there are four gathered together in Beckett, whether in his name or not, they never yield the *I.* "That brings us up to four, gathered together. I knew it, there might be a hundred of us and still we'd lack the hundred and first, we'll always be short of me" (*Trilogy,* 311). What is the *I* doing in here, then, one might ask, if we are always "short of me," and the answer is, "This *I* is not I; it's really he, and we are all of us as dissociated as ever." This answer, though Fraser stays with other pronouns than the *I* for 170 out of 185 pages, is not one he is finally willing to give, and so in his book, as in his therapy, I should say that Fraser succeeds rather than failing as no other dare fail.

The problem Maxine Hong Kingston has in saying the *I* in *Woman Warrior*[19] one would judge to be fleeting in light of the frequency and seeming ease with which she deploys the pronoun throughout the book. Nevertheless, there was a period in her childhood, Kingston claims, when she found it virtually impossible to recognize *I,* to articulate it and associate it with herself. "When I went to kindergarten and had to speak English for the first time, I became silent," she says (p. 191), and a couple of pages on,

> It was when I found out I had to talk that school became a misery. . . .
>
> Reading out loud was easier than speaking because we did not have to make up what to say, but I stopped often, and the teacher would think I'd gone quiet again. I could not understand "I." The Chinese "I" has seven strokes, intricacies. How could the American "I," assuredly wearing a hat like the Chinese, have only three strokes, the middle so straight? Was it out of politeness that this writer left off strokes the way a Chinese has to write her own name small and crooked? No, it was not politeness; "I" is a capital and "you" is lower-case. I stared at that middle line and waited so long for its

19. Maxine Hong Kingston, *The Woman Warrior: Memoirs of a Girlhood among Ghosts* (New York: Vintage Books, 1977). Further citations appear in the text.

black center to resolve into tight strokes and dots that I forgot to pronounce
it. (P. 193)

There are many things to be said about this passage, most of which Kingston
says, implicitly or explicitly, elsewhere in the book. When she writes of
"the way a *Chinese* has to write *her* own name small and crooked," we
understand that the difficulty she points to is both gender and culture specific, and we recall that she has earlier informed us that "[t]here is a Chinese
word for the female *I*—which is 'slave.' Break the women with their own
tongues!" (p. 56). For the Chinese woman, we could say, adapting Rimbaud, "*I* is a slave"; for her to use the *I* would be to accept that less-than-
person status. But for the schoolgirl the American *I* was scarcely, if at all,
better, for while the Chinese *I* was unacceptable, the American *I* was unrecognizable. And Kingston makes it clear that the dilemma was not hers alone:
"The other Chinese girls did not talk either, so I knew the silence had to
do with being a Chinese girl" (p. 193).

In addition to culture and gender, there is another determinant, which
we might term "geographic," for Kingston's *I/not I* quandary. Immediately
after telling how perplexed she was by the American *I,* Kingston proceeds
to an account of the word that seems to have joined with *I* to make her
life in school miserable. "The other troublesome word was 'here,' no strong
consonant to hang on to, and so flat, when 'here' is two mountainous ideo-
graphs. The teacher, who had already told me every day how to read 'I'
and 'here,' put me in the low corner under the stairs again, where the noisy
boys usually sat" (pp. 193–94). I suppose we are to understand by this that
the young girl could not read or say *I* and assert an undivided identity
because she both was and was not "here." Had she been "there," in China,
she would have had an all-too-clear *I* (= slave); had she been wholly American, rather than Chinese-American, she would presumably have been able
to read *I* because she would have been fully and at home "here." Given this
impossible "I-here/I-there" situation, Kingston adopts the only strategy
evidently available, which is to project a number of Beckettian avatars, a
series of *she*s in whom her *I* can both hide and realize itself. There is her
mother, who passed on to Kingston as a legacy the power of "talking-
story"; there is Ts'ai Yen, who made and sang the "Song for a Barbarian
Reed Pipe" that "has been passed down to us" (p. 243); and there is most
of all Fa Mu Lan, the Woman Warrior herself, whose story, borne literally
on her back, Kingston narrates in the first person, for—more than a mere
surrogate—Fa Mu Lan becomes Maxine Hong Kingston, merging with
her and conferring on her the *I* achievable neither in its Chinese nor its
American form (both essentially *not I*'s) but only in the form of writing.

Kingston is the one who writes her mother's story, writes Ts'ai Yen's story, writes Fa Mu Lan's story, and their stories thereby coalesce as her own, their *shes* becoming her *I* as a writer.

Patterns of Childhood[20] is a much longer book than either *Woman Warrior* or *In Search of a Past,* and in it Christa Wolf eschews the *I* more tenaciously and for many more pages certainly than Kingston but even than Fraser, allowing the first-person pronoun to surface tentatively, and with uncertain stability, only on the last of 407 pages. Wolf's reasons for being so chary of the *I*—which, like all the book's techniques and procedures, she analyzes at great length—are quite different from Fraser's, as is the assignment of the various pronouns. *Patterns of Childhood* is constructed as three interconnected narratives, more nearly concentric than parallel. The core is the story of a girl named Nelly, born in 1929, growing up in Nazi Germany (for what it is worth, the same years Fraser was growing up in Amnersfield: 1933–45), and an enthusiastic member of the Hitler Youth; surrounding this, but frequently crossing over it in the structure of the book, is the narrative of an adult—probably middle-aged—writer, without name but assigned the pronoun *you,* returning for a visit, with her daughter ("Lenka"), her husband ("H."), and her brother ("Lutz"), in 1971 "to L., now called G.," the town in which *you,* the adult narrator, was born and grew up; and finally, the outer shell, again crossing over the two inner narratives, that describes the writing of this book, in the midst of political, social, and psychological upheaval, from November 3, 1972 (p. 3) to May 2, 1975 (p. 406). The child, then, is "she" or "Nelly," the adult, as both narrator and writer, is nameless and "you," and the only rapprochement between the two is effected in two or three brief paragraphs at the end, which begin—this is the first appearance of the *I*—with a thoroughly Beckettian statement of aporia and ignorance: "I don't know." And indeed, this is the spirit of the entire book: tentative, questioning, uncertain, deeply exploratory, with few or no conclusions to offer the reader. Although like Beckett in this way, Wolf is different from him in almost everything else; in particular, the weighty Germanic seriousness of *Patterns of Childhood* is worlds removed from the Franco-Hibernian humor and the swift, light touch of Beckett's texts. Both, however, show a thoroughly modern spirit in their wariness about asserting an unequivocal *I* for either past or present identity and especially about asserting it as anything like an assured bond between two such identities. Given the utter dissimilarity between them

20. Christa Wolf, *Patterns of Childhood,* trans. Ursule Molinaro and Hedwig Rappolt (New York: Farrar, Straus and Giroux, 1980). Further citations appear in the text.

on other matters, the agreement of Wolf and Beckett about the *I,* leading to their mutual avoidance of the pronoun—whatever the differing literary, psychological, and philosophical reasons they may have for that avoidance—seems significant.

In *The Quest for Christa T.,* published eight years before *Patterns of Childhood,* Wolf experimented with the pronominal shifts she would develop much more fully in the later book. The Christa T. of the title is a schoolmate of the narrator who dies young, and the narrator's "quest" is to get inside the life of her friend, to know her, as the epigraph to Rousseau's *Confessions* has it, *intus et in cute,* "within and under the skin." But ultimately the narrator's motive in trying to enter into her friend's life is to understand better her own (which, it may be recalled, is what Rousseau, on occasion, claimed would be the great benefit of his book: offering readers a total, interior knowledge of another life to hold up against their own). *The Quest for Christa T.* exists somewhere in the shadowland between fiction and memoir. As a character, Christa T. is based on a schoolmate of the author (whether "Christa T." is a pseudonym is not clear), and the narrator is evidently a somewhat fictionalized stand-in for the author herself.[21] What the narrator attempts is to discover her own *I* in the *she* of Christa T., and at a second remove Wolf, as author, would construct an *I* for *herself* through the *I/she* conjunction of narrator and Christa T. One of the narrator's judgments about Christa T.'s life is of particular relevance here. It is that she never quite came into her own as a writer (which the narrator sees as the true vocation for both of them) because, though she may in time have succeeded, in her too brief life she could not fully articulate an *I* for herself. The conclusion of *Christa T.* revolves about what the narrator, picking the phrase up from Christa T., calls the "difficulty of saying 'I.'"[22] Far from being a danger or an impossibility in this early work, saying *I*—an act difficult but just possible and therefore courageous—is taken to be the sine qua non of the committed writer, and Wolf is intent on working out her *I* in the process of considering the reasons Christa T. was unable to do the same. What Wolf has done in *The Quest for Christa T.* is to write a kind

21. In what may be considered a further blurring of the lines between fiction and nonfiction, Wolf introduces Christa T., under the same name, into *Patterns of Childhood* (p. 227). If "Christa T." is a pseudonym, this merely continues the fiction from one book to another; if it was her real name, then bringing Christa T. into the midst of a host of fictional names would be to make her, as Emily Dickinson says of herself in a very different context, "the only Kangaroo among the Beauty."

22. *The Quest for Christa T.,* trans. Christopher Middleton (New York: Farrar, Straus and Giroux, 1970), 174.

of "biography" of her friend, making judgments as biographers will do and—as many of them also do—spelling out her own identity as a writer (though with a difference) in the life of her subject.[23] What she does in *Patterns of Childhood* is more radical. Instead of taking another for the other, she takes her younger self.

Because *Patterns of Childhood* is to a great degree about the writing of *Patterns of Childhood*, Wolf provides her reader with a good deal of analysis of the nature of pronouns and their place in the making of the book. "What is past is not dead," the text begins; "it is not even past." There is no reason for Wolf to cite them, but in reading these lines one assumes that Wolf is deeply familiar with books 10 and 11 of Augustine's *Confessions* and with the opening lines of Eliot's *Four Quartets*, each a major exemplar of life-writing in its time. Wolf continues with regard to the past: "We cut ourselves off from it; we pretend to be strangers." The observation is undoubtedly intended to introduce some of the themes of *Patterns of Childhood*, but it also offers, in the form of aphorism, a glimpse of how the book will be written, how it will work. For what better way to cut ourselves off from the past or pretend to be strangers than to change our name and substitute the nonperson *she* for the all-too-personal *I?* "People once remembered more readily," Wolf writes: "an assumption, a half truth at best. A renewed attempt to barricade yourself." Here we must pause to observe that one decision has clearly been taken before it is announced—viz., that the narrator and the writer within the narrative (if I may distinguish, for the moment, between the writer within the book and the author of the book, who remains outside it, writing of the struggle of the writer inside) will be designated by the pronouns *you* and *yourself*. This, then, brings up the question of the appropriate pronoun for *you* at an earlier stage. It can hardly be *I* (though Benveniste says that *I* and *you* are reversible, he does not mean it in this sense), and it is not clear that repetition of *you*, for past as well as present, would serve much purpose; it would not, that is, imply the continuity of consciousness and subjectivity that *I/I* would, nor would it disjoin the past and present in the manner of *I/she*. "Gradually, as months went by, the dilemma crystallized: to remain speechless, or else to live in the third person. The first is impossible, the second strange. And as usual, the

---

23. As Wolf writes in a piece called "Interview with Myself," in response to the self-addressed remark that "you are writing a sort of posthumous résumé of her life," "That's what I thought at first. Later I noticed that the focus of my tale was not, or was no longer, Christa T.—not in a clear-cut way. Suddenly it was *myself* I was confronting" ("Interview with Myself," in *The Author's Dimension: Selected Essays*, ed. Alexander Stephan, trans. Jan van Heurk [Chicago: University of Chicago Press, 1995], 16).

less unbearable alternative will win out" (*Patterns of Childhood,* 3). It would
be attractive to imagine that in the second of these three sentences Wolf is
referring to grammatical first and second persons; unfortunately the original
German will not permit such a reading. What she clearly means is that it
is impossible to remain speechless ("the first" alternative), yet strange to
live in the third person ("the second"). Nevertheless, the misreading en-
couraged by translation has its own pertinence, freed up in the confusion
engendered by the movement between languages, for the first person *is*
impossible for Wolf, and the second person *is* strange, as it situates her and
her narrator in an anticategory between the sharply distinguished categories
of nonperson (*she*) and person (*I*).

Wolf plays with the impossibility of first person and the strangeness of
second person throughout *Patterns of Childhood,* perhaps most teasingly in
the note signed "C. W." that stands before the text proper. "All characters
in this book are the invention of the narrator," the note begins, surprising
us with "narrator" when we might have expected "author" and stirring up
a wasps' nest of questions: What is the relationship between "C. W." and
the narrator? Are the narrator's initials "C. W." also? If yes, can the narrator
thus step out of the frame to address the reader directly in this note? If no,
does "C. W." have no part in the creation of characters in *Patterns of Childhood?* And, since the narrator is a major character in the book, is she an
"invention of" herself? Is the confusion of author and narrator, creator and
character but another instance of the Beckettian devised deviser devising
it all . . . not, evidently, in *Patterns of Childhood* for company, but for anxiety?
I'm not sure all these questions are or can be answered in the text, which
is another way of saying that Wolf's intent here as elsewhere is to complicate her material and any attitude she might be thought to express toward
it rather than to offer neat solutions. The problem is compounded by the
fact that there is no *I* in sight—not for "C. W.," not for the narrator, not
for the young girl, not for anyone. When "C. W." goes on to inform the
reader that no character "is identical with any person living or dead. Neither
do any of the described episodes coincide with actual events," it is deeply
unsettling, because one of the reiterated intentions of the book is to explore
and correct for the capacity of the German nation to forget. ("You imagine
a nation of sleepers, a people whose dreaming brains are complying with
the given command: Cancel cancel cancel. A nation of know-nothings
who will later, when called to account, assert as one man, out of millions
of mouths, that they remember nothing" [p. 149].) How will this be accomplished if neither character nor event corresponds with any actuality?
"C. W." responds that anyone imagining "a similarity between a character

in the narrative and either himself or anyone else should consider the strange lack of individuality in the behavior of many contemporaries." This could be fairly taken to mean, I believe, that "many contemporaries" (a good instance of the psychologically and ethically distanced third person) have shown themselves incapable of speaking a sufficiently examined, morally tested and proven *I*. But then, puzzlingly, we encounter what appears to be the same phenomenon in *Patterns of Childhood* itself.

Before looking at the passage that I take to be the most anguished formulation of the necessity of "Not-I" in *Patterns of Childhood,* we might consider reasons given by Wolf outside the text for assigning the nonperson pronoun to "Nelly." "I don't think that I ever hide the fact that the book is, so to speak, autobiographical," Wolf has said. "I admit this. But this 'so to speak' is very important because I do not feel identity with my character. There is . . . a sense of alienation from this period."[24] From the period one can understand, but from herself? With her "so to speak" Wolf throws the reader back into that uncertain area between fiction and autobiography that we find in *The Quest for Christa T.;* but to be alienated from herself, given the subject matter of *Patterns of Childhood,* has more troubling resonances than the separation (which is anyway not long maintained) between Christa T. and her narrator. This "mental alienation," as Benveniste calls it, is, Wolf implies, a historically determined condition ("perhaps one of the peculiarities of my life story, though others of my age may have the same experience"), but if for her, one wonders, why not for all others—which would result in total exculpation on grounds of total alienation? In any case, Wolf writes that "[f]rom a definite moment, which one cannot trace to the exact day but certainly to the exact period, one is no longer the same person. I no longer feel that it was I who had thought, said or done those things. And that's what I wanted to express through the third person." Once again, like the tongue unable to keep away from the aching tooth, Wolf returns to the sore spot: "above all," she says, she experienced "an uncanny feeling of alienation. As if I would be deceiving both myself and the reader if I called this being 'I' "; and then, in words that recall nothing so much as Henry Jekyll's forecast of things to come, "[I]t was exactly this feeling which I wanted to express by using the third person, because another result of this often disrupted life story is that several people wander around inside our bodies, and it is not at all easy to work out how to relate to all of them."

In *Patterns of Childhood,* Wolf does not attempt to come to terms with

---

24. *The Fourth Dimension: Interviews with Christa Wolf,* trans. Hilary Pilkington (London: Verso, 1988), 45. Further citations appear in the text.

all the people wandering around inside her body, but we do encounter, as perhaps the two principal residents, "Nelly" (or "she") and "you." The most telling, most tormented moment in the book—the crux of the matter, I think, for Wolf—comes when "you" tries to recall the meetings of "Nelly's Jungmädel unit" of Hitler Youth. "You" remembers clearly the "backs of the column. The pavement of the streets. The housefronts. But not a single face. Memory fails you in the most incredible, downright embarrassing way. No names either, neither of the leaders nor of those under them" (p. 229). That "you" has no name and "Nelly" only a pseudonymous one is relevant here, as is the implication that if there were an "I" the faces and names might well come back to the one remembering. In a remarkable passage of self-examination, which shows Wolf at her best as writer, as thinker, as analyst of the moral condition of our time, "you" considers why memory should fail so thoroughly but so selectively at just this critical juncture:

> You weren't prepared for this. The school, the street, the playground offer up bodies and faces which you could paint to this day. Where Nelly's participation was deepest, where she showed devotion, where she gave of herself, all relevant details have been obliterated. Gradually, one might assume. And it isn't difficult to guess the reason: the forgetting must have gratified a deeply insecure awareness which, as we all know, can instruct our memory behind our own backs, such as: Stop thinking about it. Instructions that are faithfully followed through the years. Avoid certain memories. Don't speak about them. Suppress words, sentences, whole chains of thought, that might give rise to remembering. Don't ask your contemporaries certain questions. Because it is unbearable to think the tiny word "I" in connection with the word "Auschwitz." "I" in the past conditional: I would have. I might have. I could have. Done it. Obeyed orders. (Pp. 229–30)

The imperatives bear no pronoun here, but of course implied in such commands as "Avoid certain memories" and "Suppress words" is always the *you,* in this instance the *you* speaking as it were to herself. *You* is compelled to absorb the pressure put upon it by the recalled activities of *she* but, at the cost of sanity, cannot assume the *I.* One need seek no further for an explanation of Wolf's adherence to the Beckettian *not I.* The sole question remaining is the legitimacy of the *I* when at last it does appear. In a public forum the year before *Patterns of Childhood* appeared, Wolf said, "Somebody asked how the book ends. It ends with the voices of the third person, Nelly, and the second person which is also in there, coming together and forming a single person, the 'I'" (*The Fourth Dimension,* 45). Or, maybe more to the point, in *Patterns of Childhood* the narrator tells how, having fallen into a serious illness while struggling with her book, she felt a "serious temptation to break off. After all, it isn't a story that must necessarily lead to a precise end." But in the hospital she has a clear feeling for what the end must be: "the final point would be reached when the second and third person were to meet again in the first or, better still, were to meet with the first person. When it would no longer have to be 'you' and 'she' but a candid, unreserved 'I' " (*Patterns of Childhood,* 349). When the meeting does occur on the final page, one must ask if there has been any satisfactory answer to the question of placing *I* and *Auschwitz* together in the same sentence. The only thing I believe we can say is that if the use of *I* has been earned and validated, then it is because it is precisely *not* "a candid, unreserved 'I' " but instead a most cautious, contested, and uncertain *I* that has not been long enough in the world to know what or why it is.

> The child who was hidden in me—has she come forth? Or has she been scared into looking for a deeper, more inaccessible hiding place? Has memory done its duty? Or has it proven—by the act of misleading—that it's impossible to escape the mortal sin of our time: the desire not to come to grips with oneself?
>
> And the past, which can still split the first person into the second and the third—has its hegemony been broken? Will the voices be still?
>
> I don't know. (P. 406)

Whether candid or not, that "I" sounds very reserved to me—and the better for it. Moreover, what is most important in the sentence is not the bare *I* but what is predicated of it. It is an unassuming *I*—so much so that, like the blizzard of "I don't know"'s that one gets in the final pages of *The Unnamable* (indeed throughout Beckett: from the Trilogy on, "I don't know" becomes like a mantra), it seems scarcely different from the *not I* that has ruled for 406 pages of *Patterns of Childhood* and that prevails, as the only pronoun available for our time, in writing across the twentieth century.

On the comparatively rare occasions when Primo Levi (in such books as *Survival in Auschwitz, The Reawakening, The Periodic Table, Moments of Reprieve,* and *The Drowned and the Saved,* and in his *Collected Poems*) avoids the *I* or doubts the pronoun's ability to reach back to embrace past consciousness, it is never because he felt, in Christa Wolf's words, "I would have. I might have. I could have. Done it. Obeyed orders." On the contrary, moments of pronominal uncertainty never come to him as a result of what, in the conditional, he might or could have done to others but rather of what, in the declarative, others did to him. Grammatically the

difference could be said to be that between the nominative and the accusative, the subjective and the objective. In an altered key, then, but still, like
Wolf, interrogating the capacity of the *I* to bind the past to the present,
and questioning in particular whether "the tiny word 'I' " can sustain itself
at all in proximity to "Auschwitz," Primo Levi writes on one such occasion,
"At a distance of thirty years I find it difficult to reconstruct the sort of
human being that corresponded, in November 1944, to my name or, better,
to my number: 174517."[25] Having been once stripped of his name and, in
effect, his *I* by his German captors at Auschwitz, having been reduced to
a number inked into the flesh, less even than *he,* the pronoun designed for
nonperson but still human status, Levi contemplates the effects of this both
on the *I* that stretches across time (if it does so stretch) and on the *I* that
may signify richly individual being at any moment. His conclusion is stark
and cheerless: full restoration is not possible. Though he seems to want to
disagree with Jean Améry, described as "the philosopher who committed
suicide and a theoretician of suicide," with whom he crossed in Auschwitz,
Levi cannot find fault with what he quotes from Améry in the preface to
The Drowned and the Saved: "Anyone who has been tortured remains tortured. . . . Anyone who has suffered torture never again will be able to be
at ease in the world, the abomination . . . is never extinguished."[26] To the
SS who handled prisoners at Auschwitz, Levi says, anyone not speaking
German was incapable of human communication and *eo ipso* was to be
treated as less than human (a minor but telling indication: "In Auschwitz
'to eat' was rendered *fressen,* a verb which in good German is applied only
to animals" [*The Drowned and the Saved,* 99]). Though he everywhere claims
something like a photographic memory for all that happened in Auschwitz,[27] there are isolated moments in Levi's writing when the human unre-
ality—or the inhuman reality—of the experience seems to submerge memory, and with it the *I* that might recall and be recalled. "Today, at this very
moment as I sit writing at a table, I myself am not convinced that these

25. Primo Levi, *The Periodic Table,* trans. Raymond Rosenthal (New York: Schocken
Books, 1984), 139.
26. *The Drowned and the Saved,* trans. Raymond Rosenthal (New York: Simon and
Schuster, 1988), 25.
27. Cf., for example, this passage in *Moments of Reprieve:* "Of my two years of life
outside the law I have not forgotten a single thing. Without any deliberate effort, memory
continues to restore to me events, faces, words, sensations, as if at that time my mind had
gone through a period of exalted receptivity, during which not a detail was lost. I remember,
for example, as they would be remembered by a tape recorder or a parrot, whole sentences
in languages I did not know then, and don't know now" (*Moments of Reprieve,* trans. Ruth
Feldman [New York: Viking Penguin, 1987], 11).

things really happened."[28] But for Levi the question of the *I* and its capacity to order and express experience is not a literary one, as it might be said to be with Stein or Wright, nor is it a matter of individual and family psychology as with Fraser. The logic of Levi's *I* is closer to Wolf's than to these others, but turned precisely inside out. Forgetting is something Wolf must work against constantly, both in herself and in the German people; Levi, too, sets his face bitterly against forgetting—

> Consider that this has been:
> I commend these words to you.
> Engrave them on your hearts
> When you go to bed, when you rise.
> Repeat them to your children.
> Or may your house crumble,
> Disease render you powerless,
> Your offspring avert their faces from you[29]

—but it is a warning to others, not himself, for he can never, Levi says, *not* remember Auschwitz. What is remembered, however, is the not being there as himself, not being seen, not being an *I* or even a *he*—to the guards, certainly, but also to the scientists in the laboratory where Levi, a chemist, was put to work for a time. After he emerged from the camp, Levi tells us in *The Periodic Table,* one of his most persistent wishes was to meet with one of those who would not or could not see him when a prisoner: "To find myself, man to man"—*I* to *I* as it were—"having a reckoning with one of the 'others' had been my keenest and most constant desire since I had left the concentration camp" (*The Periodic Table,* 215). That Levi, who had been so thoroughly "othered" as to be treated as being of another species, should now think of anyone who so treated him as "one of the 'others'" has a kind of justice about it. "The encounter I looked forward to with so much intensity as to dream of it (in German) at night," Levi writes, "was an encounter with one of them down there, who had disposed of us, who had not looked into our eyes, as though we didn't have eyes" (p. 215). One wishes that the pun in English on "eyes" and "I's" were there in the Italian, but it is not; even so, the psychology of the situation permits the formulation—the camp officials, including their scientist-"colleagues," looked on Levi and his fellow prisoners as if they had neither

28. *Survival in Auschwitz,* in *"Survival in Auschwitz" and "The Reawakening": Two Memoirs,* trans. Stuart Woolf (New York: Summit Books, 1986), 103.

29. "Shemà," in *Collected Poems,* trans. Ruth Feldman and Brian Swann (London: Faber and Faber, 1988), 9.

eyes nor *Is*. The encounter, when it comes with one Doktor Müller, is not what Levi might have wished, for his antagonist is neither vicious and evil on the one hand nor someone whose human sensibilities have been heroically transformed on the other but merely an everyday bumbler both as professional and as moral being. Müller's letter, according to Levi (and this is a shrewd comment, coming in a text as sharply written as *Periodic Table*), "was visibly the work of an inept writer: rhetorical, sincere only by half, full of digressions and farfetched prose, moving, pedantic, and clumsy: it defied any summary, all-encompassing judgment" (p. 219). The conclusion to which Levi comes, sadly echoing Wolf's general verdict on her own and an older generation of Germans, is that Müller willed himself not to know all that was going on, and part of that not knowing was not seeing the person—who would be an *I*—in front of him. "[A]t that time, among the German silent majority," Levi says, "the common technique was to try to know as little as possible, and therefore not to ask questions. He too, obviously, had not demanded explanations from anyone, not even from himself, although on clear days the flames of the crematorium were visible from the Buna factory" (p. 221). What we are concerned with at the moment, however, is not the person of Dr. Müller but the person of Primo Levi. When asked how he had survived Auschwitz, Levi responded that he willed himself to survive "with the precise purpose of recounting the things we had witnessed and endured." That he did this recounting with great force and eloquence no one could deny. Beyond the necessity to survive so that he might record, Levi says, "I was also helped by the determination, which I stubbornly preserved, to recognize always, even in the darkest days, in my companions and in myself, men, not things, and thus to avoid that total humiliation and demoralization which led so many to spiritual shipwreck."[30] In the face of all attempts to deny him his *I*, Levi tells the reader, he succeeded in maintaining it. But the circumstances of the end of his life compel one to wonder whether Primo Levi's optimism or Jean Améry's darker vision ("Anyone who has been tortured remains tortured . . .") came nearer the reality.

Gertrude Stein, according to her vice-exister Alice Toklas, "always was, she always is, tormented by the problem of the external and the internal," and one form this torment took for her was the certainty that "after all the human being essentially is not paintable"; yet, says Alice, Stein believed "that if you do not solve your painting problem in painting human beings you do not solve it at all" (*Autobiography of Alice B. Toklas*, 119).

30. Afterword to *"Survival in Auschwitz" and "The Reawakening,"* 397.

This sounds very much like Beckett's "nothing to express, nothing with which to express, nothing from which to express, no power to express, no desire to express, together with the obligation to express." Though both Stein and Beckett were speaking specifically of painters and painting, their remarks undoubtedly apply also to the written word. For the writer, Stein decided, it was all a question of the inside and the outside, and at a certain point, "Toklas" says, Stein changed her tactics: "Hitherto she had been concerned with seriousness and the inside of things, in these studies [which became *Tender Buttons*] she began to describe the inside as seen from the outside" (*Toklas,* 156). Her solution might not commend itself to everyone, but Stein's statement of the problem is as good as any, and it was a conundrum faced by every writer we are considering. How does one, how can one, depict—in paint or in words—the inner being of a living person, whether oneself or another? Is it possible for the artist to render accessible to observer or reader that inner, real, essential—whatever we want to call it—state or being or process that all of us experience, that indescribable and indescribably vague congeries of feelings and thoughts, desires and discernments, that we call, in a term as imprecise as the thing in question, the "self" or the "*I*"?

Moreover, though Stein, in the interests of simplification, pushed it aside by declaring memory hopeless and any previous self absolutely beyond reach, the issue is further complicated for the writer who would attempt to capture the self not only in the present but also in a past moment. In "A Sketch of the Past," after setting down the date of writing—"2nd May"— Virginia Woolf lays her quite un-Steinian hopes and intentions before the reader: "I write the date, because I think that I have discovered a possible form for these notes. That is, to make them include the present—at least enough of the present to serve as platform to stand upon. It would be interesting to make the two people, I now, I then, come out in contrast."[31] Interesting, yes, but possible? Stein and Beckett, I take it, would say no. But Woolf understood the difficulties, perhaps almost as well as her two— older and younger—contemporaries. "Here I come," Woolf writes, "to one of the memoir writer's difficulties—one of the reasons why, though I read so many, so many are failures. They leave out the person to whom things happened. The reason is that it is so difficult to describe any human

---

31. "A Sketch of the Past," in *Moments of Being: Unpublished Autobiographical Writings,* ed. Jeanne Schulkind (New York: Harcourt Brace Jovanovich, 1976), 75; cited hereafter as *Moments of Being.* Christa Wolf seems to have been influenced in *Patterns of Childhood* by the "method" Virginia Woolf demonstrates here of making the present moment of writing a major presence in the narrative of the past.

being" (*Moments of Being,* 65). And after giving an account of being sexually molested by her half-brother, Gerald Duckworth, and of the instinctive feeling of resentment, thousands of years old, that she then felt, Woolf continues: "[T]his throws light not merely on my own case, but upon the problem that I touched on the first page; why it is so difficult to give any account of the person to whom things happen. The person is evidently immensely complicated. . . . In spite of all this, people write what they call 'lives' of other people; that is, they collect a number of events, and leave the person to whom it happened unknown" (p. 69). For reasons of difficulty, as Woolf would have it, biographers abandon their subject's *I,* autobiographers abandon their own.

Staggering as the difficulty may be and tempting as it might be to give over the effort, I do not believe that any of the writers considered in this chapter can be said to have forsaken the project of the *I* simply because it was so hard. Indeed this is what, at bottom, each of them is about. When one or another resorts to the "Not-I" it is either because the *I,* for whatever reason and for however long a time, is not possible (which is different from being merely difficult), or because it is imagined that through the "Not-I" itself one might attain to the *I.* I have suggested that each writer had distinctive reasons for engaging the *I/not I* issue. I suggest now that Samuel Beckett offers the paradigmatic case: i.e., he shares the motives of the others and has a few of his own in addition. His is the quintessential and comprehensive instance of the writer who would say *I,* would say the self—and did say it, especially early on—but who discovered that it was not the task of a moment or a single book but a life's work, which could be accomplished only by *not* saying I and which, in the end, was destined to be an endless series of failures, their only redeeming feature being that each failed in a new way. I take Beckett at his word: he did not, as some critics would have it in order to soften the blow for the gentle reader, succeed by failing; he failed by failing. His would be a lesser example in going on were it otherwise. And failing and going on was, after all, his lesson for the age. How could Beckett *not* have failed when, as I believe, he took on himself all the separate reasons for the extreme difficulty if not impossibility of saying *I* adduced and enacted individually by Gertrude Stein, Nathalie Sarraute, Ronald Fraser, Maxine Hong Kingston, Christa Wolf, Primo Levi, and Virginia Woolf—not to say Henry Jekyll and Emile Benveniste? Stein's reasons might be said to have been artistic and stylistic, Sarraute's psychological and literary, Fraser's familial and psychiatric, Kingston's cultural and womanist, Wolf's historical and political, Levi's personal and historical, and

Woolf's aesthetic and philosophic. These reasons were each and all implicated in Beckett's theory and practice (yes, even Kingston's womanist
motive: consider *Not I, Footfalls, Rockaby, Ill Seen Ill Said,* and—in another way—*Embers* and *Eh Joe*), which together compose a very complex
tale stretching from *More Pricks Than Kicks* of 1933–34 to *Stirrings Still* of
1988–89.

I will not attempt to tell the entire story of Beckett and the *I*—to do
so would require another book of many pages—but in skeletal form it
might go like this: after the moderately conventional third-person narratives
of *More Pricks Than Kicks* (with one story, "Ding-Dong," in first person)
and *Murphy,* Beckett wrote a series of experimental fictions in which first
and third person mixed to such a degree that the *I* can disappear for long
periods of time only to resurface in the most astonishing way, claiming to
have been there all the time (*Watt* and *Mercier and Camier*), or the *I* is supposed to belong to someone dead before the story starts ("The Calmative"
and "The End"), or the *I* is merely a puppet for a *he* who gives the *I* speech
and who is thus an *I* beyond the *I* of the text (*How It Is*), or, in the Trilogy
(*Molloy, Malone Dies,* and *The Unnamable*) and in *Texts for Nothing,* all of
the foregoing—the *I* that comes and goes, the *I* that may be dead before
beginning, and the *I* that is merely one in an infinitely regressive series of
hes and *Is*; thereafter Beckett could be said to have achieved the voice his
explorations had been inexorably leading him to, a voice always in the third
person but with an undeniable and overwhelming pressure of the first person behind it—I will cite only *All Strange Away; Imagination Dead Imagine;
The Lost Ones; Company; Ill Seen Ill Said; Worstward Ho;* and *Stirrings Still.*
While this story was playing itself out in the fiction, Beckett of course was
also writing plays, which were undertaken in part to try to circumvent the
whole problem of the *I* and point of view. Instead of doing away with the
dilemma, drama only shifted it, and—to make this a radically brief account—Beckett came, after *Krapp's Last Tape,* to essentially the same solution, i.e., a disembodied voice (though occasionally from the mouth of a
character in the play) speaking, as in *Company,* to a listener, someone figuratively if not literally "on his back in the dark," telling of a life lived or
not lived and now near its end—thus (with slight variations) *Krapp's Last
Tape; Embers; Cascando; Eh, Joe; Not I; Footfalls; That Time; A Piece of Monologue; Ohio Impromptu;* and *Rockaby.* At a critical point in this history, when
Beckett had finished struggling through the dense bramble of the Trilogy
and turned for relief to writing *Waiting for Godot* (which proved to be no
relief at all), he told Israel Shenker of the *New York Times,* "At the end

of my work there's nothing but dust—the namable. In the last book—
'L'Innommable'—there's complete disintegration. No 'I,' no 'have,' no
'being.' No nominative, no accusative, no verb. There's no way to go
on."[32] Beckett did, however, go on, and thirteen years further along we
find him saying, in similar accent but with slightly different inflection,
"Writing has led me to silence. . . . Still, I have to continue. I am facing
a cliff, yet I have to move forward. Impossible, isn't it? Still one can move
forward. Advance a few miserable millimeters." And seven years later, to
the same interlocutor (Charles Juliet): "Finally one no longer knows who
is speaking. The subject disappears completely. That's where the crisis of
identity ends."[33] The subject—the nominative case, the first person—does
disappear from the late work, but paradoxically, and precisely because of
this disappearance, Beckett's *I* is stamped all over his drama and fiction—
probably more so than with any other contemporary writer. With the final
words of *Company* Beckett declines to give us at last, in the manner of Wolf
or Fraser, the *I* that has been resolutely denied throughout the book but
that has been evidently and heroically won through to in the end. He stays
with one of his two other pronouns—*you,* the voice of memory, rather
than *he,* the nonperson—and finally, which is important, it is both *you* in
the present and *you* as *you* has always been ("And you as you always were").
In 1975—twenty-five years after the Trilogy and five years shy of *Company*—Beckett spoke once again of the problem with pronouns, but *you*
is significantly not among those he specifies as being of no use: "But how
to say this: . . . there are no pronouns. The *I, he, we*—none of that works"
("Meeting Beckett," 26). In remaining faithful to the *you* and not yielding
to the allure of the *I,* Beckett implicates the reader—whose *I* is in a reversible relationship with the *you* of the text—in the isolation of *Company's*
conclusion, he transforms the condition into a universal human one, and
he evades the charge (which Vivian Mercier, for one, directed against him)
of whingeing. But behind the *you,* nevertheless, is all the exigency and
desire and anguish of *I.* Without the grammatical *I,* there is all the same
in Beckett from the Trilogy on the one ceaseless, mesmerizing voice, always
coming to an end, never coming to an end, telling, like the "wings . . .
leaves . . . sand . . . leaves . . . ashes . . . leaves" of *Waiting for Godot,* "my
old stories, my old story" of birth "astride of a grave and a difficult birth.

32. Israel Shenker, "Moody Man of Letters," *New York Times,* May 6, 1956, sec. 2,
1–3.

33. Charles Juliet, "Meeting Beckett," trans. Suzanne Chamier, in *TriQuarterly,* 77
(winter 1989/90), 13, 22.

Down in the hole, lingeringly, the gravedigger puts on the forceps. We have time to grow old. The air is full of our cries." Accompanying this elimination of the subject, as everyone recognizes, is what has been variously called a compression, a reduction, an intensification of the text— something akin to the ever-diminishing size of Alberto Giacometti's sculpted figures, a phenomenon that occurred without Giacometti's willing it and even quite contrary to his will—nowhere better realized than in the lyrical little prose piece called "neither," where the old story is told in only a few lines and where Beckett's voice and his unmistakable *I* are there the more in not being there. According to Carlton Lake in *No Symbols Where None Intended,* Beckett "wrote 'neither' in September 1976 to be set to music by Morton Feldman";[34] no doubt Feldman's composition provided fitting company for "neither," but I should think that no better, more lonely company could be found for it, if one might turn from music to the plastic arts, than in Giacometti's "Figurine entre deux boîtes qui sont des maisons" (see figure):

34. Carlton Lake, *No Symbols Where None Intended: A Catalogue of Books, Manuscripts, and Other Material Relating to Samuel Beckett in the Collections of the Humanities Research Center* (Austin: Humanities Research Center, 1984), 164.

neither

To and fro in shadow from inner to outershadow
from impenetrable self to impenetrable unself by way of neither
as between two lit refuges whose doors once neared gently close,
once turned away from gently part again
beckoned back and forth and turned away
heedless of the way, intent on the one gleam or the other
unheard footfalls only sound
till at last halt for good, absent for good from self and other
then no sound
then gently light unfading on that unheeded neither
unspeakable home[35]

35. This is the text as published in *The Complete Short Prose,* 258.

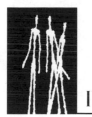

IV

NARRATIVE

A figure between two houses, between two thieves, between birth and the grave, between light and dark, and walking, always walking, but never arriving: this is the structural skeleton and the dynamic of all Beckett's narratives from the time of his revelation "that memorable night in March, at the end of the jetty, in the howling wind, never to be forgotten, when suddenly I saw the whole thing. The vision at last" (*Krapp*, 220). In an earlier version of *Krapp's Last Tape* Beckett referred to this moment in Dublin in 1945 not as "the vision" but as "the turning point, at last,"[1] and as a turning point it was for him as dramatic and as determinative as the conversion in a garden of Milan for Augustine or the illumination on the

---

1. *No Symbols Where None Intended,* 48. In *Damned to Fame: The Life of Samuel Beckett* (New York: Simon and Schuster, 1996), James Knowlson, on Beckett's authority, has corrected some of the details of this experience as dramatized in *Krapp's Last Tape* (the vision was not at Dún Laoghaire or at "the end of the jetty," for example, but in his mother's room), but he leaves it untouched as an actual revelation or turning point in Beckett's life. See *Damned to Fame,* 318–20.

There is considerable confusion about the year of Beckett's Dublin "vision." Knowlson does not specify a date, nor does Deirdre Bair; to Richard Ellmann, Beckett wrote in 1986, "All the jetty and howling wind are imaginary. It happened to me, summer 1945, in my mother's little house, named New Place, across the road from Cooldrinagh" (quoted in *Damned to Fame,* 686 n. 55). Charles Juliet, on the other hand, claims that on two different occasions Beckett told him it was in 1946. There are a number of reasons for being suspicious of Juliet's account, including the vivid description he gives—as being from Beckett's mouth—of "his experience in Dublin one night at the end of a jetty in the midst of a raging storm" and again of "the night in Dublin when, walking alone at the far end of a storm-whipped pier. . . ." See Charles Juliet, *Rencontre avec Beckett* (Montpellier: Fata Morgana, 1986), 16, 29–30; trans. Suzanne Chamier as "Meeting Beckett," *TriQuarterly,* 77 (winter 1989/90): 12, 18. Because of my sense that Juliet is rather casual about facts in the service of what he takes to be a higher, more poetic truth, I have opted in the text, but without feeling any certainty, for 1945.

road to Vincennes for Rousseau. This was not, however, the only or even the first turning point Beckett imagined for himself, as we may gather from what the ironic but highly autobiographical voice C says to the aged, immobile "Listener" in *That Time:* "turning-point that was a great word with you before they dried up altogether always having turning-points and never but the one the first and last that time curled up worm in slime when they lugged you out and wiped you off and straightened you up . . ." (*Complete Dramatic Works*, 390).[2] If this is the original turning point, then it requires little ingenuity to fix the final one, and it is between the two, while attempting to encompass both, that Beckett's narratives take on their characteristic form. My interest at the moment is not in these terminal turning points, however, but in the very concept of turning points within a life and in the way these may be felt to shape both the life or career of an artist and the narrative account the artist might give of that life.

Jean Starobinski, in one of his finely tuned essays on Rousseau, has said that a necessary condition for writing an autobiography is that there should have been a conversion of some kind in the life: "one would hardly have sufficient motive to write an autobiography had not some radical change occurred in his life—conversion, entry into a new life, the operation of Grace."[3] To this we might add that if the "conversion, entry into a new life," or turning point is a real one, it will alter entirely the understanding both autobiographer and reader will have of any experience occurring either before or after that point. This is crucial in the narratives of Augustine and Rousseau: the *Confessions* of the former exists on the knife-edge division that separates before from after, the way to perdition from the way to salvation, and no one reading the account can forget it any more than Augustine could in writing it; the *Confessions* of the latter would separate as decisively the memories of edenic existence from the fall into a world of writing, of striving, and of sorrow, for "Here begin," as Rousseau says again and again, the host of troubles that ensued upon his venturing forth publicly in language. Beckett's conversion was as different in substance from Augustine's or Rousseau's as was his vision of his own and human existence in general, but in form and in its formal relationship to narrative it was exactly the same. "When in Ireland," Charles Juliet tells us, "Beckett experienced . . . an upheaval that radically changed his approach to writing and his conception of narrative." Asked whether his altered view

2. Beckett, *The Complete Dramatic Works* (London: Faber and Faber, 1986).

3. Jean Starobinski, "The Style of Autobiography," trans. Seymour Chatman, in James Olney, ed., *Autobiography: Essays Theoretical and Critical* (Princeton: Princeton University Press, 1980), 78; cited hereafter as *Autobiography*.

came gradually or suddenly, Beckett, according to Juliet, spoke of dramatic change in a time of crisis, and continued, of the Dublin experience, "Until then, I had thought I could trust knowledge. That I was supposed to prepare myself intellectually. That day, everything collapsed." And once more, as earlier in meetings with Juliet, Beckett "describes the night in Dublin when . . . everything suddenly seemed to fall into place. Years of searching and questions, of doubts and failures, suddenly took on meaning. As he approached forty years of age, he clearly saw, as in a vision, what he would have to do." In Beckett's own words, "I glimpsed the world that I had to create in order to be able to breathe."[4]

In the text that accompanies the catalogue of Beckett materials at the Humanities Research Center in Texas (*No Symbols Where None Intended*), Carlton Lake makes much of Beckett's 1945 experience in Dublin, specifying with greater assurance than anyone else what was revealed to Beckett on that occasion. "He suddenly realized," Lake writes, "he had one subject—himself—and henceforward he would tell that story, with all its dark side, directly, through a narrator whose voice would always be his own. What he had recorded over the years, he would now play back" (p. 49). From *Krapp's Last Tape*, of course, we never know the nature of the revelation because the sixty-nine-year-old Krapp, hearing the self-satisfied crowing of his younger self, furiously fast-forwards the tape to avoid this portion and get on to the scene with the girl in the punt. I have no particular quarrel with Lake's interpretation. What surprises me a little, however, is his neglect of an earlier event that many—I think rightly—take for an equally important turning point. I have in mind the late night in January 1938 when Beckett was accosted in the streets of Paris by one Prudent, a pimp he knew slightly; Prudent demanded money, Beckett refused, and Prudent stabbed him in the chest, coming very close to killing Beckett. In a characteristic twist, it was not the near death that made the experience significant, casting a light backward and forward over Beckett's life and work, but rather the thoroughly noncommittal response he received when, thrown together with Prudent before the trial, Beckett asked the reason for the assault and was given the nonanswer, "I don't know, monsieur." I have already commented (in the previous chapter) on the flood of "I don't know"s at the end of *The Unnamable,* but the truth is "I don't know" or equivalent expressions are everywhere in Beckett from this point on. The best-known instances are probably in *Waiting for Godot,* where "I don't

---

4. Quotations are from "Meeting Beckett," 18; for the original French, see *Rencontre avec Beckett,* 29–30.

know" mingles with "Nothing to be done" from the first page to the last (and the boy, in his two brief appearances as Godot's messenger, repeats Prudent's words verbatim five times: "I don't know, Sir"). It is important to recognize that "I don't know" is not, as some would have it, an expression of nihilism or even of despair. It does not say that there is nothing to know, for, as Beckett pointed out on more than one occasion, this would be to make a presumptuous and unwarrantable claim to knowledge, even if it be the negative knowledge that there is nothing to know. After telling Tom Driver that it was the copresence of the two thieves, the mixture of light and dark, the uncertainty whether there is anything to know or not, that makes the human situation so unendurable (and yet one must go on), Beckett concluded, "The key word in my plays is 'perhaps'" ("Beckett by the Madeleine," 23). Neither "yes" nor "no," situated between hither and yon, between assertion and denial (which is itself an assertion of the negative), "perhaps" has the same epistemological valency as "I don't know," and it repeats in another form what Jack MacGowran says Beckett told him (as he told so many others: that two of them, Harold Hobson and MacGowran, manage to punctuate the four-clause, two-sentence sentence in exactly the same way is of no little interest) about *Waiting for Godot:* "There's a sentence from St. Augustine that reads, 'Do not despair; one of the thieves was saved. Do not presume; one of the thieves was damned.' Beckett said that is the key to the whole play."[5] The paired Augustinian thieves, "perhaps," and "I don't know," establish the moral, intellectual, and emotional tone of everything Beckett wrote from *Watt* through *Stirrings Still* and *what is the word* (where the title, being indeterminably either a statement or a question, enacts the same drama of in-betweenness and uncertainty).

If "I don't know" rules the end of *The Unnamable,* the beginning of that book provides good philosophical and rhetorical—and comic—reasons for it. Starting from the old issue of the *I/not I* and the question of who is speaking, Beckett gives us this at the outset: "I seem to speak, it is not I, about me, it is not about me. These few general remarks to begin with. What am I to do, what shall I do, what should I do, in my situation, how proceed? By aporia pure and simple? . . . I should mention before going any further, any further on, that I say aporia without knowing what it means. Can one be ephectic otherwise than unawares? I don't know" (*Trilogy,* 267). Being at a loss, not knowing how to start would be a reasonable definition of *aporia,* so that Beckett supplies us with both the word

5. "MacGowran on Beckett," in *On Beckett: Essays and Criticism,* 215.

and an illustrative example on the first page of *The Unnamable*. More than this, *aporia* comes from the Greek *a-* + *poros* —the alpha-privative prefix indicating negation attached to a word meaning a pathway, a passage through, a means of performing a journey, and (in the neuter plural) provisions for a journey: thus, "being without provisions for a journey." In the Beckettian narrative, which nearly always has a journey at its center, to proceed without any means for passage—"by aporia pure and simple"— would lead to situations of profound vexation; to be without the provision of even knowing what *aporia* means doubles and redoubles the dilemma. Likewise of *ephectic*, which the *Oxford English Dictionary* defines as "holding judgment in suspense: said of the ancient Skeptics," from the Greek *ephekteon*, "practicing suspense of judgment," and, in a definition particularly pertinent to the world constructed by Beckett, "immobile." Thus we set out on the journey of *The Unnamable*, along with the narrator, in a condition of ephectic aporia. Moreover, in *Malone Dies*, the previous volume of the Trilogy, the narrator has given a hint of the lay of the land when, apropos of the question of whether he must finish or not, he says, "After all it is not important not to finish, there are worse things than velleities" (*Trilogy*, 182). The double negative, coupled with *velleities*, suggests immobility in body and soul. *Velleity*—"a very low degree of desire or volition, not leading to action"—is a word and a condition common (for example) in T. S. Eliot's male protagonists (Prufrock, Gerontion, the young men in "Portrait of a Lady," "La Figlia che Piange," and *The Waste Land*), and, brought together with *aporia* and *ephectic*, it characterizes very nicely the prevailing state of the human spirit in Beckett's work after the dual turning points: a spirit willing to engage the world only by way of aporetic, ephectic velleities with "maybe," "perhaps," "I don't know," and "consider the two thieves in St. Augustine's wonderful sentence." After all . . . there are worse things than velleities, there have been worse things in our time: among them the certainty that there is nothing to know; more prominent among them, and much worse, the fanatical certainty that there is something to know and that I alone—or, more to the point, *we* alone—know it.

With these few remarks on the significance of a turning point in how the course of a life is perceived and recounted, I want to proceed, for the remainder of this chapter, to a consideration of certain issues bearing on the narrative act—the representational properties of narrative, narrative and life-history, narrative and the self, narratives finished and unfinished, and the specific forms of twentieth-century narrative—not, as in the previous chapter, with regard to Beckett and a constellation of other life-writers, but in respect of three artists I take to be definitive for the century: Samuel

Beckett (of course), Alberto Giacometti, and Franz Kafka. I should think that no objection would be raised about the first and last of these, but I can imagine the question, "Why Giacometti? What had he to do with narrative?" Briefly, I will argue not only that Giacometti did turn his hand to it in something like "The Dream, the Sphinx, and the Death of T."—and was fascinated with what narrative could and could not do, as we can see in the metanarrative he constructed around that piece—but also (and more important) that the terms in which he discussed so readily and at such length the problems of the draftsman, the painter, and the sculptor are no different from those in which critical discourse about narrative has been conducted in recent years. What Giacometti said in interviews, conversations, letters, catalogue notes, and occasional essays about the intentions, the difficulties, the successes and failures of his paintings and sculptures (and what Beckett and Kafka said of their fictions) is mutatis mutandis what Paul Ricoeur, Gérard Genette, Jacques Le Goff, W. B. Gallie, Louis O. Mink, Roy Schafer, Steven Marcus, Arthur Danto, Hayden White, Donald Spence, Jerome Bruner, Wayne Booth, Nelson Goodman, Wolfgang Iser, Robert Jauss, Edward Said, Barbara Herrnstein Smith, Frank Kermode, Robert Scholes, et al. (not to mention Aristotle and many, many others between him and the twentieth century) have been telling us these past years about narrative. And Giacometti's comments have the added virtue of coming from one immediately engaged with producing the narrative meanings and effects he talks about. My trio requires him for what Stephen Dedalus would call wholeness, harmony, and radiance (a set of qualities, I recognize, not always available or even desirable in narratives of the past seventy or eighty years—but that is a part of the story to come).

"And now the last evening that Thornton Wilder was in Paris last winter we wandered about together and I told him that what worried me was narration . . ." (*Everybody's Autobiography*, 107). The worry was not Gertrude Stein's alone, but her solution—to abolish time, memory, causality, consecutiveness, development, and all forms of linearity in one fell swoop, leaving only the *punctum temporis* of now that Augustine demonstrated could not exist (so that in Stein we get this: "But first we are going to London to see The Wedding Bouquet and then it will be today. . . . And so tomorrow is going to be the day. . . . It was tomorrow which was yesterday and it was exciting . . . ," etc. [315, 317])—seems to have been adopted by no one but herself. While Beckett, Giacometti, and Kafka could none of them be called Steinian, they would all have agreed with her that narration was a matter of very great worry; indeed, each came to the conclusion—

not once but again and again—that for many and complex reasons there was no way to succeed in the narrative act that lay at the heart of his creative endeavor. Theodor Adorno (who once told Beckett that the reception given his Beckett's—work was based on a misunderstanding, to which Beckett, in giving an account later of their conversation, responded, "That's pretty much my opinion")[6] presented the narrative artist's consternation and aporia in the starkest terms. In "The Position of the Narrator in the Contemporary Novel" Adorno writes, "Today that position is marked by a paradox: it is no longer possible to tell a story, but the form of the novel requires narration."[7] Not possible but required: this is nothing other than a restatement, in the critic's terms, of what Beckett says in the dialogues with Georges Duthuit about the artist's obligation to express while lacking all means, desire, and power to express and what he says again and then once more and again in *Molloy, Malone Dies,* and the *Texts for Nothing.* "Perhaps I had better abandon this story," Malone says in the midst of the inane three stories and an inventory he promised at the beginning—stories that go nowhere, pertain to nothing, and are regularly punctuated with the narrator's "what tedium" and "this is awful"—"Perhaps I had better abandon this story and go on to the second, or even the third, the one about the stone. No, it would be the same thing" (*Trilogy,* 174). And no doubt it would be the same, that is, a story without shape, without beginning or end (and a middle that resembles chaos), directionless, as far as Malone can see, plotless, pointless, and tedious. But necessary, absolutely necessary. "[O]n with the losing game," Malone tells himself, "it's good for the health. And all I have to do is go on . . ." (p. 214). Though this may do for the why, *how* to go on remains a question: "There I am back at my old aporetics. Is that the word? I don't know" (p. 166).

As the title of Adorno's essay suggests, one issue at stake here (but not the only one, as will become apparent) is the tangled and conflicted matter of *I* and *not I* treated in the preceding chapter. When Beckett says there is "No 'I,' no 'have,' no 'being' . . . no nominative, no accusative, no verb," he might as well be saying "no narrator, no narration, no narrative"—and no possibility of any of it. "Name, no, nothing is namable," we read in

6. See André Bernold, *L'Amitié de Beckett, 1979–1989* (Paris: Hermann, 1992), 55: "Mais il [Beckett] répétait volontiers ce qu'Adorno lui aurait dit un soir, aux Îles Marquises, que 'l'accueil fait à mon travail repose sur un malentendu.—C'est un peu mon avis,' disait Beckett. . . ."

7. Theodor W. Adorno, "The Position of the Narrator in the Contemporary Novel," in *Notes to Literature,* ed. Rolf Tiedemann, trans. Shierry Weber Nicholsen (New York: Columbia University Press, 1991), 1.30.

the eleventh of the *Texts for Nothing,* "tell, no, nothing can be told, what then, I don't know, I shouldn't have begun" (*Complete Short Prose,* 144).[8] This does exceeding well as representation of an aporetic, ephectic velleity. With Malone, it is not his *I* alone but his very existence—like the existence of all the Trilogy's narrators (and there are many of them . . . or only one . . . or none)—that is in doubt. For starters, we don't know, as he doesn't know, whether he is alive or dead; beyond this, we cannot be sure whether he is a "real" fiction of the author or the fictional fiction of some other fiction, an uncertainty that denies the reader any purchase in the world of the narrative. (What Thomas Messer says of the figures of Giacometti's mature sculpture, one could say also of Molloy: "Fragile and insubstantial, often no more than a streak in space, the standing or walking personages suggest a merely conditional existence.")[9]

The vertigo that afflicts the reader in contemplating Malone as narrator is both a demonstration and an effect of the impossibility of narrative as experienced in Beckett. If we consider *Malone Dies* in terms of its presumed narrator, the question becomes one of perspective. How can we locate ourselves in this farrago of stories, coming from we know not where and refusing to form themselves into a single story with a subject and a subjectivity—stories that will not cease nor cease proliferating but that will not offer us any focus of being either? Giacometti experienced this same difficulty both when he attempted the narrative of "The Dream, the Sphinx, and the Death of T." and when he returned to working from life in his sculptures and paintings. It was a question, as he put it, of how to situate himself in relation to his subject and of how the reader or observer would be situated with regard to the narrative taking place in time or to the sculptural object existing in its properly created space. "The Dream, the Sphinx, and the Death of T."—which is more about the manner of its own making than anything else—concerns a rather garish dream about spiders Giacometti had one night in 1946; the closing of a brothel he frequented called the Sphinx, where, more or less simultaneous with his dream, Giacometti contracted a venereal infection; and the deaths, which merge in this account, of T. (Tonio Pototsching, caretaker of the apartment building in Paris where Giacometti had his studio) and Van M. (Peter van Meurs, an elderly

---

8. *Samuel Beckett: The Complete Short Prose, 1929–1989,* ed. S. E. Gontarski (New York: Grove Press, 1995).

9. Preface to the catalogue of a 1974 Giacometti retrospective at the Guggenheim Museum (New York: Solomon R. Guggenheim Foundation, 1974), 10; hereafter cited as "Guggenheim catalogue."

Dutchman who had died in Giacometti's presence in Madonna di Campiglio, a remote village in the Italian Alps, some twenty-five years before T.'s death, the dream, the closing of the Sphinx, and the time of the story).[10] Giacometti's narrative problem is no doubt clear from this brief description: how to link these and other apparently unrelated events scattered here and there in time and space to one another and to a central consciousness, located in a Paris café, seeking some kind of ordering for them all. "Sitting in the café on Boulevard Barbès-Rouchechouard, I was thinking about all these things and looking for a way to express them. Suddenly, I had the feeling that all the events existed concurrently all around me. Time became horizontal and circular and it was also, simultaneously, space. I then tried to draw it" ("The Dream, the Sphinx," 56). And indeed there are the drawings, three of them, as part of the story, each with a different perspective on the narrative events, one horizontal, another vertical, and a third horizontal but with vertical panels—a three-dimensional representation, in other words. Not only were the events inclined to shift and change places, but Giacometti himself, placed in the café at the center, was forever moving. So he added at the beginning of the story a piece (headed "May 1920," the year before Van M.'s death and many years before any of the titular events) that purports to have been written a few days after the original composition and that begins thus:

> Tonight, going back to the article that I had started writing the other day, I no longer find myself relating in the same manner to what I wanted to express. There's been a kind of shift, the facts no longer have the same importance for me, or rather, they've slid to a different plane, a different place, and I myself am no longer quite the same, I am no longer at the same point in regard to things, their meaning has a different color, everything has passed into a different light, but the things that have changed most are the distances between myself and the things that have changed, time is no longer the same. (P. 50)

And he concludes, "But now, all these things have shifted during the past few days: there is something else, but I don't exactly know where I am" (p. 51). If Giacometti doesn't know where he is, his reader, like the reader *and* narrator of *Malone Dies* ("But what matter whether I was born or not,

10. The story first appeared as "Le Rêve, le Sphinx et la mort de T." in *Labyrinthe,* no. 22–23 (December 15, 1946): 12–13; translated by Joachim Neugroschel, it appeared in *Tracks* (November 1974): 50–59. Citations in the text are to the *Tracks* translation. The best account of the circumstances behind the story is to be found in James Lord's *Giacometti: A Biography* (New York: Farrar, Straus and Giroux, 1985); cited hereafter as *Giacometti.*

have lived or not, am dead or merely dying, I shall go on doing as I have always done, not knowing what it is I do, nor who I am, nor where I am, nor if I am" [*Trilogy,* 207]), is in no better shape. Now it may be said— and I would concur—that Giacometti is being playful here, but playfulness, as any reader of Beckett should readily understand, does not rule out being serious at the same time; and Giacometti in these passages says some things about position and perspective, about perception and distance from the subject (or object), and about the relationship of detail to the whole that, as we shall see, he took very seriously in his practice and theory of sculpture.

It was a matter of perspective, after all, of trying to realize in sculpture the way we perceive a figure receding in the distance, that produced in Giacometti the emotion he called "terror" in the letter written to Pierre Matisse before his New York show of 1948: "But wanting to create from memory what I had seen, to my terror the sculptures became smaller and smaller, they had a likeness only when they were small, yet their dimensions revolted me, and tirelessly I began again, only to end several months later at the same point. A large figure seemed to me false and a small one equally unbearable, and then often they became so tiny that with one touch of my knife they disappeared into dust."[11] Beckett would have understood, for he too could not keep his figures from disappearing into dust, and so would Kafka, whose late obsessional stories have to do with figures of constantly diminishing size: they are about the "Mouse Folk" and Josephine, their great singer (or is her singing only the piping that all the mice produce?); or about a speciesless creature who lives an increasingly constricted life of terror both inside and outside its burrow; or about the proud hunger artist who fasts on, past anyone's notice or memory, until the overseer must poke around in the dirty straw of his cage to find the hunger artist's wasted and pitiful, virtually nonexistent body, ready, like Giacometti's sculptures, to crumble into dust at a touch. Being the optimist (sunk usually in profound pessimism, it's true) that he was until almost the end, Giacometti goes on to say to Matisse, "All this changed a little in 1945 through drawing," but— as if he has spoken too soon—"This led me to want to make larger figures but then to my surprise, they achieved a likeness only when tall and slen- der." Only, one might say, when they took on the proportions of the hun- ger artist himself. As Giacometti elsewhere puts it with helpless anguish:

11. The letter to Matisse, first published in the catalogue of the 1948 show, is reprinted in the catalogue for a Giacometti retrospective at the Museum of Modern Art, New York, in 1965; the quoted passages appear on page 29 in a reproduction of Giacometti's original letter and on page 28 in translation. Cited hereafter as "1965 MOMA catalogue."

"After 1945 I swore to myself that I wouldn't allow my statues to keep getting smaller, not one iota smaller. But what happened was this: I was able to keep the height, but they became thin, thin . . . tall and paper-thin."[12] Sometimes, as Beckett said, it was all the fault of the pronouns; other times it seems to have been all the fault of perspective; in the end, however, it may be that pronouns and perspective come to much the same thing, both acting to complicate the life of anyone intent upon creating figures endowed with "reality" (Giacometti's term), whether in sculpture or in narrative. "In fact, the contemporary novels that count," Adorno writes in "The Position of the Narrator in the Contemporary Novel," "those in which an unleashed subjectivity turns into its opposite through its own momentum, are negative epics. They are testimonials to a state of affairs in which the individual liquidates himself, a state of affairs which converges with the pre-industrial situation that once seemed to guarantee a world replete with meaning" (p. 35). This is a bleak picture, bleaker than I think necessary in that it carries the conceptual bases of the art of Beckett, Giacometti, and Kafka to logical conclusions without crediting the creative achievements of their work, achievements that, precisely in being creative, exist quite beyond and aside from—or in surplus of—the conceptual grounding of the work.

Issues of perspective and of the *I/not I* quandary—or, as Adorno has it, "the position of the narrator"—almost insurmountable as they may have been, were not the only factors in storytelling that exacerbated the difficulties of the narrative act to the point of near impossibility for Beckett, Giacometti, and Kafka. It was not only (to put it in rather crude terms) point of view but also plot and characterization that provoked and hindered them until all three thought failure not only inevitable but something not far from desirable. It should be borne in mind that for each of them challenging the impossible, though it promised certain failure, was not a declinable proposition, for failure was no more certain—indeed, in a sense was less so—than the necessity (whence imposed, who knows?) of going on. Jean Genet once wrote, after watching Giacometti working over a long period of time on one of his portraits of Isaku Yanaihara, "During the entire time he battled with the portrait of Yanaihara . . . I had before me the touching spectacle of a man who never deceived himself, yet always lost his way.

---

12. Jean Clay, "Alberto Giacometti: Le dialogue avec la mort d'un très grand sculpteur de notre temps," *Réalités,* no. 215 (December 1963); quoted in Reinhold Hohl, *Alberto Giacometti: Sculpture, Painting, Drawing* (New York: Harry N. Abrams, 1972), 277.

He penetrated ever deeper into impossible regions from which there was
no way out."[13] There was no way out (*sans issue:* dead end), and he always,
no matter what, *always* lost his way. What Genet says rings true, and of
Beckett and Kafka as well. In advance, they were altogether clear eyed
about the impossibility of the task they entered upon, yet they chose the
impossible and not once but over and over again. "I know," Giacometti
said, "I know that it is utterly impossible for me to model, paint or draw
a head . . . as I see it, and, still, this is the only thing I am attempting to
do. All that I will be able to make will be only a pale image of what I see
and my success will always be less than my failure. . . ."[14] But wherein lay
the impossibility? Each of them might choose different phrasing here, but
I believe the most comprehensive expression of what all three faced (and
understood would eventually spell failure) is the observation Beckett made
to Tom Driver (quoted in chapter I) that "the task of the artist now" is to
"find a form that accommodates the mess."[15] Though the form must be
single and must exhibit (to quote, for convenience, Stephen Dedalus again)
wholeness, harmony, and radiance, the mess is irrepressibly and irreducibly
multiple, and it must be accommodated, not denied. Moreover, the mess
is not just in the world out there—though it is that too—but has made
its way into the ordering consciousness as well. Calling the mess "a buzzing
confusion" (perhaps a recall of William James's "blooming, buzzing confusion"), Beckett says, "The confusion is not my invention. We cannot listen
to a conversation for five minutes without being acutely aware of the confusion. It is all around us and our only chance now is to let it in" ("Beckett
by the Madeleine," 22). This is a desperate proposal, but as Beckett seldom
offers even the one chance it is as fair an opportunity as we will get from
him. But the problem is compounded if we think of the kind of life-writing
we are considering as self-writing, for the self as subject—and object—is
as much a part of the confusion as anything in the external world. Kafka,
who thought in just these terms—i.e., equating autobiography with the
writing of the self—sometimes claimed that if he were free of the office
where he worked he could turn with joy to autobiography, which would

13. "Durant tout le temps qu'il a lutté avec le visage de Yanaihara . . . j'ai eu le spectacle
émouvant d'un homme qui ne se trompait jamais mais se perdait tout le temps. Il s'enfonçait
toujours plus loin, dans des régions impossibles, sans issues," in Jean Genet, *L'Atelier d'Alberto
Giacometti* (Décines: Marc Barbezat, 1958), 41.

14. Giacometti's response to a question from Peter Selz about his "artistic intentions
concerning the human image," in Peter Selz, *New Images of Man* (New York: Museum of
Modern Art, 1959), 68.

15. Driver, "Beckett by the Madeleine," 23.

prove the easiest and most successful of all writing and would make him loved by everyone ("Then . . . the writing of the autobiography would be a great joy because it would move along as easily as the writing down of dreams, yet it would have an entirely different effect, a great one, which would always influence me and would be accessible as well to the understanding and feeling of everyone else").[16] Most of the time he knew better. Mixing, on one occasion, hope for the ease of autobiographical writing with a more hardheaded awareness of how it was likely to turn out, he wrote:

> Writing denies itself to me. Hence plan for autobiographical investigations. Not biography but investigations and detection of the smallest possible component parts. Out of these I will then construct myself, as one whose house is unsafe wants to build a safe one next to it, if possible out of the material of the old one. What is bad, admittedly, is if in the midst of building his strength gives out and now, instead of one house, unsafe but yet complete, he has one half-destroyed and one half-finished house, that is to say, nothing. What follows is madness, that is to say, something like a Cossack dance between the two houses, whereby the Cossack goes on scraping and throwing aside the earth with the heels of his boots until his grave is dug out under him.[17]

Beckett could have pointed out Kafka's mistake (only a momentary one, as Kafka understands that the outcome of the effort will be digging his own grave), for his Molloy, Moran, and Malone have no success at all in constructing themselves out of "the smallest possible component parts." The idea that you can cobble a self or a sculpted figure out of an old, failed one would have been an error also for Giacometti, whose method was to model and destroy, start over and destroy, again and again, until either artist or model—or both—could bear no more, then perhaps, in despair, let it be cast in metal—or destroy it, in its permanent imperfection, one last time.

Students of autobiography have been saying for a quarter century now that a self is created in the stories it tells to and about itself. (I find myself, for example, saying in a book published in 1980—and with apparent confidence—that "the act of autobiography is at once a discovery, a creation, and an imitation of the self" [*Autobiography,* 19]). Beckett and Kafka (and Giacometti in a slightly different way) test this proposition. *Molloy* and *Ma-*

---

16. *The Diaries of Franz Kafka,* ed. Max Brod, trans. Joseph Kresh and Martin Greenberg with the cooperation of Hannah Arendt (Harmondsworth: Penguin, 1964), entry for December 16, 1911, 140. Cited hereafter as *Diaries.*

17. This is among "Fragments from Notebooks and Loose Pages," in *Dearest Father and Other Writings,* trans. Ernst Kaiser and Eithne Wilkins (New York: Schocken Books, 1954), 350.

lone Dies begin alike with Kafka's "unsafe house" (the body and the self) and any putative new house both in a state of collapse. There is no more refuge in either of Kafka's or Beckett's houses than there is for the lonely being in Giacometti's *Figure in a Box between Two Boxes Which Are Houses* (as Giacometti called the sculpture in the catalogue for the 1950 show at the Pierre Matisse Gallery in New York). They are all homeless, wasted and yet still wasting away, these figures of Giacometti, Beckett, and Kafka, going back and forth, as in Giacometti's *Figure* and Beckett's "neither," endlessly "between two lit refuges whose doors once neared gently close, once turned away from gently part again." To the reader of Kafka this can only recall that great parable, "Before the Law"—so great that even Kafka was compelled to acknowledge his satisfaction in its making[18]—in which a man comes again and again over a long lifetime seeking admittance to the Law, but is turned away every time by the doorkeeper, who on each occasion repeats, "It is possible, but not at the moment." Finally, when his eyesight is failing and he is so weak "he can no longer raise his stiffening body," the man calls to the doorkeeper with one final question: "Everyone strives to reach the Law . . . , so how does it happen that for all these many years no one but myself has ever begged for admittance?" The answer is the same, one supposes, as the woman in Giacometti's sculpture or the man in Beckett's "neither" (or is it a woman? there is no indication, and it does not matter: this is not sexually differentiated man or woman but simply Lear's "poor, bare, fork'd animal") would receive before the gently opening, gently closing door: "The doorkeeper recognizes that the man has reached his end, and, to let his failing senses catch the words, roars in his ear: 'No one else could ever be admitted here, since this gate was made only for you. I am now going to shut it.'" *Life's Little Ironies,* as Thomas Hardy—who preferred to be called a meliorist rather than a pessimist—put it in the title of one of his books.

Speaking of his bad leg, which serves as a kind of synecdoche for the disintegration of his whole being, Molloy says, "I had so to speak only one leg at my disposal, I was virtually one-legged, and I would have been hap-

---

18. Typically, however, Kafka could not register his satisfaction without a reckoning of what it would cost him in both present and future misery. See diary entry for December 13, 1914: "Instead of working—I have written only one page (exegesis of the 'Legend') [i.e., 'Before the Law']—looked through the finished chapters and found parts of them good. Always conscious that every feeling of satisfaction and happiness that I have, such, for example, as the 'Legend' in particular inspires in me, must be paid for, and must be paid for moreover at some future time, in order to deny me all possibility of recovery in the present" (*Diaries,* 321).

pier, livelier, amputated at the groin. And if they had removed a few testicles into the bargain I wouldn't have objected" (*Trilogy,* 34). On pages 61–
62 we have the strange scene of Molloy's bodily dispersal, the arms and
hands, legs and feet no longer his, no longer related to one another or to
any whole body image. Likewise, in the second part of the book, Moran
(who may or may not be the same person as Molloy; in any event, both
are avatars and vice-existers) awakes one night as "a fulgurating pain went
through my knee." The next morning he is in the same condition as Molloy, one-legged in effect, but even more bizarre in his presenting symptoms:
"It was not painful. It simply refused to bend. . . . I fiddled with the knee-
cap. It felt like a clitoris" (p. 139). Some faulty workman, it would seem,
has taken used parts from an unsafe house (a previous effort at rebuilding)
and put them where they do not quite belong in the new (now old) house
called Moran. From the beginning Malone is much worse off than either
Molloy or Moran. Bedridden, he has use only of his arms, and even these
"I find it hard to guide. . . . My body is what is called, unadvisedly perhaps,
impotent. There is virtually nothing it can do. . . . My sight and hearing
are very bad," etc. (p. 171). And the Unnamable and his avatars are yet
more advanced in physical deliquescence than Molloy or Malone or any
other predecessors: the Unnamable evidently has no body at all; Mahood
lives, armless and perhaps gelded,[19] in a jar with only his head showing;
and Worm represents, at best, one of the lowest of life forms. What kind
of house could be constructed from these materials? What kind of narrative
could be pieced together from these old stories in a state of collapse, and
what kind of self would be the by-product? Such, however, is the strategy
of Beckett's narrators, as it is the proposed strategy in the Kafka passage.
They would collect these separated parts and attempt, with the puppet figures they construct out of the fragments, to tell a story that will create a

---

19. I say "perhaps" because Mahood seems not to know whether he has been the
beneficiary of the surgery to remove "a few testicles" that Molloy says he would have wel-
comed. As Mahood thinks about what would happen should he be asphyxiated by the
cement collar around his neck, he shows a considerable uncertainty about his sexual condition, also a confusion about just which parts would have been lost in the event that he has
been "gelt":

> The blue face! The obscene protrusion of the tongue! The tumefaction of the penis! The penis,
> well now, that's a nice surprise, I'd forgotten I had one. What a pity I have no arms, there might
> still be something to be wrung from it. No, 'tis better thus. At my age, to start manstuprating
> [thus, unaccountably, in the British ed.; neither the OED nor *Webster's Unabridged* knows the
> word *manstuprating;* the American ed. reads "masturbating"] again, it would be indecent. And
> fruitless. And yet one can never tell. . . . Heaven, I almost felt it flutter! Does this mean they
> did not geld me? I could have sworn they had gelt me. But perhaps I am getting mixed up with
> other scrota. Not another stir out of it in any case. (P. 305)

new, coherent alter ego, a new house for dwelling. What is described here is the bare-bones activity of narrating: making the disjunct pieces of experience shape themselves to a preexisting yet always changing form, a followable (to borrow Paul Ricoeur's term) story with, in some sense, a beginning, middle, and end. Beginning, middle, and end have existed as objective descriptive terms since Aristotle, but every age has had the task of defining for itself what could constitute a beginning, what would function as a middle, what might satisfy as an end. What we find in Beckett, as in Kafka, is that these new-old narratives just will not do: the stories refuse to come together; the old house is destroyed, but a new one never materializes. And at the end of *Malone Dies* we get another version of the Cossack's mad dance as Malone sets about killing off all the characters he has created, then proceeds to his own demise in the final words—

> or with it or with his hammer or with his stick or with his fist
> or in thoughts in dream I mean never he will never
> or with his pencil or with his stick or
> or light light I mean
> never there he will never
> never anything
> there
> any more

"What follows," as Kafka says, "is madness, that is to say, something like a Cossack dance between the two houses, whereby the Cossack goes on scraping and throwing aside the earth with the heels of his boots until his grave is dug out under him." We are unlikely to get anywhere a better description of Beckettian narrative than in these ruminations of Kafka on the probable nature and the almost certain result of his own imagined excursion into autobiographical narration.

The difficulties Giacometti encountered were not dissimilar. When he attempted verbal narrative in "The Dream, the Sphinx, and the Death of T." he found, as David Sylvester puts it, "that the shape of a continuous narrative unfolding in time does not correspond to the shape in time of the complex of events to be represented." This revealed slippage between verbal representation and the events to be represented is but another way of describing what had already proved for Giacometti so formidable a problem in sculpting and painting: what are the conditions, the means, and the limits of representation? What Giacometti had come up against, Sylvester goes on to say, "points to flaws in the convention current in representing reality in a given medium, and takes it for granted that a sense of responsibility towards representing reality entails a state of doubt as to the validity of the means of communication."[20] It would surely be fair to say that Beckett and Kafka felt the burden of this "sense of responsibility," entailing "doubt as to the validity of the means of communication"; or, to put it more plainly, in Beckett's terms (altering them only slightly), we could phrase the "doubt" in this way: "The representation that there is nothing to represent, nothing with which to represent, nothing from which to represent, no power to represent, no desire to represent, together with the obligation to represent." For Giacometti (probably for Kafka also—and, in truth, for Beckett as well) we should drop "no desire to represent," but otherwise, and in his own language, Giacometti said the same sort of thing many times throughout his career. In the previously quoted letter to Pierre Matisse, for example, Giacometti described his early experience working in Bourdelle's studio in Paris (1922–25) in these terms: "Impossible to grasp the entire figure (we were much too close to the model, and if one began on a detail, a heel, the nose, there was no hope of ever achieving the whole)" (1965 MOMA catalogue, 17, 16). Giacometti later came to feel that he could achieve the whole in a detail if he got the detail right (the eyes and the gaze, for example), or at least that this was an ideal to aspire to (*if* I could create a nose, I would have it all, he said . . . *if*);[21] but looking back on this early point in his career, he agreed with Kafka that it is futile to imagine that the whole individual reality can be constructed out of "the smallest possible component parts," for his strength—any artist's strength—would surely give out.

For a number of years (say, 1938 to 1945) Giacometti found the attempt to realize the whole figure while letting the details take care of themselves no more satisfactory than gradual construction from parts, since this meant putting the model at a greater distance; what happened then, as we have

20. David Sylvester, *Looking at Giacometti* (New York: Henry Holt and Co., 1996), 75.

21. See Giacometti's remarks to Carlton Lake in 1965 (in "The Wisdom of Giacometti," *The Atlantic* [September 1965]: 125): "When I want to do a head in sculpture, I limit myself to an attempt to understand the function of the nose. Because if I understand that a little bit, I'll understand the rest, too." Earlier in the conversation, however, Giacometti had already told Lake that to understand even the nose "a little bit" was "impossible." Before sculpting the whole head, he said, you must have some understanding of the nose, the skull, the inside of the head, but even then . . . : "So if you don't concern yourself with what's inside, you'll never bring off the outside. Impossible. Everything is impossible, but without that, it's more than ever impossible" (p. 123). Giacometti himself seems to have been—though with high good humor—a little bit impossible. Peggy Guggenheim admiringly described his "conversations and behavior" as "extremely Surrealist and whimsical, like a divertimento of Mozart" (Hohl, *Alberto Giacometti,* 275).

seen, was that the figures became dismayingly small, diminishing in size as their subjects receded in the distance, until many dwindled to nothingness. "In 1940, to my utter horror, my statues began to shrink," Giacometti told the critic Jean Clay. "Inexorably, all of my statues wound up just a centimeter tall. One last touch . . . oops! the statue disappeared. Only later did I understand this: I was instinctively reducing the size of my sculptures to reflect the real distance at which I had seen a person. A girl fifteen meters away was not eighty centimeters tall, but about ten. And, to grasp a whole and keep from drowning in details, I had to be far away. Details always bothered me. . . . So, I backed up further and further, until everything was on the verge of disappearing."[22] (It is said that when Giacometti returned to Paris after the war he carried with him the results of three years of hard, exploratory work in six matchboxes.)[23] This perceptual phenomenon grown out of his experiments in sculpture eventually came to affect Giacometti's normal visual experience as well. "And then, very gradually, and especially since the war, it has become so much a part of my nature, so ingrained, that the way I see when I'm working persists even when I'm not working," Giacometti told David Sylvester in 1964.

> I can no longer get a figure back to life size. Sometimes, in a café, I watch the people going by on the opposite pavement and I see them very small, like tiny little statuettes, which I find marvellous. But it's *impossible* for me to imagine that they're life size; at that distance they simply become appearances. If they come nearer, they become a different person. But if they come too close, say two metres away, then I simply don't see them any more. They're no longer life size, they have usurped your whole visual field and you see them as a blur.[24]

What Giacometti says here not only accounts for much in his sculpted figures; it also describes exactly all the pullulating figures of Beckett's Trilogy and later fiction, who, seen at a distance, are doll-like mannequins, puppets, worms; up close, on the other hand, they are not seen at all but (like the narrator of *The Unnamable,* for example) swarm all over you, usurping "your whole visual field and you see them as a blur."

22. Jean Clay, "Le dialogue avec la mort . . . ," *Réalités;* quoted in Hohl, *Alberto Giacometti,* 275.

23. See Albert Skira, "Alberto Giacometti in Genf 1942–1945," *Du* (Zürich), no. 252 (February 1962): 16: "One morning after the war had just ended I visited Alberto in his hotel room. He was to return to Paris the next day. I asked him: 'Have you shipped your sculptures yet?' He replied: 'No, I'm taking them with me.' He pulled six matchboxes from his pockets. In them was the work of those years." Quoted in Hohl, *Alberto Giacometti,* 276.

24. Interview included in Sylvester, *Looking at Giacometti,* 127.

What lay behind all this effort of Giacometti's, both early and late, was what we might understand not only as a basic principle of his sculpture but also as the first necessity of narrative: to find a form to accommodate the perceived, living reality of the subject. "I saw anew," Giacometti says, "the bodies that attracted me in reality and the abstract forms which seemed to me true in sculpture, but I wanted to create the former without losing the latter . . ." (1965 MOMA catalogue, 27, 26). This, no doubt, is the desire of every artist, but can it be done? When he faced that question, Giacometti more often answered "no" than "yes," which means only that he, again like Beckett and Kafka, was, in Genet's words, "a man who never deceived himself, yet always lost his way" as he penetrated "ever deeper into impossible regions, *sans issues.*" For Kafka, one of the impossible regions was metaphor, a linguistic figuration he could not, as a writer, avoid but one that inevitably dragged him down from a pure world of formal cerebration into the very impure world of people, objects, and events. "Metaphors are one among many things which make me despair of writing," he noted in his journal in 1922. "Writing's lack of independence of the world, its dependence on the maid who tends the fire, on the cat warming itself by the stove; it is even dependent on the poor old human being warming himself by the stove. All these are independent activities ruled by their own laws; only writing is helpless, cannot live in itself, is a joke and a despair" (*Diaries,* 398). Yearn after abstract forms as he might, Kafka, like any artist, had to descend into the Yeatsian foul rag-and-bone shop of the heart, had to find some way to accommodate the mess, had (in Giacometti's phrase) to try to create the reality of bodies without losing the inherited, abstract forms of his art.

The artist whose chosen mode is life-writing—and I would argue that Beckett became this with "the siege in the room," if not earlier; that Kafka was this from at least 1912 onward; and that Giacometti was always this, if we understand "life-sculpting" to be an exact analogue for "life-writing"—must seek an image or series of images that will provide a sufficient metaphor for a life; must seek, more specifically, a narrative that will adequately imitate—not in the sense of copying (a notion Giacometti flatly rejected) but of realizing in a different form, a different medium—a self-existence and a life-history. The reason for the frequent occurrence of the word "impossible" in this chapter is, perhaps, now becoming apparent. It is not immediately obvious that a narrative can "equal" a life or (which is a little less) that it can be expected to represent the course of a life-history—or should even aspire to (I add the rider in view of the fact that Beckett, Giacometti, and Kafka, knowing what they knew, yet aspired to make it do so, while regularly acknowledging that failure was certain). The one is shaped and molded, the other is not; how will the former be fitted to the latter, or the latter to the former? A large part of the point of the dialogue in Nathalie Sarraute's *Childhood*—especially that of the skeptical voice employing the pronoun *you*—is that if one is foolish enough to make the contents of memory (which is, after all, the material of the life-writer) the substance of narrative, one will likely end up with something as essentially antiartistic, as unordered and unorderable, as the soft, amorphous stuffing in an upholstered settee the *I* remembers slashing into as a child, bringing "something flabby, grayish."[25] What a mistake it is, the *you* says, to let memories come crawling and bawling out like that. She never intended, she claims, to push the *I* to commit an act of this sort, so antiaesthetic as to be virtually obscene. "I didn't for a moment dream of obliging you to lay yourself bare, to disclose what you are filled with, what you hold back, what you only ever allow to escape in dribs and drabs, you might have let it trickle out just a little bit . . ." (p. 48). What the *you* voice says makes sense, as we can see most persuasively in the funny account *I* gives of the essay she wrote for her French class called "My First Sorrow"—an account that may be intended to show what goes on in many instances of life-writing. What *I* produced was a perfectly elegant little piece, lovingly shaped and patterned, exhibiting the requisite building action, climax, and dénouement, full of affect and brilliant verbal touches . . . and with not one word of historical fact. All the truth of narrative, none of the truth of life. You can reproduce the mess, would seem to be the message *you* and *I* have for the life-writer, or you can make a fine and comely narrative, but not both.

The narrator of *The Unnamable* is scarcely concerned with making anything comely. What he spews out can be as ugly as homemade sin if only he can be certain it is his story, his life, and that there is an *I* there within. "I must have forgotten them," he says, "I must have mixed them up, these nameless images I have, these imageless names . . . , and this word man which is perhaps not the right one for the thing I see when I hear it, but an instant, an hour, and so on, how can they be represented, a life, how could that be made clear to me, here, in the dark" (*Trilogy,* 375). But it is all "blank words" for the "Unnamable," words disconnected, without relation to any pattern, to any followable, hence meaningful, narrative: "that's all words, they're all I have, and not many of them, the words fail, the

25. Nathalie Sarraute, *Childhood,* trans. Barbara Wright (New York: George Braziller, 1984), 6.

voice fails . . . quick now and try again, with the words that remain, try what, I don't know, I've forgotten, it doesn't matter, I never knew, to have them carry me into my story, the words that remain, my old story . . . perhaps it's I, perhaps somewhere or other it was I, I can depart . . . it's not I, that's all I know, it's not mine . . ." (pp. 380–81). It is not I, not my story, indeed not a story at all. The "Unnamable" cannot proceed from disjunct words (disjunct from one another and also from any nonlinguistic reality) to connected narrative, from the internal mess of subjectivity to the externalized form. How can we expect the product to represent an instant or an hour, much less a life? Kafka had in mind this conventional notion that a work or body of work could be understood to represent the author's entire being or constitute an *apologia pro vita sua* when he wrote, in a characteristically despairing letter to Max Brod, "I am not enclosing the novels [*Amerika* and *The Trial*]. Why rake up old efforts? Only because I have not burnt them yet? . . . Where is the sense in keeping such work which is 'even' bungled from the aesthetic point of view? Surely not in the hope of piecing a whole together from all these fragments, some kind of justification for my existence, something to cling to in an hour of need? But that, I know, is impossible; there is no help for me there."[26] Kafka, with his "even" wrapped in quotation marks, implies, like Sarraute, a clear distinction between what we might term "aesthetic" writing and life-writing, suggesting that *The Trial,* for example, might have succeeded "from an aesthetic point of view" (though, according to Kafka, it did not) and still have been the failure it was (in Kafka's view) as a "justification for my existence." What Kafka mentions with some scorn in his letter—the idea that writing, turned to autobiographical ends, might piece together a whole out of fragments and offer justification for a life—was a prime motive in life-writing from St. Augustine (where it is seen as certainly feasible, in no way a futile hope) through Rousseau (who, whatever we may think of the result, was originally more sanguine even than Augustine about the possibility of achieving the desired end). No doubt a large element of apologia continues in twentieth-century autobiography—even, I would say, in our three skeptics. What does not remain for them is much hope of success, at least not according to the very rigorous—impossible?—criteria they establish for determining success; and this seems to be the conclusion of those

---

26. *Letters to Friends, Family, and Editors,* trans. Richard and Clara Winston (New York: Schocken Books, 1977), 184. In the passage above, I have chosen to adopt the wording of Kafka's letter given by Max Brod in his postscript to the first edition of *The Trial* as being more germane to my purposes. See *The Trial,* trans. Willa and Edwin Muir, "Revised Definitive Edition" (London: Secker and Warburg, 1956), 295–96.

who have thought most deeply and explored most tenaciously in life-writing in our time.

Curiously enough, the insurmountable problems encountered by Beckett, Giacometti, and Kafka in narrative representations of experience may be seen to have parallels to the semipathological difficulties recorded by A. R. Luria in his two classic case histories, *The Man with a Shattered World* and *The Mind of a Mnemonist.* The first book, subtitled "The History of a Brain Wound," tells of a man who suffered an injury in World War I that destroyed his memory to the degree that he could neither connect words with things, and so construct a bridge to the world, nor connect words with words, and so make sentences to record his experience of the world. With what seems a compensatory strengthening of a function to replace the lost memory, Zasetsky (as the injured man is named) shows an incredibly strong will to tell the story of his wound and thus of his life, for the wound has become the center of his unrecoverable life-story, and everything now relates to it. The second book, subtitled "A Little Book about a Vast Memory," tells the inverse story of a professional memory person capable of retaining everything he experiences by storing each item, as it were, in an eidetic image, to which he can refer when he wishes to recall whatever it may be. Blessed or cursed with this bizarre memory, S. (as he is known in the book) cannot forget, and the consequence is that his memory is so overloaded, unable to discard through forgetting what has no significance for living his life, that he values nothing more than anything else and seems without a normal functioning of will that would cause him to choose this rather than that. There are many psychological lessons to be drawn from these twin books, but the important one for our purposes now is that a memory off the human scale at either end, being virtually nonexistent through physical trauma or so hypertrophied that it renders its possessor nearly impotent to act, will lead to an incapacity affecting both faces of the narrative act, i.e., the ability to tell a story and the ability to follow a story. Zasetsky, who Luria says had a rich perceptual and imaginal experience (he was normal or above in sensory reception), could not find words to associate with those images flowing from the world without, nor could he connect words to one another in ever larger units—clauses, sentences, paragraphs—to arrive at a fully articulated narrative. Nor could he follow a narrative, and for the same reason: the connections that make a narrative coherent or followable were not available to his ruined memory. And S. likewise but in reverse. He was able, despite having no Italian, to memorize several stanzas from the beginning of *The Divine Comedy*—"Nel mezzo del cammin di nostra vita / Mi ritrovai per una selva oscura / Che la diritta via era smarrita / Ah quanto a dir qual era è cosa dura": the prototypical narrative of the Western tradition, one might say, or the archetypal turning point in that narrative—not by referring to any meaning the lines might have, which he understood nothing of, but by breaking the lines down into words, words into syllables, syllables into sounds, and sounds into yet more basic images that he could revisit in memory whenever he wanted. "[H]e was able to use his technique and reproduce several stanzas . . . not only with perfect accuracy of recall, but with the exact stress and pronunciation. Moreover, the test session took place fifteen years after he had memorized these stanzas; and, as usual, he was not forewarned about it."[27] But S., as Luria makes clear, had no sense that what he was reproducing was narrative, and had it been presented to him as such, rather than as material to be reduced to what would be to anyone else a chaotic heap of images, he would have been utterly incapable of following it. With his shattered memory, Zasetsky could not move from images to words to sentences to narrative, and so could not follow a story made of those essential parts; with his excess of memory, S., too, because of the reductive procedure his mind automatically adopted, was left, stranded, at the starting point of images.

In Zasetsky and S. we have a narrative incapacity caused by skewed faculties; but what is intensely interesting, I think, and relevant is that the same sort of incapacity we find in their case histories we can also find, presented as the normal if unfortunate state of things in our time, all across life-writing of the twentieth century. "Ideally," Christa Wolf writes in *Patterns of Childhood,* but of course one is aware that nothing is ideal in the world she describes, "Ideally, the structure of the experience coincides with the structure of the narrative. This should be the goal: fantastic accuracy. But there is no technique that permits translating an incredibly tangled mesh, whose threads are interlaced according to the strictest laws, into linear narrative without doing it serious damage" (*Patterns of Childhood,* 272). A couple of points cry out for attention here. First, is not the "incredibly tangled mesh" the same thing as Beckett's "mess," and if so, would it be desirable, even if possible, which it is not, to translate the mess/mesh into "linear narrative"? Is Beckett not correct when he says we must find a form to *accommodate* the mess rather than a way to translate or transform it? And second, can we be so sure that the threads of the incredibly tangled mesh are interlaced according to the strictest laws? How do we know that? And

27. A. R. Luria, *The Mind of a Mnemonist,* trans. Lynn Solotaroff (Cambridge: Harvard University Press, 1987), 45.

whence those laws? Are they laws of nature? God's laws? Human laws? It will not do to say, "I don't know"; or rather it will do, but only if said at a prior stage—thus: "I don't know" that there are strict laws; also "I don't know" that there are not strict laws. "I no longer know what to think about anything," Giacometti said.[28] Wolf herself, because of narrative's failure, is compelled to say, "We can no longer tell exactly what we have experienced" (*Patterns of Childhood,* 362). When Pozzo asks, in *Waiting for Godot,* "What happened?" Vladimir, convinced that we can no longer tell exactly—or even approximately—what we have experienced, is both outraged by the question and incredulous: "Will you stop it, you! Pest! . . . Did you hear him? He wants to know what happened!" (*Complete Dramatic Works,* 77); and Estragon, seemingly unable to believe his ears and offended that anyone would ask such a question, responds a few moments later to Pozzo's "What happened exactly?" with an emphatic and scornful, "Exactly!" (p. 81).

What theorists tell us is that narrative is a powerful aid to "meaning-making"; that by "emplotment" it can produce the significance of "configuration" out of the insignificance of "succession"; that it is an indispensable component in the essential human "effort after meaning"; that it renders what we have experienced "followable" and thus understandable; that it is "capable of forming meaningful sequences and ordered connections" that in turn will do no less than redeem our sad and wasted lives,[29] and so on: many, many more could be cited to the same or similar effect. I have no quarrel with any of this. Indeed, I think it all true and spoken by some of the best thinkers we have. But what if narrative, with all its vaunted powers, is beyond you or me or anyone, as Beckett certainly says and as Giacometti and Kafka, I believe, agree? It obtains little that narrative

28. "En fait, je ne sais plus quoi penser de quoi que ce soit. . . .": See Alberto Giacometti, *Écrits,* comp. Mary Lisa Palmer and François Chaussende (Paris: Hermann, 1990), 97.

29. Quotations, in order, from Jerome Bruner, *Acts of Meaning* (Cambridge: Harvard University Press, 1990), passim; Paul Ricoeur, "Narrative Time," *Critical Inquiry,* vol. 7, no. 1 (autumn 1980): 178, and *Time and Narrative,* 3 vols., trans. Kathleen McLaughlin, Kathleen Blamey, and David Pellauer (Chicago: University of Chicago Press, 1984, 1985, 1988), passim, esp. 1.155–61; Frederic C. Bartlett, *Remembering* (Cambridge: Cambridge University Press, 1932), passim; Ricoeur, *Time and Narrative,* passim, esp. 1.149–55; Ricoeur, "The Question of Proof in Freud's Psychoanalytic Writings," in *Hermeneutics and the Human Sciences,* ed. and trans. John B. Thompson (Cambridge: Cambridge University Press, 1981), 253; and *Time and Narrative,* passim, esp. 1.161–74. As this brief listing may indicate, I find Paul Ricoeur, especially with the three-volume *Time and Narrative* and the more recent *Oneself as Another* (Chicago: University of Chicago Press, 1992), the most stimulating thinker—although he is one of many—on questions of narrative.

can do all these things and more if it is not possible. And who could talk about meaning-making, emplotment, configuration out of succession, successful effort after meaning, followability, meaningful sequences, and ordered connections after reading *Molloy* or *Malone Dies* or *The Unnamable* or *The Trial* or "A Country Doctor" or *The Castle* or even "Le Rêve, le Sphinx et la mort de T.," seeking in all good faith a followability that just does not offer itself? It is one thing to talk about followability in Dickens or George Eliot, Tolstoy or Thomas Mann, another thing to talk about it in Beckett or Kafka.

When we are told that emplotment—which we are to understand as a modernized version of Aristotle's mimesis, not as copying but as a plastic, creative, transformative imitation of, say, the course of a life ("Mimesis, in this sense, is a kind of metaphor of reality")[30]—is the key; and if we then study the mess for possibilities of exercising emplotment, or even for bare signs of any inherent plottability, we will come up, as Beckett sees it, very short. Plot, in any traditional sense, denies itself to the contemporary writer. To look back for a moment, one might say that a plot for St. Augustine was nothing more nor less than God's eternal design working itself out in time and human destiny. In quintessential form—perfectly mysterious to us because of the unnegotiable gap between divine intention and human understanding—it was the story, infinitely rich in hermeneutic possibilities, of the creation in Genesis 1.1–27. The duty of the reader for Augustine was to interpret this divinely emplotted story, and to emplot one's own life, so as to fit the individual plot to the all-encompassing, supervenient plot of God's mind. For Rousseau, per contra, plot was all too human, the reverse of divine, and as such both comprehensible and incomprehensible. To the beleaguered Jean-Jacques, plot was the conspiracy designed by enemies who were invisible but no less powerful for their being (mostly) unknown. When Rousseau accords them the ironic honorific of the uppercase "M" in "ces Messieurs," it is not to suggest that these plot makers are divine, but it does imply, among other things, that to Rousseau's troubled mind they appeared to possess the godly attributes of ubiquity and omnipotence (though certainly not beneficence). Plot, among contemporary life-writers, and especially the Augustinian-Ricoeurian ability to emplot, seems to have largely disappeared. Plot is certainly no longer a matter of divine intention, as with Augustine, nor is it a question of human conspiracy, as with Rous-

---

30. Paul Ricoeur, "The Narrative Function," in *Hermeneutics and the Human Sciences,* 292; in the same volume, in an essay titled "Metaphor and the Problem of Hermeneutics," we are told that "*mimesis* does not mean the duplication of reality; *mimesis* is not a copy; *mimesis* is *poiesis,* that is, construction, creation" (p. 180).

seau. The situations of K. in *The Castle* or *The Trial,* of Gregor Samsa in *Metamorphosis* or Georg Bendemann in "The Judgment," of Molloy, Moran, Malone, and the Unnamable in Beckett's Trilogy, of Didi and Gogo in *Waiting for Godot* or Winnie in *Happy Days* or Hamm and Clov in *Endgame* are no more the doing of God or some hidden "Messieurs" than their own doing—but vice versa also: they have not brought isolation and unhappiness on themselves any more than God or human enemies have. In a universe where plot scarcely obtains at all—where, effectively, it either does not exist or is indistinguishable from chaos—there can be no discernible, determinable, or shapable meaning.

All the foregoing is not intended to make the claim that narrative, even of a fairly conventional sort, has disappeared among modernist and post-modernist writers, or that the desire and need for narrative are no longer present and acute. Beckett, Kafka, and Giacometti may indeed be the most moving and convincing witnesses to the contrary. Each would have given his life for narrative—and, in a real sense, each did. But possibility and desirability do not always or necessarily coexist, and that is the reason, on their own accounting, for the Beckettian, Kafkaesque, Giacomettian incessant, failed struggles. On the other hand there have been writers of our time who have found, as Beckett, Kafka, and Giacometti could not, traditional modes that proved not only powerfully seductive but altogether satisfactory for their purposes. For some, in fact, the narrative drive is so compelling, so irresistible, that its dynamic usurps what we would normally take to be the function of memory—i.e., recall of what once happened.

Before citing cases, I want to mention two psychologists whose early studies of memory bear on the issue of the place of narrative in remembering, viz., Hermann Ebbinghaus and Frederic Bartlett. In *Memory* (1885), Ebbinghaus published the results of experiments he had designed to determine what material subjects could remember and how long they could remember it after it was presented to them for retention under strict conditions. Since Ebbinghaus was among the first to want to make a natural science of psychology, he put together rigorous, not to say astringent, quantifiable experiments that excluded anything not controllable in the laboratory. Thus, instead of giving his subject (singular, because Ebbinghaus was himself the sole subject) words to remember—for words would have meanings that would affect the findings and invalidate them as scientific data—Ebbinghaus used only nonsense syllables, which, he thought, would prevent the distractive possibility of their being related to the subject's nonlaboratory, real-life experience. What Ebbinghaus wanted to avoid, in other words, was the opportunity to incorporate words into larger verbal structures such as clauses, sentences, and—especially—narratives. In *Remembering* (1932), Bartlett rejected this approach, arguing that to make memory a phenomenon of the laboratory rather than of lived experience might transform psychology into a science but a jejune, irrelevant one at best. Instead of nonsense syllables, therefore, Bartlett gave his subjects stories, preferably somewhat strange stories from cultures other than their own, to remember . . . or whatever they might do in addition to or other than remembering them. And he found pretty much what he expected: in recollection the subjects first altered the stories in ways that would make them seem more familiar, that is, in content more like stories they already knew; and then they introduced elements of internal coherence and followability they apparently felt were lacking in the originals. In subtle and not so subtle ways, the subjects adapted the stories to their own, already known narratives, and thus made them both individually and culturally followable.

One thing we can see going on in Bartlett's experiments is narrative overriding memory, which is what I suggest we see also in the episode from Richard Wright's *Black Boy* (mentioned in chapter III), when Uncle Hoskins terrifies the boy by beginning to take the horse and buggy into the Mississippi River. It is narrative and its demands that drive that scene, not memory. Or perhaps a better way of putting it is that, caught up by the onward impulse of narrative, Wright comes to adopt as memory what he remembers *narrating* rather than what he remembers *happening*. (That this is not an unknown or even uncommon phenomenon has been argued by skeptical critics of "repressed memories," who maintain that people who "recover" memories of sexual abuse that never happened are transferring a memory back from the real scene of telling the story to a nonexistent scene of occurrence. In moments of heightened emotion and need, narrative can thus both displace and replace memory.) An instance of such substitution that is perhaps more interesting because seldom noticed occurs in Mary McCarthy's *Memories of a Catholic Girlhood* as she describes her father, who, together with her mother, died in the influenza epidemic of 1918, when McCarthy was six years old. Roy McCarthy, according to his daughter, was not only a storyteller but the frequent subject of stories told by others, and McCarthy's account of him is filled with anecdotes of a more or less glamorous, romantic nature. He had a bad heart, McCarthy tells us, brought on by a football injury, and doctors told him it would be dangerous to marry, but he went ahead anyway, and "They were very much in love . . . ," and "He was a recklessly extravagant man. . . . And I remember his coming home one night with his arms full of red roses for my mother"; he "was so tall that he could not get through a door without bending his head," he "had been captain of the Minnesota football team" and a member of Delta Upsilon fraternity, and he "was at the head of his class in law school." But her father, McCarthy says, "was a romancer, and most of my memories of him are colored, I fear, by an untruthfulness that I must have caught from him. . . . [T]here was a romantic aura surrounding him, a certain mythic power that made people want to invent stories about him." This acknowledgment comes amid a host of stories McCarthy has already told—for example her father's drawing a revolver on the train conductor during the fatal journey from Seattle to Minneapolis—stories that McCarthy at least feigns to want to retract; but once made part of a larger narrative, it becomes impossible to withdraw them, to expunge them from McCarthy's consciousness or neutralize their effect on her or her reader. In one such story she says of her father, "He wore his gray hair in a pompadour and carried a stick when he walked. He read to me a great deal, chiefly Eugene Field and fairy tales, and I remember we heard a nightingale together, on the boulevard, near the Sacred Heart convent. But there are no nightingales in North America."[31] A father who wears his hair in a pompadour and carries a walking stick, who reads fairy tales to his daughter and takes her to where she can hear nightingales—it is very much of a piece, and all "untrue," McCarthy suggests. But why, then, "I remember"? In part, it is the same as with Wright, who says, "Whenever I saw his face the memory of my terror upon the river would come back vivid and strong. . . ." "I remember" gives the strongest sort of belief support available to what is being said. "I think I remember" would not do, nor would "I was told that." "I remember" carries an assurance of continuity and the authenticity of an event whose status cannot be doubted since it has resided all this while, unaltered, in the protective recesses of memory.

In addition to this, however, I believe that McCarthy was in fact remembering—not a songbird in Seattle, but something of much later date. The nightingales, if such there were in North America, would have been singing to her and her father circa 1915, let us say, when McCarthy was three or four years old. *Memories of a Catholic Girlhood* was published in 1957. The forty-plus intervening years were filled with a very different kind of experience from the backwater schoolgirl days described in *Memories:* there was first the heady atmosphere of Vassar College, and after that the excitement of coming out in New York into the social, literary, and political activity swirling around *Partisan Review* that McCarthy recounts in *Intellectual Memoirs: New York 1936–1938.* "In that circle," Elizabeth

31. Mary McCarthy, *Memories of a Catholic Girlhood* (New York: Harcourt Brace Jovanovich, 1957), 9–12.

Hardwick tells us in her foreword to *Intellectual Memoirs*, "the Soviet Union, the Civil War in Spain, Hitler and Mussolini, were what you might call real life but not in the magazine's pages more real, more apposite, than T. S. Eliot, Henry James, Kafka, and Dostoyevski."[32] While the last three were dead, Eliot was very much a living presence from 1936 to 1938: he figures at one point in *Intellectual Memoirs* as the focus of a dispute about religious matters between McCarthy and Philip Rahv. But he also figures, as it were proleptically, in *Memories of a Catholic Girlhood*—once directly, once allusively. "To read Dante and Chaucer or the English Metaphysicals or even T. S. Eliot, a Catholic education is more than a help," McCarthy says in the prefatory "To the Reader"; and turning it around—to prove the help that Eliot could be for someone engaged in describing a Catholic education—McCarthy terms the schoolmates she so warmly despised "damp, confidential souls," a phrase that would immediately recall to one of McCarthy's sophistication the lines from Eliot's "Morning at the Window": "I am aware of the damp souls of housemaids / Sprouting despondently at area gates." And this, I believe, indicates surely enough how McCarthy "remembers" hearing a nightingale "on the boulevard, near the Sacred Heart convent": she recalls not a nightingale where there could not have been one but rather the final stanzas of Eliot's "Sweeney among the Nightingales," which she first read, it may be, at Vassar and then read and reread, perhaps even memorized, during the years in New York and after:

> The host with someone indistinct
> Converses at the door apart,
> The nightingales are singing near
> The Convent of the Sacred Heart,
>
> And sang within the bloody wood
> When Agamemnon cried aloud
> And let their liquid siftings fall
> To stain the stiff dishonoured shroud.

The much later *reading* memory has imposed itself in place of whatever happened or did not happen, whatever was heard or not heard, on the boulevard near the Sacred Heart convent years before in Seattle. The lesson taught us by Wright's Uncle Hoskins and McCarthy's father and the nightingale is clearly one about memory, but it is also—no doubt less clearly but perhaps more importantly—about the power of narrative. Both pas-

32. Mary McCarthy, *Intellectual Memoirs: New York 1936–1938,* with a foreword by Elizabeth Hardwick (New York: Harcourt Brace Jovanovich, 1992), p. x.

sages occur in highly thematized, carefully constructed narratives, where the author is in full control of the textual surface and nothing occurs there without design. Wright intends to say something about the incessant, inevitable betrayal of trust that for him spelled a southern childhood. He presents the theme and prepares the illustrative scene with meticulous care; he carries the reader through the rising action to the climax on the river and the conclusion, draws his moral, and ties a nice little knot around the narrative bundle. It reads almost like a copybook lesson in how to do effective narrative. Likewise with McCarthy: it would be hard to find a better example of *New Yorker* style and structure—with an intriguing sentence or two to pique the reader's curiosity at the beginning, through a graceful, never obvious development of theme about sensitive, upper-middle-class coming of age in the middle, to an exquisite dying fall at the end—than in every one of the episodes in *Memories of a Catholic Girlhood*. If, in the course of the thematic development of either book, *Black Boy* or *Memories of a Catholic Girlhood,* memory should get in the way or, more to the point, should provide insufficient grist for the mill, then narrative, with its superior, many-times-proved powers of organization, must take over.

It was not, then, the unavailability of traditional narrative in the years they were working that caused Beckett, Giacometti, and Kafka to despair of it as a satisfactory mode. It was rather the demands they made on narrative, and the perceived insufficiencies of its prestructured, quasi-structuralist forms in the face of an unstructurable mess, that made them turn away and speak of failure and impossibility. When Beckett concludes the story "The End" with his narrator saying, "The memory came faint and cold of the story I might have told, a story in the likeness of my life," it may not sound to the reader a hopeless aspiration—"a story in the likeness of my life"— but Beckett unquestionably thought it so, and not only because his narrator is at this point either dying or dead. In Beckett's view, and in Giacometti's and Kafka's, it could not be done—as simple as that. A life, "my life," any life, just could not be molded to the contours of a story or into the shape of a likeness. Giacometti, by all accounts, was brought time and again to misery and half-madness by the attempt, yet he was no worse off than Beckett or Kafka; indeed, it would appear that it was only in reading Beckett, or in listening to him and to his silences, that Giacometti found the language to express his despair as painter and sculptor, for in speaking of his own failure he more than once echoes phrases from *Malone Dies* and *The Unnamable* and observations about art and the artist from Beckett's dialogues with Georges Duthuit. There are so many heads to the impossibility of the artist's project as conceived by Giacometti that it is hard to know which one to seize on. He wanted to capture the "reality" of the subject, he said, the living presence of the model, but there was no way to do this directly, no way to transfer what was seen to canvas or sculpture because of the gap in time between seeing and consciousness of seeing on the one hand and molding or painting the figure on the other. So what he was left to paint or to sculpt was not what was seen, not a vision, but, as he put it in a 1962 interview with André Parinaud, the "residue of a vision." "One might imagine," Giacometti explained, "that realism consists in copying . . . a glass just as it is there on the table. In fact, one never copies anything but the vision that remains of it each moment, the image that forms itself in consciousness. You never copy the glass on the table; you copy the residue of a vision."[33] But this is nowhere near the end of the complexities and frustrations involved in representing reality as Giacometti conceives that task, for beyond the slippage between looking and recording there is the continual flux and flow of appearances that is the only reality we can see; beyond that is the necessity of representing not just the flow of appearances in the subject but one's own sensations in response to the subject reality; and beyond that once more is the continuous alteration in the brain, the sensibility, the registering and recording organism itself. "Every time I look at the glass," Giacometti continued to Parinaud, "it seems to remake itself, its reality becomes indefinite, because its projection in my brain is indefinite, or only partial. One sees it as if it were vanishing . . . returning . . . vanishing . . . returning . . . that is to say, as if always it were indeed situated between being and nonbeing. And that is what one wants to copy."[34] Giacometti could not have supposed that this was a difficulty never enountered before, since in philosophic terms it is at least as old as the fragments of Heraclitus and the dialogues of Plato; and when intellectuals, picking up on fashionable Sartrean formulations, began to mutter about existential anguish, Giacometti would have none of it: "Everyone's talking

33. "On peut s'imaginer que le réalisme consiste à copier . . . un verre tel qu'il est sur la table. En fait, on ne copie jamais que la vision qu'il en reste à chaque instant, l'image qui devient consciente. . . . Vous ne copiez jamais le verre sur la table; vous copiez le résidu d'une vision." (André Parinaud, "Pourquoi je suis sculpteur," Arts [Paris], no. 873 [June 13, 1962]: 5.) This piece has been reprinted in Écrits under the title "Entretien avec Giacometti: Pourquoi je suis sculpteur"; the quoted passage occurs on p. 273. Further citations will be given as "Arts" and "Écrits" with page numbers.

34. ". . . [C]haque fois que je regarde le verre, il a l'air de se refaire, c'est-à-dire que sa réalité devient douteuse, parce que sa projection dans mon cerveau est douteuse, ou partielle. On le voit comme s'il disparaissait . . . resurgissait . . . disparaissait . . . resurgissait . . . c'est-à-dire qu'il se trouve bel et bien toujours entre l'être et le non-être. Et c'est cela qu'on veut copier" (Arts, 5; Écrits, 273–74). My translation.

so much about this existential fear and anxiety as if it were something new! On the contrary, everybody at every time has felt it. Just read the Greek and Latin classics" (quoted in Hohl, *Alberto Giacometti*, 187). Nevertheless, the dilemmas of representation and the issue of what is being represented did seem to Giacometti particularly troubling and defeating for the modern artist, and here one recalls what Beckett had to say about the hopeless confusion of light and dark now as against the sharp distinction available to an earlier time. "The entire undertaking of modern artists," in Giacometti's words, "lies in this wish to seize, to possess something that constantly slips away. They want to possess the perception they have of reality more than the reality itself."[35] Which lands one right back in the mess of Beckettian subjectivity and the question of how the artist can represent it—how, in Steinian terms, the artist can devise a narrative that will make the inside outside and the outside inside.

Who can doubt that this was the project—the simple-sounding one of telling "a story in the likeness of my life"—that locked Beckett in a room for the three or four years it took to write the Trilogy and *Godot*, the same project that teased and tormented Kafka into writing "The Judgment," *The Metamorphosis*, "In the Penal Colony," "A Country Doctor," "A Hunger Artist," "The Burrow," "Josephine the Singer, or The Mouse Folk," and the great and mad "Letter to His Father"? In all these it is the indistinct self behind the life whose likeness is to be taken that becomes both subject and object of the pursuit. If Giacometti could complain that a drinking glass was forever remaking itself, vanishing and returning, and that it was impossible to grasp it in its perpetual moment-to-moment transit from being to nonbeing, how much more dire the prospects for capturing, in a single gesture and artifact, both the glass and the self's responses to it. Then replace the glass with a human model, for preference someone with whom there has been an extended and rich emotional relationship—Annette or Diego or Caroline—and the terms of the wager rise to impossible levels. When Giacometti speaks of recording his perceptions of the model in front of him, we must understand the infinite complexity on both sides of that encounter. His perceptions were on the one hand formless and indistinct, Giacometti said, and on the other, part of a tangle of everything he had seen and felt, all he knew and intended. And looking

35. "Toute la démarche des artistes modernes est dans cette volonté de saisir, de posséder quelque chose qui fuit constamment. Ils veulent posséder la sensation qu'ils ont de la réalité, plus que la réalité elle-même" (*Arts,* 5; *Écrits,* 274).

to the other side of the creative engagement, Giacometti was determined to give to the painted or sculpted figure that special, indeed unique, presence or subjectivity or life—whatever it should be called—that he experienced as the very heart of the model's being. Could this be done? Of course not, and hence the frequent expressions of despair, the curses and mutterings and rages described by Giacometti's sitters, the trashing of years of work as worthless. But hence, too, the feeling every day of his life that tomorrow might be the day. . . . In a journal entry dated "vers 1960" Giacometti spelled out the circumstances leading to both his assured despair and his infinitely deferred hope, with what he says and how he says it sounding like Beckett or one of Beckett's creatures—Malone, let us say, or the Unnamable:

> I no longer know who I am or where I am, I no longer see myself, I think my face must look like a dim, shapeless, whitish blob, which barely stays together, held up by formless scraps that fall to the ground. Blurred apparition. I no longer [see] myself, nor what surrounds me: drinking glasses, windowpanes, faces, colors here and there, yes some very vivid colors, a saucer on a table, the back of a chair. Objects seem the most real, the glass much less fleeting than the hand that holds it, lifts it up, puts it down, vanishes. Objects have their own consistency about them. The heads, the people are nothing but continual movement from within and without, they ceaselessly remake themselves, they have no real consistency. . . . They are neither cube nor cylinder nor sphere nor triangle. They are a moving mass . . . , an ever-shifting form, never entirely graspable. And yet they are as if held closely together by an internal center that gazes at us through the eyes and that seems to constitute their reality, a measureless reality in a limitless space, which seems different from the space that contains the cup in front of me or the space created by that cup. And they have no definable color at all.[36]

36. "Je ne sais plus qui je suis, où je suis, je ne me vois plus, je pense que mon visage doit apparaître comme une vague masse blanchâtre, faible, qui tient tout juste ensemble portée par des chiffons informes qui tombent jusqu'à terre. Apparition incertaine. Je ne me [vois] plus, ni ce qui m'entoure: des verres, des vitres, des visages, des couleurs par-ci, par-là, oui des couleurs très éclatantes, une soucoupe sur une table, le dos d'une chaise. Surtout les objets me semblent réels, le verre bien moins précaire que la main qui le tient, qui le soulève, le repose, disparaît. Les objets ont une autre consistance. Les têtes, les personnages ne sont que mouvement continuel du dedans, du dehors, ils se refont sans arrêt, ils n'ont pas une vraie consistance. . . . Elles ne sont ni cube, ni cylindre, ni sphère, ni triangle. Elles sont une masse en mouvement . . . , forme changeante et jamais tout à fait saisissable. Et puis elles sont comme liées par un point intérieur qui nous regarde à travers les yeux et qui semble être leur réalité, une réalité sans mesure, dans un espace sans limites et qui semble être autre que celui dans lequel se tient la tasse devant moi ou créé par cette tasse. Elles n'ont, non plus, aucune couleur définissable" (Écrits, 218). My translation.

This absence of a sustaining body image and dissolution of any sense of physical cohesiveness or definition that Giacometti says he experienced in or as himself is dramatized throughout Beckett's postwar fiction. "It is in the tranquillity of decomposition," Molloy says, "that I remember the long confused emotion which was my life, and that I judge it, as it is said that God will judge me, and with no less impertinence" (*Trilogy,* 25). How could judgment of such a life—ceaselessly agitated, in continuous movement from within and without, shapeless and ungraspable—be anything but impertinent? "My life, my life," Molloy says, with a kind of aporetic skepticism about the whole affair, "My life, my life, now I speak of it as of something over, now as of a joke which still goes on, and it is neither, for at the same time it is over and it goes on, and is there any tense for that?" (p. 35). The question implies its answer: there is no tense, no temporal narrative scheme, that can do justice to that which is over and done, yet at the same time is going on and going on.

For such a situation, where life is over and the joke still goes on—a situation we have learned to call "Kafkaesque"—and where there is no possibility of narrative, there also cannot be any summative judgment, at least not without impertinence. Which does not mean that either Beckett or Kafka ceased to attempt the life narrative with its summary reflection or ceased to judge the results, quite the contrary; and the judgments they brought to bear on "their lives, their lives," as lived and as written, were seldom less than devastating. To his young friend Gustav Janouch, whom he felt he had shocked with the sincere observation "I am as old as Jewry, as the wandering Jew," Kafka said, "But I really do envy youth. The older one grows, the larger one's horizon. But the possibilities of life grow smaller and smaller. In the end, one can give only one look upwards, give one breath outwards. At that moment a man probably surveys his whole life. For the first time—and the last time."[37] What he would likely see in that moment of looking up (and the direction of the gaze is not without significance) Kafka seemed pretty confident he knew: thoroughgoing, overwhelming, suffocating, soul-destroying guilt would probably not be far off as a characterization of the feeling induced by such a survey. K. thinks at one point in *The Trial* that if he is "to meet an unknown accusation . . . , the whole of one's life would have to be recalled to mind, down to the smallest actions and accidents, clearly formulated and examined from every angle" (p. 144). He decides against such an effort, with the thought that

37. Gustav Janouch, *Conversations with Kafka,* trans. Goronwy Rees, 2d ed. (New York: New Directions, 1971), 161–62.

it is "an occupation for one's second childhood in years of retirement, when the long days needed filling up." But surely there is a reason closer to home: were he to undertake such a clear formulation and examination, he would himself have to pronounce the guilty verdict better left to the mysterious others to render. To Milena, who evidently had hazarded some small criticism of "The Stoker" (the first chapter of *Amerika*)—a response that naturally produced spasms of guilt in Kafka for inflicting the piece on her— he wrote, "I'm glad to be able to make a small sacrifice with the few remarks you suggested about the stoker, it will be a foretaste of that eternal damnation which consists in having to go once more through one's life with the eye of knowledge, wherein the worst is not the insight into obvious misdeeds but into those deeds one once considered to be good."[38] As with the fond and foolish satisfaction (mentioned earlier) that he took in the writing of "Before the Law," Kafka was certain that to consider any of one's deeds "good" would lead invariably to agony when they are revealed in their true light and viewed by the pitiless eye of knowledge. Moreover, knowing what is to come, one should not wait, according to Kafka, but should begin a sort of anticipatory suffering now.

"Guilt," of course, was ever the great word with Kafka and something that, in his view, one can hardly have too much of. Supreme moments of passion in his diaries, letters, and fiction find Kafka or his protagonists saying not, as in some other authors, "I love you" but "I am guilty." Kafka could write in his journal that it would be "incorrect to say that I have known the words, 'I love you' " (*Diaries,* 413), but he could never write the same about professions of guilt. Not that the former expression has no place at all in his journal, but when it occurs it goes something like this: "I love her [Felice] as far as I am capable of it, but the love lies buried to the point of suffocation under fear and self-reproaches" (*Diaries,* 228). This Kafka follows, under the same date (August 14, 1913), with one of his most bizarre, if characteristic, observations on the subject: "Coitus is punishment for the happiness of being together. Live as ascetically as possible, more ascetically than a bachelor, that is the only possible way for me to endure marriage. But she?" Good question. We have no indication, unfortunately, of what Felice's feelings might have been.

The question of love does not come up often in Beckett either; or rather it does, but seldom in conventional dress, and this is surely part of the point: that the conventional resolutions of eighteenth- and nineteenth-

---

38. *Letters to Milena,* ed. Willi Haas, trans. Tania and James Stern (London: Penguin, 1983), 24–25.

century novels are hopelessly anachronistic in fiction at the end of the twentieth century. We might cite as examples three instances of love rearing its
head in Beckett, one in each volume of the Trilogy: Molloy's one experience of "true love" (if indeed it was that) with Ruth or Edith (he is uncertain about the name); Malone's vicarious experience of love as he watches
a couple performing an act of some kind in a window across the way; and
the preposterous, inane, and very funny story designed to teach the narrator,
near the end of *The Unnamable,* the various emotions swirling around the
word *love.* Before looking at these passages, I would suggest that the Trilogy
characters are doing much the sort of thing Kafka told Janouch everyone
does in the final moment—i.e., attempting a survey of the whole life. Here
is how Malone puts it a couple of pages into his narrative: "All my life
long I have put off this reckoning, saying, Too soon, too soon. Well it is
still too soon. All my life long I have dreamt of the moment when, edified
at last, in so far as one can be before all is lost, I might draw the line and
make the tot. This moment seems now at hand" (*Trilogy,* 167). Drawing
the line in this fashion and making the tot implies at least a modicum of
comprehensible narrative structure to the life, else the reckoning would be
inappropriate, wildly wrong, or simply impossible. What have the narrators
discovered, then, about the humanly crucial issue of love in the course of
what they are occasionally moved to call their lives? Of his sexual engagement with Ruth (or Edith), Molloy says, "I would have preferred it seems
to me an orifice less arid and roomy," for that, he supposes, "would have
given me a higher opinion of love. . . . But love," he goes on to speculate,
"is no doubt above such base contingencies. And not when you are comfortable, but when your frantic member casts about for a rubbing-place,
and the unction of a little mucous membrane, and meeting with none does
not beat in retreat, but retains its tumefaction, it is then no doubt that true
love comes to pass, and wings away, high above the tight fit and the loose"
(p. 54). The reader, made suspicious by the incongruous language at the
end ("wings away, high above," etc.) and by the overassertive repetition
of "no doubt," will no doubt doubt this as an altogether serious presentation
of "true love." And indeed, Molloy himself is not sure that he knew true
love on that occasion, for it is unclear whether Ruth (Edith) was a man
or a woman and unclear, therefore, what the exact nature of the "rubbing-
place" he found with her (him) might have been. "But there is one thing
that torments me, when I delve into all this, and that is to know whether
all my life has been devoid of love or whether I really met with it, in Ruth.
What I do know for certain is that I never sought to repeat the experience,
having I suppose the intuition that it had been unique and perfect, of its

kind, achieved and inimitable, and that it behoved me to preserve its memory, pure of all pastiche, in my heart, even if it meant my resorting from time to time to the alleged joys of so-called self-abuse" (p. 55). For Beckett, one of the first duties of a fiction writer would seem to be to destroy by parody and mockery conventional narrative modes of the past that have no effective currency for the present. Here and elsewhere he sets about the task with impolite and rowdy zest.

Malone's understanding of love is acquired from a different kind of source, but in the end it proves as incomplete, as puzzling, and as unsatisfactory as Molloy's. While Molloy wonders whether he ever knew true love, Malone, at a narrative remove from the experience he observes, is left to speculate about what the couple in the window opposite are actually doing; and the reader, even more in the dark than Molloy or Malone, cannot be certain whether anything at all has taken place, or if this is not simply a story Malone tells himself—"the kind of story he has been telling himself all his life, saying, This cannot possibly last much longer" (*Trilogy*, 219). In any case, what Malone claims to see is a couple (or possibly three people) who "cleave so fast together that they seem a single body. . . . But when they totter it is clear they are twain, and in vain they clasp with the energy of despair, it is clear we have here two distinct and separate bodies, each enclosed within its own frontier. . . ." It is a very pretty fable, we seem to hear Malone saying, the one Aristophanes tells in Plato's *Symposium* about lovers having been divided into two, then destined to seek forever the separated half in order that the two might again become one body— pretty, but in practice false. So what is it, then, makes them clasp "with the energy of despair"? "Perhaps they are cold, that they rub against each other so," Malone thinks, "for friction maintains heat and brings it back when it is gone. It is all very pretty and strange, this big complicated shape made up of more than one . . . but rather poor in colour." (It is not irrelevant to recall Giacometti's remark about the people in the café, that they have "no definable color at all"; nor to point out that for a time Giacometti could not avoid gray in painting portraits ["As I was working I had to eliminate one color after another, no—one color after the other dropped out, and what remained? Gray! Gray! Gray!"][39] and that gray, as being an indistinguishable mix of black and white, of dark and light, is the pervasive noncolor laid over everything in *Godot,* the Trilogy, and all of Beckett's late work.) Malone realizes that, since the night is warm, the explanation for their rubbing "against each other so" cannot be the cold: "So it is not

39. Giacometti to Gotthard Jedlicka, quoted in Hohl, *Alberto Giacometti,* 225.

cold they are, standing so lightly clad by the open window. Ah how stupid I am, I see what it is, they must be loving each other, that must be how it is done. Good, that has done me good." I suppose we can take Malone at his word, though it is hard to see exactly what good his voyeurism has done him. But then the pair cease rubbing together, which causes more puzzlement and mixed reactions: "They are right up against the curtain now, motionless. Is it possible they have finished already? They have loved each other standing, like dogs. Soon they will be able to part. Or perhaps they are just having a breather, before they tackle the titbit. Back and forth, back and forth, that must be wonderful. They seem to be in pain. Enough, enough, goodbye" (pp. 218–19). Inconclusive as this secondhand experience may be in showing the effects of love ("that must be wonderful. They seem to be in pain . . ."), it seems designed to constitute one kernel in a comprehensive, narrative totting up of the experiences of a lifetime, and viewed in that regard, its inconclusiveness can be seen to be symptomatic and, paradoxically, definitive. Conclusions do not follow from any of the bits and pieces of the one embracing life story Malone feels compelled to tell, and were he able to tell that tale in the likeness of his life, still nothing would follow from it. "I have only to open my mouth for it to testify to the old story, my old story," Malone says, and he speaks the truth, for everything in the book testifies to a life that is, in the most literal sense, inconsequential. "And if I ever stop talking it will be because there is nothing more to be said, even though all has not been said, even though nothing has been said" (p. 216).

The Unnamable gives a third lesson in love and "the nature of emotion," a lesson delivered in a brisk and mindless, probably American story that announces itself as such—"there's a story for you"—three or four times in less than a page. It has everything we could want in a narrative: numerous characters—more, in fact, than it knows what to do with; an unbelievable amount of action for a story so brief; plot all over the place; it begins, as we know an epic should, *in medias res,* and ends . . . well, in a shambles, but there is an explanation for that; and it has paradox and irony enough to gladden the heart of the New Critic in us. "They love each other"— this is how it starts, in midparagraph, with no forewarning, no indication of who "they" might be, no tie to anything before or after, and no hint that we are about to be harrowed by emotion of indescribable intensity, laid on very thick:

> They love each other, marry, in order to love each other better, more conveniently, he goes to the wars, he dies at the wars, she weeps, with emotion, at having loved him, at having lost him, yep, marries again, in order to love

again, more conveniently again, they love each other, you love as many times as necessary, as necessary to be happy, he comes back, the other comes back, from the wars, he didn't die at the wars after all, she goes to the station, to meet him, he dies in the train, of emotion, at the thought of seeing her again, having her again, she weeps, weeps again, with emotion again, at having lost him again, yep, goes back to the house, he's dead, the other is dead, the mother-in-law takes him down, he hanged himself, with emotion, at the thought of losing her, she weeps, weeps louder, at having loved him, at having lost him, there's a story for you. . . .

Indeed it is a story, rather a breathless one, one would say, except that the narrator has thoughtfully provided for breath pauses with forty-three commas strewn almost at random. Almost at random, but not quite: it may be noticed that each time *emotion* occurs, it is set off by commas so that the asserted fact of emotion bears no relation to the insanely speeded-up activity of the verbs. Yet, as the narrator says, "that was to teach me the nature of emotion," and in a sense it does teach him about the place of emotion in a certain kind of narrative fiction, and about a lot of other things besides: "that was to teach me the nature of emotion, that's called emotion, what emotion can do, given favourable conditions, what love can do, well well, so that's emotion, that's love, and trains, the nature of trains, and the meaning of your back to the engine, and guards, stations, platforms, wars, love, heart-rending cries, that must be the mother-in-law, her cries rend the heart as she takes down her son, or her son-in-law, I don't know, it must be her son, since she cries. . . ." Suddenly, out of this harum-scarum narrative jumble (though the ostensible narrator is surely unaware of what he is producing) there emerges a comically rendered *Pietà*, and as readers we find ourselves back in the neighborhood of the two thieves from St. Augustine's "wonderful sentence." There's a story for you, and no doubt, but it cannot detain us, for the narrator, caught up by his obsessional concern with a Kafkaesque door that will or will not open to him when he finishes with all his words and all his stories, is intent on hurrying readers on from the mother or mother-in-law and the son or son-in-law or whatever they may be to an end that he knows will give him trouble because it has always given him trouble in the past. "[A]nd the door," he says,

the house-door is bolted, when she got back from the station she found the house-door bolted, who bolted it, he the better to hang himself, or the mother-in-law the better to take him down, or to prevent her daughter-in-law from re-entering the premises, there's a story for you, it must be the daughter-in-law, it isn't the son-in-law and the daughter, it's the daughter-in-law and the son, how I reason to be sure this evening, it was to teach me how to reason, it was to tempt me to go, to the place where you can come

to an end, I must have been a good pupil up to a point, I couldn't get beyond
a certain point, I can understand their annoyance, this evening I begin to
understand, oh there's no danger, it's not I, it wasn't I, the door, it's the door
interests me, a wooden door, who bolted the door, and for what purpose, I'll
never know, there's a story for you . . . (Pp. 374–75)

There are I believe at least two, perhaps three, narratives going on here:
one might be called a pseudonarrative, the original story about lovers, hus-
bands and wives, mothers and mothers-in-law, trains, and so on, a parodic
version of a tale of love, jokingly designed "to teach me the nature of
emotion"; the second is the narrative whose lesson—that he doesn't know
how to make an end of it—the narrator begins to intuit as his attention
becomes fixed on the door he will talk about for the remaining half-dozen
pages of the book; and the third we might term the narrative of narratives,
that is, the story of Beckett's attempt to tell a story in the likeness of his
life as the maker of *The Unnamable,* and before it of *Murphy, Watt, Mercier
and Camier, Molloy, Malone Dies,* and *Waiting for Godot,* and after it of *Texts
for Nothing, Endgame, All That Fall, Krapp's Last Tape, How It Is, Happy
Days, All Strange Away, Imagination Dead Imagine, Not I, That Time, Company, Ill Seen Ill Said, Worstward Ho, Stirrings Still,* and a host of other short
fictions and plays. If the lesson to be drawn from the first narrative is a
parodic joke and that from the second is by way of being an aporetic conundrum, the lesson of the final narrative is serious, moving, and exemplary,
one we can read into and out of the lives of Giacometti and Kafka as well
and that pertains specifically, in all three instances, to their lives as artists.

   The shape of a creative career, the form taken by the struggle to give
form to the mess—this is the ultimate narrative to which Beckett, Giacometti, and Kafka devoted their lives. And I mean "devoted their lives" to
be read in this dual sense: first, that they worked unceasingly at their craft;
and second, that they made this unceasing work at the craft the stuff of
their art. Every volume in Beckett's body of work, every story and every
uncompleted novel composing Kafka's oeuvre, every painting, sculpture,
and drawing Giacometti did—each of them tells a small part of the one
story; or perhaps one should say "of the three stories," which are so astonishingly alike, however, that they could well be taken for only one. While
all the mininarratives along the way, all the various experiments, the renewed assaults on the medium, the turning points, and the new starts came
to failure, it is important to recognize that we cannot say the same of the
example Kafka, Beckett, and Giacometti left in the completed image of
the life of the artist. In a brilliant and deeply moving 1921 letter to Max
Brod—a letter studded with "impossibilities" and rich in proleptic echoes

of Beckett speaking with Georges Duthuit—Kafka outlined the mad project to which he had committed his life. He first rejects the psychoanalytic model as being, for himself, unsatisfactory and then proceeds to what is surely—in his instance and in general—a more expressive image for the situation of the Jewish writer in German and, as a corollary, for the artist in the modern world. "Psychoanalysis lays stress on the father-complex and many find the concept intellectually fruitful. In this case I prefer another version, where the issue revolves not around the innocent father but around the father's Jewishness. Most young Jews who began to write German wanted to leave Jewishness behind them, and their fathers approved of this, but vaguely (this vagueness was what was outrageous to them). But with their posterior legs they were still glued to their father's Jewishness and with their waving anterior legs they found no new ground. The ensuing despair became their inspiration" (*Letters to Friends, Family, and Editors,* 288–89). Here we see Kafka as it were stepping back from the story to take the long view (not unlike Giacometti, and in more than one sense) of the artist's creative life and at the same time choosing from among possible images one that had served him well at a specific, crucial stage, in one particular story. The story I have in mind, of course, is *The Metamorphosis,* written nine years before the letter to Brod, a fiction that, at the time he was composing it, Kafka, in a letter to Felice (this in the very early days of their courtship), called "this exceptionally repulsive story. . . . infinitely repulsive," but of which he also said—and in the same letter—"on the whole I am not too dissatisfied. . . . and the nights can never be long enough for this business [of writing] which, incidentally, is highly voluptuous."[40] The bizarre mix of emotions that the act of writing induced in Kafka in the instance of *The Metamorphosis* was very much in character, and I use that last word deliberately: no reader, I should think, doubts that in the Gregor Samsa of *The Metamorphosis,* as in the K. of *The Trial* and *The Castle* and the Georg Bendemann of "The Judgment," Kafka was writing about himself and his life. (In fact, as to the last of these, Kafka himself, as I will point out later, establishes the identity between author and protagonist at some length in his *Diaries.*) What is particularly interesting about the 1921 letter to Brod is that in it we see Kafka taking a retrospective look back to one of the first pieces about which he could feel "not too dissatisfied," back to what could be seen in 1921 as very close to the beginning of his life as a writer, to reinvoke an image that had been effective at an early

40. *Letters to Felice,* ed. Erich Heller and Jürgen Born, trans. James Stern and Elisabeth Duckworth (New York: Schocken Books, 1973), 58.

stage and that now appears equally effective as an emblem for the writer's situation throughout his life. When he appropriates this image in taking what I have described as the long view, Kafka succeeds in saying something not just about the way he may have felt with regard to, for example, his parents ("I felt like some monstrous, unloved vermin") but, more significant, about the writer's relationship to the language and the culture in which he is compelled—self-compelled as much as anything—to do his work. "The ensuing despair became [his] inspiration": this might be the motto for Kafka's career, the device to be stamped on all his works—if not, as in "In the Penal Colony," inscribed on his body. It was also, as it happens, the advice Samuel Beckett gave Alberto Giacometti during their long postmidnight walks in the streets of Paris when the latter, "who did most of the talking," spoke "indefatigably" of the "anguish he felt at not being able to do what he wanted to do." Beckett's counsel was that Giacometti should accept "the impossibility of what he was struggling to achieve and . . . [should] develop the inner nature and exploit the natural resources of that very impossibility."[41] Thus the despair ensuing upon the perceived impossibility of the artist's task might become Giacometti's or Beckett's or Kafka's inspiration. "An inspiration as honorable as any other," Kafka goes on to say in the letter to Brod,

> but on closer examination showing certain sad peculiarities. First of all, the product of their despair could not be German literature, though outwardly it seemed to be so. They existed among three impossibilities. . . . These are: The impossibility of not writing, the impossibility of writing German, the impossibility of writing differently. One might also add a fourth impossibility, the impossibility of writing (since the despair could not be assuaged by writing, was hostile to both life and writing; writing is only an expedient, as for someone who is writing his will shortly before he hangs himself—an expedient that may well last a whole life).

It is clear that Kafka is writing in this passage for and about himself and others like him, "young Jews who began to write in German," equally clear that he could not be writing for or about either Giacometti or Beckett, yet there are frequent observations in both of the latter that have precisely the same impetus as what Kafka had to say. It was impossible for Beckett not to write ("you must go on, I'll go on"), impossible for Giacometti not to paint and sculpt ("Giving up painting and sculpture seemed to me such

---

41. This is the account James Lord gives from an interview with Beckett at the time that Lord was preparing his biography of Giacometti: *Some Remarkable Men: Further Memoirs* (New York: Farrar, Straus and Giroux, 1996), 289. Cited hereafter as *Some Remarkable Men*.

a very sad idea that I didn't even feel like getting up in the morning and eating. So I started work again");[42] impossible for either of them to work in the insuperably difficult medium of his choice and impossible not to; impossible and unthinkable to work in any different way, for they would not be Giacometti and Beckett if they tried that (moreover, for all their failures, none of the three doubted that his work was superior to other work of the time); and impossible, utterly impossible to write anything, to paint anything, to sculpt anything. It is an instructive experience to read a book like James Lord's *A Giacometti Portrait,* where we hear Giacometti on virtually every page declaring the impossibility of his undertaking— "Impossible, impossible, impossible"—and what could he have been thinking anyway when he started the portrait? " 'It's hopeless,' he muttered. 'At that distance it's hopeless. . . . The simple fact is that I don't know how to do anything. People think I'm affected when I say that, but it's simply the truth."[43] It was simply the truth that, without affectation, Beckett and Kafka felt and said the same. This bewildering farrago of impossibilities did not prevent Kafka, however, from concluding the letter to Brod with an image for the situation and activity of the Jewish writer in German that, if anything, surpasses the one of posterior legs glued to the father's Jewishness and waving anterior legs that find no new ground. "[W]hat resulted," Kafka says, "was a literature impossible in all respects, a gypsy literature which had stolen the German child out of its cradle and in great haste put it through some kind of training, for someone has to dance on the tightrope. (But it wasn't even a German child, it was nothing; people merely said that somebody was dancing)"[44] In this brief passage (broken up in my presentation, but only about half a page in length) Kafka compresses into two stunning images and half a dozen lines of discursive explanation the life of the Jewish writer in German, which of course was his own life as caught in one summary look back.

By all accounts, Giacometti was a great talker who loved nothing so much as repeating to interviewers and gallery owners and anyone who would listen (and they were legion) the story of his career, which, at least as he told it, fell into clearly delineated stages ordered by an overall sense of narrative progression. He reached turning point after turning point, at

42. Quoted in Hohl, *Alberto Giacometti,* 172.

43. James Lord, *A Giacometti Portrait* (New York: Farrar, Straus and Giroux, 1980), 61.

44. The letter breaks off at this point without punctuation: *Letters to Friends, Family, and Editors,* 289. The notion of Kafka's art as dancing on a tightrope finds an echo in a number of late stories, e.g., "First Sorrow," "Josephine the Singer, or The Mouse Folk," and "A Hunger Artist."

each of which he had a revelation about something in his project that started him off in a new direction . . . and so again a few years later . . . and once more a few years on . . . etc. Whether it was the repeated telling that brought out and fixed the clear lines of a career or whether it was really that way is hard to say. We do know that Giacometti was not opposed to changing a good story into a better one, or one more suited to the moment of telling, when the narrative fit was upon him. However that may be, one can discover in many sources accounts given by Giacometti of such signifi-cant moments in the life of the artist—of *this* artist—as the following: draw-ing pears with his father and finding it impossible to draw them as large as his father thought they should be; viewing in succession a group of Tintoretto paintings, a number of Giotto frescoes, and then two or three girls in the street and being turned and turned and turned again in his perception of what the reality of the artist should be; the death of Peter van Meurs ("my life was changed that day"); the decision in 1935 to work from life, which caused a break with the Surrealists and an entirely new aesthetic for Giaco-metti; the experience of seeing Isabel walking away from him on the Boule-vard Saint-Michel, receding and diminishing in size but retaining her wholeness of identity; coming out of a cinema in Montparnasse and, seeing faces in the street after viewing the flashing images on the screen, having the sense that reality was something other than he had ever imagined; etc.; etc. There are more of these markers that established the contours of Giaco-metti's life both in the living and the telling, but there is only one that, by its nature and timing and because of Giacometti's odd, lifelong attitude toward it, demands further attention. This is the automobile accident that occurred late one night, early one morning when Giacometti was struck as he was walking along the Place des Pyramides after leaving his friend Isabel at her nearby hotel. Giacometti suffered broken bones in one foot, spent a week in a clinic recovering, came out on crutches, and limped slightly for the rest of his life, but it was what he said of the experience that made it so remarkable. According to James Lord, Giacometti referred to it as "one of the most important and propitious experiences of his life-time" (*Some Remarkable Men,* 223), and, in a phrase even more peculiar than "important and propitious," told Jean Genet that "he had been very happy when he learned that his operation—after an accident—would leave him lame."[45] Nor was Genet uniquely favored in being thus taken into Giacometti's confidence. "It was not long," Lord writes, "before he started

---

45. *L'Atelier d'Alberto Giacometti,* 28: "Il me dit qu'il a été très heureux quand il a su que son opération—après un accident—le laisserait boiteux."

telling his friends, as he told them again and again in later years, that he had been glad when he realized that he would remain permanently lame" (*Giacometti*, 204). In fact, Giacometti became so proprietary in his feeling for *his* accident (even though—or perhaps because—his versions of it altered over the years)[46] that he broke definitively with Sartre when, in *The Words,* the latter published an incorrect account of what had happened (locating the accident in the Place d'Italie, for example, rather than the Place des Pyramides). But why did Giacometti place such emphasis on this event? There were many other turning points besides this one, at least some of which would seem to have considerably greater significance in the progress of his career. One explanation might have to do with the date of the accident—October 1938. This date, give or take a year, would establish the dividing line for many commentators on Giacometti's work—on one side the early, Surrealist and Cubist Giacometti, on the other the mature, Giacomettian Giacometti. Moreover, on October 18, 1938, Giacometti had just turned thirty-seven (born October 10, 1901), which is by convention right at life's midpoint; it is also the age at which "reminiscence" typically begins, according to psychologists who have thought up a new term, "autobiographical memory," to describe the ways of a specifically adult memory that imagines life not as a heap of snapshotlike moments but as constituting a connected narrative sequence.[47] And beyond this there is the fact that 1938 was something of an annus mirabilis for violent turning points

46. Different friends had different stories to tell about the accident, all of them claiming Giacometti as their authoritative source. The one furthest from the known facts is given by Giorgio Soavi in *Giacometti: La ressemblance impossible / Resemblance Defeated / Unerreichbare Ähnlichkeit* (Milan: Éditions André Sauret, 1991), 209: "1938 Alberto is run over by a car in the street. His foot is injured and he is forced to spend several months at the Hôpital Bichat in Paris. The artist comes close to being amputated. Fortunately his foot is saved but he was to remain lame all his life. He is badly shaken by the incident and becomes obsessed with the notion of balance. Twenty-five years later, in *Les Mots,* Jean-Paul Sartre gave an account of the accident and its consequences. This version was disproved by Giacometti." Admittedly, some of the more bizarre expressions are due to a very bad translation (the third sentence, for example, reads, in French, "On envisage une amputation, finalement évitée," and the final clause reads, "une version des faits que Giacometti contestera"), but faulty translation cannot be responsible for the claim that Giacometti spent "several months at the Hôpital Bichat"—he spent two nights in the hospital and one week in the Rémy de Gourmont Clinic—or that there was any question of amputating a foot or leg, much less of amputating the artist himself. One cannot know whether Giacometti told Soavi the story in this form or Soavi (who presents himself as a very close friend of Giacometti) improved on the story as received from Giacometti. Both seem distinct possibilities.

47. See, for example, *Autobiographical Memory,* ed. David C. Rubin (Cambridge: Cambridge University Press, 1986).

in the streets of Paris: Beckett was stabbed by the pimp Prudent late one night, early one morning in January while walking on the Avenue d'Orleans; Giacometti was hit by a car driven by a Chicago woman named Nelson late one night, early one morning in October while walking along the Place des Pyramides. I would not suggest this as a complete explanation, of course, but Giacometti (like most people) was more than a little superstitious, and when it came to interpreting his accident, which to others might not appear to have any interpretable significance, he understood it to be hardly less than providential, a major link in the chain of his destiny. If we believe Reinhold Hohl when he says that Beckett's thought and his moral presence were more important to Giacometti than anyone else's ("Camus's authority in Giacometti's thought was exceeded only by that Samuel Beckett had from 1952 on" [Hohl, *Alberto Giacometti,* 208]), that "Giacometti was very much affected by Beckett's words from the beginning,"[48] and that "he felt a deep sympathy for Beckett's writings," it may not be farfetched to imagine that in interpreting his accident in the street he would recall Beckett's similar trauma, for this is what narrative always does: provides contexts and patterns through which we can read, understand, rerealize, and transmit our experience. Without the example of narrative, how would any of us make sense of our lives? And with Giacometti's enduring pleasure in being lame and in retailing the incident of his injured leg, one helplessly recalls the similar problems Molloy and Moran had with the same limb— narratives that Giacometti could not have known when his accident occurred but that he knew well in the years when he told about it.

But here the paradox dramatized simultaneously in the lives and works of Giacometti, Beckett, and Kafka returns with added force: every work, they said as if in chorus, every painting and sculpture, every novel and story

48. Just when that "beginning" was is an interesting question. Beckett said that he met Giacometti in the Café de Flore "sometime before the war." Commentators tend to guess at a year—1938, 1939—without offering any reasons for the guess. In *No Symbols Where None Intended,* Carlton Lake describes a card written by Beckett to George Reavey dated March 6, 1935, about the publication later in the year of *Echo's Bones and Other Precipitates* and notes that on the other side of the card "are the name and address of the sculptor Alberto Giacometti (in Giacometti's hand), raising at least the possibility that there may have been some thought of asking Giacometti to illustrate the book" (p. 29). As Beckett was not in or around Paris in 1935, I assume that the name and address must have been acquired by Reavey, who seems to have frequented the same Montparnasse cafés as Giacometti (and Beckett as well, both when he lived in Paris from 1928 to 1930 and after his return in 1937)—the Closerie des Lilas, the Sélect, the Dôme, La Coupole. At any rate, it is interesting to speculate from this that Giacometti may have come into Beckett's ken, one way or another, earlier than previously supposed.

and play, was a failure in its attempt to represent the unrepresentable—
or, in the words of Arsene in *Watt*, "to utter the unutterable, to eff the
ineffable"[49]—yet out of the lifework of each of them can be drawn a narrative, a self-conscious narrative self-consciously realized, that is a more than
adequate representation of a life in motion. I stress this last element because,
as each made clear, it was this continuous movement, life's incessant sliding
and flowing, its propensity for making, unmaking, and remaking itself
ceaselessly, that, taken at any single point, made it so maddeningly unrepresentable. It is, however, precisely the sense of motion in time inherent in
the narrative act, the sense of movement implied by coming to a dead end,
finding a new start, reaching a turning point, and going on anew that renders the whole life representable in the whole body of work. Giacometti
spoke always of "work in progress," Beckett of "going on" (when he was
not speaking of "work in regress," which has to do with movement all the
same). The notion of achievement—I do not say success but achievement—in failure, of making despair one's inspiration, of "developing . . .
the natural resources . . . of impossibility" became the hallmark of the various lifeworks and life-writings of Beckett, Giacometti, and Kafka.

That there were turning points in the works as in the lives of the three
is apparent to anyone who listens closely to them talking about what they
were doing. In *Oneself as Another* Paul Ricoeur cites Wilhelm Dilthey's
"concept of *Zusammenhang des Lebens* (the connectedness of life)" and says
that Dilthey took this "to be equivalent to the concept of life history"
(p. 141); I would turn this around to suggest that Beckett, Giacometti, and
Kafka perceived or constructed a narrative sequence in their lifeworks that
was then taken to be an imitation of the connectedness of their lives as
artists. That Beckett thought in this way we can see from a pair of remarks
about *Watt*, the novel (or antinovel) written in Roussillon during the war
years (finished on December 28, 1944, according to James Knowlson:
Damned to Fame, 310) but not published until 1953. Writing to George
Reavey, Beckett described *Watt* as "an unsatisfactory book, written in dribs

---

49. "Not that I have told you all I know," Arsene says to Watt, "for I have not, being
now a good-natured man, and of good will what is more . . . , and perhaps also because
what we know partakes in no small measure of the nature of what has so happily been
called the unutterable or ineffable, so that any attempt to utter or eff it is doomed to fail,
doomed, doomed to fail" (*Watt*, 62). There is a lot of joking, of course, in the manner of
speech Beckett gives Arsene, but Beckett is altogether serious in *Watt* about the nature of
what we know and the question of whether it can be "effed" or not. His view, like Arsene's,
is that "it is doomed to fail, doomed, doomed to fail." This is why he turns away from any
attempt to represent the unrepresentable, choosing instead to dramatize a life in continual
pursuit of the impossible.

and drabs, first on the run, then of an evening after the clodhopping, during
the occupation. But it has its place in the series, as will perhaps appear in
time" (*No Symbols Where None Intended,* 75). Though it took a long time
for anyone else to perceive it, particularly in the case of *Watt* with its nine
years in limbo, there was clearly a structure to the whole body of work in
Beckett's mind as there was to any individual piece of the puzzle. And in
Molloy, written and published while *Watt* was still in search of a publisher,
Molloy speaks of his journeys through strange places, none stranger than
the town where they have never heard of Watt: "So there was no way of
coming at my town directly, by sea, but you had to disembark well to the
north or the south and take to the roads, just imagine that, for they had
never heard of Watt, just imagine that too" (*Trilogy,* 71). It is virtually
inconceivable, this ignorance about a character and a book—never mind
that they exist only in manuscript notebooks—that have their place "in
the series, as will perhaps appear in time." The logic is clear: without Watt,
the Beckettian (that one can use the adjective and expect to be understood
makes the point in another way) landscape is not fully peopled; without
Watt, Beckett's body of work remains incomplete. I use the phrase "body
of work" deliberately to invoke the organic metaphor of limbs, organs, and
so on, all contributing in distinct and necessary ways to the functioning of
the whole. The "series," as Beckett calls it, the "body," as I have termed
it, was missing an essential item until *Watt* was permitted to take its place
after *More Pricks Than Kicks* and *Murphy* but before—this is crucial: *before*—
*Molloy, Malone Dies, The Unnamable, Waiting for Godot, Endgame, Happy
Days, How It Is, Company,* and a dozen shorter pieces, to take its place in
"the complete consort dancing together"[50] that composes the lifework of
Samuel Beckett.

"Life is in continual evolution," Giacometti said to Carlton Lake, and
this simple—but also complex—fact presents a problem for the painter or
sculptor who yearns to fix life's reality in an unchanging form at an instant
of that "continual evolution." It presents a problem, but viewed in another
perspective it also offers a narrative opportunity that Giacometti was happy
to avail himself of throughout his career. That he intended to embody a
life story in individual works and more particularly in the evolving arc described by the connectedness of those works is clear in all that Giacometti
had to say about himself and his art. Leaving aside such sculptures as *Man
with Pointing Outstretched Hand, Man Walking in the Rain, Man Crossing a*

---

50. Although Beckett never warmed to T. S. Eliot, this phrase from *Little Gidding*
seems peculiarly fitting here.

Square on a Sunny Morning, Man Staggering, and *Walking Man 1* of 1960 as
being too obviously determined by some internal self-image, one might cite
works that have been identified by critics, with Giacometti's agreement, as
self-portraits that do not at first glance seem to be such: in *The Artist's
Mother,* Charles Juliet says, Giacometti "painted his mother and, at the same
time, made a self-portrait in which he was able to express, for the first time,
what haunted him";[51] in busts of Diego it has been claimed, again with
Giacometti's concurrence, that the artist realized his own image much more
truly than his brother's; and when Jean Genet expressed surprise that *The
Dog* should have entered among the figures of Giacometti's sculpture, the
latter responded, "That's me. One day in the street I saw myself like that.
I was the dog" (*L'Atelier,* 24). To others Giacometti said that when walking
in the rain one day he imagined himself that pitiable creature of the streets
("For a long time I'd had in my mind the memory of a Chinese dog I'd
seen somewhere. And then one day I was walking along the rue de Vanves
in the rain, close to the walls of the buildings, with my head down, feeling
a little sad, perhaps, and I felt like a dog just then. So I made that sculpture"
[Lord, *Giacometti Portrait,* 34]). This is only half of the story Giacometti tells
of his life, however; the other half, seen so clearly by him and outlined for
interviewers and other interested parties countless times, is in the evolution
from the hard, cold violence of the Surrealist images; through the painting
of his mother and the *Apple on a Sideboard;* to the sculpted individual figures
and groups of three (*Three Men Walking*), four (*Four Women on a Pedestal*),
five (*City Square* and the arrangement for the Chase Manhattan Plaza), seven
(*The Forest*), nine (*The Glade*), or a shifting number of figures (groups of
four, five, six, or nine—up to fifteen—composing the *Women for Venice*)
and sometimes separate body parts (*Head on a Rod, The Nose, The Hand,
The Leg*) of the late '40s and the '50s; to, finally, the late paintings of Yanaihara, Annette, and Caroline and the late busts of Diego and Elie Lotar. In
no single work, by his estimation, was he ever successful in capturing what
he saw, his response to it, and the vision that resulted from the two coming
together. "In December 1965"—that is, a month before his death—"Giacometti said he would never attain the goal that he had set himself; for
thirty years he had gone on thinking that he would get there the next
day."[52] Yet we see, of course, what Giacometti saw when he stepped back

51. Charles Juliet, *Giacometti* (New York: Universe Books, 1986), 45.
52. Peter Schifferli, quoted by Angela Schneider in "As if from Afar: Constants in the
Work of Alberto Giacometti," *Alberto Giacometti,* ed. Angela Schneider (Munich: Prestel,
1994), 71.

a little from the immediate piece in hand: that he had advanced, if only millimeter by millimeter as Beckett said of himself and of Giacometti,[53] had advanced through turning point after turning point, without concern for success or failure, to realize in his work a life, and life itself, in continual evolution.

"Every day," Kafka wrote in his 1911 diary, "since I seem to be completely finished—during the last year I did not wake up for more than five minutes at a time—I shall either have to wish myself off the earth or else, without my being able to see even the most moderate hope in it, I shall have to start afresh like a baby" (*Diaries,* 36). Eleven years on, things seemed hardly better, but then back in 1911, of course, he could not "see even the most moderate hope" in any new fresh start, so there was little reason to expect a great bursting-forth. "In the Great Account of my life," he writes in 1922, "it is still reckoned as if my life were first beginning tomorrow, and in the meantime it is all over with me" (*Diaries,* 413–14). What both these diary entries suggest is the notion of a turning point that is at once a beginning and an end—not, however, in the usual sense of the end of movement in an old direction and the beginning of movement in a new one. Instead the beginning *is* an end and the end a hopeless beginning. Like so much in Kafka, the paradox constitutes a desperate and self-defeating in-turning upon himself, seemingly designed to foreclose any future. Yet there was a moment between 1911 and 1922, fully recorded in the *Diaries,* when Kafka felt that a major turning point had been accomplished and that thereby his future as a writer (if nothing else) was assured. Kafka being Kafka, this does not mean that he began to write with ease and without misgivings or that he immediately produced masterpiece after finished masterpiece; nor does it mean that he saw his way to taking equal pleasure in living and writing—as for this latter, quite the contrary. But as significant fruit it did bring forth "The Judgment," one of the few pieces that Kafka remained satisfied with and that resonated throughout the work from 1912 on. "It is easy to recognize a concentration in me of all my forces on writ-

53. Speaking to Charles Juliet in 1968, Beckett said (as quoted in the previous chapter), "Impossible, isn't it? Still one can move forward. Advance a few miserable millimeters" ("Meeting Beckett," 13); talking with James Lord in 1970, he used virtually the same words but in reference to Giacometti rather than himself: "Giacometti was determined to continue with his struggle, trying to progress even if it was only by so much as an inch, or a centimeter, or a millimeter" (*Some Remarkable Men,* 289).

For a vastly expanded account of the narrative aspect of Giacometti's life work see Yves Bonnefoy's *Alberto Giacometti: A Biography of His Work,* trans. Jean Stewart (Paris: Flammarion, 1991).

ing," Kafka says in the diary entry for January 3, 1912. "When it became clear in my organism that writing was the most productive direction for my being to take, everything rushed in that direction and left empty all those abilities which were directed towards the joys of sex, eating, drinking, philosophical reflection, and above all music. I atrophied in all these directions. . . . Naturally, I did not find this purpose independently and consciously, it found itself . . ." (*Diaries*, 163). This reads like a birth announcement: Birth of the Writer Franz Kafka. After running through some of the sacrifices his vocation will entail—the joys of love and appreciation of music, the pleasures of eating and drinking ("on New Year's Eve I dined on parsnips and spinach, washed down with a glass of Ceres"), the delights of philosophizing—Kafka concludes that "the compensation for all this is clear as day. My development is now complete and, so far as I can see, there is nothing left to sacrifice; I need only throw my work in the office out of this complex in order to begin my real life in which, with the progress of my work, my face will finally be able to age in a natural way." Given what he once told Max Brod ("I shall never grow up to be a man, from being a child I shall immediately become a white-haired ancient"),[54] the final phrase of the entry is—coming from Kafka—uncharacteristically hopeful.

The hopefulness of the remark, untypical as it may be, is validated and justified, after many intervening disappointments, in a pair of diary entries—the first one nine months after the January 1912 entry—about the throes, both sexual and birthing, involved in bringing "The Judgment" into the world.

> 23 September. This story, 'The Judgement', I wrote at one sitting during the night of the 22nd–23rd, from ten o'clock at night to six o'clock in the morning. I was hardly able to pull my legs out from under the desk, they had got so stiff from sitting. The fearful strain and joy, how the story developed before me, as if I were advancing over water. Several times during this night I heaved my own weight on my back. How everything can be said, how for everything, for the strangest fancies, there waits a great fire in which they perish and rise up again. . . . As the maid walked through the ante-room for the first time I wrote the last sentence. Turning out the light and the light of day. . . . Only *in this way* can writing be done, only with such coherence, with such a complete opening out of the body and the soul. . . . Many emotions carried along in the writing, joy, for example, that I shall have something beautiful for Max's *Arkadia*, thoughts about Freud, of course. . . .
>
> I, only I, am the spectator in the orchestra. (*Diaries*, 212–13)

54. Max Brod, *Franz Kafka: A Biography*, 2d ed. (New York: Schocken Books, 1960), 37.

That in this experience of a single night he found "compensation" for the sacrifice of love and music, of philosophy, food, and wine is evident in the ecstasy of Kafka's language, especially in the climactic last line that suggests a sexual performance in which he is both of the partners in congress, the only begetter and spectator of it all, indeed even the theater in which the drama takes place. The emotional rush of that night is confirmed in what Kafka told Brod about the conclusion of the story ("Do you know what the last sentence means? When I wrote it, I had in mind a violent ejaculation" [*Franz Kafka,* 129], and it returned in force when Kafka read proofs six months after writing "The Judgment" and chose to spell out the ways in which it is through and through a life story. "While I read the proofs of 'The Judgement', I'll write down all the relationships which have become clear to me in the story as far as I now remember them. This is necessary because the story came out of me like a real birth, covered with filth and slime, and only I have the hand that can reach to the body itself and the strength to do so" (*Diaries,* 214). Kafka proceeds to write of the relationship of father and son, central to his life and this work, then tacks down the identities in the story: "Georg has the same number of letters as Franz. In Bendemann, 'mann' is a strengthening of 'Bende' . . . , [which] has exactly the same number of letters as Kafka, and the vowel *e* occurs in the same places as does the *a* in Kafka. Frieda has as many letters as F. [Felice] and the same initial . . . ," and so on (p. 215). The crucial place "The Judgment" occupied in Kafka's life as a writer we may judge from the diary entry in which he tells of reading the story to a group of friends and Max Brod's journal remarks at the time about Kafka's state of mind. "Yesterday read at Baum's," Kafka writes under date of September 25. "Towards the end my hand was moving uncontrollably about and actually before my face. There were tears in my eyes. The indubitability of the story was confirmed" (*Diaries,* 214). This is quite astonishing self-praise on Kafka's part and virtually unique in his reflections on his work. Brod, meanwhile, noted in his friend mental states unknown either before or (sad to say) after. "September 29: Kafka is in ecstasy, writes whole nights through. . . . October 1: Kafka in unbelievable ecstasy. October 2: Kafka is still greatly inspired" (*Franz Kafka,* 128). It was not to be repeated, this experience Brod calls ecstasy, and probably no one should have expected it to be, but the certainty that he was a writer and that his life *was* his writing never left Kafka, whatever the failures or bad days there were to be. "The tremendous world I have in my head," he exclaims in his diary. "But how free myself and free it without being torn to pieces. And a thousand times rather be torn to pieces than retain it in me or bury it. That, indeed, is why I am here, that is quite clear to me" (*Diaries*, 222). Talk as he would about the misery and futility of being a writer, Beckett would not have disagreed with this sentiment of Kafka's (whether he would have expressed it publicly is another matter); and certainly Giacometti was as committed—fanatically committed—to the role of the artist as Kafka or anyone else has ever been.

All three experienced turning points that established narrative structures to their lives, Giacometti most frequently but Beckett and Kafka richly also. It was with beginning that the latter two had difficulty and with finishing that all three struggled (which is not to say that the in-between was problem free, for it was not; but the in-between offered, as it were, more of a donnée with which to work rather than being inherently and simply inconceivable). It is a curious and revealing feature of their life stories that Beckett and Kafka shared the peculiar feeling of not having been properly born. Kafka notes the condition in his diary of 1922: "Hesitation before birth. If there is a transmigration of souls then I am not yet on the bottom rung. My life is a hesitation before birth" (*Diaries*, 405). Two months later he repeats the same sense of prenatal being/nonbeing in the world: "Still unborn and already compelled to walk around the streets and speak to people" (*Diaries*, 417). As Kafka had only a little over two years to live from the date of this second entry, one must suppose that, according to his notion, he never did succeed in being born before he died. In an earlier letter to Felice (October 1916) Kafka makes it clear that this feeling of an unsuccessful and therefore infinitely-to-be-repeated birth was closely related to an obsessive but impossible need to trace his guilt to a point of origin:

> Any relationship not created by myself, even though it be opposed to parts of my own nature, is worthless; it hinders my movements, I hate it, or come near to hating it. . . . Yet, I am my parents' progeny, am bound to them and to my sisters by blood. . . . Sometimes this too becomes the object of my hatred; at home the sight of the double bed, of sheets that have been slept in, of nightshirts carefully laid out, can bring me to the point of retching, can turn my stomach inside out; it is as though my birth had not been final, as though from this fusty life I keep being born again and again in this fusty room; as though I had to return there for confirmation, being—if not quite, at least in part—indissolubly connected with these distasteful things; something still clings to the feet as they try to break free, held fast as they are in the primeval slime. (*Letters to Felice*, 525)

With Kafka's final phrase one cannot but recall the hopeless, pathetic image of the son's posterior legs glued to the ancestral past while his waving anterior legs find no new ground, which suggests that the attempt to trace back from one's present, unhappy state through a series of causes and effects to

some nonexistent natal point from which all the misery springs is as desperate and futile as the effort of young Jewish writers to express their deepest
truths in the German language. Yet what else can he do if his "birth ha[s]
not been final"? One might note the ingenious way Kafka's phrasing
("birth" and "final") contrives to bring together beginning and end but
precisely on the ground that neither one exists. Kafka had wise words to
offer Milena (wiser than he was ever able to recognize for his own case)
about the futility of this kind of search for an Original Cause when she
was entangled in mutual recriminations with her husband. "But one of the
most senseless things in this wide world is the serious treatment of the problem of guilt, at least so it seems to me" (*Letters to Milena*, 154). Coming
from someone else, the observation would be both unexceptionable and
unsurprising, but it is not what one would ordinarily look for from Kafka.
"It's not the uttering of reproaches that seems to me senseless," he continues; "but that one should consider it possible to argue about it as about
any ordinary arithmetical problem which is so clear that it produces results
for daily conduct, this I don't understand at all. Of course you are to blame,
but then your husband is also to blame and then you again and then he
again, since it cannot be otherwise in the living together of human beings
and the blame piles up in endless succession until it reaches the grey Original
Sin, but what use can it be for my present day or for the visit to the doctor
in Ischl to rummage about in eternal sin?" Unexpected as this may be at
first glance, it makes a good deal of sense, and not only in itself but for
Kafka's practice as well. What we see in his fiction, his letters, his journals—
in his "Dearest Father" letter, to whatever genre *that* may belong—is that
a feeling of guilt is endemic and pervasive: it is specific to the human condition. But there is no point in arguing or reasoning about it, no point in
trying to think through a logical chain from the present effect to an ultimate
cause. Nor (though he once told Milena, "[S]ometimes I believe I understand the Fall of Man as no one else did" [p. 142]) does it serve any purpose,
according to Kafka, to utter the mantra "Original Sin" or to rummage
about in that—to him—meaningless doctrine. I add the qualification "to
him" because, of course, the doctrine had all sorts of meaning to (for example) St. Augustine, who found in it a comprehensive and sufficient explanation for the state of the world. And it was because Rousseau (being in this
much closer to the modernist writer than to Augustine) did not subscribe
to Original Sin but to a contrary belief in Original Goodness that he was so
baffled in his attempt to trace, hand over hand through a linear, connected
narrative, back to a beginning for all his woe. It was Rousseau's misfortune
(or good fortune, some would think) to be neither fully of the ancient nor

of the modern world. As a child of the Enlightenment, he could not, like St. Augustine, believe in Original Sin; but neither could he, like Kafka or Beckett, abandon belief in the power of reason (but when Rousseau says "reason" he usually means "feeling") to return him to a fixed source that would permit him to say, with unquestioned confidence, "In the beginning. . . ."

Had he ever set out to write an autobiography, Beckett would have been in no position to avail himself of the conventional (though more honored in the breach than in the observance) opening for such a book—the opening that even Rousseau could adopt: "I was born at such a place on such and such a date." The feeling that he had never been fully or properly born was even odder in Beckett than in Kafka, for, speaking both in propria persona and through his characters, Beckett on more than one occasion claimed to remember being born and, what is more, to remember his prenatal existence in the womb—neither of which, according to his testimony, was a pleasant experience. Nor was old age, if we are to believe Charles Juliet's account in *Rencontre avec Samuel Beckett*. After he asked Beckett about his health, Juliet says, the conversation turned to aging, but he discerned that Beckett "prefers not to think about this period of his life. He talks about tunnels, about a state of mental twilight." Then, with no transition, Beckett, as Juliet tells it, switched from the end to the beginning of life—or the nonbeginning: "I have always sensed that there was within me an assassinated being," Beckett said. "Assassinated before my birth. I needed to find this assassinated person again. And try to give him new life. I once attended a lecture by Jung in which he spoke about one of his patients, a very young girl. After the lecture, as everyone was leaving, Jung stood by silently. And then, as if speaking to himself, astonished by the discovery that he was making, he added: In the most fundamental way, she had never been really born. I, too, have always had the sense of never having been born."[55] The experience of the Jung lecture is transferred, with minimal alterations, to Mrs. Rooney (who does not recall Jung's name, referring to him instead as "one of these new mind doctors," not a "lunatic specialist" but merely a specialist in "mental distress") in the radio play *All That Fall* (*Complete Dramatic Works*, 196); and in abbreviated form it turns up once more among the addenda to *Watt*: "never been properly born" (p. 248). This feeling subverts the possibility of any linear account of a life: the first, most elemental piece of the narrative is simply not there. Moreover, it helps

---

55. Charles Juliet, *Rencontre avec Samuel Beckett*, 14; for convenience, I have used the translation by Suzanne Chamier, cited earlier.

not at all if Beckett remembers being born and being before that in the womb. Such recollection merely pushes any putative beginning further and further back until it is out of sight, not only invisible but inconceivable. And that, I take it, is part of his intention, to demonstrate the morphological dissimilarity or inequality between a neat, beginning-middle-and-end narrative and the mess that currently goes under the name of life.

Philosophers and historians of a certain persuasion (Jacques Le Goff is a good example) argue that the "reversibility of time" is a necessary principle for the activity of history-writing and further that, "on condition that they later restore history's true movement," historians can profit from reading it backward.[56] This principle and practice have long been central to both the writing and the reading of autobiography, but Beckett does all he can to show their impossibility for life-writing and life-reading in our time. A passage in *The Unnamable* parodies this dual notion of the reversibility of time and of reading one's history first backward then forward; the narrator says of Worm, one of his own earlier incarnations on the ladder of evolution, "Of what is it time to speak? Of Worm, at last. Good. We must first, to begin with, go back to his beginnings and then, to go on with, follow him patiently through the various stages, taking care to show their fatal concatenation, which have made him what I am. The whole to be tossed off with bravura. . . . Please God nothing goes wrong. Mahood I couldn't die. Worm will I ever get born? It's the same problem. . . . But let us go back as planned, afterwards we'll fall forward as projected. The reverse would be more like it. But not by much. Upstream, downstream, what matter . . ." (pp. 323–24). As I pointed out earlier, the regress, being infinite, allows for no possibility of getting back to any real beginning: before Mahood there will be Worm; before Worm there will be Jones; before Jones there will be someone with another name or with no name— "Upstream, downstream, what matter?" This is the same thing Mahood is said to have discovered when he set about trying to determine the extent and significance of his Kafkaesque sense of guilt:

> And without knowing exactly what his sin was he felt full well that living was not a sufficient atonement for it or that this atonement was in itself a sin, calling for more atonement, and so on, as if there could be anything but life, for the living. And no doubt he would have wondered if it was really necessary to be guilty in order to be punished but for the memory, more and more galling, of his having consented to live in his mother, then to leave her. And

56. See Le Goff's *History and Memory*, trans. Steven Rendall and Elizabeth Claman (New York: Columbia University Press, 1992), especially the chap. 1, "Past/Present"; the quoted passage occurs on p. 19.

this again he could not see as his true sin, but as yet another atonement which had miscarried and, far from cleansing him of his sin, plunged him in it deeper than before. (*Trilogy*, 220)

And in a conclusive observation, which stands as a kind of reproach to Milena or Rousseau or anyone else who would try to reason about sin and guilt or attempt to trace existential effect back to metaphysical cause, the text informs us that "truth to tell the ideas of guilt and punishment were confused together in his mind, as those of cause and effect so often are in the minds of those who continue to think" (p. 220).

So much for the possibility of any true beginning for narrative or any reliable connectedness between present and past, but what about an end? It depends, we learn in *The Unnamable*, on what you are working on when you consider the question: "It's the end that is the worst, no, it's the beginning that is the worst, then the middle, then the end, in the end it's the end that is the worst . . ." (*Trilogy*, 363). In any case, the search for an end, like the search for a beginning, as Arsene might say—as Giacometti, Beckett, Kafka *do* say—"is doomed to fail, doomed, doomed to fail." Not only were the three of them temperamentally incapable of finishing anything and letting it be, but they went further, to make it not a question of temperament but a tenet of their art that no project could or should be finished. This may not appear to be as true for Kafka as for Giacometti and Beckett, but even Kafka would have felt that if he successfully finished a story or a novel he had not raised the stakes high enough in the beginning, and his failure to do so would be proved—so to say, tautologically—by his ability to finish the piece successfully. I am not saying that we as readers or viewers judge his, Giacometti's, or Beckett's work this way, but that they all, individually, did so judge their work. Indeed, stories like *The Metamorphosis*, "The Judgment," or "A Hunger Artist," or a parable like "Before the Law"; sculptures like any number of Giacometti's figures and busts, paintings like *Apple on a Sideboard*, *The Artist's Mother*, and the portraits of Yanaihara, Annette, Caroline; pieces like *Company* or *Not I* or *Rockaby*, not to mention *Murphy*, *Watt*, or the Trilogy—these all seem supremely finished, achieved works, but not according to Kafka, not according to Giacometti, not according to Beckett. Kafka finished none of the three novels for which he is known and only a handful of the stories. Reading the regretful, quasi-apologetic notes accompanying so many of the stories in the Schocken *Complete Stories*[57] one becomes aware of something like a compulsive inabil-

57. Franz Kafka, *The Complete Stories*, trans. Willa and Edwin Muir and others, ed. Nahum N. Glazer (New York: Schocken Books, 1971).

ity to finish a work: "unfinished," we read of "Description of a Struggle"; "Wedding Preparations in the Country" is "fragments of a novel"; "The Village Schoolmaster" is "unfinished" and "the one gravely incomplete story in the book"; "Blumfeld" is "incomplete," "The Great Wall of China" is "apparently a fragment," "Investigations of a Dog" is "virtually complete," and "The Burrow" is "virtually finished." The point might be made in another way by considering the introduction that Thomas Mann— by contrast with our three, a compulsive finisher of novels and stories— contributed to *The Castle,* wherein he finishes the novel on behalf of the lamentably inconclusive author. What Beckett said of himself and Joyce could be said with equal justice of Kafka and Mann. The difference between his work and Joyce's, Beckett told Israel Shenker, "is that Joyce was a superb manipulator of material—perhaps the greatest. . . . The kind of work I do is one in which I'm not master of my material. The more Joyce knew the more he could. He's tending toward omniscience and omnipotence as an artist. I'm working with impotence, ignorance" (Shenker, "Moody Man of Letters," 3). The great manipulator and controller vs. the artist of the mess: as Joyce to Beckett, so Mann to Kafka. Thus we get at the end of Mann's introduction ("Homage") this: "*The Castle* is not quite complete. . . . The author gave his friends a version of the ending by word of mouth. K. dies—dies out of sheer exhaustion. . . . The villagers stand about the stranger's deathbed—when, at the very last moment, an order comes down from the Castle: . . . not in consideration of his honest efforts, but owing to 'certain auxiliary circumstances,' it is permitted to him to settle in the village and work there. So, at the last, grace is vouchsafed."[58] And so, at the last, a conclusion is vouchsafed for the novel Kafka never could, never would finish. One must wonder, however, if any reader ever yearned for a conclusion before Thomas Mann provided his. Kafka's response to Gustav Janouch, who remarked that Kafka's art may well be a foretelling of the future—"You are right. You are certainly right. Probably that's why I can't finish anything. I am afraid of the truth" (*Conversations with Kafka,* 150)— is in one respect correct, in another not: his art, we can now see, has foretold the future, and he could not finish anything; but his not finishing is not out of fear of the truth any more than Beckett's or Giacometti's inability to conclude is motivated by their being frightened of the truth. It is the intractability of the material and the hugeness of the task—trying to formal-

58. *The Castle,* trans. Willa and Edwin Muir (New York: Alfred A. Knopf, 1964), p. xvii.

ize all reality, subjective and objective, in the work—that resulted in their being artists of the incomplete.

Beckett, like Giacometti, recognized very early on that this was how it had to be. His lifelong project was premised on the impossibility of finishing. How could there be any end to *Waiting for Godot?* Even the title, with the meaning of "to wait" and use of the present participle indicating a continuing action, would give the lie to any attempt at closure. In choosing the progressive tense form, Beckett virtually announces that, as Giacometti said of each of his sculptures and paintings, his would be a work in progress, never ending, perpetually going on. "Shall we go?" Vladimir asks; "Yes, let's go," Estragon responds, anticipating already the ongoing going on of the end—which is not really an end—of *The Unnamable.* All of *Malone Dies* is an attempt to come to an end, but just as the voice of that volume, issuing from a disintegrating body, seems about to succeed, we turn the page and hear the entirely disembodied voice—the tormenting whirr and buzz of consciousness—take up the ceaseless monologue again in *The Unnamable.* In *Time and Narrative* Paul Ricoeur, though not referring directly to Beckett, describes well enough what we find on the last pages of *The Unnamable,* when he characterizes "the situation of contemporary culture and literature, . . . where crisis replaces the end, where crisis becomes an endless transition" (*Time and Narrative,* 2.24). Elaborating on this in *Oneself as Another,* Ricoeur points out how the disintegration of character in the contemporary novel goes hand in glove with the loss of narrative structure and of movement toward any necessary or even possible end. "To see more clearly the philosophical issues in this eclipse of the identity of the character," Ricoeur writes, "it is important to note that, as the narrative approaches the point of annihilation of the character, the novel also loses its own properly narrative qualities, even when these are interpreted . . . in the most flexible and most dialectical manner possible. To the loss of the identity of the character thus corresponds the loss of the configuration of the narrative and, in particular, a crisis of the closure of the narrative" (*Oneself as Another,* 149). This describes quite exactly what we get in all of Beckett's fiction from the Trilogy—or even earlier: from *Watt* and *Mercier and Camier*—right through *Stirrings Still,* with the anguished, inconclusive conclusions to each of its three parts:

> Then all as before. The strokes and cries as before and he as before now there now gone now there again now gone again. Then the lull again. Then all as before again. So again and again. And patience till the one true end to time and grief and self and second self his own.

So on unknowing and no end in sight. Unknowing and what is more no wish to know nor indeed any wish of any kind nor therefore any sorrow save that he would have wished the strokes to cease and the cries for good and was sorry that they did not. The strokes now faint now clear as if carried by the wind but not a breath and the cries now faint now clear.

Such and much more such the hubbub in his mind so-called till nothing left from deep within but only ever fainter oh to end. No matter how no matter where. Time and grief and self so-called. Oh all to end.[59]

It is more than a little hard to understand how Beckett can achieve such lyricism, such rhythmic beauty and such beauty of phrasing out of the desperate wish to end and the impossibility of it. It is as if in despairing of an end he achieves his end. I use such a strange word as "beauty" advisedly— and I would use it in speaking of Giacometti's sculptures, paintings, and drawings too, and of course Kafka's stories—knowing that Beckett himself, very late in life, availed himself of the same term. John Montague records visiting Beckett less than a fortnight before his death in the bizarrely named Tiers Temps retirement home—or "old crock's home," as its most illustrious inhabitant called it—and hearing Beckett describe what he was reading: "I've been reading Keats's 'Ode to a Nightingale.' It's very beautiful," Beckett says. To which Montague responds that he has "never heard him use the word 'beautiful' except in connection with Yeats. He nods. 'Ah, yes, yes, beautiful, too.' "[60] I am assuming that the Yeats here is W. B. (although it could be Jack, to whose paintings—and to whom personally— Beckett, by 1989, had been devoted for well over fifty years); in any case, it is certainly not John Butler Yeats, but the elder Yeats, too, could delight Beckett on occasion. André Bernold tells of a conversation with Beckett when the latter happened to be reading William Murphy's biography of John Butler Yeats, in which, among other things of interest to Beckett, Murphy tells of J. B. Yeats's great self-portrait, which he worked on for eleven years only to leave unfinished at his death.[61] Beckett's "eyes shone

59. *Stirrings Still,* in *The Complete Short Prose,* 261, 263, 265.

60. John Montague, "A Few Drinks and a Hymn: My Farewell to Samuel Beckett," *New York Times Book Review,* April 17, 1994, 24.

61. What Murphy has to say of the Yeats self-portrait is altogether relevant to the discussion above. John Quinn commissioned the painting, as a way to give continuing support to Yeats, eleven years to the day before Yeats's death. There were those who finally thought of his dabbling away at the painting for so long a kind of sad joke, but as Murphy writes, "It was to prove the ultimate example of John Butler Yeats's belief that as things constantly change, nothing is ever really finished. . . . To imagine that John Butler Yeats would ever have 'finished' it would be to misunderstand all that he stood for. It didn't

with admiration when he spoke of" Yeats père, according to Bernold, who goes on to quote Beckett's exclamatory enthusiasm for the Yeatsian example: "He never finished anything! He messed up his entire career! What *they* call messing up!"[62]

Giacometti could hardly have said it better, but he did say it about as well and many times, sometimes with glee, sometimes with anguish. To James Lord, while working on Lord's portrait, Giacometti declared, "It's impossible to paint a portrait. Ingres could do it. He could finish a portrait. It was a substitute for a photograph and had to be done by hand because there was no other way of doing it then. But now that has no meaning." When Lord objects that "there have been portraits since Ingres. Cézanne painted some pretty good ones . . . ," Giacometti comes back with words almost identical to those of Beckett on J. B. Yeats: "But he never finished them. After Vollard had posed a hundred times the most Cézanne would say was that the shirt front wasn't too bad. And he was right. It's the best part of the picture. Cézanne never really finished anything. He went as far as he could, then abandoned the job. That's the terrible thing: the more one works on a picture, the more impossible it becomes to finish it" (Lord, *Giacometti Portrait*, 11–12). Giacometti describes the situation as "terrible," yet one wonders if his eyes may not, like Beckett's, have shone when he said, "Cézanne never really finished anything"; indeed, a few pages later (p. 29), on the same subject, Giacometti says that "the fact that he [Cézanne] never finished his paintings, or considered them finished, is very appealing." Annette and Diego and Caroline were devoted to Giacometti and so were willing to put up with the impossible demands made on them as models— the same demands Cézanne imposed on Vollard and J. B. Yeats on himself—but others were driven nearly mad by Giacometti's insistence that, once they began to pose for a painting, they make their life over to him for the duration, which had no fixed or fixable date. Poor Professor Yanaihara, for example, who thought he had to get back to his students and classes in Japan, was told it was not possible for him to leave since Giacometti needed him to continue sitting for the portrait, which the painter himself had no expectation of finishing nor any desire to finish. "I find it harder

---

matter where the portrait stopped. As a work of art it was always complete and incomplete at the same time, as a moment is a thing in itself and yet only a sequel to what went before and a prelude to what would come after" (William M. Murphy, *Prodigal Father: The Life of John Butler Yeats (1839–1922)* [Ithaca: Cornell University Press, 1978], 385, 538–39).

62. André Bernold, *L'Amitié de Beckett*, 55: "ses yeux brillaient d'admiration lorsqu'il disait de lui: 'Il ne finissait jamais rien! Il a raté sa carrière! Ce qu'on appelle rater!' "

and harder to finish my things," Giacometti said. "The older I get, the more I find myself alone. I suppose in the end I will be entirely alone."[63] ". . . [H]ow words are coming to an end. . . . And how better in the end. . . . And you as you always were. Alone." Besides being an eerie anticipation of the conclusion of Beckett's *Company,* Giacometti's remark introduces another, deeply personal reason for preventing Yanaihara from returning to Japan and for keeping Annette, Diego, Caroline, and Elie Lotar on constant call as sitters: they constituted company, a momentary stay against aloneness and mortality. "The more you try to finish" a painting, Giacometti told Carlton Lake, "the more you find yourself beginning all over again. With sculpture it's the same thing" ("The Wisdom of Giacometti," 120). And so all the models for Giacometti's late work had to yield to his emotional, psychological, professional, and moral need to begin all over again and again. "Giacometti's last sculptural work was a life-size half-figure of Elie Lotar, seated," Reinhold Hohl writes. "This, too, remained 'unfinished', though the word here has no meaning, since, for Giacometti, no work was ever really 'finished' and, by the same token, might be regarded as 'finished' at any stage" (in Schneider, *Alberto Giacometti,* 40).

In the same way that they can find no absolute beginning for their narrative constructions, so modern artists cannot hope to arrive at any clear end. They are left, instead, to struggle *nel mezzo del cammin di nostra vita,* in the middle of the journey of our life. With this pervasive fact of the unfinished in contemporary life-writing we come full circle, for we must recall that Augustine never finished his *Confessions* and that Rousseau, as if obsessed with unfindable endings, went on from book to book in a vain search for some kind of closure, some form of absolution. The difference one might see, however, between Augustine and Rousseau on the one hand and Beckett, Giacometti, and Kafka on the other is that while the former pair were frustrated in their attempt to finish, the latter trio exacerbated or elevated the fact of incompletion—perhaps it would be better to say incompletability—to a principle of narrative: narrative as such, and a fortiori if it is the narrative of a life, cannot be finished. Not, at least, from within. But the paradox is that we, as readers of the lives spread out across dozens of unfinished works, can and do finish the larger, comprehensive project, constructing our narratives of the lives out of the detritus left behind as failed works.

63. Gotthard Jedlicka, "Alberto Giacometti zum sechzigsten Geburtstag," *Neue Zürcher Zeitung* (October 10, 1961); the passage is quoted in Hohl, *Alberto Giacometti,* 283, and in Lord, *Giacometti: A Biography,* 427. Hohl's and Lord's versions differ somewhat; the quotation above is a combination of the two.

"The silence, I am alone here, outside the night, everything is still and sleep takes me again. I don't know who I am, nor what I am doing, nor what I desire, I don't know if I am old or young, perhaps I still have hundreds of thousands of years to live until my death, my past sinks in a gray abyss. . . ."[64] This happens to be Giacometti, but it could well have come from either Beckett or Kafka: silence, the loneliness and isolation, the past sinking in a gray abyss—these are themes shared in full measure by all three. Jean Genet, in *L'Atelier d'Alberto Giacometti*, focuses these related themes in one that he terms "solitude" and that he finds preeminently in the figures of Giacometti's sculpture. "Regarding his sculptures," Genet writes, "yet another impression: these are all very beautiful beings, but it seems to me that their sadness and their solitude are akin to the sadness and solitude of a deformed man who, suddenly naked, would see his deformity put on public show, but who, at the same time, would display it to the world as a special sign of his solitude and his splendor. Inalterable."[65] Some pages earlier, as a guard against being misunderstood—and I quote it for the same reason—Genet has specified the sense in which he intends "solitude": not the miserable state understood by many as the plight of insignificant men and women of the present time but something quite different. "Solitude, as I use the word, is not a wretched condition but rather a secret royalty, profound separateness but at the same time more or less dim awareness of an unassailable singularity."[66] I don't suppose that Giacometti or Beckett would want to use these grand words to describe either their art or their state in life, but with the words in mind I think we can better understand why Beckett so prized the times he could be by himself, alone but not

64. "Le silence, je suis seul ici, dehors la nuit, tout est immobile et le sommeil me reprend. Je ne sais ni qui je suis, ni ce que je fais ni ce que je veux, je ne sais si je suis vieux ou jeune, j'ai peut-être encore quelques centaines de milliers d'années à vivre jusqu'à ma mort, mon passé se perd dans un gouffre gris. . . ." From *Paris sans fin*, republished in *Écrits*, 93. This text was designed to accompany a collection of 150 original lithographs of Paris scenes that were particularly significant to Giacometti. Commissioned by the publisher (and longtime Giacometti friend) E. Tériade in the early 1960s, it was left unfinished at Giacometti's death and was published by Tériade posthumously in 1969 with the title *Paris sans fin, 150 lithographies originales*.

65. "En face de ses statues, un autre sentiment encore: ce sont toutes de très belles personnes, pourtant il me semble que leur tristesse et leur solitude sont comparable à la tristesse et à la solitude d'un homme difforme qui, soudain nu, verrait étalée sa difformité que, dans le même temps il offrirait au monde afin de signaler sa solitude et sa gloire. Inaltérable" (*L'Atelier*, 47). My translation.

66. "La solitude, comme je l'entends, ne signifie pas condition misérable mais plutôt royauté secrète, incommunicabilité profonde mais connaissance plus ou moins obscure d'une inattaquable singularité" (*L'Atelier*, 26). My translation.

lonely, at his hideaway in Ussy and can understand too what he meant when he wrote in the journal he kept while traveling for six months in Germany, "How I ADORE solitude," accompanying the exclamation with a description of the walk in the Tiergarten in Berlin that occasioned it, watching the "ducks in dusk, taking wing from the water with the sound of consternation and settling again with a long liquid râle, flying fiercely in pairs down the axes of water, so different in the air than afloat."[67]

Solitude of this sort was a necessary state of the soul and a thematic element common to Beckett, Giacometti, and Kafka. But there are other mutual themes that I think go beyond those of silence, solitude, and isolation or that encompass them and can serve as a corrective to images of the isolated, solipsistic artist filled with anxiety, in love with the void, indifferent to the concerns of common humanity, and so on. Giacometti absolutely refused any such attitudinizing, as in the following: "While working I have never thought of the theme of solitude. I have absolutely no intention of being an artist of solitude. Moreover, I must add that as a citizen and a thinking being I believe that all life is the opposite of solitude, for life consists of a fabric of relations with others. The society in which we live in the West has made it necessary in a sense for me to pursue my activities in solitude. For many years it was hard for me to work isolated from society (but not, I hope, from humanity)" (quoted in Lord, *Giacometti,* 309–10). "But not, I hope, from humanity" would serve very well as an emblem for the work and the intention behind it of all three artists. Kafka, despairing of the effect of his writing but making the same high demands of it that Giacometti would of his painting and sculpture or Beckett of his fiction and drama, told his young friend Janouch, "One must be silent, if one can't give any help. No one, through his own lack of hope, should make the condition of the patient worse. For that reason, all my scribbling is to be destroyed. I am no light. I have merely lost my way among my own thorns. I'm a dead end" (*Conversations with Kafka,* 150). Kafka's anguish at his perceived inadequacy to the great task we may think mistaken, but he cannot be faulted for his belief that one must either be of help to the suffering patient or should fall silent.

But Beckett may be the most moving witness of the three to the artist's human responsibilities in his piece, intended for Irish radio but apparently never broadcast, on Saint-Lô, "The Capital of the Ruins." "Saint-Lô was bombed out of existence in one night," Beckett writes as he attempts to describe the devastation encountered by the personnel who came from Ire-

---

67. Quoted in Knowlson, *Damned to Fame,* 218–19.

land to Normandy to establish "the Hospital of the Irish Red Cross in Saint-Lô, or, as the Laudiniens themselves say, the Irish Hospital." What was in the beginning a "provisional" hospital, Beckett suggests, will become permanent, or as permanent as anything can be "in this universe become provisional." The Irish Red Cross with its hospital brought much to Saint-Lô, he writes, and will be remembered for it; and he speculates that "to the end of its hospital days it will be called the Irish Hospital, and after that the huts, when they have been turned into dwellings, the Irish huts. I mention this possibility," he says, in these remarks intended for an Irish audience,

> in the hope that it will give general satisfaction. And having done so I may perhaps venture to mention another, more remote but perhaps of greater import in certain quarters, I mean the possibility that some of those who were in Saint-Lô will come home realising that they got at least as good as they gave, that they got indeed what they could hardly give, a vision and sense of a time-honoured conception of humanity in ruins, and perhaps even an inkling of the terms in which our condition is to be thought again. These will have been in France.[68]

That Beckett shared with Giacometti and Kafka this "vision and sense of a time-honoured conception of humanity in ruins" and that he, like they, devoted his life to discovering "the terms in which our condition is to be thought again" cannot be doubted. This is what their lives and their works teach us, insofar as we are capable of receiving it. Of the enlarged scale of the figures intended by Giacometti for the Chase Manhattan Bank Plaza— "the only larger than life-size figures of his entire career"—Dieter Honisch writes, "If Giacometti himself saw a meaning in this enlargement of scale, we can only assume this to have been the desire to create a monument that was not a memorial in the traditional sense: not an exaltation of the victors, but of the victims, the maltreated and the nameless."[69] In his characterization of those commemorated by Giacometti's sculpture, Honisch might as well be describing any number of figures in Beckett's fiction and drama, even to the Beckettian adjective he uses—"the nameless," *The Unnamable*. Another such nameless being Giacometti memorializes in *Figure*

68. "The Capital of the Ruins" has been published a number of times; the version above is from Gontarski, *The Complete Short Prose*, 275–78. For a richly pictorial account of the Irish Hospital and Beckett's involvement, see Eoin O'Brien, *The Beckett Country: Samuel Beckett's Ireland* (Dublin: The Black Cat Press, in association with Faber and Faber, 1986), 314–42.

69. Dieter Honisch, "Scale in Giacometti's Sculpture," in Schneider, *Alberto Giacometti*, 68.

in a Box between Two Boxes Which Are Houses. It is with considerable interest that one can read in Reinhold Hohl's *Alberto Giacometti* or again in his catalogue to the 1974 Guggenheim retrospective that "it is not improbable" that in the figure in the box Giacometti is recalling a 1945 newspaper photograph of a "naked Jewish woman being driven across the open space between the prisoners' barracks and the gas chambers. . . ."[70] This is that "humanity in ruins," hurried endlessly from closed door to closed door— or, in this case, worse: to the open door of the gas chamber—for which Giacometti, Beckett, and Kafka, immersing themselves in the mess of the middle way, sought terms of exaltation and celebration.

I think it is more than trivial to learn, from James Knowlson's biography of Beckett, that in old age he returned to reading Franz Kafka (and quoting his *Diaries* from memory)—Kafka, whose art, he had earlier said to Israel Shenker, was really quite different from his own. When Beckett and his wife got away to Italy for a brief holiday in 1982, Knowlson tells us, "Beckett spent much of his time reading Kafka and kept up his Italian by reading *La Stampa*"; in early 1983, he wrote to a friend, "I remember an entry in Kafka's diary. 'Gardening. No hope for the future.' At least he could garden. There must be words for it. I don't expect ever to find them." And perhaps the most revealing of all, when he went into the Tiers Temps "old crock's home," he took with him for reading a couple of biographies of Irish figures (Oscar Wilde and Nora Joyce) and "some Kafka" (*Damned to Fame,* 599, 601, 615), both the Irish biographies and the Kafka being, though in different senses, a revisiting of worlds familiar to Beckett.

But it was Beckett's relationship with Giacometti that was particularly intriguing and, I believe for both of them, emotionally charged. There is first of all the account given by Giorgio Soavi of the long night the two of them spent mulling over the stage set, consisting only of a moon and a tree, that Beckett asked Giacometti to do ("It would give us all enormous pleasure," he wrote to Giacometti) for the Jean-Louis Barrault revival of *Waiting for Godot* at the Théâtre de l'Odéon in 1961. "It was supposed to be a tree," Giacometti told Soavi, "a tree and the moon. We experimented the whole night long with that plaster tree, making it bigger, making it smaller, making the branches finer. It never seemed right to us. And each of us said to the other: Maybe."[71] The tentative meeting of two minds, not in "yes," not in "no," but in the in-between of "maybe" (*forse:* maybe,

---

70. Hohl, *Alberto Giacometti,* 304; Guggenheim catalogue, 26.
71. Giorgio Soavi, *Il mio Giacometti* (Milan: All'Insegna del Pesce d'Oro, 1966), 59; translation is from Hohl, *Alberto Giacometti,* 210.

perhaps, probably)—there could hardly be a better linguistic marker for the shared vision of Giacometti and Beckett: standing on either side of the tree, they are Didi and Gogo, they are the two thieves of Augustine's sentence. Or more precisely, declining to remain on opposed sides of the tree, each takes into himself both Didi and Gogo, both of the thieves, both the light and the dark, the whole mess "between being and non-being" (in Giacometti's phrase) that is the middle. "*E uno diceva sempre all'altro: forse. And each of us said to the other: perhaps.*" Translating *forse* as "perhaps" one recalls Beckett's precise comment to Tom Driver: "The key word in my plays is 'perhaps.' "

Beckett once told an interviewer that Giacometti was a friend, but not "a good friend," someone he didn't feel close enough to for the latter phrase. One must honor Beckett's sense of their relationship, of course, but it seems not entirely in keeping with comments and gestures he made at various times. When Beckett traveled to the United States for the first and only time, for the making of *Film*, he brought with him, according to Deirdre Bair, a Giacometti drawing intended as a special gift to commemorate the occasion of his being the first guest in Jean and Alan Schneider's new home.[72] Knowing how strong were Beckett's feelings for Alan Schneider, one can only think that this was a carefully thought-out gift. It was in mid-1964 that Beckett carried Giacometti's drawing to the Schneiders, just eighteen months before Giacometti's death. When news of that event reached Beckett, he wrote to Jacoba van Velde in the broken, elegiac rhythms of a person in emotional distress: "Giacometti dead. George Devine dead. Yes, take me off to the Père Lachaise, tearing through the red traffic lights."[73] And there is finally the account given by Sorel Etrog of his 1971 meeting with Beckett in Etrog's Paris hotel—"Hotel l'Aiglon, Boulevard Raspail, corner of Edgar Quinet."[74] There is some slight mystery, as Etrog tells the story, about why Beckett, who suggested their meeting place, should have chosen this hotel when it was well known that Beckett met everyone who came to him in a bar or a café. After greeting one another, the two of them proceed up to Etrog's floor: "Third floor corridor, narrow, darkly lit, old red carpet. Beckett stops, stares for some time at the

72. Deirdre Bair, *Samuel Beckett: A Biography* (New York: Harcourt Brace Jovanovich, 1978), 575.

73. Quoted in Knowlson, *Damned to Fame*, 482; in a note (p. 720), Knowlson gives the original French: "Giacometti mort. George Devine mort. Oui, conduis-moi au Père Lachaise, en brûlant les feux rouges."

74. Sorel Etrog, "Tribute," in *As No Other Dare Fail* (London: John Calder, 1986), 101.

end of the corridor. He was there before." In Etrog's room, which he has supplied with "a bottle of Bushmills, two plastic glasses, an ashtray," the two chat about Etrog's lithograph illustrations for *Imagination Dead Imagine,* drink a couple of whiskies, fall silent.

> Unexpectedly Beckett moves. He actually gets up, turns towards the window just behind me, and faces the traffic lights on Boulevard Edgar Quinet. Behind it, like a backdrop, is the cemetery of Père Lachaise,[75] with the gravestones losing some of their shape in the mists of nightfall. . . .
>
> Beckett's dark silhouette against the window pane looks like a Matisse cut-out, or perhaps like the silhouette of the Auditor in *Not I.* Then in a barely audible voice, which this time seems as if it were coming from outside the window,
> 'It reminds me of times I visited Giacometti in this hotel.'
> 'Perhaps that's the reason you suggested that we meet here.'
> Short silence. Still facing the window, Beckett says, 'How sad . . . the tree was destroyed. The tree at the Odéon was destroyed in sixty-eight. Giacometti's tree.' Adding, as he returns to the chair, 'The Godot tree.'

In the solitude of memory Beckett rejoins his lost companion as, later in the Tiers Temps, he was to rejoin Kafka through the act of reading—or more precisely, through the act of rereading, which carries with it the memory of first reading. In the end—but this is not yet the end, for in Etrog's account Beckett is still remembering, which is an act not of an absolute end but of the middle and of going on—there are the narratives of the three individual lives, each embracing the totality of a career and its informing vision, what we term Beckettian, Giacomettian, Kafkaesque, and there is also the subsuming narrative of Beckett, his two fellow artists, and their conjoint making of an image sufficient to the day: "a vision and sense of a time-honoured conception of humanity in ruins, and perhaps even an inkling of the terms in which our condition is to be thought again."

75. "Père Lachaise" is clearly a mistake for Montparnasse Cemetery. In retrospect, Beckett's looking out on Montparnasse Cemetery in his moment of reverie has a richer emotional charge to it than if it were Père Lachaise since he and his wife Suzanne are now buried in Montparnasse Cemetery.

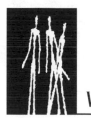

V

MEMORY

"I suppose all is reminiscence from womb to tomb," Samuel Beckett wrote to James Knowlson in 1972 a propos of the numerous literary reminiscences scattered through Winnie's near–monologue in *Happy Days*.[1] Many things could be meant by Beckett's apparently simple (though, grammatically speaking, complex) sentence, and, being Beckett, he no doubt intended them all. The sentence could mean that there is no perception and no cognition that is not altered by the intervention of memory. Before a perception can be registered in consciousness and thus become to us a perception, time will have passed and thrown it into memory, where other memories will affect and transform it. This is what Antonio Damasio has in mind when he writes, "Present continuously becomes past, and by the time we take stock of it we are in another present, consumed with planning the future. . . . The present is never here. We are hopelessly late for consciousness."[2] Herbert Read said that we truly experience a color or a sound only once, the first time, and that any subsequent experience of the color or sound will be altered by this first encounter. Going beyond Read, one could argue that even this first time is not pristine; yet we will never know, because we cannot remember any such first time as the one Read indicates. Likewise when Giacometti talks about painting from life, whether it be the glass on the table or one of his preferred sitters, he is soon thinking of painting from memory, for the one immediately, automatically becomes the other. In the instant when he looks away from the glass or the face to the canvas, the pure perception in a nonexistent now—already an impossi-

1. James Knowlson, "Beckett's 'Bits of Pipe,' " in Morris Beja, S. E. Gontarski, and Pierre Astier, eds., *Samuel Beckett: Humanistic Perspectives* (Columbus: Ohio State University Press, 1983), 16.
2. Damasio, *Descartes' Error,* 240.

bility—becomes distant, ghostly—a memory. Or perhaps it becomes clearer and more fixed as a memory. In any case it becomes something other than unmediated perception, which it never was anyhow and never could be. Winnie's meditation on herself past and present in *Happy Days* points up the same dilemma in different terms: "Then . . . now . . . what difficulties here, for the mind. (*Pause.*) To have been always what I am— and so changed from what I was. . . . deep trouble for the mind" (*Complete Dramatic Works,* 161). The difficulties that "then" and "now" represent for Winnie's poor mind are surely a major contributor to what Beckett terms "the hubbub in his mind so-called," speaking of the figure in *Stirrings Still* who "would sometimes lift . . . his past head a moment to see his past hands" (*Complete Short Prose,* 265, 260). Another thing Beckett's remark suggests is that the vast in-between "from womb to tomb" is memory's true medium, established by memory and feeding back into it at the same time. Beckett and others have claimed to remember the womb experience, but taken all together they do not compose a sufficient number for a sig- nificant sampling; and no one would seriously maintain (except in a figura- tive sense I will touch on later) that it is possible to "remember" the tomb experience. In any case, it seems clear that by "womb to tomb" he means to establish the limits of memory, and this ground between, I say again— and surely Beckett would agree—is the distinctive province, the rich ter- rain, of memory with all its wondrous recollections and imaginings, its errors and confusions, its failures and overcompensations for failure, its capacity for transformation, distortion, ordering and reordering. *This* is where memory does what it does, and what it does is to constitute nothing less than what we—each of us—are. St. Augustine said it first and best: "Great indeed is the power of memory! It is something terrifying, my God, a profound and infinite multiplicity; and this thing is the mind, and this thing is I myself" (*Conf.,* 10.17, 227). It *is* terrifying, and Beckett was fully aware of that fact: "Such and much more such the hubbub in his mind so- called. . . ."

The context in which the Beckett-to-Knowlson sentence occurs serves both to limit and to extend its significance in very interesting ways. Knowl- son seems to have asked about certain allusions in *Happy Days,* in particular Winnie's expression "I call to the eye of the mind . . . ," which appears to be borrowed from the Musicians' speech at the beginning of W. B. Yeats's *At the Hawk's Well* ("I call to the eye of the mind / A well long choked up and dry . . ."). In response to Knowlson's query, Beckett wrote, "I simply know next to nothing about my work in this way, as little as a plumber of the history of hydraulics. There is nothing / nobody with me when I'm writing, only the hellish job in hand. The 'eye of the mind' in *Happy Days* does not *refer* to Yeats any more than the 'revels' in *Endgame* (refer) to *The Tempest*. They are just bits of pipe I happen to have with me. I suppose all is reminiscence from womb to tomb. All I can say is I have scant information concerning mine—alas."[3] There is much more going on in this passage than mere acting out by an author reluctant to comment on his work for an academic critic. If one attends closely to what Beckett says, then the "all" that is "reminiscence from womb to tomb," the "all" that provides the Beckettian writer with the "bits of pipe" that make a play or a novel a functional work, comprehends not only such tags as "the eye of the mind" but any and every recollection that is knocking about in the author's mind, now to be deployed in his writing. Moreover, when we take note of the fact that the literary reminiscences in (for example) *Happy Days* are not just of works by Shakespeare, Milton, Keats, Herrick, Yeats, and many others (Knowlson gives a very good account of the borrowings in the play) but of works by Beckett himself—writings both earlier *and later* than *Happy Days*—the wealth of material available as "bits of pipe" takes on a wholly new significance. And one step further: if we reflect that this self-referential system, wherein phrases, figures, and themes are swapped about among Beckett's many works, some of them recollections of earlier appearances, others projections of later appearances, is by no means restricted to *Happy Days* but is the modus operandi—I would say almost the modus vivendi—for Beckett from at least *Murphy* through *Stirrings Still,* we will have an increased understanding of the multidimensionality, the ubiquity, and the enormous importance of memory in his thought and his practice and, it may be, in the thought and practice of other writers of our time as well.

"A poet," Yeats says in what he calls "The First Principle" in his great, summative essay, "A General Introduction for My Work," "writes always of his personal life, in his finest work out of its tragedy, whatever it be, remorse, lost love, or mere loneliness. . . ."[4] This reads almost as if Yeats in 1937 were looking ahead with Beckett to the thematic "bits of pipe"— remorse, lost love, mere loneliness—or the memories that Beckett had to work with throughout his career. I intend "had to" in two senses: they were what was available to him; and they imposed themselves as something he could not refuse. They were to turn up again and again in novel after novel, story after story, play after play, until finally they bound the body

---

3. Knowlson, 16.
4. W. B. Yeats, *Essays and Introductions* (New York: Macmillan, 1961), 509.

of work together as a single image, a representation of the writer's life as writer. This is not precisely the same as the "story in the likeness of my life" that the narrator of "The End," like all Beckett's characters, fails to be able to tell. Or if it is the same, it is so only at a remove where the narrator's failed attempt at "a story in the likeness of my life" is included within the writer's achieved story in the likeness of his life. I would separate as clearly as possible the remorse, lost love, and mere loneliness of Beckett's life—which no doubt existed, but they went when he went—from the emotions that bear the same names but now exist only as deployed thematic material in novels, stories, and plays. It would be foolish to deny that Beckett is remembering something from his life when, for example, he retails three or four times the mother's cutting remark to her son about the apparent or real distance away of the sky. But it is very much to the point to observe that the tellings are strikingly different one from another and that Beckett was undoubtedly hyperaware of this difference from telling to telling. In other words, as a man Beckett no doubt remembered, probably in a rather blurred manner, whatever happened (or didn't happen) thirty years or sixty years earlier between himself and his mother; as a writer, however, what he remembers is that he has placed the "memory" as a thematic bit at carefully chosen, significant spots in different works. Recalling and tracking the occurrences of such a motif, we are able to follow the course of Beckett's career.

It is Beckett's evolution as a writer that I wish to trace in this chapter with an emphasis throughout on the place of memory, both as means and as substance—for Beckett was not only subject to memory, he also made it his subject, memory thus becoming simultaneously the "by which" and the "about which" of his writing—in that evolution. To put it otherwise, what I intend is a case study of twentieth-century literary memory across the body of Beckett's work, amplified by thought (both my own and others') about the nature of memory, its place in life-writing, and particularly, its availability and usefulness to the contemporary life-writer (I would insist that if one seeks a generic label for what Beckett does, "life-writing"—or an equivalent term like Porter Abbott's "autography"—is as close as we can come). I will pursue the case study in a somewhat unusual way, a way determined by what I conceive to be the operant mode of memory itself, imitating my subject as I study it. In the previous chapter I mentioned the principle of the reversibility of time, whose corollary is that one may profitably read history backward before reading it forward. I pointed out that this procedure of historians has been common, too, in life-writing and life-reading. I now suggest that a backward and forward reading of experience is by way of being an accurate characterization of memory's functioning, and should provide a model for our own practice as we turn our attention to memory as a crucial feature in a largish body of life writing. What I intend, then, after some further reflection on this backward-forward aspect of memory's working, is to look closely at what I take to be Beckett's last major piece of writing—*Stirrings Still*—in which we can discern phrases, images, motifs, and themes reprised from works all the way back to the Trilogy (and even earlier), before returning to the earliest works to make our way forward and so back to *Stirrings Still*. Proceeding thus we will be imitating memory, which lays out the text of our lives for continual rereading, backward and forward, forward and backward. When Beckett's figures attempt this, they fail; but then we are in a different position from Malone, say, and a more favorable one, a different position from the speaker of "First Love" or even the "he" of *Stirrings Still*, and the texts we have to deal with, while difficult enough, are not, as theirs are, unfollowable or impossible to construe.

Memory, as St. Augustine's great passage on reciting a psalm makes clear, is both recollective and anticipatory. It looks forward to what is to come even as it drops what has been recited into the past, whence it can be recalled to be looked forward to once—and more than once—again. Memory, at least in part, is an adaptive function, with a self-adjusting and self-defining plasticity about it, turning back to the past so as to position itself and us for what is to be dealt with in the future: it adapts continuously to changing circumstances, external and internal, to constitute the self as it is at any given instant. "The neural basis for the self," according to Antonio Damasio, a neurologist who is as expert a guide as we have to the workings of the brain and its partnerlike relationship to the body, "resides with the continuous reactivation" not of fixed memory traces or inalterable images but of the adaptive potentialities Damasio terms "dispositional representations." These dispositional representations form out of "key events in an individual's autobiography, on the basis of which a notion of identity can be reconstructed repeatedly." With their reference to the past and to major autobiographical motifs, these representations provide the self an evolving stability in the face of the Heraclitean flux in all things; part of that stability depends, of course, on our recent past history, but another part of it relates to our imagined or anticipated future. Memory reaches toward the future as toward the past, and balance demands a poised receptiveness in both directions. We have available "in recent dispositional memory," Damasio writes, "a collection of recent events, along with their approximate temporal continuity, and we also have a collection of plans, a number of imaginary events we intend to make happen, or expect to happen. The plans and imaginary events constitute what I call a 'memory of the possible future.' It is held in dispositional representations just like any other memory" (*Descartes' Error*, 238–39). There might well be some who would object to the use of the word *memory* when speaking of the future, but St. Augustine, who talks of "a present of things past, a present of things present, and a present of things future," all of which "do exist in the mind" and thus in the memory (*Conf.*, 11.20, 273), would not be one of them; nor, I am sure, would Samuel Beckett, who demonstrates in and for his work an uncanny foreknowledge of what will be, which is the reverse side of an exact recollection of what has been. The elements repeated time and again in Beckett's writings are the dominants of his imagination, which is to say the dominants of his creative memory.

The life-writer who draws on memory does so in full awareness that the temporal position he or she occupies is the present moment of the past and that an excursion into history can begin only with a backward reading from that point. Autobiography, according to Georges Gusdorf, "is a second reading of experience, and it is truer than the first because it adds to experience itself consciousness of it."[5] It is through memory and its repetitional, restorative capacity—but repetition and restoration always with a difference, in part due to the most immediate previous repetition—that the second, and beyond that, third, fourth . . . readings of experience are performed. It is, as I have suggested, as if memory spreads out the text of our lives for us to read again and again, but I would recall and reemphasize the etymological origin of *text* in *texere*, "to weave," for the text is never fixed or single: it is ever rewoven, constantly renewed or reconstructed, constantly evolving, a story and a work in progress. Wilhelm Dilthey says that we all perform the act of autobiography all the time, not in the sense of writing it down, of course, or sending it into the world for publication, but in the sense of—as Beckett puts it and performs it so often—drawing the line and making the tot. But the tot will be different each time, for memory and the self will have altered with circumstances, and these—self and circumstances—taken in adaptive conjunction, will determine the new tot. We can see such a totting up of a career, of necessity provisional and incomplete, as early as 1948, in a letter Beckett wrote to George Reavey: "I am now retyping, for rejection by the publishers, *Malone Meurt*, the last I hope of the series Murphy, Watt, Mercier & Camier, Molloy, not to

5. Georges Gusdorf, "Conditions and Limits of Autobiography," in Olney, *Autobiography: Essays Theoretical and Critical,* 38.

mention the 4 Nouvelles & Eleuthéria" (*No Symbols Where None Intended*, 53). Hope on, is one's immediate reaction, for *Malone Meurt* was not, of course, to be the last of the line or anything like it. Certainly *The Unnamable*, *Waiting for Godot*, and *Texts for Nothing* must be additions to the series, however defined, and I would argue that *everything* after *Malone Dies*, up to and including *Stirrings Still* (and going back to catch up *Molloy* and *Malone Dies* as well), was part of a single, grand series. One might also glance at the confidence, masked by the apparent derogation of "retyping, for rejection by the publishers," involved in Beckett's including the unpublished and, as of July 1948, seemingly unpublishable *Watt, Mercier et Camier, Molloy*, "4 Nouvelles & Eleuthéria," in his list of classics-to-be. And just as intriguing is the certainty that from a later perspective Beckett would have deliberately excluded *Eleuthéria* as being no longer a worthy item in the series. Not only does the totting up demand to be done over and over, but it will produce a subtly different reckoning each time.

It would be unreasonable to dispute Beckett's accounting in his early look backward and forward, but we should distinguish all the same among some of his titles to convey the sense that though every published book, at least, ought to be included in a comprehensive summing-up, there still might be miniseries within the inclusive Series. I have in mind a title Beckett does not include, although the book was published well before 1948 (*More Pricks Than Kicks*), and one not published in his lifetime, which I believe Beckett would not have included whether in 1948 or 1988 (*Dream of Fair to Middling Women*), as well as three works securely on the list: *Murphy, Watt, Mercier et Camier*. The reasons one might want to think of these final three as being of a different miniseries from, say, the Trilogy and immediately surrounding volumes are several. That *Murphy* was completed by 1936, was thus prior to what I have described as the turning point of 1938 and well before the one of 1945, and was written in English sets it apart somewhat from post-*Molloy* works; that *Watt*, too, was written in English, after the 1938 stabbing but before the "revelation" of 1945, argues for a special status for it; and that *Mercier et Camier*, while written in French, exists on the cusp between the two languages and right on the divide that the 1945 Dublin experience marks in Beckett's relationship to his work, makes it a transitional volume that might belong to an earlier or a later series—or, of course, to both simultaneously, since there is much of the arbitrary about establishing "periods" of a writer's work in this way. In doing so, however, I take my cue from Beckett himself, even if, from a perspective fifty years from 1948, my perception of the points of demarcation differs somewhat from Beckett's.

I have already implied that in looking back from 1988, the year of
Stirrings Still, what one sees as crucial moments and decisions in Beckett's
life as a writer are the 1938 stabbing, the 1945 "revelation" in Dublin, and
the switch from English to French, which began with the writing of *Mercier
et Camier* in 1946 and (as I see it) came full-blown into its own with *Molloy*
in 1947. Thereafter, as Beckett once put it to an interviewer,[6] *Malone Dies*
came out of *Molloy, The Unnamable* out of *Malone Dies,* and *Texts for Nothing*
out of *The Unnamable* as if by a natural, inexorable process of gestation and
birth. Once set in motion, the whole career, if one is looking back from
the end of it, seems inevitable, for all the elements are there in the last
work, gathered together one final time. But what, one must ask, set the
career in motion? What distinguishes the work after *Molloy* from *Murphy,
Watt, Mercier et Camier*—to leave it with just those three titles, all from
Beckett's list and each in its way a remarkable achievement? I will offer a
simple answer before attempting the requisite complications. There is first
of all, for *Murphy* and *Watt,* the matter of language; there is second, for all
three of the earlier works, the question of perspective, of where we are
situated as readers; and third and finally, as a natural consequence of the
first two issues, there is the matter of what the books are about, of what
their subject is or what their subjects are. Having separated these elements
for the purposes of simplification, I must now take them up together, for
they are interrelated in complex and significant ways.

If it is true, as has been asserted by Charles Juliet, James Knowlson,
and Carlton Lake among others, that in the "revelation" of 1945 Beckett
realized that he had but one subject—himself—and that he was to let the
dark in to become the critical element in his work—struggling to find a
form to accommodate the mess, as I have argued—then the chief means
at hand for realizing that subject of the self would, of necessity, be memory,
memory in all its complexity, relating to the future as to the past, and at
its best capable, as Damasio claims, of moment-by-moment reconstruction
of the self in its encounter with the world inside and outside. At the same
moment that Beckett made memory both the means and the subject of his
writing, he shifted from English—to be more precise, from Irish English—
to French. He gave many explanations (some more nearly evasions than
explanations) for the switch, but I suggest that one overriding reason has
to do with the tangled and intimate relationship that binds together, in a

---

6. Interview with Gabriel d'Aubarède in *Nouvelles Littéraires,* February 16, 1961; reprinted in Lawrence Graver and Raymond Federman, eds., *Samuel Beckett: The Critical Heritage* (London: Routledge and Kegan Paul, 1979), 216.

single package, memory, language, and emotion. We hardly needed them to tell us, since we all know that memory is emotion laden and emotion bedeviled, but neuroscientists (e.g., Gerald Edelman in *The Remembered Present* and *Bright Air, Brilliant Fire*), neurologists (e.g., Antonio Damasio in *Descartes' Error*), neurobiologists (e.g., Steven Rose in *The Making of Memory*), theoretical neurophysiologists (e.g., William J. Calvin in *How the Brain Thinks: Evolving Intelligence, Then and Now*), psychologists (e.g., A. R. Luria in *The Man with a Shattered World* and *The Mind of a Mnemonist,* Elizabeth Loftus in *Eyewitness Testimony* and *The Myth of Repressed Memory,* and Israel Rosenfield in *The Invention of Memory*), psychiatrists (e.g., J. Allan Hobson in *The Chemistry of Conscious States* and Daniel Schacter in *Searching for Memory*), and even journalists (e.g., Philip J. Hilts in *Memory's Ghost* and George Johnson in *In the Palaces of Memory*) have for some years been demonstrating in convincing detail (some of it, perhaps, repetitive) how the amygdala, the hippocampus, and the hypothalamus—indeed, the entire limbic system, which is the center of emotional activity and response in the brain—are implicated in every act of memory. And we hardly require linguists to inform us that language is as closely bound up with and by emotion as is memory itself. (I might mention here the passage from Kafka in the previous chapter, on young Jewish writers who choose, or are compelled, to write in German: "what resulted was a literature impossible in all respects, a gypsy literature which had stolen the German child out of its cradle and in great haste put it through some kind of training, for someone has to dance on the tightrope.") It was with the intention, I believe, of clothing memories in a language that had for him no tentacular roots *in* memory, a language that was therefore safer, more formal and abstract than the intensely charged medium of English, that Beckett decided, when memory became in all ways central to his work, to write in French. There is an apparent, but I think not real, paradox here. If he wished to indulge in memory, why did Beckett not choose to remain in what was for him the language of memory? But precisely—he did *not* wish to indulge in memory: he had no choice but to take it on as subject along with the self. English both was and was not Beckett's language; he had no love of the English mentality (responding to the question "Are you English?" with "Au contraire"), and when the language of that somewhat alien people assumed the form of Irish English, with its suffocating richness in sentimental, stereotyping turns of phrase, this could hardly make the language more appealing to someone of Beckett's astringent reserve. Besides, an Irish-inflected English was the language of Joyce (and Beckett from early on knew he had to get out from under that oppressive figure), of Yeats and

Synge and O'Casey and many others. Beckett had every reason to want to disburden himself of a language in which every word, every phrase, was loaded with a memorial freight both personal and cultural. Even when he was writing in French, however, and then translating himself into English, there never ceased to be Irishisms in Beckett's work, which means, I suppose, that there was an ineradicable Irishness—a memory of Irishness, one might say—in the author, operating beneath or beyond his choice of language. But French served Beckett well, especially in its capacity, acting as a kind of fine-woven linguistic mesh, to filter out emotion-drenched localisms that would have little or no affect in French but more than enough in Irish English. *Murphy* is a wonderful book, as rich in Irish humor and Irish spirits as anything Beckett ever wrote, but he could not continue in that vein, not if he was to heed what he took to be the lessons of his turning points of 1938 and 1945.

I believe that those experiences had rather differing lessons for Beckett (and here I part ways with those who either do not perceive a difference between the two or simply disregard the earlier event, feeling that the 1945 "revelation" carried all the meaning for Beckett). It is on this ground that I would distinguish *Watt* from *Murphy* although both are written (or appear to be at first glance) in English. One (but as I see it only one) thing he learned from the two experiences that serves to separate *Watt* from *Murphy* we can intuit from what Beckett said to Knowlson—pretty much repeating what he had earlier told Israel Shenker—in an attempt to describe how his work differed from Joyce's: "I realised that Joyce had gone as far as one could in the direction of knowing more, [being] in control of one's material. He was always adding to it; you only have to look at his proofs to see that. I realised that my own way was in impoverishment, in lack of knowledge and in taking away, in subtracting rather than in adding" (*Damned to Fame,* 319). This realization, as Beckett calls it, we can see being put to work in *Watt. Watt* is—in a way that *Murphy* is not—a radical questioning of how and whether, sunk in the human condition as we are, we can know anything; the answer the novel gives is profoundly skeptical and helps one understand what Beckett means when he says that his way is "in lack of knowledge and in taking away, in subtracting rather than in adding." The epistemological skepticism of the novel is dramatized in Watt's absolutely futile attempt to know anything of Mr. Knott and is conveyed even in the negativity of Knott's name. Porter Abbott points up the contrast between *Watt* and *Murphy* well when he says, of the protagonists' attitudes toward the two figures, Endon and Knott, who so fascinate them, that with the latter, "The effort is no longer to *be* him but to comprehend him."[7] This effort to comprehend Knott, or in fact to comprehend anything in the world of *Watt,* is "doomed to fail, doomed, doomed to fail." *Watt* thus points to Beckett's way of nonknowing. Another significant difference between the two books lies in their language: *Murphy* is replete with Irish expressions; *Watt,* on the other hand, has few Irishisms, at least after the first pages, and seems to be written in no known language. Beckett once declared that he had chosen French because it was possible to write in that language (not, obviously, for the French but for someone Irish like himself) "sans style." Without switching to French, Beckett nevertheless comes, in *Watt,* as close as anyone could to writing *sans style,*[8] even making commas serve to deprive the book of anything that would ordinarily go under the name of style:

> Watt, reflecting on this, heard a little voice say, Mr Knott, having once known a man who was bitten by a dog, in the leg, and having once known another man who was scratched by a cat, in the nose, and having once known a fine healthy woman who was butted by a goat, in the loins, and having once known another man who was disembowelled by a bull, in the bowels, and having once frequented a canon who was kicked by a horse, in the crotch, is shy of dogs, and other four-footed friends, about the place, and of his inarticulate bipedal brothers and sisters in God hardly less so, for he once knew a missionary who was trampled to death by an ostrich, in the stomach, and he once knew a priest who, on leaving with a sigh of relief the chapel where he had served mass, with his own hands, to more than a hundred persons, was shat on, from above, by a dove, in the eye. (P. 91)

When we are told in the next sentence that "Watt never knew quite what to make of this particular little voice, whether it was joking, or whether it was serious," we cannot be altogether surprised, but so it is throughout the book: we can never know whether any little voice is joking or is serious and indeed can never know anything about anything else either. Beckett, in writing in a language that abandons normal syntactic logic, seems intent on showing the folly of employing reason and logic in an attempt to know the world or any denizens of it. But there are also peculiar intimations of

---

7. H. Porter Abbott, *The Fiction of Samuel Beckett: Form and Effect* (Berkeley and Los Angeles: University of California Press, 1973), 59.

8. For a brilliant treatment of language and knowing in *Watt* from a slightly different point of view see Marjorie Perloff, *Wittgenstein's Ladder: Poetic Language and the Strangeness of the Ordinary* (Chicago: University of Chicago Press, 1996), esp. chap. 4, "Witt-Watt: The Language of Resistance/The Resistance of Language," 114–43.

French even in this styleless book, as if Beckett were inhabiting a strange no-man's-land, no longer Irish English, not Standard English either, and not yet French in any meaningful sense. A trivial instance of French looming in the distance—but as yet far away—occurs when Mr. and Mrs. Nixon and Mr. Hackett are discussing the figure (Watt, as it turns out) who has just come off the tram: "But does the penny fare end here, said Mr Nixon, at a merely facultative stop?" *Facultatif*, when used in the vicinity of a tram stop, would not give a French speaker pause, but *facultative* in the same sense is not, I should think, in common English usage, even among Irish speakers. Beckett rises, if only momentarily, out of the nonlanguage of *Watt* to announce the imminent arrival, at this "merely facultative stop," of a new tongue—"but not yet," as St. Augustine said in a rather different context, "not yet."

Watt, then, in my reading of it, is concerned with one of the two lessons Beckett derived from (1) being stabbed by Prudent on a Paris street, and (2) having a vision in his "mother's little house, named New Place, across the road from Cooldrinagh"; and coming, as it did, between these events, we may conclude that the impress the book bears is a result of the first of them. Knowledge of the world and of other people is not, in any significant sense, possible in *Watt,* which does not mean that the search immediately turned inward for Beckett or for his characters. Watt is avid to know Mr. Knott, but he exhibits little interest in turning that search for knowledge back on himself. The achievement of *Watt* is a great one and essential to what Beckett would eventually do, yet that achievement is almost entirely negative: he shows why one way of proceeding—the way of knowing—must be rejected, but offers little by way of an alternative. Point of view is likewise pertinent here: for the first hundred pages or so of *Watt,* an omniscient and objective author seems responsible for everything presented; there is never any suggestion, as will become the standard after *Molloy,* that we are inside the skull of the protagonist (or someone situated just behind the protagonist and mimicking being inside his skull). In fact, we have as little knowledge of the inside of Watt's head as we have of Mr. Knott. It must come as a surprise to most readers of *Watt* to discover, far into the book, that there is a narrator of all this material who is also a character in the book—someone who cannot possibly be aware of most of what has been narrated and who, we learn, is at least as much in the dark about Mr. Knott as Watt is. We are made aware of his presence only when he ("Sam") intrudes on the narrative in the most bizarre ways, as in the following, where he thrusts his head up and out of an ostensibly third-person narrative: "But that does not at all agree with my conception of Mr

Knott. But what conception have I of Mr Knott? None" (p. 120). I cannot imagine a reader who would not be astonished at the sudden entry of an *I* not known to exist before; but if "Sam"—nameless at this point—appears abruptly, he disappears with equal dispatch, and the next sentence, clothed in the objectivity of the third person, begins, "Watt wondered if Arsene, Walter, Vincent and the others had passed through the same phase as that through which Erskine then was passing . . . ," etc. If Carlton Lake is right when he writes that Beckett "suddenly realized he had one subject— himself—and henceforward he would tell that story" (*No Symbols Where None Intended*, 49), then that realization came after *Watt*, not before it, and (I am inclined to say) after *Mercier et Camier* as well.

One reason I would place *Mercier et Camier* before the great divide, though it was written in what I have described as being for Beckett the memoryless language of French, is that it has, perhaps even more strangely than *Watt*, an absentee first-person narrator whom Beckett produces at the outset but then whisks away almost before we can take account of his exis- tence. The narrator begins with the confidence of full presence, claiming knowledge of all that has happened on the journey of Mercier and Ca- mier—"Le voyage de Mercier et Camier, je peux le raconter si je veux, car j'étais avec eux tout le temps": "The journey of Mercier and Camier is one I can tell, if I will, for I was with them all the time"[9]—and then disappears from the text more completely even than "Sam" from *Watt*, not leaving behind so much as the trace of a name. This looks forward in one way, it may be, to the narrators of the Trilogy, whose identities are forever being called into question, but what seems beyond doubt in the Trilogy, especially in *The Unnamable*, but not in *Mercier et Camier*, is that the voices all issue from inside a head, whosesoever it may be. "And sometimes I say to myself I am in a head," we hear from the voice of *The Unnamable*, "surrounded on all sides by massive bone" (*Trilogy*, 322). Uncertain though one may be about the voice on other matters, it seems to have it right on this one. A passage to similar effect occurs in *That Time* where C, sounding very much as if he were giving a brief rundown of Beckett's career, comes to what I take to be the period of the Trilogy: "when you started not knowing who you were from Adam trying how that would work for a change not knowing who you were from Adam no no notion who it was saying what you were saying whose skull you were clapped up in whose moan had you the way you were . . ." (*Complete Dramatic Works*, 391).

9. *Mercier et Camier* (Paris: Les Éditions de Minuit, 1970), 7; *Mercier and Camier* (New York: Grove Press, 1974), 7.

Being clapped up inside someone's skull—and it does not take too much imagination to say that the skull is ultimately, beyond the infinite regress of other possibilities, other avatars, Beckett's own skull—is the condition of the voices in all his fiction from *Molloy* on—but not before. Another reason for excluding *Mercier et Camier* from the arc as I will draw it of his career is that not only does the book not constitute a part of the *Molloy–* through–*The Unnamable* "series," it also came to seem to Beckett himself (and here I am in full agreement) not to belong to what we might call the canonical works. In 1948, as the letter to Reavey indicates, *Mercier et Camier* was clearly a part of Beckett's rudimentary conception of how the body of work should look when completed. And it appears to have remained so throughout the period of composing *Molloy, Malone Dies,* and *The Un-namable,* for in all three volumes Mercier and Camier, separately or to-gether, appear as members in good standing in "my troop of lunatics" (*Trilogy,* 282), the band Beckett elsewhere calls "my people." By the time *Mercier et Camier* was published, however (1970 in French, 1974 in English), Beckett had strong misgivings and said, on more than one occasion, that he was sorry he had ever granted the book his imprimatur. It is not a ques-tion here of a miniseries or whatever we might call it, for Beckett never disclaimed *Murphy* or—perhaps a better test case—*Watt.* It is my guess also that he came to be slightly embarrassed by the French of *Mercier et Camier,* which has about it something of the neophyte showing off some of the choicer pieces in his recently acquired vocabulary. It is pertinent to observe that the English version differs quite markedly from the original and that Beckett hated translating the book, as if the whole production caused him unbearable chagrin. I will admit to one twinge of regret in excluding *Mercier et Camier* from the tot, a twinge that comes with the final words, as Camier goes off and leaves Mercier alone: "Seul il regarda son ciel s'éteindre, l'om-bre se parfaire. L'horizon englouti, il ne le quitta pas des yeux, car il connais-sait ses sursauts, par expérience. Dans le noir il entendait mieux aussi, il entendait des bruits que le long jour lui avait cachés, des murmures hu-mains, par exemple, et la pluie sur l'eau": "Alone he watched the sky go out, dark deepen to its full. He kept his eyes on the engulfed horizon, for he knew from experience what last throes it was capable of. And in the dark he could hear better too, he could hear the sounds the long day had kept from him, human murmurs for example, and the rain on the water" (*Mercier et Camier,* 210; *Mercier and Camier,* 122). *Seul:* Alone—this could be the one on his back in the dark of *Company* or the "he" of *Stirrings Still.* Beckett did not shy away from translating anything in the passage, did not cut or compress as he did many other parts of *Mercier et Camier;* too, in this final passage there are many anticipations of the strongest parts of the later work: alone, watching the sky go out, dark deepening to its full, the engulfed horizon, the last throes, sounds in the dark, the long day, human murmurs—these turn up over and over. It is as if Beckett had caught a glimpse for just a moment of all that was to come.

Having permitted myself to cite a favored passage in *Mercier et Camier* while at the same time attempting to decanonize the book, perhaps I may proceed further in boldness and use the book as a springboard all the way forward to *Stirrings Still*. What we have at the beginning of *Stirrings Still* is a situation that, in various forms, dominates all of Beckett's post-*Murphy* writing, including *Watt* and *Mercier et Camier:* that is to say a situation in which the protagonist (if that is the right word—Beckett's writing does not accommodate itself easily to standard or old-fashioned literary terminology) is being watched by a known or unknown other. In the case of *Stirrings Still* the observer is well known to the observed because they are one and the same—"One night as he sat at his table head on hands he saw himself rise and go"—but this is merely a culmination and intensification of the condition of virtually all Beckett's characters. It may not be apparent that it is so in *Mercier et Camier,* but consider the claim made by the narrator: "The journey of Mercier and Camier is one I can tell, if I will, for I was with them all the time." That the *I* immediately disappears from view does nothing to alter the assertion that he has observed Mercier and Camier throughout their journey; what in fact his disappearance does is to make him akin to that indistinct or invisible figure, called "the old bastard," "the foul brute," and other similar names, who looms behind the narrators of the Trilogy and who becomes the devised deviser devising himself and others for company in the 1980 *Company*. In his review of *Company* ("The Voice of Language"), Raymond Federman is at pains to deny that memory plays any part in the book or indeed that *Company* shows traces of life-writing at all. "[T]he text of Beckett's new work of fiction," Federman writes, "asks us to imagine a voice reaching someone in the dark. But this is not the voice of memory—Beckett does not need memory (biography/autobiography) to sustain his fiction. . . ."[10] Federman's insistence, which protests much more than the occasion demands, suggests that he is arguing an untenable case: this *is* the voice of memory. And whether Beckett does or does not "need" memory is a dead issue; it is so central to what he is doing that it becomes the very subject of that doing. "To murmur, Yes I

10. Raymond Federman, "The Voice of Language," *American Book Review* 3, no. 3 (March–April 1981): 10–11.

remember. What an addition to company that would be! A voice in the first person singular. Murmuring now and then, Yes I remember" (*Company*, 16). It may be, as Federman says, that *Company* is "all *words, words,*" but those words are about memory, its return on itself, its repetitions, reenactments, and alterations. Though it could be argued that Beckett is merely teasing the reader with the fifteen passages that recount memories of some sort belonging to someone, we must keep in mind that the same or very similar memories have been produced to tease us out of thought in other works. Given that we do remember these memories, it is unclear to me how things would be altered or improved by calling them "memories" rather than memories.

"Do you think God sees me?" Estragon asks Vladimir in *Waiting for Godot;* and later in the play Vladimir addresses the question in a way that glances back to Estragon's query and forward to the "he" sitting "at his table head on hands" in *Stirrings Still:* "At me too someone is looking, of me too someone is saying, he is sleeping, he knows nothing, let him sleep on" (*Complete Dramatic Works,* 71, 84). The observed/observer situation is so common in Beckett that it is hard to know where to start or where to stop citing instances. *Film*'s raison d'être is to dramatize the Berkeleyan *esse est percipi,* "to be is to be perceived," and to test the frightening proposition (sounded in other works but not resolved in any of them) that one's existence may be dependent, or may be thought to be dependent, on nothing more than solipsistic self-perception. "It will not be clear until end of film," Beckett writes in his general directions for *Film,* "that pursuing perceiver is not extraneous, but self," and what we get at "end of film," when Buster Keaton as the pursued and observed realizes that the eye pursuing and observing is his own, are these directions to the filmmakers: "He sits, bowed forward, his head in his hands, gently rocking. Hold it as the rocking dies down" (*Complete Dramatic Works,* 323, 329). Whether this is Beckett's memory looking back to what has been done in *Happy Days* (Winnie: "Strange feeling that someone is looking at me. I am clear, then dim, then gone, then dim again, then clear again, and so on, back and forth, in and out of someone's eye" [*Complete Dramatic Works,* 155]), in *Krapp's Last Tape* (where Krapp is self-hearer and self-heard rather than seer and seen), in *Waiting for Godot,* and in the Trilogy or is Beckett's memory looking forward to what will be done in *Eh Joe, That Time, Company, Rockaby,* and *Stirrings Still* is of little import since the forward glance of one moment becomes the backward glance of the next and, taking the long perspective, we must see that the two come to pretty much the same thing. The voice of the woman that speaks to Joe in *Eh Joe* and the three voices of the one self that speak to that self in *That Time,* although disembodied, are all to be imagined as having their addressees under direct observation, just as we, the audience, see Joe and "Listener"—hold them in our eyesight— throughout the plays. It is his feeling of being constantly seen, his feeling that his memories are visible to "Woman's Voice" and to the eye of the camera, that makes Joe search his room obsessively in the futile attempt to ensure that it has been sealed against intrusive observation. But what happens in both plays is that the lone figure, Joe or "Listener," is compelled not only to be watched but to be the watcher, to observe himself and to remember his past, and through that dual act of perception, by way of viewing and by way of memory, to be as he now is, to exist as he now exists.

To return to *Stirrings Still:* I have said that the piece is a culmination and intensification of this situation so common in Beckett, by which I mean that, while not different in kind from earlier instances, the focus has been tightened by eliminating other figures, voices, camera eyes, everything else, leaving us with only the "he" who watches himself rise and go. *Stirrings Still,* as I see it, completes the other works by gathering into itself these memories of its own earlier occurrences; or, looking in the other direction, we could say its predecessors were preparations, anticipations, "memories of the future" that would reach their full term only with *Stirrings Still.* Christopher Ricks too reads the book as an end but with a somewhat different emphasis. For him the piece is an attempt to imagine one's own death rather than, as it is for me, a memory and a reviving of all its own previous incarnations. *Stirrings Still,* Ricks writes, "begins with simple finality. 'One night as he sat at his table head on hands he saw himself rise and go.' "[11] Ricks asks a series of questions about this opening—"He saw himself go out of this life? go out of his body? and go out of his mind?"—and then reflects on what would usually be the foolishness of an attempt to prefigure one's death. "People imagining 'their own Deaths': an unthinking writer sinks into folly here." Beckett, of course, was anything but an unthinking writer (as Ricks is fully aware), which makes me believe that he is doing more even than imagining death, dramatic and difficult as that may be. I would say yes and no to Ricks's formulation: yes, the language has about it that simplicity and finality arrived at only by a lifetime's effort; but no, *Stirrings Still* is less the imagination of death—or it is less that alone—than a vast exercise in recalling all that Beckett has been and done as a writer,

---

11. Christopher Ricks, *Beckett's Dying Words* (Oxford: Oxford University Press, 1993), 46.

distilled into a very few words, all of them simple in the way that only Beckett could achieve simplicity. And any "simple finality" in Beckett's first sentence is thoroughly undone by the Yeatsian recall in the phrase "rise and go" (actually "rise and go" in *Stirrings Still* could be seen as a recollection of an earlier recollection of Yeats in *Texts for Nothing 5:* "I'm going to rise and go . . ." [*Complete Short Prose,* 120]), by the fact of the watcher watching himself, and by that final word "go," which echoes from work to work in Beckett until it becomes something like an identifying signature. The "rise and go" phrase, which is neither complete nor exact as a quotation but is more in the nature of a memory, Beckett cannot have written without thought of Yeats, who, in his old age, took on an emblematic importance for Beckett in *his* old age. "I always wanted to be poised for action in old age," Beckett told Charles Juliet. "One's being can burn brightly while the body decamps. I've often thought about Yeats. He wrote his best poems after age sixty."[12] Beckett resisted Yeats for much of his life, but by 1988 he was prepared to make common cause with the poet of "The Lake Isle of Innisfree." Yeats was par excellence the creator who went on, who would "rise and go," and when this occurs in *Stirrings Still* one has the feeling of Yeats watching Beckett "go" as Beckett also watches Yeats "go." This is, in effect, to extend memory outside the single writer's work to embrace a longer tradition, one that had earlier to be declined but that could now be incorporated in the richer project. "I shall arise and go now" has language in it that could come from either Yeats or Beckett; for the latter it was one of those "bits of pipe" lying about when he wrote *Stirrings Still,* and it was out of just such bits of pipe, of his own and others' making, that Beckett put together the body of work bearing his name.

Let us pick up a few more bits of pipe, humble and grand at the same time, from *Stirrings Still.* The following phrases and clauses will, I think, do us well: "stirrings still"; "cries now faint now clear"; "same hat and coat as of old when he walked the . . . back roads"; "stop dead and stand stock still . . . and . . . sink his head as one deep in meditation"; and "so on . . . all to end." The "stirrings" of the title we can trace back, if we want to choose a ribald line, to the sudden and unexpected fluttering Mahood (in *The Unnamable*) feels in his genital region in spite of his suspicion that "they had gelt me": "Heaven, I almost felt it flutter! Does this mean they did

12. "Meeting Beckett," 10; the original French, somewhat more vigorous than the English, imitates a bit better what Beckett was talking about: "J'ai toujours souhaité avoir une vieillesse tendue, active. . . . L'être ne cessant pas de brûler alors que le corps fout le camp. . . . J'ai souvent pensé à Yeats. . . . Ses meilleurs poèmes, il les a écrits après soixante ans . . ." (*Rencontre avec Beckett,* 13).

not geld me? I could have sworn they had gelt me. But perhaps I am getting mixed up with other scrota. Not another stir out of it in any case. I'll concentrate again" (*Trilogy*, 305). Nothing comes of his concentration here, but that there were stirrings still almost forty years later for a Beckett figure is surely a promising sign. The voice of someone undecidable speaking to an undecidable someone in the third of the *Texts for Nothing,* after redoubling itself so that speaker and spoken-to are the same ("What matter who's speaking, someone said what matter who's speaking"), urges the hearer and speaker to be up and stirring: "Start by stirring, there must be a body, as of old . . . , I'll say I'm a body, stirring back and forth, up and down, as required. With a cluther of limbs and organs . . . , I'll call that living, I'll say it's me, I'll get standing, I'll stop thinking, I'll be too busy, getting standing, staying standing, stirring about, holding out, getting to tomorrow, tomorrow week, that will be ample, a week will be ample, a week in spring, that puts the jizz in you" (*Complete Short Prose,* 109). If language can ever imagine itself to be self-generating, it does so here and in a double sense, for it claims to be capable not only of setting itself in motion but of jump-starting the self it is about. In other words, though the passage constitutes a parody of the extravagant claim, its language suggests a simultaneous generation of *it*self and *the* self. The reason there is much less "jizz" in the language of *Stirrings Still* than here is to be sought less in the mere passage of time (though that too plays its part) than in the "still" part of the *Stirrings Still* title. The "stirrings" of *Texts for Nothing* (which is among the first "series" in French, coming out of the Trilogy as an attempt to deal with some of the problems encountered in those books) is a parodic version of starting out and revving up; the "stirrings" of *Stirrings Still,* by contrast, is an elegiac modulation into stillness. The two exist, however, on a continuum, one at either pole, that describes the arc of Beckett's engagement with language and of his literary career. An equation for this curve would be a very complex proposition since there is always a bending back on the curve, and it would be necessary to factor in, among other things (increasing age, intervening experience, accumulating texts), the switch in the late '40s from Irish English to French (modified by Beckett's translation of *Texts for Nothing* back into a "jizzy" English) and the return in the late '80s to his language of origin and memory (modified, yet again, by his translation of *Stirrings Still* into the French of *Soubresauts,* a title Christopher Ricks describes nicely when he says it "makes a sudden leap, is less stirring"—more "jizzy" perhaps).

To complicate the situation further, we must notice that even as there is a lessening of energy in the later "stirrings" that continue yet but are becoming "still," there are compacted into the latter word a host of literary echoes, from Beckett and others, that compensate in weight for what may have been lost in rambunctious energy. Beckett provided a kind of guide to the possible uses and meanings of "still" in "Fizzle 7," which, unlike all the other fizzles except number 8, bears a title: "Still." "Fizzle 7" reads like a two-finger exercise and preparation for the intensely compacted richness of *Stirrings Still*. We are shown a figure (pronouns are assiduously avoided, so there is no knowing whether woman or man) "sitting quite still at valley window," watching "the sun low in the southwest sinking." "Always quite still" in "small upright wicker chair with armrests," the figure sits on. "Eyes stare out unseeing till first movement some time past close though unseeing still while still light. Quite still again then all quite quiet apparently till eyes open again while still light though less." Even as the meanings of "still" accumulate, proliferate, and turn back on themselves with suggestions of continuing negative action ("unseeing still") bound to an opposite sense of yet-ness ("while still light"), both of them balanced and reversed by the fixity of motionlessness and silence ("Quite still again"), meanings that are in turn undermined by the modifiers "quite" and "again," it is revealed that we have been wrong about everything we thought to be the case: "Quite still again then at the open window . . . though actually close inspection not still at all but trembling all over. Close inspection namely detail by detail all over to add up finally to this whole not still at all but trembling all over. But casually in this failing light impression dead still even the hands clearly trembling and the breast faint rise and fall" (*Complete Short Prose*, 240). Because they can both coincide and differ widely in sense, "still" and "even," locked in an embrace at the heart of this verbless sentence, create a profusion and confusion of meanings for the entire linguistic sequence. The placing of "still" makes for added difficulty: there is no indication whether it should be attached to "dead" or to "even" or should remain in the isolated splendor of its own multiple meanings. Does the failing light give the impression that the figure is "dead still," placing an equal accent on both words to make a compound adjectival phrase meaning absolutely immobile or absolutely silent or both? Should a greater emphasis fall on "still," so that the impression is that the figure continues to appear dead? Should mental commas be placed around "still," separating it from "dead" on one side and from "even" on the other and enforcing a pause both before and after the word in its poised status between? Which of its half-dozen meanings (continuation of an action; to become motionless or to render motionless or silent; immobile; silent; yet; nevertheless; an intensive stressing the comparative degree; apparatus for distillation; etc.) should we ascribe to "still," which of its three or four to "even" (still; although; an intensive stressing the comparative degree or the unexpected; trickle down in minute drops; etc.)? In combination and permutation these two slight words, especially in Beckett's late manner, which eliminates pronouns and, for the most part, finite verbs, produce a bewildering number and variety of meanings.

When Beckett largely avoids finite verbs in a piece like *Stirrings Still* and when he does a dance around the word "still" in "Fizzle 7," he is not only developing a signature stylistic tendency but is also adhering to certain qualities in Irish English—by which I mean an English that shows the effects of a substratum of Gaelic (whether the writer knows Gaelic or not)— qualities that separate it from all of the other worldwide varieties of English. "Still," in its use denoting a continuing action, joins itself with a predominance of iterative and durative tenses in Irish, a language that has no equivalent of the perfect tense and so a reduced capacity for presenting completed action. Or to turn the matter to its positive face: the ghostly presence of Gaelic in Irish English makes the latter, in writing as in speech, a language of the still-continuing present rather than of the finished past. And here it becomes significant that Beckett chose to return to English for *Stirrings Still* (and, as far as he was concerned, English was the only language for the immediately preceding *Worstward Ho,* which he could discover no way to translate into French). No exclusive, settled meaning is possible for the second word of Beckett's title, which might signify any—and probably does signify all—of the following: Stirrings Yet; Stirrings Nevertheless; Stirrings Even; Stirrings Quiet; Stirrings Immobile; Stirrings Continuing. When he settled on *Stirrings Still*—or hovered above it, for it was not a quick or easy choice of title—Beckett made available to himself both his own earlier explorations in the meanings of "stillness" and those of other writers in the English tradition. I think primarily of Keats, Yeats, and Eliot, recalling that Beckett declared the poetry of the first two "beautiful" and disregarding, because not to my purposes, his failure to say the same of Eliot's verse. "Thou still unravish'd bride of quietness, / Thou foster-child of silence and slow time. . . ." If Beckett was reading Keats's "Ode to a Nightingale" shortly before his death and returning, as John Montague puts it, "to the pleasant discoveries of boyhood," I should think he could not have failed to note the poised and pregnant meanings Keats achieves with the word "still" in the first line of "Ode on a Grecian Urn." Yet-ness, quietness, silence, and continuing through ever-during time—these are the same uses to which Beckett put the word and that he would no doubt have found "beautiful" in Keats's poem. The repeated, nearly compulsive coupling of "still" and "light" in "Fizzle 7"—"still while still light," "still light," yet again "still light," "failing light quite still," and "just less light still"—suggests to me no one so much as the Eliot of *Four Quartets*. We are told that in translating *How It Is* from French Beckett felt that "the English language had seduced him . . . into saying more than he meant to say";[13] I wonder if translating "Fizzle 7" into English and composing *Stirrings Still* in that same language might not have seduced Beckett, in like manner, into a greater intimacy with the language and the sentiments of the *Quartets* than he would have found altogether comfortable.

> At the still point of the turning world. Neither flesh nor fleshless;
> Neither from nor towards; at the still point, there the dance is,
> But neither arrest nor movement.

Neither arrest nor movement is the very condition of "stillness," and "At the still point of the turning world" might be the location of any of Beckett's late fictions; but it is later, in "Burnt Norton," that Eliot joins "light" and "still" in ways that Beckett must have found pertinent:

> After the kingfisher's wing
> Has answered light to light, and is silent, the light is still
> At the still point of the turning world.

And in the last section of "Burnt Norton" Eliot repeats the trick—which he certainly knew from Yeats if he didn't learn it from him—of balancing "still" at the end of a line so that it enacts its multiple and conflicting meanings of stopped-motion-yet-continuing-on in the pause the reader must give to "still" before moving on to the next line.

> Only by the form, the pattern,
> Can words or music reach
> The stillness, as a Chinese jar still
> Moves perpetually in its stillness.

When in "East Coker" we are told that we "must be still and still moving / Into another intensity / For a further union, a deeper communion"— profoundly akin at the deepest layers of language to Beckett's "it will be the silence . . . , in the silence you don't know, you must go on, I can't go on, I'll go on" in *The Unnamable* and "So on till stayed. . . . now to press on regardless now in one direction and now in another" in *Stirrings Still*—we can only imagine that Beckett was attentive to what Eliot had been doing in the war years when he (Beckett) was preparing to leave the language to which he would fully return only forty years later. In "Fizzle

13. See John Pilling, "How It Is," in James Knowlson and John Pilling, *Frescoes of the Skull* (London: John Calder, 1979), 78.

7," of the one "quite still again. . . . staring out at nothing just failing light
quite still. . . . Quite still then . . . of course not still at all," it is said in
the end, "Leave it so all quite still or try listening to the sounds all quite
still head in hand listening for a sound." This is the same stilly, silent and
intent activity, the listening for a word or a sound, that we have in *Stirrings
Still* ("So on till stayed when to his ears from deep within oh how and
here a word he could not catch it were to end where never till then") and,
I suggest, the same as in "Little Gidding," the last of the *Quartets:*

> When the last of earth left to discover
> Is that which was the beginning . . .
> Not known, because not looked for
> But heard, half-heard, in the stillness
> Between two waves of the sea.
> Quick now, here, now, always—
> A condition of complete simplicity
> (Costing not less than everything). . . .

Eliot's "stillness" here is Beckett's, or Beckett's is Eliot's; and if Beckett is
not recalling the "still light" and the "light still" of *Four Quartets* in "Fizzle
7" and *Stirrings Still,* then Eliot is doing the much more difficult thing of
preimagining Beckett's "still light" and "light still" forty-five or fifty years
on from the *Quartets.*[14] After half a lifetime of refusing a poetic tradition
in English that featured Keats and Eliot, Beckett ended by embracing it,
the pivot word "still" being for him the point of turning and returning.

In one important way, however, Beckett's language was neither Keats's
nor Eliot's. Though Eliot was demonstrably and deeply influenced by Yeats
in *Four Quartets,* his English, unlike Yeats's and Beckett's, is not inflected
by the ghostly presence of Gaelic. It is all very well for Beckett to give us
the following exchange in *All That Fall,* a radio play of 1956:

> MRS ROONEY: No, no, I am agog, tell me all, then we shall press on
> and never pause, never pause, till we come safe to haven.
> *[Pause]*
> MR ROONEY: Never pause . . . safe to haven . . . Do you know,
> Maddy, sometimes one would think you were struggling with a dead
> language.

14. As I am dealing with recollections of instances of "still" in earlier work, it is perhaps
fitting that I should recall that I devoted an extensive section of my chapter on Eliot's *Four
Quartets* in *Metaphors of Self* to the occurrence of the word and its conceptual extensions
in that set of poems. See *Metaphors of Self* (Princeton: Princeton University Press, 1972),
278–84.

MRS ROONEY: Yes indeed, Dan, I know full well what you mean, I of-
ten have that feeling, it is unspeakably excruciating.
MR ROONEY: I confess I have it sometimes myself, when I happen to
overhear what I am saying.
MRS ROONEY: Well, you know, it will be dead in time, just like our
own poor dear Gaelic, there is that to be said.
[Urgent baa.]
MR ROONEY: *[Startled]* Good God!
MRS ROONEY: Oh the pretty little woolly lamb, crying to suck its
mother! Theirs has not changed, since Arcady. (*Complete Dramatic
Works,* 194)

Maddy shows herself not only surprisingly conversant with Rousseau's *Essay on the Origin of Languages* ("Theirs has not changed, since Arcady" is
perfectly in keeping with Rousseau's ideas about a natural language of innocence and beauty, still available to our woolly friends but not to us since
our fall into society), but she also appears to exhibit in her speech rhythms,
her vocabulary, and her syntax traces of "our own poor dear Gaelic," long
dead though it be. (As instances one might offer three brief passages: "Will
you get along with you, Mr Rooney, Mr Tyler I mean, will you get along
with you now and cease molesting me? What kind of a country is this
where a woman can't weep her heart out on the highways and byways
without being tormented by retired bill-brokers?" "Stiff! Well I like that!
And me heaving all over back and front." "Cissy Slocum! That's a nice
way to refer to your betters. Cissy Slocum! And you an orphan!") However
it may be with Mrs. Rooney, it is unquestionably the case that Yeats developed a language designed to accommodate rather than to expel from its
inner reaches the ghost of Gaelic ("What moves me and my hearer," Yeats
wrote in "A General Introduction for My Work," "is a vivid speech that
has no laws except that it must not exorcise the ghostly voice" [*Essays and
Introductions,* 524]); and that Beckett, in his late pieces especially, gladly
shared elements of that Gaelic–haunted language with Yeats. Something of
Beckett's attitude on this issue can be seen in his response to a request that
he join in a tribute to George Bernard Shaw on the occasion of the cente-
nary of Shaw's birth; ever recalcitrant, however, Beckett goes out of his
way to give tribute not to Shaw but to Yeats and other writers associated
with the Abbey Theatre and the Irish Literary Revival: "I wouldn't suggest
that G. B. S. is not a great playwright," Beckett wrote to the organizers,
"whatever that is when it's at home [which is itself a nice Irishism by way
of Molly Bloom's soliloquy]. What I would do is give the whole unupset-
table apple–cart for a sup of the Hawk's Well, or the Saints', or a whiff of

Juno, to go no further."[15] The references to Yeats's *At the Hawk's Well,*
Synge's *The Well of the Saints,* and O'Casey's *Juno and the Paycock,* and by
implication to the poetry of those plays as against the prosaic manner of
Shaw's drama, can be taken as a fair indication of how Beckett felt about
the resources of Irish English. When he adopted "still" as a word trailing
rhythmic and syntactic clouds of glory from Gaelic, it was most often Yeats
who came to Beckett's mind. There is a curious echo of Yeats at the end
of "Fizzle 2," when, after the speaker's claim that it was "athletics" that
ruined him—"all that jumping and running when I was young"—he concludes with this sentence, haunted not only by Yeats's Irish English and
by a Yeatsian "still" but by the poet himself: "My fortieth year had come
and gone and I still throwing the javelin." The first phrase conflates two
passages, five lines apart, from a single poem, "Vacillation":

> No longer in Lethean foliage caught
> Begin the preparation for your death
> And from the fortieth winter by that thought
> Test every work of intellect or faith . . .
> My fiftieth year had come and gone,
> I sat, a solitary man,
> In a crowded London shop,
> An open book and empty cup
> On the marble table-top.

That Beckett misremembers his Yeats, or, more likely, tips a wink to the
reader as he deliberately alters the year that has come and gone, does nothing to diminish the status of the sentence as a Beckettian recollection of a
predecessor who knew well his eminent place in the tradition of English
poetry, delicately nuanced in the specific instance by Gaelic undertones.
And as for the second phrase, it is pure Yeats of the Old Man on the Boiler
period if it is not pure Irish English of the Dublin streets. I ask the reader
to refer to the instances given earlier of Maddy Rooney's speech and to
the syntax of the "Fizzle 2" sentence before considering what Yeats says
about the style and attitude he sought in his mature work. "I tried to make
the language of poetry coincide with that of passionate, normal speech.
I wanted to write in whatever language comes most naturally when we
soliloquise, as I do all day long, upon the events of our own lives or of
any life where we can see ourselves for the moment. I sometimes compare
myself with the mad old slum women I hear denouncing and remembering;

15. Quoted in Eoin O'Brien, *The Beckett Country,* 277.

'How dare you,' I heard one say of some imaginary suitor, 'and you without health or a home!' " Of which of Beckett's figures might it not be said that they soliloquize all day long? And when their soliloquies are cast in such phrases as "Stiff! Well I like that! And me heaving all over back and front," or "Cissy Slocum! And you an orphan!" or "My fortieth year had come and gone and I still throwing the javelin," there can be little doubt that Beckett's language has its source in the same place as Yeats's—when that source, indeed, is not Yeats himself.[16] Beckett in his last works, like Yeats in the poetry and drama one thinks of as most distinctively Yeatsian, appears concerned first of all, and whatever else he might do, never to "exorcise the ghostly voice."

More telling instances of a Beckettian durative "stillness" out of Irish English occur in Yeats's "Leda and the Swan" and "The Wild Swans at Coole."

> A sudden blow: the great wings beating still
> Above the staggering girl, her thighs caressed
> By the dark webs, her nape caught in his bill,
> He holds her helpless breast upon his breast.

One of the most remarkable things about this most remarkable poem is its rigorous avoidance, until the question at the end ("Did she put on his knowledge with his power . . ."), of any tense suggesting a finished action or suggesting that any of this is of the past. As in "Fizzle 7" and the very title of *Stirrings Still,* the dominant verbal mode of "Leda and the Swan" (and of Irish English) is the present participle ("beating . . . staggering . . . loosening") or a participle that, while past in form ("caressed . . . caught . . . terrified . . . feathered"), is present in its descriptive effect ("her thighs [are being] caressed . . . her nape [is] caught . . . her fingers [are] terrified . . . his glory [is] feathered"). The intense, overwhelming *presentness* of the poem, caught and carried in "the great wings beating still," allows for no escape, no looking aside, with the "wings beating still" as multifarious in meanings of "stillness" as Beckett's "stirrings still." Leaving "still" to hang

---

16. The Yeats quotation is from "A General Introduction for My Work," 521. I record with gratitude my debt to Laura O'Connor for suggestions about Beckett's English, deriving from her own deeply interesting study of Celtic resistances to anglicization, in particular for information about the extensive use of anacoluthia (phrases that are logically, but not grammatically, connected) and a corresponding frequency of afterthought locutions in Irish English. This leads to a general effect, as in the passages cited in the text, of someone thinking in Irish and speaking in English. On Beckett's English, see the excellent essay by Mary Lydon, "Stretching the Imagination: Samuel Beckett and the Frontier of Writing," *Journal of the Midwest Modern Language Association* 30 (spring 1997): 1–15.

at the end of the line with no punctuation yet with the certainty that the correct reading requires a clear, hovering pause, the poem remains resolutely in the continuing now, its action repeated ("A shudder in the loins *engenders* there / The broken wall, the burning roof and tower / And Agamemnon dead") throughout a history that issues now and always in the present. The first line—a sort of marker of this continuing action in an ongoing present—is and is not enjambed, which is what "still" both means and does.

This strategic line-end placing of "still" is employed also in the earlier "Wild Swans at Coole"; but as that poem is in mood very unlike "Leda and the Swan" so the meanings drawn out of "still" correspondingly differ.

> The trees are in their autumn beauty,
> The woodland paths are dry,
> Under the October twilight the water
> Mirrors a still sky. . . .

"Ah, yes, yes, beautiful, too," one seems to hear Beckett murmuring of these lines as he did when John Montague brought up Yeats's name. Such is the effect of an autumnal still sky mirrored in still water, and such is one of the effects—not the only, but an important one—of the "still" in *Stirrings Still*. "Unwearied still, lover by lover," the swans of Yeats's poem "paddle in the cold / Companionable stream or climb the air," and the poet imagines them miraculously endowed with stillness in all its forms, tenses, and meanings:

> Their hearts have not grown old;
> Passion or conquest, wander where they will,
> Attend upon them still.
>
> But now they drift on the still water,
> Mysterious, beautiful. . . .

That such stillness, such yet-ness and constancy, such immobile movement and speaking silence, is not humanly possible (or, truth to tell, avianly possible, but that goes against the conceit of the poem) is part of the statement of "The Wild Swans at Coole," and it is one of the things that one imagines would have drawn Beckett to the poem. But its mere impossibility hardly means that a writer like Beckett might not thematically yearn for it in works recalling other works doing the same. And this, I propose, is what Beckett does with the phrase "stirrings still," in which he recalls what he has done earlier in a career now coming to its close and what others—Keats, Eliot, Yeats—have done in a tradition now residing, for the moment, in Beckett's own body of work.

Stirrings Still is thus a revisiting by Beckett of his career as a writer, which involves a revisiting of writers feeding into that career, and it has all the iterative quality one might expect in such doubled and redoubled revisitings. "As when he disappeared only to reappear later at another place. Then disappeared again only to reappear again later at another place again. So again and again disappeared again only to reappear again later at another place" (*Complete Short Prose,* 259–60). It is a little like joining the author watching the author through the wrong end of a telescope, surfacing and vanishing and resurfacing at different points along the progress that brings him eventually to this final work. The iterativeness that the passage above illustrates is not a phenomenon only of Beckett's writing but is the way of memory itself, for what is memory but repetition . . . or the ghost of repetition, failed repetition? "There had been a time he would sometimes lift his head enough to see his hands," we are told of the "he" in *Stirrings Still.* "At rest after all they did. Lift his past head a moment to see his past hands. Then lay it back on them to rest it too. After all it did." Just so—it is the present gazing back to the past, the past to the more distant past, the more distant past to . . . and so on: this is the activity and its textual representation that we are offered in *Stirrings Still.* The repetitions of *Stirrings Still* are those of memory, but memory's repetitions are, so to say, substanceless, the experience of a revenant, virtually in a dream; for the return is not real, and we do not, in memory, become a child again even for a night. Or if we think we do and jump from bed imagining we are eight years old, aching bones will soon provide a reality check. This is why Krapp is so anguished in his remembering, because he has only his tape player to embrace and not the girl in the punt. This thinned-out, spectral version of experience that can nevertheless be emotionally ravaging is dramatized in *Stirrings Still* in the man who, much like Krapp on his successive birthdays, watches his shadow self repeating over and over the events of memory, hearing the strokes and "the cries now faint now clear," the strokes and the cries of memory.

If one wishes to maintain, as I do, that *Stirrings Still* constitutes a kind of memorial résumé of Beckett's canonical production, and if one further situates the beginning of that production in the immediate postwar years with the four *Nouvelles,* the Trilogy, and *Waiting for Godot,* it is extraordinarily interesting that the memories should go back to experience from the time of "The Capital of the Ruins" (dated June 10, 1946 on the final page of the typescript). What I have in mind is the death of Dr. Arthur Darley, who was at Saint-Lô with Beckett in 1945 and whose death from tuberculosis in December 1948 (at age thirty-five) Beckett memorialized in the poem "Mort de A. D." This friend of forty years earlier comes into *Stirrings*

Still as "Darly," as if memory for the name were somewhat faint by "The same place and table as when Darly for example died and left As when others too in their turn before and since. . . . A clock afar str the hours and half-hours. The same as when among others Darly once die and left him. Strokes now clear as if carried by a wind now faint on the still air" (*Complete Short Prose,* 260). The repetition in the text mimics the repetition in memory, but what is especially significant about Darley as a representative focus for these memories from the start of the period when Beckett became Beckett is that Darley was one of a group—the Irish Red Cross contingent in the Saint-Lô hospital—to which Beckett also belonged and with which he showed strong emotional ties and allegiances. What Beckett evokes at the end of "The Capital of the Ruins" is a collectivity, one community in relation to another, the Irish of the Red Cross giving to and even more receiving from the French of Saint-Lô something of inestimable human value ("some of those who were in Saint-Lô will come home realising that they got at least as good as they gave, that they got indeed what they could hardly give, a vision and sense of a time-honoured conception of humanity in ruins, and perhaps even an inkling of the terms in which our condition is to be thought again" [*Complete Short Prose,* 278]). What I would say is that Darley came to focalize for Beckett a redoubled collective memory: first, of the Irish and the French who met in Saint-Lô; second, the collective memory Darley represents as one of the cast of figures—almost the first of them—who people Beckett's fiction and drama from 1946 on. For Darley, by the time of *Stirrings Still,* is both a fictive character and a real person, long since dead but stirring still in Beckett's memory of his own oeuvre. I take it Beckett refers to himself in the final phrases of "Mort de A. D."—"témoin des départs / témoin des retours"— and what he wrote in 1948 is hardly different from what he set down in *Stirrings Still* in 1988: "witness of departures / witness of returns." Moreover, when "cries now faint now clear" sound in the ear of the one with his head on his hands in *Stirrings Still,* they issue from figures in earlier work even back to "The Capital of the Ruins." In *Waiting for Godot* Vladimir, reflecting on the whole course of a life, says, "We have time to grow old. The air is full of our cries" (*Complete Dramatic Works,* 84); the narrator of *From an Abandoned Work* as he leaves home looks back to see his mother "still in the window waving, waving me back or on I don't know, or just waving, in sad helpless love, and I heard faintly her cries" (*Complete Short Prose,* 156); and Winnie, in *Happy Days,* anticipates in a number of ways the cries now faint now clear of *Stirrings Still* when she imagines she hears Willie crying out: "Perhaps he is crying out for help all this time and I do

ar him! *[Pause.]* I do of course hear cries. *[Pause.]* But they are in
...ead surely. *[Pause.]* Is it possible that . . . *[Pause. With finality.]* No,
., my head was always full of cries. *[Pause.]* Faint confused cries. *[Pause.]*
hey come. *[Pause.]* Then go. *[Pause.]* As on a wind" (*Complete Dramatic
Works*, 163–64). They may be in Winnie's head, but these cries of "sad
helpless love," of suffering and woe, are very real too, the audible accompaniment to *lacrimae rerum*. The cries of the inhabitants of Saint-Lô Beckett
does not mention in "The Capital of the Ruins" because he has no need
to: the entire piece is the cry of "humanity in ruins" and reaches easily the
ear of the one on his back in the dark in *Company*, "numb with the woes
of [his] kind" (pp. 44, 57, 59), and the ear of the one with his head on his
hands in *Stirrings Still*, who "would have wished the strokes to cease and
the cries for good and was sorry that they did not. The strokes now faint
now clear as if carried by the wind but not a breath and the cries now faint
now clear" (*Complete Short Prose*, 263).

It is important to recognize that this most distant memory drawn from
the work—i.e., the memory from "The Capital of the Ruins"—should
be collective in nature. In his classic work on collective memory, Maurice
Halbwachs writes of various groups that might be thought capable of it—
religious communities, social classes—but the model of the group that
forms and is informed by collective memory, as one might expect, is the
family. The Irish Red Cross was not, in any literal sense, a family, nor were
the French living in Saint-Lô, but for Beckett the two groups clearly stood
for something like the family of humankind. Having spoken of the reconstruction of the past that inevitably occurs in remembering, Halbwachs goes
on to demonstrate how this occurs in the family situation:

> A given scene which took place in our home, in which our parents were
> the principal actors, and which has been fixed in our memory . . . does not
> reappear as the depiction of a day such as we experienced it in the past. We
> compose it anew and introduce elements borrowed from several periods which
> preceded or followed the scene in question. The notion we have at this mo-
> ment of recreation of the moral nature of our parents and of the event itself—
> now judged from a distance—imposes itself on our mind with so much power
> that we cannot escape being inspired by it. The same is true regarding those
> events and figures that arise out of the totality of family life, which summarize
> it and which serve as landmarks for whoever wishes to localize details and
> circumstances of lesser importance.[17]

17. Maurice Halbwachs, *On Collective Memory*, ed. and trans. Lewis A. Coser (Chicago:
University of Chicago Press, 1992), 61.

I have already commented on the way memories shape and reshape themselves as we remember, as we then remember remembering, and so on, a characteristic feature of Beckett's drama and fiction. What Halbwachs does is to add to the multilayered complexity of the process by showing not only that each of us individually reconstructs the past in light of earlier and later times, especially in light of a present that is already contemplating the future, but also that we collaborate with other family members in a collective reconstruction that has much more to do with subsequent relationships between children and parents and among siblings than with anything that could be called a historical, factual past. The continually altering and currently held sense we have of our parents, for example, derived in part individually and in part collectively, we read back into any particular scene remembered from twenty, thirty, forty years ago. Darley, of course, was not a parent to Beckett, but the memory Beckett produces of him in *Stirrings Still* is in large part determined by the fact that both of them were members of the Irish Red Cross "family" in Saint-Lô in 1945; and that Darley died three years later while Beckett was engaged in his "siege in the room" reconfigures Beckett's memory of him as surely as the deaths of his father and mother reconfigured their images in his memory.

I deliberately bring Darley into conjunction with the image of the father in Beckett because that is how they are placed in *Stirrings Still*. The two references to Darley's dying and leaving "him" surround the following paragraph as if they were the opening and closing of a parenthesis, making all references thereby the more collective: "Seen always from behind whithersoever he went. Same hat and coat as of old when he walked the roads. The back roads. Now as one in a strange place seeking the way out. In the dark. In a strange place blindly in the dark of night or day seeking the way out. A way out. To the roads. The back roads." In the first instance this is the "he" or his alter ego seen as he disappears and reappears, but it is also the familiar compound ghost who, throughout the fiction, sets out endlessly to walk "the back roads," halting at intervals to tot up the number of steps, yards, miles, or leagues covered in a lifetime of walking: "Halted too at your elbow during these computations your father's shade. In his old tramping rags. Finally on side by side from nought anew" (*Company,* 15). So familiar is this figure in Beckett's work that when we hear in *Stirrings Still* of the "same hat and coat as of old" we know not only that the hat is a "battered once buff block hat" and the coat a greatcoat that covers the walker from chin to boots but also that the coat, originally green, is now "stiff with age and grime" (*Company,* 24, 23). Moreover, the shade of the father has been so often at the elbow of the walker or just "to right and a little to the rear" on "that dear old back road" (*Company,* 23) that father and son become virtually indistinguishable one from the other; and as the father's shade ceases to accompany him, the son too thins out to a shade walking the back roads only in memory. "Hand in hand with equal plod they go," we are told of two like shades in *Worstward Ho.* "Backs turned both bowed with equal plod they go. . . . Backs turned. Both bowed. Joined by held holding hands. Plod on as one. One shade. Another shade."[18] When we are informed that such as these are not "real" memories and that Beckett had no "need" for memory, I am at a loss to know what to make of the claim. It may be that Beckett did not need memory, but memory certainly needed him—else he would not have used a word like "obsessional," as when he told James Knowlson that the image of an old man walking hand in hand with a child was "the most 'obsessional' of his childhood memories" (*Damned to Fame,* 594); nor is it an image difficult to trace in the fiction. Perhaps the quarrel has to do with genre and comes from the notion that fiction, as against autobiography, has no use for memory. Leaving aside the issue of autobiography as a merely distracting question of conventional expectations, I see no reason to suppose that life-writing and the making of fiction are mutually exclusive acts or that memory should be restricted to one and denied to the other, imagination restricted to the other and denied to the one. It would be more comfortable, no doubt, for both Beckett and his reader if it could be said that everything in *Company, Ill Seen Ill Said, Worstward Ho,* and *Stirrings Still* were the product of memoryless imagination. What a subtraction from company that would be! A voice in the third-person singular. Murmuring now and then, Yes he imagines. But this fanciful recension of the text of *Company,* denying the hold of memory, is nowhere to be found, nowhere to be sought. Instead, what we get in *Ill Seen Ill Said* of the "old so dying woman" is this: "If only she could be pure figment. Unalloyed. This old so dying woman. So dead. In the madhouse of the skull and nowhere else. . . . Cooped up there with the rest. Hovel and stones. The lot. And the eye. How simple all then. If only all could be pure figment."[19] If only this old so dying woman were entirely imaginary, the creation merely of nonreferential words strung together, how simple all then. Whoever the old so dying woman may be or have been, Beckett could hardly be clearer than he is here. We can call it fiction or, it makes little difference, but whichever designation we choose, we have to recognize that Beckett's work is as memory bound, as memory

18. *Worstward Ho,* in *Nohow On* (New York: Grove Press, 1996), 93.
19. *Ill Seen Ill Said,* in *Nohow On* (New York: Grove Press, 1996), 58.

determined, as any writing of our time and that while the memory at issue is in one of its aspects specific and individual, in another it is collective in nature.

Thinking about the place of memory in writing like Beckett's, one would have to say that terms like "real" and "accurate"—as in "this is or is not a real memory" and "this memory is or is not accurate"—lose all sense through being attached to memory; indeterminateness is of its very nature. No one can say with assurance that any given memory is accurate (I am of course aware that appearances suggest the contrary and that people pronounce with assurance all the time: I *know* this is the way it happened). If memory is filtered through all subsequent experience, as it surely is, then the question forces itself upon us: "Accurate with regard to what?" To indenture it to its own first perception of how things are would be to deny memory's evident plasticity and its capacity for adaptation, and it would go against everything that we have learned—I am tempted to say since St. Augustine but will content myself with saying in the past sixty-five or so years. Frederic C. Bartlett was the first modern psychologist of memory (by psychologist I mean a practicing scientist) to insist on its profoundly constructive nature and to make of that a first principle for understanding what it does. The single-word participial title of his book—*Remembering*—is wonderfully well chosen to point up the durational process that we tend to still with the word *memory*. From his "preface" to his "Summary and Some Conclusions," Bartlett maintains one essential point: "Everybody would agree that it would be a disastrous matter if all common opinions turned out to be wrong," Bartlett says in his forthright and commonsense manner, "and of necessity a psychologist works in a field in which popular opinions are numerous. However, some widely held views have to be completely discarded, and none more completely than that which treats recall as the re-excitement in some way of fixed and changeless 'traces'."[20] This is what one might term (without irreverence, since it is a model that occurs in St. Augustine) the "treasure-house theory" of memory; it is just such a notion of memory that I take it Beckett parodies (irreverently) in *Mercier et Camier*: "On cultive sa mémoire, elle finit par être passable, un trésor, on se balade dans sa crypte, sans chandelle, on revisite les lieux, on se re-mémore les bruits (très important), on finit par les savoir par coeur . . . quel disque se jouer": "You cultivate your memory till it's passable, a treasure-bin, stroll in your crypt, unlit, return to the scenes, call back the

---

20. F. C. Bartlett, *Remembering: A Study in Experimental and Social Psychology* (Cambridge: Cambridge University Press, 1932; reissued 1995), p. xviii.

old sounds (paramount), till you have the lot off pat . . . what old jingles to play back" (*Mercier et Camier,* 188–89; *Mercier and Camier,* 108). A storehouse of riches where nothing is ever lost and nothing changes, a place one can revisit at will and with impunity—this Beckett laughs (or shudders) at and Bartlett rejects out of hand. The model of memory Bartlett favors is one of process, not fixity, and its constructive essence is all in the service of what he terms "effort after meaning": "I shall call this fundamental process of connecting a given pattern with some setting or scheme: *effort after meaning*" (*Remembering,* 20; cf. similar passages on 44–45, 84–85, 227–38). Given a more contemporary, computer-age focus, the view of memory that Bartlett initiated presents itself as an argument about the brain and consciousness. The brain, according to those who follow Bartlett's line of thought, is not analogous to a computer, nor is artificial intelligence—AI, in the jargon—the equivalent of human intelligence; and for consciousness (which is to say for memory also and for the *I*) these philosophically inclined scientists and mathematicians tell us there can be no knowable or discoverable algorithm. Taken together, these two horns of the argument mean that there are no predictive, computational procedures adequate to the indeterminacy and complexity of human memory, consciousness, and the self. "The brain/computer metaphor fails," one scientist writes, "because the neuronal systems that comprise the brain, unlike a computer, are radically indeterminate. . . . [B]rains and the organisms they inhabit, above all human brains and human beings, are not closed systems, like the molecules of a gas inside a sealed jar. Instead they are open systems, formed by their own past history and continually in interaction with the natural and social worlds outside, both changing them and being changed in their turn."[21] It seems odd, but is perhaps in the nature of scientific advance, that

21. Steven Rose, *The Making of Memory: From Molecules to Mind* (New York: Doubleday, 1992), 89. The quotation from Rose is like a summary of various summaries. For expansion—sometimes vast expansion—of ideas Rose here summarizes, see the following: Gerald Edelman, *The Remembered Present: A Biological Theory of Consciousness* (New York: Basic Books, 1989) and *Bright Air, Brilliant Fire: On the Matter of the Mind* (New York: Basic Books, 1992), for an evolutionary theory of consciousness based on what Edelman terms "neuronal group selection"; Israel Rosenfield, *The Invention of Memory: A New View of the Brain* (New York: Basic Books, 1988), for a popularization if not idolization of Edelman's theories; and Roger Penrose, *The Emperor's New Mind: Concerning Computers, Minds, and the Laws of Physics* (Oxford: Oxford University Press, 1989) and *Shadows of the Mind: A Search for the Missing Science of Consciousness* (Oxford: Oxford University Press, 1994), for a spirited (and lengthy) refutation by a mathematician and physicist (basing himself largely on Gödel's theorem) of the possibility of an algorithm for human consciousness.

These are all lively and, in differing degrees, engaging books, but the most intelligent and, at the same time, accessible of publications on the subject (after Bartlett's *Remembering*)

what had to be presented by Bartlett in 1932 as contrary to common sense—that recall is a constructive and adaptive process rather than reactivation of fixed, changeless traces in the brain—should now appear to be the commonsense consensus not of scientists alone but of all who think seriously about the subject.

Another consensus among scientists who study memory—but not only among them, for it was well known to Augustine and Rousseau and has been obvious to laypeople of their time and ours—is that memory always involves the deepest kind of emotional engagement. "Recollections without affect are not recollections," Israel Rosenfield says flatly. "Emotions are essential to the creation of a memory because they organize it, establishing its relative importance in a sequence of events much as a sense of time and order is essential for a memory to be considered a memory, and not a thought or a vision at some particular instant, unrelated to past events" (*Invention of Memory*, 72). Rosenfield's point closely parallels Bartlett's view that remembering is to be associated with "effort after meaning" (the "fundamental process of connecting a given pattern with some setting or scheme"); moreover, if we recall that Plato, in discussing anamnesis, claims that all cognition is recognition, we will be prepared to understand that what Rosenfield says is much the same as Steven Rose's observation that "cognition cannot be divorced from affect, try as one might" (*Making of Memory*, 38). Daniel Schacter gives a local habitation and a name—"Amygdala"—to the emotional component of memory when he writes that the "amygdala is a critical structure in the brain network that regulates emotions—including emotional aspects of memory. It has become increasingly apparent that the amygdala plays a vital role in the emotionally charged memories that wield such a potent influence in our mental lives."[22] The extraordinary importance of the emotion-organizing amygdala and of the entire limbic system is most apparent in the work of Antonio Damasio, who maintains that because the limbic system is positioned both in the

---

are Rose's *The Making of Memory* and Antonio Damasio's *Descartes' Error*. I would feel remiss, however, if I failed to mention the entertainment to be derived from Edelman's polyphiloprogenitive terminology, which loves to reproduce itself in lavish quantity, and Penrose's extreme fondness for the word *indeed* (scarcely a paragraph in either of his books is without at least one *indeed,* and some have five or six) and for emphatic italicization and the exclamation point: "Is there any direct evidence that the phenomenon of *consciousness* is related to the action of the cytoskeleton, and to microtubules in particular? Indeed, there *is* such evidence. Let us try to examine the nature of this evidence—which addresses the issue of consciousness by considering what causes it to be *absent!*" (*Shadows of the Mind*, 369).

22. Daniel Schacter, *Searching for Memory: The Brain, the Mind, and the Past* (New York: Basic Books, 1996), 213.

cerebral cortex and subcortex—situated as it were between the two structures and partaking of both—it is uniquely able to mediate between raw
desire and intelligent choice. "[E]motion and feeling," he writes, which
are "central aspects of biological regulation . . . provide the bridge between
rational and nonrational processes, between cortical and subcortical structures" (*Descartes' Error,* 128). For Damasio it is not just simplistic but plain
wrong to consider emotion the opposite of reason; properly seen, emotion
is an essential ally of reason, both of them necessary collaborators in an
effort at adjustment to the human situation.

It hardly needs saying, before returning to Beckett and the issue of
emotion-as-memory/memory-as-emotion in his work, that the feelings
that memory ineluctably draws in its wake are not always pleasurable or
jolly. Paul Valéry states a very powerful, not to say distressing, proposition
when, in the course of abjuring all interest in remembrance of things past,
he writes:

> No, I have no fondness for memories, which to me are images already
> used, a dreary useless waste. Bad memories remain bad, still wounding and
> confounding us; the good ones are atrocious. Long ago I wrote this verse,
> which is redolent of that far away time:
>
> > *Nos plus chers souvenirs mordent nos coeurs dans l'ombre . . .*
>
> The Hades of the Ancients (a true and noble compound of psychological
> symbols far superior to the monstrous contrivances of our foul Hell) lacks a
> sufferer, akin to Tantalus and Sisyphus, who would be condemned to rewitness
> (which is not the same as reliving) the happiest moments of his life. Hades also
> lacks another miserable creature whose torture would be a memory constantly
> unfolding to him the tableau of missed opportunities. . . .[23]

To paraphrase the Winnie of *Happy Days* (who, apropos of what she terms
"sadness after intimate sexual intercourse," says to her husband, "You
would concur with Aristotle there, Willie, I fancy")—Beckett would concur with Valéry there, I fancy. For is it not a Beckett speaker who, in "The
Expelled," says to himself: "Memories are killing. So you must not think
of certain things, of those that are dear to you, or rather you must think
of them, for if you don't there is the danger of finding them, in your mind,
little by little. That is to say, you must think of them for a while, a good
while, every day several times a day, until they sink forever in the mud.
That's an order" (*Complete Short Prose,* 46–47). And the line of verse Valéry

quotes from an earlier time—"Our dearest memories ravage our hearts in the darkness"—might have been written if not by Krapp at least for him. The logic of Valéry's "the good ones are atrocious," like the logic of Beckett's "Memories are killing" and "those that are dear to you," is unbearable but undeniable: to say "once upon a time" is also to say "never again, never again in the same way"; and who would care to deny that "bad memories remain bad, still wounding and confounding us"? Not Beckett surely. Valéry's line as written describes Krapp's situation exactly; if one might alter it slightly to replace "chers" with "mauvais" or "pénibles," it would be exactly fitting, even as to the darkness, for nearly all the figures in Beckett's later fiction. Perhaps we cannot say that Beckett himself was such a "sufferer, akin to Tantalus and Sisyphus," but surely the characters he created would be at home in Valéry's reimagined Hades of the Ancients. "No, no!" Valéry exclaims. "It is no pleasure to retrace in my mind those old paths of my life. I am not one to pursue remembrance of things past!" ("Moi," 288). Such retracing in the mind can hardly have been a pleasure for Beckett either, but as an artist he seems to have been condemned to make that his obsessive subject even as, in a manner of speaking, he steps outside it. He offers us a string of more or less tormented figures retracing the paths of their lives, and at the same time he gives us the picture of himself retracing, through the body of his work, those recurrent figures recurrently retracing their old paths.

"Not possible any longer except as figment," the narrator of *Ill Seen Ill Said* declares of the image of the "old so dying woman" . . . . "Not endurable" (p. 65). Yet it is endured once more, as it had been before, as it would be again in *Stirrings Still*. When we hear in the second section of *Stirrings Still* of "one hastening westward at sundown to obtain a better view of Venus," we are meant to and must recall the beginning of *Ill Seen Ill Said:* "From where she lies she sees Venus rise. On. From where she lies when the skies are clear she sees Venus rise followed by the sun. Then she rails at the source of all life. On. At evening when the skies are clear she savours its star's revenge. At the other window" (p. 49). Later we see her in the westward aspect at sundown: "She reappears at evening at her window. When not night evening. If she will see Venus again she must open it" (p. 77). The view of Venus rising is obscured, however, by what we soon learn is not exactly a curtain nor, as at first surmised, the fall of night, but "a black greatcoat." There may be more than one greatcoat floating around in the world of Beckett's fiction, but I think it is reasonable to assume that Beckett would have his readers recall the omnipresent greatcoat that, originally green, gets darker with each reappearance until it would be at least likely for it to appear black by the time of *Ill Seen Ill Said.* In any case, this is a work in which everything tends to merge with everything else, and there can be little doubt about the greatcoat, accompanied by block hat, that the old so dying woman sees being worn by one of the twelve whose function in life seems to be to watch her: "Dark greatcoat reaching to the ground. Antiquated block hat" (p. 60). It is not difficult to recognize this greatcoat upon appearance, for it has been reaching to the ground, dark and getting darker, accompanied by a more and more antiquated block hat, since the time of the Trilogy, and (though this goes beyond the canon as I would have it) before that in *Watt,* where we are given a remarkable and significant genealogy for the greatcoat.

Before turning to that genealogy and the greatcoat's many appearances, I want to look again at the passages in *Ill Seen Ill Said, Worstward Ho,* and *Stirrings Still* in which Beckett and his reader must be conscious of drawing up behind them this garment of such antiquity and ubiquity. I would like to establish the emotional affect that accompanies reference to the greatcoat and that increases with each instance since the affect is produced not by the image alone but by memory of all its earlier surfacings. By the time of *Stirrings Still*—that distillation of previous work into the briefest compass that even Beckett attempted—it requires only one word to set off the train of emotions: "same" provides the trigger ("Same hat and coat as of old when he walked the roads"), for in memory everything is always the same and nothing is ever the same. In *Worstward Ho* the child who holds the old man's hand is a ghost of the past as much as the old man himself is, and even as we see them merge and trade places we have to be aware that this is all being remembered by someone who was once the boy, child to the father, is now an old man yet still a boy, both always and neither ever. "The child hand raised to reach the holding hand. . . . Slowly with never a pause plod on and never recede. Backs turned. Both bowed. Joined by held holding hands. Plod on as one. One shade. Another shade" (*Worstward Ho,* 93). Of course the two-in-one are dressed as we might expect them to be: "Black greatcoats to heels. . . . as one dark shade [they] plod unreced-ing on" (p. 95). It is not the boy and the old man alone who plod on as one, however, for there is yet another shade merged with their shades— or rather there are two more shades in addition to the "one dark shade" of the man and the boy. There is the one in whose head all of this occurs, himself as much a shade as the others, and there is the bowed figure that advances and recedes and, it is eventually determined, is the shade of an old woman. When the speaker at one point declares that this "narrow field" is "rife with shades" (p. 101), he is both right and wrong. The field, which is inside the speaker's skull, is unquestionably a place haunted by many ghosts, yet in the end there is but one ghost, the ghost of him who dreams on all the others.

A similar situation is presented in the first of *Texts for Nothing,* where the narrator recalls the stories his father told him—or story, rather, for it was always the same, "about Joe Breem, or Breen, the son of a lighthouse keeper, evening after evening, all the long winter through." Now in age dreaming back to that time, he says, "Yes, I was my father and I was my son, I asked myself questions and answered as best I could, I had it told to me evening after evening, the same old story I knew by heart and couldn't believe, or we walked together, hand in hand, silent, sunk in our worlds, each in his worlds, the hands forgotten in each other. That's how I've held out till now" (*Complete Short Prose,* 103). In *Worstward Ho* we begin with the old man, then the boy ("First one. Then two"), or we begin with the old man and the boy, who then merge ("Or first two. Then one. Or to-gether"); but finally the old man and the boy, the old woman with bowed back and the one remembering and imagining them into existence are "all again together. The bowed back. The plodding twain. The skull. The stare. All back in the skull together. Unchanged. Stare clamped to all" (p. 102). The same merger of the same shades is effected in *Ill Seen Ill Said* where the existence of the old woman, as later of the old man, depends entirely on what can only be this same "staring eye" (p. 69) of the speaker's mem-ory. What is most remarkable about the merger, however, is that it is ac-complished by wrapping the old woman, the old man, and the boy in a single black greatcoat capable of covering them all. As I have already men-tioned, the old man makes his appearance in a dark "greatcoat reaching to the ground" (*Ill Seen,* 60), which, we must suppose, also covers the boy, for as we recall from *Worstward Ho* (remembering ahead the better to remember back), the two of them are outfitted in "[b]lack greatcoats to heels" and "as one dark shade plod . . . on." When it comes time "for a turn in the pastures," the old woman "for some reason covered her head" in something resembling a mantle so that "head included she lies hidden," and she walks out in a "long black skirt" that claws the "limp grass strangely rigid under the weight of the rime." By the time she arrives at her destination—the cromlech-like stones that "gleam faintly afar"—to find some but not all of the twelve guardians there, her headdress and long black skirt seem to have blended and metamorphosed into nothing else but a man's greatcoat: "The guardians—the twelve are there but not at full muster. . . . Simply note how those still faithful have moved apart. Such ill seen that night in the pastures. While head included she lies hidden. Under on closer inspection a long greatcoat. A man's by the buttons" (p. 74). This capacious coat provides hiding space and protection and a semblance of collective existence for the old woman, the old man, and the boy who in some sense is a child of both. Near the end of *Ill Seen Ill Said* remembrance is evoked "till all recalled," and the first, most important item to remember is a pair of greatcoats: "Suddenly enough and way for remembrance. Closed again to that end the vile jelly or opened again or left as it was however that was. Till all recalled. First finally by far hanging from their skirts two black greatcoats" (p. 81). Admittedly, by this point in *Ill Seen Ill Said* there is a great deal going on: when, for example, we find reference two pages later to a nail at "the place of the skull . . . [o]ne April afternoon," we might guess that it was Augustine's pair of thieves who left behind the "two black greatcoats," since "the place of the skull" is simply a translation of "Golgotha." But however many other things we discover going on here, we have to recognize that the two greatcoats have been well established as the special property of the old man and the old woman, and as such they figure in the memory of the boy-become-an-old-man as something akin to the paternal and maternal principles. The affect associated with repeated, layered memories of an old green greatcoat, now nearly black from age and from being so often processed through recollection, would only be increased by extending its reference to include the mother along with the father.

It can scarcely be doubted that the image of a greatcoat called up so often by Beckett had a profound personal meaning for him, but I suggest that as it figures in the work—and at the time it begins to figure—it had a historical, collective, and cultural significance as well. The garment generally designated a greatcoat in the English versions of Beckett's work is termed in the French editions a "manteau," which a French-English dictionary defines as follows: "cloak, coat, overcoat, U.S. top coat (en général)"; but as an item with specifically military significance, "manteau" translates, according to Larousse, as "Great coat," and in a figurative sense it means "mantle, cloak, veil." As soon as we think of the greatcoat as a mantle and as an item of military dress (but worn, as in Beckett, in a non-military context), it takes on an immense suggestiveness. Much is made in *Ill Seen Ill Said* of the properties of the greatcoat that allow the old woman to lie hidden within it, and we learn more about its hiding capacity from both *Molloy* and *Malone Dies*. In the former, when he is transferring his sucking stones around from pocket to pocket, Molloy says he devised a plan that required leaving the left pocket of his greatcoat empty, but he then immediately corrects and explains himself: "empty of stones that is, for its usual contents remained, as well as occasional objects. For where do you think I hid my vegetable knife, my silver, my horn and the other things that I have not yet named, perhaps shall never name" (*Trilogy*, 67). And it is from its hiding place under his cloak ("cape" in *Malone Meurt*) that Lemuel produces the hatchet at the end of *Malone Dies* and begins to lay about him. The significance of this for an Irishman of Beckett's time, place, class, and education will be clearer if we look at the beginning of Maria Edgeworth's *Castle Rackrent,* where Thady Quirk introduces himself to the reader as one known for wearing a greatcoat: "My real name is Thady Quirk, though in the family I have always been known by no other than *'honest Thady'*—afterwards, in the time of Sir Murtagh, deceased, I remember to hear them calling me *'old Thady;'* and now I'm come to *'poor Thady'*—for I wear a long great coat* winter and summer, which is very handy. . . ."[24] There is an incipient social history in these lines, and Edgeworth takes the occasion to fill it out with a wonderfully illuminating footnote marked by the asterisk: "The cloak, or mantle, as described by Thady, is of high antiquity.—Spencer [i.e., Edmund Spenser], in his 'View of the State of Ireland,' proves that it is not, as some have imagined, peculiarly derived from the Scythians, but that 'most nations of the world antiently used the mantle . . .' "; after quoting Spenser on evidence for the mantle among the Jews, the Chaldees, the Egyptians, the Greeks, and the ancient Latins and Romans, Edgeworth adds the sly observation that "Spencer knew the convenience of the said mantle, as housing, bedding, and cloathing," and proceeds to provide witness from *A View of the Present State of Ireland:*

> Iren. Because the Commodity doth not Countervail the discommodity; for the inconveniences which thereby do arise, are much more many; for it is a fit house for an outlaw, a meet bed for a rebel, and an apt cloak for a thief.—First, the outlaw being, for his many crimes and villainies, banished from the towns and houses of honest men, and wandering in waste places, far from danger of law, maketh his mantle his house, and under it covereth himself from the wrath of Heaven, from the offence of the earth, and from the sight of men. When it raineth, it is his pent-house; when it bloweth, it is his tent; when it freezeth, it is his tabernacle. In summer he can wear it loose; in winter he can wrap it close; at all times he can use it; never heavy, never cumbersome. Likewise for a rebel it is as serviceable; for in this war that he maketh (if at least it deserve the name of war), when he still flieth from his foe,

---

24. Maria Edgeworth, *Castle Rackrent* (Oxford: Oxford University Press/World's Classics, 1964; first published 1800), 7. Laura O'Connor first made me aware of the pertinence of *Castle Rackrent* for a historicized reading of Beckett.

and lurketh in the *thick woods, (this should be black bogs,)* and straight passages waiting for advantages; it is his bed, yea, and almost his household-stuff.

Spenser is well known to the Irish for recommending in this same book not only that mantles or greatcoats be forbidden as dress in Ireland—because "the Comodytie doth not Countervaile the discomoditie" and "the inconveniences which thereby doe aryse, are much more manye"[25]—but that the Gaelic language should be outlawed as well, for it too is capable of hiding all too many things from the English settler class—and, too, the practice of using Irish women for wet nurses (or worse yet, intermarrying with them) since the settler children would, Spenser thought, take in much too much of the Irish spirit along with their "sucke."[26] One has only to

25. Edmund Spenser, *A View of the Present State of Ireland,* "Edited, principally from MS Rawlinson B478 in the Bodleian Library and MS 188.221 in Caius College, Cambridge, by W. L. Renwick" (London: Scholartis Press, 1934; first published 1596), 67. Irenius (i.e., Spenser) says he "would thincke yt meete to forbydd all mantells," but especially he would outlaw them for women:

> For some of them that bee these wandring weomen . . . yt is half a wardrobe: For in Sommer ye shall fynde her arayed comonlye but in her smocke and mantle to bee more readye for her light seruices: In winter and in her travell, yt is her cloke and saifgard and also a coverlett for her lewde exercyse. And when she hath fylled her Vesell, vnder yt shee can hyde both her burthen and her blame, yea and when her bastarde is borne yt serues in steade of all her swadlinge cloutes. . . . And as for all other good women which loue to doe but lyttle worke, how hansome yt is to lye in and sleepe, or to louse them selues in the sunshine, they that haue bene but a while in Ireland can well witnesse. (P. 69)

Spenser's ire is aroused by mantle-wearing men of Irish affiliation but to a much greater degree by the women of that country.

26. When Eudoxus expresses surprise that English settlers would adopt the Irish language and "take more deleight to speake that language then there owne, whereas they should, (mee thinckes) rather take scorne to acquainte theire tonges thereto for yt hath bene ever the vse of the conqueror to dispise the language of the conquered, and to force him by all meanes to learne his," Irenius responds thus:

> I suppose that the cheif cause of bringinge in the Irishe language amongst them was speciallie theire fosteringe and marryinge with the Irishe which are twoe most dangerous infeccions, for first the child that sucketh the milke of the nurse must of necessitie learne his first speach of her, the which beinge the first that is envred to his tonge, is [ever] after most pleasinge vnto him insomuch as though he afterwardes bee taught Englishe, yett the smacke of the first will alwayes abyde with him and not onelie of the speach, but of the manners and Condycions: for besydes the yonge children bee lyke Apes, which will affecte and ymitate what they see done before them speciallie by theyre nurses, whom they loue so well, they moreover drawe into them selues togeather with theire sucke, even the nature and disposition of theire nurses, for the mind followeth much the temperature of the bodye: and also the wordes are the Image of the mynde, so as they proceding from the mynde, the mynde must bee needes effected with the wordes: So that the speach beinge Irish, the harte must needes bee Irishe, for out of the aboundance of the heart the tonge speaketh.

And of the monstrous notion of intermarriage with Irish women Irenius says, "[I]ndeed how can such matchinge but bringe forth an evill race, seinge that comonlye the child taketh most of his nature of the mother . . . ; therefore are these ij [i.e., "2" in roman numeral]

think of the many uses to which figures in Beckett put their greatcoats— some of them not far removed from "a fit house for an outlaw, a meet bed for a rebel, and an apt cloak for a thief"—to realize that memories associated with the greatcoat were for Beckett collective in a cultural and historical as well as in a familial sense. And when Beckett describes the old woman in *Ill Seen Ill Said* taking a turn in the pastures ("While head included she lies hidden. Under closer inspection a long greatcoat. A man's by the buttons"), is there not a recollection of Spenser's animadversion on mantle-wearing Irish women: "And as for all other good women which loue to doe but lyttle worke, how hansome yt [the mantle] is to lye in and sleepe, or to louse them selues in the sunshine"?

It is familial evocations that are most prominent in the history of the Beckettian greatcoat given in *Watt*. As he prepares to leave Mr. Knott's house, Watt appears before his successor, Micks, "with in each hand a small bag, that is to say, two small bags in all." It is not, however, the two bags, the way of numbering them, and the manner in which Watt holds them that are of special interest (though we get four paragraphs devoted to these matters); what draws our attention instead is Watt's mode of dress. "Watt wore a greatcoat, still green here and there. This coat, when last weighed by Watt, weighed between fifteen and sixteen pounds, avoirdupois, or a little more than a stone." After some detail about how Watt managed the weighing of his greatcoat, the narrator—presumably "Sam," but in this novel one never knows (as we are informed anent another issue in an earlier footnote, "Haemophilia is, like enlargment of the prostate, an exclusively male disorder. But not in this work")—continues with, as it were, the "begats," the lineage, and the generational treatment of this particular item:

> This coat was of a very respectable age, as such coats go ["of high antiquity," in Maria Edgeworth's words], having been bought at secondhand, for a small sum, from a meritorious widow, by Watt's father, when Watt's father was a young man, and motoring in its infancy, that is to say some seventy years before. This coat had not, since then, at any time been washed, except imperfectly by the rain, and the snow, and the sleet, and of course occasional fleeting immersion in canal water, nor dry-cleaned, nor turned, nor brushed, and it was no doubt to these precautions that its preservation, as a unit, was due. The material of this coat, though liberally scored and contunded, especially in the rear, was so thick, and so strong, that it remained exempt from perfora-

evill customes, of fosteringe and marryinge with the Irishe, most carefullie to bee restrayned, for of them twoe the thirde that is the evill custome of language, which I spake of cheyflie procedeth" (pp. 88–89).

tion, in the strict meaning of the word. . . . The skirts were not divided . . .
(*Watt,* 217–18).

We cannot fail to be attracted by the piquancy of logic in the phrase "and
of course occasional fleeting immersion in canal water," but more than mere
piquancy is the certainty that this garment, unwashed "except imperfectly
by the rain, and the snow, and the sleet," is none other than the mantle
so feared and maligned by Spenser nearly four hundred years earlier. And
that it came down to Watt from his father would suggest that the generational drama is a unit within the historical sweep that goes back to the time
of troubles in the sixteenth century and back much, much earlier to the
Scythians, the Chaldees, the Greeks, and so on.

Watt's greatcoat is not, however, the only thing of interest to "Sam"
and the reader about his clothing. There is a hat to be considered, there
are boots (or a boot and a shoe), and there are small and other clothes
hidden by the greatcoat. And there is something very like a philosophy of
clothes that moves "Sam" to exclamatory excitement and to philosophy
and poetry.

> Watt wore, on his head, a block hat, of a pepper colour. This excellent
> hat had belonged to his grandfather, who had picked it up, on a racecourse,
> from off the ground, where it lay, and carried it home. Then mustard, now
> it was pepper, in colour.
>
> It was to be observed that the colours, on the one hand of this coat, on
> the other of this hat, drew closer and closer, the one to the other, with every
> passing lustre. Yet how different had been their beginnings! The one green!
> The other yellow! So it is with time, that lightens what is dark, that darkens
> what is light.
>
> It was to be expected that, once met, they would not stay, no, but con-
> tinue, each as it must, to age, until the hat was green, the coat yellow, and
> then through the last circles paling, deepening, swooning cease, the hat to be
> a hat, the coat to be a coat. For so it is with time.
>
> Watt wore, on his feet, a boot, brown in colour, and a shoe, happily of
> a brownish colour also. This boot Watt had bought, for eight pence, from a
> one-legged man who, having lost his leg, and a fortiori his foot, in an accident,
> was happy to realize, on his discharge from hospital, for such a sum, his unique
> remaining marketable asset. He little suspected that he owed this good fortune
> to Watt's having found, some days before, on the sea-shore, the shoe, stiff
> with brine, but otherwise shipshape. . . .
>
> Of Watt's coat and waistcoat, of his shirt his vest and his drawers, much
> might be written, of great interest and significance. The drawers, in particular,
> were remarkable, from more than one point of view. But they were hidden,
> coat and waistcoat, shirt and underclothes, all hidden, from the eye.

There can be little question that it is the greatcoat's oft-cited capacity for concealments that is alluded to comically in the final sentence. I have quoted at length from this initiatory moment in the history of the Beckettian greatcoat for several reasons. There is first of all the pleasure in reading the peculiar prose (presumably a reflection of "Sam's" mind) that insists on taking account of every permutational possibility in any situation. There is next the evident intent, at this point in Beckett's career, to satirize the hopelessly naive manner of conventional, realistic narrative. And there is finally the fact that at this stage, after the encounter with Prudent in the Paris street but before the revelation of Dublin—i.e., after he had perceived that not-knowing should be the mode of his writing but before he had determined that his subject should be himself and therefore memory—the only emotion Beckett associates with the greatcoat is humor, even though the greatcoat is descended from the father and the buff-colored hat from the grandfather. That Watt's greatcoat is in every sense a worthy successor to Spenser's (or Edgeworth's) mantle and a worthy ancestor of all the greatcoats in Beckett gives it, nevertheless, an obvious cachet.

To resume the order of what I take to be Beckett's canonical works, "The End" (the first extended fiction written in French) begins with a Kafkaesque "they," not otherwise identified, who "clothed me and gave me money." When the narrator protests that he wants certain of his own clothes back, "they" are unmoved: ". . . the hat was a bowler, in good shape. I said, Keep your hat and give me back mine" (*Complete Short Prose*, 78). Though the narrator gives no further specifics, I think we can fairly assume that the lost hat was buff (or, as in *Watt,* mustard) in color and block in shape. After his plea for its return, the narrator continues: "I added, Give me back my greatcoat. They replied that they had burnt them, together with my other clothes. I understood then that the end was near, at least fairly near." His understanding proves all too accurate, and without a greatcoat as make-do and resource for all seasons, he soon finds himself, as Spenser would have wished and Edgeworth feared, without "housing, bedding, and cloathing." To deprive him of his greatcoat, and of his hat as well, is for this narrator literally the beginning of the end. Two or three times during his decline he imagines, delusionally, that he has his coat back, and there is real poignance when he is compelled to correct himself: "no, I had no greatcoat now. . . . what's the matter with me . . ." (p. 92). In "The Expelled" the narrator speaks once of his greatcoat, but nowhere else in the *Nouvelles* does it have the thematic and emotional significance it bears in "The End."

It is with *Molloy* and *Malone Dies* that Beckett takes to the greatcoat with purpose. After the passage about the pair whom he calls A. and C. ("they wore greatcoats. They looked alike, but no more than others do" [*Trilogy,* 10]), Molloy gives us details of his own clothing shortly before he sets out on his journey to his mother. He tells of his hat and his greatcoat, but then stops himself—yet with an implicit promise, which will be fulfilled in time, to speak of both: "But it is neither of my hat nor of my greatcoat that I hope to speak at present, it would be premature. Doubtless I shall speak of them later, when the time comes to draw up the inventory of my goods and possessions. Unless I lose them between now and then. But even lost they will have their place, in the inventory of my possessions. But I am easy in my mind, I shall not lose them" (p. 15). And indeed he does not lose them, any more than Beckett does, nor does he fail to pass them on to his descendants or successors. The pockets of Molloy's greatcoat, as I have pointed out, are essential to the scheme that allows him to be reasonably certain of sucking each of his stones turn and turn about without error, and at least one of those pockets provides the kind of hiding place Spenser would have liked to deny to someone with a name like Molloy. The most interesting appearance of the greatcoat in *Molloy,* again with a little Spenserian kick to it, comes when Molloy describes how he withstands the rigors of Irish weather. "And in winter, under my greatcoat," he says, "I wrapped myself in swathes of newspaper, and did not shed them until the earth awoke, for good, in April. The *Times Literary Supplement* was admirably adapted to this purpose, of a never failing toughness and impermeability. Even farts made no impression on it" (p. 29). It is perhaps not too much to suggest that the *Times Literary Supplement* is chosen for this honorific position under the greatcoat as being the major organ of the English literary, cultural, and intellectual imperialism for which Spenser may be thought of as a principal spokesman in his time. Even Irish farts make no impression on it.

But Molloy is less concerned with the greatcoat in itself—its color, fabric, antiquity—than with its specific uses as shelter in winter and as repository for sucking stones. It is left to Malone in the Trilogy to provide a conceptual and practical disquisition, which occurs, significantly, when Malone is imagining into being a vice-exister, an incarnation for himself into whose body he thinks he may slip undetected. "And there he is," Malone says, the result of his—Malone's—efforts in imaginative creation, "as good as gold on the bench, his back to the river, and dressed as follows, though clothes don't matter, I know, I know . . ." (p. 208). But of course they do matter—not all clothes, perhaps, but these particular ones. "He has had them a long time already, to judge by their decay," according to Malone. "But most remarkable of all is his greatcoat, in the sense that it covers him completely and screens him from view. For it is so well buttoned, from top to bottom, by means of fifteen buttons at the very least, set at intervals of three or four inches at the very most, that nothing is to be seen of what goes on inside." Just as Spenser said, but even worse, for "the tails of this coat literally sweep the ground and rustle like a train . . . , and the hands too are hidden." Who knows what anti-English mischief those hidden hands may be about? "Now as to the colour of this coat, for colour too is an important consideration, there is no good denying it, all that can be said is that green predominates. And it might safely be wagered that this coat, when new, was of a fine plain green colour, what you might call cab green, for there used to be cabs and carriages rattling through the town with panels of a handsome bottle green, I must have seen them myself, and even driven in them, I would not put it past me" (p. 209). I suppose one could do an analysis of the cultural and historical resonances of the color green, making obligatory reference to Yeats's "Easter 1916"—

> For England may keep faith
> For all that is done and said.
> We know their dream; enough
> To know they dreamed and are dead;
> And what if excess of love
> Bewildered them till they died?
> I write it out in a verse—
> MacDonagh and MacBride
> And Connolly and Pearse
> Now and in time to be,
> Wherever green is worn,
> Are changed, changed utterly:
> A terrible beauty is born.

—and such an analysis would no doubt contribute much to our understanding of what Beckett is up to with his tirelessly repeated description of a greatcoat once bottle green in color but now dark and grimy. Useful as this exercise would be—and it should not be neglected—I do not believe it would get us all the way to the bottom of what Beckett is doing. If we are to find depths of Irish meaning in the greenness of the greatcoat, then we must ask ourselves whether there is any corresponding importance in the buffness of the hat. Could Yeats just as well have written the lines

"Now and in time to be / Wherever buff is worn"? I shouldn't think so, not with the same effect, but Malone in fact goes on to assert of his avatar's head covering, "And were there nothing more to be said about the structure of this hat, the important thing would still remain unsaid, meaning of course its colour, of which all that can be said is this, that a strong sun full upon it brings out shimmers of buff and pearl grey and that otherwise it verges on black, without however ever really approaching it" (p. 210). This has much of Beckett's characteristic humor about it, but in addition to the humor and any historical or cultural significance the two items may bear, there is, to adopt Beckett's term, something pretty clearly "obsessional" about the once-green greatcoat and the buff-colored hat. There seems to me, moreover, an alteration over time in the kind and degree of obsession involved in these recurrent items, which is to say a change in their import. To put it another way, one might not discover anything very obsessional in the two images as they occur progressively in *Watt, Molloy,* and *Malone Dies;* but if one thinks backward from *Stirrings Still, Worstward Ho, Ill Seen Ill Said, Company,* and some intervening dramatic pieces, where the images bear a vastly greater psychological charge, then we will be tempted to feel that Beckett has—as it were ex post facto—invested them with obsessiveness as they occur in the earlier works. Beckett is intensely conscious at all times not only of what he is doing but also of what he has done, and meaning in his work is often a result of projecting backward—when it is not a question of projecting forward.

We get a tiny clue to what I have in mind in *The Unnamable,* where the greatcoat turns up once only and the hat, though more often, always in a single context. This sudden disappearance is accounted for largely by the fact that the Unnamable is not only unnamable but also unbodied and unseeable, therefore without the same need as Molloy and Malone have for protection against the weather and the prying eyes of the colonizers. The one appearance of the greatcoat and the two or three of the hat are always in the context of the Unnamable's seeing a figure from a previous book and attempting to identify him by his dress, and it is precisely Molloy and Malone whose identities are in question. "Malone is there," the Unnamable says. "I am almost sure it is he. The brimless hat seems to me conclusive. . . . Sometimes I wonder if it is not Molloy. Perhaps it is Molloy, wearing Malone's hat. But it is more reasonable to suppose it is Malone, wearing his own hat. Oh look, there is the first thing, Malone's hat" (*Trilogy,* 269). But the small—very small—hint of what has been happening over the course of the previous half-dozen books comes when greatcoat and hat come together: "But what makes me say I gaze straight before me?"

the Unnamable asks, and proceeds to respond, "This question in any case is secondary, since I see nothing. Am I clothed? I have often asked myself this question, then suddenly started talking about Malone's hat, or Molloy's greatcoat, or Murphy's suit" (p. 279). The Unnamable is remembering his predecessors by their dress, just as Beckett is remembering, from the vantage point of *The Unnamable,* what he had done in works up to that final volume of the Trilogy. Murphy, being in the earliest of the novels, was not granted a greatcoat but is instead pictured "stalking about London in a green suit" and "a perfectly plain lemon made-up bow tie." There is, in fact, some question about the greenness of the suit ("The suit was not green, but æruginous"), but it is interesting in any case to observe that its color has progressed in a direction contrary to that of the greatcoat, for the suit was black "the day it was bought" and is now either green or æruginous, while the greatcoat, once green, is now barely distinguishable from black. The point I would make is that if you are in a Beckett book before *Watt* you do not get a greatcoat, and even with *Watt* and after there are still distinctions to be made. Mercier and Camier, in the novel that proved ultimately unsatisfactory to Beckett, have only a raincoat ("un imperméable") between them, which they discard—as no one in Beckett would do a greatcoat—midway through the novel (leaving in the pocket, according to Camier, "[p]unched tickets of all sorts, spent matches, scraps of newspaper bearing in their margins the obliterated traces of irrevocable rendez-vous, the classic last tenth of pointless pencil, crumples of soiled bumf, a few porous condoms, dust. Life in short" [*Mercier and Camier,* 66]). Furthermore, in *Watt* and even in *Molloy* and *Malone Dies,* the latter two securely within the canon, there is little or no emotion discernible when the greatcoat comes into view, and this will not be true in later works. This is to say that Beckett himself perceived an emotional significance about that article of clothing only after a certain point, but then, remembering what he had done earlier and being endowed with an appropriately opportunistic memory, he tied the earlier works in with the later to effect an unbroken line of greatcoats from *Watt* to *Stirrings Still;* or one might better say that a single greatcoat is passed on from book to book until, by the end, it has become virtually mythic in its dimensions.

If I had to specify a date when the change in kind and degree of obsessiveness with regard to the greatcoat occurred, it would be 1958, the year of *Krapp's Last Tape,* which, not irrelevantly, was Beckett's first full exposition and dramatization of memory as the essential ground and agent of identity. It is also important to recall that it was in *Krapp's Last Tape* that Beckett rendered an account, however altered for the purposes of effective dramatic presentation, of his revelatory experience in Dublin in 1945, as a consequence of which, I am claiming, Beckett was thrown back on self and on memory as his dual sole subject. I choose 1958 and *Krapp's Last Tape* as the year and the play of the greatcoat transformation in full awareness that there is no mention at all here of a greatcoat or of a father who would have worn it. I maintain that in light of the works that follow *Krapp* and as a consequence of memory's retroactive power for investing earlier events with later understanding—this on behalf of both Beckett and his reader—the greatcoat and a father to wear it (and pass it on to the son) are the more present in *Krapp's Last Tape* for their being absent. Having mentioned that play, however, I am going to skip over it to look at later works in which the emotional complex I have been detailing becomes fully operative, before returning to consider how *Krapp's Last Tape* functions as a nodal point in what I see as (from after the fact) a lifelong commitment to a literature of memory. In *Cascando* (1961), the play that combines music with voice for its effects, the sheer repetition of "same old coat . . . same old coat . . . same old coat . . . same old broadbrim . . . same old coat . . . same old coat . . . same old coat" (*Complete Dramatic Works*, 297–302) serves to transform the item by rhythmic and musical means into something other than, something more mythic and more archetypal than, the same old coat. It resonates like a fairy tale or a bedtime story for children in which repeated phrases establish a feeling of security through fulfilled expectations; indeed it has much the same effect as that claimed for the stories told by the father to his son in *Texts for Nothing 1,* "the same old story. . . . evening after evening, all the long winter through. . . . it ended happily, it began unhappily and it ended happily, every evening, a comedy for children" (*Complete Short Prose,* 103). Thus the stories of childhood but not, alas, of adulthood, for though the same old coat may connect us with the past, it also and inevitably signifies loss as being the garment of the one who told the childhood stories and is there no longer. Once upon a time my father told me a story every evening that began "Once upon a time. . . ."

This sense of shifting perspectives and values, the effect of time's passage and memory's ability to evoke a ghost of the past but not the past itself, informs *That Time,* a brief play in which "Listener"—"Old white face, long flaring white hair as if seen from above outspread"—listens silently to three voices, all the same voice ("Voices A B C are his own coming to him from both sides and above"), remembering three different periods in his life. Voice A recalls his futile effort in maturity to return to a place ("Foley's Folly") associated with an event from childhood; Voice B recalls a love that he "gave up for good" when he decided he had to let the dark in; Voice C recalls his failure as an old man attempting something we might imagine to be the artist's project. From this brief description it will be evident that *That Time* (1975) is both a thematic redaction of *Krapp's Last Tape* (1958) and a thematic anticipation of *Company* (1977–79), the three of them representing a working, a reworking, and a preworking of the old man–young man–child trio and, from that, the old man–child–old woman trio that are so prominent in Beckett's very late, post-*Company* writing. "[W]as your mother," Voice C asks Listener, "was your mother ah for God's sake all gone long ago all dust the lot you the last huddled up on the slab in the old green greatcoat with your arms round you whose else hugging you for a bit of warmth to dry off[?]" Voice C, representing Listener at his oldest, thus reveals that in age he still wore the same greatcoat he had worn when, according to Voice A, he "went back to look was the ruin still there where you hid as a child." Unable to get anywhere near Foley's Folly because both the tram and the railway of his childhood had long since stopped running, he sat, in Voice A's description, "huddled on the doorstep in the old green greatcoat in the pale sun with the nightbag needless on your knees not knowing where you were little by little not knowing where you were or when you were or what. . . ." It should come to the reader as no surprise when Voice A, telling how the frustrated attempt to get to Foley's Folly concluded and specifying the provenance of the greatcoat, says, "back down to the wharf with the nightbag and the old green greatcoat your father left you trailing the ground . . . not a thought in your head only get back on board [the ferry] and away to hell out of it and never come back. . . ." That the greatcoat came to Listener from his father reminds readers of what they might forget—that Listener's earlier selves, like the father who has left the greatcoat empty, like the mother whose warmth is inadequately replaced by the greatcoat's embrace, are no more than memory's ghosts haunting the reveries of Listener, himself hardly more than a ghost. And thus Voice C's darkly shaded conclusion, replacing the separate "that time"'s of Voice A, Voice B, and Voice C by the "no time" of memory's failure to make the past ever be again: "not a sound only the old breath and the leaves turning and then suddenly this dust whole place suddenly full of dust when you opened your eyes from floor to ceiling nothing only dust and not a sound only what was it it said come and gone was that it something like that come and gone come and gone no one come and gone in no time gone in no time." When Listener, whose sole action throughout the play has been to close and open his eyes three times, now manages, after an eighteen-second silence, a "smile, toothless for preference," one can only ponder his—and Beckett's—humor.

However one interprets Listener's smile, the prevailing emotion of *That Time* and in particular the emotion associated with the image of "the old green greatcoat" is what I would call "post–*Krapp's Last Tape*"—i.e., somber, elegiac, deeply felt, often lyrical. And this is how I would describe the mood of *Company* as well: not that it is without humor—nothing of Beckett's is—but its humor is very different from that of *Murphy* or *Watt,* say, very different even from the humor of the Trilogy or *Waiting for Godot,* and I cannot see that such humor as there is in *Company* ever attaches itself to scenes in which the father and the greatcoat come together. I should pause here to say that I am unaware of any evidence that either Beckett or his father ever owned or wore a greatcoat. There may be such evidence, but I have not seen it. This seems to me to matter not at all. The greatcoat is there and doing a great many things throughout Beckett's work. Lack of evidence that would make mentions of a greatcoat merely or largely biographical is one reason (not the only one) why I think it circumspect, necessary, and desirable to refer always to *the* father, *the* mother, *the* son, never to Beckett's father, Beckett's mother, Beckett. It may be that Beckett was thinking of his father, his mother, himself, but it is not of these people the work is thinking. I would invoke Yeats once more: "A poet writes always of his personal life, in his finest work out of its tragedy, whatever it be, remorse, lost love, or mere loneliness." And no doubt Beckett did just this. But Yeats goes on to say that even so the poet (and, in his late works especially, Beckett fits very well what Yeats means by "the poet") "never speaks directly as to someone at the breakfast table, there is always a phantasmagoria . . . ; even when the poet seems most himself . . . , he is never the bundle of accident and incoherence that sits down to breakfast; he has been reborn as an idea, something intended, complete" (*Essays and Introductions,* 509). So we must understand the figures of *Company, Ill Seen Ill Said, Worstward Ho,* and *Stirrings Still.* The memory I am concerned with, then, is that of the artist and the work—and the memory of the artist *for* the work—more than it is the memory of the man. In the first section of the first chapter of this book I quoted Beckett, on the occasion of his seventieth birthday, writing John Calder that in old age work would be his company, an observation that bears obvious meaning for the book of that title. I wonder if one might suggest that Beckett may have had in mind not only work yet to be accomplished (the pieces just cited) but also the work already out in the world, his oeuvre to that time. This is not entirely different from the more obvious interpretation, but it adds a new dimension to that understanding. Could we not say that in the pieces Beckett wrote after 1976 he was creating company for himself with the new work but that a large part of that work consisted of returning to, revisiting, and gathering in old friends and company in the form of earlier work? I would not want to push the analogy too far, but I believe it would here be useful to recall St. Augustine, who, late in life (about Beckett's age when he wrote *Company,* seventy-two or seventy-three), went back over the body of his writings in the *Retractations* and made company for himself by, in effect, performing a second act of life-writing on top of the first. This, at any rate, is what Beckett does—throughout his career (note the reappearance of Murphy, Watt, and Mercier and Camier in the Trilogy, of Molloy, Malone, and Moran in *The Unnamable,* and so on), but supremely in the works from *Company* through *Stirrings Still.*

Had *Company* been Beckett's last work, as for a time it seemed like being, that book would have occupied (and very handsomely) exactly the same position and role I have been claiming for *Stirrings Still,* i.e., the recollective, summative crown to everything before, the condensed memory of the entire body of work. The only difference, since Beckett did *not* stop with *Company,* is that *Stirrings Still* can include within itself memory of *Company*'s memories as well as memory of everything previous and subsequent to *Company.* One can be sure that had Beckett not died shortly after finishing *Stirrings Still* and had he possessed the physical strength to go on, he would have produced another piece admirably suited to the summative role. In a very suggestive passage about the late paintings and thought of Édouard Manet, the authors of a little book called *The Last Flowers of Manet* write: "Death is always arbitrary and yet the mind imposes the sense of an ending, the closing of a curve. Perhaps particularly in the case of an artist with whom the stages of growing and self-understanding—features of anyone's life—are imprinted on the work he leaves behind and are hardly to be separated from our understanding of it. . . . The imagination moves through time backward and forward and can as little guard itself from doing this as the body can guard itself from the flow of time in one direction." The editors go on to speak of the romance that early death casts retrospectively over an artist's work, and then of those like Manet who die in their middle years. Such an artist as the latter "is cheated of the flares of an early death and the glow of old age. . . . Manet's life does not describe a curve but the beginning of one, broken with an ugly jerk."[27] Beckett, of course,

27. Robert Gordon and Andrew Forge, *The Last Flowers of Manet,* with translations from the French by Richard Howard (New York: Harry N. Abrams, 1986), 9.

grumble as he might that the end could not come soon enough, escaped such a fate, and he took advantage of his final years—years he claimed he would decline if he could—to perfect the work.

> The intellect of man is forced to choose
> Perfection of the life, or of the work,
> And if it take the second must refuse
> A heavenly mansion, raging in the dark.

So Yeats declares, and the phrase "raging in the dark" can only remind us of Beckett, who in his last years, besides writing always of figures in the dark, was given to reading *Lear* and the Book of Job. What interests me at the moment is the part memory plays in the process of perfecting the work. For an artist like Keats, let us say, memory as regards a body of work can have little or no temporal extension; it is like the flashbulb memories of early childhood, described by psychologists, that the child cannot yet articulate into narrative and into a life story. Of the way such eidetic images may eventually be transformed into connected life-histories Steven Rose writes:

> The transition from childhood to adult memory is dramatic, from imaged and timeless to linear and time-bound. In most adults, memories seem to be formed in orderly sequence and undergo a series of transformations from the time when they are first acquired to their later, more permanent form. Only a few individuals seem to retain in adulthood the eidetic memory of their childhood, a sort of arrested development, like a tadpole that won't metamorphose into a frog. We marvel at their talents, perhaps recalling our own childhood eidetic capacities—but usually fail to see at what cost such talents are bought. *'Idiots savants'*, miracle calculators or professional stage performers impress us all—but no-one would wish to suffer the fate of Shereskevskii [in Luria's *The Mind of a Mnemonist*] or Funes [in Borges's "Funes the Memorious"]. Better to submit to the linearities of time that the transition to maturity brings. (*Making of Memory*, 106)

The poet cut off at twenty-six has no extended memory of earlier work that would permit meaningful anticipation of later work, while the painter dead in middle life presents the image of a career that seems to be gathering the momentum of memories only to be broken off before its memory of the future can be realized, a little like the Pont Bénézet in Avignon, which is firmly grounded on one side but then stops abruptly in the middle of the river, never to reach the other side. Had Beckett died, like Keats, at twenty-six, there would be nothing to remember; had he died, like Manet, at fifty-one, there would be a smallish, enigmatic body of work, apparently going somewhere—but just where would be impossible to say. Yeats again supplies the text as, for Beckett, he did so often in old age:

> 'The work is done,' grown old he thought,
> 'According to my boyish plan;
> Let the fools rage, I swerved in nought,
> Something to perfection brought;'
> *But louder sang that ghost 'What then?'*

The ghost of Plato urges the artist, in Beckettian phrase, always to go on. The curious thing to consider, from Yeats's poem as from Beckett's career, is that it is memory of what has been done that requires the artist to go on to what must be done. What was started in "The Capital of the Ruins," the Trilogy, and *Godot* demanded completion in "neither," *Company,* and *Stirrings Still.*

What began with *Murphy*-like humor in *Watt*—"The coat had not . . . at any time been washed, except imperfectly by the rain, and the snow, and the sleet, and of course occasional fleeting immersion in canal water"— concludes (but only momentarily) with *Stirrings Still*–like emotional gravity in *Company,* describing memories of the last walk out in the greatcoat before resignation to stillness and the dark: "You lie in the dark with closed eyes and see the scene. As you could not at the time. . . . The skirts of the greatcoat resting on the snow. In the old bowed head in the old block hat speechless misgiving. Halfway across the pasture on your beeline to the gap. The unerring feet fast. You look behind you as you could not then and see their trail. A great swerve. Withershins. Almost as if all at once the heart too heavy. In the end too heavy" (*Company,* 38). It is through looking back in memory, with closed eyes, that the one on his back in the dark can see what he could not then see: the ghost of himself, but indistinguishable from the ghost of the father; and it is just this indistinguishability, together with the present absence of both, that produces the great swerve withershins, "as if all at once the heart too heavy. In the end too heavy." The quoted lines occur at the end of *Company*'s longest section, which comes at the precise center of the book—twenty-eight pages from the beginning, twenty-eight pages from the end. With all the totting up and calculating that go on in *Company,* I cannot believe that there is anything unintentional about either the length of the passage or its placement. This is the emotional heart of the book, and it seems as if, looking back to *Molloy* and *Malone Dies* if not indeed to *Watt,* that heart were become "all at once too heavy. In the end too heavy" to bear, experiencing and anticipating the last word in the book: "Alone."

"The last time you went out the snow lay on the ground," the voice tells the one lying on his back in the dark. "You now on your back in the dark stand that morning on the sill having pulled the door gently to behind you." This is the third of five times that the voice speaks of walks taken in the greatcoat, and it is here that the father is said to have disappeared even as a shade. The first memory has the one on his back in the dark doing the "giant tot in miles. In leagues. How often round the earth already. Halted too at your elbow during these computations your father's shade" (*Company,* 15). The second likewise: "Nowhere in particular on the way from A to Z. Or say for verisimilitude the Ballyogan Road. That dear old back road. . . . Head sunk totting up the tally on the verge of the ditch. Foothills to left. Croker's Acres ahead. Father's shade to right and a little to the rear. So many times already round the earth" (p. 23). But on the third occurrence, before the "great swerve. Withershins," it is different: "Your father's shade is not with you any more. It fell out long ago." Whether that shade really fell out long ago or only penetrated deeper to the bone is unanswerable, but in any case this third instance of remembering lies at the midpoint between the one on his back in the dark of the first line of the book and the aloneness of the last line, midway between solitude and solitude, between dark and dark. The last time the voice reminds him of solitary walking, it is well after the final excursion: "Out no more to walk the little winding back roads and interjacent pastures now alive with flocks and now deserted. With at your elbow for long years your father's shade in his old tramping rags and then for long years alone. Adding step after step to the ever mounting sum of those already accomplished. Halting now and then with bowed head to fix the score. Then on from nought anew" (p. 61). This periodic halting "with bowed head to fix the score" or "head sunk totting up the tally" represents memory's recurrent review of life, and it brings us eventually not only to the end of *Company* but to *Stirrings Still,* where once more, and again with head sunk, life is reviewed and the work reprised: "the best he could do was stop dead and stand stock still which after a moment of hesitation he did and of course sink his head as one deep in meditation which after another moment of hesitation he did also" (*Complete Short Prose,* 263). How many tottings up from across the range of Beckett's work this ultimate one recalls and repeats: *Stirrings Still* is the totting up of tottings up.

Some pages back I suggested that one should take note of the time—the historical moment—when the greatcoat rises to the surface of Beckett's consciousness and his fiction. Through backward and forward movement I then attempted to show that Darley (and by way of him Saint-Lô) should be seen to be associated with the greatcoat figure, which, by this and other means, assumes something of a collective significance. Immediately before the Saint-Lô experience and the writing of "The Capital of the Ruins," Beckett had spent the war years in Roussillon struggling with *Watt,* the book in which, toward the end, the greatcoat makes its first glorious appearance. I believe these are all interrelated parts of a single imaginative and memorial vision in Beckett. The description he gives of Saint-Lô reads like a particularized version of a general scene that could be observed—and had been observed by Beckett—all across France and indeed Europe: "Saint-Lô was bombed out of existence in one night. German prisoners of war, and casual labourers attracted by the relative food-plenty, but soon discouraged by housing conditions, continue, two years after the liberation, to clear away the debris, literally by hand" (*Complete Short Prose,* 277). Demobilized soldiers and displaced civilians were a familiar sight everywhere in Europe after the war, a great many of them decked out in trousers, shirts, boots, jackets, caps and hats, *manteaux* and greatcoats, vaguely—or actually—of military provenance. (In *Reawakening* Primo Levi gives a vivid account of his own nearly endless shuttling through Poland, the Soviet Union, Romania, Hungary, Czechoslovakia, Austria, and Germany as he tried to make his way back to Turin after liberation from the concentration camp at Buna. Many of the figures he describes along the way—their dress, their bewilderment, their going on in the face of the impossibility of going on—could easily have come out of Beckett.) This was the scene that Beckett presumably saw in making his way from Roussillon back to Paris, then again when he visited bombed-out London, and most of all during the months he spent in Saint-Lô; it is in many ways the scene that we have come to think of as and to call Beckettian, the landscape of *Waiting for Godot, Endgame, Happy Days.* But what was in the beginning an image for a devastated Europe and a homeless humanity—"a time-honoured conception of humanity in ruins"—gradually took on a much more personal meaning. Not that the original meaning was not personal enough or accompanied by strong emotion—surely it was—but imperceptibly, as Beckett came back again and again to the figure in a greatcoat, it assumed the contours and dimensions not of a generalized humanity nor of the universal human condition but of the primary family group: mother, father, child—which, of course, is universal in its way but starting, so to say, at home and returning there again and again, in memory if not in reality: "then gently light unfading on that unheeded neither unspeakable home" ("neither," *Complete Short Prose,* 258). "Why, for all of us," T. S. Eliot asked in the Norton Lectures at Harvard, "out of all that we have heard, seen, felt, in a lifetime, do certain images recur, charged with emotion, rather than others? . . . [S]uch memories may have symbolic value, but of what we cannot tell, for they come to represent the depths of feeling into which we cannot peer."[28] Why the greatcoat, once green, now dark? Why man and child hand-in-hand? No one can say, for they do represent ineffable "depths of feeling into which we cannot peer"; but neither can anyone deny—however much one may wish to honor Beckett's "no symbols where none intended"— that these images have powerful emotional significance and, yes, "symbolic value," both for Beckett (one must assume) and (more specifiably) for the work in which they figure so prominently and so often.

Krapp's Last Tape is the work in which I have located the essential change in the emotional valency of the greatcoat image, but as I have pointed out there is no reference to such a coat in the play nor to the father who might wear it. It is not there except for the author who spoke of the obsessional memory of the child and father hand in hand, not there except for readers who know an obsessional image when they see one—even when they see one not there in literal fact. It is there, I believe, for Beckett and for such readers as I have posited, in this passage near the end of the play: "Ah finish your booze now and get to your bed. Go on with this drivel in the morning. Or leave it at that. *[Pause.]* Leave it at that. *[Pause.]* Lie propped up in the dark—and wander. Be again in the dingle on a Christmas Eve, gathering holly, the red-berried. *[Pause.]* Be again on Croghan on a Sunday morning, in the haze, with the bitch, stop and listen to the bells. *[Pause.]* And so on. *[Pause.]* Be again, be again. *[Pause.]* All that old misery. *[Pause.]* Once wasn't enough for you" (*Complete Dramatic Works,* 223). When Beckett chose to translate "Lie propped up in the dark—and wander" as "Installe-toi là dans le noir, adossé aux oreillers— et vagabonde," he gave a hint to interpretation with the final word ("vaga- bonde"), which takes one back to the figure in a military greatcoat wander- ing the face of Europe; but it is with his recollection of "the dingle on a Christmas Eve" and of "Croghan on a Sunday morning," of stopping and listening to the bells, that Beckett causes the reader familiar with *That Time, Company, Ill Seen Ill Said, Worstward Ho,* and *Stirrings Still* to sense the pres- ence of a ghostly walker in a greatcoat in *Krapp's Last Tape.* It is conve- nient—but not, I would say, decisive—to learn from Enoch Brater's *Why Beckett* that in 1955 (three years before *Krapp's Last Tape*) Beckett wrote

---

28. T. S. Eliot, *The Use of Poetry and the Use of Criticism* (London: Faber and Faber, 1964), 148.

his old friend Susan Manning, remembering walks with his father of thirty
and more years earlier, "If there is a paradise, father is still striding along
in his old clothes with his dog. At night, when I can't sleep, I do the walks
again and stand beside him again one Xmas morning in the fields near
Glencullen, listening to the chapel bells."[29] The melding in *Krapp's Last
Tape* of "the dingle on Christmas Eve" with "Croghan on a Sunday morning," crossing Christmas morning with Christmas Eve and Croghan with
the dingle, is a nice if minor instance of imagination shaping memories to
its own creative ends.

More important for my purposes in the letter to Susan Manning is the
opening phrase, "At night, when I can't sleep. . . ." This, of course, is what
the sixty-nine-year-old Krapp imagines as a more appropriate activity than
trying to record the previous year's events ("Leave it at that. Lie propped
up in the dark—and wander. Be again . . ."); and it is not at all far removed
from the one lying on his back in the dark to whom a voice comes in
Company, or from the other (same?) one who, in *Stirrings Still,* "One night
as he sat at his table head on hands . . . saw himself rise and go." The half-
remembering, half-dreaming figure lies at the center of much of the drama
after *Krapp*—*Embers, Cascando, Eh Joe, That Time, A Piece of Monologue,
Rockaby,* for example—and in the late fiction, the voice such figures hear
("this murmur of memory and dream," the narrator of the twelfth of *Texts
for Nothing* calls it [*Complete Short Prose,* 149]), can be taken to represent
the sound of consciousness itself. Beckett, in directing Pierre Chabert in
Krapp's Last Tape, spoke of the "dreams" or dreaming that goes on in the
play and specified that the state of consciousness he wanted dramatized was
what he called "rêverie": "Strictly speaking we are talking about rêverie.
. . . This is a state of rêverie rather like that of someone reading: the face
looks up from the book and the look seems to be miles away."[30] Reverie
is par excellence the mental condition of "in-between": between being
here and being "miles away," between consciousness and unconsciousness,
between waking and sleep, between willed recollection and vagrant dreaming; and it is the state that prevails in *Krapp's Last Tape.* I return once more
to a pertinent quotation from Yeats's "General Introduction for My
Work," in which he describes as the most deeply affecting sort of poetry

29. Enoch Brater, *Why Beckett* (London: Thames and Hudson, 1989), 10.

30. Pierre Chabert, "Samuel Beckett as Director," trans. M. A. Bonney and J. Knowlson, in *Samuel Beckett: Krapp's Last Tape, A Theatre Workbook* (London: Brutus Books, 1980),
105, 97.

that which combines "passionate, normal speech" with ancient metrical and stanzaic forms: "What moves me and my hearer is a vivid speech that has no laws except that it must not exorcise the ghostly voice. I am awake and asleep, at my moment of revelation, self-possessed in self-surrender" (*Essays and Introductions,* 524). This is the state in which Krapp listens to his own ghostly voice on the tape player, reverie-possessed, speaking a memory of thirty years earlier:

> . . . upper lake, with the punt, bathed off the bank, then pushed out into the stream and drifted. She lay stretched out on the floorboards with her hands under her head and her eyes closed. Sun blazing down, bit of a breeze, water nice and lively. . . . I asked her to look at me and after a few moments— *[Pause.]*—after a few moments she did, but the eyes just slits, because of the glare. I bent over her to get them in the shadow and they opened. *[Pause. Low.]* Let me in. *[Pause.]* We drifted in among the flags and stuck. The way they went down, sighing, before the stem! *[Pause.]* I lay down across her with my face in her breasts and my hand on her. We lay there without moving. But under us all moved, and moved us, gently, up and down, and from side to side. (*Krapp,* 221)

The passage is compact with memories for the reader of Beckett—first, of what was to be later, in *Happy Days,* when Winnie recalls to Willie the "sunshade you gave me . . . that day . . . *(pause)* . . . that day . . . the lake . . . the reeds"; second, of *Waiting for Godot,* where Estragon responds to Vladimir, who thinks he hears a sound that might be Godot arriving, "Pah! The wind in the reeds." And here we have Beckett not only "recalling" his own later work but also remembering *The Wind Among the Reeds,* Yeats's volume of poems of 1899, now become one of Beckett's "bits of pipe."

    Krapp's reveries also contain literary memories more distant in time (but nearer in spirit). I have in mind the fifth promenade of Rousseau's *Reveries of the Solitary Walker* and will pause over the title just long enough to remark that it fits Beckett's writing and what we know about his life almost better than it fits Rousseau's work and life. In an early letter (1931) Beckett wrote that on walks "the mind has a most pleasant and melancholy limpness, is a carrefour of memories, memories of childhood mostly, moulin à larmes" (*Damned to Fame,* 137). I stress the date of this letter only because the remark is so unlike what one would expect of Beckett later— it may, I would suggest, be important to bear in mind that Beckett's father, the silent companion of his walks, was still living in 1931. However that may be, the letter, like the passage from *Krapp's Last Tape,* contains sentiments very like those of Rousseau in the *Reveries.* In the following, for example, the floating and drifting described could as well be Krapp's as Rousseau's: "I would make my escape and install myself all alone in a boat, which I would row out into the middle of the lake when it was calm; and there, stretching out full-length in the boat and turning my eyes skyward, I let myself float and drift wherever the water took me, often for several hours on end, plunged in a host of vague yet delightful reveries . . ." (French, 85; Pléiade, 1.1044). These edenic experiences on "the Island of Saint-Pierre in the middle of the Lake of Bienne" took place twelve years before Rousseau wrote of them[31] and are thus doubly determined by reverie: the reverie of the walking/drifting time, the reverie of the writing time. Krapp, too, engages in dual, treble acts of reverie: the reverie while drifting with the girl in the punt, the reverie of the thirty-nine-year-old reviewing the previous year, and the reverie of the sixty-nine-year-old casting back over both events as he lies propped up in the dark, wandering. This is not all, however, for with Beckett we have, beyond all these reveries and circumscribing them all, the reverie of the writer dreaming on all he has made and on the shape his making describes. "As evening approached," Rousseau says of his habitual activity on the Lake of Bienne,

> I came down from the heights of the island, and I liked then to go and sit on the shingle in some secluded spot by the edge of the lake; there the noise of the waves and the movement of the water, taking hold of my senses and driving all other agitation from my soul, would plunge it into a delicious reverie in which night often stole upon me unawares. The ebb and flow of the water, its continuous yet undulating noise, kept lapping against my ears and my eyes, taking the place of all the inward movements which my reverie had calmed within me, and it was enough to make me pleasurably aware of my existence, without troubling myself with thought. . . . [S]oon these fragile impressions [of the instability of things] gave way before the unchanging and ceaseless movement which lulled me [*me berçoit*] and without any active effort on my part occupied me so completely that even when time and the habitual signal called me home I could hardly bring myself to go. (French, 86–87; Pléiade, 1.1045)

In his own translation of *Krapp's Last Tape*, Beckett rendered the last lines quoted above in a rhythmic imitation of the movement of the water in ways that can only recall Rousseau: "Nous restions là, couchés, sans remuer. Mais, sous nous, tout remuait, et nous remuait, doucement, de haut en bas,

---

31. "Looking back later on the experience" of the Island of Saint-Pierre in the *Reveries,* Maurice Cranston tells us, Rousseau "depicted it in brighter colours" than in letters written at the time. See of Cranston's biography of Rousseau, *The Solitary Self: Rousseau in Exile and Adversity,* 3 vols. (Chicago: University of Chicago Press, 1996), 3.134.

et d'un côté à l'autre."[32] The repeated "ou" sound of "Nous . . . couchés
. . . sous nous . . . tout . . . nous . . . doucement," punctuated regularly
by "remuer . . . remuait . . . remuait" catches nicely the gently repetitive,
lapping, lulling effect the water has on the mind, as does Rousseau's "le
flux et reflux de cette eau, son bruit continu mais renflé par intervalles
frappant sans relache mon oreille et mes yeux" that induces in him "une
réverie delicieuse" (French, 86–87; Pléiade, 1.1045). Moreover, when
Beckett gave to his French version of Rockaby the title Berceuse, which translates as "lullaby," "cradle-song," "swing-cot," and "rocking chair," Beckett
caught much the same rocking, lulling, cradling sense, appropriate both for
the beginning and the end of life, as Rousseau with his phrase "l'uniformité
du mouvement continu qui me berçoit."

Reverie, as we can gather from Beckett as from Rousseau, represents
a lowered state of consciousness but a heightened state of receptivity, of
memory formation, and of connection making. The way sleep investigators
and psychologists of memory have been putting the matter in recent years
is to speculate that it is during sleep and dreaming that short-term memories
are processed to become long-term memories; it is then (in Steven Rose's
terms) that single-occurrence eidetic images are either discarded—if insignificant or not amenable to sequential development—or are transformed
into a continuous, linear narrative to provide the meaningful infrastructure
of one's life story. "I believe, though I can't yet prove it," J. Allan Hobson
writes, "that the brain-mind traverses the states of non-REM and REM
sleep in part to reinforce and reorganize memory. . . . Though still speculation, there is mounting evidence that one of the reasons we need sleep at
all is to permanently encode our memories. We sleep, and the past day's
memories are reactivated as we dream, which changes their status; it advances them from short-term memory into long-term memory. . . .
[D]ream scenes are random and we impose a plot. In doing so, we are
cementing memories and linking them to action programs."[33] Daniel

32. La dernière bande, translated from the English by Beckett (Paris: Éditions de Minuit,
1959), 25–26.

33. J. Allan Hobson, The Chemistry of Conscious States: How the Brain Changes Its Mind
(Boston: Little, Brown, 1994), 114–17. Gerald Edelman, in his own language (where "the
letter C standing before a parenthesis stands for 'categorization of . . .' and implies reentrant
function. Boldface C stands for 'conceptual categorization of. . . .' I stands for interocep-
tive input and W for exteroceptive or world input; a dot between symbols means linkage
through neural connectivity or synaptic change"), means much the same as Hobson when
he writes, in The Remembered Present, "Given a reasonable amount of experience,
$C[C(W) \cdot C(I)]$ can interact with even slight amounts of W inputs to sustain some degree
of awareness. . . . Sleep may, in fact, be obligatory in organisms with primary consciousness

Schacter, too, claims only speculative force for what he says, but thinks it likely that "during sleep, when the brain is not so preoccupied by the continual barrage of external stimulation that occurs during waking, it works through the experiences of the day, discarding the trivial and saving the significant. . . . It now seems likely that as we sleep, our brains are working hard to save the experiences that we will carry around with us for much of our lives. . . . Our conscious activities during waking probably conspire with unconscious happenings during sleep to shape and sculpt the stories that we tell about our lives" (*Searching for Memory,* 88). Since this matter of sleep, dreaming, and short- and long-term memories is yet but speculative, I feel free to add my own thoughts, which are derived not from laboratory experience but from a reading of richly memoried texts like Beckett's. If we believe, with Schacter, that consciousness during waking conspires with unconsciousness during sleep to shape our stories, then we are justified in calling this sequence-producing activity "reverie," for therein precisely is consciousness joined indistinguishably with unconsciousness. I would like to emphasize the repetitive nature of this activity, so repetitive as to be virtually compulsive or obsessional, but always with alterations and transformations and tending ever toward the summative. Adopting yet again a phrase from Yeats but changing the context, I suggest that Beckett engages continually in what, in *A Vision,* is termed "dreaming back"; and that though Beckett's dreaming back may well be to his childhood, it is more certainly dreaming back over the work he has done that brings him to this point of reverie. The supreme instance of dreaming back (for my purposes) is *Stirrings Still,* and that piece has about it a strong feeling of reverie, and ultimately of vision.

Vision occurs in moments of sleeping wakefulness, when the unconscious feeds into and vastly expands the boundaries of consciousness; and it realizes itself in the artwork as style. Beckett may—as he claimed—have chosen to write in French because he could do so "sans style," but the truth is that his post-1945 writing is as distinctive in style as any one can think of—and the longer he continued with it, the more Beckettian it became. Vladimir Nabokov's aphorism that a writer's truest autobiography is the story of his style is fully borne out in Beckett's case. During the same period when Beckett was working through the "sans style" of *Watt* toward

for a number of reasons, the most important being to maintain the match required in conscious animals between the greatly disparate C(I) and C(W) systems of categorization. . . . Sleep may therefore be required in evolution in order to reduce C(W) drive periodically, thus allowing *alternative* C(I) and C(W) systems to be replenished biochemically and synchronized" (*The Remembered Present,* 155, 169–70).

his middle and late manner, Giacometti was making similar theoretical and practical discoveries with regard to sculpture. Asked by André Parinaud what had sent him back to sculpture in the late '40s after the "terrifying" diminution of every figure he attempted in the early part of the decade, Giacometti responded first with a question, then a paradox: "Have you noticed that the truer a work is, the more style it possesses? This is strange, since style is not the realism of appearances; and yet the heads I find most like people I might meet in the street are the least naturalistic—Egyptian, Chinese, archaic Greek, Chaldean sculptures. For me, the freest inventiveness is allied with the closest resemblance. I notice this particularly in the summer, when I see unclad women who resemble Egyptian paintings— that is to say, the most symbolic, the most artificial, and the least direct art imaginable."[34] He follows this with the remark quoted in the previous chapter about painting a drinking glass: "You don't copy the glass on the table," he says—"you copy the residue of a vision." In thus coupling vision and style, Giacometti conceives of creative sources deeper and "truer" than surface realism can reach or comprehend, and he points us in the direction of those late Beckett pieces in which vision and style rise out of reverie and merge with it as the substance and mode of the work.

I have written of reverie and dreams as close kin, but there is an important distinction to be drawn. However lowered the state of consciousness, it is never entirely absent in reverie as it is in sleep and dreams. The former merges consciousness with materials from the unconscious, but always on the home ground of consciousness; the latter remains wholly in the unconscious realm. Since will is a function of conscious mind, it plays a significant role in reverie but not in dreams. Reverie can avail itself of will as resource and ally, and as a result is capable of the articulated view backward and forward over a life or a career that dream as such—without the supplementation of conscious control from outside—cannot command. Dreams, that is to say, like the "snapshot" memories of early childhood, possess neither will nor sequentiality, but reverie has the potential for both, and this capability has signal importance for the narrative act that has its source in mem-

34. *Arts,* 5; *Écrits,* 273: "Avez-vous observé que plus une oeuvre est vraie plus elle a du style. Ce qui est étrange puisque le style n'est pas la vérité de l'apparence, et cependant les têtes que je trouve les plus ressemblantes avec les têtes de n'importe qui que je rencontre dans la rue, sont les têtes les moins réalistes, les sculptures égyptienne, chinoise ou grecque archaïque, ou chaldéenne. Pour moi, la plus grande invention rejoint la plus grande ressemblance, cela me frappe l'été, quand je vois les femmes nues, elles ressemblent a des peintures égyptiennes, c'est-a-dire a l'art le plus symbolique et le plus reconstitué, le moins direct." My translation.

ory. Beckett's characters, I have argued, exist in a condition of velleity, a near absence of volition: they typically have just enough will to "go on," but no more than that. We must not infer from this, however, that their creator is equally subject to velleity. Everything tells to the contrary. An "effort after meaning," which Bartlett posits as the motivating force behind every conjoint act of memory and narrative, runs all through Beckett's work and demonstrates a strenuous, unremitting exercise of will, especially in a time that seems to make the attainment of such meaning impossible. The Beckettian artist—who has the "obligation" but not the means, the power, or the desire to express—is not permitted to relinquish the effort after meaning merely because it will prove fruitless.

St. Augustine made the will (significantly also termed "love" in his lexicon) coequal with memory and understanding in a trinity of the mind, and one feels its articulative capacity everywhere at work in the narrative of the *Confessions*. It is pertinent to remark that volition is nowhere more fully engaged in the *Confessions* than in the account of the reverie-like vision shared by Augustine and his mother at Ostia—shortly after the conversion that made his diseased and divided will single, whole, and healthy. In terms of the present discussion, we might say that Augustine's unconscious contributed its portion to the working of his conscious mind, thus deepening and expanding its reach. There is no suggestion in Augustine's account that consciousness was obliterated during his experience of the mystic vision; on the contrary, he indicates that through a merger of consciousness with the unconscious a state of hyperconsciousness was attained. About Rousseau's description of his experience on the Island of Saint-Pierre, on the other hand, there is a distinct sense of consciousness lowered almost to the point of oblivion and of a will so relaxed it might as well be absent. And this Rousseauvian sort of reverie, as I have indicated, is also what we get in Krapp—*but not in Krapp's creator*. There is something like an iron will that keeps Beckett going on in the face of impossibility and certain failure. But it is failure at the level of dream and of Krapp's reverie, not at the level of the body of work and the writer's career. Beckett thus avails himself of Rousseau's sense of reverie for his subject matter, of Augustine's for his way of proceeding.

Like Krapp, both the one who rises and goes in *Stirrings Still* and the one with his head on his hands who watches him rise and go are revenants, ghosts visiting and revisiting their pasts. A quick consultation of the dictionary will reveal that no etymological relationship can be claimed between *reverie* and *revenant*, but I think there is nevertheless, in Beckett's work, a significant bond forged between the two at just that subliminal level where reverie plays itself out. And what does this reverie of the artist produce but broken dreams on the one hand, a coherent body of work—sequential, integral, and summative—on the other? Let the broken dreams go with other detritus of short-term memory; the body of work remains as the story told and retold, the creation and the complement of long-term memory, and finally, actually, almost miraculously brought to its end: "Such and much more such the hubbub in his mind so-called till nothing left from deep within but only ever fainter oh to end. No matter how no matter where. Time and grief and self so-called. Oh all to end."

POSTLUDE

"Je suis froid, je suis triste, je pisse mal," Jean-Jacques Rousseau wrote to his Amsterdam publisher, Marc-Michel Rey, as the winter of 1762 was coming on in Môtiers, the town in the Swiss canton of Neuchâtel where Rousseau had sought asylum when he fled France after the storm raised by *Émile* and *The Social Contract:* "I am cold, I am sad, I piss badly." Three years later, having been chased first from Môtiers and then from his blessed haven on the Island of Saint-Pierre, he wrote to Thérèse, who remained behind on the island, that he had arrived in Basel (on his way eventually to England) "with a sore throat, fever, and death in the heart": "J'arrive aujourdui Mercredi dans cette Ville sans grand accident, mais avec un mal de gorge, la fiévre, et la mort dans le coeur."[1] The expressions are thoroughly characteristic of Rousseau and could be duplicated a hundred times over from his correspondence, but they might equally well have come from any of the "heroes" of Beckett's Trilogy or *Waiting for Godot* or *Krapp's Last Tape,* all of whom are conscious of being in an advanced state of physical wreckage. Rousseau was only fifty years old when he wrote the first of these letters, fifty-three when he wrote the second. Krapp, or Krapp's creator, could have told him there would be much worse to come. "What's a year now?" the sixty-nine-year-old Krapp asks, then answers himself: "The sour cud and the iron stool," meaning, as Beckett told Patrick Magee (the actor for whom the play was written), "rumination and

---

1. The two letters are in the *Correspondance complète de Jean-Jacques Rousseau,* ed. R. A. Leigh, 51 vols. (Geneva and Oxford: Voltaire Institute, 1965–95), the first, number 2219, at 13.183, the second, number 4777, at 27.197. Both are cited in Maurice Cranston's biography of Rousseau (*The Solitary Self*), 3.40, 3.140. The phrase about "death in the heart" is one that found considerable favor in Rousseau's mind: see the cited letter to Rey in which, referring to the way his countrymen had treated him in forcing him to leave Yverdon for Môtiers, Rousseau writes: "Voila le coup qui m'a porté la mort au fond du coeur"; *Correspondance complète,* 13.182).

constipation." Now St. Augustine, as I pointed out in chapter I, writes of ruminant activity as a metaphor for the process of memory, but I have sought through his writings in vain for any expressions similar to those of Rousseau or of figures from among Beckett's "troop of lunatics." I have discovered precious little in Augustine about being cold or sad or suffering from constipation, nothing about pissing badly or having death in his heart. There are no doubt many reasons for this, most of them irrelevant to present purposes, but one explanation of why Rousseau and Beckett write this way and Augustine does not is entirely pertinent and bears directly on the question of what we can understand life-writing to have been for Augustine as against what it was for his two lineal descendants.

To put it briefly, these stylistic variants point to widely different attitudes about the proper orientation, focus, and subject matter for the life-writer. Rousseau—to take him first because it is with him that a radical reorientation occurred, bringing with it a host of consequences affecting all subsequent writers in the tradition—assumed that his correspondents cared whether he pissed well or badly because Rousseau cared so very deeply himself. The bizarre and incomprehensible thing is that those correspondents did care—or feigned to—about Rousseau's urinary problems, so successful was he in making his concerns the only ones that should matter to anyone. On the other hand, I am not aware of a single passage in Rousseau's voluminous correspondence (fifty-one volumes), in the three volumes of autobiography, or in any other source that would indicate that he had the least interest in the success or unsuccess of someone else's micturition (unless it be Turc or Sultan, but the two dogs were mere extensions of himself and therefore deserving recipients of Rousseau's solicitous tendance). The stated principle of the *Confessions,* carried out to the letter in execution, is that nothing is too trivial, too shameful, or too puerile to find its place in the book so long as it relates to Jean-Jacques Rousseau (and as readers of that book are aware, references to urination and catheters and Armenian robes to cover the problem abound). From that relationship and that one alone, which makes Rousseau the center of all attention and all affection, the trivial becomes important, the shameful natural, and the puerile praiseworthy. Again, we should not fail to note Rousseau's faithful execution of his plan: the *Confessions,* the *Dialogues,* and the *Reveries* are filled with the trivial, the shameful, and the puerile; whether they are transformed into their opposites by the simple fact of having issued from Rousseau is for every reader to decide. Rousseau, at any rate, has done what he promised, which is to make his books center on one subject and one subject alone: "Oui, moi, moi seul" (Pléiade, 1.1149).

Rousseau, as I pointed out in chapter II, drew what he intended to be a careful and exact distinction between amour de soi ("love of self") and amour-propre ("self-love"). He first broached the subject in the second discourse ("On Inequality") as a way to describe the origins and evil effects of social inequality; he enlarged on the idea in *Émile;* he brought it to bear as an explanation for his own woes in the first and second dialogues of *Rousseau juge de Jean Jaques;* and he returned to it in the eighth promenade of *Reveries* to claim that he had transcended amour-propre by recovering his original amour de soi. But the distinction that Rousseau worked out so carefully in theory vanishes in his autobiographical practice, and the two amours are collapsed into one in such a manner that any reader of the *Confessions* or the *Dialogues* would have difficulty in discerning the effects of one from the other. Briefly, what Rousseau's theory says is that amour de soi, which is a kind of life instinct or instinct for self-preservation, is present in all people in the mythical state of nature. Existing in complete solitude (which is necessary so that there be no jealousy arising from competition), such creatures do not need to worry about loving and being loved by others but instead are free to enjoy and to love themselves to their heart's content and in total innocence. Amour de soi is absolute and an absolute good for Rousseau. When *l'amour des autres* (to create a phrase that does not occur in Rousseau) comes into the picture, meaning both the infected love one has for others and the equally infected love others have for oneself, it inevitably brings with it contentiousness, vanity, jealousy, artificiality, pride, and hatred, for each of us in the fallen state of society wants to be loved more than anyone else is loved, and in that condition our pleasure comes not simply in being and in loving ourselves but rather in winning the competition with others to be the most loved of all. Thus, amour-propre, which is for Rousseau an evil the social world instills and encourages in all of us. It would be wrong to call amour-propre an absolute evil, however, in the sense that amour de soi is an absolute good, since it is the nature of amour-propre to be relative and dependent and to exist only where rivalry is fostered by the presence of others. Hence the exaltation of solitude in the *Reveries,* where Rousseau dramatizes his recovery of amour de soi after years of having been diverted from his true nature and misled by so-called friends—Grimm, Diderot, and the like—into exercise of amour-propre. Likewise, the first half of *Émile* is given over to an education (devised and executed by Émile's tutor, Jean-Jacques) the goal of which is to prevent the boy's amour de soi from turning into amour-propre, making of him in the book's latter half a prodigy who can live in society while yet remaining natural man, independent, free, innocent, and good. And this is what Rousseau believed about himself: that in his deepest being, no matter what his deeds might seem to tell to the contrary, he was really another Émile—not by education but by innate genius and good fortune—and that the amour-propre he appeared to exhibit was merely superficial, momentary, and illusory, foisted on him by the world in which he moved.

Whether or not we accept this reading by Rousseau of his character and of his *moi,* it is one of the true greatnesses of the *Confessions* and one of the mad triumphs of the *Dialogues* that in those two books he gives us, not in the theoretical terms of the second discourse nor in the fictional guise of *Émile* but in propria persona, the portrait of a man in whom amour de soi and amour-propre are present in the highest degree and utterly indistinguishable. He loves himself lovingly as if still in the state of nature, and he seeks to be first in the love of everyone he encounters, from the highest reaches of the aristocracy to the lowest street urchin he charms with cakes and candies. This is not theory and it is not fiction; it is truth to the life, and brilliantly done as no one before could have done it, as no one since has succeeded in doing it. I suspect Rousseau would have disavowed any such intention or accomplishment, but to readers at the end of the twentieth century his presumed disavowal can only appear to be an uncharacteristic instance of modesty. And as surely as the first *Confessions* inaugurated a new mode of writing in the Western world, the second *Confessions* altered the course of the inherited Augustinian tradition of life-writing, sending it veering off withershins (in the phrase from *Company*) from Rousseau's time to ours.

What Augustine would have thought of this new direction in life-writing we can surmise from what he writes in his summary of the character of his two cities, the earthly and the heavenly, in the conclusion to book 14 of *The City of God:* "We see then that the two cities were created by two kinds of love: the earthly city was created by self-love [*amor sui*] reaching the point of contempt for God [*contemptum Dei*], the Heavenly City by the love of God [*amor Dei*] carried as far as contempt of self [*contemptum sui*]" (*City of God,* 14.28, 593). By *amor sui* Augustine unquestionably means both amour de soi and amour-propre; because he was concerned with the larger contrast between love of self and love of God, Augustine would never admit such nice theoretical, autobiographical, and ad hoc distinctions as Rousseau wanted to make between love of self and self-love. Indeed, with his balanced opposites of *amor sui / contemptum Dei* and *amor Dei / contemptum sui,* Augustine introduces terms that will lead directly on to Pascal's famous *pensée,* "Le moi est haïssable": "The self is hateful," a doctrine that I believe Rousseau's rather tortured sundering of amour de soi from amour-propre was designed to circumvent or defuse. But if we consider the grounds on which Pascal's hatred of the self was founded, it seems almost as if he anticipated Rousseau's strategic move: "I hate the self," he writes, "because it is injust in wanting to make itself the center of everything. Briefly, the self [le moi] has two characteristics. It is injust in itself in that it makes itself the center of everything. It is pernicious to others in that it wants to subjugate them, for every self is the enemy and would like to be the tyrant over all the others."[2] This reads like a prevenient strike against Rousseau's century-later distinction, for making the self the center of everything is what Rousseau would claim is the benign desire of amour de soi, while taking every other self for the enemy and wanting to tyrannize over all others is the malign activity driven by amour-propre. Pascal, in his hatred of le moi and in his reasons for it, disallows Rousseau's differentiation as firmly as Augustine would have done. I say all this to suggest that in making "moi, moi seul" the all and everything of the life-writing project, Rousseau introduced complications and even impossibilities into the venture that Augustine was able—and careful—to avoid but that no one coming after Rousseau could fail to grapple with and try to find terms to accommodate if not to overcome.

Samuel Beckett was at least as severe in his attitude toward the self as St. Augustine or Pascal (which may be in part what Jean Anouilh meant when he called Waiting for Godot "a great music hall sketch of Pascal's Pensées as played by the Fratellini clowns"),[3] but that severity in no way relieved him of the necessity of acknowledging what Rousseau had done or of accepting that the self and all the mess attending it were unavoidable as the subject of post-Rousseau life-writing. In an early draft of this book I wrote the following sentence, intending it to figure near the end of the section called "The Children of Jean-Jacques": "I am not aware that Samuel Beckett ever commented directly on Rousseau—my guess is that he would thoroughly disapprove of Rousseau if he ever took notice of him—but in spite of that and in spite of his demonstrable admiration for Augustine there

2. "Le moi est haïssable. . . . Je le hais parce qu'il est injuste qu'il se fasse centre de tout. . . . En un mot le moi a deux qualités. Il est injuste en soi en ce qu'il se fait centre de tout. Il est incommode aux autres en ce qu'il les veut asservir, car chaque moi est l'ennemi et voudrait être le tyran de tous les autres": Pascal, Oeuvres complètes, ed. Louis Lafuma (Paris: Éditions du Seuil, 1963), 584; my translation.

3. Jean Anouilh, Arts-Spectacles, no. 400 (February 27–March 5, 1953): 1. It is interesting to note that, according to James Knowlson, one of Beckett's "Mirlitonnades" was sparked off by his reading of Pascal's "I seek only to know my own nothingness" (see Damned to Fame, 569).

is no way to get from the antiquity of St. Augustine to the modernity/
postmodernity of Samuel Beckett but through Jean-Jacques Rousseau."
The sentence has been deleted for a number of reasons, not the least of
which is the information conveyed in Knowlson's biography that amid a
large body of reading Beckett did in 1934, "[s]ome books came alive for
him in a special way—Rousseau's *Confessions* and the *Rêveries du promeneur
solitaire,* for instance." Attached to the passage is an endnote telling the
reader that "[t]his letter [from Beckett to Tom MacGreevy] contains a remarkable critique of Rousseau 'as a champion of the right to be alone and
as an authentically tragic figure' . . ." (*Damned to Fame,* 204, 660 n. 110).
Now this letter is very early—before either of the events I see as turning
points in Beckett's career and well before he had a clear sense of what his
lifelong subject was to be (which may have come indeed only toward the
end)—but it is good to have all the same. One cannot say what Beckett
intended by "an authentically tragic figure," nor can we know how much
his views might have changed over time, and it is a pity that he took no
note of the *Dialogues,* which could not have failed to interest him; nevertheless the letter to MacGreevy places the young Beckett on a course that
would bring him to confront and even, to a considerable degree, accept
Rousseau's radical reorientation of the Augustinian tradition while still
holding to the sense that Augustine offered the terms in which one might
accommodate (but not deny) the mess that followed upon identifying the
self as the sine qua non of the life-writing project.

Not only did St. Augustine not love the self and exalt it à la Rousseau—
he neither could nor would have—but he also never conceived of it as,
in any sense, the center of his attempt at writing his life. In the passage
from book 11 of the *Confessions* about reciting a psalm and narrating a life
that I have cited so frequently as the Augustinian paradigm of life-writing,
there is no suggestion that he or anyone could make a narrative out of the
self. I have argued elsewhere that if we take the word "autobiography"
apart we can understand the central term *bios* in a number of different ways.
Perhaps the primary meaning from the Greek—and this would be the one
first to occur to Augustine—would be "lifetime" or "the course of a life."
Understood this way, with time as a crucial element, *bios* assumes a clear
historical dimension, even a quasi-objective one, and memory becomes the
indispensable faculty for discovering, creating, or re-creating the narrative
pattern implied by "the course of a life." Though for Augustine this complex remembering-and-narrating process was deeply interesting, as we can
see from the practice of books 1 through 9 and the wondering speculations
of books 10 and 11 of the *Confessions,* it was not a disturbingly problematic

affair; and to write a life, though he may be said to have been the first to do it, never seemed to him an impossible undertaking. According to his view (and Vico's, I might add), the referential capacities of language are fully equal to describing events, movements in time, developments in social, intellectual, and psychological states of being because these are all things of our own making, therefore can be known by us, therefore can be narrated by us. Looking back, and especially back over the divide that was his conversion experience, Augustine, through the esemplastic power of his memory, was able to find words that would recall events in such a way that they fell into the pattern we signify by the phrase "a lifetime" or "the course of a life." And language was capable of doing even more than this, for though Augustine says that "this is hard labor, hard labor inside myself, and I have become to myself a piece of difficult ground, not to be worked over without much sweat" (*Conf.*, 10.16, 226), he nevertheless gives an ordered account of his perceptions, his faculties, his thoughts and feelings in response to the world lying outside himself. Even when he tells us of the pleasure he takes in songs and a well-trained voice, of his joy in eating and drinking, of his love of sounds and colors and light ("For light is the queen of colors, and wherever I am in daytime she is suffused over everything visible; she glides up to me in shape after shape, cajoling me when I am doing something quite different and am paying no deliberate attention to her. But she makes her way so forcibly into my mind that, if light is suddenly withdrawn, I look for it again with longing, and if it is absent for long, my mind grows sad" [*Conf.*, 10.14, 243])—even then, when working the "difficult ground" that is "inside myself," Augustine is not concerned with what, in a world post-Rousseau, we mean by *le soi, le moi,* the self, or the *I;* and that being the case, hard as the labor may be, he can and does find the words for telling "in order the stories of so many things" (*Conf.*, 11.1, 257).

Consider then the task Rousseau set for himself: to make his inner being—that which was unique, invisible, intangible, most secret and unreachable, a chaos of confused emotion and feeling without color, sound, or shape—to make this, his very self, transparent to the reader's eye, and to do it, moreover, "without the cold intermediary of words." It is true that in the *Confessions* Rousseau attempts his portrait of a self in the form of narrative—"Je suis né," etc.—but he tells us repeatedly that these narratable externals are nothing to his real purpose. Augustine looks back, with feeling but with equanimity, to events of the past; Rousseau does not look back on past events so much as he reexperiences in the present the unresolved emotional tumult that for him constitutes the past . . . and the present. And

what, it must be asked, does one *see* when one sees the self? The closest
we get to a hint comes when Beckett, in *The Unnamable,* refers to "[t]hat
tiny blur, in the depths of the pit" (*Trilogy,* 329). A blur, a smear, something
come and gone before any image can form itself on the retina, before any
shape emerges that one could hope to transform into words. This, however,
is only the beginning of the difficulty for writers who commit themselves
to the medium of time, memory, and narrative. If the self cannot be seen
in the close-up of the present, then how much less can it be discerned across
the distance of time; and this is the reverse of the case with autobiography as
the course of a life, for with the aid of memory, which discards what is of
no use and reshapes everything else to tell its story, the course of a life
becomes more distinct, not less, over time. One might be said at least to
"feel" what one's self is at the present moment; I cannot quite imagine
saying the same of a past self (though admittedly this is what Rousseau
seems to claim). One consequence of positing the self at the center of the
life-writing act, as we can see in Rousseau one way, in Beckett another,
is to disorient both memory and narrative and to vex the latter to the point
of impossibility. It was with such impossibility that Rousseau concluded
his *Confessions* and *Dialogues* and that Beckett began all his post-1945 efforts.

Can the self remember itself? The answer, I believe (and it is crucial
in any consideration of the intimate interrelation of memory and narrative),
must be no, at least if by "remember" we mean the same sort of thing as
when we say, "I remember doing thus and so," or, "I remember meeting
this person on that occasion in such and such a street." For the self to
remember itself would be to isolate it so absolutely that there would be
nothing else in the world. Time would be abolished and change also; the
self then and the self now would be identical, but not through any act of
memory, which, like narrative, requires time and change and some degree
of self-difference, which carries with it the possibility—indeed the certainty—of a slippage in congruity between then and now. Whence the
necessity, implicitly recognized by Rousseau in the *Dialogues,* explicitly by
Beckett everywhere, of splitting off into an other to depict the self. If the self
were capable of remembering itself it would be involved in an absolutely
unsharable activity, precisely analogous to a sleeper engaging in acts of
memory within a dream—which is again, I believe, not a tenable conception. Maurice Halbwachs, opposing the notion that memory can ever be
an absolutely individual act in the way I have described it as having to be
if the self were to remember itself, argues that this Rousseauvian condition
of being *enlacé de moi-même* ("intertwined with myself") inside memory is
little more than an illusion, yet dangerous all the same: "If recollections

were preserved in individual form within memory, and if the individual could remember things only by forgetting human society and by proceeding all by himself—without the burden of all the ideas that he has acquired from others—to recapture stages of his past, he would become fused with this past; that is, he would have the illusion of reliving it. I have shown that there is indeed one case in which people become fused with the images that they represent to themselves, that is, where the person believes he is living what he imagines all by himself. But this is also the only moment in which he is no longer capable of the act of memory: when he dreams" (*On Collective Memory*, 169). What Halbwachs describes in monitory terms is nothing other than the condition to which Rousseau aspires in the *Reveries*—and not only aspires to but claims to have attained. But we must remember that the *Reveries* represents the third and last move in his autobiographical trilogy and comes only after he has proposed himself as an other to all readers in the *Confessions* and then divided and redivided himself against himself in the *Dialogues*.

At the outset of this venture, Rousseau's confidence in his ability to make his soul fully visible to the reader would appear to have been complete, yet the logic of his procedure even at the beginning—and much more when he passes on to the *Dialogues*—suggests considerable doubt about the possibility of any such integral and unmediated self-revelation. For what he says in his preamble and in the "Ébauches des Confessions" he intends to do is to offer himself as an other so that readers may have a "piéce de comparaison" by means of which they might know themselves. Whoever you may be, Rousseau says, you cannot know yourself without another self to serve as a foil bringing out your true colors and character. Rousseau obviously, if illogically, makes an exception for himself, since he plainly believes that he needs no other in order to know himself; but the wholesale division of the self that takes place in the *Dialogues* subverts any such claim to self-sufficiency in self-knowledge. However much it might go against the grain of Rousseau's conscious and characteristic way of thinking, his procedure is straightforward enough and its meaning clear: the self can be apprehended not directly and in itself but only as and through an other. The practice that postcolonial and cultural critics in recent years have bitterly condemned of creating an other or others through whom our own identity can be established and asserted is exactly what Rousseau proposed as the benign and ideal effect of his *Confessions*. But more to the point is the fact that the self-division that shows itself as disordered memory and narrative first in the *Confessions* ("I have so confused a memory of this whole affair that it is impossible for me to impose any order or connexion

on the ideas which come back to me" [Cohen, 579; Pléiade, 1.627]) and
then in the *Dialogues* ("It is impossible for me to retain anything, collate
two sentences, and compare two ideas" [Masters/Kelly, 6; Pléiade, 1.665])
has become the prevailing condition of life-writing in the twentieth century. Beckett adverts to it even more frequently than Rousseau, and his
characters, from Didi and Gogo and the speakers of the Trilogy to the
voice of *Stirrings Still,* hardly talk of anything else than tormented, obsessive
memories and confused, shapeless stories that resist telling in any followable
form. At the point in his narrative when he is approaching his conversion
in the garden in Milan, Augustine pauses in the onrush of events to discourse on the divided will that, he says, is our inheritance from Adam and
Eve, but on this side of the conversion—in the narrative itself—he shows
no sign of a divided will, and neither the story he tells nor the memory
that brings it back to him in order shows any confusion or disfigurement.
But then Augustine, though he shared in the fallen human nature be-
queathed by Adam and Eve, had not the post-Rousseau modern self, with
its susceptibility to internal division, to contend with, and he knew nothing
of the Beckettian need for avatars, vice-existers, and puppets in recalling a
narrative that would be an adequate representation of his life. There was, of
course, an other necessary for Augustine's self-knowledge, but that other was
genuinely other rather than being as "Rousseau" would be to his readers or
as all the avatars might be to "the old bastard" behind them in Beckett.

Another alteration effected by Rousseau (but still intimately tied to an
insistence on *le soi / le moi* as the primary subject) was to make autobiography
a fully literary genre—this in spite of the fact that Rousseau never tired of
inveighing against *littérateurs.* It had not been this before, and certainly was
not for St. Augustine (though we may think we can see, looking back, that
the seeds were there in what he accomplished); but as critics too numerous
to name have been arguing for thirty years now, when memory and narrative conspire together to produce a written text, it falls to their lot to deal
with it rather than to theologians, psychologists, sociologists, or historians.
Consider what brought Rousseau to the point of writing the *Confessions,*
then the *Dialogues,* then the *Reveries.* The autobiographical trilogy might
well be seen to have grown out of an earlier three-part group: *Julie, ou la
Nouvelle Héloïse, The Social Contract,* and *Émile.* The first and last of these
present themselves as novels, accompanied and bolstered, however, by
Rousseau's theories about the origins of nearly everything in the human
world; *The Social Contract,* on the other hand, offers its theory neat, abandoning the veil of fiction thrown over the *Nouvelle Héloïse* and *Émile.* It
can be unsettling to a latter-day audience, raised on New Critical notions of

pure and impure literature, to contemplate the degree to which Rousseau's novels of sentiment are really novels of ideas—especially unsettling in light of his acknowledgment that for him thought was as slow and difficult as feeling was impetuous and spontaneous. But it would probably be fair to say that for most readers of Rousseau there is the impression (and not only in the two novels) of thought being generated by and filtered through emotion. In any case, when it was borne in upon Rousseau, by the call from his publisher and others for his memoirs[4] and by the revelations about children and the Foundling Hospital made by Voltaire, that his next project should be what materialized in time as the *Confessions,* Rousseau was coming immediately from his experiments in creating a literary form for revealing what the human world was in the beginning and what the moral state of its inhabitants, how it comes to be what it is now, and how we ought to act in the dual light of that ideal past and the far-from-ideal present. For these purposes, he created in Émile a character whose every thought, feeling, and motive was known to the author as his "onlie begetter" and whose destiny to the last detail lay in the hands of his creator (or, as Beckett would have it, his deviser); and Rousseau doubles his authorial control (again in a way similar to Beckett) by cloning himself in the character of "Jean-Jacques," the tutor who arranges the model education to which Émile is subjected. This is to say that when Rousseau set about portraying himself as he was "inside and under the skin," where he believed he was as unknown to others as those others were to themselves, he had in front of him as model the novel *Émile,* which differed from the project he was about to undertake only in this: that in *Émile* Rousseau was the author and Émile his character while in the *Confessions* Rousseau occupied both roles, being

---

4. David Hume, who accompanied Rousseau from Paris to London as sponsor of his stay in England, wrote perceptively and amusingly of Rousseau's response to Hume's insistence that he should write his memoirs. The letter was written immediately upon their arrival in London, well before the bitter public quarrel that divided the two men, and reflects only Hume's good feeling toward the one he calls his "pupil":

> My companion is very amiable, always polite, gay often, commonly sociable. He does not know himself when he thinks he is made for entire solitude. I exhorted him on the road to write his Memoirs. He told me, that he had already done it with an intention of publishing them. At present, says he, it may be affirmed, that nobody knows me perfectly any more than himself; but I shall describe myself in such plain colours, that henceforth every one may boast that he knows himself, and Jean-Jacques Rousseau. I believe, that he intends seriously to draw his own picture in its true colours: but I believe at that same time that nobody knows himself less. (*Correspondance complète,* 28.203, letter no. 4990)

The observation that "nobody knows himself less" than Jean-Jacques Rousseau anticipates the consensus judgment of two centuries of readers, but this only makes his achievement the more astonishing and to be wondered at.

thus the devised deviser of it all for company. Émile is the hero of a novel; Rousseau is the hero of an autobiography, but one that is possessed of all the properties of the novel that preceded it. The argument that Rousseau was the first to make autobiography a full-blown literary genre may seem to contradict what I said a few paragraphs back about the *Confessions* being neither theory nor fiction, but this is merely another way of stating the dilemma that Rousseau created for himself and his successors. In taking his self for his subject, in attempting to render his subjectivity in characters on a page (characters in the dual sense), and in making his self-feeling the center and circumference of the act of life-writing, Rousseau merged auto-biography with the novel and wrote what could well be seen—what, in-deed, Rousseau *did* see, but without using these words—as both the defin-itive and the ultimate Romantic text. What is revealed in Rousseau's autobiographical practice but elided or unrecognized in his theory is that words, even strung together as narrative, cannot adequately represent the self. Emile Benveniste would say that there is no reference for *I* outside the present instance of discourse, and this is precisely what Rousseau's volumes demonstrate. Adopting once again the Vichian principle of *verum-factum,* one could say that we have made, therefore can know and can narrate, the course of our lives; the same cannot be said of the self. One of the lessons of Freudian psychology, surely, is that the self is not self-made. The Rous-seauvian self, not hateful as Pascal said but lovable as Rousseau claimed, has thus proved itself capable of doing great mischief to the Augustin-ian tradition of life-writing, as later practitioners—left to pick over the pieces—might testify.

But Rousseau, not content with devastating the earlier tradition by installing the Romantic self at the heart of the project, made everything yet more difficult for subsequent life-writers by taking up in turn the three narrative forms—linear, dialogical, circular—that would seem logically suited to the task; and then, as if this appropriation of all available forms were not provocation enough, he demonstrated, by their successive failures in his hands, the inadequacy of any and every form for representing the self, the *I*, or subjectivity. This does not mean, of course, that there have not been many autobiographers since who have adopted the linear mode of the *Confessions,* the dialogical mode of the *Dialogues,* and the meditative, circular mode of the *Reveries,* but it does mean that writers like Henry Adams or Gertrude Stein, who thought much about these matters, turned away instead of following Rousseau, and it means also that someone as devoted to wresting form from chaos as Beckett was declared the task im-possible and then took that impossibility rather than the self for the truest

and the deepest subject of life-writing ("develop the inner nature and exploit the natural resources of that very impossibility," was, we recall, Beckett's advice to Giacometti). What Rousseau did, in Beckett's terms, was to
fail as none before him had dared to fail, and then, to close out the possibility
of anyone surpassing him by failing better or worse or in a new way, he
proceeded to fail in every conceivable narrative form, leaving Beckett to
say that not success and not even possibility but failure constituted the artist's highest calling. It would be a nice matter to decide whether in the end
Beckett succeeded at failure or failed at it; whichever it might be, one
would have to say that he kept the faith, such as it was.

Beckett kept faith not with St. Augustine's theology of the divine nor
with Rousseau's theology of the self but with the dogma that declares memory and narrative to be inseparable, indispensable, and in some ways indistinguishable partners in the making—the living and the writing—of a life.
When Malone, trying to get on with some kind of story in the likeness of
a life, exhorts himself with "That's it, reminisce" and "That's it, babble"
(Trilogy, 185), and when the voice of the Unnamable, apparently having
picked up the trick of this locution from Malone, says to himself, "That's
right, weave, weave" (Trilogy, 312), they are both invoking the twin powers, however diminished, however suspect they may have become in our
time, of memory and narrative. It has been the argument of this book that
memory and narrative, together and alike, are the two major epiphenomena
of consciousness, the dual defining conditions of our being human and not
something else. Memory has, both in theory and practice, changed from
Augustine's time to ours; we think about it differently, and (to a degree)
we do it differently. The same is true of narrative. Yet the words suffice
to indicate a pair of activities or processes continuous and recognizably the
same, however altered their colors may be, for the extended period we are
thinking about. For Augustine, Rousseau, and Beckett, memory enables
and vitalizes narrative; in return, narrative provides form for memory, supplements it, and sometimes displaces it. These reciprocal relationships have
not essentially changed in sixteen centuries. In chapter I, I discussed two
metaphors Augustine employs to characterize memory as a process—the
first, weaving; the second, rumination. Earlier in the postlude, I mentioned
the very un-Augustinian way Beckett treats of rumination in Krapp's dis-
missive reference to "the sour cud and the iron stool." There is a passage
in the eleventh book of Rousseau's Confessions that represents something
like a halfway house between Augustine and Beckett in this matter and
that reveals the gradual transformation in thought about memory from 397
to 1766 to 1988. Book 11, like the concluding book that follows (which

begins, as so much in Rousseau does, with "Ici commence l'oeuvre de tenebres dans lequel depuis huit ans je me trouve enseveli": "Here begins the work of darkness in which I have been entombed for eight years past" [Cohen, 544; Pléiade, 1.589]), consists mostly of a litany of the woes descending on him from all sides, but midway in his list of miseries Rousseau pauses to give an account of the psychology of his memory. He never remembers sorrows once they have passed, Rousseau says, and certainly never thinks vindictively about those responsible for them, because his heart was formed not for such negative responses but only for remembering happiness. "The more I suffer in anticipation," Rousseau writes, "the easier I find it to forget. Whereas, on the other hand, I am continuously preoccupied with my past happiness. I remember it and chew it over, so to speak, in such a way that I can enjoy it afresh at will": "Je le rapelle et le rumine, pour ainsi dire, au point d'en jouir derechef quand je veux" (Cohen, 540; Pléiade, 1.585). If we leave aside for the moment the ease with which he claims to forget unhappiness (a claim that strains credulity if we even slightly recall the episodes involving a broken comb, a stolen ribbon, unjust punishments, Wintzenried, five children and the Foundling Hospital, Voltaire, Grimm, Diderot, etc., etc.), we can see that this strikingly resembles Augustine's description of the mind's capacity for snatching something from the passing moment, swallowing it into the first belly of memory, then periodically bringing it up as a cud to chew over again at will. The great difference between Rousseau and Augustine (and this is why the former's proclaimed ease in forgetting unhappiness could be left aside only momentarily) lies precisely in this little matter of will: in Augustine, will enjoys an equal status with memory and understanding, the three composing a trinity in which no one partner rules or annuls either of the other two. It is quite otherwise in Rousseau, where memory usurps all powers to itself, working its will on will and imposing its understanding on understanding. When Augustine exclaims, "Great indeed is the power of memory!" he does not mean to characterize it as autonomous, all-powerful, free of any corrective or directive constraints, which is pretty much what memory becomes in Rousseau's experience; nor would Augustine have imagined memory to be obsessional as it is with Beckett and his characters. It is merely a sign of the times that "rumination," which was such a brilliant activity of the mind in Augustine and still an attractive pursuit in Rousseau, has become in the twentieth century a more or less technical term referring (in the language of Campbell's *Psychiatric Dictionary*) "to the persistence of some content of mind that has ceased to serve any adaptive purpose, the inability to turn one's attention from dominating, unpleasant ideas, and/

or an obsessive preoccupation with ideas, recollections, or plans." This, I judge, is not far from Beckett's understanding of the matter, both in *Krapp's Last Tape* and in general.

The other activity Augustine used as an analogue for both memory and narrative—weaving—has had a somewhat happier role to play in the history of life-writing, even down to the Unnamable's "That's right, weave, weave." Both rumination and weaving are processual in nature, and in that sense would be fully in keeping with the way scientific investigators, like their literary counterparts, are today thinking about memory and narrative. The less favorable sense given to rumination at present no doubt follows upon the perception that it is primarily an in-turned and private pursuit, all too likely to become stuck in the manner of a gramophone needle, while weaving may be thought to maintain something of a free and adaptable, mediatorial position between the inner and the outer, the private and the public, the fixed and the changing. In any case it is easier to see memory and narrative as symbiotic activities if we think of them both as akin to weaving; in so thinking we also lay the ground for an ongoing hermeneutic procedure that would be the counterpart of the process of weaving. More-over, at just the point where memory and narrative may be thought of as subsets of weaving, another collocation and quasi identification suggests itself—that of memory and imagination. As weaving has little of the rote about it, so also with memory, which is more imaginative in its operation than mechanical, more adaptive than simply or only reactive. The justifica-tion for bringing interpretative practice together with the operation of memory and the making of narrative lies in the Latin *contexo,* "to weave together," which permits us to speak of a text of memory and a text of narrative, both woven forms amenable to interpretative unraveling and re-raveling in the pursuit of meaning. To grant the weaving/text metaphor its full weight we must conceive of it, for any author, in terms not of an isolated passage or single volume but of the entire body of work, which we may call, in keeping with such phrases as "a lifetime" and "the course of a life," a lifework. This is not enough, however, for with the kind of tradition I have been concerned to delineate in this book, no author's con-tribution can be wholly contained within one text, even if, as we must, we expand the parameters of *text* to mean a body of work. St. Augustine's full significance in the tradition will be understood only if read in the light of Rousseau and Beckett, Rousseau's only if read in the light of Augustine and Beckett, Beckett's only if read in the light of Augustine and Rousseau. This is the kind of hermeneutical generosity, weaving back and forth and in and out among texts at every conceivable level, demanded by the tradition of life-writing emergent in the Western world over sixteen centuries. Where, then, do we find ourselves now in our narrative? What is life-writing about at present?

We can say, if we want, that after the revelation in Dublin of 1945, Beckett "realized he had one subject—himself—and henceforward he would tell that story" (*No Symbols Where None Intended,* 49), but the truth is that for Beckett the *I* or the self has no narrative, or at least none we can grasp or put to use. It was Rousseau's great passion to find his way back to an original state—to where everything started—even if that origin was merely ideal and mythical; but Beckett makes it his job to demonstrate by every means—parody, satire, imitative failure—that there is no way to trace back, hand over fist, through effect and cause to an originary moment; nor did he discover any satisfactory means for bringing narrative forward from such a nonexistent beginning to the muddle of present time. The futility of the effort in *The Unnamable* to "go back to his [Worm's] begin-nings and then . . . follow him patiently through the various stages, taking care to show their fatal concatenation, which have made him what I am" (*Trilogy,* 323) is both patent and paradigmatic. If it is reasonable to say (as I believe it is) that Rousseau exhausted the narrative forms for representing the self and that he drove that exhaustion home for later writers by his seriatim failures, then one should also observe that by Beckett's time, the Rousseauvian, Romantic exaltation of the self had long since spent itself and offered no possibilities to the life-writer working at the cusp of modernism/postmodernism. Rousseau inherited from St. Augustine a tra-dition of life-writing that in its own terms was healthy and flourishing; Beckett inherited from Rousseau a tradition in ruins and was left with no option but to call for, to yearn for, the death of the self responsible for bringing life-writing to this hopeless point: "the one true end to time and grief and self and second self his own. . . . Time and grief and self so-called. Oh all to end."

Finally, I think one must recognize that the self was for Beckett only the ostensible subject of life-writing—a kind of decoy, as it were: "self so-called"—with the career of the life-writer as his real subject. Which is not to say that his exasperated observations about the chaos of the self and the impossibility of representing it constituted a coy fiction behind which he could go merrily about his business. On the contrary, Beckett wrestled in dead seriousness with the subject of the self again and again; but as he persisted with the effort, realizing and demonstrating its hopelessness time after time, he gradually shifted focus to include in the picture not only the self but also, in the background, the artist struggling to represent it. Like

Velázquez in *The Maids of Honor (Las Meninas,* a painting Svetlana Alpers justly terms "one of the most subtle and powerful experiments in representation in all of Western art"),[5] like Goya in *The Family of Charles IV (La Familia de Carlos IV),* or like Courbet in *Studio of a Painter: A Real Allegory Summarizing My Seven Years of Life as an Artist (L'Atelier du peintre, allégorie réelle déterminant une phase de sept années de ma vie artistique),* Beckett is both inside and outside his work: he writes and depicts himself writing. Surrounded by his "troop of lunatics," as Velázquez is by court figures, Goya by the royal family, and Courbet by various models for his paintings, Beckett produces something like "a real allegory summarizing my forty years of life as an artist." He might not have been comfortable with this language, but it has to be said that in the end Beckett becomes the protagonist, even the hero, of his work. The phenomenon is far from uncommon among twentieth-century writers, who—to hazard a general rule—selfconsciously take their writing for their ultimate subject. This was no doubt one meaning behind Beckett's remark that in old age work would be his company: it had been for forty years; no reason to think this would change after the age of seventy. If one looks more closely, however, it becomes apparent that what Beckett was doing (and no doubt other writers followed the same logic) was to give over the Rousseauvian project as hopeless— and hopeless in thoroughly unproductive ways—in favor of a return to the Augustinian course-of-a-life model for life-writing; but folded into that "new" program all the same, as a failed but necessary component, was the agenda of the self that Rousseau introduced. We might put it like this: time and again, in the Trilogy, *Texts for Nothing,* and so on, Beckett played out Rousseau's futile project—to represent the self directly. But at the same time another drama, another project, was opening itself up under Beckett's watchful eye and careful direction: that of the writer chasing the Rousseauvian chimera, failing and going on, failing and going on, until the failures add up to a lifetime of effort and—that effort's twin—a body of work that is, at last, a more than sufficient representation of the life. This is the special mark of Beckett's genius, corresponding to the genius of St. Augustine in initiating a tradition of life-writing that would endure for centuries and to the genius of Rousseau in transforming the genre in ways that had the most profound consequences.

Setting out when he did, Beckett could no more have adopted unaltered the confessional Augustinian mode (*"Great art thou, O Lord, and greatly*

---

5. Svetlana Alpers, *The Art of Describing* (Chicago: University of Chicago Press, 1983), 69.

to be praised; great is thy power, and thy wisdom is infinite") than he could have begun where Rousseau did, with his solipsistic claim about showing "to my kind a man in all the truth of nature, and that man will be myself": "ce sera moi. Oui, moi, moi seul." But if Beckett could find his voice neither in the accents of Augustinian self-abasement nor of Rousseauvian self-exaltation, he nevertheless could not disregard what his two predecessors had done, and he had in some way both to come to terms with their examples and reconfigure them to the conditions and exigencies of his own era and vision. This is precisely what I see Beckett as having done, moving, as it is put in "neither," "to and fro in shadow from inner to outershadow/ from impenetrable self to impenetrable unself by way of neither." And I would recall, one final time, Beckett's repeated return to the great progenitor: "I take no sides. I am interested in the shape of ideas. There is a wonderful sentence in Augustine: 'Do not despair; one of the thieves was saved. Do not presume; one of the thieves was damned.' That sentence has a wonderful shape. It is the shape that matters." The sentence does have a wonderful shape, and so too the sentence that began this postlude: "Je suis froid, je suis triste, je pisse mal." The first—in which antithetical syntax and logic mirror one another—is as characteristic of Beckett's thought and expression as of Augustine's; the second—in which simple parataxis replaces both syntax and logic—is thoroughly Rousseauvian, while also sounding as if it might have come from one of Beckett's characters. This two-tiered mode of linguistic representation—Augustinian on the level of the maker, Rousseauvian on the level of the made—is Beckett's way of reconciling and encompassing the two antagonistic ancestral voices. He succeeds in wrapping himself in a mantle that seems sometimes a legacy from Augustine, other times from Rousseau, but that is always, finally, Beckett's own, cut to his pattern and to no one else's. It was the shape that mattered for Beckett as for Rousseau and Augustine, the shape of a life as remembered, the shape of a life as narrated; the exquisitely complicating factor for Beckett was that he had not only to delineate a shape in a time he felt was inimical to form, but also to respond to and accommodate the shapes bodied forth with such grandeur by his predecessors. I have written about Beckett as if he were the end, but of course he is not; or if he is, then only for the moment. There will be new forms, as yet unimagined and unimaginable, for the life-writing enterprise, but if these are to be true to the task as presently evolved, they will have to take into themselves the intricate, composite lessons of Beckett as well as those of Augustine and Rousseau.

INDEX